Veterinary Notes
for Cat Owners

EDITED BY
Trevor Turner BVetMed, MRCVS
and Jean Turner VN

Stanley Paul
LONDON

First published in the United Kingdom in 1994 by
Stanley Paul & Co Ltd
Random House, 20 Vauxhall Bridge Road,
London SW1V 2SA

Random House Australia (Pty) Limited
20 Alfred Street, Milsons Point, Sydney,
New South Wales 2061, Australia

Random House New Zealand Limited
18 Poland Road, Glenfield, Auckland 10, New Zealand

Random House South Africa (Pty) Limited
PO Box 337, Bergvlei, South Africa

Random House UK Limited Reg. No. 954009

A CIP catalogue record for this book
is available from the British Library

ISBN 0 09 177627 9 (cased)
0 09 175103 9 (paper)

Set in Linotron Sabon by SX Composing Ltd,
Rayleigh, Essex
Printed and bound in Great Britain
by Richard Clay Ltd, Bungay, Suffolk

ACKNOWLEDGEMENTS

The majority of the photographs in this book were provided by Trevor
Turner and the authors. For allowing the use of additional photographs,
the editor, authors and publishers would like to thank Stephe Bruin (figures
3 and 152) and Alan May, Glasgow Veterinary School (figures 93 and
95-99 inclusive); also Dr K.C. Barnett of the Animal Health Trust and Dr
S.C. Crispin of the Bristol Veterinary School for providing the colour plates
depicting conditions of the eye.

Chapter 6 Behaviour Problems by Peter Neville first appeared in *The
Behaviour of Dogs and Cats* published in 1993 by Stanley Paul.

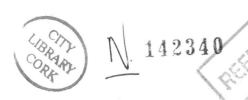

CONTENTS

Anatomy and Physiology

Organ Systems

Infectious Diseases

Feline Immunology

Poisoning and First Aid

Veterinary Nursing

Breeding and Genetics

The Show World

ABOUT THE AUTHORS

Dr DIANE ADDIE, BVMS, PhD, MRCVS
Diane Addie qualified as a veterinary surgeon from Glasgow University in 1979 and worked in small animal practice for eight years. In 1982 she won the clinical paper category of the Willows Francis Literary Award with a paper on feline leukaemia virus.

Diane Addie returned to Glasgow University in December 1987 to study with Oswald Jarrett. She conducted the first long-term longitudinal survey of cats in the field naturally infected with feline coronovirus and in 1992 was awarded a PhD for her thesis, 'Studies on the humoral immune response to feline coronovirus'.

Interested in the welfare of cats, as well as their diseases, Diane sits on the Council of the Cats' Protection League. She has written four CPL disease information leaflets, and an A-Z of cat disease in the CPL book *A Passion For Cats*.

Diane Addie works at Glasgow University where she continues her research into feline coronavirus.

ALISON ASHFORD, FZS
Alison Ashford was born in the Transkei, South Africa, and came to Britain when she was ten to commence her formal education. She left school at sixteen to begin training for the Certificate of the Tuberculosis Association, which she gained despite suffering from the disease herself; she later became a Registered General Nurse.

It wasn't until after the birth of two daughters that the gift of a Siamese kitten brought entry into the Cat Fancy and the real start of her interest in animals. She became a successful breeder of Siamese and a pioneer breeder of Cornish and Devon Rex. A founder member of the Colourpoint, Rex-coated and Any Other Variety Club, Alison was later elected a Delegate to the Governing Council of the Cat Fancy (GCCF). She became a correspondent for *Cats* magazine and was appointed Fellow of the Zoological Society in recognition of her work.

Alison, who underwent major surgery for cancer in 1980 and who still battles with the disease, currently breeds Persians. She also serves on the Executive Committee of the GCCF.

PATSY BLOOM, Associate Member BSAVA

Patsy Bloom, founder of Pet Plan, the UK's leading animal insurance specialists, was born in London in 1940.

She began her career in advertising and worked on major accounts such as Oxfam and the Mary Quant range of cosmetics before moving into publishing – firstly as Promotions Manager for *Queen* magazine and then Publicity Manager for Sphere. Later, when working for a major charity and facing mounting vets' bills for her sick dog, Patsy first had the idea of pet insurance.

Having completed a programme of extensive research into the viability of such a project Patsy, together with David Simpson, launched Pet Plan in 1976. Offering an entirely new concept in pet insurance, the company rapidly grew, forcing Patsy to devote her full energies to its marketing.

Seventeen years on, Pet Plan has gone from strength to strength with over 51% of the small animal insurance market, a major slice of the leisure horse market plus a successful Thoroughbred division 'Bloodlines', insuring over 350,000 animals. Plans for 1994 include the formation of the Pet Plan Charitable Trust – expected to make a significant contribution to animal welfare in the next decade.

Patsy is an Associate Member of the British Small Animal Veterinary Association and a Fellow of the RSA; she was Veuve Clicquot Business Woman of the Year in 1992.

HEATHER BRIGGS, BVMS, MRCVS

Heather Briggs graduated in Veterinary Medicine and Surgery at the University of Glasgow in 1957 and started work in the surgery department at the Royal Veterinary College. On leaving there, a period was spent in veterinary practice in Yorkshire, during which time she became involved with the Cat Fancy, and on leaving the North she became an honorary life member of the Northern Siamese Cat Club.

The next few years were spent in the Virology Department of the Wellcome Research Laboratories, working on cat and dog diseases, and the production of vaccines. After another period in small animal practice, she was appointed as Head of the Veterinary Nursing Department at the Berkshire College of Agriculture. Whilst there, she began writing, and contributed to the standard textbook for veterinary nurse training. She was also involved with the production of the first correspondence course in veterinary nursing.

She now works freelance; lecturing, writing and tutoring for GCSE Human Biology courses for the National Extension College. She is in veterinary practice part time, where she undertakes clinical work with cats, and is able to devote more time to veterinary assistance at cat shows.

Dr BARRY M. BUSH, BVSc, PhD, FRCVS

Barry Bush qualified from the University of Liverpool in 1961 and worked in small animal practice before moving to the Royal Veterinary College where he became Senior Lecturer in Small Animal Medicine. In addition to teaching commitments he acted as a consultant in the referral hospital of the Royal Veterinary College. After retiring from London University he joined Hill's Pet Nutrition, where he is currently Senior Veterinary Advisor for Northern Europe. His main interests are internal medicine, laboratory medicine, clinical nutrition and first aid for dogs and cats. He has published several books and was responsible for establishing the first organized courses for the education of veterinary nurses and continues to be associated with their training and examination.

JOHN E. F. HOULTON, MA, VetMB, DVR, DSAO, MRCVS

John Houlton qualified from the University of Cambridge Veterinary School in 1970 and subsequently spent six years in practice before returning to Cambridge as Assistant University Surgeon. He is a double Diploma holder of the Royal College of Veterinary Surgeons, obtaining the Diploma in Veterinary Radiology in 1982 and the Diploma in Small Animal Orthopaedics in 1991. Now University Surgeon at the Cambridge Veterinary School he is responsible for the Orthopaedic lecture course and referred orthopaedic cases.

In 1985 he was awarded the British Small Animal Veterinary Association Simon Award for outstanding contributions to Veterinary Surgery, and is currently recognized by the Royal College of Veterinary Surgeons as a Specialist in Small Animal Surgery (Orthopaedics).

SID JENKINS, MRIPHH

Sid Jenkins joined the RSPCA in 1973 and rose through the ranks to become Superintendent. During his service he was awarded a Bronze Medal and three bars for animal rescues together with many certificates of merit and commendations. He was also awarded the RSPCA's Media Award, Long Service Medal and Special Services Medal – the latter for bringing to justice those involved in organizing dog fights.

In 1990, after leaving the RSPCA to allow himself greater freedom to campaign for animal welfare on radio, television and in the press, Sid visited the then Soviet Union to see the situation of animal welfare for himself. He has since returned to Leningrad (now St. Petersburg) on thirteen occasions and is a member of the St. Petersburg Animal Protection Society, which now boasts a committee of 12 and over 400 members.

He appeared in the six-part BBC series *Animal Squad* and has made personal appearances on *Wogan, Live from Piccadilly* and numerous other TV and radio shows. His views on animal welfare matters are often called for by Yorkshire TV's *Calendar News* programme and BBC's *Look North* and he broadcasts regularly on local radio.

Sid writes a weekly column for the *Yorkshire Evening News* entitled *Animal World* and writes monthly for *Cats* magazine. His latest book on *Animal Rights and Human Wrongs* was published in July 1992.

NORMAN W. JOHNSTON, BVMS, MRCVS, FAVD

Norman Johnston qualified from the Royal School of Veterinary Studies, University of Edinburgh in 1976. Following a short period of mixed practice in Yorkshire, he returned to Edinburgh to join his 'home' practice in 1977. He became a partner in 1982 in what is now a four vet hospital practice and referral centre. The practice was the first in Scotland to attain hospital status which it did in 1989.

Norman Johnston first became interested in veterinary dentistry about 10 years ago in tandem with a local dentist who happened to be a client. He is a charter member of the British Veterinary Dental Association and has served as President since 1991. He is also a Charter Member of the European Veterinary Dental Association and currently serves on its board of Directors. In 1991 he was awarded a fellowship by the American Academy of Veterinary Dentistry becoming the first person from the UK to receive this honour.

His current research interests include the role of micronutrients in the maintenance of collagen and their role in the prevention of periodontal disease.

HELEN A. LAWSON, BVMS, MRCVS

Helen Lawson graduated with Honours from Glasgow University in 1992 and spent one year as House Surgeon in the Department of Veterinary Surgery at the same establishment.

She is currently a Clinical Scholar with special interests in Oncology and Radiology and is studying for a Certificate in Veterinary Radiology.

Dr IAN S. MASON, BVetMed, PhD, CertSAD, MRCVS

Ian Mason graduated from the Royal Veterinary College, University of London in 1981. After three years in general practice, he joined the Dermatology Unit at the Royal Veterinary College to study factors influencing the development of pyoderma in dogs with atopic dermatitis. In 1987 he was appointed as Leverhulme Resident in Veterinary Dermatology at the RVC.

Awarded a PhD for studies on bacterial skin disease in dogs in 1990, Ian is Treasurer of the British Veterinary Dermatology Study Group and Editor of the Bulletin of the European Society of Veterinary Dermatology. As a member of the American Academy of Veterinary Dermatology he has presented numerous papers at scientific and clinical conferences throughout the world including both World Congresses of Veterinary Dermatology.

Ian is the author of several scientific papers and editor of two textbooks. He is currently co-writing a textbook on veterinary dermatology and runs a referral dermatology practice in south-east England.

S. E. MATIC, MA, BVSc, MRCVS, DVR, DSAC

After qualifying as a veterinary surgeon in South Africa, Sue Matic returned to Britain and worked in general small animal practices in the south-east for seven years. She moved to Cambridge in 1982 where she gained the Diploma in Veterinary Radiology from the Royal College of Veterinary Surgeons (RCVS) and went on to teach Small Animal Medicine at the Cambridge Veterinary School. Whilst Sue is no longer in clinical practice, she maintains an interest in Veterinary Cardiology, having gained the RCVS Diploma in that subject in 1989. She is currently Chairman of the Veterinary Cardiovascular Society.

JULIA MAY, BVetMed, BSc, MRCVS

Julia May has worked as a veterinary surgeon in small animal practice since qualifying from the Royal Veterinary College, London in 1968. Julia bred her first litter of Siamese in 1970 and has been breeding Siamese and Orientals and, more recently, Angoras ever since. A very active member of the Cat Fancy, she has been Secretary of the Red Point & Tortie Point Siamese Cat Club since 1972, a member of various other Cat Club Committees, a Delegate to the Governing Council of the Cat Fancy (GCCF) since 1978 and a Show Manager since 1981.

In addition she is a member of the GCCF Veterinary Sub-Committee, Genetics Committee, Disciplinary Committee, Executive Committee and Supreme Show Committee, and from 1994 will be the Show Manager of the GCCF Supreme Show, but still finds time to show her own cats.

HELEN S. MUNDAY, BSc (Hons) MSc

Helen graduated in Agricultural (Animal) Science from Leeds University in 1986. She was awarded her MSc for research in Meat Science from Nottingham University in 1987. Helen joined Pedigree Petfoods in 1987 in the Material Development Department, initially working on the control of raw material quality. She then moved to the Waltham Centre for Pet Nutrition in 1989 in the role of Project Scientist. In 1991 Helen was promoted to her current position of Nutritionist in which she has responsibility for research in the optimum feeding of cats through the life stages.

Professor ANDREW NASH, BVMS, PhD, CBiol, FIBiol, MRCVS

Andrew Nash qualified from the Glasgow Veterinary School in 1967, gaining the silver medal in clinical veterinary medicine, and spent the next five years in general practice in North Devon. He returned to Glasgow in 1973, as a house physician in the Department of Veterinary Medicine, taking responsibility for a small animal clinic run by the Veterinary School in conjunction with the Glasgow Dog and Cat Home.

In 1975 he became a lecturer in small animal medicine and in 1985 was promoted to senior lecturer, having completed a PhD degree in 1984 on renal biopsy in dogs and cats.

In 1993 he was promoted to Titular Professor in veterinary medicine and more recently has been appointed Director of the University of Glasgow Veterinary Hospital. His major research area has been kidney disease and since 1985 he has taken a special interest in juvenile nephropathies in dogs. Other interests include anaemia in dogs and cats, endocrine diseases, infectious diseases of cats, and, more recently, problems associated with obesity and hyperlipidaemia in dogs.

He has published widely on many aspects of small animal internal medicine and is a regular speaker at professional and lay meetings at home and abroad. In addition, he is President of the International Society for Veterinary Nephrology and Urology, a board member of the Glasgow Dog and Cat Home, and Honorary President of the Scottish Cat Club.

PETER NEVILLE, BSc (Hons)

Peter Neville graduated with an Honours degree in biology from the University of Lancaster in 1979. This was followed by postgraduate studies on feral cat, mole and seal behaviour and human/companion animal relations during three years spent as Research Biologist for the Universities Federation for Animal Welfare. His doctorate was awarded by the Etologisk Institut, Denmark, for studies of feline behaviour and the development of treatment for feline behaviour problems. He is the author of many scientific/veterinary papers on pet and feral cat behaviour, and has lectured on four continents on pet behaviour therapy.

Currently Visiting Animal Behaviour Therapist at the Department of Veterinary Medicine, Bristol Veterinary School, Peter is also in practice for the referral and treatment of behaviour problems in pets. He is co-founder and Honorary Secretary of the Association of Pet Behaviour Counsellors.

Author of the internationally bestselling books *Do Cats Need Shrinks?*, *Claws and Purrs* and *Do Dogs Need Shrinks?*, his latest book *Pet Sex* was published in May 1993.

Dr IAN H. ROBINSON, BSc, PhD

Ian Robinson graduated from the University of Durham in 1983 with a degree in Zoology and obtained his PhD for studies on olfactory communication at the University of Aberdeen in 1987. During this time he also conducted research on lynx behaviour in France and Spain.

From 1987, Ian spent 18 months working in the Flavour Group of Unilever Research, investigating the perception of odour and flavour. Thereafter he joined the Waltham Centre for Pet Nutrition in 1988 as an Animal Behaviourist, studying the feeding behaviour of dogs and cats. In his current position he is involved in studies of the human/companion animal bond and is particularly interested in the health benefits associated with pet ownership.

Working with Universities throughout the world, Ian has established a number of projects designed to investigate both the psychological and physiological benefits which can be obtained from pet ownership, and the possible mechanisms behind these effects.

Dr ANDREW SPARKES, BVetMed, PhD, MRCVS

Andrew Sparkes graduated from the Royal Veterinary College in 1983. After spending four years in general practice, he joined the staff at the University of Bristol Veterinary School as the Feline Advisory Bureau (FAB) Scholar in feline medicine. Andrew remained at Bristol after completion of his year as FAB Scholar, and has undertaken studies in feline dermatophytosis for a PhD. He is currently the FAB Lecturer in Feline Medicine in the Department of Veterinary Clinical Sciences at Bristol University.

Dr MARTIN SULLIVAN, BVMS, PhD, DVR, MRCVS

Martin Sullivan graduated from Glasgow University in 1978 and, apart from a short time in general practice, has been a member of staff in the Department of Veterinary Surgery at Glasgow University. He holds a Diploma in Veterinary Radiology and is a Charter Member of the European College of Veterinary Surgeons. His main clinical interests lie in the upper respiratory tract of the dog and cat and he has published a number of articles and contributed to a number of books pertaining to this area.

Dr SARAH R. TOTH, DVM, PhD

Sarah Toth was born and educated in Hungary and studied at the Veterinary School of Budapest where she graduated as Doctor of Veterinary Medicine. After working in practice in Hungary and West Germany, she joined the University of Glasgow Veterinary School and carried out research relating to feline leukaemia virus infection leading to a PhD in 1980.

Lecturer in the Department of Veterinary Pathology since 1979, and in charge of the Diagnostic Haematology and Cytological Services, Sarah is currently involved in various research projects, including acquired and experimental infection of cats with feline immunodeficiency virus (FIV) and investigation of the role of genes and viruses in the development of T-cell and B-cell tumours in mice.

JEAN TURNER, VN

Jean Turner was a secretary/PA in a large organization and after marriage and children, sought a new challenge. This was fulfilled with veterinary nursing and she qualified in 1971. She speaks and writes widely on veterinary nursing matters with particular reference to cats. She regularly contributes to various veterinary and veterinary nursing publications as well as the cat press. She was an examiner for the veterinary nursing examinations RCVS scheme for seven years and served on the British Veterinary Nursing Association (BVNA) Council for 16 years.

Jean is now an honorary member of the BVNA and enjoys living with, breeding and showing her cats who live in harmony with a couple of Irish Wolfhounds and a Basset Griffon Vendeen . . . and numerous other little people who pass through their home.

SALLY TURNER, MA, VetMB, MRCVS

Sally Turner comes from a veterinary family and was brought up surrounded by a menagerie of cats, dogs and various 'small furries'. She expressed a desire to become a veterinary surgeon at an early age and qualified from the University of Cambridge in 1991. She worked in general small animal practice for two years before taking up her present position as GDBA Fellow at the Animal Health Trust, Newmarket, where she is pursuing an interest in ophthalmology, leading to a Royal College of Veterinary Surgeons certificate in the subject.

TREVOR TURNER, BVetMed, MRCVS

Trevor Turner qualified from the Royal Veterinary College in 1958. Brought up with dogs, he established a small animal practice in Northolt a few months after he qualified. This practice is now a veterinary hospital approved by the Royal College of Veterinary Surgeons and employs over 30 people. Together with Jean he started breeding cats over a quarter of a century ago. He started with a domestic shorthaired white mongrel cat and ultimately bred and successfully exhibited pedigree Long Haired Silver Tabbies.

Currently the home is shared with two Maine Coons and a 15-year-old Long Haired Silver Tabby. A member of several cat clubs he is currently President of the Russian Blue Breeders Association and Vice-President of the Herts and Middlesex Cat Club. He regularly vets-in at shows ranging in size from small breed club shows to the National Championship Show – the largest cat show in the world.

Trevor writes and speaks widely on feline topics. He has been honoured by the British Small Animal Veterinary Association as the recipient of the prestigious Melton Award and by the Royal College of Veterinary Surgeons for forging links with breeders and members of the pet-owning public and for service towards the advancement of small animal practice. He has also received the William Hunting Award for the best clinical presentation in the Veterinary Record. He is editor of the companion volume, *Veterinary Notes for Dog Owners* as well as author of several books and numerous articles on feline and canine topics.

LORRAINE WATERS, BVetMed, MRCVS

Lorraine Waters graduated from the Royal Veterinary College, London in 1990 and stayed on for a year as a small animal House Surgeon. She was involved in work with both cats and dogs and was able to gain a good grounding in both medicine and surgery. After this she went to the University of Bristol to spend a year as the Duphar Fellow in feline medicine. She worked closely with the Feline Advisory Bureau Scholar and was responsible for producing the *Feline Update* magazine. During these two years Lorraine developed a strong interest in both ophthalmology and feline medicine.

After leaving Bristol Lorraine worked in a small animal practice in Peterborough. In January 1993 she joined the comparative ophthalmology unit at the Animal Health Trust, as the Cosmo-Cran Scholar, studying for a Royal College of Veterinary Surgeons Certificate in Ophthalmology as well as undertaking work on corneal disease leading to a PhD.

Dr SIMON J. WHEELER, BVSC, PhD, MRCVS

Simon Wheeler graduated from the University of Bristol in 1981 and took up a position as House Surgeon at Glasgow University Veterinary School. Following a year in general practice in Wales, he was appointed Clinical/ Research Assistant in Neurology at the Royal Veterinary College, London. He received a Veterinary Research Training Scholarship from the Horserace Betting Levy Board and a grant from the BSAVA Clinical Studies Trust Fund to pursue his interest in neurological disorders, particularly peripheral nerve and spinal conditions.

Simon was awarded a PhD by the University of London in 1988. From 1988–1992 he was Assistant Professor of Neurology at the College of Veterinary Medicine, North Carolina State University. Currently he is Lecturer in Neurology, in the Department of Small Animal Medicine and Surgery, at the Royal Veterinary College. He has published research and continuing education articles, and textbook chapters in the USA and Great Britain. He is Vice-President of the European Society of Veterinary Neurology.

Dr JOSEPHINE M. WILLS, BVetMed, PhD, MRCVS

Jo Wills qualified from the Royal Veterinary College, London, in 1981, and then spent two years in small animal practice, where an interest in feline medicine developed. She then joined the department of veterinary medicine at Bristol University, where her work on chlamydia infection in cats led to a PhD in 1986.

After a period of postdoctoral research at the University of Manchester Medical School, she joined the Waltham Centre for Pet Nutrition in 1988. Jo was Scientific Editor for the *Bulletin of the Feline Advisory Bureau* for five years and is now Scientific Affairs Manager at the Waltham Centre for Pet Nutrition.

Dr SUSAN YEO, BVetMed, PhD, MRCVS

Sue Yeo qualified from the Royal Veterinary College in April 1981. She spent two years working in a very mixed practice on Dartmoor, after which she spent the next four years in the Department of Veterinary Medicine of the University of Bristol, first as House Physician and later studying the development of the respiratory tract immune system in young calves, for which she was awarded a PhD in 1987. She now works in general practice near Bristol.

INTRODUCTION

Veterinary Notes for Cat Owners joins two previous volumes, *Veterinary Notes for Dog Owners*, published in 1990, and *Veterinary Notes for Horse Owners*, first published in 1877 and now in its 17th revised edition. The same principles which guided the first two books have been applied to the present volume which is, as the title indicates, a collection of veterinary notes intended to inform, guide and assist all those involved with the care and welfare of cats. It is not intended to be a do-it-yourself manual nor a feline encyclopaedia.

Explanations have been kept as simple as possible, but the temptation of over-simplification has, I hope, been resisted. The reader may find some chapters heavy going and, for this, I am sorry. I did not intend the book to be over-erudite but certain subjects, e.g. feline viruses, are complex and over-simplification would only result in distortion of the facts. Some repetition will be found throughout the book but for this I make no apology. This is a book of notes which are meant to advise rapidly, concisely and effectively. To fulfil this role some repetition is unavoidable.

Thirty-three chapters written by 26 authors, all eminent in their particular fields, present up-to-the-minute facts relating to cats and their management. Like the two companion volumes, the book is divided into specific sections. It opens with a section on the new owner which discusses the responsibilities of owning a cat. Chapters are devoted to the fast growing field of feline behaviour, both normal and abnormal. Catteries and cattery management are discussed in depth as is the role of the veterinary nurse in feline nursing. Useful information on nursing the sick cat complements chapters on administration of medicines and first aid. The section on feline infectious disease is deliberately comprehensive and is as up-to-date as deadlines allow. In this section will be found the very latest information. Feline neurology as distinct from feline orthopaedics is another newly established discipline which is fully described in the appropriate chapter.

Symptoms are the patient's subjective impression of the disorder and thus strictly can only be used in connection with conditions involving

Figures 1 and 2 Trevor and Jean Turner were not short of enthusiastic feline co-operation in the preparation of this book

humans. In animals we have to depend on observation of the signs of the disease since the patient's symptoms are not communicable to us.

Exciting new diagnostic methods and treatments are attaining a previously inconceivable level of precision. These however often involve considerable cost and it is for this reason that a chapter has been included on the advantages of pet health insurance which, like man, horse and dog, is available for cats too. It is worth consideration.

As a book of notes, I am sure omissions will come to light. I will be glad to learn of them and will do my best to rectify any faults in the future. I hope the book will be of value and interest to all who live with cats, be they breeders or pet owners, not to mention those veterinary surgeons and veterinary nurses looking for authoritative, easily understood, up-to-the-minute explanations of sometimes complex issues.

I am grateful to my co-authors for making it all possible and above all to Jean, my wife, whose nimble fingers and inexhaustible patience ensured that deadlines slipped little.

Trevor Turner
Mandeville Veterinary Hospital
1994

The New Owner

1

SHOULD I HAVE A CAT?

Growing up in a small leper colony on the African veldt, the companion I most longed for was a cat, but my parents were adamant in their refusal, for they believed that a cat would carry the leprosy bacteria. The only cats I ever saw were thin little brown cats known as 'Kaffir cats', which roamed from hut to hut; we never discovered if they had more illustrious forbears. The Xosa tribe loved them, and they survived on the scraps they were thrown.

It was not surprising that a cat was the first thing I wanted when we settled in England. With nobody to advise us, we visited a pet shop in the main street of Folkestone, the town where my father was appointed to work. Crouched in a rather dirty pen was a tiny black kitten, crying piteously. I was allowed to hold him, and he snuggled into my coat – he'd obviously decided he was coming home with me! My father paid the princely price of 2s 6d for him (about 15 pence these days!), and we took him, shivering, on the bus to our home near the sea-front.

I certainly learned cat care the hard way, for Sooty was infested with fleas and worms. We managed to find a vet, who was rather contemptuous about cats – but in 1937 the care of cats was low on the list of veterinary studies. However, he gave us tablets for the worms, powder for the fleas and informed us that Sooty also had mange, a horrible skin disease which needed months of care before he was finally fit to live a normal life!

Needless to say, I had not thought much about the practical side of owning a cat, as I ought to have done. After all, with proper care, a cat should be a companion for at least 15 years. It needs regular feeding, grooming, a certain amount of exercise and, most important of all, *love*. Today, it can cost as little as £5, or as much as £600. Food costs about £3 a week and vaccinations about £40 a year. These are the very basic costs, but if there is illness, or if the cat is entered for shows, then of course the costs rise dramatically.

If you have considered all this, and are *sure* you want a cat – then go ahead. You could not have a more loving companion, one who will always want you, and who will be loyal and, sometimes, possessive. Added to these is the bonus that today medical opinion believes that stroking a cat helps reduce stress, and even lowers blood pressure.

Complete novices at cat buying usually think of the pet shop as the obvious place to find a cat, but actually there are other sources, e.g. breeders. Nevertheless, a pet shop MAY be able to help, even if they have no cats. These days the best pet stores do *not* keep kittens in cages, waiting to be sold, because of the risk of infection in such situations, and of those stores that do many are unfortunately not entirely honest about the kittens' ages. Many are taken too young from the mother, and no amount of love from an owner can compensate for the mother's care.

The better sort of pet store will probably supply details of people who have litters, both 'moggies' and pedigrees, whose homes you can visit. Also, most local newspapers carry advertisements for kittens. And by far the best way to find a pedigree kitten is to look in the pages of Britain's two specialist cat magazines, the weekly *Cats*, which is the official journal for the Governing Council of the Cat Fancy, or the monthly *Cat World*. Both have columns of cats and kittens for sale, and both contain useful and interesting articles.

Then must come the decision – shall I buy a cat or a kitten? My own advice is always choose a kitten. Firstly, because a young kitten (the ideal age is 12 weeks) will 'bond' with its new owner, and the two will gradually learn each other's ways. Secondly, because if an adult is for sale, the question must be asked: 'Why is an adult cat being sold?' Unwary buyers commonly find that the cat is dirty, not a good breeder, or, worst of all, has an incurable disease.

The ideal is to buy two kittens, for they settle down more quickly, do not grieve for their mother so much, and, if the owners go out to work, amuse each other while they are away. Then must come the decision, long or short hair? If the litter is a non-pedigree there is not a great deal of difference as the 'longhairs' never have a very long coat, and grooming is usually simple. There may be longhairs *and* shorthairs in one litter, for the longhaired gene, being recessive, can be 'carried' by both parents, resulting in a 'mixed' litter. With pedigree cats, however, there is a vast range of coats and temperament which can be broadly divided into three categories, Longhairs, Semi-Longhairs and Shorthairs. The different pedigree types will be discussed in a later chapter.

Basically, a longhaired cat may be Persian, with the full, rather flat face, or non-Persian, where the coats are less profuse and heads are longer. A Persian's temperament is almost always placid and gentle, while a non-Persian, or Semi-Longhair, is sometimes more temperamental. Both types are affectionate and fun loving, but Persians *must* be well-groomed daily if they are to remain free of tangles. The Persian coat-length is man-made, longer-haired coats having been chosen for breeding in each generation

Figure 3   Persian kittens are animated fluff balls

until today's wonderful fluffy Persians appeared. The very first 'Persians' are believed to have been the semi-longhaired Angoras brought to Britain in the eighteenth century, which were bred with the household cats of that time. It has taken nearly three centuries to reach today's standard for Persians, the best of which are massive-bodied cats with large round heads, tiny ears, snub noses and fantastic coats in every possible colour. The breeders of today study genetics in order to understand fully what they are doing, though unfortunately some still have no idea as to which factors are dominant and which recessive. The long hair in itself is due to a recessive gene, whilst many of the colours are 'dilutes' of the original dominant blacks and tabbies. This complex subject will be dealt with in another chapter (see Chapter 31, Genetics).

Curiously, also classified as 'Longhairs' are the Exotics, which are Persian-type cats with short coats! This variety is comparatively new, and is the result of careful planning. Good Persian types were bred to the 'chunkiest' British Shorthairs. The F1 generation was, of course, entirely shorthaired, but of indefinite type. The project needed several breeders with different lines to cooperate to widen the gene pool. After five generations there are now a few really good Exotic types being bred, so that in future it will be possible to breed Exotic to Exotic with good-type kittens being born.

The Semi-Longhairs are very beautiful. Several of them come from other countries, while others are simply longhaired varieties of pedigree Shorthairs. Those imported to Britain are the massive Maine Coon cats from the USA; the strangely limp-limbed Ragdolls, also from the USA; the

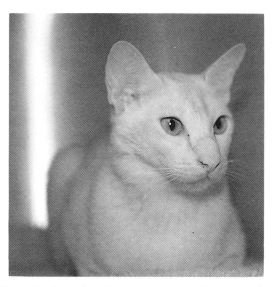

Figure 4 Some breeds are elegant and short coated, like this Abyssinian

large graceful Norwegian Forest Cats; the magnificent Sacred Cats of Burma, known as Birmans; and the silky-coated, auburn-tailed swimming cats from Turkey. That they enjoy swimming is absolutely true, as I have watched them enjoying a dip! All these cats have fascinating histories, which will be told in Chapter 31, Genetics.

The Semi-Longhairs derived from the Shorthairs are:

(a) The Somalis, bred from Abyssinians. Having the same lithe grace as the Abyssinians, they are becoming very popular.
(b) The Tiffanies. These are from the recessive genes in the Burmillas, which are themselves Shorthairs and the result of breeding Burmese to Chinchillas.
(c) The Balinese, bred from Siamese.
(d) The Angoras, bred from Orientals.

Shorthairs are divided into British and Foreign.

I previously mentioned the British Shorthairs. These sturdy cats are truly the 'Bulldog' of the cat world. Short in body and legs, with round, neat-eared heads and fairly short tails, they have been bred from the original non-pedigree house cats of former years. Their coats are crisp, and, like the Persians, they now come in every possible colour. Not as placid as Persians, they are great companions and live to a good age. Classified with the British Shorthairs are the Manx, the little tail-less cats which originated on the Isle of Man. They will always be few in number, as they do not breed easily, carrying a lethal gene which often results in deformed kittens when bred like-to-like. It takes a brave person to breed Manx, as it is heart-breaking to watch a litter born knowing that some will not survive.

Foreign Shorthairs are those breeds which have long bodies, legs and tails, thus being distinctly different from the British. Their varieties are many, and all are equally fascinating. They are possibly more excitable than the Persians and British but are highly intelligent, making devoted pets. Abyssinians are said to derive from Egypt, but, with their tawny, lithe bodies, always remind me of lions. As with all the Foreign Shorthairs, they are fine-boned yet muscular. Their coats are sleek, with three bands of 'ticking', and their heads are of medium length with expressive gold or green eyes. They seem to be always on the move, and are happiest when they have a garden where they can play.

Truly 'Foreign' are the Russian Blue cats, which came to Britain from Russia in the 1800s. The early Russian Blues were noted for their thick blue coats, which resembled sealskins. Sadly, due to the fact that they had to be bred with other breeds, their coats are no longer so plushy, although breeders are working hard to improve them. They are extremely elegant, with large, high-set ears and brilliant green eyes. Some breeders are now producing Black or White Russians, which seems to me a pity as they are *not* typical.

Another lovely blue cat from foreign parts is the Korat. Imported to Britain from the USA, they originated in the Far East. Although they are fine-boned, they do not have the length of the other Foreigners, having short cobby bodies and a beautiful heart-shaped face with huge round eyes of a brilliant, almost luminous, green. They are still uncommon cats, since breeders are strictly forbidden to outcross them to any other breeds.

In 1950 came a great surprise for cat-lovers in the form of a *natural* genetic mutation. Amongst a litter of ordinary farm kittens bred by Mrs Ennismore of Bodmin Moor, Cornwall, was a red and white male with a distinctly curled coat. Her veterinary surgeon stated, after examining the kitten, that it was probably a natural mutant, which was proved by mating this male back to his mother, an ordinary Shorthaired Tortoiseshell, when two more curly coated kittens were born! By this time the media had picked up the story, and Mrs Ennismore was persuaded to breed all known relations to the original curly coated male, named Kallibunker. As would be expected with so much indiscriminate mating, more curly coated kittens were born, but many were weak and failed to survive. Fortunately, a very knowledgeable member of the Cat Fancy, Brian Stirling-Webb, offered to take up the cause of these unique cats, and, with a group of friends, and by judicious outcrosses, he managed to breed some healthy curly coated kittens, which became known as Rex cats, as they closely resembled the Rex rabbits.

In 1960, another curly coated kitten was born to a semi-wild female living near a tin mine in Buckfastleigh, Devon. The finder, Miss Beryl Cox,

Figure 5 The curly coated Rex could almost have been permed. Devon Rex kitten

had read of the Rex cats of Cornwall, and, assuming that this recent find (a mole-grey male) must be a relation, contacted Mr Stirling-Webb. He, together with Mrs A. Watts, bought the new kitten, which was, in due time, mated to a third generation offspring of Kallibunker. To the great disappointment of all concerned, three similar matings only produced straight-coated kittens, and it was decided that the Devon Rex, Kirlee, was a completely different genetic type.

Since then, these two distinct varieties, now named Cornish and Devon Rex, have been bred completely separately, and are classified as Foreign Shorthairs. This seems an anomaly to many people, since the breeds originated in England, but they had the long bodies and fine bones of Foreign-type cats, and the Governing Council of the Cat Fancy decided that the Foreign category was right for them. They are still expensive to buy, but are extremely popular as they are very 'people-orientated', need very little grooming and are particularly good with children.

Burmese cats originated in Burma, where they were owned by the wealthy and by the Keepers of the Temples. They were sleek-coated brown cats of medium size and very distinctive golden eyes. In 1930 an American psychiatrist managed to purchase one. A student of genetics, he was able to prove that the Burmese were, in fact, a hybrid variety of Chocolate-pointed Siamese. Careful selective breeding produced more Brown Burmese, which were known as sable in the USA. As a matter of fact, similar cats had been bred in England from Siamese since the late 1800s! However, the breed was not properly established in Britain until Mr and Mrs France, who were already breeding Siamese, imported one male and two female Burmese in 1949. In 1955, after a long struggle, the Burmese Cat Club was founded and the Governing Council of the Cat Fancy gave official recognition. Now these delightful, very mischievous cats are bred in all colours. They are wonderful show cats and make delightful family pets.

As I have mentioned, the beautiful, graceful Siamese were first brought to Britain in the mid-1800s. More has been written about them than about any other pedigree cat; and at one time, if a pedigree cat was mentioned, the usual reply was, 'Oh, you mean a Siamese'. The original ones were Sealpoints, their colouring depending on a colour-restriction gene. In other words they are, basically, dark brown cats with the colour restricted to the points (ears, mask, paws and tail). It is a fact that the first Siamese did come from Siam (now Thailand) but much of their history remains shrouded in mystery. Soon after the Sealpoints were recognized, Bluepoints (being the dilute of black) appeared in a litter, and today there are Siamese-pointed cats in every possible colour.

In the early days Siamese had long elegant bodies, fine legs and long whipped tails. Their heads were gentle wedges and their ears were large. Due largely to the wishes of our judges, the type is now greatly changed, the top Siamese having long, triangular heads with completely straight profiles. The eye colour is still a brilliant sapphire and the shape is very Oriental. These cats are superb, though many people wanting pets still prefer the gentle 'old-fashioned' look.

From the Siamese have come the Orientals, slim cats of Siamese type but without the colour restriction. Much hard work has gone into the production of these dainty cats, which combine the intelligence of the Siamese with the added bonus of fascinating colours.

Finally there are the 'rarities'.

The Ocicats are the result of matings between British-type cats, Abyssinians and Siamese, that have resulted in an attractive, medium-sized, golden-spotted cat. In England, the Asian cats are derived from the breeding of Burmese with Chinchillas, producing the Burmillas ('ticked' cats of Burmese type) and the Tiffanies (Semi-Longhairs with a shadowy-tabby pattern).

The almost-naked Sphynx cats, resembling Devon Rex without a coat, have also been imported into Britain in the 1980s. Said to have been a natural mutation in North America, they are not yet officially 'recognized' by the Governing Council of the Cat Fancy but a number are now being bred. What they lack in coat they compensate for in character, as they have extremely affectionate personalities.

The Singapuras are now making their appearance in Britain, but they are *not* the same as the true Singapuras which roam the streets of Singapore.

Those imported come from the USA and are the result of mating true Singapuras with Abyssinians. They are attractive, but are not the same as the pale-coated, large-eyed street cats of Singapore.

Many of the pedigree cats are outside the average family's purse, as they can cost up to £1000, due to the high cost of importation and quarantine. However, many people nowadays prefer to have pedigree cats as they can then be certain of the temperament a cat will have.

Those owners of one cat who are uncertain whether or not to introduce a new one into the family need not worry. I always think that two cats is ideal. They usually become inseparable companions, and, if the owners have to be out to work, are quite happy to be left alone, whereas one cat may become lonely and neurotic.

Before leaving the subject of choosing a new pet, I must add a word of warning about kittens reared in outside catteries. These may be beautiful and healthy, but they will *never* have the loving personality of a home-reared kitten, due to the fact that they probably only see a human three times a day. Cats are *not* pack animals and respond badly to being reared in a 'farming' habitat.

The new kitten

Having decided that a cat is the right pet, the decision whether to choose a 'moggie' or a pedigree must be made. If it is to be a 'moggie', the local veterinary surgeon is the first person to approach. In any case, it is wise to meet the vet who will treat your pet, as some vets are known to be 'good' with cats, whilst others are really not interested. Obviously the vet should be located as near as possible to the client in order that as little time as possible is lost in getting there when there is an emergency. It is easy to make enquiries. If neighbours or your doctor own cats, ask which vet they consult. If this fails, the secretary of the Feline Advisory Bureau* can usually advise for most vets and cat owners belong to this most helpful Bureau. It is a non-profit-making organization, formed in 1961 by a dedicated cat lover, which has gradually become a worldwide organization. I was a founding member and have received much valuable advice over the years.

Most vets keep details of families who have kittens or cats which need homes and it is sensible to approach your local practice. It is still important to visit the home where the cat or kitten lives if at all possible. On entering the house, there should be no 'catty' smells, a sign that the place is not hygienic. The room in which the cats are kept should be warm and

* Feline Advisory Bureau, 235 Upper Richmond Road, Putney, London SW15 6SN. Tel. 081 789 9553.

Figure 6   Kittens should be well fed, bright-eyed and bold

comfortable. It is wonderful if, on entering the room, one of the cats or kittens comes up to you, so 'choosing' its new owner. Quite often, it will turn out to be the best pet for you.

Sometimes, one kitten in a litter may be tiny and frightened. Such a kitten is very appealing but it is not wise to choose such a 'runt'. Often it has failed to grow because of an internal problem such as persistent diarrhoea or a faulty heart. If the litter is a 'moggie' one, the father is usually not available, but if it is a pedigree litter, it may be possible to see the father, who, if home-owned, will probably be in his own, warmed stud house (see Chapter 30, Breeding).

The mother should be with her offspring and it is important to note if she is fit and friendly. Each kitten should look well-fed and bright-eyed. Having chosen one, or been chosen by a kitten, it should be carefully and gently examined. The eyes should be bright, the legs strong and the rear end clean, with no trace of faeces sticking to it. The teeth should be even, the tongue clean and there should be no trace of 'snuffling' nose or mouth ulcers. Both the last mentioned are signs of one of the cat flu types of illness. If a kitten or cat has any such symptoms, it should not be chosen, as it will probably become really ill under the stress of moving house.

Examine the coat carefully for signs of dirt, which may indicate the presence of fleas. It is very difficult to keep kittens completely free of fleas.

An odd one is acceptable but flea dirt is the sign of a real infestation. To test for flea dirt, comb the coat over a piece of damp paper. If the tiny black flecks turn to tiny spots of red, this is a sure sign of infestation as flea faeces contain dry blood. With modern preparations flea control is relatively simple and your veterinary practice will advise you.

If the choice is for a pedigree kitten, it is a good idea to obtain a copy of the official Standard of Points which costs £3 and is obtainable from the Governing Council of the Cat Fancy.* This little book provides all the information any owner could need and gives a good idea of how the cat should look.

View the kittens with a critical eye. If the breeder is honest, he or she will point out the good and the bad points. Sadly some breeders are only anxious to sell their stock and will swear a kitten will grow out of a certain fault. This is unlikely to be true and it is not worth taking a risk, especially if the kitten is intended for showing. If intended merely as a pedigree pet, some faults are acceptable but they should be pointed out, discussed and accepted at purchase.

Ideally, no kitten should leave home before it is 12 weeks old, and should be fully vaccinated against feline infectious enteritis and cat flu. If a kitten is bought for breeding it is also advisable to have it vaccinated for chlamydia (a nasty infectious eye disease) and for feline leukaemia, which is also contagious. To have all the vaccinations can cost as much as the kitten, and they all have to be annually renewed. I personally only vaccinate against chlamydial infection if I want to breed. On the other hand, the vaccinations against flu and enteritis are essential for the infection is found almost everywhere.

If the new kitten has a pedigree it is the breeder's responsibility to supply a Governing Council of the Cat Fancy pedigree and an official transfer form. This has to be completed by the new owner and sent to the GCCF office as soon as possible. The breeder may have registered some of the kittens on the non-active list. This means that those kittens may not be used for breeding. The reason for this may be that there is a genetic fault which does not affect the kitten but might be passed on to its offspring, or it may simply be that the breeder feels that, in today's economic climate, it is unwise to breed more kittens.

In any case, the breeder should provide a diet sheet for each kitten for it is important that the kitten continues to have the same diet it has been weaned on to otherwise a gastric upset may ensue. The breeder should also provide a vaccination certificate, even if the kitten has only had its first 'shot', and a note to say when it was last wormed. (I shall discuss this in another chapter.)

* Governing Council of the Cat Fancy, 4–6 Penel Orlieu, Bridgwater, Somerset TA6 3PG. Tel. 0278 427575

Up to now I have not mentioned the question of sex. This is always a difficult problem for a pet owner. Both sexes make delightful pets although I have found that males are usually the more affectionate of the two. Finance may influence the decision. A pet kitten may be neutered from about 5 to 7 months of age. It is usually cheaper to neuter a male than a female. However, if you are considering using a male for exhibition and breeding, think carefully. A male will need his own stud house and run and suitable accommodation for his ladies, plus heating for both. Stud fees seldom cover the cost. *Think carefully!*

It may take several weeks to make the final decision on the type of cat or kitten. Most breeders take pride in showing their kittens to prospective buyers. One piece of advice is worth remembering. If there are any sickly kittens offered for sale, not only is it unwise to buy one, it is criminal to visit another breeder before changing your shoes and washing your hands. This may sound unusually fussy but I have known whole litters of kittens actually to die after being visited by a prospective buyer who had previously visited sick kittens. This is also worth remembering if, in time, the new owner decides to breed, when the same precautions prevail.

When the final decision has been made and a date fixed for the collection of the cat or kitten, the preparations for the newcomer must be made. Most good pet shops these days have a selection of beds for cats. If quite a small kitten has been chosen, probably the favourite bed (apart from the owner's!) is a 'beehive' shape made of a soft synthetic material with a washable cover. A larger cat will probably prefer a round beanbag type of bed. Again these should have washable covers. Since all cats drink a fair amount of water, it is advisable to buy a deep non-tippable bowl plus several plastic dishes for food. For grooming, shorthaired cats need strong bristled brushes and narrow toothed combs. Longhaired cats need a brush with widely spaced hard plastic bristles and both fine and wide toothed combs. A supply of good canned cat foods should be bought, remembering that cats prefer variety. Modern dried foods such as Hill's Science Diet or Iams (Eukanuba) are excellent and are often appreciated for at least one meal of the day. They are excellent for dental care and for this reason I always mix a fine puppy biscuit with all canned or fresh food as this ensures good teeth in old age. It must be well mixed with the moist food as all cats and kittens are crafty and will cunningly push aside the biscuit and eat only the meat.

Very important in the preparations are the litter and litter trays. Many types of litter are now available and are sold in supermarkets and pet stores. It is wise to budget for the larger sizes of cat litter since in the long run it is cheaper than buying small bags. Litter trays should measure about 24 × 18 inches (60 × 45 cm) at least and should be at least 2 inches (5 cm) deep. If the trays are shallow, the cat or kitten will spread the litter everywhere, causing much unnecessary mess! The litter tray should be kept reasonably close to the bed at first, so that a kitten knows immediately where to go. If the house is fairly large, it is wise to keep one tray upstairs and one downstairs. I personally have always used the white 'Fuller's earth' type litter granules, the only disadvantage being the weight. There are now lightweight litters available made of compressed wood shavings. These are probably not suitable for longhaired cats as the granules tend to stick in the coat. All in all, the choice of litter is very much a personal decision both for the cat and the owner.

When buying the litter, it is wise to buy a couple of scoops, one for lifting up the clean litter and another perforated scoop for removing damp lumps of litter or faeces. It is not necessary to discard a tray of litter when cleaning it. The 'used' lumps should be removed and put in a refuse sack, the clean litter tipped into a plastic washing up bowl and the litter tray washed, disinfected with Domestos or household bleach and the 'old' litter plus a top-up of fresh litter put back into the tray. If the newcomer is a kitten it is kind to position one tray in the kitchen and one on the upstairs landing. An older cat should manage with one tray provided the house is not too large.

So, the great day comes for the arrival of the new addition to the household. As yet I have not mentioned a carrier for the cat or kitten. Whilst a strong cardboard carrying box as supplied by the RSPCA or your veterinary surgeon will suffice, I always think it wise to buy a stronger type of carrier as there will be many times when it will be needed. I always use a carrier with a top opening lid. These come in many sizes, are hard wearing and easy to disinfect. However, nowadays the plastic carriers with front opening doors are much favoured. These are fairly light and easily disinfected but the front opening door causes problems since, if the cat is disinclined to come out, it is much harder to remove him. Another choice is the all-wire basket. Similar in appearance to the original wicker baskets, they are very strong but need to be given a protective cover when used in winter.

The first weeks

Sceptics may laugh, but it is no exaggeration to say that the first introduction of a new cat or kitten to its owner is as exciting as the arrival of a first baby! Each has so much to learn from the other and the gradual 'bonding' of a new relationship is very rewarding.

On arrival the new pet should be taken from its carrier and given much cuddling and affection. However frightened it may be, it will slowly respond and want to curl up in your arms.

If there is already another pet in the house, too rapid a confrontation should be prevented. The new arrival should be shown the litter tray and then be allowed to explore. When the survey is completed, the newcomer should be shut in the room with the litter tray whilst the other cat or dog is allowed to smell around the rest of the rooms to pick up the scent of the newcomer. When each appears satisfied, the two should be introduced at feeding time when both will probably be more interested in the food! 'Neutral ground', a room not normally used by either, is a good first meeting place.

Hopefully the two will then be weary and decide to have a sleep. This is the time to show the kitten the bed when it will usually fall into an exhausted sleep. The new owner, too, will be somewhat tired and should relax over a drink whilst the future is planned.

From now on I shall refer to the new arrival as a kitten, as a new older cat will need less attention but just as much tender, loving care. As previously mentioned, it is very important to follow as closely as possible the diet to which the kitten has been accustomed. Any completely different food will probably result in an attack of diarrhoea.

A reasonable diet for a kitten between 3 and 5 months would be as follows:

8 a.m.	Two tablespoons raw minced beef or cooked chicken, mixed with a dessertspoonful of puppy meal.
12 noon	Two tablespoons good canned kitten food mashed with a few pieces of puppy meal.
7 p.m.	Two tablespoons cooked fish or chicken mixed with a little puppy meal.

Alternatively one of the complete kitten foods can be offered. These are available both dry and canned and it should be emphasized that today dry complete foods do not cause urinary problems.

Last thing at night I usually offer a small saucer of undiluted evaporated milk unless the breeder has advised against it. Milk gives some kittens diarrhoea, although this is usually cow's milk. The mother's cat milk is far richer than ordinary cow's milk, which is why evaporated milk is the nearest substitute.

Alternatives to this diet can be given with advantage. Raw liver contains taurine, a very important amino acid necessary for a cat's growth. This is now added to many commercial diets. Too much liver can cause problems due to excess of vitamin A. Cheese contains important protein, fats and minerals. Fish, given occasionally, contains protein and vitamins. The oily fish, such as herrings, mackerel, pilchards, sardines, sprats, tuna and salmon, are excellent as they contain protein, taurine, fats and vitamins. However, too frequent feeding of fish is not good and occasionally kittens may be allergic. This usually shows in a skin rash but it really is rare.

Calcium is an important part of a kitten's diet as it, together with phosphorus, is responsible for the rigidity, or strength, of bones. Milk and cheese are rich in calcium, while phosphorus is found in red meat. Poultry, fish and dairy products are reasonable sources of calcium and phosphorus. Since lack of calcium can cause problems, most proprietary canned foods today contain calcium, phosphorus and added vitamins.

Veterinarians often suggest the addition of cooked rice to a kitten's diet. This provides carbohydrates, as does puppy meal. With a varied diet it is not usually necessary to add extra vitamins to the food except in cases of added stress, such as pregnancy or after illness.

Dried cat foods such as Hill's Science Diets or Iams are complete meals and need no additives except water to be drunk but I have found cats and kittens become bored with an all-dry diet. If the kitten has to be left alone for some hours, a saucer of dried food can be left without fear of contamination by flies. In the early days of dried cat foods there was a rise in the number of male cats who developed blockages of the urethra causing great difficulty with the passing of urine. This is feline urolithiasis syndrome, now known as feline lower urinary tract disease (FLUTD). The problem was traced to the high magnesium content in dried foods. This was corrected and all types are now safe. However, the animal should always have access to fresh water.

Quite often, on hearing all this advice, people comment, 'It's strange that a lot of cats exist quite well on table scraps'. Probably the word 'exist' is the important one for it is true that cats can eke out an existence on scraps but they are usually sickly animals who have short lives.

The first night in a new home is always traumatic for a kitten, which will be missing its mother and littermates. It is important to start off in the way in which you, the new owners, want to continue. If you are happy to have the little kitten on your bed then all is well – everybody will be happy! However, if you feel that the kitten should sleep in a bed provided in the kitchen then firmness is the answer. The kitten can be tucked up with a hot water bottle and the door closed. There will be cries for a short time but kittens are highly intelligent and soon learn the rules. If, at first, the kitten urinates or defecates in the wrong place, it must be firmly placed in the litter tray. Kittens are amazingly intelligent and mistakes are relatively few. They are inherently clean. Whatever happens, a kitten must not be smacked. This destroys trust and creates stress. Where an 'accident' has occurred the area should be washed as soon as possible with either weak household bleach or a biological detergent.

When the kitten has had a couple of days to settle, it should be taken to the owner's veterinarian for a general health check and, if necessary, vaccination. Most breeders do not sell their kittens until the vaccination programme is at least under way. The usual programme consists of two injections of vaccines against feline infectious enteritis and the cat flu syndrome. The first injection should be given at 9 weeks of age and the second at 12 weeks. It is *essential* that every kitten has the full vaccination

Figure 7 Laid back, longhaired Smokes arrive for their first veterinary check-up

course. Without the full course the kitten is unprotected and will almost certainly be vulnerable to infection from any passing stray. Once the course of two injections has been given only an annual booster is necessary and your veterinarian will provide a certificate of vaccination which gives a date for the first booster.

All young kittens should be wormed by the breeder but it is important that further worming is carried out. This should be discussed on the first meeting with the veterinarian and at the same time as should any queries regarding vaccination, feeding, neutering, and so on.

The serious business now over, there comes the time of enjoyment for any new owner and kitten. Both have so much to learn from each other. In these first weeks, the kitten's character is formed. There is a saying that owners grow to look like dogs and it is certainly true that a kitten's personality grows to be like its owner's! A 'nervy' owner will produce a jumpy, nervous kitten which could grow into a spiteful cat. It is very important to speak gently to the new arrival, to allow time for games with it and time for it to tell you its needs. After 30 years as a breeder I still feel the same thrill at the arrival of a new kitten as I did as a novice and it's a wonderful feeling.

The adult cat

It is impossible to say exactly when a cat becomes adult although it is officially called an adult when it is over 9 months of age. The Foreign Shorthairs tend to mature more quickly than the Longhairs and I have known a precocious 5-month-old Siamese successfully to mate his first queen! Each cat matures in its own time and the Longhairs are generally slower. Most Longhair males of 8 months still think flirtatious queens are there for games but there is no hard and fast rule. A male destined to be a stud cat should not be allowed to run freely with the girls after the age of 5 months.

At 9 months kittens should have shed their temporary teeth for strong, healthy adult teeth. Occasionally temporary teeth will interfere with the growth of the permanent dentition and the vet will probably advise removal of the old tooth to allow normal dentition to proceed. This is not cosmetic surgery and should never be confused with it as cosmetic surgery is *not* allowed by the Governing Council of the Cat Fancy.

If the kitten has been bought solely as a pet, neutering must be considered. Known as castration for males and spaying for females this operation is usually carried out when the kitten is mature, as it can be from as young as 5 months, but more frequently at 6–7 months of age. At this age all the hormones should be in 'working order' and neutering will cause no great problems. Many people argue that it is better to spay a queen after having a litter but this is arguable. Equally it could be said that it only means that there are yet more unwanted kittens to be homed! With male kittens it is said that he is being deprived of his natural instincts. Again this is absolute nonsense. An entire male will begin to roam outside his usual territory and other tomcats will attack him, often giving him bites that abscess, so it is clearly kinder to neuter the kitten.

The vet will advise that the kitten is not allowed any food or drink after midnight on the night before the operation. He will probably arrange that the kitten is brought to the surgery early in the morning. A consent form for the operation will need to be signed and the kitten should be ready for collection later in the afternoon. It may be slightly wobbly after the operation and only a light meal should be offered that evening. On the following day all should be back to normal and the kitten will grow to be a happier, more contented pet.

Here I must add a brief word of warning. It is important when a routine operation is carried out that the owner makes certain that the type of operation is clearly written on the veterinary consent form and retains a copy. *Very occasionally* tragic mistakes have been made, for example a cat left for a blood test under anaesthetic has been mistakenly castrated. When a cat is a valuable stud, the sad consequences can be imagined, but such an occurrence is very very rare. However, it is protection for both parties if everything is clearly written down.

If a kitten is taught to play with the owner when young it will keep these playful ways until comparative old age. Pet stores sell myriads of toys and there is never any need for a cat to be bored. They soon learn to retrieve light objects just as well as a dog. They also learn to walk on a lead and most love to ride in cars, providing they start at a young age. One of the most important items to buy – or make if the materials are handy – is a solid scratching block. This saves the furniture providing the cat is shown how to use it at an early age. These scratching blocks are expensive to buy yet all that is necessary is a solid tree trunk about 8 inches in diameter fixed to a heavy block of wood which stands firmly on the floor. Thick cord is wound around the trunk to which can be fixed wooden arms on which toys and balls can be hung. This provides hours of pleasure as well as keeping the claws honed down.

By using some imagination, many types of home-made toys can be produced, one of the favourites being a set of cardboard boxes made into a maze. Kittens will spend countless hours running round the many 'passages' made by the boxes.

This brings to mind the question of exercise. All cats and kittens need a certain amount, and plants to nibble. If a garden is available, so much the better. However, even cats who live in high-rise apartments can have this need met. Most pet shops now sell trays of cocksfoot grass seed, which is the ideal type of grass for cats, being high in minerals and vitamin C. If the seeds are well soaked before being planted they germinate quickly, so a succession of trays can be grown. In addition to minerals and vitamins, grass does, of course, provide the fibre necessary in all diets, human and feline. Failing this, modern complete foods will provide all the necessary nutrients.

If a cat has access to a garden there are problems to be considered. The first one is safety, for in the crowded Britain of today, few suburban gardens are very far from traffic. In my village in Kent very few cats are allowed their freedom for there have been countless deaths on the roads. If possible it is a good idea to wire in part of the garden allowing a run for the pets. A strong mesh wire such as Weldmesh is excellent for this purpose. This can be fixed to concrete posts built 8 feet apart. The wire must be 8 feet high with an overhang of 3 feet held rigid by horizontal posts. This overhang not only prevents the cat from escaping but also prevents unwanted cats from paying visits. If these overhangs are placed along the entire fenced-in area there is no need for a complete roof of wire, which adds considerably to the cost. If just one cat is kept, purely as a pet, there need not be too much concern about infectious diseases being carried in by stray cats, but if several cats are kept for breeding then the possibility of infection becomes a real danger. I will discuss this later in the chapter on breeding (see Chapter 30).

If the pet cat decides to use the garden for toilet purposes, the area must be regularly dug over as it soon becomes contaminated and may also be a source of roundworm re-infestation. All cats should be wormed every 4–6 months in order to ensure adult egg-laying worms are eradicated from the bowel and the passage of infected eggs into the environment is reduced. It is usually only necessary to treat for roundworms (*Toxocara cati*) but if the cat has access to wild birds or mice then it may well also be infected with tapeworms and will need to be treated for these as well. Tapeworms are usually diagnosed by the presence of tiny pale-coloured segments (looking rather like rice grains) adhering to the hairs around the anus. These unpleasant worms are formed of numerous segments, some of which are passed in the faeces while the head of the worm remains buried in the wall of the intestine. Modern treatment causes no discomfort. Worms can cause irritation and loss of condition in the cat but actually cause the owner more problems since they are aesthetically unpleasant.

The years pass quickly, hopefully without any real health problems, and the kitten grows to be a loving adult, a part of the family circle. Although the Cat Fancy quotes a cat as being adult at the age of 9 months, it continues to grow until it is over 1 year. It is usually fully mature by the age of 2. At 6 months, two good meals a day are usually adequate and I have always given two meals throughout my cats' lives. When they are pregnant or nursing, they do, of course, need extra meals. There is no definite rule as to how much a cat needs at each mealtime. This must depend on the size and breed of the cat. Whilst treats such as pieces of cheese or proprietary treats may be given as rewards, it is a bad practice to offer titbits when the family eats as a cat can easily become a nuisance and even good friends may decide to stay away if an unwanted cat makes a nuisance of itself on the meal table.

However frequently a cat may be groomed, if it has access to grass where rabbits or other cats wander, contamination with fleas is always possible in summertime. Daily grooming should involve a check for fleas and flea dirt and if either are found the cat should be treated with a preparation prescribed by the vet. I emphasize this because there are some flea preparations for use on other animals which can cause illness and even death to a cat. This is a very important point to remember. DDT and BHC are both poisonous to cats, although safe with dogs, so it is always important to read the ingredients in any spray or powder. Flea collars are sometimes used on cats but generally should be used with care as cats can be allergic to the ingredients in the collars. The new generation 'pour-on' products are generally well tolerated.

If fleas or mites are present, it is useless to treat only the pets. The entire house needs treatment, however annoying this may seem. There are now several effective house sprays obtainable from veterinarians, who will advise using the spray on all floors, curtains and bedding. When I use these I treat one room at a time, keeping it closed for at least 12 hours. This may seem annoying but it is the only way to keep an insect-free household.

Remember, fleas only live for approximately 10 per cent of the time on the animal; the other 90 per cent is spent infecting the carpets!

The Cheyletiella mite, normally found on rabbits, has become almost endemic in many catteries. It is invisible to the naked eye but if a cat or kitten looks 'scurfy' and constantly licks, the presence of the mite should be suspected. Since it also affects humans, most veterinarians ask the owners if they have noticed any skin irritation. If the answer is 'yes' then the cat almost certainly has the mites. Unfortunately these annoying creatures are resistant to many of the usual insecticides, although selenium will kill them. A weekly bath using a preparation from your vet will rid the cat of the pests, although several weeks of treatment may be necessary.

Grooming

A daily groom is necessary for all cats and kittens. If it is made a pleasurable experience in the beginning the cat will really enjoy the daily brush. I always give a treat as a reward when the task is completed so that it becomes a pleasurable routine. Shorthaired cats need only a quick brush and comb but a longhair, especially a Persian, will often take a lot longer. I use a nylon bristle brush which is really strong enough to tease the hairs. Two types of combs are necessary and those with handles are easiest to use. A wide-toothed comb will deal with the odd knot, which can be gently teased until it comes away. The fine-toothed comb is useful for the 'furnishings' around the ears and also where fleas may be suspected. Brushing and combing should always be done in an upward movement, rather like back-combing, so that a well-groomed Persian resembles a powder puff in appearance.

Grooming must also include a gentle cleaning of the ears as ear mites (*Otodectes cyanotis*) may be picked up during any encounter with other cats, especially at shows. They also are almost invisible to the naked eye although they can be clearly seen through a magnifying glass as tiny white wriggling 'dots'. Their presence can be suspected if the cat constantly scratches or shakes its head. There may also be a dry waxy discharge which should always be regarded with suspicion. If present, the ears should be treated by drops supplied by your vet. I can clearly remember the time when my young queen collected mites during her first visit to a stud cat. Unfortunately I was blissfully unaware of the possibility of mites and it was not until I had actually sold the kittens and had irate calls from the new owners complaining that their new kittens had ear mites that I understood what I had done. I was terribly ashamed, but my vet was very calm and said this happened to all breeders at some time or other. He examined all my cats with an auriscope and all had ear mites. It took 6 months finally to eradicate them from the last cat so it was a lesson learned the hard way.

By the time a cat is about 8 years of age it can be considered middle aged. This is usually a time when entire queens have fewer kittens in their litters but a stud usually remains active and fertile for several more years.

Assuming that no emergencies arise, a regular annual or bi-annual visit to the vet is all that is necessary. This visit will be for the annual booster injections and at the same time the vet will give the cat a general health check to ensure there is nothing seriously wrong. As a cat ages its teeth tend to become coated with a build-up of tartar. If this is not removed the gums become infected with bacteria, cavities form in the teeth and they fall out if they are not extracted (see Chapter 14, Dentistry).

It is now possible to obtain special pleasant-tasting toothpastes for cats. If the cat has its teeth cleaned once a week and is regularly given some hard food, it is possible that the teeth will be retained until old age. Sometimes cats will resent any interference with their teeth and in this case your vet will suggest scaling the teeth under an anaesthetic.

As mentioned briefly earlier, it is very important to register with a vet who understands the problems of cats. As with human medicine, there are some vets who are wonderful with cats whilst others have not studied more than their basic needs.

Skin problems are not unusual in middle-aged cats. Eczema is quite common. The cat develops bare patches which cause irritation. A veterinarian must diagnose the cause since a hairless patch could be due to diverse causes, such as fleas or a hormone deficiency. Even with hormonal eczema control is often possible with a dosage of the necessary hormone. This can produce wonderful results with the cat regaining both its composure and lustrous coat. Unfortunately in some individuals these drugs can cause side effects. Remember fleas are by far the most common cause of eczema.

As the cat grows older its habits change. Though it will still enjoy games with its owner, it tends to sleep more. Sometimes a cat develops a seemingly unquenchable thirst. This may be a sign of diabetes or of kidney disease, both of which can be treated if the cat is taken to the veterinarian as soon as the symptoms are noted. Treatment is usually with special diets although diabetes mellitus may need daily injections.

Even if no disease develops, the cat's diet often needs to change slightly. If there are dental problems, it will probably not want to chew any pieces of meat, preferring instead a variety of good canned foods. Extra vitamins are also needed at this time, especially B vitamins, which are water-soluble vitamins that are often flushed out of circulation by the high fluid turnover due to the failing renal function.

If the cat seems to have difficulty in digesting food, and if the vet finds no specific illness, this may sometimes be a sign of simple old age, in which case a digestive aid such as Pro-zyme powder may be tried. Made by Univet, this is palatable and I have not yet found a cat which objects to half a teaspoonful mixed into the food. Pro-zyme is a mixture of enzymes and probiotics and should be obtainable from your veterinarian. In any case it is worth discussing the problem with him.

With approaching old age, a cat becomes less fussy about its own cleanliness. A normally fastidious animal, constantly washing itself, becomes a rather pathetic, untidy little creature. It is at this time that it most needs its owner gently to 'top and tail' it, generally helping with the necessary cleaning and reassuring it with gentle words. A younger pet in the house will sometimes take over as 'nursemaid' but every owner should be prepared to do everything to make the final years as happy, comfortable and warm as possible.

Eventually the old cat may find itself unable to crawl to its litter tray and may become dirty in the house. It is at this time the owner has to answer the question, 'Is it kind to keep my cat alive?' If the quality of life has become too poor then the answer *must* be 'no'. There is no particular age when a cat can no longer cope. Some may live well into their twenties whilst others seem to give up around 17 or 18 years.

The owner, who has been so close to the cat through all the years, will instinctively know when the time has come to make the decision. Sometimes a cat will die peacefully in sleep but others struggle on in misery. If it is too hard to make a final decision, rely on your veterinarian. It is not easy for a vet to advise euthanasia but most vets become family friends over the years at least to the pet if not the owner. No vet will say, 'You must put this cat to sleep,' but will quietly discuss the pros and cons of the case. When I have had to make this decision, I have found my vet to be a tremendous help as I am sure the reader will.

If the decision to end a cat's life is made the vet will usually allow the owner to hold the cat whilst an injection of an overdose of an anaesthetic is given. Within minutes the little cat is at peace. The vet will check the heart to make certain that life has gone. It is surprising how peaceful one's pet looks when life is done and the struggle is over. Remember that cats do not close their eyes when life has gone.

There is one final decision to be made and that is what to do with the body. Most veterinarians can arrange cremation or you may prefer burial in the garden. I used to bury my pets when I was young but in later life I feel that cremation is best as nobody can know what will happen to a garden when a house changes hands. Cremation services often have a facility for returning the ashes and these can, of course, be buried or scattered.

There are also several pet cemeteries throughout the country where your pet or the ashes can be buried. Most veterinarians have particulars. Some owners find it comforting to know where their pet's last resting place will be. However, such graves do have to be maintained and this can be costly.

After the death of a pet, an owner feels utterly bereft and this will only pass with time. I believe when the first hurt has eased it is a wise idea to choose another kitten or cat. It is not being disloyal to the first pet and a new kitten brings real joy. It is worth consideration.

2

CATS AND THE LAW

Cruelty

It will come as a surprise to many cat owners that there is very little legislation laid down to protect the felines who share our lives. In fact it was as recently as 1988 that the cat, along with other animals, ceased to be a second-class citizen to the dog in the eyes of the law. Prior to this, while a person could be disqualified from keeping a dog upon being convicted of an offence, it needed a second offence before they could be disqualified from keeping a cat.

Unlike the dog, the cat did not have to be licensed, and this seems to have very much influenced the attitudes of our legislators towards them. A change of approach only came about when the government scrapped the dog licence.

The Act of Parliament that provides the main source of protection for cats is the Protection of Animals Act 1911 (as amended). This Act, like all others, is broken down into sections, which spell out the legislation. For example, section 1 deals with the various offences that come within the scope of this Act and provides the penalties for those who are found guilty of such offences.

In all cases of cruelty brought under this Act it has to be proven that any suffering caused to a cat was *unnecessary suffering*. Unless this can be shown, any case brought before the court will fail.

Basically there are three ways in which offences may be caused to cats under this Act: (1) acts of commission; (2) acts of omission; and (3) the owner permitting acts of commission or omission.

1. *Acts of commission.* These are acts whereby a cat is caused unnecessary suffering as a result of someone's positive act, such as beating, kicking or torturing. It is also an act of commission to inflict *mental suffering* on a cat by a positive act.
2. *Acts of omission.* Perhaps the best example of such an act is that given in the Act itself, which is 'causing unnecessary suffering by

unreasonably failing to provide a cat with food, water, or veterinary treatment'.

3. *The owner permitting acts of commission or omission.* The first two offences have in common the fact that they can be committed by any person, not just the owner. This third type of offence can only be committed by the owner of a cat. A company or firm who own a cat can be prosecuted under this section.

The courts usually require the statement and evidence of an expert witness to prove that unnecessary suffering has been caused. This is usually the veterinary surgeon who examines the cat. Therefore, should your cat ever have the misfortune to be caused unnecessary suffering, you are advised to ensure that it is examined at the earliest possible moment.

Any person found guilty of causing suffering to a cat under this Act is liable upon summary conviction to a maximum penalty of imprisonment for a term not exceeding 6 months or to a fine not exceeding level five on the standard scale, *or both*. The courts also now have the power to disqualify a person convicted of cruelty from owning any animal for such a period of time as they deem fit.

Abandonment

Surprisingly, when one considers how traumatic it must be for a cat that has lived in a home, abandonment of an animal was not an offence under the Protection of Animals Act 1911 as originally passed. This omission was not rectified until 1960, with the passing of the Abandonment of Animals Act. This made it an offence for any owner or person having control of any animal to abandon it, 'whether permanently or not, without reasonable cause or excuse, he or she shall be guilty of an offence of cruelty within the meaning of the principal Act'. The 'principal Act' referred to is the Protection of Animals Act 1911, and the penalties upon conviction are the same as for it. Moreover, like most Acts, this is only in relation to offences committed in England and Wales. There are separate but similar Acts for Scotland and Northern Ireland.

In the case of abandonment, as can be judged from this wording, proof that unnecessary suffering has been caused is not required. It is enough to prove that suffering is *likely* to be caused. It should also be noted that the abandonment does not have to be permanent. A cat left in a basket in a car in hot weather, or left at home for a couple of days to fend for itself, could be considered as cases of abandonment.

The stealing of cats

The fear of having their cat stolen is a potent one among owners of both show and pet animals, the more so because of stories that those who have reported their cats missing or stolen have been told by the authorities that nothing can be done because they cannot be classed as property. On the contrary, this is quite untrue. Under the Theft Act 1968 'a person is guilty of theft if he/she dishonestly appropriates property belonging to another with the intention of permanently depriving the other of it'. The definition of property includes all creatures that by habit or training live in association with man, e.g. domestic animals, including cats and dogs. It is therefore clear that cats can be stolen, and owners should not allow themselves to be fobbed off, but should press for action to be taken by quoting this Act. A person guilty of theft can be sent to prison.

Threats and damage to pets

It is not uncommon for there to be dispute between cat owners and others, notably neighbours, who do not want cats near or in their gardens. Of course it is to be hoped that the responsible cat owner will do all he or she can to limit the annoyance their cat causes to others, but there are times when, despite everything done to placate those who complain, threats are made against cats, which can be very distressing. Should the situation get out of hand and actual attempts at harm be made, there is justice available via the Criminal Damages Act 1971. Amongst other things, this Act makes it an offence 'deliberately or recklessly to kill or injure domestic and captive animals which belong to or are in the care, control or charge of others'.

It is also an offence within the meaning of this Act to 'threaten to kill or injure such an animal', provided it can be shown that the threatening is done in such a way as to make the so-threatened fear that it will be carried out. In cases of this sort the court can order compensation to be paid.

Unforeseen owner absences

'What will happen to my cat should I have to go into hospital?' is a question often asked by worried elderly cat owners and people living alone. Discuss the possibility with a friend, who should contact the Social Services Department of your local authority if an emergency occurs and you are rushed into hospital. They have a duty to care for all goods and chattels belonging to a person admitted to any hospital or institution, animals being classed as belongings.

Section 48 of the National Assistance Act 1948, when read in conjunction with section 79 of the National Health Services Act 1946, calls upon local authorities 'to take reasonable steps to prevent or mitigate loss or damage to property' of any person admitted as a patient to any hospital.

Figure 8 Cats roam freely

The council are empowered to enter the home of the person who is confined in hospital at all reasonable times so that they can carry out this duty, and may recover any reasonable expenses as a civil debt.

It is a good idea for those who live on their own to carry a card stating they have a cat or cats at home that will require attention in an emergency. Most local authorities have contracts with local catteries to cover such emergencies.

Further legislation

I stated earlier that it was not until 1988 that cats, together with other animals, came to enjoy the same protection in law as dogs. However, although there has been an improvement in relation to acts of cruelty, our feline friends are still far behind in the legislative stakes on the issue of animal welfare. Examples are the Riding Establishments Act, and Codes of Conduct for the Guidance of Farmers keeping Cows, Sheep, Goats, Pigs, Turkeys and Chickens, but there is nothing for cats. Again, there is a Breeding of Dogs Act, which lays down the requirements to be met for dog breeding, but there is no similar legislation for cats. It seems to me that the legislators have failed to provide a fair deal for cats. Why the cat is considered not as worthy of protection as the dog is unclear. Indiscriminate breeding can give rise to deformed and unhealthy animals threatening the future of the breeds we have come to love whether they be cats or dogs.

The breeding and selling of the non-pedigree cat is also not regulated. This results in thousands of kittens being born and then destroyed through the lack of available homes.

When all this is taken into account, it is clear that there is an obvious need for immediate legislation to assist those who breed cats, and not least the cats themselves. Responsible breeders should be given at least the same status as dog breeders enjoy as a result of the Breeding of Dogs Act. Cats and those who care for them are not second-class citizens, and the sooner this fact is recognized the better. For example, at present, when a cat is injured or killed on the roads, it is left to individual police forces to decide whether or not they wish to be involved. It is time there was an umbrella Act in place that encompasses all animals.

When this subject has been broached in the past, one of the reasons given for treating cats as inferior to dogs was the fact that dogs were licensed. With the abolition of the licence this is not a valid argument. Since this is no longer so, I can see no valid reason for thinking in this way.

Death

The death of a pet can be very traumatic, and is likely to cause great grief. This is quite natural, since it is likely that it shared your life, home and relatively straightforward matter, either by burial in a pet cemetery or in the garden, or by cremation.

However, it is a fact little known by cat owners that once buried it is against the law to exhume a carcass without an order issued by the Ministry of Agriculture, Fisheries and Food. There are also a number of other documents required from the local authority, and from the owner of the land, should you not own the plot yourself.

The appropriate legislation is Article 13 of the Anthrax Order 1938. This has to be read in conjunction with other legislation and it is easier if owners just remember that an exhumation order is required if they want to remove any remains from the ground.

The Ministry of the Environment recently confused things even more by introducing the Control of Waste Regulations 1992. These were introduced to work in conjunction with the already existing Environment Protection Act 1990. These Regulations concern pets alive and dead and place certain restrictions upon cat and other pet owners together with veterinarians in respect of the disposal of *clinical waste*, which is defined in the Regulations as:

(a) '. . . any waste which consists wholly or partly of human or *animal* tissue, blood or other body fluids, *excretions*, drugs, or other pharmaceutical products, swabs or dressings or syringes, needles or sharp instruments, being waste which unless rendered safe may prove hazardous to any person coming into contact with it.'

(b) '. . . any other wastes arising from medical, nursing, dental, *veterinary*, pharmaceutical or similar practice, investigation or research, or the collection for blood transfusion, being waste which may cause infection to any person coming into contact with it.'

Careful study of these Regulations makes one realize that they place a burden of responsibility on cat owners. For example, the faeces of cats undergoing treatment can be classed as *clinical waste*, as can the soiled litter from used litter trays of such animals. It is no longer legal within the meaning of the Act and Regulations for a veterinary surgeon to return the body of a euthanased animal to its owner, and the veterinarian and owner can face prosecution because the Regulations forbid the burying of dead pets 'within the curtilage of a dwelling'.

This is how the law stands at present. However, the Environment Minister has stated in a letter to the British Veterinary Association, 'I am saddened by this unforeseen side effect of the Environment's Protection Act. The pet remains the owner's property and so they still have the right to bury it themselves.'

This letter has been circulated to all local authorities, in order that they may act with discretion. However, the law is the law and that is how it stands at present.

Deterrents

The fact has to be faced, not everyone likes cats. Some people go to extraordinary lengths to dissuade them from going into their gardens, in some cases resorting to the use of broken glass on top of their walls, spikes and even barbed wire. Those of us who own and care for cats feel that the use of such things is wrong, but they are not ruled out in law, it being generally accepted there that any person has a right to protect their land from trespassers, including cats, which often damage well-kept gardens.

What, if anything, can be done if a cat becomes injured as a result of these deterrents? At first glance, very little. However, a closer look reveals that there is some protection for pets.

The Highways Act 1980 states:

> where barbed wire is used on land adjoining a highway and constitutes a nuisance, the appropriate authority is empowered to require by notice the occupier of the land to abate the nuisance within such time, not being less than one month and not more than six months from the date of service of the notice, as may be specified therein.

Further reading of this Act reveals that 'barbed wire shall be deemed to be a nuisance to a highway if it is likely to be injurious to persons *or animals* lawfully using the highway'.

As there is nothing unlawful about a cat using a highway, should your cat become injured on barbed wire on a house that adjoins a highway, then it appears that the way is open for you to take action in the courts.

The Occupiers Liability Act 1984 can also be of assistance to the cat owner, even if a pet is considered to be unlawfully trespassing. The original Act of 1957 did not cover potential damage to trespassers, but this Act was built upon and expanded by judges via case law also to apply to intruders. As a result Parliament brought in the 1984 Act, which 'imposes a duty on an occupier to take such care as is reasonable in all circumstances to see that any uninvited entrants do not suffer injury by reason of any risk of which he is aware or has reasonable grounds to believe exists'.

Having looked closely at this legislation, and having discussed the matter with members of the legal profession, I believe the word 'trespasser' can apply to felines as well as humans. Therefore, should a cat be injured by these 'defences', then it could be argued that the occupier has a case to answer, and it just may be worth taking legal advice.

Unfortunately I can find no record of any such case being taken before a court under this particular Act.

In my opinion, it is always worth trying to come to an agreement before resorting to the law. Be conciliatory. Explain to your neighbours that you realize how much work they have put into their garden, that you understand how not everyone enjoys the company of cats and offer to pay for or replace any plants your cat digs up and destroys. If all else fails, it is worth remembering about these Acts. Sometimes just the threat of legal action works wonders.

Sadly, very few in the legal profession know the intricacies of the law when it comes to animal welfare.

I fervently hope that the hotch-potch of animal welfare is soon tidied up and made easier for all to understand.

3

HEALTH INSURANCE

Today's health care

Cats began the twentieth century very much as the poor relations of dogs, the favoured pets of Her Majesty Queen Victoria and her family. In those days, cats were relegated to the role of mouse-catcher and very often not fed beyond a saucerful of milk, because hunger was thought to make them better hunters. Consequently, the majority of cats led short lives of very poor quality, with disease, poor nutrition and lack of human compassion bringing them to an early death.

How different is the feline world in the closing years of this century! True, the cat now has a terrible enemy in the shape of the motor car, and there are a number of new epidemic diseases to contend with, but the cat is about to overtake the dog as the most popular domestic pet, because it is particularly suited to modern lifestyles. Today's cats are cosseted in a way their Victorian ancestors never dreamed of. Nowadays a multi-million-pound industry caters to Britain's 7 million cats, providing 545,000 tons a year of daintily packaged foods, some ready-to-eat from disposable saucers, toys and luxurious beds, carpeted towers to climb on and smart plastic carriers for the journey to the veterinarian's surgery for their vaccinations and necessary treatments. Cats are booked into professional grooming salons and boarded in five-star grade catteries. And an ever-increasing number of owners insure their cats so that in time of crisis they can always have the best veterinary treatment modern small animal practice has to offer.

Over the last 50 years there has been a tremendous expansion in the scope and expertise of small animal practice, particularly in the surgical and medical treatment of cats. Moreover, in recent years a completely new expertise has appeared in the veterinary world, the giving of advice and treatment of feline behaviour problems.

Surgical, medical and psychological conditions which were considered untreatable a few years ago can now be successfully dealt with thanks to major advances in anaesthesia, drugs and specialized equipment. Specialist vaccines have been evolved and improved to protect pet cats from the infectious diseases which are so easily passed from cat to cat; tests have been devised to identify the infectious diseases which were previously major causes of death.

However, probably the most spectacular advances have been made in the surgical repair of feline victims of road accidents. For instance, a glancing blow from a speeding car will often break a cat's jaw. A few years ago such an injury would have been untreatable, but now many a cat has its jaw repaired, its broken limbs stabilized by pins or plates, and is sent back to its owners to live a happy and active life, preferably on the home side of the road.

Less obvious but equally important advances have been made in the treatment of chronic illnesses, which inevitably involve maintenance of the cat on medication for long periods, often for life. Veterinary medication is expensive, mainly because of the low volume of production and sales compared with similar pharmaceuticals for treatment of humans. Today, small animal veterinary surgeons have at their disposal a multitude of diagnostic aids which were undreamt of 30 years ago.

Unfortunately there is no National Health Service for pets, so there is no help from the State if a cat needs urgent veterinary treatment at a time when the owner is most short of money.

Animal charities are now able to help only the most disadvantaged owners, who must fulfil stringent means-tested conditions before they are granted assisted treatment. There is nothing more heart-rending than having to request euthanasia for a beloved pet which could be saved if treatment could be afforded. This is particularly so when there are children in the family. Pet owners are responsible for the full cost of diagnosis and treatment of any illness their pet suffers, that is unless they have been wise enough to take out pet insurance cover in anticipation of times of unexpected accident and illness.

Knowing a client has insurance cover for their pet also frees the veterinary surgeon from the worry of wondering whether or not to suggest an expensive course of treatment that may only prolong the pet's life for a relatively short time. On the other hand, if it turns out to be six more months of enjoyable life, which is a good-sized proportion of most pets' lifespans, the owner will have had a very special and precious bonus.

The philosophy of pet health insurance

This type of insurance does not, and was never intended to, cover the complete maintenance and running costs of your cat. These costs can be reasonably predicted and budgeted for. It is those events that bring about

Figure 9 Healthy, innocent and adorable – an ideal age to insure

unexpected medical expenses – the traffic accident, a poisoning episode, a cat fight abscess or sudden onset of debilitating disease – that veterinary fee insurance is there to cover.

None of the pet insurance policies available covers preventative treatment, e.g. primary vaccinations, annual boosters and the neutering of male or female cats, but if there is a disease condition present which makes such an operation necessary, then most companies' policies will cover the cost.

Hundreds of thousands of pet owners (the number increases every week) realize that having insurance cover is the only practical way to ensure that their cat will always have the veterinary care it needs right up to the end of its life. They know their pet need never suffer from any lack of ready cash at the time it is ill or injured. According to the level of cover that is chosen, veterinary bills of up to £2,000 will be covered, and the owner just has to contribute a few pounds at the time of the claim.

The insured cat is generally brought to the surgery at the first sign of illness, while the cat without insurance protection may well have its visit deferred until the condition is well advanced and so more difficult to resolve. Insured cats also undoubtedly enjoy a better standard of veterinary care when expense is not an immediate consideration.

The Royal College of Veterinary Surgeons, the British Veterinary Association, the British Small Animal Veterinary Association, the Society of Practising Veterinary Surgeons, the British Veterinary Nursing Association, the Governing Council of the Cat Fancy and all the major animal charities agree that having a pet cat insured is part of responsible ownership.

Specialist insurance companies

In recent years several specialist pet insurance companies have put forward practical proposals to cover unexpected heavy veterinary bills, as well as providing a wide range of other benefits to help cat owners in times of trouble. Pet insurance companies pay out millions of pounds in claims every year. Here are just a few examples of claims paid in 1993 by one company:

Name	Age (years)	Breed	Condition	Amount paid (£)
Holly	14 months	Tabby	Recurrent cystitis	119
Jack	3	Birman	Blocked intestine	228
Ron	3	Moggie	Road traffic accident	202
Yubi	2	Burmese	Fell three storeys	185
Smuffin	13	L/h Domestic	Chronic kidney failure	169
Teazle	4	Tabby	Major stomach obstruction	317
Pussie	8	Moggie	Virus infection	200
Wispa	2	Burmese	Broken hindleg	126
Thomas	9	Moggie	Abscess due to cat fight	175

Cover for veterinary fees and other benefits is usually available for different amounts, reflecting the level of premium the owner wishes to pay.

Complementary medicine

Leading pet insurance companies now offer an additional amount of cover for complementary medicine, including physiotherapy, acupuncture and herbal or homoeopathic treatment. This is because many owners who have experienced the benefits of complementary medicine themselves want their cats treated in the same way. There are in fact an increasing number of veterinary surgeons who have studied and use this type of therapy. It is reassuring to know that some insurance companies will cover these claims up to the level appropriate to the premium paid.

What are the advantages of insuring a cat with a specialist pet insurance company rather than getting an extension of a household policy from one of the larger well-known companies? The cat field, with its very special ways, illnesses and veterinary needs, may be a relatively unknown one to the claims department of a multi-faceted company, and so there may be more queries and delays in paying claims than with a specialist pet insurance company. In fact several of the bigger pet insurance companies employ qualified veterinary nurses in their customer care departments, and they also have access to veterinary surgeons in practice who act as advisers. Specialist pet insurance companies are indeed very close to the world of the animals they serve.

How United Kingdom pet insurance works

Britain is probably unique in the world in having the longest established and most successful pet insurance schemes. The leading company began its business in close consultation with the small animal veterinary profession and now enjoys the confidence of nearly every practice in the country.

The procedure for insuring a cat is as simple as it can possibly be. Any cat can be insured from 8 weeks old, and initial insurance can be taken out at any stage of its life until it is 10 years old. Although that is the top age of entry, the insurance cover can be continued for the whole of the cat's life, although the death from illness benefit is not payable after 8 years old.

Insurance proposal forms can be picked up at any veterinary surgery, or can be obtained direct from the companies listed at the end of the chapter. No initial veterinary examination is needed when a cat is enrolled, although any past and present conditions must be declared, and it may be that any further treatment for some conditions will be excluded – at least during the first year of the insurance.

If your veterinary surgery stocks proposal forms for more than one company, it may be helpful to discuss your needs with the veterinary surgeon, the nurse or the receptionist. Over years of use, they will have gained experience of the quality of service of the various companies, especially with regard to speedy, trouble-free payment of claims.

The premiums for cats are usually significantly lower than those for dogs. There is no difference between premiums for pedigree or household pet cats, or even for cats obtained from rescue homes. Some companies provide facilities for paying premiums in monthly instalments, and many owners find this more convenient than annually paying a lump sum.

MAKING A CLAIM

When your cat seems ill, or has an accident, you need not hesitate to take it to the veterinary surgery immediately. Treatment can begin at once without asking the permission of the insurance company. The veterinary surgeon has complete freedom to carry out whatever treatment he or she feels is necessary, or even to refer the cat to someone who specializes in an area of disease. At the end of the course of treatment, the client pays the bill and the veterinary surgeon completes and signs the insurance claim form. A cheque for the amount less the statutory excess is then sent direct to the client within a very short time.

Figure 10　Pedigree or moggy, kittens can be insured from 8 weeks of age

THE EXCESS PAYMENT

In common with all other types of insurance, e.g. motor policies and household insurance, the insured pet owner is required to pay a small amount towards each claim. This amount is deducted from your claim cheque before it is sent to you.

The other benefits

Most insurance plans offer additional benefits relating to emergency situations. Probably the most useful to cat owners is the cover for advertising and reward if your cat 'goes missing', as many a cat will do at some stage in its life.

Advertising in local newspapers, getting posters made and photographs reproduced to give the best chance of recovering a cat can be an expensive business. It is helpful to know that pet insurance companies will contribute towards the cost, probably allowing you to offer a significant amount for a reward, which may be the crucial factor in getting your cat returned. And if that good fortune does not happen, and your cat is stolen or is never returned to you, many insurance plans will refund the purchase price.

An optional benefit which tends to go along with higher premium plans is death benefit, to refund the purchase price of the cat if it dies from accident at any age or illness before it is 8 years old.

Another benefit which can be invaluable to the caring owner, particularly those who live alone with their cats, is the sum allowed for boarding cattery fees or home care with a friend if the owner has to go into hospital for more than 4 days. This lump sum can be a real blessing, leaving an owner with just his or her own health to worry about until they can be united with their pet again.

If you are booked to go on holiday and are forced to cancel it because your beloved cat suddenly needs emergency surgery, or perhaps runs into trouble while you are away, necessitating your return, the insurance company will pay your travel company or hotel the cancellation fee.

Every pet owner has different needs, and you may feel it is unlikely that you will need death benefit, or boarding cattery fees in the event of your hospitalization. It is therefore sensible to read carefully the small print of the policy you are considering, and also to clarify with the insurance company the meaning of any wording which is not clear to you. You are then more likely to get the insurance policy closest to your own particular needs, but it is always wise to check your choice with the staff at the veterinary surgery.

The leading pet health care insurers are:

Pet Plan Ltd, FREEPOST Pet Plan House, 10/13 Heathfield Terrace, London W4 4BR. Tel. FREEPHONE 0800 282 009.

Paws, City Plaza, Temple Row, Birmingham B2 5AB. Tel. 021 633 3377.

Pet Protect Ltd, 55 High Street, Epsom, Surrey KT19 8DH. Tel. 0372 739490.

Dog Breeders Insurance, 9 St Stephens Court, St Stephens Road, Bournemouth BH2 6LG. Tel. 0202 295771.

4

CATTERIES

Introduction

Mention of the word 'cattery' to most cat owners surely brings to mind immediately the problem of ensuring puss is properly looked after while they jet off to some far-flung place, and that puss also has something of a holiday. Many boarding catteries have capitalized on this last concept and actually call themselves cat hotels or pet holiday centres. Nonetheless, they are boarding catteries, of which they are the largest, but by no means the only, group. A cattery is in effect a cat kennels, a place where cats are congregated for one purpose or another. There are also breeding catteries, which may be used to house the entire breeding stock or just the stud cat and his visiting queens. This aspect is covered in Chapter 30, Breeding.

In Britain today we still have strict quarantine regulations, and so have quarantine catteries in which any imported cat has to reside for a period of 6 calendar months. There are also rescue catteries, which, on sheer numbers of inmates, statistically are probably the most popular catteries, although sadly not by choice.

Some of these catteries, i.e. boarding and quarantine catteries, are controlled by law whereas others are not.

Boarding catteries

Let us look at catteries that are popularly considered the most common type, the boarding cattery – the 'cat hotel'.

Anyone wishing to board cats, or for that matter dogs, must be licensed by the local authority for that purpose under the Boarding of Animals Act 1963. The licence is renewed annually and the premises are subject to inspection by the local authority, usually in the person of the environmental health officer, although some enlightened local authorities employ veterinary surgeons. The Act lays down requirements regarding the size of individual accommodation, feeding, heating, lighting, waste disposal and care of the animals in fairly general terms, and these are open to individual interpretation. This creates some concern among cattery owners since there appears to be wide variation in interpretation of the legislation from one local authority to another. Nevertheless, licensing by the local authority does at least give some assurance of control and a guarantee that some level of inspection has been carried out. It should not be regarded by owners as any sign of endorsement of the cattery by the local authority. Some cattery owners actually incorporate the fact that they are licensed by the local authority on their notepaper. This is pointless since they would not be allowed to trade if they were not so licensed.

The choice of the cattery is still the responsibility of the cat owner. The purpose of this chapter is to help you make an informed choice, and to indicate how you can find a cattery and assess it in relation to your needs.

CONSTRUCTION

The Boarding of Animals Act only lays down broad outlines regarding construction in terms of the welfare of the animal, prevention of the spread of infection, etc. There are no specific size recommendations or indications regarding materials to be used in construction or shape, configuration, etc. Recently the Institute of Environmental Health Officers has produced a set of model licence conditions for kennels and catteries. Working within the framework of the Act, these guidelines also take into account more recent legislation, such as the Health and Safety at Work Act of 1974 and the Environmental Protection Act of 1990, so that it does appear that a more stringent attitude will be taken by inspectors in the future. Today catteries are available in all shapes and sizes, and some local authorities will accept those of wooden construction, provided exposed woodwork is maintained in good condition and regularly treated to prevent the spread of infection. However, the current trend is to have catteries constructed of more durable materials, although wood has the great advantage of being warm and giving a rural atmosphere, often synonymous with holiday boarding. Local authority interpretation of the legislation is largely that the unit must be constructed in such a way that exposed surfaces are impervious and easily cleaned. Modern units are constructed of a variety of such materials. The most popular are:

1.   Traditional brick or structural blocks suitably rendered and plastered.
2.   Stainless steel.
3.   Modern fibreglass and plastic materials.

Security is a high priority. All units, both sleeping and exercise accommodation, must be securely roofed, and partitions should be of solid

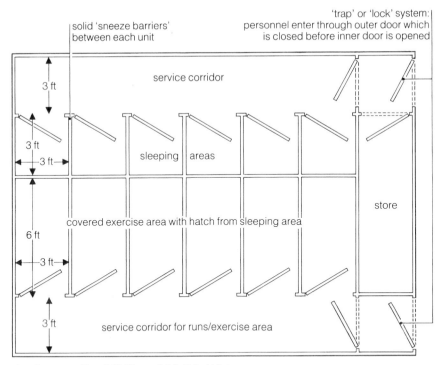

solid 'sneeze barriers' between each unit

'trap' or 'lock' system: personnel enter through outer door which is closed before inner door is opened

service corridor

3 ft

3 ft

3 ft

sleeping | areas

store

covered exercise area with hatch from sleeping area

6 ft

3 ft

3 ft

service corridor for runs/exercise area

sleeping area – 9 sq ft (0.85 sq m) 3 ft (0.9m) high
exercise area – 18 sq ft (1.7 sq m) 6 ft (1.8 m) high

Figure 11 Plan of typical 'corridor'-type cattery

construction and extend to the roof. This is to prevent the possibility of the spread of airborne viruses, of which the flu viruses are an important example in this context. Ventilation is important. It must be adequate in both summer and winter, and must not result in either overheating or chilling. Many modern catteries have controlled extraction or intake facilities in the form of fans, often ducted into each individual unit.

Ventilation has to be considered with heating. Heating in wintertime in Britain is always an expensive undertaking. To heat a whole building, possibly accommodating 10–20 individual units, when only two or three are occupied may give an impression of cosiness to visiting owners, but it can financially ruin the operator. Today the trend is towards individual hot-spot heating, occupied units being heated individually. This can be in the form of radiant heat, e.g. infra-red etc. This does not give such a cosy appearance to the casual observer walking down a service corridor, but without doubt is eminently acceptable to the occupant. After all, it is just like being at home and lounging against the radiator!

Lighting is the other major consideration. This again has to be adequate. It is often considered with ventilation and heating. The common practice

Figure 12   Cattery with outside covered run and service passage

Figure 13   Cattery showing solid wall construction to lower part with impervious translucent sneeze barriers on door and partitions. Note washing-up bowl as a bed and individual infra-red heater

today is to have transparent/translucent panels let into the roof. However, in summertime, if these are too plentiful, overheating problems can result. To some extent these can be counteracted by increasing the ventilation and the number of air changes per hour, but care is needed for this not to lead to draughts.

According to the Act, artificial lighting must be adequate; again, the interpretation of this is left to the local inspector. My criterion has always been quite simple. After dark, the lighting should be sufficient for the personnel to see both what they and the boarders are doing.

Service passages to sleeping accommodation and to runs must be as secure as the accommodation itself. Some cats are great escapists – and great climbers too. Safety glass and transparent plastic materials are ideal for partitions between kennels and for door apertures etc., since cats are extremely social animals and like to see what is going on around them.

Cattery design has progressed tremendously over the last few years. Very few commercial catteries now employ what I call the 'bin' type of construction, where cat cages, often of generous dimensions, are stacked one above another and enclosed in a wired, roofed enclosure. This used to be the most common method of construction 20 or 30 years ago, when respiratory viruses were rife and it was essential that as much ventilation as possible was afforded to the inmates without them having paw or nose contact. Today design can vary from individual chalets with sleeping and run accommodation attached, and a group of chalets secure within a wire-roofed compound, to the more conventional design, where several units are built side by side with adjoining runs, and both sleeping and exercise areas are serviced from secure passageways. These have a double entry system, the so-called 'trap' or 'lock' system, whereby one door has to be closed before the next can be opened.

These then are just a few of the points which you can check when you visit your chosen cattery.

One final point which is of course of concern to many owners is the question of exercise accommodation. Most commercial catteries today do provide individual runs for their boarders for exercise. However, it is my experience that, with the exception of kittens and sometimes cats housed together, very few short-term boarders, i.e. 2–3 weeks, take advantage of their exercise accommodation.

Veterinary practice catteries seldom have exercise accommodation, and this sometimes concerns owners who have to leave cats at a practice for any length of time. My experience has been that the lack of a run seems to bother the occupant not at all, provided the animal's personal space is sufficient to accommodate food, litter tray and comfortable bed. The fact that a cat is active when at home does not necessarily apply when boarded or hospitalized. After all, our exercise patterns and lifestyles change while we are on holiday, and so do those of our pets.

The beds and bedding should be clean and adequate. Plastic washing-up bowls provide good, hygienic, warm beds, and often cats like to curl up in them completely empty of any bedding. They can be easily cleaned and disinfected after use, and the shape of the oval bowls appears to be particularly comfortable for cats. Many catteries use acrylic bedding of the 'VetBed' type, and this is easily laundered and is acceptable to the majority of cats, although a few prefer to sleep on the backing rather than the furry surface. Cardboard boxes also make excellent beds for boarders. Most cats like them; a few even try to eat them! They are hygienic in that they are totally disposable.

Finally there is the question of the cat's own bed. It is always worth checking with your cattery. The majority, you will find, are more than happy to accept the pet's bedding, provided it is not too bulky, but it has to be correctly labelled, and return to owners can sometimes be a problem.

Feeding bowls, like everything else associated with cattery construction and management, should be designed to minimize the spread of infection. They should be capable of thorough disinfection and easily cleaned. Stainless steel is an excellent material for water and food, although many catteries today use disposable cardboard dishes, which are less labour-intensive in respect of washing up and disinfection. Many cats prefer plastic feeding dishes, and these again are acceptable provided they are easily cleaned and disinfected. Unfortunately hard plastic tends to become brittle and crack, while the softer forms (polythene) tend to get scuffed and can harbour infection. Some catteries are more than happy to accept an owner's own dishes, but my experience has always been that labelling and safe return can present problems. Often puss can be returned in superb condition after boarding, but loss of a feeding bowl can cause untold acrimony.

Litter trays and litter fall into the same category as the feeding dishes. They must be hygienic and easily cleaned/disposable. Many catteries use disposable litter trays, and although initially more expensive they do save on labour costs. However, they are not without their disadvantages since they are often chewed and tend to be more unstable than the more durable varieties. Because of the problems of infection, few catteries employ reusable litter, although I have had requests from owners to use a particular brand which the owner was perfectly prepared to provide since kitty "would tolerate nothing else". I am still not convinced it is a good idea, although I concede that some cats will only use one type of litter. Any well-run cattery is aware of this and often keeps several varieties on hand, and will change litter if it is noted the animal has not used the tray after 24–48 hours.

Over the last few years safety in the workplace has become of paramount importance and this affects catteries as much as any other type of workplace. Control of Substances Hazardous to Health (COSHH) has had

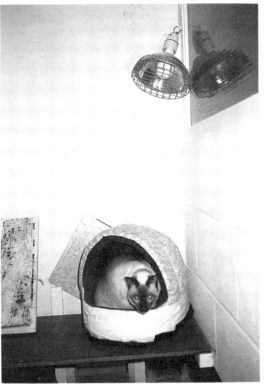

Figure 14 Sleeping area with raised platform for bed, (hatch below to outside run), and infra-red heater

great impact on catteries since there are precise regulations regarding the safe use of even relatively common household products when they are being used in a commercial sense. Bleach is one of these. It is a particularly safe and effective disinfectant for use in catteries but its use is now rigorously controlled. This also applies to many other substances used in cattery management which in turn has led to the development of disinfectants such as Trigene which fulfil COSHH regulations in that they are non-hazardous both to the cats and personnel and are also extremely effective. Fire regulations and the provision of fire extinguishers with adequate fire drills are all part of the same aim, that of protecting personnel in the workplace, and in this case it has an undoubted advantage for the boarder as well.

Waste, its handling and safe disposal is another area which the average owner of a holiday boarder would hardly consider but which is now of great importance and which is considered seriously when licensing a cattery. This subject is, strictly, without the original Boarding

Establishments Act, except in general terms, but is nevertheless very much part of the current Environmental Protection Act 1990 and the Control Waste Regulations 1992 (see Chapter 2, Cats and the Law).

These then are broadly the requirements for the commercial cattery. How do you find and select one?

FINDING A CATTERY

Personal recommendation from another cat owner is by far the most preferable method, but this is often easier said than done. However, cat owners at the local veterinary practice are a great source of information and your veterinarian can usually supply names and addresses of local catteries but will not recommend any particular one since individual standards and facilities are often unknown to the practice. Where else can you seek information? Yellow Pages are a useful source of information since kennels and catteries are listed. The Feline Advisory Bureau, 235 Upper Richmond Road, Putney, London SW15 6SN, telephone 081 789 9553 (restricted hours) will supply a list of FAB catteries and there well may be one in your area. Also it is worth contacting the local authority. They, after all, license all the local boarding establishments!

Having secured some names and addresses, the next stage is to select those within reasonable access and telephone for a brochure and price list. How your request is received and actioned often gives an indication of the efficiency of the enterprise, but do make allowances, you may have telephoned at a particularly bad time.

You have now accumulated information from which it should be possible to select a few catteries in which you are interested. When making this preliminary selection distance should not be the prime consideration. After all, how far are you prepared to travel for your holiday? Equally, cost has to be evaluated and you will find boarding fees will vary. The smaller, family-run concern often has a turnover below the level necessary for registration for VAT purposes, and so their prices will be significantly lower than the larger units. However, the larger units have probably only become so as a result of efficient service and facilities; so, you pay your money and take your choice. Payment at current rates is likely to be at least 17.5 per cent higher if VAT is added at the current rate.

INSPECTIONS

Once you have a preliminary list, next comes cattery visiting. The majority of cattery owners are more than happy to show their facilities and answer questions from the owners of prospective boarders, but it is only reasonable to make an appointment. This is not in order to allow the cattery owner to prepare for your visit but to enable the visit to be fitted into a busy work schedule. Unfortunately, in my experience, there are still far too many owners who arrive with their cats for the first time and are quite put out if they cannot have an in-depth discussion of the facilities and services offered by the cattery. This really should be assessed well in advance of the boarding date. After all, if you don't like what you see, what can you do about it if it is the morning of your departure?

I hope the foregoing will have given some indication of the facilities you should expect in a modern boarding cattery, but it may still be worth making out a check-list in order to ensure you do not omit something important. Many owners ask to see the specific accommodation their cat is likely to occupy, and sometimes this is not possible if the visit has been arranged some time before the boarding. In all honesty the personnel themselves may not be sure, particularly if the boarding is at a peak period. It is worth checking whether all the accommodation you see is of the same standard, and, if you are boarding more than one cat and wish them to be together, seeing the size of family units if these are available. Check the heating, lighting and ventilation, the type of dishes provided, litter, bedding and beds as already described. Discuss grooming, especially if you have a longhaired cat, and ask what the facilities are for coping with illness. Is veterinary attention readily available? Are routine veterinary calls made to the kennels or does the animal have to be taken to the vet in case of illness? In this connection, check the question of insurance.

Many pet health insurance companies today provide specific policies to cover kennels in the event of illness of any of the boarders. Does this particular cattery offer such a scheme, and is it included in the boarding fees, or do you pay extra for it? Many owners find it particularly irritating to be faced with a large veterinary bill on collecting their cat from a boarding cattery if the animal is now once more restored to perfect health. Under these circumstances a boarding cattery insurance policy is a boon, both to the cattery and the owner alike.

Check the method of booking. Do you have to fill in a booking form and sign it so that it in effect becomes a contract between you and the cattery? Do you get a copy of this and what sort of information do you have to supply? These are pointers to the standard of efficiency of the administration. Details required should include owner and animal and also contact addresses and telephone numbers. The owner's holiday address and telephone number may be requested, but if this is not available then you may be asked for the telephone number and address of a responsible person e.g. a member of the family or friend. The request for this information is the sign of a caring management. Emergencies can occur and most owners in my experience appreciate being informed as soon as possible. Similarly a caring cattery will request the name and address of the boarder's veterinary surgeon, along with details of inoculation.

Most catteries today insist upon up-to-date vaccination status against feline enteritis and flu. There are some that also require proof of vaccination against the other feline diseases, e.g. feline Chlamydia disease or feline leukaemia. These are, at present, not as important as flu and enteritis. Flu and enteritis vaccinations should be boosted prior to boarding if they are near to their due date. In this way you can ensure that the cat has the best possible immunity when boarded. Ideally, these vaccinations should be carried out a minimum of 14 days prior to boarding.

A trip to the veterinarian at this time is worthwhile in other respects. Prior to vaccination the veterinarian will give your cat a thorough health check, and, if you mention your cat is due to be boarded, he will be happy to discuss any points and worries you may have. He will also check ears and trim nails if required, which is something many owners expect catteries to do as routine. Do remember that, although many catteries will carry out simple 'maintenance jobs', it is not within their remit, with the exception of normal grooming.

Does the booking form request details of food preferences and normal diet? If an animal is taking time to settle, caring cattery owners will ensure that food as near as possible to the normal diet is offered in order to hasten the settling-in process.

If the cat is old or has a chronic condition which involves continuous medication, check that the cattery is prepared to carry out the necessary treatment during the boarding period. Even the most exclusive hotel is not a nursing home and similarly the best-run cattery is not a veterinary hospital. The staff are trained to look after healthy animals, not sick ones. The administration of tablets to Felix at home may be a doddle, but administration by a stranger in a strange environment can be something quite different. It is always helpful to discuss these matters prior to boarding. If there is any doubt discuss the question of hospitalization with your veterinary surgeon.

In this connection remember that most pet health insurance policies, particularly those covering boarding animals, have exclusions for pre-existing conditions and for elderly animals. No matter how healthy the cat appears to be, if it is aged, the stress of a strange environment can precipitate problems, the cost of treatment for which you may have to be responsible for. Forewarned is forearmed; budget for such eventualities.

Infection in catteries is controlled by individual housing, up-to-date vaccination, adequate ventilation, which is equally important as heating, and, of course, no contact between cats from different families. In well-constructed catteries each cat is virtually in isolation, so in the case of illness the cat can usually stay in its familiar environment rather than be removed to another area, which will disturb it further. Obviously, if a serious infectious disease is diagnosed, the animal may have to be moved into isolation or hospitalized at the veterinary surgeon's.

Following the preliminary visit you should by now have settled on a cattery. If your cat has not been boarded before, it may be worthwhile running a trial boarding weekend at the cattery to assess if the animal will settle. If more than one cat is involved, board them all for the weekend, make arrangements that they can be kept together, if that is what you require, but ensure that the cattery has facilities to separate them should the need arise. It is surprising how many cats who live in perfect harmony at home will disagree when boarded, particularly at mealtimes. This may be due to the stress of change of environment and confinement, but it is important they can be separated if necessary.

Owners frequently telephone next day to find out if the cat has settled, eaten, etc. Cats often take over 24 hours to settle, and provided they are drinking and seem comfortable and unperturbed it is seldom a cause of worry that they have not eaten for the first 24 hours or even 48 hours. In the cattery the cat is not getting the exercise it is used to at home and therefore food requirements will be less. It is the same phenomenon as us not sleeping very well in a strange bed the first night we are away.

If your cat has any 'peculiarities' which are likely to worry the cattery owner, do pass them on although they may not have been specifically requested. Some cats worry about storms, telephones or people with long hair or glasses; some prefer men to women and vice versa. If the animal is a little nervous anyway, and is stressed by the boarding environment, these little idiosyncrasies can become major behavioural problems. The cattery staff will be pleased to learn of Felix's funny little ways before you are hundreds of miles away. This is all part of the communication game so necessary for the welfare of the cat.

Generally the majority of cats settle very well and take boarding in their stride. Most cats are very accommodating, and provided they are warm, fed and watered, have a clean litter tray and somewhere to move around a little, they seem quite unconcerned that they are confined to what is a relatively small area compared with their own home and garden. Many cats today live in flats and seldom, if ever, go out, and these animals are even less bothered with the cattery environment, except that they can be stressed by noises they do not encounter at home.

Indoor/outdoor animals, on the other hand, who may be used to a cat flap and the ability to go as they please, seem seldom worried by strange noises, but very occasionally get bored with a cattery after a couple of weeks.

I have been involved with cat boarding for nearly 30 years and during that time I can recall only one occasion when owners have had to be contacted because their cat was fretting and inconsolable. On this occasion he was boarding on a three-day trial basis so his owners were not on holiday. He had been boarded merely to see if he would settle with us. Since he did not, the owners, not in the least surprised, collected him and decided he must stay at home in future with a house-sitter known to him. He was a particularly sensitive cat but definitely an exception.

That, then, is the boarding scene. What of the other types of cattery accommodation?

Breeders' catteries

Cattery accommodation for breeders or stud cat owners (see Chapter 30, Breeding) is a completely different need and here licensing is not a consideration. Many stud cats are accommodated outside in wooden units with wire mesh-roofed runs. The whole reason for such units is that entire male cats, particularly those used at stud, have strong-smelling urine, so a good supply of fresh air is essential. Many stud cats are brought up as 'outside' cats, but their owners always ensure they have draught-proof indoor sleeping quarters and adequate bedding. Others are kept as pets and only occupy the stud house when visiting queens are imminent.

Catteries for breeding cats can follow similar lines. Modern vaccination has ensured that virus diseases are not the problem they once were but nevertheless too many animals kept together in close proximity indoors is likely to lead to the spread of infection, particularly the flu or upper respiratory viruses. This is less of a problem if the cats are housed in outside catteries. However, it must be said that kittens reared outside without close human contact are frequently more nervous and less sociable than kittens brought up in the hurly-burly of a family home.

Rescue catteries

These cater for a totally different need. Here the cats are unowned or unwanted for many reasons. The saddest are those who were once loved pets, discarded because their owners no longer want or are unable to keep them. Many are much-loved pets who may have wandered off or been frightened away, had a near miss with a car, been injured and run away blindly . . . we often never know.

However, the majority are genuinely unwanted animals and the largest proportion of these are kittens. The only way to tackle this problem is by more responsible ownership and ensuring that, unless required for specific breeding purposes, pet cats are neutered. Only in this way can we ensure the population does not continue to increase.

Rescue organizations are inundated with cats requiring homes. Accommodation may have to be arranged for a few days or for the rest of the cat's life. These organizations are always short of funds, and the problem is greater than the resources available. They just have to do the best they can for the animals in their care. Some organizations are able to foster cats out to private homes and others have neutering policies for feral cats, who are then returned to their original environment and live out their lives without the problem of continuous litters of unwanted and often diseased, maladjusted kittens.

Never be critical of a rescue cattery. On inspection the standard may fall far short of the boarding establishment, but remember the staff are doing their best under difficult circumstances and any help or support you can give is always welcome. Food, of any sort, is always gratefully received. Many of the staff in rescue catteries are volunteers doing the job because of their love of cats. They are usually inundated with requests to take in cats and find it difficult to refuse, so the rescue cattery is not infrequently overcrowded, which in itself can lead to further problems as has already been touched on.

Quarantine catteries

The catteries designed to fulfil the present quarantine regulations in Great Britain are another group entirely. The requirements for a quarantine cattery are strictly laid down by law. At present, any cat entering the United Kingdom from abroad has to undergo a statutory 6 calendar months quarantine period in a licensed quarantine kennels. These establishments are licensed by the Ministry of Agriculture, Fisheries and Food (MAFF) and the licence is issued to a veterinary surgeon appointed by the Ministry who may not be the owner of the kennels. The veterinary surgeon or his appointed and approved deputy must make a daily visit to the kennels 6 days a week and on Sundays if required. Strict rules control the minimum size of sleeping and run accommodation and the unit should be so constructed that each cat is unable to make paw or nose contact with another. They are kept in the same pen for the statutory 6 months and cannot be visited by the owners for the first 2 weeks of the quarantine period. Vaccination against rabies is compulsory on arrival. Even transporting your cat from the place of entry into the country to the quarantine kennels must be in a vehicle licensed for that purpose by the MAFF. Communal exercise areas are not allowed and all units must be on one level. Each cat must have a bench or sleeping bed, and partitions and walls for sleeping and exercise areas must extend from floor to ceiling and be constructed of solid material. Each block of kennels must have a double door (trap or lock system) at the entrance and the doors should open inwards and be self-closing. Locks must be fitted to all doors and gates, and premises must be kept locked when no staff are available.

The licensed carrying vehicles must be able to enter the secure quarantine area for unloading to take place.

Regulations control the type of construction of the units, the washing facilities available for staff, disinfection, etc. Owners are able to visit their animals after the initial 2 weeks 'settling-in' period but they have to be accompanied by a member of staff or consent to be locked into the accommodation with their animals. They can only visit their own animals.

When reading these formidable requirements one can sympathize with those who fail to understand why quarantine is necessary in Britain, particularly since cats and dogs appear to live happily on the Continent where rabies is a fact of life and vaccination routinely carried out. However, it should be remembered that rabies is communicable to man and the disease is not curable. For many decades quarantine has been shown to be effective in keeping the virus out of this country. Vaccination might well protect our pet but will do nothing for our wild life, infected members of which could be inadvertently condemned to a particularly horrible death should present regulations be lifted.

Behaviour

5

NORMAL FELINE BEHAVIOUR

Cats have been closely associated with man for many thousands of years, and have become extremely popular as companion animals during this century. Despite this long association, interest in the behaviour of domestic cats has only developed relatively recently. This is probably because the traditional role of cats has been the control of vermin, and cats are well adapted to this task, requiring no training by man. This contrasts with the dog, where man has selectively bred and trained the animal to perform a variety of tasks. It is only recently, with the growth of the cat fancy and the development of modern breeds, that various breed characteristics and behavioural traits have become of interest and, consequently, the scientific investigation of these differences is still in its infancy.

This chapter provides a general discussion of the social and developmental behaviour of the domestic cat. Those who require more detailed information will find suggestions for further reading listed at the end of the chapter.

Social behaviour of the domestic cat

Members of the cat family are generally considered to be solitary animals although lions, which form groups called prides, are usually seen as the classic exception to this rule. However, the social organization of many small cat species is unknown, owing to the difficulties involved in observing animals that live at low densities in difficult and remote terrain. Pet cats are often forced to be group living, if owners choose to keep more than one cat in the house, and most adapt well to this situation provided that introductions of new cats are managed properly. If allowed access out of the house, female cats tend to move over an area which includes their house and garden and any surrounding, undefended space (normally called a home range). Male cats, both neutered and entire, tend to have home ranges approximately ten times as large as those of the female, and these ranges may overlap with the females and with each other. The social organization of feral domestic cats (i.e. domestic cats that have returned to a free-living state) is largely determined by the availability and distribution of food. Studies have shown that feral cats can live either singly (usually when food is scarce) or in large social groups (when food is plentiful and concentrated) and densities of between 1 cat per square kilometre and approximately 2000 cats per square kilometre have been recorded. Where groups do form, they usually consist of adult females (which are often related) with their kittens, and many groups revolve around the cooperative rearing of kittens by the females. Male cats may be loosely attached to groups and when conditions allow, they will roam between different groups of females. Thus, the social behaviour of the domestic cat is very flexible which probably accounts for their ability to adapt to a variety of human living conditions.

Social interactions between cats

When cats meet they can respond in various ways. Their familiarity with each other, and with the surrounding environment, largely determines their behavioural response. When strange cats are first introduced to each other in an unfamiliar environment, their priority is, in general, to explore their surroundings before they begin their investigation of each other. Initial investigations between cats usually begin nose to nose (normally without touching) with the head and neck extended and the body slightly arched. From this position, a cat can retreat rapidly if the other cat makes a sudden attack. Both animals will attempt to sniff along each other's neck and flank before finally smelling the other's anal region while trying to prevent investigation of its own.

If one cat behaves in a more confident manner by sniffing a particular region before the other is ready, then this sequence may break down and the second cat may respond in a defensive manner by crouching and moving sideways slightly. Persistent investigation by the more confident cat will cause the less confident cat to hiss and strike defensively with its paw and eventually move away. The confident one will then sniff the area where the other cat was crouched before resuming its investigation of the other cat. This sequence may be repeated several times until either the confident cat stops its investigation attempts, the other cat capitulates and allows itself to be investigated, or the confident cat attacks the other.

When strange cats are introduced in a room which is familiar to both cats, investigations proceed as described above, except that the initial investigation of the surroundings does not occur. However, when only one cat is familiar with the room, this cat initially becomes the more confident animal, as the unfamiliar cat tries to avoid an encounter and concentrates on exploring its surroundings. The 'familiar' cat may follow the 'explorer' and attempt to sniff its anal region, but such advances are usually rejected with a hiss or a defensive paw strike. This behaviour is of relevance when a pet cat is introduced to a new home. It is suggested, therefore, that a new cat should be allowed to explore a room before meeting any resident animals; alternatively the cat can be housed within a secure playpen or large cage, which will allow safe introductions to occur, but will allow the newcomer to withdraw if necessary.

Cat communication

The maintenance of a complex social structure, whether it is between cats or cats and humans, relies on good communication. Cats communicate in a variety of ways, and quickly learn how best to communicate with their owners.

Visual communication

Cats can communicate their mood by facial expressions and body postures. They tend to use such body language to communicate at short range, with ear and eye shape being the main indicators of mood. Figure 15a shows the normal relaxed facial expression of the cat and Figure 15b shows a cat which is alert and inquisitive, with both the ears and the whiskers pointed

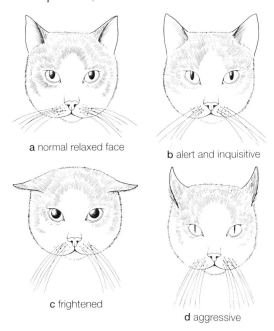

a normal relaxed face

b alert and inquisitive

c frightened

d aggressive

Figure 15

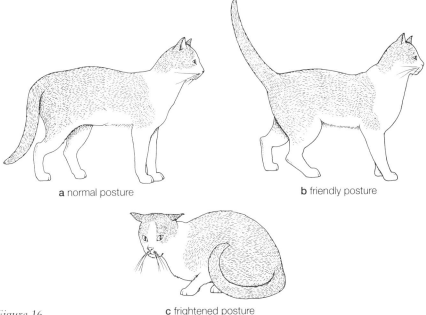

a normal posture

b friendly posture

Figure 16

c frightened posture

forward relative to the relaxed position. Frightened cats lower their ears (Fig. 15c) and a really frightened cat will hold its ears flat against its head. In an aggressive cat the ears are erect, and turned in from their normal posture showing more of the back of the ear (Fig. 15d).

Body posture can also indicate a cat's mood. Figure 16a shows a normal body posture for a cat whereas a cat that is greeting a known individual usually raises its tail in a distinctive manner (Fig. 16b). Frightened cats will crouch and flatten their body against the floor (Fig. 16c). The posture of an arched back with an erect bushy tail is seen in very frightened cats, often after a shock. However, this posture may also be seen in kittens during social play.

In addition to body posture and facial expression, cats may use other forms of visual communication. For example, by scratching on trees, posts or furniture, cats can leave a clear visible sign of their activity although it is possible that this also serves to attract other cats to investigate secretions that may be deposited by special glands in their paws. Furthermore, cats are thought to scratch objects to keep their claws in good condition, as a visual sign of dominance in the presence of subordinate animals, or during interactions with humans as a general indication of excitement.

Vocal communication

Domestic cats produce a wide range of vocalizations. Some are well known and unambiguous, such as the calling of a female in oestrus or the distress howl a cat makes when trapped or injured. Other vocalizations, such as purring, are also well known but are much less understood. Purring is generally regarded as a sign of contentment in pet cats, although it can also occur when an animal is in pain, when it tends to be deeper and louder than the cat's normal purr. The function of purring is not clearly understood nor, until recently, was the precise way in which the sound is produced. It is now known that purring is a true vocalization in that it is controlled by the vocal apparatus. The sound is due to a sudden build-up and release of pressure, as various sections of the vocal apparatus are rapidly moved by the laryngeal muscles.

Purring first occurs in kittens at about 1 week of age, and may indicate to the mother that the kittens are warm and not hungry. The occurrence of purring in adult cats during cat to cat or cat to human interactions may simply be the retention of infantile behaviour in adult life. This suggestion is supported by observations of adult cats purring and producing the foot treading behaviour seen in suckling kittens. In some cats this behaviour may be accompanied by drooling as though in anticipation of milk. However, purring in adult cats may be used to communicate that the individual is relaxed and unlikely to attack.

The miaows of pet cats when demanding food or attention are well known to cat owners. Many cats will vocalize in response to their owners talking to them. It is generally believed that pet cats are more vocal than their feral counterparts, as pet cats quickly learn that vocalization can produce responses from their owners in the form of a vocal reply, petting or the provision of food. Owners and cats tend to train each other. For example, if a cat miaows and the owner then provides food, the cat will quickly associate its vocalization with the arrival of food and will use the sound to solicit food on further occasions. In the same way, if the owner uses the same words or tone of voice when asking the cat if it wants food, the cat will also learn to associate these sounds with the arrival of food and will tend to perform food-soliciting behaviour such as miaowing and leg rubbing when it hears that sound.

Olfactory communication

The sense of smell (olfaction) provides an important form of communication in cats and signalling in this way has a number of advantages over other forms of communication. A scent deposited in the environment (scent mark) can provide information for long periods of time in the absence of the producer and therefore provides a record of its movements. Olfactory signals can also be used when visual or acoustic signals may be difficult to detect, such as at night, or in dense vegetation. The information conveyed in a scent mark is still largely unknown, and many suggestions have been made as to the function of these scent marks, which may vary for different species of animals. These marks may help to deter other animals from intruding into an occupied area, or may enhance an animal's confidence by surrounding it with a familiar smell. Another theory suggests that an animal can be identified as the resident of an area if its body odour matches that of scent marks distributed throughout the area.

In cats, as in other animals, urine provides an important means of scent marking, and cats will spray urine backwards on to visually conspicuous objects. Urine marking often occurs at regular places in a cat's range but tends to be deposited over old marks. Studies have shown that cats can discriminate between the urine odour of different individuals, and can also discriminate between sprayed urine and that deposited during a normal urination. This latter observation supports the suggestion that during spraying, cats may eject some anal sac secretion into the urine stream. The exact function of urine marks is unknown, but one suggestion is that they act like 'railway signals' which inform other cats if a cat is in a particular area. A fresh urine mark would be the equivalent of a red light since this would mean that a cat had just used the area and that confrontation was possible. An old scent (green light) would indicate that no animal had recently used the area and it was therefore safe to proceed. In this way, a sort of 'time sharing' system could be set up, where several cats may use the same area, but at different times.

In female cats, urine can also provide information on their sexual receptivity. The levels of oestrogens in urine reflect those in the blood and these vary during the oestrous cycle. Tomcats appear to respond to urine from females which are in oestrus. Cheek gland secretions of female cats may also provide information on their hormonal status. Cheek rubbing may, therefore, have a role in sexual signalling in addition to providing a means of visual and tactile communication.

Faeces may also be important for cats in olfactory communication, although, as for urine, the exact function or message conveyed is unknown. Observations of feral cats which defecate away from their home area have shown that they often leave faeces exposed, but will cover or bury them when at home. It is thought that some wild cat species may leave faeces in specific locations, where other individuals are most likely to encounter them.

Tactile communication

Cats often rub parts of their body against objects, other cats and humans. This behaviour is sometimes interpreted as a form of olfactory communication (mediated by the sense of smell) since glandular secretions from the cat's body may be deposited on the object, but rubbing may also serve as a means of tactile communication (using the sense of touch) within social groups. Rubbing with the cheek glands appears to be more likely to occur from a subordinate to a dominant individual and this behaviour may help to reinforce social position. The sense of touch is the most developed sense at birth and this is obviously important for young kittens to enable them to locate their mother and littermates.

Reproductive behaviour

Breeding is discussed in detail in Chapter 30, and so this section is only concerned with the broader aspects of reproductive behaviour. In reproductive terms the female domestic cat is seasonally polyoestrous, meaning that she has a breeding season within which there are several periods of sexual receptivity (oestrus) interspersed with periods of sexual inactivity (dioestrus); at the end of the breeding season the cat undergoes a longer period of sexual inactivity (anoestrus). The timing of this breeding season is controlled by the length of the day, with 12–14 hours of light tending to bring queens into oestrus. This fact is sometimes exploited by cat breeders in order to produce kittens at convenient times of the year. Queens subjected to a reduced day length of around 9 hours for a few weeks, and then an increased day length of about 14 hours, will come into oestrus even during the winter months. Surveys of cat breeding in the United Kingdom suggest that the breeding season generally extends from January until September, but that many cats do not undergo an anoestrous period. This lack of anoestrus is possibly due to artificial lighting in homes, which can interfere with the normal control of the reproductive cycle.

There are suggestions that tomcats also undergo seasonal changes in sexual activity, with a peak of activity in the spring, which declines throughout the rest of the year. This observation may be a function of the greater number of receptive females during the spring, but some studies indicate a higher sperm count in spring and summer than during the rest of the year, suggesting that the reproductive cycle may also be controlled by day length. Male cats can, however, be sexually active at any time of year, and experienced 'stud' cats will copulate and successfully produce kittens throughout the year.

Female cats undergo behavioural changes during the oestrous cycle and owners often note an increase in 'affection' shown by their cat in oestrus, as the cat increases the amount of head and flank rubbing directed on to objects, and the amount of time spent vocalizing and rolling on the floor. These behaviours intensify as the oestrous cycle progresses until at the peak of oestrus, the female will adopt a mating posture in front of its owner, another cat, or any other familiar animal. This posture consists of the front half of the body resting on the floor with the forelegs extended and the head often lying stretched out on the forelegs. The rear of the body is raised but the hindlegs are bent so that the knees are close to the ground. Once in this posture the cat curls its tail around one side of its body exposing its genitalia, and the hindlegs tread up and down rocking the body (Fig. 17).

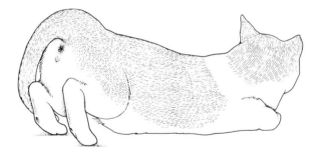

Figure 17   Cats often show lordosis when in oestrus

This position is often referred to as lordosis, and pet cats in oestrus can be induced to adopt this posture by being stroked along the lower half of their back.

Maternal behaviour

Female domestic cats do not usually build nests to give birth, but tend to make use of whatever shelter is available. Some pet cats prefer to use dark, quiet places and will reject suitably prepared areas in favour of a cupboard or garden shed; others, which are more confident, may choose a familiar sleeping place, such as the owner's bed, on which to give birth. Feral cats have been observed to build nests in grass, but will also use suitable structures in the environment. For feral cats the nest site serves to keep kittens warm, and helps to protect them against predators, which could include male cats.

The queen cleans herself before giving birth and as each kitten is born, she removes the amniotic sac surrounding the kitten, severs the umbilical cord and licks the kitten clean, which also serves to stimulate its breathing. She then nuzzles the kitten towards her mammary glands. Occasionally, abnormal behaviour occurs around birth and a queen may reject one or more kittens, making no attempt to remove the amniotic sac or to clean them. Sometimes, she will remove the sac correctly but after biting through the umbilical cord may go on to kill and eat the kitten. Such behaviour is more common in females having their first litter, although some cats never make good mothers.

In feral cat groups, related females (usually mother and daughters or sisters) may often share a common nest site and suckle each others' young. Although there may be certain disadvantages to this behaviour, such as an increased disease risk from meeting a number of adults, one benefit is that more than one adult is available to protect the kittens from predators or infanticidal males. During the later stages of pregnancy and especially after giving birth, females become increasingly aggressive to both familiar and unfamiliar males and to other species, such as dogs, which may threaten their nest.

Behavioural development

Once the kittens are born, they develop relatively rapidly, and there have been a number of studies investigating this process. Cat development can be divided into a number of stages, although these stages are less well defined in the cat than in other domestic species such as the dog.

From birth to around 2 weeks of age, kittens are in the neonatal period, which is dominated by eating and sleeping. At this stage, the kittens are completely dependent on their mother for survival. Although the eyes and ear canals remain closed for the first 7–10 days of life, the senses of smell, touch and thermal perception are partly functional and these enable the neonatal kitten to detect and move towards its mother and littermates, for food or warmth. The next stage is the transitional period, which lasts from the end of the neonatal period until about 3 weeks of age, and as its name suggests is when kittens change from being totally dependent on their mother to having a degree of independence. Following the transitional period is the socialization period. The kittens are now seen to participate in increasing periods of social play. The socialization period is also an important time for human contact. Studies have shown that kittens who are not handled during this period rarely grow up to be friendly adult cats, and so contact with people is essential at this stage. The peak time for socialization is between 2 and 7 weeks of age, and although socialization can continue beyond this time, it is never as effective.

Coordination and balance gradually improve and by 5 weeks, kittens may attempt complex activities such as walking on narrow surfaces or balancing on an object. The famous 'air righting reflex' which enables a cat to land on its feet after a fall is fully developed by 6 weeks of age (Fig. 18).

The juvenile period spans the time between the end of the socialization period and the onset of sexual maturity. The length of this period may vary between breeds. For example, the Oriental breeds tend to reach sexual maturity much earlier than others. During this period, the kitten's behaviour patterns do not alter significantly, but there is a gradual improvement in its physical skills which are associated with the increase in muscular development and improvement in coordination. Vision continues to improve as the kitten matures until around 16 weeks of age, when sharpness of vision appears to be fully developed.

Figure 18   How cats fall and land on their feet

The development of feeding and predatory behaviour

During the first 3 weeks of life, kittens are dependent on their mother's milk for their total nutrition. To ensure they obtain this supply of nutrients, newborn kittens possess a rooting reflex (which causes them to burrow into warm objects) and a sucking reflex. Whilst suckling, kittens often show a treading action with their forepaws and this activity is believed to stimulate the flow of milk. Studies have shown that on average, kittens will spend 4 hours per day engaged in suckling. This drops to around 3 hours per day by the end of the second week and to 2 hours per day in the third. Time spent suckling can vary considerably between individuals, with some kittens spending up to 8 hours per day engaged in suckling during their first week. Such studies, however, do not measure food intake, and increased time spent at a nipple may reflect reduced availability of milk from that nipple. By the third week of life, kittens begin to show an interest in solid food, but at this stage they may only spend around 1 minute per day in their attempts to consume the food. By 4 weeks of age, this will have increased to about 25 minutes per day, and by 6 weeks to about 50 minutes per day. Once the kittens start to consume solid food, the queen begins the process of weaning. This is accomplished by the queen spending more time away from her kittens and by adopting postures in which her nipples are not accessible. Weaning is a period of conflict between the queen and her kittens, with the queen attempting to reduce the dependency of her kittens while they attempt to maintain it. Kittens have a very strong drive to consume the same food as their mother and during weaning, they will normally sample any food their mother is consuming and therefore learn what is safe to eat. Kittens reared by free-living or feral cats learn to consume prey whereas kittens of house cats normally learn to eat prepared pet food. Individual taste preferences shown in the adult cat may be established during the period of weaning.

Cats are born with an innate predatory ability and even those individuals who have never had to hunt to survive will still exhibit predatory behaviour when presented with an appropriate stimulus. However, this innate ability must be developed and improved with practice and experience before the cat can become an efficient and successful hunter. In free-living cats, the teaching of rudimentary predatory behaviour by the queen commences at around 4 weeks of age, when she will encourage the kittens to investigate and consume prey which she has caught and delivered to the nest. Although certain skills acquired as kittens may influence the cat's predatory ability as an adult, it is still possible for kittens with no hunting experience to develop into efficient predators as adults.

Play behaviour

Play is an activity which most people are able to recognize, but which is very difficult to define as a behaviour, and its exact functions are not fully understood. Play behaviour in cats can be categorized as either *locomotory, social,* or *object play*. In kittens, locomotory play may be social or solitary and includes running, rolling, jumping or climbing. Object play may also be social or solitary and is defined as play involving an object. Social play includes wrestling, rolling and biting with other kittens or cats, although a human hand may often be accepted as if it were another kitten.

By 4 weeks of age, kittens have already started to engage in social play with their siblings and mother, and this may continue at a high level until 14 weeks of age. Social play can be quite rough, but kittens gradually learn to reduce the intensity of their attacks since inducing pain in others will invariably lead to a reciprocal response. Many postures adopted during social play resemble those seen in adults displaying predatory behaviour, but some postures mimic those observed in bouts of conflict between cats. Social play usually takes place between kittens, but adults will sometimes respond to playful approaches by kittens. Social play between adults is rare but when it occurs, may develop into more serious fighting.

Object play includes pawing, stalking and biting of objects and is commonly observed in kittens and many adult cats. Such play also tends to be regarded as simulating aspects of the predatory sequence and cat owners often allow their cats to indulge in this activity by providing a variety of 'prey-like' toys. Object play is commonly thought to provide practice for predation and studies have shown that cats which have access to play objects will acquire predatory skills at an earlier age than those which do not, although the lack of play objects will not prevent the development of predatory behaviour.

Cats and man

In recent years, there has been increasing interest in the interaction between animals and their owners, particularly in the understanding of what is termed the *human–companion animal bond*. As one of the most popular companion animals, a number of studies of the human–cat relationship have been conducted, and several have focused on factors which may cause the relationship to break down. A discussion of cat problem behaviour can be found in Chapter 6.

A number of factors have been identified which may influence the cat and also the human–cat relationship. These include the general housing conditions within which a cat is kept, the behaviour of the owner, and the behaviour of the cat. In the first of these categories, the quantity and quality of space available to the cat, the number of cats in the household, and the human family structure may all influence the human relationship with the pet cat. Behavioural problems are more commonly observed in cats kept indoors than those with free access outside the house, but this in itself does *not* show that keeping cats indoors is bad for them. Certain aspects of cat behaviour may only be considered a problem if they occur indoors. Cats with access to outdoors may therefore have an identical behavioural repertoire to indoor cats, but may never cause problems for their owners because all potentially problematic behaviour occurs outside the house. Also, pedigree cats tend to be kept indoors more often than 'moggies' and so some problem behaviour may have a genetic rather than an environmental basis.

There are no firm recommendations for the minimum amount of space required by a cat in a house to prevent problems arising. However, a good rule of thumb is that as the size of the space occupied by the cat is reduced, so the quality of its environment should be increased, although this is difficult to quantify in absolute terms. A cat that has access to a large area, including the house and garden, has a wide variety of places to visit and various spatial levels to occupy such as window sills, walls and trees. Such cats also have much to occupy their attention, for example other cats in the area, the movement of birds or the activities of people. A small two-roomed multi-storey apartment provides much less space for a cat but can be similarly enriched by providing several hiding and sleeping places; by allowing access to furniture or shelves at different heights in the rooms; and through regular interactive play with the owner.

The majority of cat owners keep only one cat and in general, this causes no problems for the cat or its owner, especially if the cat has access to outdoors or frequently interacts with the human family. However, when confined to a small area with the owners absent for a large part of the day, the resulting lack of environmental stimulation may cause problem behaviour to arise. In such situations, even if the living space is small, it may be preferable to keep two cats rather than one, although this may present difficulties if the animals are not sociable towards each other. However, careful selection of individuals, possibly by taking two kittens from the same litter, should minimize any problem. Observations of feral cat social structure suggest that taking two females from the same litter should be the best approach.

Most people who own more than one cat would consider that although there are gross similarities in the behaviour of cats as a species, there are many aspects of behaviour which may be peculiar to the individual, so that two cats may be as individually distinct as two people. Differences between individuals in any species can be caused by genetic differences or by environmental influences, or a combination of both. However, the relative importance of each effect is difficult to ascertain since most behavioural traits are the result of a complex interaction of many factors. An individual's behaviour may also vary according to the context in which it finds itself. For example, a normally docile female may become aggressive when she gives birth; or a cat which is subordinate in most situations may become dominant in competition for food when it is hungry.

Environmental factors can influence the kitten's rate of development. Early stroking and handling by humans can produce more rapid physical development and will make the kittens more responsive to humans. Longer periods of handling will also increase their attachment to humans. The most sensitive period for socialization in cats appears to be from 2 to 7 weeks of age. However, a small percentage of animals seem to resist socialization, irrespective of the amount of handling they receive.

Although little is known about the genetic influences on individuality in cats, it is likely that these will have a significant effect. However, the genetic contribution of the parent will also affect its appearance, which can indirectly influence its behaviour. For example, kittens of certain colours (controlled by genetics) may be preferred by owners and therefore handled more often, an experience which is likely to make the kitten more friendly. Some cat breeds are thought to exhibit breed-specific traits (such as the vocal and extrovert nature of Siamese cats) and pedigree kittens are often selected with these characteristics in mind. Some recent studies have shown that there may be a genetic aspect to cat friendliness, in addition to early handling experience. Kittens from friendly fathers were found to be quicker to approach, touch and rub both familiar and unfamiliar people, and novel objects, than cats from unfriendly fathers. Thus the father's temperament must be seriously considered before selecting a stud tom for breeding.

Studies of the human–cat relationship have confirmed a number of issues which many cat owners have always suspected. For example, the more often a human initiates an interaction with a cat, the shorter is the total interaction. However, the more often the *cat* initiates the interaction, the longer the total interaction time. Furthermore, when the owner responds favourably to the cat's desire to interact, then the cat is more likely to reciprocate when the owner wishes to interact.

When selecting cats as pets, owners usually choose a kitten on the basis of its colour or visual appeal, but the development of a good cat–human relationship depends on the cat satisfying other criteria. Temperament may be more predictable in pedigree cats, where certain breeds are considered to be more extrovert than others; however for the average pet cat, the temperament of its ancestors may be unknown. Therefore, owners requiring a cat with a specific personality should obtain as much information as possible about the socialization conditions of the kitten, the behaviour of its parents (if possible) and its current behaviour to ensure a good match. Luckily, cats are very flexible creatures and can readily adapt to a wide variety of living conditions, an ability which helps to explain their popularity as pets.

Further reading

For cat owners who are interested in more detailed information on cat social, developmental or reproductive behaviour, excellent accounts by a number of cat biologists can be found in the following books.

The Waltham Book of Dog and Cat Behaviour, edited by Chris Thorne (Pergamon Press, 1992)

The Behaviour of the Domestic Cat, John Bradshaw (C.A.B. International, 1992)

The Domestic Cat: the biology of its behaviour, edited by Dennis Turner and Patrick Bateson (Cambridge University Press, 1988)

The Wildlife of the Domestic Cat, Roger Tabor (Arrow Books, 1983)

6

BEHAVIOUR PROBLEMS

Introduction

Domestication is said to occur when the breeding, care and feeding of an animal is under the control of man. It therefore implies some genetic manipulation by man to produce docility. This involves a reduction in wild characteristics – both behavioural, such as aggression, and physical, such as size – and an adaptability to different human domestic environments. For companion animals such as cats, stability of a sociable character and retention of infantile behaviour characteristics into adulthood both are appealing to the nurturing/mothering emotions in man and enhance docility and handleability – key factors in the successful evolution of any species as a pet. These factors are very different from the demands on animals domesticated for food purposes. Cats are, however, different from other domesticated species such as the dog in that they do not relate to their owners as part of an organized social or hunting group. The cat retains its ability to hunt as a solitary animal and continues to do so away from the shared human den, even when well fed and cared for. It also retains a high level of adaptability and can survive in a wide range of environments, from sub-antarctic islands to semi-deserts, as a wild creature deriving no benefit from man. Indeed, recent evidence suggests that what is nowadays regarded as the domestic cat genetically varies very little from its ancestor, the African Wild Cat.

In our homes, the cat as a pet is apparently simply occupying a favourable niche without compromising its ability to survive, reproduce and exploit almost any other opportunity in the world where an adequate year-round supply of food and water is available.

The cat has succeeded in remaining a wild animal in our homes because of its willingness to engage in social, friendly and affectionate behaviour with us, despite not being dependent on such social relations. Predatory behaviour or territorial aggression is usually restricted to the surrounding gardens and our pet cats happily return for rest, affection and security in our homes. The human–pet cat relationship is, despite this somewhat straightforward opportunism on the cat's part, based on many, often contrasting factors. Indoors the cat is valued for its cleanliness, affection and playfulness, and admired for its highly evolved play behaviour. Although not a group hunter, the cat retains an enormous capacity to be sociable and accepts the benefit of living in the human family and den without compromising its general self-determining and independent behaviour. Outdoors, that lack of compromise in the domestication of the cat is reflected in its ability and desire to hunt, even when well fed. The cat views its human family partly as social counterparts and partly as maternal figures, continuing much of its kitten behaviour into adulthood when with them. This frequent demonstration of extremely affectionate responses of an infantile character helps to build an extremely strong bond between owner and cat, one that is essential to bear in mind when treating medical or behavioural problems.

Most cat owners will tolerate a much higher level of disruption to their social life and household hygiene than will dog owners when their pets present behavioural problems, and are far less likely to apportion blame to a cat for its actions than a dog. Cat owners are often very sensitive to their cat's emotions and accept that, as the legacy of the cat's adaptability, they may vary from day to day or even hour to hour. Even though some breed characteristics of temperament have been enhanced almost coincidentally in breeding and selection for physical appearance, such as docility in long-hairs or responsiveness and attention demanding in the Burmese, the cat's basic character is largely unaffected by domestication. Most owners understand that pet cats are not easily trained to perform set tasks and so accept that, when behaviour problems arise, their cats may not be deliberately causing difficulties.

Behaviour problems

Behaviour problems discussed are based on the author's caseload. Owners of high value breeds were more likely to seek help than owners of crossbred cats. While only 8 per cent of British cats are of recognized breeds, 44 per cent of the caseload involved pedigree strains, 14 per cent first cross pedigree strains and 42 per cent domestic Short- and Longhairs. Of the pedigrees, 24 per cent were Siamese, chiefly referred for problems of indoor urine spraying; 20 per cent Burmese, chiefly for problems of aggression towards other house cats or, if allowed access to the outdoors, towards local rival cats; 13 per cent Abyssinian, mainly for sudden breakdowns in relations between several Abyssinians sharing a home, and 13 per cent Longhairs (Persians), almost exclusively for serious house-training problems. Representatives from 17 breeds were referred. Just over half the cases referred (56 per cent) were male and only fourteen un-neutered cats were treated. The average age of cats presented was 3 years and 10 months, though this is somewhat skewed by the presence of five cats over 14 years of age treated for loss of house training and excessive night-time vocalization. Most of the cats seen were between 1 and 5 years old, divided as 1–2 years (25 per cent), 2–3 years (21 per cent), 3–4 years (18 per cent) and 4–5 years (11 per cent). The most common case profile is therefore a neutered 1–2-year-old male domestic Shorthair or Siamese cat which lives with one other cat and sprays or soils inappropriately indoors. The implication of this finding may be that would-be owners should avoid keeping such types of cat, but the great majority of cats, even of this type, do not present behaviour problems and make excellent trouble-free pets. In any case, as yet there is no firm evidence to suggest, as there is with dogs, that many such problems could be avoided through improved breeding, character assessment or selection of the pet when young. Some kittens simply seem to turn out more reactive, sensitive or problematic as adult cats despite careful breeding, the best of husbandry and attention to social development.

The emphasis on referral of pedigree strains may be because an owner will often have paid a relatively large sum of money for their cat and so be less willing to reject it because of a behaviour problem than if they owned a crossbred cat which would be cheaper to replace. Pedigree strains are also more likely to be housed permanently indoors (and so more likely to present noticeable problems due to being more reactive to change within the home) or because the most popular breeds such as Siamese, Burmese and longhaired breeds are often reported by owners and breeders as being generally more 'sensitive' or emotional.

Very few feline behaviour problems have simple answers and, in diagnosis and treatment, most necessitate the detailed recording of a complete problem history, relevant medical history, lifestyle and relationship data within the family. The nature of the home environment is crucial both to the cause of many problems and, through modification of access, in the treatment of most. Treatment of behaviour problems exclusively with drugs of any kind is rarely curative and usually inhibits learning. The use of drugs often has to be based on a trial and error approach as there are marked variations in response between breeds and individuals. Where used, drugs are offered as a short-term vehicle to facilitate the application and acceptance by the cat of management, husbandry or behaviour modification techniques and to facilitate learning by degree during systematic desensitization.

INDOOR MARKING (scratching, spraying, middening)

Chin, head and flank rubbing are normal forms of feline scent marking and social communication and are encouraged by most owners. Other types of marking behaviour may not be well tolerated indoors. Scratching to strop claws can usually be transferred from furniture to an acceptable sisal-wrapped post, hessian- or bark-faced board by placing this in front of the furniture and then steadily moving it to a more convenient location. Scratching as a marking behaviour is usually more widespread in the home and appears to be performed as a dominance gesture in the presence of other house cats. It should be treated in the same light as other forms of marking such as urine spraying, associative urination and defecation away from the litter tray. The latter two actions are usually performed on beds or chairs, or sometimes even on or in hi-fi headphones where the owner's smell is most concentrated and from which the cat presumably perceives the benefit of associating its smell with that of a protecting influence against challenges, real or imagined. The event most commonly cited by owners is toileting on the bed when they go on holiday and leave friends or minders to care for their cats. Associative marking can also occur on doormats, where challenging smells may be brought in on the owner's shoes from the outside, and, unusually, on electrical appliances such as video and washing machines, perhaps because of a scent association.

In contrast, urine spraying is a more normal and frequent act of marking practised by most cats outdoors, both male and female, entire and neutered. Cats usually have no need to spray indoors because their lair is already perceived as secure and requires no further endorsement. Spraying occurs from a standing position and usually a small volume of urine is directed backwards against vertical posts such as chair legs, curtains, etc. It has also been suggested that cats which spray indoors may also be more restless generally and more active nocturnally than non-spraying cats. They may also be relatively more aggressive towards the owner.

Of the indoor spraying cases treated by the author in 1990/91 (see Fig. 19), 47 per cent came from two-cat households; only 10 per cent were solo house cats and 17 per cent came from three- or four-cat households. Most were male neuters (61.5 per cent) indicating perhaps some social inability of males especially to accept the presence of another cat in the home territory up to some variable threshold, beyond which there may be some suppressing effect on the need to spray urine. This contrasts with the previously generally held view that the greater the number of cats sharing a house, the more likely that one at least would spray. The author has visited one three-bedroom home in London used as a rescue centre for stray and unwanted cats and which houses over 140 resident pet neutered cats in addition to a continuous input of new arrivals and departures when individuals are found new homes. The owner reports that few of her cats have ever sprayed and her home does indeed smell relatively cat free! Other cats seem peculiarly specific in the objects that they spray in the home. One famous sprayer only ever anointed a picture of the Czar and Czarina of Russia hanging on the stairway wall, a feat achieved by the cat by reversing

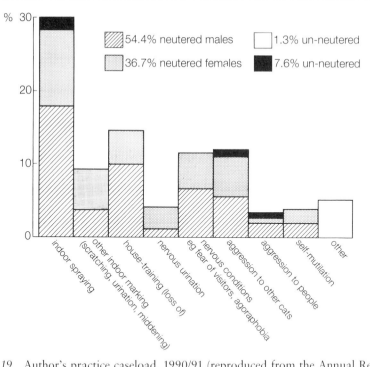

Figure 19 Author's practice caseload, 1990/91 (reproduced from the Annual Report of the Association of Pet Behaviour Counsellors 1990/91)

his rear end through the landing balustrade and targeting a jet of spray some 3 feet across the stairs!

When such marking occurs indoors it is usually a sign that the cat's lair is under some challenge. The challenge may be obvious, perhaps the recent arrival of another cat, a neighbour's small dog, a new baby, or an increased challenge from a cat outdoors, or it may result from moving or changing furniture, redecorating, family bereavement, having guests to stay, bringing outdoor objects anointed by other cats into the house, bringing in novel objects (especially plastic bags) and, most commonly of all, following the installation of a cat flap. This can totally destroy indoor security even without the obvious challenge of a rival cat or even a neighbour's small dog entering the inner sanctum of the home. Protest spraying is observed particularly in some highly manipulative and social individuals of certain Oriental breeds when frustrated or denied the attention of the owner.

Treatment

Spraying and other marking should not be considered as having a purely message function for other cats or challenges even though feral cats are clearly able to distinguish between urine marks deposited by males, females, and neutered or entire individuals. The response of other cats to a spray mark is often to investigate it but then to continue normally rather than run away or show a fearful reaction, and, invariably, to overmark it with their own spray. Indoor marking may help the perpetrator feel more confident by surrounding him or herself with his or her own familiar smell. Hence cats which spray indoors may be trying to repair scent or security 'holes' in their own protective surroundings caused by change, the arrival of new objects or the addition of strange smells on new objects, cats or people, or the loss of a contributor to the communal smell that helps identify every member of the den. Spraying after cat flap installation probably occurs because the outdoors is then perceived as continuous with the indoors and the cat feels that the home therefore needs to be re-anointed in similar manner to identify his occupancy and ensure that he encounters his own smell frequently. The cause should be identified if possible and the cat's exposure to any physical challenges controlled. Cat flaps should be boarded up to define den security, sprayed or middened areas should be cleaned as outlined in the 'House soiling' section (see pages 78–79) and baited similarly with dry food. The cat should never be punished, either at the time or, worse, after the event, as this furthers indoor insecurity and increases the need to mark. However, confining the cat to one room when unsupervised can create a new safe 'core' that needs no further identification by spraying. The best 'cores' are usually warm draught-proof beds sited close to radiators or safe heat sources where a cat would often naturally choose to relax and sleep. In severe cases, the core can even initially take the form of such a bed in an indoor pen, with the cat only released to the secure surrounding room under supervision. Once the cat relaxes in the room and ceases to spray, his access through the house can be expanded gradually by one cleaned, baited room at a time under the supervision of the owner at each stage. During treatment, and perhaps for ever more, all local rival cats should be chased out of the garden to avoid upset or challenge to the patient.

Protest sprayers should be ignored and the whole relationship between owner and cat restructured so the cat only receives contact, food, affection, etc. at the owner's initiation, in a manner similar to the treatment of over-demanding or dominant dogs. This type of spraying may worsen initially before responding positively to treatment. Drug support is very much case-dependent but a tapered prescription by the veterinary surgeon of oral progestagens or sedatives for 3 to 4 weeks may assist treatment.

HOUSE SOILING

Inappropriate urination and defecation as acts of normal toileting or as a result of nervousness should first be distinguished from deliberate acts of marking by urine spraying described earlier or associative marking by urination and middening. Most cats instinctively tend to use loose

Figure 20　Queens initially stimulate their kittens to eliminate by licking them

substrate such as cat litter as their latrine when first venturing from the maternal nest, and learn by experimentation and observation of their mother that litter is a surface on and in which to excrete. Prior to this they are unable to excrete without physical stimulation from the mother. Initially this is carried out in the nest and the action enables the mother to clean all waste and prevent the kittens from soiling the nest. This process is developed when the mother carries the kittens out of the nest and licks them to stimulate excretion, or they wander out and their own movements produce the same result. The result is that the majority of cats learn early in life never to soil their own bed. The house is often seen in adulthood as an extension of the bed and a feeding lair. Excretion therefore normally takes place away from it, or it remains specifically targeted into a litter tray.

Poor maternal care can disrupt this latrine-association learning process and occasionally kittens are weaned without becoming house-trained, especially some longhair strains. For others, medical or emotional trauma, especially during the cat's adolescence, decreases the security of home and an initial breakdown in hygiene may then continue long after the source of the problem has disappeared or been treated. Cats that are generally nervous or incompetent may repeatedly excrete indoors rather than venture outside, and the siting and nature of the litter tray and type of litter offered can all affect toileting behaviour. Being offered food too close to the tray will deter many cats from using it, and positioning of the tray in a site that is too busy, open or otherwise vulnerable may also cause cats to

Figure 21 Cats normally eliminate in a secluded area on a soft substrate

seek safer places. Some cats that are normally fastidious in their personal hygiene are reluctant to use soiled or damp trays, or to share with other cats. Trays may need to be cleaned more frequently or more trays may need to be provided. Certain compressed wood pellet litters appear to be less comfortable for cats to stand on, especially for cats living permanently indoors which may have more sensitive pads to their feet than cats whose pads are toughened up by an outdoor lifestyle. Litters which release deodorizing scents when damp have also been implicated in deterring cats from urinating in the tray, possibly because they irritate the pads of the feet when damp. Inflammation and cornification of the pads should be looked for in such cases. Litters containing chlorophyll are also reported as being unattractive to some cats and so should be swapped when problems arise.

Cats may also associate pain and discomfort with their tray if suffering from cystitis, feline urological syndrome or constipation. They may seek alternative surfaces and then continue to find carpets or beds more attractive as latrines. Other cats sometimes simply forget where the tray is, get 'caught short', or become arthritic or perhaps a little lazy in old age and need more trays or easier access to them.

It is often worth trying a finer grain commercial litter or fine sterile sand, which cats, perhaps because of their semi-desert ancestry, seem to find more attractive to use as a latrine than woodchip pellets or coarse grain litters. The position of the tray should be checked, especially relative to the position of food bowls and for security. Placing the tray in a corner or offering a covered tray, or, if the cat is unwilling to be enclosed, at least a tray with sides but no roof may help to improve the security of the latrine. It should not be sited in active areas of the house or those disrupted by children or the family dog. The tray should be cleaned a little less frequently than previously to allow the smell of cat's urine to accumulate as this improves its identification and association as a latrine. As with dogs, the smell of urine may stimulate the cat to urinate, but the whole litter surface should not be allowed to get too dirty or too damp, as this may also deter the cat. Once per day cleansing per cat is usually adequate. For outdoor cats, up to 50 per cent soil from the garden can be added to the litter or sand. Transfer of the use of the litter tray completely outdoors over a period of 2 to 3 weeks can be achieved by moving the tray progressively nearer the door and then out on to the step and finally into the garden.

For serious cases, confinement in a small room for a few days may help to reduce the opportunity for mistakes. Confinement in a pen where a simple choice between tray and bed can be provided may ensure that any early learning is reinforced. The cat can steadily be allowed more freedom indoors, one room at a time, when able to target excretion into the tray. Previously soiled areas in the house must be thoroughly cleaned but never with an agent that contains ammonia as this is a constituent of urine and

Figure 22   Offering food too close to the tray will deter many cats from using it

may endorse the idea of the cleaned area being a latrine. Many proprietary agents/cleaners may only mask the smell to the human nose and not be effective for the cat. Instead, a warm solution of a biological detergent may be followed by a wipe or scrub down with surgical spirit or other alcohol. Certain dyes in fabrics may be affected and so should be checked first for colour fastness under this cleaning system. Cleaned areas should be allowed to dry thoroughly before allowing the cat supervised access. Bowls of dry cat food (with the food glued down if necessary to prevent consumption) may act as a deterrent to toileting at cleaned sites for a few days and the cat can also be fed its main meals longer term at previously regularly soiled areas, provided, of course, that the family dog can be prevented from consuming them!

The cat should never be punished, even if 'caught in the act'. This makes cats more nervous and more likely to excrete in the house and even in the presence of the owner. Instead the cat should be calmly placed on its tray or outside the house and accompanied for reassurance if it appears that this helps. Timing of feeding can help to make faecal passage time more predictable in kittens and young cats and enable the cat to be put in the right place at the right time. Drug support is only usually helpful in cases of inappropriate toileting caused by nervousness. Prescription by the veterinary surgeon of oral sedatives or progestagens for 1 to 2 weeks, in addition to management changes, may be beneficial in such cases.

ATTACHMENT/BONDING DIFFICULTIES

The critical time for socializing kittens to humans, other cats, dogs and a normal household environment is between 2 and 7 weeks of age. Most problems of nervousness and incompetence in adult cats would never have arisen had they been handled intensively by at least four people during this period and exposed to a wide range of stimuli and experiences. Between 4 and 12 weeks (prior to completion of vaccination courses) they should be subjected to as complex and active a home environment as possible. Imprinting on humans in the few hours after birth probably also occurs through smell, and handling then may help produce a friendlier, more tractable pet at weaning. Recent Anglo-Swiss research suggested that there may be two distinct character types in cats, one with a high requirement for social contact and one for which such contact may be tolerated but not seen as an essential feature of the quality of life. The latter group seem to have a higher requirement for social play and predatory activity rather than affectionate interactions. A cat may therefore either need to live with other cats and be less competent socially on its own, or need to lead a solitary life and be less able to be sociable with other cats. It is suggested that, as a result, in its relations with human owners, a cat will either have a high requirement for physical contact and petting from the owner, or will never

Figure 23   Most problems of nervousness and incompetence in adult cats would never have arisen if they had been handled intensively between 2 and 7 weeks of age

appreciate it, even if the owner is very insistent at trying to provide it. Cats more typical of this second category may well prove less rewarding as pets, especially to those owners seeking a very affectionate relationship based on physical contact with the cat. However, these categories take little account of temperament changes of cats in adulthood, or those resulting from personality differences between one owner and the next. Nor do the studies consider the fact that most cats become far more affectionate towards their owners after, for example, intensive nursing following trauma or during illness. Furthermore, improvements may also result from trying to treat individual aggressive or nervous conditions. However, if a particular cat is rather shy and unresponsive to attempts to improve its self-confidence, it is usually comforting for the owner to know that the origins of the problem may be largely genetic and beyond their influence. Perhaps their cat is closer in character to his uncompromised and reactive ancestors whose speed of reaction to challenge defined their chances of survival.

UNDER-ATTACHMENT

Cats perceived by their owners to be 'under-attached' are often intolerant of the owner's proximity or approach, especially of handling, and fail to relax when held. Causes may include a lack of early socialization, over-enthusiasm on the part of the owner, trauma or necessary invasive handling during illness.

Treatment

This involves increasing the bond with and the cat's dependence on the owner, and a major feature is feeding frequent, small, attractive meals preceded by much vocal communication and encouraging of the cat to follow the owner for its food. Feeding at table level while attempting gentle handling along the cat's back only is the next step. Actions such as steadily increasing the frequency and intensity of handling, offering treats at other times and occupying favoured resting positions on the floor by the fire/radiator so that the cat comes to sit on the owner to gain access may all improve the cat's perception of the owner as rewarding. Owners should discontinue all efforts to chase the cat with a view to handling, especially if the cat seems to be of a more predatory and less affectionate character. The more owners try to initiate contact with this type of cat, the less time will actually be spent in contact with them. If, however, owners make themselves more attractive to their under-attached cats by offering food, titbits and toys or by lying passively in front of favourite resting places, and allow the cat to initiate the interaction, then the total time spent with the cat will usually increase. In severe cases the cat can be penned for a short time to accustom it to close human presence, and though it may seem a little bizarre, owners should try to approach the cat head first to stimulate the greeting behaviour observed between friendly cats and slowly introduce hands (perhaps otherwise viewed as threatening weapons) afterwards. It is essential that owners always respond positively with affectionate touch and a calm, gentle voice to any initiating gesture that the cat may make in approaching them in the home, especially for cats which are allowed outdoors. Drug support is usually not necessary except with severely traumatized cats or those unhandled before about 8 weeks, but tapered prescription of progestagens may help.

OVER-ATTACHMENT

Typically such cats are of pedigree strains, kept on long after weaning in the breeder's home when they should have been developing new social attachments with other cats and people and developing their behavioural repertoire in response to new challenges in new environments. They are also more likely to be cats of any breed or crossbreed which are kept permanently indoors and so are more dependent on their owners for stimulation and social contact. Over-attached cats may follow their owner constantly, perhaps crying regularly in an effort to engage them in physical contact. This is often the case in elderly cats when left alone and feeling insecure during the night. Once the owners have responded to the cat's distress calls by getting up, perhaps because they suspect some medical problem in their pet, the cat, reassured, often simply settles down to sleep.

The over-attached cat may be agitated or nervous when isolated. Often such cats demonstrate prolonged infantile behaviour when with their owners by sucking their clothes or skin. Owners may then feel guilty about rejecting the cat's affection or fear loss of contact if they do not respond. Where the cat fails to lose sucking and other nursing responses after weaning, this is often the result of the owner encouraging close association. It may also occur after intensive nursing during illness or during old age with its associated increased dependence on the owners.

Treatment

This involves detachment by non-punishing rejection of the cat's advances together with periodic physical separation and replacement by alternative forms of affectionate contact for short periods of time that are initiated by the owner. Provision of novel objects helps the cat learn to explore. Aversion therapy using loud startling noises or a jet of water can be used in severe cases. Old cats can be offered a secure, warm bed in the owner's bedroom and will usually then remain reassured and quiet throughout the night without needing to cry out to gain immediate physical attention.

NERVOUSNESS, PHOBIAS, SEPARATION ANXIETIES

These conditions can be presented as a range of problems. They can include the cat failing to adapt to 'normal' household events such as noise and visitors, lack of confidence in individual family members, failure to cope when away from the owner, and in some cases, agoraphobia. Cats may be shy and fearful if not exposed to a range of experiences and handling between the ages of 2 and 7 weeks. This is particularly likely if they are of the social play/predatory type of character (see page 79) and they are pursued too frequently or handled too roughly at any stage. Behaviour includes becoming withdrawn and secretive, moving with a low crouching gait, reluctance to enter open space or go outdoors, inappetence or psychogenic vomiting in very severe cases. Low threshold flight reactions and defensive (fear) aggression may occur if the cat is unable to avoid the challenge. Cats with such fears may have suffered a lack of early experience or a trauma such as agoraphobia caused by fear of attacks by cats outdoors. Indeed, agoraphobia is the only recognized genuine phobia encountered in cats. Old age and its associated loss of competence may also be a factor in the development of nervous conditions.

Treatment

Systematic desensitization is carried out by means of controlled exposure to known problem stimuli in low but increasing doses, while denying the opportunity to escape, so providing the possibility for habituation to the problem. With general nervousness/incompetence this is often best

Figure 24   Penning helps a new or nervous cat to adjust quickly to other animals in the household

achieved by penning the cat indoors (or outdoors for agoraphobic cats if coupled with chasing other cats away) and forcing it to experience 'normal' household events such as the proximity of visitors, the family and other pets while protected. The cat may thus come to learn that their presence is not threatening and often does so very quickly. Frequent short meals should be offered by an increasing number of people, including visitors. Detachment from any one over-favoured member will encourage the cat to spread its loyalties to more people. Drug support is often helpful. Progestagens can be administered as before and oral sedatives during desensitization may help. Alternative medicine such as certain homoeopathic treatments and Bach Flower Remedies may also be helpful for longer term support of cats which are generally hyper-reactive to common stimuli and nervous.

OVER-GROOMING AND SELF-MUTILATION

Most cats groom their flanks or back when confused, immediately after some mild upset or when unable to avoid general threatening stimuli. The behaviour seems to have little effect on the layering or quality of the coat but has a stress relieving function. This may be mediated, as in social monkeys, by the release of opiates from grooming and repetitive self-interested behaviour patterns. The behaviour is usually harmless, but occasionally a cat will over-groom in response to continued 'stress', such as the presence of too many cats in the house, acquisition of a dog, isolation from its owner, physical punishment or harassment by the owner for other behaviours such as house-soiling, or in response to an emotional disturbance between family members. Grooming may progress to the point of breaking hairshafts and producing a balding appearance to the flanks, the base of the tail, on the abdominal area or on the legs. In severe cases of unresolved stress or in particularly sensitive or incompetent individuals, the cat may actually pluck out large quantities of fur causing large bald patches. Often this is a secretive behaviour in its initial stages as the cat may feel more comfortable in the owner's presence and so refrain from the behaviour. In the later stages the cat may mutilate itself in their presence as well. This is an area where behaviourists and dermatologists are now conferring as it is thought that these reactions may also be triggered as the result of flea allergy and sensitivity to diet, and occasionally from allergy to household dust, but go far past the normal groom or scratch behaviour because of some underlying 'stress'.

In my experience, actual self-mutilation of body tissue is extremely rare but it is described as a common clinical condition in Canada by Professor Donal McKeown at the Ontario Veterinary School. Such severe self-inflicted damage is usually directed at itchy infected plucked areas or, less explicably but typically, at the tail or mouth. In these cases the behaviour is usually manic and occurs in frequent or occasional episodes. The behaviour may be self-reinforcing because of the euphoria engendered by the release of opiates. Many cases, such as sporadic clawing at the tongue, which was presented approximately every 6 months by one Burmese cat in the UK, have no obvious clinical cause. Other obsessive compulsive disorders have been described in cats, such as air licking, prolonged staring, air batting, jaw snapping, pacing, head shaking, freezing, paw shaking and aggressive attacks at the tail or feet accompanied sometimes by vocalization.

Treatment

Any dermatosis, such as flea sensitivity, atopy or dietary allergy, or other possible medical cause, should initially be investigated by the veterinarian. Only when such potential causes have been ruled out, or tackled as associative treatment, can behaviour therapy be considered.

Building the competence of a cat to cope alone by restructuring relations with the owner is required if separation anxiety is suspected. Stimulation with novel objects and situations, and controlled change of husbandry patterns can also be offered.

Self-mutilation can sometimes be resolved in single cats by the acquisition of another cat. The use of an Elizabethan collar for a short time may also help healing and perhaps break any learned behaviour patterns. The cat may also be distracted by sudden movement, loud noises or jets of water during severe episodes of mutilation. Generally increased levels of contact initiated by the owner may also help to define relations better and to offer more security in the home without the cat becoming over-dependent on the owner's presence.

Sedatives such as diazepam or amitryptaline may be given as immediate treatment to control severe episodes of self-mutilation and on a lower dose during lifestyle modification lasting several weeks. Anti-convulsants, anti-depressants and anti-anxiety drugs have been employed with some success in cats and dogs in Canada. Morphine antagonists such as naloxone may also inhibit the behaviour perhaps by enabling the animal to feel the pain of its self-mutilation. The effectiveness of any drugs at treating such problems is believed to be influenced by the length of time during which the behaviour has been expressed and the presence and ability of the owner to control conflicts and stresses in the cat's lifestyle and home environment.

AGGRESSION

Towards other cats

Aggression towards other cats may vary from occasional or frequent hissing or scuffling between two individuals in multi-cat households to serious physical attack of all cats on sight, indoors or out. Despotic aggression, victimization and, most commonly, persisting intolerance of new feline arrivals in the household are all quite common and have given rise to the widely held belief that most cats are highly individualistic, territorial and intolerant of other cats. In fact the cat is one of the most socially 'elastic' mammals on earth and can adapt its social tolerance according to circumstances and the individual nature of other cats it encounters. Hence vast numbers of cats can be found living peaceably together in 'feral' colonies in a wide range of environments around the world, including some in which food and shelter are in short supply and should have led to increased social competition and levels of aggression. When individual pet cats don't get on, the aggression by one cat towards another may include violent physical attack, low threshold arousal in response to the sight of movement of other cats or a total lack of initial investigatory or greeting behaviour. The cat may also be generally hyperactive and territorial. Nape biting and mounting, particularly of younger and unfamiliar or passive cats, may also be observed. Aggression rarely seems to be a defensive reaction, but occasionally attack becomes a learned policy to avoid investigation by other cats. Depending on its early experiences, a cat may have an emotional need to share a home base with other cats or be more solitary. In the latter case, the cat may be able to tolerate other house cats, but never form close social ties based on mutual grooming and resource sharing. Causes may include individual dislike or intolerance of one or more individual cats or lack of social learning or contact with other cats when young. There may be marked territorial defence reactions with failure to recognize and respond to friendly or neutral reactions of other cats, which may compound the success of early assertive or rough play with siblings. Territorial defence reactions and mutual intolerance of entire male cats, and defence of kittening areas by fertile queens or those in oestrus, or kitten defence by mothers are normal and expected forms of aggression and are not regarded as treatable. Finally, medical conditions such as hyperthyroidism, brain lesions and diet sensitivity can also cause aggression problems, but diagnosis and treatment clearly lie in the hands of the veterinarian.

Treatment

This has to be highly variable in order to suit particular situations. Controlled frequent exposure to new arrivals by housing the original cat and the new arrival alternately in an individual pen to allow protected introductions is one technique. Distraction techniques such as bringing cats together when feeding, modification of owner relations (especially with more 'rank-conscious' Oriental breeds) by instilling a hierarchy favouring the top cat in all greeting and play have all been known to help. In severe cases, a highly aroused protagonist can sometimes be deterred from attack by a spray of water from a plant mister, and thereafter may become more tolerant of the presence of another cat in the home, but such tactics are usually labour intensive and may require repeated carefully managed introduction sessions to achieve lasting results. In severe cases, rehoming may be the only safe and kind option.

Drug support includes tapered doses of progestagens, anti-androgenic injectables which may calm the aggressor (even if neutered), and sedatives. Some alternative treatments such as Bach Flower Remedies may be tried and may help a traumatized victim relax more during controlled inductions.

Towards visitors and owners

Cats may attack people, grabbing them with their claws and biting, though this is rarely accompanied by vocalization. The behaviour is often sudden and unpredictable and may be triggered by sudden movement, such as passing feet, or occasionally by certain high-pitched sounds. Defensive aggression to prevent handling is often caused by a lack of either early socialization or gentle human contact. Predatory chasing of feet and other moving body targets, territorial defence, especially in narrow or confined areas (only seen so far in Oriental breeds), hyper-excitement during play, dominant aggression towards people who are lying or sitting, i.e. vulnerable, occasionally food guarding and kitten defence against owners by nursing mothers have all been recorded. However, most problematic is the case of redirected aggression by very territorial cats agitated by the sight through a window of rivals outdoors. Owners who unwittingly approach to pacify their cat may inadvertently stimulate an attack because of the attraction of their movement. 'Petting and biting syndrome' also occurs in many cats, but this is usually tolerated or avoided by the owner. Initially the cat accepts affection but it may then suddenly lash out, grab and bite the owner, and then leap away to effect escape. The threshold of reaction is usually high and injury slight.

Treatment

This must always be carefully considered in relation to the members of the family most at risk, likely to be those with jerky or unpredictable movement patterns such as children and elderly relatives. Controlled exposure to habituate the cat to normal family movements and activities can help. However, stimulation in the form of another carefully introduced cat (preferably a kitten, which may be less threatening than a more socially, territorially or sexually competitive adult), together with opportunity to go outdoors (free-ranging where possible, or perhaps on a harness and lead in urban areas), frequent presentation of novel objects and concentrated play sessions (predatory chase, capture) of half an hour per day are all highly therapeutic. The use of a moving target such as a ball or string to attract the safe release of aggression will help an excited or frustrated cat and make owner intervention afterwards less risky. Diet sensitivity and its effect on feline behaviour are little understood but may be empirically investigated by withdrawing all canned foods for two weeks and replacing with fresh chicken/fish plus subsequent vitamin-mineral supplementation if matters improve. Certain modern complete dry diets may also be employed without a return of problems, and with greater convenience than preparing fresh diets. This treatment has been particularly valuable for those problem behaviours occurring after a change from a standard canned diet to an apparently better quality canned or 'cooked in foil' prepared diet. Access to catnip toys should be denied during treatment to preclude concomitant excitability in sensitive cats. Drug support using progestagens for 3–6 weeks may help and some 'alternative' medicinal approaches have produced excellent response in easily agitated Oriental breeds in particular. Burmese cats seem to respond especially well to certain Bach Flower Remedies.

PICA

This is the depraved ingestion of non-nutritional items. It is usually unexplained, although the eating of some house plants may be due to the desire to obtain roughage or a source of minerals and vitamins. Occasional cases are reported of cats eating rubber and electric cables but the main problem concerns the ingestion of wool and other fabric. Wool eating was first documented in the 1950s and was thought to be limited to Siamese strains but a recent survey of 152 fabric-eating cats by Dr John Bradshaw of Southampton University and myself shows the behaviour to be more widespread. Responses to the survey showed that fabric eating was presented most by some Siamese (55 per cent of responders) and Burmese (28 per cent) cats, occasionally by other Oriental strains and, more rarely, by crossbred cats (11 per cent). Males were as likely as females to present the problem and the majority of responders of both sexes in the survey were neutered. The typical age of onset for fabric eating is 2–8 months. Most cats (93 per cent in the survey) start by consuming wool, perhaps attracted by the smell of lanolin, but later transfer to other fabrics. Cotton was eaten by 64 per cent and synthetic fabric by 54 per cent.

While some fabric eaters chew or eat material on a regular basis, others only do so sporadically. Many consume large quantities of such materials as woollen jumpers and cotton towels, underwear, furniture covers, etc. without apparent harm, although surgery is required in a few cases to clear gastric obstructions and impaction of material. Some have presented such a level of economic damage to their owner's property that they have been euthanased, but most owners of fabric-eating cats seem remarkably tolerant of their behaviour.

The exact cause of the behaviour is unknown but a variety of factors have been suggested including genetic. Wool eating is suggested to be a largely inheritable trait, rarely expressed, caused by a physiologically based hyperactivity of the autonomic nervous system. Such neuronal disturbances could affect the control of the digestive tract and thereby produce unusual food cravings and inappropriate appetite stimulation, although the exact mechanism is unclear.

Another suggestion is that the desire to suck and knead wool and then other fabric is a continuing redirected form of suckling behaviour resulting from the failure of the cat to mature fully. Some cats grow out of the behaviour at maturity, but others will eat all unattended fabric despite good nutrition and husbandry. The behaviour is usually more prevalent in cats housed permanently indoors. Fabric eating is sometimes secretive, but it is usually blatant and unaffected by punishment. While most cats will consume fabric at any time, some will take a woollen item to the food bowl and eat this alternately with their usual diet, and only at mealtimes.

Some fabric-eating cats have caused hundreds of pounds worth of damage to designer jumpers, carpets and tweed-covered furniture! Fabric-eating behaviour may sometimes be triggered by some form of stress, perhaps in the form of medical treatment, or the introduction of another cat to the household. A significant number of cats in the survey first exhibited fabric eating within one month of acquisition. Insufficient handling of kittens before adoption or separation from the mother at too early an age may also lead to stress and trigger the behaviour. Only 15 per cent of cats in the survey were acquired before 8 weeks of age. This may be earlier than is often recommended for maximizing full emotional development, particularly for the later maturing pedigree Oriental strains. Over half of the pedigree cats in the survey were acquired by their owners at or beyond the minimum age of 12 weeks recommended by the UK Governing Council of the Cat Fancy, suggesting that the age at which a kitten is taken from its mother may not be the only influence on the subsequent development of fabric eating.

Continuing infantile traits, such as over-dependence on the physical presence of the owner, can lead to separation anxiety when the owner departs and cause the cat to start eating fabric. The behaviour may become triggered as a learned pattern, even in response to previously tolerated influences. The best hope for the treatment of fabric eating probably rests with cases where the relationship between owner and cat can be modified so that the cat is made less dependent on its owners for emotional security, thus reducing the need to eat fabric as a form of anxiety-relieving displacement behaviour.

Fabric eating also seems to form part of a prey catching/ingestion sequence otherwise usually unexpressed in the day-to-day repertoires of the pet cat fed prepared and often very easily digested food. Indeed, 40 per cent of the cats reported in the survey had little or no access to the outdoors and hence restricted or no opportunity to develop exploratory and hunting behaviour, including ingestion of small prey.

Treatment

Currently, treatment involves a combination approach of social restructuring with the owner (see Over-attachment, page 81), increasing the level of stimulation for the cat through play, increased activity at home, opportunity to investigate novel stimuli and, where possible, the opportunity for indoor cats to lead an outdoor life. This can mean allowing free access or housing in a secure pen or accustoming the cat to being walked on a lead and harness.

Increasing the fibre content of the diet by offering a dry diet and/or gristly meat attached to large bones to increase food (prey) handling and ingestion time has also brought improvements in many, and even total cures in a few cats. Others have improved by being offered increased fibre in the form of bran or chopped undyed wool or tissue paper blended in with their usual wet canned diet. Such tactics presumably help because the higher fibre intake keeps the cat's stomach active and reduces any appetite-related motivations to fabric eating. Remote ambushes may be employed using aromatic taste deterrents such as eucalyptus oil or menthol applied to woollen clothes. Traditional deterrents using pepper or chilli powder seem only to broaden the cat's normal taste preferences! Remote aversion tactics using touch-sensitive cap exploders under clothes (or under non-current carrying cable for electric cable chewers) deliberately made available can deter some cats. This treatment must only be employed under the careful guidance of the veterinary surgeon or referred behaviourist. It is never used with nervous cats or those suffering from certain medical conditions, e.g. cardiac problems. Some cats may be safely channelled into chewing only certain acceptable items provided at meal and resting times. Owners of such cats have found in these cases that, to preserve clothes and household items, the cat has to be kept supplied with a cheap supply of its favourite fabric. No drugs are as yet recognized as being helpful with treatment.

Nutrition
and Feeding

7

NUTRITION AND FEEDING

Cats need to eat in order to live and to remain healthy. The components of food which provide all the energy and raw materials to fulfil this task are called *nutrients*. Unless the diet provides the correct amount and balance of these nutrients, the cat is unable to sustain a long, healthy, active life, but the cat's specific requirement for each individual nutrient varies at different stages of its life cycle.

Nutritionally speaking, the cat is an unusual animal. Throughout its history of evolution, the cat has adhered to a strictly carnivorous diet and therefore there has been no reason for it to evolve alternative metabolic pathways in order to adapt to a changing diet. We shall see how this affects the nutritional needs of the domestic cat and how these requirements mean that the cat is an *obligate carnivore* whose diet must be derived, at least in part, from animal tissues.

The nutrients in food are eaten or *ingested* by the cat and subsequently *digested* in the guts, *absorbed* into the bloodstream, and processed or *metabolized* by the body to fulfil the cat's needs. Each of these will now be considered in turn, and particular attention given to the cat's special requirements.

Nutrients

The major classes of nutrients are:

(a) proteins
(b) fats
(c) carbohydrates
(d) vitamins
(e) minerals
(f) water

Proteins are made up of *amino acids*, which are the basic building blocks of the body and important for cell and tissue growth, maintenance and repair. They can also be metabolized to provide energy and this is an important function of proteins in the cat. With its natural 'all-animal' diet, which is not a rich source of carbohydrate, the cat would have depended on protein for a large proportion of its energy source. It therefore uses a certain amount of protein in the diet to provide energy and the dietary protein requirement for cats is considerably higher than that for other species, such as the dog. At least 25 per cent of the dry matter of the cat's diet should come from proteins.

When proteins have been utilized by the body, they are broken down in the liver prior to excretion. Some of the products of this breakdown, such as ammonia, are toxic. Most of these are processed in the liver to form *urea* and then flushed out of the body in the urine. The cat requires around 20 amino acids. Eleven of these cannot be synthesized in the body and are therefore known as *essential amino acids*; the remainder are called non-essential since they can be manufactured by the cat. If the diet is lacking in certain of these essential amino acids, notably taurine and arginine, special disease syndromes may occur. The cat must have animal tissue in its diet, since little taurine is found in tissues of plant origin.

Fats are the other major source of energy in the cat, and should form a minimum of 9 per cent of the dry matter of the diet. When they are digested by the body, they are broken down to *fatty acids* and *glycerol*. Again, some of these fatty acids cannot be synthesized by the cat and they are called *essential fatty acids* or *EFAs*. The main function of fat is as an energy source, but it is also a provider of the fat-soluble vitamins A, D, E and K. Fatty acids also have a structural function in all cell membranes, particularly nervous tissue; are part of many of the body secretions; and are necessary to maintain coat condition. The essential fatty acids linolenic acid and the longer chain arachidonic acid are required in the cat's diet since they cannot be synthesized in the body. Arachidonic acid is almost entirely absent from plant tissues, so the cat must have some dietary source of animal fat.

Carbohydrates are a major source of energy in most species. However, animal tissues provide very little in the way of soluble carbohydrate and the cat has evolved so that it can survive without any carbohydrate in the diet, using protein instead to make up the shortfall in energy intake. Many cat diets do, nevertheless, contain a significant amount of carbohydrate and there are times where a ready supply of energy is beneficial to the cat, e.g. during growth, pregnancy, lactation and at other times of stress. Complex, insoluble carbohydrate is otherwise known as *fibre* and this is not digested by the animal. It provides the bulk for faeces and is important for keeping the digestive system in good working order. In the wild, fur and feathers provide the necessary fibre in the cat's diet, whereas in other species, plant fibre is an important dietary component.

Vitamins are required in microscopic amounts and are either water-soluble or fat-soluble. The water-soluble vitamins are the 'B-group' vitamins and vitamin C (which the cat can synthesize itself) and the fat-soluble vitamins are A, D, E and K. Once the body's requirement has been met, there is no benefit in providing large excesses, and indeed, excess fat-soluble vitamins are stored in the liver and other fat depots where they can accumulate and lead to problems of toxicity.

Minerals have many functions in the body and are usually divided into two groups depending on their concentration in the diet. The major or 'macro' minerals are usually present in amounts which can be measured in milligrams (1/1000 g) and include calcium, phosphorus, sodium, potassium and magnesium. The trace elements or 'micro-minerals' include iron, copper, zinc, manganese and iodine and the quantities of these in the diet can usually be measured in micrograms (1/1,000,000 g). It is vitally important that these minerals are not only present in the correct *absolute* amounts, but they must also be present in the correct amounts *relative* to each other. This is particularly important in the case of calcium and phosphorus in the growing kitten, as we shall see later.

Water is also considered a nutrient and it is vital for many functions within the body. Although the body can survive for weeks without food, a total lack of water can result in death within days. The amount of water the cat needs to drink depends on the moisture content of its food; fresh meat and canned cat foods have a high water content (about 75 per cent) whereas dry cat foods may only be around 8 per cent water. Another source of water is the *metabolic water* produced in the body from the metabolism of carbohydrates, fats and proteins. The kidneys of the cat are extremely efficient at conserving water, presumably because of its desert origins, and the cat often does not need to drink much water to meet its requirement, particularly when a moist diet is fed. However, water intake will rise under certain conditions, such as high environmental temperatures, activity, during lactation and in certain diseases.

The digestive system

The process by which food is broken down into a simple form which can be absorbed and used by the body is called *digestion* and in mammals this process takes places in the digestive or *alimentary* tract (see Chapter 8 Anatomy and Physiology). This may be thought of as a tube through which the food passes while being acted upon by secretions from organs that discharge into the tube. These secretions contain digestive *enzymes*, which speed up the process of *hydrolysis* by which food is broken down by water. The three major classes of food that require digestion are carbohydrate, protein and fat.

MOUTH

Digestion of food begins when the cat first *ingests* or takes food into the mouth. The teeth of the cat are particularly suited to a meat eating lifestyle and are adapted to the efficient killing of prey and the tearing of flesh, rather than chewing. As they cannot chew effectively, cats reduce their food to pieces small enough to swallow by tearing or cutting. These actions begin the breakdown of food in the mouth, and this process is helped by the secretion of saliva which coats the food with mucus and facilitates swallowing. Saliva also contains *ptyalin*, an enzyme which digests starch, although this is of little importance to the cat.

STOMACH

When food is swallowed, it passes down the *oesophagus*, whose muscles contract with a 'wave' motion called *peristalsis*, and arrives at the stomach within a few seconds. The stomach has several functions. It is a storage organ, allowing food to be taken in as meals rather than continuously; it is a mixing bag, where more digestive enzymes are added to the food; and it is a regulator valve that controls the rate of flow into the small intestine. The stomach secretions contain a number of digestive enzymes; hydrochloric acid, which creates an acid environment for the proper functioning of certain enzymes; and mucus, which again lubricates the food and protects the lining of the stomach wall from being digested by its own enzymes. The secretion of acid, mucus and enzyme depends on the composition and quantity of food eaten and is regulated by both hormones and nerves.

The wall of the stomach is muscular, particularly in the *pyloric region*, and a series of peristaltic waves mix the stomach contents and push it towards the *pyloric sphincter*. By this time, the mixture is a thick milky liquid called *chyme*, and its passage into the small intestine is controlled by the pyloric sphincter.

THE SMALL INTESTINE

The acid chyme that arrives in the *duodenum* (the first part of the small intestine) is neutralized by secretion from the *pancreas*, which contains sodium bicarbonate, which is alkaline. Pancreatic juice also contains digestive enzymes that further break down fats, carbohydrates and proteins. The pancreas also secretes the hormone *insulin* into the bloodstream to control blood sugar levels. The regulation of pancreatic enzyme release is largely under the control of two hormones, *secretin* and *pancreozymin*, which are secreted from cells in the wall of the duodenum and small intestine.

The liver is the other major organ associated with the small intestine. *Bile* is produced in the liver, stored in the gall bladder and passed into the gut via the bile duct. The salts contained in bile emulsify the fat into tiny globules that can then be processed by the lipase enzymes in pancreatic juice. It is the pigments in the bile that give faeces their characteristic colour. In most mammals bile salts are manufactured in the body by the combination of bile acids with either taurine or glycine (another amino acid), but in the cat only taurine can be used in significant amounts. This creates an unusually high demand for taurine and it must be supplied in the diet as the cat is unable to synthesize enough of this amino-sulphonic acid to fulfil its needs.

The digestion of food is completed in the small intestine and, once it has been broken down to its simplest form, it can be absorbed across the wall of the intestine and into the blood. The end products of digestion are thus carried to the liver, where they are metabolized. Fat is absorbed into the *lymph vessels* and is later transferred to the bloodstream. The cat's intestines are short in comparison to the dog and are therefore slightly less efficient at digesting food. The shorter intestine may have evolved as the result of being an advantage in the wild. The wild cat species hunt by a strategy of ambush with short bursts of acceleration, in which a smaller volume (and hence weight) of guts and their contents are beneficial. At the other extreme, herbivores such as cattle and sheep are somewhat slower in their movements and their digestive systems are considerable longer and more complex, allowing them to digest the tough cellulose in plant tissues.

LARGE INTESTINE

By the time the food reaches the large intestine, most of the nutrients have been digested and absorbed. In this part of the gut, water is absorbed and in the *caecum* some fermentation of cellulose by bacteria takes place. Faeces are around 70 per cent water and 30 per cent undigested food, dead bacteria and some inorganic material. The faeces are stored in the rectum and evacuated through the anal sphincter, which is under voluntary control. Problems with control may occur in old age or during bouts of diarrhoea or other illness.

The practical feeding of cats

FEEDING THE ADULT CAT

The cat's specific requirements for certain nutrients that can only be provided by animal tissues, which must, therefore, form at least part of the cat's diet, have already been mentioned. Cats are particularly adapted to a meat eating lifestyle and this appears to apply even to their sense of taste. Although they will react to substances we think of as salt, sour or bitter, they do not respond to the sweet taste of simple sugars. However, they can distinguish the 'sweet' taste of certain amino acids and are particularly sensitive to the constituents of meat. The sense of taste together with the sense of smell seem to have the greatest influence on how the cat perceives the 'flavour' of a food. In addition, they prefer to eat food at around 35°C, which is close to their own body temperature as well as that of freshly killed prey. This preference may also be partly explained by the increase in odour as the food is warmed. Moist foods may be preferred when first offered, but the texture of the food does not affect the cat's overall food intake.

In general, cats will adjust their daily food intake in order to meet their energy requirement and unless they are fed an exceptionally palatable diet, or lead a particularly sedentary life, they seldom overeat. All nutrients in the diet must, therefore, be balanced in relation to its *calorie* (energy) content in order to ensure that the cat receives the correct amount of these nutrients. The daily energy requirement of adult cats is between 60 and 90 kcal/kg body weight, depending on the cat's level of activity, and at least 25 per cent of the diet (on a dry matter basis) must be provided in the form of protein. The cat's body is unable to adapt to a diet extremely low in protein and indeed, such a diet is likely to be completely rejected by the cat since they find low protein diets rather unpalatable. A typical canned food will supply 70 kcal/100 g.

When allowed continuous access to food, cats tend to adopt a pattern of small, frequent (usually 8–16) meals throughout the whole 24-hour period. However, cats readily adapt to different feeding schedules imposed by their owners and are commonly fed two meals per day.

Cats do seek variety in their diet, as long as the new food is not *too* different from the familiar one, or the palatability too low, but at times of stress, a familiar diet is preferred. Repeated exposure to fresh supplies of a new food not initially acceptable to the cat may encourage the cat to overcome its reticence. Furthermore, cats may sometimes detect and may reject diets that are deficient in certain nutrients, so it is important that any diet offered is nutritionally complete.

FEEDING THE GROWING KITTEN

At birth, most kittens weigh between 85 g and 120 g and in the first few weeks of life, they will increase their body weight by about 100 g/week. Males grow at a faster rate than females and by 6 weeks they are already 7 per cent heavier than female kittens. At 1 year, males can be up to 45 per cent heavier than their female counterparts and at this age most kittens will have reached their adult weights of, on average, 3–6 kg, although males take slightly longer to mature than females. In both sexes, kittens are likely to have achieved around 75 per cent of their mature weight by 6 months of age.

In the early stages of growth, kittens are largely dependent on their mother's milk to supply their nutrient requirements but by 4 weeks of age, solid food will have begun to form part of their diet. Growth rates at this

Figure 25 Grossly obese but hard to believe – do I weigh that much?

stage are extremely high and this is a very nutritionally demanding time for kittens. They need between two and four times as much energy as an adult would if it were the same weight, and they need high levels of protein for growth. Rapidly growing bones need a supply of minerals (especially calcium and phosphorus) in the correct amounts and in the correct proportions to each other to develop properly.

The energy requirement for adult cats is about 60–90 kcal/kg body weight/day, depending on their level of activity, but kittens at weaning need 220–250 kcal/kg body weight/day. As the kitten grows, this requirement gradually tails off and by 20, 30 and 40 weeks it has fallen to 160, 120 and 100 kcal/kg body weight/day respectively. The dietary protein requirement of kittens is 28 g/400 kcal as compared to 25 g/400 kcal in adults. In practice, growing kittens should be fed as much as they will eat since they regulate their food intake well, but at the same time keeping a close eye on their weight and condition to ensure that they are developing properly and not becoming too fat.

Kittens, therefore, need to eat relatively large amounts of food in relation to their body weight, but their stomachs have only a small capacity. To compensate for this, they need to be fed several small meals a day; four or five meals may be fed when they are weaned at 8 weeks but this can be gradually reduced to one or two meals by 6 months.

In order to encourage the kitten to eat enough to satisfy its nutritional needs, a diet specifically formulated for growth should be fed. This diet may be fed until the kitten is about 8–9 months old. Ideally, such diets should be:

(a) palatable, since a meal which is left uneaten has no nutritive value
(b) energy rich
(c) high in protein (of a suitable amino acid profile)
(d) easily digested
(e) low in bulk
(f) balanced in respect of vitamins and minerals as nutritional errors at this stage can have long-lasting and possibly irreversible effects.

Devising an acceptable balanced diet for growth is a complex exercise and, for most owners, commercially prepared diets offer the safest, most convenient solution. It is sometimes possible to feed an adult formulation, but the kitten must eat proportionally more of it and may not be physically capable of eating enough to meet its requirements. A typical adult canned diet for cats will provide 70 kcal/100 g compared to 90 kcal/100 g in kitten growth formulations. Additionally, not all adult formulations contain enough essential nutrients for the growing kitten.

Contrary to popular belief, milk is not an essential part of a kitten's diet after weaning, since many cats lose their ability to digest milk sugar (lactose). However, for those who can tolerate it, milk is a useful source of nutrients if fed in restricted amounts.

BREEDING QUEEN

Energy requirements are very high at this stage of the life cycle. The energy requirement of the queen increases from around 70 kcal/kg body weight/day at pre-mating, to around 100 kcal/kg/day during gestation and upward of 240 kcal/kg/day during lactation. Unlike most mammals, the pregnant queen begins to eat more and her weight steadily increases within a week of a successful mating. In other species, including the dog, the most significant weight gain occurs in the last third of pregnancy to coincide with the greatest amount of foetal growth. This unusual pattern of weight gain in the pregnant cat is due to the deposition of energy stores around the body that can be mobilized later in pregnancy and lactation when it may be difficult for the queen to eat enough to meet her requirements.

Throughout the whole period of pregnancy and lactation, sufficient food should be available to satisfy the queen's appetite. During lactation, in particular, food should also be available during the night. Frequent meals of a concentrated food, such as kitten food, are helpful since the capacity of the stomach to expand is limited when the abdomen is otherwise full of kittens. Again palatability is all important to encourage her to eat enough to meet her needs. By the fifth and sixth week of lactation, the combined food intake of the queen and her kittens may be as much as three times that of the queen before mating.

Nutrition and disease

Nutrition-related disorders can be divided into those conditions *caused* by errors in the diet and those conditions which may benefit from alterations in the diet.

DIET-INDUCED CONDITIONS

These are frequently caused by well-meaning owners with ill-conceived ideas about the cat's nutritional requirements. Over-supplementation of the diet with, for example, fish oils, or indulgence of a cat's apparent 'addiction' to a particular food may lead to imbalances in the diet. The consequences of improper feeding of cats are most apparent in cats during the 'critical' life stages, such as during growth, pregnancy or lactation or at other times of disease or stress.

Hypervitaminosis A

Although the cat must have a source of vitamin A in the diet, deficiencies of this fat-soluble vitamin are rare since cats are unlikely to eat a diet low in fat and vitamin A content (see Chapter 9, The Locomotor System). It is far more likely that they will suffer from an *excess* of vitamin A in the diet. This can occur when the diet is over-supplemented with cod (or other fish) liver oil or when they have been fed large amounts of liver, usually over a long period of time. Liver is very palatable to cats and this can lead to the rejection of other foods.

The most obvious effect of feeding too much vitamin A to cats is the production of bony outgrowths, especially on the neck vertebrae and on the long bones of forelimbs. These are extremely painful and can result in the *ankylosis* or fusing together of the bones of the joints. The cat will be very stiff, especially around the neck, and the first sign an owner may notice is that the cat is not grooming itself as normal. Sometimes, affected cats will sit in the posture of a kangaroo to avoid bearing any weight by the front half of the body. Hypervitaminosis A can also lead to liver damage.

Once diagnosed, the condition may be treated by correction of the diet and, in the early stages, pain killers may be required. If treated early, the clinical signs will be resolved and the progress of the disease will be halted. However, if ankylosis of joints has already occurred, this cannot be reversed.

Vitamin E deficiency

A deficiency of vitamin E in cats results in a painful, inflammatory condition of the fat under the skin known as *pansteatitis* or *yellow fat disease*. This condition is often associated with feeding either rancid fat or large amounts of oily fish (especially red tuna), which are high in polyunsaturated fatty acids. Vitamin E is an anti-oxidant and is therefore rapidly depleted in diets high in polyunsaturated fatty acids, which are easily oxidized.

The fat deposits under the skin of an affected cat become hard, painful and lumpy and, in the later stages of the disease, assume a yellow colour. The cat is usually off food, has a fever and resents being touched anywhere on the body.

Treatment is again aimed at correction of the basic diet, but it is also necessary to administer oral vitamin E supplements to replace the body stores. Initially, anti-inflammatory drugs may be required. Recovery is slow and may demand several weeks or months of treatment. Occasionally a cat may not respond to treatment and will continue to deteriorate; sudden death may also occur although, fortunately, this is rare.

Thiamin deficiency

Thiamin (vitamin B_1) is a water soluble vitamin which can be destroyed by prolonged storage, overcooking and certain forms of processing. It is also destroyed by an enzyme, *thiaminase*, present in certain types of raw fish, but this enzyme is destroyed by cooking. Most cat food manufacturers supplement their products to compensate for possible losses but it may be necessary to supplement some home-prepared diets.

A deficiency of this vitamin can produce clinical signs within 1–2 weeks of introducing a defective diet. The signs include salivation and a failure to eat despite being interested in food. The cat may initially be unsteady on its feet and the head is held in a downward-flexed position. These neurological signs progress to short seizures, circling and spasms of the limbs, which give the impression that the cat is 'walking on its toes'. In the terminal stage, the cat is in semi-coma, continuously crying and convulsing, before death eventually supervenes.

Provided the cat is not in this final stage, the response to treatment is quite dramatic. The signs may improve within 24 hours of the administration of thiamin either by mouth or by injection. The defective diet must subsequently be corrected.

Hypervitaminosis D

Vitamin D *toxicity* can be produced relatively easily in the cat and is usually the result of overzealous dietary supplementation with, for example, cod liver oil, which is rich in vitamin D. This leads to resorption

Figure 26 Food allergy in a 2-year-old domestic cat. The cat improved on a chicken and rice diet

of bone and deposition of calcium in soft tissues causing weakness, brittle bones and a failure of a number of organs, particularly the kidney. Affected cats do not always recover, but treatment is aimed at alleviating the cat's symptoms and encouraging it to eat a normal diet, without supplements. A deficiency of vitamin D can lead to the development of 'rickets', but in the cat, this is rare provided it has access to some sunlight.

Taurine deficiency

We are becoming increasingly aware of the importance of taurine in the cat and a deficiency of this amino-sulphonic acid is now known to be associated with retinal degeneration in the eye, heart disease, reproductive failure and developmental abnormalities in kittens. The cat's unique dietary requirement for taurine stems from its exceptionally high physiological demand for this nutrient together with its inability to manufacture sufficient taurine to meet these demands. As taurine is only present in negligible quantities in plant tissues, this again emphasizes the cat's special need for animal tissue in its diet.

Nutritional secondary hyperparathyroidism

This condition is the result of feeding a diet deficient in calcium; the deficiency may be absolute or relative, where the concentration of phosphorus in the diet is excessive in relation to calcium. The correct ratio of calcium to phosphorus in the diet should be approximately 1.1:1. Mineral imbalances are likely to have their greatest effect on growing kittens and, typically, this condition is seen in young animals which have been fed an all or predominantly muscle meat diet. Muscle and organ meats have relatively low levels of calcium, but relatively high levels of phosphorus. Some of these tissues give rise to a disastrous calcium to phosphorus ratio of 1:15 or even 1:20.

The body attempts to restore levels of calcium in the blood by a variety of means, including an increased resorption and decreased formation of bone and subsequent replacement of bone with fibrous tissue. This results in pain, lameness and skeletal deformities, and sometimes pathological fractures. Treatment is aimed at correction of the dietary imbalance and provision of a nutritionally balanced diet for the cat's needs. Additional calcium supplementation may be required initially when the disease is advanced, and pain killers may also be of some help to start with, although pain is usually relieved fairly rapidly once the diet has been corrected. Most cases respond well to treatment, but an affected kitten may be left with skeletal deformities and stunted growth. Prevention of the condition is therefore preferable to a cure.

Before the availability of commercial kitten foods it was not uncommon for this condition to be regularly seen, especially in Siamese kittens. Breeders would often wean them using raw meat and water rather than milk since it was believed that Siamese kittens could not tolerate lactose or milk sugar in cow's milk. It was not unusual for veterinarians in feline practice to see whole litters of kittens of 2–3 months of age affected with the condition that was often erroneously diagnosed as rickets by the owner, who would not infrequently attempt to correct the condition prior to presentation to the veterinarian by the administration of large doses of vitamin D in the form of cod liver oil.

Essential fatty acid deficiency

Cats have a particular dietary requirement for the essential fatty acids linolenic acid and arachidonic acid, which they are unable to synthesize from linolenic acid. As arachidonic acid is almost entirely absent from plant tissues, the cat must be provided with a source of animal fat in the diet. It may take several months before any signs of a deficiency are seen, but these may be evident as listlessness with the appearance of a dull, dry, scurfy coat that is greasy to the touch. The condition responds well to supplementation and correction of the diet.

Obesity

Not traditionally a problem in cats as most cats will regulate their energy intake to their requirements. However, a significant proportion of the cat population can be considered overweight (6–12 per cent in the UK; 20–25 per cent in the USA).

Obese cats tend to be neutered, over 3 years old and confined indoors. Although cats may not suffer the complications of obesity to the same extent as dogs and humans, definite links have now been made between obesity and the occurrence of feline lower urinary tract disease, diabetes mellitus and hepatic lipidosis. Furthermore, the condition may reduce the cat's quality of life and presents difficulties in grooming, which can result in skin problems.

Two stages are apparent in the development of obesity: an initial 'dynamic' phase in which the cat's energy intake exceeds its requirement resulting in the deposition of fat; and a subsequent 'static' phase in which the cat remains fat, but the body weight is fairly stable and appetite is normal or even reduced. Overweight kittens may always be at risk of obesity since overfeeding during the growing period leads to an increase in fat cell *numbers* (which have a measurable volume below which they cannot shrink) as opposed to a reversible increase in cell *size* in the mature animal.

An animal is considered obese when its body weight exceeds the normal by 15 per cent or more and in cats fat is commonly deposited in the groin to form an 'apron'. There is usually also a large amount of fat in the abdominal cavity, but this must be distinguished from other causes of abdominal enlargement such as the accumulation of abdominal fluid, pregnancy or abdominal organ enlargement.

Weight loss can be achieved by a programme of controlled calorie reduction and should be carried out in consultation with your veterinary surgeon. An initial target weight should be set that should either be the ideal weight or, if the cat is more than 15 per cent overweight, should represent a 15 per cent loss in weight. A weight loss of 15 per cent can realistically be achieved in 18 weeks by feeding a diet that provides 60 per cent of the calories the cat would need if it was at its target weight. An average cat requires 60–90 kcal/kg/day and the energy requirements for weight reduction in cats of different weights are shown in Table 1.

In some cases, it is sufficient to feed less of the normal diet, but this may lead to a relative deficiency of other nutrients and the cat may feel hungry since a smaller volume is fed. Commercially prepared low calorie diets

Table 1 Calculation of energy requirements for weight reduction in cats

Target body weight (kg)	Maintenance energy requirements (kcals)	60% of energy (kcals)
3.0	210	125
3.5	245	145
4.0	280	170
4.5	315	190
5.0	350	210
5.5	385	230
6.0	420	250

address these issues and provide a convenient and effective means of achieving weight loss in cats.

DIET-RESPONSIVE CONDITIONS

These conditions are not actually caused by dietary errors but their treatment usually involves an element of dietary modification.

Kidney failure

Many of the signs associated with chronic renal failure result from the build-up of the toxic products of protein breakdown in the body. Many cases will respond if the protein in the diet is restricted to the cat's actual needs, and also if the level of phosphorus is reduced. However, the cat must have a certain amount of protein in its diet and is unable to adapt to an excessively low protein intake. In any case, cats do not find very low protein diets palatable and they will not eat them. Limited amounts of high-quality protein are needed in the diet, and fat (such as strips of bacon fat) may provide a useful source of energy, which will also help to augment the palatability of the diet.

In chronic renal failure, the output of urine is usually high and can also result in a loss of water-soluble vitamins, especially the B-group vitamins. A number of commercially prepared diets suitable for cats with renal failure are available through the veterinary profession that are balanced for all nutrients, but if a diet is to be prepared at home, cooked egg, cottage cheese and chicken are good sources of high-quality protein. This can be supplemented with rice or pasta which will provide calories with minimal vegetable (low quality) protein. Veterinary advice should be sought and observed if a diet is to be formulated at home.

Feline lower urinary tract disease (FLUTD)

This condition is also known as feline urological syndrome, urolithiasis and 'Blocked Cat' and is a complex condition characterized by a number of clinical signs that include the presence of blood in the urine, increased frequency of urination and difficulty or pain in passing urine. It is often, but not always, associated with a urinary obstruction due to the accumulation of granular *struvite* crystals and a gelatinous matrix, particularly in males. If not treated quickly, this can lead to acute renal failure, which is life threatening.

Early studies suggested that diet was a primary cause of this condition, but it is now thought more appropriate to view diet as merely one of a number of different contributory factors, which may include viruses or bacteria as well as individual susceptibility to the condition. However, manipulation of dietary factors has been shown to be important in the management of FLUTD, particularly where struvite urolithiasis is involved.

It appears that the acidity of the urine is the most important factor in the development of struvite urolithiasis, and struvite crystals are more likely to form when the urinary pH is higher than 6.5 (i.e. the urine is alkaline). In addition, when the volume of urine is low, it becomes more concentrated and this may also encourage struvite to crystallize out of the solution. Very high levels of magnesium (higher than those in commercial cat foods) can also promote struvite urolithiasis, since this mineral is a major constituent of struvite. However, this is probably dependent on the form in which magnesium is given as this can also affect the acidity of the urine.

The pattern of meal feeding may affect the urinary pH. A regime in which there is continuous access to food results in a constant, but slightly more alkaline, urine. Where separate, distinct meals are fed, the urine experiences a wave of alkalinity, the *alkaline tide*, approximately 3–4 hours after a meal. It is not yet clear which method of feeding provides the lowest risk of struvite deposition.

Cats which are fed a predominantly dry diet tend to have a lower water intake and a slightly greater water loss in the faeces than those on canned or semi-moist foods, but there is a considerable variation in the amount that individual cats will drink voluntarily. This is compounded by other environmental and metabolic factors such as obesity, inactivity, infrequent urination patterns or limited access to water with the result that the risk of developing FLUTD varies enormously between individual cats.

Dietary management of cases of FLUTD will help to prevent recurrence. Moist, highly digestible foods should be provided and extra water may be added to make them even wetter; drinking water should be freely available; excessive dietary magnesium should be avoided; oral urinary acidifiers may be administered and if these are given at the time of feeding, the effects of the 'alkaline tide' will be minimized. Urinary acidifiers can be toxic in high doses and their use should be monitored by a veterinary surgeon.

Reputable pet food manufacturers have modified their feline diets to provide lower levels of magnesium and have addressed factors such as those which influence water intake, urine acidity and faecal volume in order to minimize the risks associated with dry diets.

Food intolerance and food allergy

Dietary sensitivity is a term that describes any abnormal reaction of the body to a food substance which has been eaten, and includes conditions caused by true dietary *allergy* and those caused by what we call food *intolerance*. Food allergies are the result of an abnormal response of the immune system to a particular nutrient, especially proteins. In the cat, this reaction usually results in the production of intensely itchy skin lesions, particularly around the face and neck, but vomiting and diarrhoea are occasionally seen. Many basic food ingredients may cause allergic reactions but the most common proteins associated with food allergies in cats are those found in cow's milk, beef and fish. Once an offending ingredient has been identified, this protein must be eliminated from the cat's diet for the rest of its life. Identifying the culprit can however involve much effort both on the part of the owner and the veterinarian.

Food intolerance occurs when the body is unable to process a particular food item. A classic example of this is the *lactose intolerance* seen in about 10 per cent of the cats in the UK. Once kittens have been weaned, their digestive systems become progressively less efficient at digesting lactose, the sugar in milk, and in some cats this ability is lost completely. Additionally, any form of inflammation can impair the cat's ability to digest a variety of food components, including lactose. The result is that undigested lactose accumulates and can by osmosis and fermentation produce diarrhoea.

Feeding inappetent cats

Cats are notoriously fastidious feeders even when healthy and this problem is exacerbated when the cat is inappetent through illness. By exploiting their known preferences and natural feeding habits it may be possible to tempt a sick cat to eat. The following strategies may be attempted:

(a) Ensure that food is palatable and fresh with a strong smell.
(b) Remove uneaten food after 10–15 minutes.
(c) Warm the food to around 35°C but not over 40°C.
(d) Offer frequent, small meals to expose repeatedly the cat's senses to fresh stimuli.
(e) Feed wet foods rather than dry foods as the former are more palatable.
(f) Introduce a new or veterinary diet gradually until it becomes familiar to the cat.
(g) Appetite may be improved if the utensils, dishes, attendant, diet and feeding time are all familiar.
(h) Some cats respond to being fed by hand.
(i) Unless there is a good reason not to, feeding in a group may encourage an inappetent cat by providing competition for food.

If the cat refuses to eat despite these measures, syringe or tube feeding may become necessary. In any event, it is preferable to offer foods which are concentrated and easily digested in order to obtain maximum benefit from the small amount of food that may be accepted.

Anatomy
and Physiology

8

ANATOMY AND PHYSIOLOGY

The average cat owner has little interest in the anatomy and physiology of their pet. Nevertheless, some understanding of basic anatomy and physiology is essential in order to appreciate some of the problems discussed in later chapters of this book. Moreover, with a working knowledge of feline anatomy and physiology owners have a considerable advantage when it comes to rendering first aid or discussing a problem with their vets. For example, the reasons for the provision of fluids to cats with enteritis in frequent, small quantities are apparent with an understanding of the physiology of dehydration. Similarly, a knowledge of anatomy would help an owner to understand the theory of nursing a cat with a joint injury. Confinement to restrict exercise with the limb unsupported to encourage use will often be advocated and may seem nonsense to the uninitiated. And lastly, the owner may really grasp that cats are not small people or small dogs, a point that some people find difficult.

Basic anatomy

The basic building brick of any living animal is the cell. A collection of cells working together to perform a particular function constitute a tissue. A collection of tissues forms an organ and a collection of organs comprises a system. The body consists of a number of systems, digestive, skeletal, reproductive, urinary, cardiovascular, lymphatic, endocrine, respiratory and nervous, which will each be discussed in turn. The skin, eyes and ears are also described.

The digestive system

The digestive system consists essentially of a long muscular tube which runs from the lips to the anus. Associated with the digestive system are a number of accessory structures including the tongue, salivary glands, liver and pancreas.

Food is taken into the mouth and passes into the digestive tract. During its passage through the digestive tract it is mechanically and chemically broken down into products that can be absorbed into the body across the wall of the gut. Once in the body these products are used for replacing the body tissues and for energy requirements. Waste products comprising those parts of the food not absorbed are transformed into faeces during passage through the gut. Faeces are stored in the rectum and pass out of the body at the anus at appropriate intervals. In the normal animal it takes up to 48 hours for the food to pass through the entire length of the gut.

Food can be taken into the mouth in comparatively large pieces. These are picked up by the front or incisor teeth, which are particularly small in the cat. Food of homogeneous consistency, such as the majority of canned foods, is taken into the mouth by the action of the tongue. If necessary food is mechanically broken down in the mouth by the crushing and grinding action of the premolar and molar teeth. However, true chewing as occurs in man does not take place in the cat.

In the mouth, food is mixed with saliva, which acts as a lubricant. Saliva is produced in four pairs of glands situated adjacent to the buccal cavity (mouth). These are the parotid glands, zygomatic glands, sublingual glands and mandibular glands. Saliva is chiefly composed of water but also contains mucus. Unlike human saliva, it does not contain digestive enzymes. Therefore, in the cat digestion does not begin until food reaches the stomach.

The tongue forms the floor of the mouth and is one of the most important structures in it. It is very muscular and contains areas of special sense called tastebuds. With these cats can differentiate between acid, sour and bitter tastes, but unlike man they cannot appreciate sweetness and thus sweet foods are wasted on them.

The roof of the mouth is formed by the palatine bones of the skull which join together to form the hard palate, which is covered with a tough mucous membrane. The hard palate separates the mouth from the nasal cavity and has an important function in separating both solids and liquids in the food from the air the cat breathes in during respiration.

In the foetus the left and right palatine bones sometimes do not correctly fuse and a defect occurs. This is called a *cleft palate* and causes problems when the kitten sucks from the queen since milk enters the nasal cavity and can drip from the nostril.

The *pharynx* is situated at the back of the mouth and it is the area between the mouth and the oesophagus or gullet. The mucous membrane of the hard palate continues the soft palate, a muscular and freely movable structure that acts as a curtain covering the larynx. This protects the airway during swallowing and ensures separation of the nasal and digestive pathways.

The pharynx seems full of holes! The following openings are the most important:

(a) The internal nares from the nasal cavity
(b) The oral cavity or mouth
(c) The larynx from the lower respiratory tract
(d) The auditory, or Eustacian tubes, from the ear. These like the nares are two in number.

When food is passing from the pharynx to the oesophagus, a part of the larynx, the epiglottis, flaps across the opening of the larynx (glottis) and thus prevents food from 'going down the wrong way', i.e. entering the respiratory system. The soft palate also plays a part here.

Food is passed from the mouth into the oesophagus or gullet by movement of the tongue and contraction of the walls of the pharynx. The pharynx is connected to the stomach by the oesophagus, a muscular tube running down the neck, passing through the chest or thoracic cavity and then through a special hole in the diaphragm which divides the thoracic cavity from the abdominal cavity.

In the abdomen the oesophagus opens into the stomach. Food is propelled along the oesophagus by a wave of muscular contractions called peristalsis. This is an involuntary action, i.e. it cannot be controlled voluntarily by the animal. It only takes about 30 seconds for the food to pass along the length of the oesophagus and into the stomach.

It is important for the veterinary surgeon to know the normal time taken for material to pass along various parts of the digestive tract and it is a help when diagnosing various conditions, e.g. if there is an obstruction in the oesophagus.

The oesophagus is connected with the small intestine via the stomach, a roughly C-shaped organ. It is very muscular and in the lining are glands that produce secretions important in digestion. Mechanical breakdown of food continues in the stomach due to muscular contraction and relaxation, the so-called 'churning'. Chemical breakdown by enzymes produced in the special glands in the lining also commences. Other glands in the lining of the stomach produce hydrochloric acid. This secretion of acid in the cat is important for not only does it enhance the enzymic action involved in the breakdown of the food but it also ensures that harmful bacteria are kept to a minimum in the stomach. Bacterial gastritis in the cat is therefore relatively rare.

The entrance to and exit from the stomach are controlled by strong bands of muscles called sphincters which act like valves. The pyloric sphincter at the exit from the stomach is very strong and food material cannot leave the stomach until it starts to relax. As a result the stomach acts as a temporary store for food. The pyloric sphincter controls the passage of the contents allowing only small amounts of material to pass intermittently, thus it takes some time for the stomach to empty completely. Usually some food starts to leave the stomach within 30 minutes of being taken in by the mouth. This is important in cases of poisoning. Although emetics to make the cat sick will often be given up to several hours after ingestion of a possible poison, it should be remembered that if the emetic is given more than 30 minutes after ingestion it is likely that some of the poison will have passed from the stomach and will be being absorbed in the small intestine. Thus although the cat may be sick as a result of the treatment, signs of poisoning may still become apparent.

The capacity of the stomach of the cat is also important. In the adult it is only about 300 ml, a capacity of just over half a pint, and it is important to remember this when feeding animals, especially if it has to be done by stomach tube. Kittens, depending on their age, obviously have a smaller capacity than the adult.

Material leaving the stomach no longer resembles the food eaten. It is a semi-fluid mass and is known as chyme.

The small intestine is another long muscular tube. it runs from the *pylorus* to join with the large intestine at the *ileo-caecal valve*. It contains many glands in its wall. There are also the openings of the bile duct, which brings bile from the gall bladder where it is stored, and also the pancreatic duct, which brings enzymes produced from the pancreatic gland. The openings of these ducts are situated in the first part of the small intestine, known as the duodenum.

The small intestine is divided into three parts, the duodenum, the jejunum and the ileum. The duodenum is connected to the stomach via the pylorus. It is U-shaped and fairly fixed in position. Within the arms of the U is the pancreas. The jejunum and the ileum are much more movable and take up a large part of the abdominal cavity. The lining or mucous membrane of the small intestine is thrown into a number of minute 'finger-like' projections or folds called villi which are important since they increase the surface area available for absorption of the products of digestion. These are absorbed either into the bloodstream or the lymphatic systems. They are then transported to other areas of the body, e.g. the liver.

Chyme, on entering the duodenum, mixes with bile from the liver that has been transported via the bile duct, secretions from the glands of the intestinal wall, i.e. the intestinal juice, and also pancreatic juice. Intestinal and pancreatic juices contain enzymes that continue the chemical breakdown of the food which commenced in the stomach.

Food essentially consists of five components:

1. proteins
2. carbohydrates
3. fats
4. crude fibre, which is the indigestible component
5. ash, which is the scientific name for the minerals.

Proteins, carbohydrates and fats are the *nutrient components* and are broken down into smaller elements or molecules which can be absorbed through the intestinal wall and conveyed to other areas of the body, mainly the liver, where they can be reassembled into components necessary for the maintenance of the body.

For example, the protein taken in with a fish diet by the cat will be broken down into its constituent amino acids by the action of the enzymes in the bowel. Some of those amino acids, after absorption through the gut wall and transport via the bloodstream, finally play their part in contributing to the maintenance of the cat's muscles. Thus the fish protein will have been effectively converted to cat protein.

The protein component of the food is broken into the constituent amino acids, some of which are essential to the cat, while carbohydrates, usually in the form of starches, are broken down into simple sugars, monosaccharides, of which the most common is glucose. Fats are partly broken down by enzymes but bile also plays an important part in their digestion. Bile salts, one of the constituents of bile, emulsify the fat globules. This makes it easier for the fat enzymes (lipases) to convert them to fatty acids and glycerol. The breakdown products of protein and carbohydrates, i.e. amino acids and monosaccharides, are absorbed into the bloodstream while the breakdown products of fats (fatty acids and glycerol) mainly pass into the lymphatics.

Bile secreted by the liver also contains pigments which play no part in digestion. These bile pigments are responsible for the colour of faeces passed from the anus. Bicarbonate is also present in all the secretions that pass into the lumen of the small intestine. This neutralizes the acid produced in the stomach. This is necessary since the enzymes in the small intestine are only active in an alkaline environment, unlike those in the stomach, which only work in acidic conditions.

Waves of muscular contraction – peristalsis – transport the chyme along the small intestine in the same way that the food is originally transported down the oesophagus to the stomach. Water is absorbed in the small intestine but the material leaving and passing into the large intestine is still of fluid consistency and known as *chyle*.

The large intestine is divided into three parts, the caecum, colon and rectum. In carnivores like the cat the caecum is very small. Since the caecum is concerned with the digestion of plant starch or cellulose, it is very large in herbivores such as the horse and rabbit but very small in the cat. In a cat it only forms a small pocket off the main digestive tube. In man, the omnivore, the caecum has in addition the appendix but this is absent in the cat.

The large intestine differs in several respects from the small intestine. It does not contain glands in its wall or have villi and it has a wider diameter and is more fixed in position. No breakdown nor absorption of nutrients takes place in this part of the tract. The main functions of the large intestine are the absorption of water and the formation of faeces. If water absorption does not take place diarrhoea is passed rather than normal faeces.

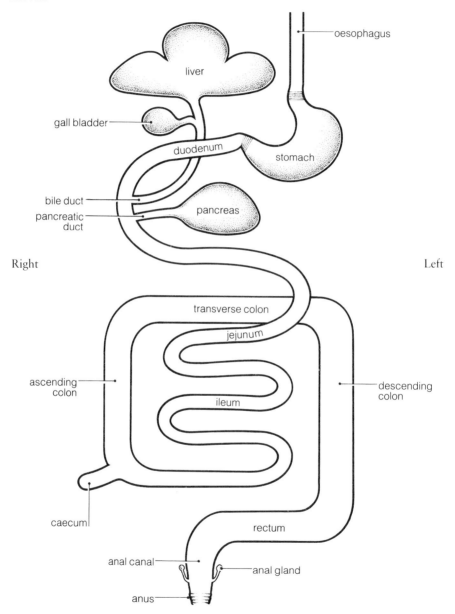

Figure 27 The digestive tract

The digestive system teems with bacteria, most of which are not disease producing. Bacterial action further breaks down the content in the large intestine. During this process gas is produced and should there be an increase in bacterial breakdown the condition of flatulence or wind occurs.

The colon is the main part of the large intestine (see Fig. 27). The end products of digestion, known as faeces, are stored in the rectum, which is a continuation of the colon, until passed through the anus at defecation. In the cat, like man and the dog, defecation is both a voluntary and involuntary function. It is because of this partly voluntary nature of the function that the cat can be house-trained.

LIVER

The largest gland in the body, situated in the cranial abdomen, between the diaphragm and the stomach. Reddish brown in colour it is divided into a number of lobes which virtually surround the stomach when it is empty. Bile is produced in the liver and stored and concentrated in the gall bladder.

On their absorption into the blood vessels in the villi lining the intestine, the products of digestion are transported to the liver by the vascular system and further processed. The liver is often called the 'chemical factory of the body', and not without good cause. Many chemical processes take place there. For example, amino acids can be reformed into proteins or converted to other amino acids of use to the cat; glucose can be converted to glycogen

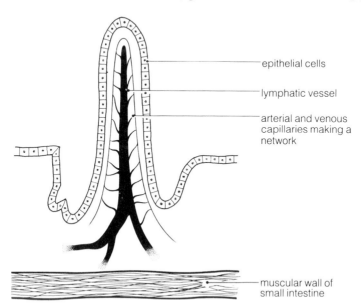

epithelial cells

lymphatic vessel

arterial and venous capillaries making a network

muscular wall of small intestine

Figure 28   The structure of a villus

or animal starch and temporarily stored in the liver. The liver can also store vitamins, e.g. vitamins A, B12 and D, and minerals such as iron and copper. The liver produces some of the factors essential in the blood clotting mechanism and very importantly it is the site in the body where poisons and drugs are detoxified.

However, the liver of the cat, compared with that of man and the dog, is, in some respects, less efficient. It cannot, for example, make the amino acid taurine so this has to be supplied in the cat's diet, which explains why cats need a different diet from dogs.

Detoxification of certain substances, especially drugs, is also less efficient, which explains why cats react in a different way if given medicaments intended for canine use. An example of this is aspirin, which takes a long time to be eliminated in the cat and therefore, if given at all, should be given in minute doses when compared with the doses we take or are given to dogs.

TEETH

When the kitten is about 3 weeks of age the teeth start to erupt (see Chapter 14, Dentistry). The kitten is then capable of lapping and starting to eat solid food. The deciduous (milk) or temporary dentition is complete when the kitten is about 8 weeks of age. Then the kitten will have 26 teeth compared with 30 in the adult.

There are four types of teeth. Starting at the front of the mouth and moving progressively backwards these are the incisors, the canines, the premolars and the molars (see Fig. 29). Molars are absent in the deciduous dentition.

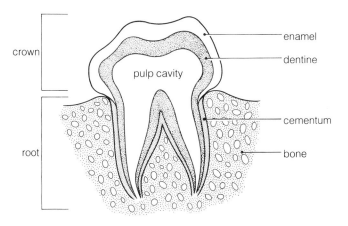

Pulp cavity contains blood vessels, nerves and lymphatic vessels

Figure 29 The structure of a tooth

Temporary teeth are lost from about 14 weeks old and the cat should have a full set of 30 permanent teeth when it is about 7 months old.

Permanent teeth can be distinguished from their temporary counterparts by their larger size, and they have longer roots. In both temporary and permanent dentition on each side of both the upper and lower jaws there are three incisor teeth, one canine, with three premolars in the upper and four in the lower jaw. Permanent dentition has, in addition, one molar on each side in both the upper and lower jaws, i.e. four extra teeth.

Dentine, similar but not identical in composition to bone, makes up the bulk of a tooth. It surrounds a cavity known as the pulp cavity in which are found blood vessels and nerves. The part of the tooth protruding from the gum is known as the crown and the dentine here is covered with enamel, which is the hardest substance in the body. The dentine comprising the root or part of the tooth embedded in the gum is covered not with enamel but with cementum, which coats the root and attaches the tooth.

Teeth have many functions other than those involved in eating. They are used for attack and defence, grooming, tearing the umbilical cord of the kitten at birth and in the male cat are used to hold the skin of the scruff of the neck of the queen at mating in order that erection and ejaculation can take place.

ANAL GLANDS

The anal glands in the cat, or more correctly the anal sacs, are a pair of sac-like structures the size of small peas that lie parallel to the lateral walls of the rectum. They open via a small duct into the terminal part of the rectum just within the anal ring. They are normally emptied by faecal pressure at defecation, the secretion being forced out by compression. The secretion is foul smelling and is used in attack and defence and for territory marking and is considered to play little or no part in digestion.

The skeletal system

This system (see Fig. 30) has many functions which include giving shape and support to the body, helping in movement by acting as levers and providing areas for the attachment of muscle. The skeleton also acts to protect such vital organs as the brain and lungs and is also a site for the production of blood cells as well as an area for the storage of minerals and fat. It comprises a large number of bones that are classified either according to shape, e.g. long, flat, irregular or short, or function, of which an example is the patella or sesamoid bone.

Long bones are the main bones forming the limbs. Long bones in the forelimb are the humerus, radius and ulna and in the hindlimb the femur,

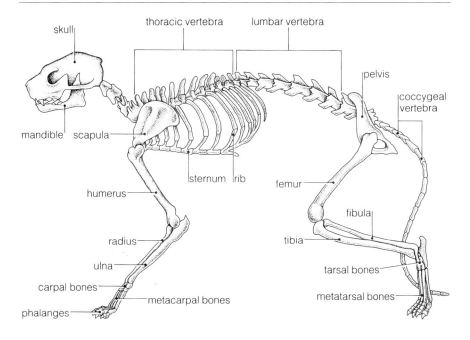

Figure 30 The skeleton

tibia and fibula. These bones are frequently fractured in accidents and are often pinned or plated by the veterinary surgeon.

Long bones (see Fig. 31) consist of a shaft or diaphysis and two ends or epiphyses. In the growing animal there is a special area at the junction of the diaphysis and each epiphysis known as the growth plate and it is the activity of this area that results in increase in length of the bone. If the bone is cut longitudinally it will be seen to be hollow. The central cavity is the medullary cavity. Surrounding this is the medullary bone which has a spongy appearance. On the outside of this there is a layer of solid bone, the cortex. In life, the medullary cavity is filled with marrow which is red in colour in the young animal, since it contains a large number of red blood cells. As the animal ages, in many bones the red marrow is replaced by fat and becomes yellow in colour.

The scapula or shoulder blade and many of the bones in the skull are *flat bones*. The skull is a complex structure made up of a large number of bones with joints between them. Unlike the hip and knee joints there is no movement between the adjacent bones of the skull. The 'joining material' is fibrous tissue that is unlike the fluid synovia found in movable joints (see Fig. 32).

The lower jaw consists of two separate parts, the mandibles, which form a synovial or movable joint with the skull on each side. The mandibles on each side are joined with fibrous tissue in the centre of the chin and this is

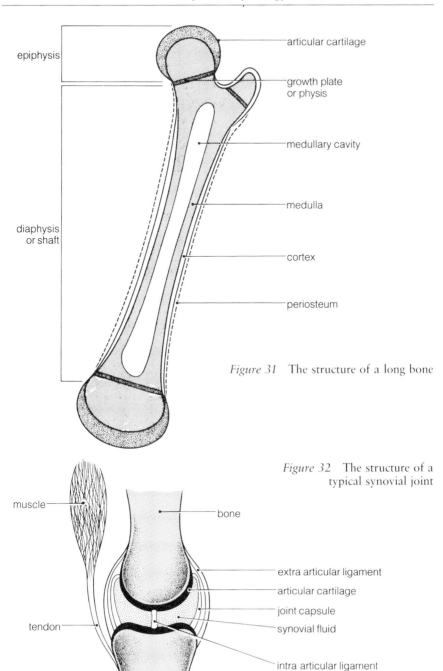

epiphysis

diaphysis
or shaft

articular cartilage

growth plate
or physis

medullary cavity

medulla

cortex

periosteum

Figure 31 The structure of a long bone

Figure 32 The structure of a
typical synovial joint

muscle

bone

extra articular ligament

articular cartilage

joint capsule

synovial fluid

tendon

intra articular ligament

bone

*The space between the ends
of the bones is much smaller
in the living animal*

known as the mandibular symphysis. It is the weakest part of the lower jaw and that most frequently fractured when a cat 'breaks its jaw' in a fall or road traffic accident.

The frontal or maxillary bones of the skull contain sinuses. These are spaces between the surfaces of the bones lined with mucous membrane. They connect with the nasal cavity and play an important part in warming air in respiration. They are important, as in some cats, like the nasal passages themselves, they can become infected, which can result in chronic discharge from the nostrils.

The vertebral column or spine is made up of a large number of small irregular bones or vertebrae. Although all different they are divided into a number of groups, the members of each group having similar general characteristics.

There are 7 cervical or neck bones of which the first and second are very specialized. They are known as the *atlas* and *axis* respectively. In the chest region there are 13 thoracic vertebrae and the ribs articulate with these. The 7 lumbar or backbones are the stoutest or strongest in the spine; the powerful back muscles attach to these vertebrae. The seventh lumbar vertebra articulates with the sacrum which comprises three sacral bones that are fused together to form the sacrum. The tail comprises 15–20 coccygeal bones.

The spinal cord passes through each vertebra to the level of the sacrum.

There is bony continuity between the vertebral column and the hindlimbs via the pelvis and sacrum. The forelimb has no direct bony articulation with the vertebral column.

The cat, unlike the dog, possesses a clavicle or collar bone, which, although not as well developed as the clavicle in man, is clearly visible on X-rays and has, on occasions, been mistaken for a foreign body.

The muscles attached to the bones are voluntary muscles, i.e. they are under the control of the will unlike some of the other muscles of the body, e.g. the gut, which cannot be controlled by the cat.

Tendons attach the muscles to the bones. They are fibrous extensions of the muscle sheath. General movement is brought about by contraction of the muscles. This control can be exercised over other functions such as defecation, since voluntary muscles at least in part control the anal sphincter. Contraction of the muscles of the abdomen, thorax and diaphragm are involved in respiration. Muscle contraction also plays a part in the opening and closing of eyelids and movements of the eyeball, ear and twitching of the skin.

JOINTS AND LIGAMENTS

Joints are formed when two bones are in apposition. They can be immovable or movable. The bones of the skull joined with fibrous tissue are examples of immovable joints whereas the hip and the elbow joints are good examples of movable joints. In movable joints the joining material is not fibrous but is a fluid known as synovial fluid, which is like a light oil in function and consistency (see Fig. 32). The articular surfaces, together with the synovial fluid, prevent friction within the joint. Movable joints are always surrounded by a fibrous joint capsule which helps to maintain the stability of the joint and also prevent escape of the joint fluid. Stability is also maintained with ligaments, which can be found either within or outside the joint capsule.

The site and disposition of the ligaments varies according to the joint. In the shoulder joint there are no true ligaments, stability being maintained by the joint capsule and the surrounding muscle mass. In contrast, the elbow, a hinge joint, working in one plane, has strong ligaments outside the joint capsule on both the lateral and medial aspects of the joint. In the case of the hip joint, which moves in more than one plane, it has an internal ligament that attaches the head of the femur to the bottom of the acetabulum or socket where it articulates. Dislocation (luxation) of this joint is a not infrequent occurrence as the result of trauma, and it often results in the rupture of this ligament. This explains why some dislocations, when put back by the veterinary surgeon, will readily reluxate.

The stifle or knee joint is a very complicated joint. Basically a hinge joint it has important ligaments crossing within the joint joining the femur to the tibia. These are the cruciate ligaments, which can be disrupted by trauma and result in acute lameness unless repaired by the veterinary surgeon. Within this joint there are also two pads of cartilage that act as shock absorbers. These are the menisci. External collateral ligaments bind the bones of the joint together forming a strong hinged joint.

The carpus (wrist) and tarsus (ankle) joints are made up of a number of short bones arranged in two rows. Many ligaments are involved in stabilizing these joints.

Sprains involve joint injury that causes stretching or damage to a ligament without displacement of the bone involved. Because of the number of ligaments involved, sprains are relatively common injuries in the tarsus, carpus and stifle joints.

Strains involve stretching or tearing of muscle.

The female reproductive system

In the female cat or queen the reproductive system (Fig. 33) consists of a uterus composed of a body and two uterine horns continued cranially to the fallopian or uterine tubes (see also Chapter 17, Reproduction and Breeding Problems). These terminate in an expanded funnel-like structure situated close to but not directly connected with the ovary on each side.

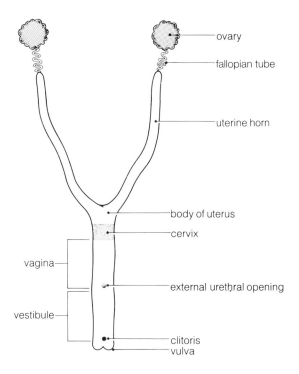

Figure 33 The structure of the female reproductive system

Each ovary is situated just posterior to the adjacent kidney. The uterine body terminates caudally at the cervix which is a valve-like structure consisting of a circular band of muscle. This muscle is normally tightly contracted except during oestrus, when it relaxes to allow free passage of the spermatazoa, and during parturition, when it allows emergence of the offspring. When contracted the cervix still has a small, central passage, which is closed with a plug of mucus. In the early stages of kittening, when the cervix is dilating, this plug can often be seen as a clear mucus discharge. Caudally the cervix opens into the very distensible vagina, on the floor of which is the opening of the urethra. Thus the vagina plays a part both in reproduction and the excretion of urine. The terminal part of the vagina opens to the exterior at the vulva, which is guarded by muscular vulval lips. Just within these, on the floor of the vulva, lies the clitoris, a small knob of specialized tissue. Stimulation of this highly sensitive area by the tom at mating leads to release of the ovum or egg from the ovary.

Cats are theoretically seasonally polyoestrous. They come into heat, oestrus, or 'on call' as it is popularly known, repeatedly during the breeding season. In the feral cat this tends to occur in late spring and summer but domestic cats will cycle throughout the year. This is due to the effect of better nutrition and also environmental conditions, particularly the number of hours of light to which they are subjected. Thus pet cats kept indoors in lighted homes in winter will continue to cycle if unspayed, unlike their feral counterparts.

The average age of puberty is approximately 6 months but the cat can start calling at anything from 4 to 18 months. Once a queen starts cycling she continues to do so throughout life unless she is spayed, i.e. an ovariohysterectomy operation is carried out by a veterinary surgeon.

The length of the cycle is approximately 21 days. The queen will only allow coitus to occur during oestrus, i.e. at a specific stage of the cycle. During oestrus, i.e. on call or calling, the queen becomes very much more vocal and inexperienced owners will often assume she is in pain because at the same time as calling frequently she will roll on the floor. She is also often more affectionate, taking up a characteristic stance with her tail held above her back rubbing her hindquarters against any convenient object, not infrequently the owner's legs.

Unlike the bitch there is no obvious vulval discharge at this time, nor are the vulval lips markedly swollen as occurs in the bitch. Detection of the right time to take a breeding queen to the stud cat can therefore be difficult for the inexperienced. Gentle stroking of the base of the tail is a useful method. If the queen is in oestrus this stimulation will cause her to deflect her tail laterally, exposing her genitalia.

Unlike the bitch the queen is an induced ovulator, i.e. eggs are not released spontaneously from the ovary, but only as a result of stimulation of the vagina, and particularly the clitoris. Because of this the length of oestrus cannot be stated precisely. It lasts about 3 days in the presence of a male cat whereas in the absence of mating it can last very much longer. It also varies according to the breed of cat.

In the kitten the surface of the ovary is smooth. Once sexually mature the ovary appears knobbly due to the swellings caused by the developing eggs beneath the surface. After the ova or eggs have been released as a result of the stimulation of mating, the follicle or cavity from which the egg has been released does not collapse but forms a structure known as the corpus luteum (yellow body) which also is responsible for some of the swellings on the surface of the ovary. The corpus luteum produces a number of hormones associated with the maintenance of pregnancy.

Once released from the ovary the eggs pass into the fallopian tubes where fertilization takes place. It takes approximately 3 days for the eggs to pass along the uterine tubes to reach the uterus. The young develop in the horns of the uterus, which are approximately five times as long as the body.

After fertilization the structure is known as a zygote or conceptus. This immediately starts dividing as it passes down the tubes until a ball of cells is formed. It remains free in the lumen of the uterus for about two weeks after ovulation has taken place, obtaining nutrients by diffusion from the secretions produced by the lining membrane of the uterus. When it becomes attached to the wall of the uterus it is still only approximately 5 mm in diameter. It is then known as an embryo.

Once the features of the living animal become visible it becomes known as a foetus. This occurs about midway (30–32 days) through pregnancy, which lasts approximately 63 days. A range of 59–67 days is considered normal.

The foetus is attached to the uterine wall by the placenta which connects the maternal blood supply to the foetus ensuring the provision of nutrients for and removal of waste products from the foetus.

The male reproductive system

This tract consists of the testes (testicles), two in number, epididymis, vas deferens (the deferent duct), urethra and penis. The prostate and the bulbo-urethral glands are accessory sex glands (see Fig. 34).

The two testes are found in a pouch of skin, the scrotum, under the tail just below the anus. This arrangement ensures that the testes are kept at a lower temperature than the rest of the body, which is necessary to ensure fertility.

In the foetus the testes develop near the kidneys but descend into the scrotum and should be present by the time the kitten is 10 weeks old. However, some cats are 'late developers' and therefore the Governing Council for the Cat Fancy (GCCF) will allow kittens to be shown that do not have fully descended testes, but the testes must be in the scrotum when the cat is eligible to be shown as an adult, which is at 9 months of age, unless he has been castrated in which case he will be shown in special neuter classes.

Spermatazoa (sperm) are produced in the testes together with a small amount of fluid for their initial development. Spermatazoa are released from the seminiferous tubules of the testes before they are mature and complete their development during temporary storage in the epididymus.

The spermatazoon is a single cell and consists of three main parts, the head and neck, middle part and tail. The head carries genetic material and counts for half the weight of the cell. The tail is used for propulsion and the middle piece contains substances necessary to release energy to drive the spermatazoon to its destination. The spermatazoon carries half the normal chromosome number, the other half being made up by the ovum at fertilization. The rest of the reproductive tract in the male consists of a series of tubes through which the spermatazoa pass on their way to the exterior. The epididymis is a convoluted duct closely adherent to the surface of the testes into which open the many blind-ending seminiferous tubules, in which the spermatazoa are produced. The epididymis opens

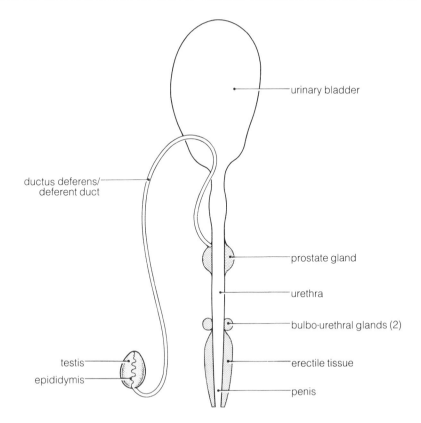

urinary bladder

ductus deferens/
deferent duct

prostate gland

urethra

bulbo-urethral glands (2)

testis

epididymis

erectile tissue

penis

Only one testis and associated ducts shown

Figure 34   The structure of the male reproductive system

into the vas deferens or deferent duct which in turn opens into the urethra near the prostate gland.

The *prostate gland* is an accessory sex gland found in all species. It produces a secretion which, during mating, passes into the urethra where it mixes with the spermatazoa to provide nutriment. This prostatic fluid forms the bulk of the ejaculate or semen. During mating it is forcibly expelled from the penis into the vagina of the queen as the result of muscular contraction during ejaculation. The immature spermatazoa leaving the seminiferous tubule have matured in the epididymis and on expulsion into the vagina are able to swim in the nutrient fluid (semen) from the accessory sex glands. This is forced up the uterus by the rhythmic peristaltic contractions initiated by mating. Fertilization as already stated takes place in the fallopian tubes.

Unlike the dog the cat has a pair of additional accessory sex glands, the *bulbo-urethral glands* (see Fig. 34). Their secretion also passes into the urethra but through openings which are more terminal than that of the prostate gland.

The urethra continues terminally to form the *penis*. It is surrounded by special cavernous erectile tissue in which blood can become trapped. This, together with small pieces of cartilage found within the tissue, aids hardening and erection of the penis at mating. The tip of the penis, or glans, is not smooth as in the dog but covered with small backward-pointing papillae rather like tiny rose thorns. Their function is to assist in holding the penis in the vagina during mating and also stimulate the clitoris, which is essential for ovulation to occur.

There are several essential differences between the urethra in the male and female. In the male the urethra carries urine from the bladder to the exterior and is joined by the vas deferens, and thus the terminal part is dual purpose in function since it carries urine and semen during ejaculation.

In the female the urethra performs the same function of carrying urine, but opens on to the floor of the vagina. Thus urine passes through the terminal part of the female reproductive tract, whereas semen passes through the terminal part of the urinary tract in the male.

Mating is a fairly short procedure. The tom mounts the queen and holds the skin of the scruff of the neck between his teeth. This stimulates him to erection. Penetration of her vagina by the penis, and the stimulation of being mounted and having her scruff held by the tom, causes the queen to ovulate, and in addition to elicit the cry known as the coital yell. These stimulatory aspects of mating in the cat are the reason that artificial insemination is extremely difficult.

Coitus lasts only a few seconds. The tom then dismounts and usually retires to a safe distance. This is because the queen will often display a 'post-coital rage' reaction, which may involve an attack on the tom together with rolling and frantic licking of the vulva. For this reason, it is wise carefully to clip the queen's nails so she does not inflict serious injury on the stud cat.

Some queens will ovulate successfully after a single mating, whereas others require several. It is important that matings take place in fairly quick succession. If cats are allowed to mate at will several matings will take place in the first half hour.

Vaginal smears, often used to establish the right time for mating in the bitch, are seldom used in the queen since the mere introduction of a swab into the vulva can result in premature ovulation.

There are some terms owners are likely to meet that are used to describe abnormalities of the reproductive system. These need to be defined.

Unilateral cryptorchid. This is a cat with only one testis descended. In the unilateral cryptorchid the retained testis, since it is subject to the higher temperature in the body, may enlarge and form a tumour and thus it should be removed.

Monorchid. This is a cat in which only one testis has developed but the term is often used, strictly incorrectly, to describe a unilateral cryptorchid. True monorchidism is quite rare in the cat. The monorchid cat is fertile but should not be used for breeding as the fault may be transmitted to offspring.

Bilateral cryptorchid. A cat in which neither testis has descended into the scrotum. It is sometimes difficult to differentiate from a castrated animal, where the testes have been surgically removed, but the latter usually have a less masculine conformation.

The urinary system

This system (Fig. 35) is responsible for removing some waste products and also excess water from the body. Other important functions include the conversion of vitamin D to a substance that can be used by the body and

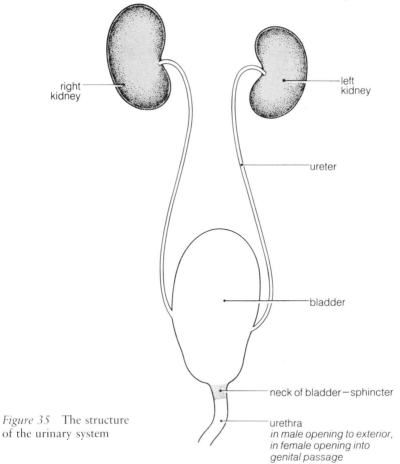

right
kidney

left
kidney

ureter

bladder

neck of bladder—sphincter

Figure 35 The structure
of the urinary system

urethra
*in male opening to exterior,
in female opening into
genital passage*

the production of erythropoietin which is involved with the production of red blood cells (erythrocytes) by the red bone marrow.

The parts of the urinary system are the same in all animals and consist of two kidneys, two ureters with a single bladder and urethra. The kidneys are the site where the functions of the urinary system are carried out, the remaining structures being purely for the passage or storage of urine formed by the kidneys until it is voided from the body. The kidneys are situated in the dorsal abdomen, caudal to the liver and just below the sublumbar spine, with the left kidney placed more caudally than the right. From each kidney a tubular urethra carries urine to the bladder which in turn opens to the exterior via the urethra. The bean-shaped kidneys have a very copious blood supply. Blood enters at the hilus via the renal artery and passes through a complex network of arteries, veins and capillaries, finally leaving from the same area via the renal vein.

The kidney is covered by a thin membrane, the renal capsule, which can easily become damaged following abdominal injury.

If a kidney is cut through longitudinally it will be seen that the substance can be divided into two distinct areas, the outer cortex and inner medulla.

Microscopically the kidney consists of thousands of renal tubules which are long, blind-ending, convoluted tubules. The blind end situated in the outer part or cortex of the kidney is known as the glomerular capsule and in this lies a knot of blood capillaries, the glomerulus (Fig. 36). The tubules, together with their closely related blood vessels, pass from the cortex into the medulla. Each kidney tubule, together with the glomerulus and associated blood vessels, is called a nephron. The tubules unite to form collecting ducts that empty into the renal pelvis and then into the ureter. While passing along the nephrons much modification of the filtrate from the glomerulus takes place before it finally arrives at the renal pelvis in the form of urine.

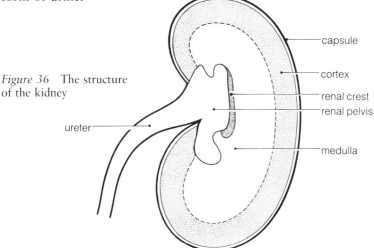

Figure 36 The structure of the kidney

Many forms of kidney disease will alter the filtration and reabsorption of water and other substances and it is for this reason that urine analysis can be so helpful in the diagnosis of many kidney conditions.

The ureters enter the bladder at an acute angle and this forms a valve which prevents the backflow of urine.

The bladder is a pear-shaped distensible organ in which the urine is stored until it is voided from the body at micturition. At the exit or neck of the bladder there is a sphincter that consists of muscles under both voluntary and involuntary control. Remember, it is those voluntary muscles of the bladder that enable cats to be house-trained.

The urethra carries the urine from the bladder to the exterior. In both sexes the terminal portion of the uro-genital system is dual purpose. In the female the urethra opens on to the floor of the vagina and so urine passes through the terminal part of the female reproductive tract. In the male the terminal portion of the urethra, from the level of the prostate where the vas deferens opens to the tip of the penis, carries both urine and semen. In the male cat the penis points backwards and thus the urethra is comparatively short compared with the male dog where, in order to point anteriorly, it has to curve around the pelvis.

The circulatory system

Two distinct transport systems exist within the cat's body to carry fluids, nutrients, waste products, etc. These are the cardiovascular system and the lymphatic system.

CARDIOVASCULAR SYSTEM

Its function is to supply the necessary oxygen and nutrients to all tissue cells and to remove waste products from them. The cardiovascular system consists of the heart and blood vessels, of which there are three types, arteries, veins and capillaries.

Arteries carry blood away from the heart and veins towards it. Arteries break down in the tissues to capillaries which are very small vessels, often with walls only one cell thick. It is from the capillaries that oxygen and nutrients diffuse from the tissues, and conversely waste products diffuse from the tissues into the blood (Fig. 37).

The heart is divided into four chambers. The two upper ones, the right and left atria, are relatively thin-walled while the two lower ones, the ventricles, have much thicker walls. The wall of the left ventricle is about three times as thick as that of the right. In the normal animal there is no communication between the right and left sides (Fig. 38).

The myocardium or heart muscle is a specialized tissue that contracts and relaxes continuously throughout the animal's life without becoming

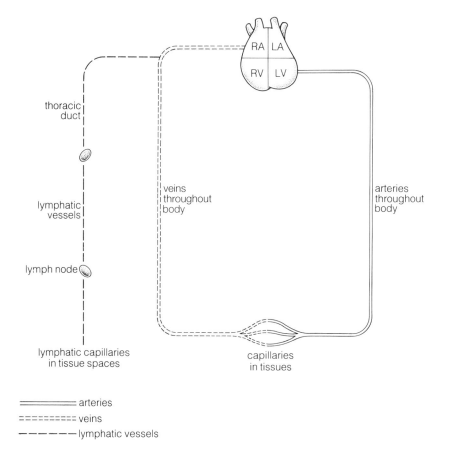

thoracic duct

lymphatic vessels

lymph node

lymphatic capillaries in tissue spaces

veins throughout body

capillaries in tissues

arteries throughout body

RA LA
RV LV

========== arteries
========== veins
– – – – – – lymphatic vessels

Figure 37 The blood and lymph circulation

exhausted. Blood returning to the heart enters an atrium and then passes into the corresponding ventricle. These contract simultaneously and blood is forced out into arteries either to the lungs for oxygenation (right ventricle) or around the body (left ventricle). There are valves between the atria and the ventricles that ensure that blood only flows in one direction. These are the atrio-ventricular valves.

In addition there is an aortic valve at the base of the aorta and a pulmonic valve at the base of the pulmonary artery, near to the heart. These are the only valves present in the arteries since arterial blood pressure is sufficient to prevent backflow of blood.

In veins the pressure is much lower and thus valves are found throughout their length (Fig. 39). Blood returns to the heart from the body via the large vein known as the vena cava which communicates with the right atrium. The blood is low in oxygen and high in carbon dioxide content. It passes

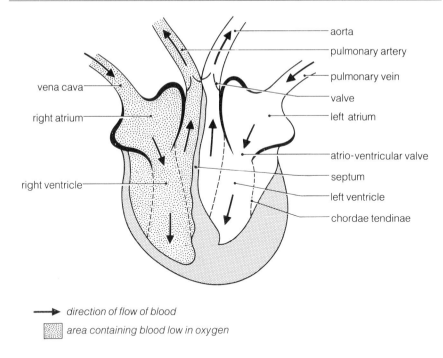

aorta
pulmonary artery
pulmonary vein
valve
vena cava
right atrium
left atrium
atrio-ventricular valve
septum
right ventricle
left ventricle
chordae tendinae

→ direction of flow of blood

area containing blood low in oxygen

Figure 38   The structure of the heart

into the right ventricle and then to the pulmonary artery which transports it to the lungs for oxygenation. The blood then returns to the heart via the pulmonary vein and enters the left atrium. The pulmonary vein is the only vein in the body carrying oxygenated blood! From the left atrium it passes into the left ventricle and then via the aorta enters the general circulation once more.

Major arteries are given off to supply individual organs, e.g. the renal arteries to the kidneys, and these arteries in turn break down into smaller and smaller branches with thinner walls until finally capillaries are formed with walls only one cell thick through which diffusion between the tissues and the blood can take place. In turn the capillaries then join up to form larger and larger veins. These eventually result in the anterior and posterior venae cavae being formed, which transport the blood back to the heart.

The cranial vena cava carrying blood from the head and neck and the caudal vena cava carrying blood from the remainder of the body join just before they enter the right atrium.

The muscle of the heart does not receive blood via diffusion but from coronary arteries that are the first branches of the aorta. If malfunction of a coronary artery occurs, serious heart disease can result. The aorta supplies arteries to the digestive tract but veins from the small intestine do not pass to the vena cava as might be expected. Blood from the small intestine

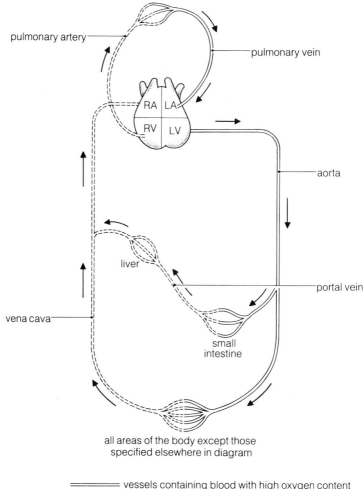

Figure 39   The blood circulation

is loaded with the products of digestion, which have to be processed by the liver. The portal venous system has been developed to shunt blood from the small intestine to the liver. Veins from the small intestine join to form the portal vein, which passes through the liver where it breaks down into capillaries where the products of digestion, in particular glucose and amino acids, diffuse out into the hepatic tissues. These capillaries then join to become veins, finally forming the hepatic vein which in turn joins the vena cava.

Blood

Blood consists of an almost colourless yellowy fluid (plasma) in which are suspended a number of cells. These include red blood cells (erythrocytes), white blood cells (leucocytes), of which there are various types, and blood platelets (thrombocytes).

Plasma consists of approximately 90 per cent water. It also contains plasma proteins, sodium bicarbonate, chloride and nutrients (particularly glucose and amino acids) and waste products (e.g. urea) together with hormones and enzymes undergoing transportation around the body.

Plasma proteins consist mainly of albumins, globulins and fibrinogen.

Albumins and globulins have many functions including control of fluid balance and antibody production, thus aiding the body's defence mechanism. Fibrinogen is one of the most important constituents for blood clotting.

Normal mature red blood cells, or erythrocytes, have no nucleus and therefore cannot be classed as true cells. They are described as 'biconcave' discs and approximately 5–10 million are found in every cubic millimetre of blood. In size they are about 1/7000 of a millimetre (7 nanometres) in diameter. They contain haemoglobin, which is responsible for oxygen transport and also imparts colour to the blood. Since iron is one of the constituents a shortage of this element can seriously impair oxygen transport and result in some forms of anaemia. Erythrocytes have a lifespan of only approximately 4 months and they are continuously being produced in red bone marrow and broken down by the liver and spleen. During breakdown iron is recycled and bile pigments are produced during haemoglobin breakdown.

Leucocytes are larger than erythrocytes. There are between 6,000 and 20,000 in each cubic millimetre of blood in the healthy animal. In bacterial conditions, their numbers can markedly increase, but viral infections often result in a decrease in the number of leucocytes. Unlike erythrocytes, they are colourless. Microscopic examination following special staining techniques reveals they can be divided into two main groups, depending on whether or not granules are visible in the cell body. Those with granules are called granular leucocytes or granulocytes and the rest are non-granular leucocytes or agranulocytes. Depending on the colour of the granules after staining, granulocytes are further divided into neutrophils (purple) eosinophils (red) and basophils (blue).

Granulocytes are often called polymorphonuclear leucocytes since the nucleus is divided into lobes or segments connected by filaments. This is most marked in the neutrophil and this cell type is referred to as the polymorph, or polymorphonuclear leucocyte.

Agranulocytes are often known as mononuclear leucocytes since the nucleus is not divided.

Neutrophils are the most common and comprise approximately 60 per cent of all leucocytes. Basophils are rare, never amounting to more than 1 per cent in a normal blood sample.

All the leucocytes play an important part in the body's defence mechanism. Lymphocytes are concerned with antibody production (B lymphocytes) or cell mediated immunity (T lymphocytes) (see Chapter 24, Feline Immunology).

Monocytes, which are the largest of the leucocytes, spend only a few hours in the circulation then enter the tissues where they mature into macrophages. These large, mononuclear cells are, like the granular leucocytes, involved in phagocytosis whereby bacteria, viruses and other foreign material are engulfed and rendered harmless within the substance of the cell. Macrophages (monocytes) play an important role in phagocytosis when viruses or fungi are involved. They are also involved in antibody production together with lymphocytes and also remove old cells, devitalized tissue and endotoxins.

Platelets or thrombocytes are cytoplasmic portions of cells called megakaryacytes. They are smaller than erythrocytes and irregular in shape and play an important part in the blood clotting process both by physical plugging of the defect and also by the release of thromboplastin, an enzyme which initiates other changes leading to the formation of a blood clot.

LYMPHATIC SYSTEM

More fluid and substances pass out of the blood capillaries than return. If some alternative transport system were not available the tissues would become waterlogged and swollen. This is the condition called oedema that occurs in some disease conditions. Oedema is avoided because the excess fluid passes into blind-ending tubes in the tissues called lymph capillaries. These, like the blood vessels, join up to form vessels of increasing size and eventually in the abdominal cavity one large collecting trunk (cisterna chyli) that passes through the diaphragm into the chest. It is then known as the thoracic duct and enters the vena cava near the heart.

Unlike blood vessels the lymphatics are not easily visible since the fluid contained is colourless and at very low pressure. The vessels are very thin-walled. Flow through the vessels is brought about by movement of adjacent muscles and is controlled by a series of valves even greater in number than in veins. This ensures a one-way system.

The lymphatic system differs from the cardiovascular system since every vessel passes through at least one lymph node between its formation and reaching the heart. These are small swellings that, in the normal animal, are virtually impossible to palpate. They act as a filter for bacteria and other foreign material. Thus in the face of infection they will often enlarge considerably, a fact often made use of in veterinary diagnosis and treatment.

Lymph nodes

These contain special lymphoid tissue that is also found in the thymus, spleen and tonsils. It is in these tissues that the important white blood cell, the lymphocyte, essential in the body's defence mechanism, is produced.

Thymus

This gland is found at the entrance to the thoracic cavity. Large in the young animal it regresses in size throughout life and has a special function in developing the animal's body defence mechanism.

Spleen

This organ is found in the abdominal cavity close to the stomach and is dark red in colour and often described as tongue-shaped. Although performing many functions it is not essential to life and can be successfully removed.

Tonsils

The tonsils are found on either side of the pharynx, near the larynx. Enlargement leads to tonsillitis. They, too, are not essential for life and can be removed if diseased.

Lymph

A colourless fluid containing small amounts of protein in which are suspended varying numbers of lymphocytes. Each time lymph passes through a lymph node further lymphocytes are added.

The endocrine system

Secretions of the endocrine system, known as hormones, are transported round the body by the bloodstream. Endocrine glands can also be called ductless glands and thus they differ from glands such as the salivary or mammary glands which convey their secretions by a specific duct to the target tissue.

There are 7 major endocrine glands:

1. thyroid
2. parathyroid
3. adrenal
4. pituitary
5. pancreas
6. ovary
7. testes.

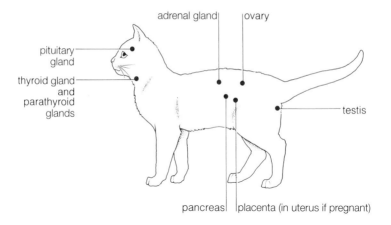

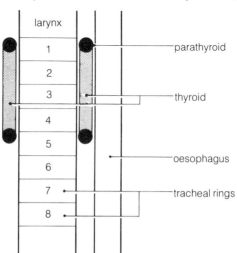

Figure 40   The sites of the endocrine glands

In addition, other organs, e.g. the stomach wall, the kidney and the placenta, also produce hormones.

Most hormones will act at a number of different sites and their actions can be very complex. Endocrine disorders therefore often exhibit complex clinical signs. Broadly, like the nervous system, the endocrine system can be considered as a regulatory system within the body.

THYROID GLAND

This consists of two distinct lobes found on either side of the trachea (windpipe) just behind the larynx (Fig. 41). These glands produce thyroid hormone which is basically a combination of thyroxin (T.4) and

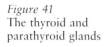

Figure 41
The thyroid and
parathyroid glands

tri-iodothyronine (T.3). Another hormone, calcitonin, is also produced by the thyroid gland. Its purpose is to lower the level of calcium in the blood. Thyroid hormone has an effect on the heart rate, blood pressure, the activity of the nervous system and is overall responsible for the normal growth of the animal. The production of thyroid hormone is under the influence of thyroid stimulating hormone (TSH) produced by the anterior pituitary gland in the brain.

PARATHYROID GLANDS

These are arranged in two pairs. They are closely associated with the thyroid gland, one pair being found at each end of each lobe. They produce the hormone parathormone which has the opposite effect from calcitonin in that it increases the rate at which calcium is absorbed through the intestinal wall and back through the wall of the kidney tubules, thus increasing the level of calcium in the bloodstream. It also decreases the amount of phosphate that is reabsorbed back into the blood in the kidney tubules.

ADRENAL GLANDS

The adrenal glands (Fig. 42) are each approximately the size of a pea. There are two adrenal glands lying close to the inner aspects of the kidney. In structure they consist of two areas, an outer cortex and an inner medulla. Each area produces a number of hormones. The cortex produces two main groups of hormones, the corticosteroids and the adrenal sex

Figure 42
The adrenal glands

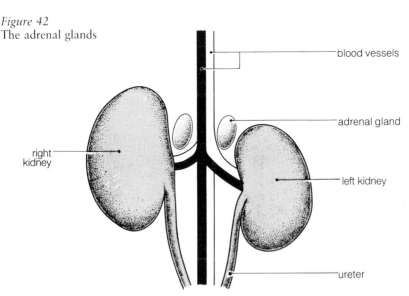

blood vessels

adrenal gland

right kidney

left kidney

ureter

hormones. Collectively these hormones are known as steroids. The corticosteroids are essential for life and can be subdivided into mineralocorticoids and glucocorticoids. The mineralocorticoids, of which aldosterone is the most important hormone, influence the reabsorption of substances in the kidneys, including water. The glucocorticoids increase blood glucose levels and reverse the effect of adrenalin produced by the adrenal medulla. They also have anti-inflammatory effects and control the body's natural immune response. The most important glucocorticoid is cortisol (hydrocortisone).

Sex hormones are produced by both males and females and their exact significance is not fully appreciated. In entire animals the amount of sex hormones produced compared with those produced by the ovary or testes is small but their importance may be of consequence in the neutered animal.

The adrenal medulla produces two hormones, adrenalin and noradrenalin. These are the 'emergency' hormones and allow flight, fright or fight reactions. They increase the level of glucose in the bloodstream, increase the heart rate and constrict many blood vessels, which in turn increases blood pressure and shunts blood from non-vital areas, e.g. the skin, to the muscles.

Production of some of the adrenal hormones is controlled by adrenocorticotrophic hormone (ACTH) produced by the *pituitary* gland. Aldosterone, however, is not controlled by ACTH but by a complex hormone system involving the kidney and the liver. This is known as the renin-angiotensin system (see page 297).

PANCREAS

This differs from the other 6 endocrine glands in that it is a mixed gland. Part of it, the Islets of Langerhans, produces hormones and is endocrine in function while the remainder is an exocrine gland, producing pancreatic juice, a digestive secretion that passes into the duodenum via the pancreatic duct. The Islets of Langerhans produce antagonistic hormones, glucagon and insulin. Insulin allows the tissues to use glucose and release energy and to convert excess glucose to glycogen (animal starch), which is temporarily stored in the liver. It also converts excess glucose to fat, which is stored in fat deposits. Insulin release is stimulated by the presence of glucose within the digestive tract.

OVARY

In addition to the production of ova the ovary has a major endocrine function, the most important hormones being oestradial and progesterone. In addition relaxin is also produced by the ovary. This causes relaxation of the ligaments of the pelvis during parturition.

Oestrodial, one of a group of hormones known as oestrogens, produces signs associated with calling (oestrus) and prepares the genitalia for mating. In addition there is a feedback effect on the pituitary gland resulting in a reduction in follicle stimulating hormone (FSH), which causes growth of the ova, and an increase in luteinizing hormone (LH), which causes formation of the corpora luteum which in turn produces progesterone.

The corpus luteum develops from the follicle once the egg (or ovum) has been shed. Progesterone prepares the wall of the uterus for implantation of the embryo and is essential for the maintenance of pregnancy.

TESTES

In addition to the production of spermatazoa the testes produce male hormones, the most important of which is testosterone. This is responsible for the development of typical male characteristics, the accessory sex glands and the maintenance of the reproductive tract.

PITUITARY GLAND

This is a small but important endocrine gland found attached to the lower surface of the midbrain. Many of the hormones it produces control the secretions of other endocrine glands. It is divided into two parts, the anterior and the posterior. The anterior portion produces the following six important hormones:

1. Thyroid stimulating hormone (TSH), which controls the production of hormones by the thyroid gland.
2. Follicle stimulating hormone (FSH), which controls the production of ova.
3. Luteinizing hormone (LH), which controls the production of the corpus luteum and thus indirectly progesterone.
4. Adrenocorticotrophic hormone (ACTH), which controls the production of hormones by the adrenal cortex.
5. Somatotropin or growth hormone (STH), which has many effects regulating normal growth of the body.
6. Prolactin, which causes growth of the mammary glands and stimulates lactation.

The posterior part of the pituitary gland produces two hormones:

1. Oxytocin, which causes contraction of uterine muscle at parturition.
2. Antidiuretic hormone (ADH), which regulates the amount of water re-absorbed by the kidney tubule. This hormone is important in maintaining correct water balance in the body.

STOMACH WALL

This produces gastrin which stimulates the production of hydrochloric acid and gastric juice in the stomach.

SMALL INTESTINE

The wall of the small intestine produces secretin which stimulates the liver to secrete bile.

PLACENTA

This produces a number of hormones. Two are of importance:

1. Progesterone, which supplements that being produced by the corpus luteum.
2. Somatotropin (growth hormone), which controls, among other things, growth and development of the mammary gland as well as controlling the growth of the foetus.

The respiratory system

The main function of this system is effective oxygenation of the blood. In addition it plays a part in heat regulation and excretion of excess water vapour. Air is taken into the body through the nostrils (external nares) into the nasal cavity, which is divided into right and left parts.

The cavity is almost filled by a number of very fine bones (turbinate bones) arranged in the form of scrolls. These are covered with a mucous membrane with a very good blood supply.

Whilst passing through the nasal cavity the air is warmed, moistened and any small foreign bodies are filtered out by structures called cilia found protruding from the cells of the mucous membrane.

The maxilla and frontal bones of the skull have cavities within them known as sinuses. These communicate with the nasal cavity and are lined with the same mucous membrane. Within the mucous membrane of the nasal cavity are nerve endings associated with smell.

The nasal cavity is separated from the oral cavity or mouth by the hard palate and opens into the pharynx via the internal nares. The pharynx is divided into the nasopharynx and oropharynx by elongation of the mucous membrane covering of the hard palate. This is known as the soft palate. The pharynx has the dual function of conducting both air and food into the body. The pharynx leads to the larynx, a complex cartilaginous structure that passes air into the trachea (windpipe).

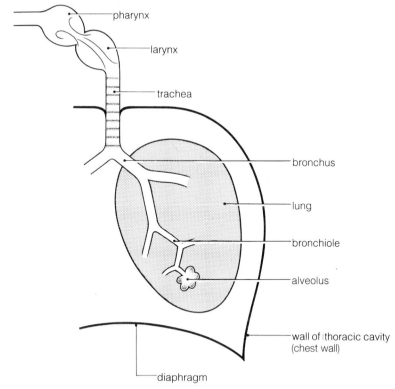

Figure 43   The respiratory system

The larynx lies parallel with the oesophagus (gullet), the opening of which is adjacent to the glottis, the opening into the larynx from the pharynx.

Food is prevented from entering the respiratory system via the glottis by movement of the epiglottis, one of the cartilages of the larynx. The functions of the larynx are to control the amount of air entering the trachea and the production of sound via the vocal chords.

The trachea is a straight, non-collapsible tube that ends by dividing into the right and left bronchii in the thoracic cavity. Its rigidity and non-collapsibility are due to a series of C-shaped pieces of cartilage. The open part of the C is situated against the oesophagus in order that boluses of food may pass down the oesophagus without obstruction from the cartilaginous rings. The arms of the C and adjacent rings are joined together by a mixture of muscle and connective tissue.

The paired lungs, bright pink in colour due to their good blood supply, occupy most of the space within the thoracic cavity. The bronchii, like the branches of a tree, divide into smaller and smaller bronchioles that end in blind air sacs, the alveoli, which in turn have their surface area increased by the development of swellings or pulmonary alveoli. Oxygen diffuses from the alveoli into the blood through the walls of the surrounding capillaries while carbon dioxide passes in the opposite direction. Normal lung tissue is soft and spongy in texture and made up of a mass of these raspberry-like air sacs supported in connective tissue.

Once an animal has breathed normal lung tissue will float in water, and this is used to determine whether a kitten was born dead.

The lungs are a passive structure and do not contain respiratory muscles. Breathing is brought about by the action of the diaphragm and the intercostal muscles between the ribs. Their combined action alters the volume of the thoracic cavity and thus the pressure so that air is either inspired or expired. Once oxygen has passed from the alveoli into the blood it combines with the red pigment haemoglobin in the erythrocytes to form oxyhaemoglobin and is transported throughout the body.

Excess water diffusing from the blood into the alveoli is breathed out in the form of water vapour and thus the lungs play a part in the water balance of the body.

The nervous system

The function of this system (Fig. 44) is to control other body systems and also to receive stimuli from the environment and enable the animal to make suitable responses.

The basic nerve cells, *neurones*, differ from other body cells in that they consist of a cell body and a number of processes. Each neurone has several short dendrites that carry impulses to the cell body. These are known as afferent or sensory fibres. One long axon carries impulses away from the cell body. This is the efferent or motor fibre. The axon has a number of short processes known as axon terminals.

Each neuron will normally communicate with many others but there is no direct contact. Adjacent processes are separated by a minute gap known as the synapse across which impulses will 'jump'.

The nervous system can be divided into the central nervous system and the peripheral nervous system.

The central nervous system consists of the brain and the spinal cord.

The brain is enclosed by the bones of the skull and covered with membrane. It is continued caudally as the spinal cord which leaves the cranial cavity through the foramen magnum, passes through the central or vertebral canal of the vertebral column and terminates in the lumbar region, dividing into a number of branches called the corda equina.

The brain is covered with three membranes or meninges. The inner membrane, the pia mater, is closely adherent to the nervous tissue of the

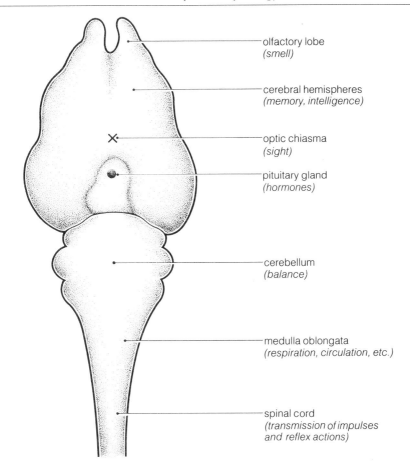

olfactory lobe
(smell)

cerebral hemispheres
(memory, intelligence)

optic chiasma
(sight)

pituitary gland
(hormones)

cerebellum
(balance)

medulla oblongata
(respiration, circulation, etc.)

spinal cord
*(transmission of impulses
and reflex actions)*

Figure 44 The nervous system

brain. The subarachnoid space, which separates the pia mater from the middle membrane or arachnoid mater, is continuous with the spaces within the brain known as the ventricles. These, and the subarachnoid space, are filled with cerebrospinal fluid (CSF), which is similar to but not identical in structure and function with lymph. Lymph vessels are not found in the central nervous system. The outermost layer of membrane is the toughest and is known as the dura mater.

Basically the brain is divided into three parts, the forebrain, the midbrain and the hindbrain.

The forebrain consists of the right and left hemispheres. Cranially there are two projections, the olfactory bulbs. Ventrally, between two cerebral hemispheres, is the optic chiasma where nerve fibres from the eye reach the brain. The pituitary gland is found in this area together with the hypothalamus, which controls the autonomic nervous system. The cerebral hemispheres are concerned with intelligence, memory and personality.

The midbrain is a small area and almost covered by the cerebral hemispheres. Movement and consciousness are under its control.

The hindbrain consists mainly of the cerebellum, which is concerned with balance and co-ordination of movement. Caudally to this is the medulla oblongata, which controls respiration, blood pressure and heart rate. This continues as the spinal cord, which has a central canal continuous with the ventricles and is also filled with cerebrospinal fluid.

Neurone bodies are found only in the brain or spinal cord. They are often referred to as grey matter. Nerve fibres constitute the white matter in the spinal cord. This matter containing the nerve fibres is found in the outer area while the grey matter, arranged in the form of an H, is in the centre. In the brain the grey matter is found on the outer surface. A pair of spinal nerves emerges from the spinal canal at the level of each vertebra from the cervical region to the lumbar. The spinal nerves are made of fibres that enter or leave the spinal cord via either the dorsal or ventral nerve roots. Sensory fibres enter via the dorsal nerve roots and motor fibres leave by the ventral root. The dorsal root has a swelling on it called the dorsal root ganglion that contains cell bodies.

Afferent or sensory fibres carry impulses towards the central nervous system, while motor or efferent fibres carry impulses away. Individual nerve fibres can conduct impulses in one direction only. A nerve is a bundle of nerve fibres united by connective tissue and usually contains both efferent and afferent fibres.

The peripheral nervous system is made up of spinal nerves together with 12 pairs of cranial nerves that arise from the brain itself and with one exception only carry impulses to and from the head. Each spinal nerve is made up of 4 different kinds of fibres, somatic sensory, visceral sensory, somatic motor and visceral motor. Somatic fibres conduct impulses to or from muscles under voluntary control while visceral fibres are concerned with involuntary action, e.g. peristalsis in the bowel. The visceral sensory and motor fibres together form the autonomic nervous system.

The paired cranial nerves all have names. For example, No. II is the optic nerve which runs from the eyeball to the brain and is concerned with sight, while VIII is the vestibulocochlear nerve which connects the ear and the brain. Both of these are mixed nerves containing sensory and motor fibres. Other cranial nerves can be purely sensory or purely motor.

The fore and hindlimbs have major nerve trunks formed from the amalgamation of the spinal nerves. In the axilla a combination of a number of spinal nerves forms a plexus that results in the formation of a major nerve trunk that divides to form the radial, median and ulna nerves. A similar arrangement in the hindleg results in the formation of the sciatic and femoral nerves.

The skin

The surface of the body is covered by skin (Fig. 45) which is continuous with mucous membrane at the natural orifices and also with the conjunctiva, which covers the outer surface of the eye (see Chapter 13, The Skin). The structure of skin differs according to the area and the amount of hair present. On the feet, for example, it is specialized to form the foot pads, which are hairless. Various types of glands are associated with the skin, e.g. sebaceous and sweat glands. Mammary glands and anal glands can also be considered specialized skin glands.

The skin consists of an outer epidermis and inner dermis that is attached to a layer of connective tissue known as the hypodermis or subcutis. The epidermis consists of several layers of cells but does not have a blood supply. The cells of the epidermis are dying or dead and are produced adjacent to the dermis. They migrate continuously to the surface where they are sloughed off in the form of scurf or dandruff. The epidermis varies in thickness over the body. It is especially tough in those areas likely to be subjected to trauma, e.g. the back, neck, etc.

The dermis consists of connective tissue in which are found blood vessels, glands, pigment cells, nerve endings, small muscles and hair follicles.

Although hairs are found over the entire surface of the body they are more abundant in some areas than others and are absent on the foot pads and around the nasal apertures.

Specialized hairs, called whiskers or vibrissae, are found on the sides of the nose and above the eye. These are connected with specialized nerve endings that are sensitive to touch.

Figure 45   The structure of the skin

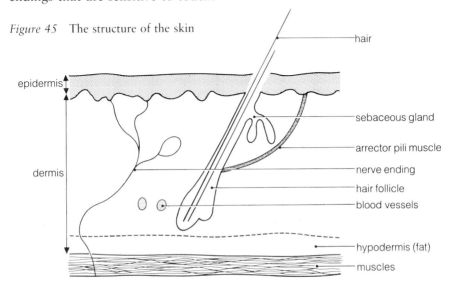

Several hairs emerge from the skin surface through one common opening. One of them is larger and stiffer than the others and is known as the guard or cover hair and the remainder are underhairs or lanuga hairs. Sometimes the guard hairs are sparse or absent as occurs in the longhaired (Persian) breeds.

Attached to the hair follicle is a small muscle, the arrector pili, which on contraction makes the hair assume a more vertical position.

Ducts from the sebaceous glands open into the hair follicles. These produce sebum, oily in consistency, which lubricates the skin and helps to keep it pliable. Sebum also contains a substance that, under the action of sunlight, is converted into vitamin D and can be taken in during grooming.

On the dorsal surface of the tail, near the anus, is a specialized area containing many sebaceous glands. This area is known as the caudal gland and it sometimes produces excessive sebum which leads to the condition of 'stud tail'. Sebaceous glands are also present in the ear canal where they are known as ceruminous glands. Their secretion is cerumen or wax.

Sweat glands in the cat are found chiefly on the feet. On each paw there are four distinct pads associated with the toes or phalanges and also a central metacarpal or metatarsal pad that is rounded in shape. This is also known as the bearing pad. The pads consist of strong connective tissue and fat forming the digital cushion. This acts as a shock absorber. The cat's narrow, pointed claws are normally retracted by the action of ligaments into a special fold of skin. This retraction can be quickly overcome by muscular action and the claws brought into use. Functions of the skin include protection, regulation of body temperature, production of certain substances and storage. It also has a sensory function and plays a part in communication. It contains nerve endings that respond to touch, pain, heat, cold, pressure and vibration, all of which contribute to making the animal aware of its surroundings.

The skin acts as a mechanical barrier to trauma and invasion by pathogenic bacteria. In addition there is a subtle protective function since the skin acts as a host for a large number of harmless bacteria that compete with the harmful disease producing bacteria for nutrients etc. Reproduction and growth of these pathogenic bacteria are thus restricted. The system breaks down in disease.

The skin also protects the body by preventing loss of water and essential salts. Fat, stored in the hypodermis, acts as a form of insulation and adds to the protective function.

The correct absorption of calcium from the intestine depends on vitamin D, which is produced in the skin. The skin also produces sebum which lubricates it and maintains its suppleness. In addition, sweat, milk and pheromes are produced. Pheromes are natural scents and are used in communication between cats. They are produced by the anal glands within the anal sacs and by some of the sebaceous glands, especially those of the caudal glands in the tail and the areas in front of the ears.

Heat regulation depends on fat in the subcutis acting as a thermal insulator. Further insulation can be provided by the erecta pilae muscles erecting the hairs. Dilation or constriction of the superficial blood vessels also increases or decreases blood flow to the skin and thus further temperature control of the body is brought into play. The production of sweat, important in man in the control of body temperature, is of little importance in the cat due to the relative paucity of sweat glands, except in the foot pads.

The mammary glands are specialized skin glands found in both sexes, but they are usually rudimentary in the male. The queen has four pairs in two rows, arranged symmetrically on the ventral body wall extending from the axilla to the inguinal region. They consist of glandular and connective tissue covered with skin. The amount of glandular tissue increases during pregnancy and lactation and also alters slightly in the various stages of the oestrous cycle. Each mammary gland opens to the surface through the teat, which, in the queen, contains between 8 and 16 orifices through which the milk is secreted. Muscle tissue in the wall of the teat prevents milk from dripping from it continuously when the queen is lactating. Each orifice leads to a group of passages and milk producing areas, which do not communicate with each other in the gland.

The glands have a good blood, lymph and nerve supply but those on each side are supplied separately and there is no connection between those on the right and left sides. This is important in some cases of breast cancer when the breasts from only one side may be removed with little risk of spread to the other side.

The eye

This is a special sense organ associated with sight (Fig. 46). Located in the orbit it is protected by the bones of the skull. Anteriorly it is protected by the eyelids and membrana nictitans (third eyelid) and also by the tears.

The wall of the eyeball is made up of three layers. The sclera is the outer, fibrous layer. Its function is to be protective. The uveal layer is the middle, vascular layer and comprises the choroid, the iris and the ciliary body. The retina is the inner layer and is the sensory layer.

The eye comprises an anterior and a posterior chamber separated by the lens and various other structures. The anterior chamber is filled with fluid, aqueous humour, and the posterior chamber contains vitreous humour which is jelly-like in consistency.

The sclera continues over the front surface of the eye as the clear cornea. The sclera, strong and white in colour, gives shape to the eyeball, and also provides for the attachment of several muscles. The transparent cornea allows the passage of light into the eye. It normally does not contain blood vessels and obtains its nourishment by diffusion from tears outside and from the aqueous humour on the inside.

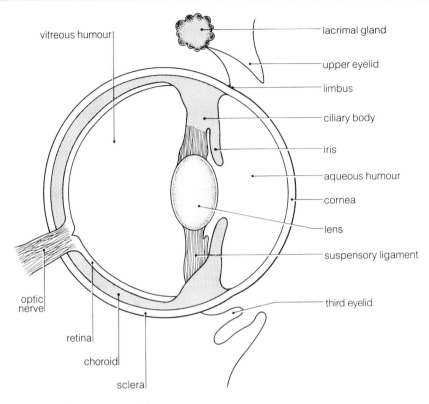

Figure 46 The structure of the eye

The uvea is usually dark brown or black in colour and consists of three parts, the choroid, ciliary body and iris.

The choroid lines the sclera in the posterior chamber but just behind the corneo-scleral junction (the limbus) it forms a projection, the ciliary body, which helps to divide the two chambers. A spur develops from the ciliary body to form the iris surrounding the lens. The suspensory or zonular ligament from the lens is connected to the remainder of the ciliary body. Within the choroid are special cells that form the tapetum which is the special reflective layer that causes the cat's eyes to shine in the dark. Its function is to increase the ability of the animal to see dimly lit objects. In the cat the tapetum is a bright metallic yellowy green colour.

The lens is slightly biconvex and the shape can be changed by contraction and relaxation of muscles found in the ciliary body. Its function is to focus light on the retina. It does this very accurately by changing its shape which is known as 'altering the accommodation'. The amount of light entering the lens is controlled by the size of the pupil, which in turn is controlled by the contraction and relaxation of the muscles of the iris lying adjacent to the anterior surface of the lens.

The retina consists of several layers of cells. It contains two distinct types of photoreceptors, rods and cones. Rods respond to light regardless of colour and function in any intensity of light. Cones respond to coloured light but function better in bright light. Cones are found chiefly in the centre and rods towards the edges of the retina.

The nerve fibres within the retina join to form the optic nerve which takes impulses to the brain and leaves the eye at the optic disc.

The upper and lower eyelids meet at the lateral and medial canthi (singular canthus). The eyelids are folds of tissue covered by skin on the outer surface and mucous membrane (conjunctiva) on the inner surface. Eyelashes are specialized hairs found on the free borders of the eyelids. The modified sebaceous glands found in the upper lids are called tarsal glands. Their ducts open either into the hair follicles or on to the surface near the hairs. The eyelids protect the eye in several ways. They can completely close and cover the cornea, while the eyelashes repel foreign bodies and constant blinking moistens the surface of the eye and flushes foreign bodies away. Lacrimal fluid, or tears, is produced chiefly by the lacrimal gland and to it are added the oily secretions produced by the tarsal glands and mucus from the conjunctiva. Excess fluid is drained away into the nasal cavity via the tear (nasolacrimal) duct situated in the medial canthus.

In addition to the upper and lower eyelid the cat has a third eyelid. This, the membrana nictitans or nictitating membrane, is a plate of cartilage covered on both its inner and outer surfaces by conjunctiva. It is situated at the medial canthus but can be rapidly moved across the cornea. Protective in function it sometimes becomes prominent in illness, when the cat is said to be 'showing its haws'.

Many muscles are associated with the eyeball. These include those found in the eyelid, those within the eyeball and those attached to the exterior of the sclera. These are responsible for rotation of the eyeball and also retraction into the orbit.

The ear

Hearing and balance are the functions of the ear (Fig. 47). Structurally it can be divided into three areas, the exterior, middle and inner ear.

The exterior or external ear consists of the ear flap (pinna) and the aural canal (auditory meatus) which ends at the eardrum (tympanic membrane). The pinna is a plate of cartilage covered on both sides by a layer of skin. It is highly mobile and its function is to direct air vibrations into the auditory canal and on to the tympanic membrane (eardrum). The auditory meatus is a canal that runs vertically and then horizontally and ends at the tympanic membrane. This is oval in shape and semi-transparent. It is not of uniform thickness, being thinnest in the centre and increasing in thickness towards the periphery, and beyond it is the middle ear.

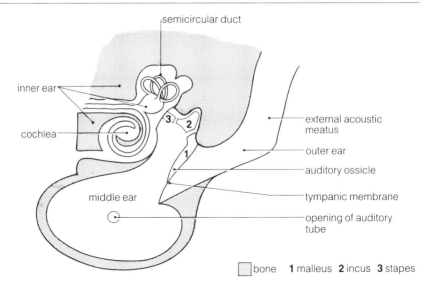

Figure 47   The structure of the ear

The middle ear houses three small bones (the auditory ossicles). These transmit the vibrations from the tympanic membrane to the vestibular window in the wall of the skull that leads to the inner ear. The bones are known as the hammer, anvil and stirrup (malleus, incus and stapes). The malleus is attached to the tympanic membrane and the stapes to the vestibular window.

The Eustachian auditory tube connects the middle ear and the nasopharynx. Its function is to maintain atmospheric pressure on both sides of the tympanic membrane.

The inner ear converts sound vibration into nervous impulses. It consists of a complex system of sealed tubes known as the membranous labyrinth suspended in a body cavity known as the bony labyrinth. The bony labyrinth is divided into the cochlea, the vestibule and the semicircular canals.

A fluid known as perilymph fills the space between the bony and membranous labyrinth. Fluid is also found within the membranous labyrinth and this is known as endolymph. The membranous labyrinth consists of the cochlear duct, the semicircular duct and the sacule and utricle which fit into the vestibule. Nerve endings connected with hearing are found in the cochlear ducts and are called the Organ of Corti. Impulses are carried from this area by the vestibulocochlear nerve to the brain.

The semicircular canals are concerned with balance. Each has a swelling at one end and in these are otoliths, minute balls containing a tuft of sensory hairs. Their position is altered with movements of the head and the impulses relating to balance are then transmitted to the brain via the vestibulocochlear nerve.

Organ Systems

9

THE LOCOMOTOR SYSTEM

The locomotor system is made up of the bones, joints, tendons, ligaments and muscles. The bones form the skeleton (Fig. 48) which protects the internal organs of the cat. It also acts as a scaffold to support the muscles, allowing them to move the various bones of the limbs and spine.

A typical long bone is composed of two expanded ends called the epiphyses, and a more cylindrical central portion, the diaphysis. The outer part of the diaphysis consists of dense, cortical bone, while the epiphyses contain a softer, more open type of bone called cancellous bone (Fig. 49).

Figure 48   The skeleton of a cat

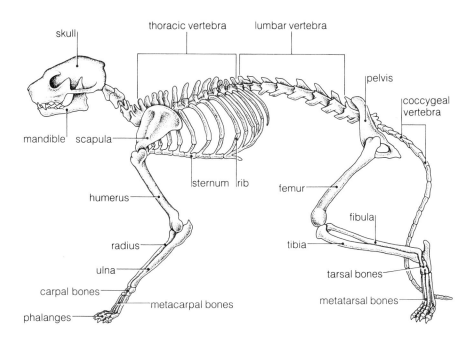

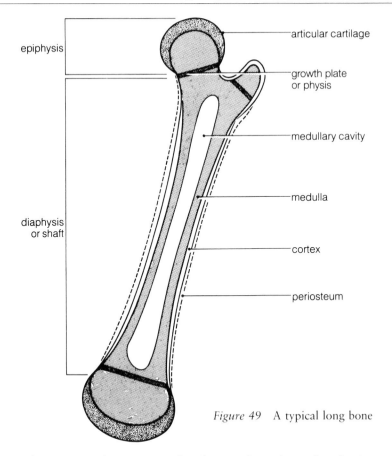

epiphysis

articular cartilage

growth plate
or physis

medullary cavity

medulla

diaphysis
or shaft

cortex

periosteum

Figure 49   A typical long bone

Long bones grow from a specialized area of cartilage, the physis or growth plate, which is situated between the epiphysis and the diaphysis.

A joint is any connection between two or more bones or cartilage. Most joints are designed to permit movement, and are called synovial joints. They contain synovial fluid, which lubricates the joint and helps to nourish the articular cartilage that covers the ends of the bones forming the joint. They are lined by a synovial membrane that secretes the synovial fluid. The combination of very smooth articular cartilage and the lubricating synovial fluid reduces frictional forces when the joint moves.

Synovial joints are covered by a fibrous joint capsule which helps to limit excessive joint movement. Further thickenings strengthen the joint capsule. These are called ligaments.

Skeletal muscles are composed of contractile, striated muscle fibres. The muscles contract by becoming shorter. They have a good blood supply and their activity is controlled by nerves running from the spinal cord to the muscle. They are attached to the surface of the bones (the periosteum) directly, or via tendons.

Tendons contain parallel bundles of collagen and are more fibrous than muscle. They have two major properties: they possess great tensile strength and they glide easily through the surrounding tissues, thereby making joint movement more efficient.

Orthopaedic problems are seen less frequently in the cat than in the dog. This is probably because cats cope well with many types of disability and because there are fewer breed-related conditions. Nevertheless, many cats are injured or killed on our roads and in our cities.

The causes of lameness in cats can be divided into diseases of bone and joints, and injuries of tendons and muscles.

Diseases of bone

METABOLIC DISEASES

Hypervitaminosis A

One of the functions of vitamin A is to help control the balance between the amount of bone produced and the amount resorbed. Cats require high levels of vitamin A in their diet because they do not absorb carotene well (carotene is converted by the cat to vitamin A). Commercial cat foods are specially formulated to contain the correct amount of vitamin A. However, if home-mixed rations are fed, it is possible to feed excessive amounts of this vitamin. This generally occurs when large amounts of liver are fed, to which cats often become addicted. The effects of excess vitamin A (hypervitaminosis A) vary according to how much liver is fed and the age of the cat eating it.

In young cats, there is a reduction in the longitudinal growth of bones due to degenerative changes in their cartilaginous growth plates. There is also a reduction in the bone formed around the diaphyses of their bones due to suppression of the cells that produce bone in this region.

In adult cats, new bone forms in the ligaments and tendons that are attached to the skeleton. This occurs particularly in the cervical and thoracic spine, but also around the joints of the limbs (especially the fore limbs), and around the rib heads and sternebrae. There is an abnormally high level of fat in the bloodstream and abnormal fat accumulation in the reticulo-endothelial cells of the liver, spleen and lymph nodes. The reticulo-endothelial cells are part of the cat's immune system, and a depletion of their numbers may predispose it to other diseases or infections.

Hypervitaminosis A is typically seen in the adult cat aged between 1 and 5 years old, although it does occur in older animals too. The condition is chronic with a gradual deterioration in the cat's condition over a period of many months. Clinical signs include anorexia, weight loss, hyperaesthesia,

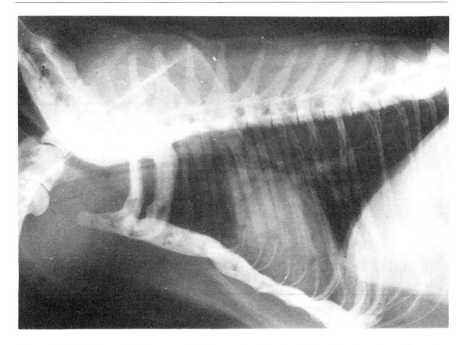

Figure 50   Radiograph of a cat with hypervitaminosis A showing fused vertebrae in its lower neck and sternum (breastbone) due to new bone formation. The first pair of ribs are also enlarged due to new bone formation

joint pain and lameness. Cats are reluctant to move and jump. They have rigid necks and spines and their coats are often unkempt since they are no longer able to groom themselves. Affected limb joints may be enlarged and painful and have a decreased range of movement. Neurological signs may develop if the new bone impinges on the nerves as they exit the spine.

Radiographically, dense bony exostoses are seen on the vertebrae, often fusing several bones together (Fig. 50). Exostoses are also found in the limb bones around the attachment of ligaments and joint capsules. In immature cats, there is decalcification of the limb bones, bone distortion and subsequent uneven growth of the bones.

Treatment must include removal of liver from the diet. Owners often find this difficult, since their cat initially refuses to eat anything else. However, perseverance is ultimately rewarded, and as the cat begins to eat other food it becomes less painful. However, the exostoses persist and may *occasionally* require surgical removal. Bony deformities in kittens persist.

Hypovitaminosis A

This condition is possibly more prevalent than recognized, because it produces non-specific neurological symptoms in young cats. Again, there is an imbalance between bone production and bone resorption, which results in distortion of the long bones and of the bones of the cranium and vertebral column.

Clinical signs are very varied. There may be neurological signs due to pressure on the brain and spinal cord, or the kitten may be lame. Other signs include anorexia, weight loss, ocular discharge, muscle weakness, impairment of sight and hearing and difficulties in parturition later in life.

Radiographically, long bones show deformities with an absence of normal cortical outline due to decreased mineralization.

Treatment is directed towards feeding a normal diet.

Nutritional secondary hyperparathyroidism

This condition, also known as juvenile osteoporosis, is seen in kittens fed on all-meat diets and little milk. The Siamese breeds are said to be more prone than domestic breeds. However, this may merely be a clinical impression, since breeders used to avoid giving milk to Siamese kittens when weaning them as they erroneously believed they could not tolerate lactose.

The condition is caused by a diet with a low calcium to phosphorus ratio. This induces a transient lowering of the blood calcium levels (hypocalcaemia), stimulating parathyroid hormone production, which in turn causes calcium resorption from the bones. Bone turnover is increased and resorbed bone is replaced by fibrous tissue. Clinical signs are seen in young kittens a few weeks or months old. They are lame due to bone pain, as the weakened bones bend and spontaneously fracture. Besides long bone deformities, deformity of the thoracic wall, sternum and pelvis also occurs. Compression fractures of the vertebrae may cause neurological signs. These can range from hindlimb weakness to total paralysis of all four limbs.

Radiographs show a generalized loss of bone density within the skeleton. The bones have thin cortices, and compression and/or folding fractures may be evident. The loss of bone density is reversible, provided the pathology is not too advanced. There is rapid improvement once the diet has been corrected. Feeding of a commercial cat food is advised or, alternatively, bone meal may be added at a rate of 15g/kg dry weight. Analgesics may be necessary. Cage rest is essential until the bones become stronger. Most cats respond within a short time, but bone deformities will persist and there may be some permanent stunting.

Renal secondary hyperparathyroidism

This condition is associated with chronic renal disease. Reduced kidney function results in phosphorus retention, elevated blood phosphorus levels (hyperphosphataemia) and a compensatory hypocalcaemia. This stimulates the release of parathyroid hormone and bone resorption. Renal damage may also affect the production of a metabolite of vitamin D in the kidney. This results in an effective vitamin D deficiency and reduces calcium absorption, thus aggravating the problem.

The older cat is most often affected. Signs associated with renal failure are seen, such as excessive drinking and frequent urination. Generalized stiffness and lameness, softened jaw bones and loose teeth may also be evident.

Radiographs demonstrate poor mineralization of the jaw, and soft tissue calcification may be seen.

Treatment involves a low protein diet with calcium gluconate/lactate and vitamin D supplements. However, since the underlying renal pathology is irreversible, the prognosis is generally poor.

CONGENITAL AND DEVELOPMENTAL CONDITIONS

Multiple cartilaginous exostoses

Multiple cartilaginous exostoses or feline osteochondromatosis is seen in mature cats of the Siamese, Burmese and DSH breeds. A progressive enlargement of several palpable bony nodules occurs, usually with no other clinical signs, although lameness may be seen if the masses interfere with joint movement. These protuberances arise from the cortex of bones and are found predominantly in the scapula, ribs, vertebrae and pelvis. Radiographically they are seen to be extensive calcified masses.

The cause of osteochondromatosis is not known, and the lesions may be due to a congenital dysplasia of the growth plate or to disordered periosteal activity. Feline leukaemia virus-like particles have been recorded in the exostoses in one case.

Affected cats have a poor prognosis. The lesions often recur after surgical excision and may undergo malignant transformation.

Mucupolysaccharidoses

These are a class of disease caused by inborn errors of glycosaminoglycan metabolism. Glycosaminoglycans are large molecules found in cartilage. Enzymes present in cells are required to break down these molecules, and the disease occurs when there is disordered activity of a specific enzyme. In the cat mucupolysaccharidoses type I and VI have been described. Clinically the two syndromes are similar with cats being affected when they are a few months of age or when they are young adults.

Type I is due to an autosomal recessive gene. Cats are often bright and alert on presentation, with near normal intelligence and normal reflexes. They often have a crouched stance with their stifles held close together. There may be pain on manipulation of the head, neck and hips.

Affected cats have a number of bony abnormalities, including facial distortion, hip dysplasia, deformed sternebrae and wide, fused cervical vertebrae. Bony proliferations may occur in the spine and long bones, their appearance being similar to hypervitaminosis A. Other abnormalities include corneal clouding and leaking heart valves.

Type VI deficiency has been reported in the Siamese, with signs similar to those of type I. Affected cats also have growth plate abnormalities accompanied by severe degenerative joint disease, atlanto-axial subluxation and hydrocephalus. The trait is transmitted by a simple autosomal recessive gene but more than one defective allele is present.

In both types of disease the signs tend to become progressively worse with age. Treatment is symptomatic.

Osteochondritis dissecans (OCD)

OCD has been reported in a one-year-old, neutered male cat, affecting its left shoulder joint. Radiography showed an erosive lesion on the caudal aspect of the humeral head, a detached flap of articular cartilage and early signs of degenerative joint disease. The detached flap was surgically removed and the lameness resolved. The lesion resembled OCD in other aspects, but it is not known if the aetiology is the same, or if osteochondrosis really occurs in the cat. It is, of course, a relatively common disease in large and giant breed dogs.

BONE TUMOURS

Both primary and secondary bone tumours are much less common in the cat, compared with the dog.

Osteosarcomas are the commonest feline primary bone tumour and usually occur in aged, female, DSH cats. In the dog, there are certain predilection sites for osteosarcomas, but this is not so in the cat. Any limb bone can be involved, although the humerus and femur are common sites.

Affected cats are lame, with swelling over the tumour, pain, and a decreased range of movement in the associated joints. Radiographic changes are variable. Osteolysis, with radiolucency of the medulla and thinning of the cortices may occur, with or without pathological fractures (Fig. 51). Alternatively, there may be periosteal new bone formation.

Osteosarcomas tend to metastasize slowly in cats, spreading to regional lymph nodes, the lungs and the kidney. Amputation of the limb is generally the treatment of choice, provided there is no radiographic evidence of secondaries.

Juxtacortical osteosarcomas are a rare tumour in the cat. They arise on the outer surface of the bone cortex and have a characteristic histological pattern.

Clinically, a hard mass, firmly attached to bone, can be palpated; sites include the limb bones, the frontal bone and the mandible. Radiography shows irregular, poorly defined masses of variable density attached to the bone cortex.

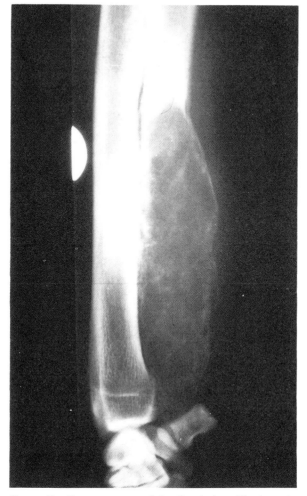

Figure 51   Osteosarcoma of the distal ulna. The bone is expanded and osteolytic. The cortices have been destroyed

The tumours do not appear to metastasize and excision of the primary tumour has resulted in a successful outcome.

Osteoclastomas are an unusual bone tumour in the cat. They affect adult animals of almost any age, causing lameness and swelling of the affected bone. Radiographically, there is a localized osteolytic area with thinning of the cortices and expansion of the medulla with a fine trabecular pattern forming a 'soap-bubble' appearance. This appearance is also seen in aneurysmal bone cysts (see below). The tumour is slow growing and may metastasize to the kidney or lung; however, resection of the affected bone has been successful where the diagnosis was established at an early stage.

Two tumour-like lesions simulating primary bone tumours are seen in the cat. Neither is numerically important, but as they have a much better prognosis than bone tumours, it is essential that they are not confused with them.

Aneurysmal bone cysts are benign lesions composed of blood-filled spaces of varying size, separated by bony and fibrous septae. These cysts can be curetted and packed with bone chips. The second condition is called fibrous dysplasia. This is a developmental abnormality that has been seen in the mandible and ulna of two cats. It consists of cellular, fibrous tissue interspersed with bony trabeculae.

Secondary bone tumours are rare, but metastatic spread from tumours of the mammary gland, bronchi and lymphosarcoma has been reported. Radiographically, both lysis and sclerosis are seen.

Other soft tissue tumours may cause lameness by growing into bone as they expand locally. The most important of these are the fibrosarcoma and the squamous cell carcinoma. Squamous cell carcinomas often involve the feet and invade the bones of the digits, appearing radiographically similar to osteomyelitis. There is loss of mineralization, with bone erosion, soft tissue swelling and periosteal new bone formation. Similarly, fibrosarcomas invade bones, causing destruction of the cortex and medulla.

INFECTIOUS DISEASES

Bone infection (osteomyelitis) is relatively common in the cat. Osteomyelitis is usually caused by bacterial infections following a bite wound from another cat. It may also follow a fracture where there is gross soft tissue damage and the bone is exposed. Infection spreads in the bone within the medulla or by tracking under the periosteum. This often results in focal areas of dead bone. The dead bone may be reabsorbed and replaced, but in extensive infections the cat's defence mechanisms may be inadequate and the dead bone becomes walled off by a ring of sclerotic bone to form a sequestrum. Radiographically, areas of lysis and sclerosis are seen within the infected bone and extensive periosteal new bone formation occurs (Fig. 52). This radiographic appearance may be confused with a tumour. Treatment comprises surgical removal of the dead bone and a prolonged course of antibiotics.

Most cat bite wounds result in abscessation and infection in the soft tissues. However, infection of the deeper tissues is always a potential complication , and as osteomyelitis is a serious condition prompt treatment of any infection is recommended.

TRAUMATIC CONDITIONS

Most feline orthopaedic problems are traumatic in origin. Fractures are particularly common since cats are frequently struck by automobiles or fall

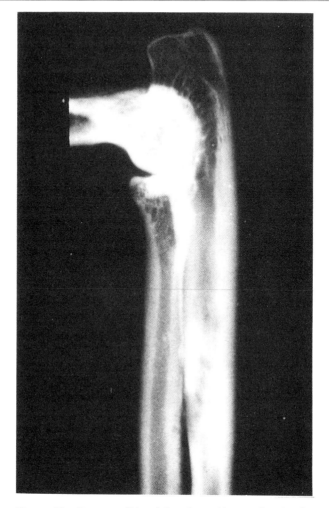

Figure 52 Osteomyelitis of the ulna with osteolysis and osteosclerosis

from heights. The femur, tibia, mandible and pelvis are commonly involved.

Feline bones heal readily and, since cats cope well with orthopaedic problems, there has been a tendency in the past to advise cage or box rest as the treatment of many fractures. In some instances, such as with certain pelvic fractures, this is still the treatment of choice. However, most long bone fractures should be repaired using internal fixation techniques. The use of Steinmann pins and cerclage wires is often successful, the straight shafts of the long bones allowing good immobilization with a well-fitting pin (Fig. 53). Small plates and screws can also be used. Fractures through the growth plate are common, particularly in castrated males, since growth

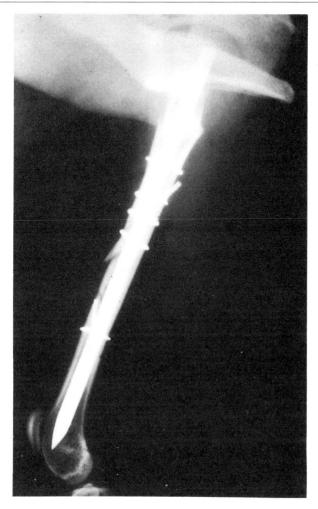

Figure 53 Fractured femur repaired with intramedullary pin and cerclage wires

plate closure occurs much later in these animals. These fractures can be repaired using small pins or wire.

Open fractures are relatively common but can generally be treated by internal fixation. Where internal fixation is inappropriate or too expensive, external fixators can often be used very successfully (Fig. 54). Indeed, in some instances they are the best form of treatment. They comprise a series of small pins drilled into the bone through the skin and connected to an external frame of further pins or methylmethacrylate. They have the advantage, when compared with conventional splints and casts, that any wounds can be dressed easily, yet the fractured bones are held rigidly together.

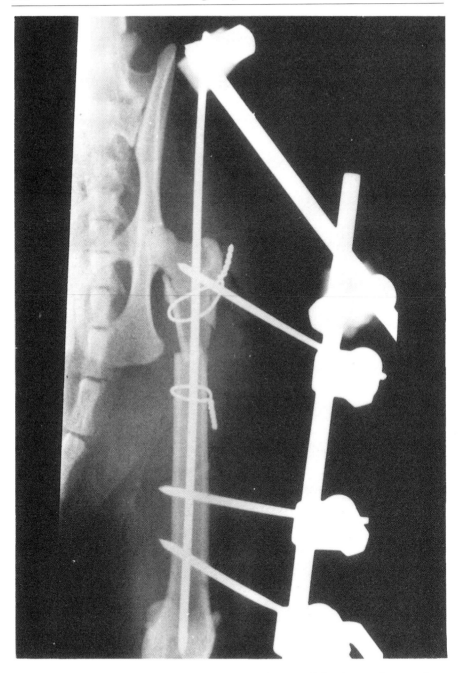

Figure 54 A combination of internal fixation and external fixation used to repair a fractured femur. A small intramedullary pin and cerclage wires are reinforced with an external fixator, where the pins are driven through the skin into the bone and connected to a frame

Diseases of joints

Joint disease in the cat can be divided into a number of categories, namely:

(a) Traumatic injuries
(b) Degenerative joint disease
(c) Inflammatory arthritis:
      Infectious:
      1. Bacterial
      2. Mycoplasmal
      3. Viral
      Immune based:
      1. Idiopathic
      2. Periosteal proliferative
      3. Rheumatoid
      4. SLE
      5. Non-periosteal proliferative

TRAUMATIC INJURIES

The two most common traumatic conditions for joints are sprains and dislocations.

Sprains

A sprain occurs when the joint exceeds its normal range of movement and its associated ligaments and joint capsule are torn. Mild falls from trees or rooftops are likely to cause sprains, whereas more serious falls are likely to result in fractures. Thus, a veterinarian will often radiograph a swollen, painful joint, even though only a sprain is suspected, in order to eliminate the possibility of an associated fracture.

Simple sprains are treated by rest and bandaging, in order to reduce the swelling. Once this has subsided, gentle exercise can be reintroduced.

Luxations

The terms luxation and dislocation are synonymous and refer to the displacement of the opposing surfaces of the bones that form the joint. Luxations may be the result of developmental or congenital problems, or they may be caused by an accident.

Traumatic luxations of the hip, stifle, hock and carpus are fairly common. Patellar luxation may occur following a traumatic incident, but there may also be a congenital predisposition to this injury. Congenital medial patellar luxation is thought to occur in the Devon Rex.

Total stifle disruption, i.e. rupture of both cruciate ligaments along with a collateral ligament, is more common than rupture of the cranial cruciate ligament alone. This is a devastating injury, but the ligaments can be reconstructed and joint function restored.

DEGENERATIVE JOINT DISEASE

This occurs as in other species, but is less commonly diagnosed because of cats' abilities to compensate for their disabilities. Treatment is more difficult than in the dog since it is harder to regulate a cat's exercise and because the non-steroidal anti-inflammatory drugs tend to be more toxic. However, there are now suitable preparations available.

INFLAMMATORY ARTHRITIS

This may be due to infections of the joint or it may be immune mediated. Infective arthritis is more common in the cat than in the dog, again because of the incidence of fighting. A cat's canine tooth may penetrate an adversary's joint and directly seed organisms in that joint, or the infection may spread from an adjacent abscess.

Viral arthritis, caused by a calicivirus, has been seen in 6–12-week-old kittens. It is, however, an unusual cause of arthritis. Similarly, a transient inflammatory reaction in a number of joints (a polyarthropathy) uncommonly occurs as a complication to vaccination.

The immune-based arthritides are referred to as non-infectious polyarthropathies. Their main pathological feature is an inflammation of the lining of several joints with, usually, a bilateral, symmetrical distribution. All types are rare. Most reported cases have been in male cats and any age of cat can be affected.

The most common form of the disease is the idiopathic, periosteal proliferative form seen in young adult males. Idiopathic means the cause is unknown, and periosteal proliferative means new bone formed from the surface of the bone. Clinical signs include fever, malaise and stiffness, pain on manipulation of the joints and swelling of the regional lymph nodes. Conjunctivitis is seen in some cats. After several weeks the fever subsides and characteristic radiographic signs are seen. There are extensive, fluffy new bone deposits around affected joints, particularly the hocks and carpii. Similar changes may also occur around the stifle, elbow, hips and the articular facets of the spinal vertebrae. New bone is also seen at the insertions of muscles and tendons. Destructive changes may also be seen, e.g. erosions in the bone around the joint, subchondral cyst-like lesions in the bone beneath the joint surfaces and loss of bone density around the affected joints. Later in the course of the disease, fibrosis of the joint capsule reduces movement and causes stiff joints. However, deformities and joint instability do not occur.

The aetiology of the disease is unknown, but it is believed to involve immune complexes in the synovial membrane of the joints. No bacteria or mycoplasma have been isolated, but there is a statistical relationship between the condition and feline leukaemia virus and feline syncitial forming virus. However, if viruses are involved, there must be some individual predisposition to the condition.

The second form is a chronic, progressive, destructive polyarthritis with many similarities to rheumatoid arthritis in man. It is seen infrequently in cats and, again, it is not known exactly what triggers the inflammatory changes. The disease is seen particularly in older male cats. It is an insidious condition, progressing slowly to a severe disabling arthritis. Multiple joints are swollen and painful, and there is joint instability and deformity progressing to sub-luxation. Radiographically, bony destructive changes are seen with severe subchondral bone erosion and irregularly increased joint spaces. In time, collapse of the joint spaces occurs with fibrous ankylosis. There is overall loss of mineralization and a coarse trabecular pattern around affected joints.

Polyarthritis associated with systemic lupus erythematosis (SLE) is occasionally seen. This is a non-erosive, symmetrical polyarthritis, associated with a multi-systemic disease. Thus, skin lesions, kidney disease, central nervous disorders and diseases of the haemopoietic system may occur in conjunction with these painfully swollen joints. To confirm the diagnosis anti-nuclear antibody (ANA) must be detected in the serum.

An idiopathic, non-periosteal proliferative polyarthritis also occurs in the cat. These cats resemble those affected with SLE but no ANA is detectable. The condition is thought to be mediated by immune complex hypersensitivity reactions.

Treatment for all the immune-based arthritides is similar. Some cats respond to corticosteroids, others require a combination of corticosteroids and chemotherapeutic drugs, e.g. cyclophosphamide or azothiaprim. Occasionally cats respond well, but clinical improvement is often short term and relapses are severe.

Muscle and tendon injuries

RUPTURE OF TENDONS

This may follow a sharp blow or laceration. Similarly, any violent contraction of a muscle against a fixed joint is likely to result in either rupture of the muscle or its tendon.

The clinical signs of a tendon rupture will vary with the site of the injury, but in general there is a loss of significant function. Many tendon ruptures require surgery to repair them, followed by a period of restricted exercise to allow the tendon to heal.

INFECTION

Most cat-bite wounds result in abscessation and infection in the soft tissues. Prompt treatment is advisable to minimize more serious complications.

10

THE EAR

Felines are well known for their acute sense of hearing. Start opening a can in the kitchen and you are likely to find your cat round your ankles, having heard you from three rooms away! As well as hearing, this complex organ is involved in balance and equilibrium. Much of its structure is hidden from view and the ear flap that projects from the top of the head is actually only a small component of a very intricate organ. There is little variation in the external appearance of cats' ears and, unlike the dog, disease problems associated with specific breed characteristics like floppy ear flaps are seldom encountered in this species. However, ear disease is still a significant and potentially serious problem which necessitates immediate veterinary attention at the first sign of disorder.

Scratching at the ear, persistent head shaking, an abnormal smell or any discharge coming from the opening of the ear are all suggestive of an ear problem. This may cause pain and discomfort to the cat, impairment or even loss of hearing and can occasionally interfere with balance.

It must be emphasized that 'do-it-yourself' cleaning with often inappropriate lotions and implements (for example cotton buds) is to be avoided. This only compounds the existing problem and causes more suffering to your pet. Prompt professional treatment should result in speedy resolution of the disorder to everyone's satisfaction, not least the cat's.

Structure of the ear

In order to understand the processes at work in ear disease, it is helpful to have some knowledge of the structure of this organ.

For simplicity's sake, the ear can be divided into three adjoining compartments: the external ear, the middle ear and the inner ear (Fig. 55). Much of the external ear can be seen, whereas the middle and inner ears are

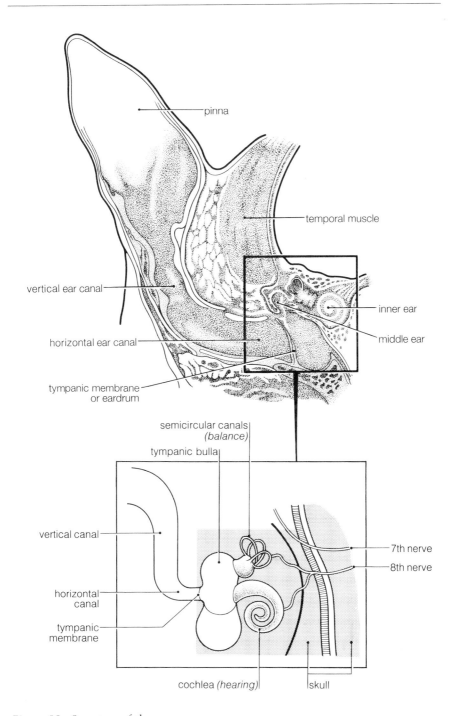

Figure 55 Structure of the ear

hidden from view within the temporal bone of the skull. Soundwaves propagated by the movement of air particles are sequentially converted into electrical energy by the structures within these three chambers. Conduction of the electrical energy to the hearing centre in the brain occurs via nerves originating in the inner ear. Once there, the impulses are interpreted and the animal 'hears' the initiating sound. Other nerves in the inner ear inform the cat about the position of its head in relation to gravity and their function is necessary for normal balance.

THE EXTERNAL EAR

The external ear consists of two parts: the ear flap (pinna) and the external auditory canal. The pinna collects sound in a manner akin to a radar dish and then channels it into the external auditory canal. This is a tube leading from the base of the pinna to the eardrum (tympanic membrane), a membrane stretched across an opening in the temporal bone.

The pinna is made of cartilage covered by skin on both sides. It is the cartilage which determines the shape of the ear as we see it. In cats it is sufficiently stiff to erect the ear at all times. Multiple small muscles can turn the pinna towards the source of the sound. Each ear can move independently and, unlike ourselves, cats do not have to turn their heads to locate noises.

The external auditory canal is a rolled tube, also made of cartilage but this time lined with modified skin that contains many wax producing (ceruminous) glands. Earwax (cerumen) is believed to trap dust to prevent it reaching the delicate eardrum. The canal has two parts: a vertical length from the pinna downwards and a horizontal portion from the bottom of this to the eardrum. This change in direction means the canal has quite a tight bend, which can hinder the drainage of wax as it has to move upwards against gravity. As all vets know only too well, it also makes conscious examination of the canal and eardrum rather awkward.

THE MIDDLE EAR

The middle ear is a small air-filled chamber (tympanic cavity) housed in the temporal bone and interposed between the external and inner ears. It is separated from the external ear by the eardrum and from the inner ear by two similar membrane-covered holes, the oval (vestibular) window and the round (cochlear) window.

The upper part of the tympanic cavity contains a chain of three very small bones, only a few millimetres in length, called the auditory ossicles. These pass from the eardrum in the outer wall of the chamber across to the oval window in the inner wall and connect the two. The first and largest ossicle is the malleus which attaches to the eardrum on one side and to the second ossicle in the chain, the incus, on the other. The incus, in turn, is joined to the stapes, the third ossicle. The base of the stapes sits in the oval window and makes contact with the inner ear through this. Soundwaves conducted via the external ear cause vibrations of the tympanic membrane. These are picked up by the first ossicle and transmitted through the chain by a lever action. The base of the stapes is set in motion, the oval window vibrates and as a result the fluid of the inner ear oscillates. Hence, sound from the environment is transmitted across the tympanic cavity to the internal ear.

Located in this part of the tympanic cavity on its inner wall is the opening to the auditory (Eustachian) tube. This is a canal passing from the middle ear to the throat; it is normally collapsed except for a short time when swallowing. Its function is in equalizing the pressure on the two sides of the delicate eardrum, which can become unbalanced, for example when taking off in an aeroplane or going through a long tunnel. The opening of the canal during swallowing permits restoration of normal pressure with a pop.

The lower part of the tympanic cavity is a bulbous expansion of eggshell-thin bone known as the tympanic bulla. Its function is not known but it is thought to improve perception of very high and low pitched sounds (Fig. 56 on page 174).

THE INNER EAR

This is certainly the most complicated part of the ear, consisting of many fluid-filled passages and cavities contained within a very hard part of the temporal bone. It is because of this complexity that it is also known as the labyrinth. Two separate systems are housed together, those channels concerned with balance (the utriculus and semicircular canals) and those involved with hearing (the cochlear and sacculus).

The fluid within the utriculus and semicircular canals is set in motion by movement of the head. Stimulation of nerve endings occurs as a consequence of this fluid movement and the resultant impulses are conveyed to the brain via the vestibular nerve. The cat is therefore aware of the position of its head and is able to balance normally.

The fluid within the cochlea and sacculus is also set in motion, this time by the rocking of the base of the stapes in the oval window. The moving column of fluid stimulates nerve endings within the lining of the channels and the electrical impulses generated are carried to the brain via the cochlear nerve. When the impulses reach the hearing centre in the brain, they are interpreted and the cat perceives the stimulating sound.

Disease may affect any one or more of the three major divisions of the ear. Inflammation is a common accompaniment to disease anywhere in the body and is termed 'otitis' when it occurs in the ear. Hence we have otitis

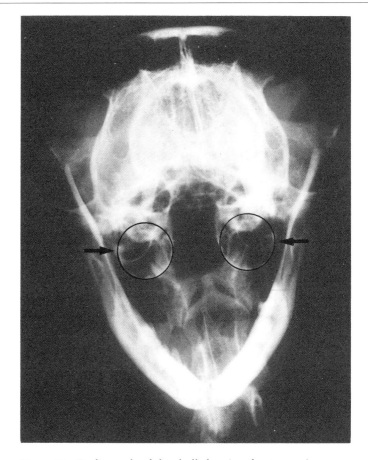

Figure 56   Radiograph of the skull showing the tympanic
bullae as air-filled chambers outlined by bone

externa, otitis media and otitis interna, disease of the external, middle and
inner ears respectively. Other disorders do not have inflammation as a
major component and will be discussed separately.

Diseases of the external ear

THE PINNA

Wounds

Tears of the pinna sustained during cat fights are a relatively common
injury. With immediate veterinary treatment, suturing under a general
anaesthetic and a short course of antibiotics should prove adequate. If left,

infection or even an abscess may develop which will be painful and cause the cat to feel off-colour. The vet may then wish to treat the infection first before repairing the ear, should this be necessary.

Aural haematoma

Damage to blood vessels in the pinna may result in leakage of blood between the skin and cartilage. This forms a localized blood-filled non-painful swelling known as a haematoma. Bleeding is probably a consequence of the head shaking and ear scratching that the cat indulges in when there is inflammation of the external auditory canal. The vet may leave the haematoma alone for several days to allow the blood clot to organize but surgical intervention is necessary to prevent the formation of a shrivelled 'cauliflower' ear. The clot is removed and the layers of the pinna are pressed together to stop further seepage of blood.

Tumours

Tumours of the pinna arise from the skin, the most common being the squamous cell carcinoma located at the tip of the ear. White cats are particularly susceptible and, as in man, its development is related to exposure to sunlight and lack of protective pigment (melanin). However, it is also occasionally seen in coloured cats. The flap becomes ulcerated and thicker than normal, and on occasion there is a proliferative lumpy growth. Amputation of the pinna is an effective treatment and will not pose a problem for the cat, although the ear may look a little odd.

THE EXTERNAL AUDITORY CANAL

Otitis externa

Inflammation of the external ear is usually secondary to an underlying primary disease but the picture can be complicated by the mutilation caused by the cat scratching and rubbing at the ear. This results in tissue damage which predisposes to bacterial and fungal infection with further pain and irritation. A vicious circle of irritation, self-trauma, infection and further irritation is established.

It is vital that the wax produced continuously by the lining of the ear is cleared at the same rate. Excess production of wax, as occurs in many diseases of the external ear, may overwhelm the normal drainage process up the vertical canal. Consequently, wax builds up and inflammation follows. The inflammation will cause swelling that will narrow the canal and further exacerbate the wax accumulation. The resulting inflammation coupled with self-trauma can make it very difficult to determine the initiator of all this damage in an ear that may look very like any other ear with otitis externa (Fig. 57).

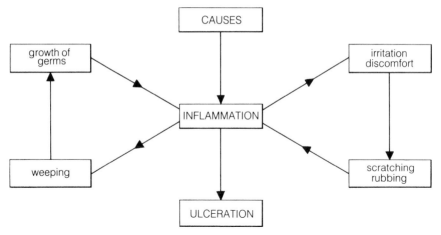

Figure 57 The vicious circle of otitis externa

So, what are the primary conditions which may lead to the end result of otitis externa?

Mites

Otocariasis is the name given to infestation with the ear mite *Otodectes cynotis*. It is also known as 'canker' although this term may be applied to any long-standing (chronic) otitis externa. Ear mites are the single most common cause of otitis externa in the cat, over 50 per cent of cases being attributable to these little beasties, which is far greater than in the dog. In fact, cats are believed to act as a reservoir of infestation for the dog. Adult cats seem able to tolerate large numbers of mites whereas just a few mites in a dog ear can cause intense irritation, perhaps as a result of an allergic reaction to the saliva or faeces of the parasites.

The mites trigger the ceruminous glands and the most characteristic sign of infestation is the excess production of thick brown wax, often with little irritation. The pinhead-sized white mites show up against this brown background but because they live at the bottom of the external auditory canal, a special illuminated cone called an auriscope is needed to see them. The light will stimulate movement of the mites which will be seen as small scurrying white points on the wax.

Treatment is fairly straightfoward with administration of an acaricidal drug into the ear canal ensuring elimination of the parasites. It is important to treat all in-contact cats and dogs even if they aren't showing signs of otocariasis in order to prevent recurrence of the condition.

Foreign bodies

Foreign bodies as a cause of otitis externa are rarely seen in the cat. Occasionally grass awns may find their way into the ear canal. A general anaesthetic will probably be necessary for the removal of any foreign material from deep in the canal.

Skin disease

It must be remembered that the covering of the external ear is skin very similar to skin anywhere else over the body. Generalized skin disease, for example allergic responses and parasitic skin infestations, can involve the ear as part of a widespread process. When this occurs, there will be changes in the skin in locations other than the ear. Sometimes an allergic reaction is localized in the ear but this is an unusual presentation. An example of this is ringworm, where lesions can be confined only to the ear.

Polyp

Chronic otitis externa can occur secondary to the growth of a 'polyp' from the middle ear. The polyp expands out through the eardrum and obstructs the ear canal causing inflammation and irritation (see Plate 22). The origin of these growths will be discussed further under otitis media so suffice to say that once the vet has identified the polyp, surgical removal will be necessary. The defect in the eardrum will heal within about 3 weeks with no impairment to hearing.

Tumours

The external auditory canal is not a common site for tumour growth (neoplasia). Tumours may be either benign or cancerous and can arise from any of the tissue types present: skin, ceruminous glands or cartilage. Although it is not generally possible to tell what type of tumour is present from looking at it, ceruminous glands are the exception because they have a distinctive appearance rather like a blue raspberry (Plate 23). Treatment of tumours in this site is invariably surgical and often the entire ear canal should be removed. The long-term outlook will very much depend on the tumour type and promptness of discovery and excision.

Micro-organisms

It is unlikely that micro-organisms have a major role to play in the initiation of otitis externa. Bacterial and fungal infection most probably occurs after inflammation has been set up by a separate condition but once it is established it plays a big part in the perpetuation of disease. Rupture of the eardrum can result from otitis externa and microbes can then gain entry to the middle ear with potentially serious consequences. It is therefore of utmost importance to get on top of a simple otitis externa before this event. An early visit to the vet will undoubtedly pay off in the long term.

Diseases of the middle ear

Otitis media

Infection of the middle ear usually arises as an extension of otitis externa following rupture of the tympanic membrane. Occasionally micro-organisms may gain entry via the Eustachian tube or be carried to the tympanic cavity by the bloodstream. Bacteria are the most common agents involved but fungi, foreign bodies, trauma and tumours must also be considered as initiators of middle ear disease.

The signs of otitis media are very similar to those that are seen with diseases of the external ear: shaking of the head, scratching at one or both ears and evidence of pain on petting. There may be tilting of the head for a short time. In some cases there is damage to the nerves that pass through the middle ear, causing for example drooping of the upper eyelid. Hearing difficulties can be difficult to assess because only one ear may be affected and the cat can hear to some extent across the skull bones anyway.

Medical management involves aggressive antibiotic therapy but otitis media is notoriously difficult to treat effectively. Surgery to remove the external ear canal and clean out the middle ear may well be required. This is a major procedure with a number of associated risks so it is far better to sort out a straightforward otitis externa before its progression to this stage.

If a tumour is responsible for the otitis media, treatment and its efficacy will depend on tumour type and how early the diagnosis is made.

Polyps

These are inflammatory growths of the lining of the middle ear that probably result from a chronic otitis media. It is a condition seen most frequently in young cats, sometimes as early as two months of age. All the layers of the lining proliferate and a number of types of inflammatory (infection fighting) cells infiltrate the mass. This is different to a tumour where there is overproduction of only one cell type. What stimulates polyp formation isn't precisely understood but by the time the signs become apparent to the owner the preceding otitis media is usually long gone. As well as growing out through the tympanic membrane, polyps can grow down the Eustachian tube into the back of the throat. The cat will be affected differently depending on the location of the mass; those in the middle and external ears can cause discharge from the ear, head shaking and sometimes a head tilt, whilst growth into the throat tends to result in coughing and difficult eating and breathing.

A general anaesthetic and removal of the polyp is necessary, because they do not spontaneously regress once the cat is clinically affected. Sometimes recurrence will require further surgery; this is usually in the same ear although some cats may develop growths in both.

Diseases of the inner ear

Inherited deafness

In cats, coat and eye colour is associated with a form of deafness that is due to degeneration of structures of the inner ear. This occurs at about 4–6 days post-natally. White cats are affected with blue-eyed white cats more frequently deaf than odd-eyed cats. Orange-eyed cats are least often affected. In a small number of cats deafness is unilateral. Despite being deaf, these animals still make very affectionate, loving pets.

Otitis interna

Inflammatory and infectious diseases of the inner ear most frequently occur as an extension of middle ear disease. Occasionally disease involving the brain spreads to the inner ear. The signs suggestive of otitis interna are those resulting from impairment of the sense of balance rather than loss of hearing and include tilting of the head, involuntary rapid eye movements (nystagmus) and falling over when attempting to walk. Treatment is usually the same as for otitis media, aggressive antiobiotic therapy. If hearing has been impaired, it will seldom return to normal but any loss of sense of balance may be compensated for eventually.

Conclusion

The message for the cat owner has to be 'better sooner than later'. The majority of cases of serious ear disease start as a simple otitis externa but late institution of therapy or, even worse, inappropriate home cleaning allow these easily managed situations to develop into something more. Seek professional help early on. This way the time and money spent and, most importantly, the cat's suffering will be minimized.

11

THE NOSE

In the dog noses vary in shape between the extremes of the Pekes and the Pointers, whereas there is little variation in the cat with the exception of a small number of breeds, good examples being the Persians' flattened features and the elongated Siamese muzzle. Feline nasal disease is not uncommon and can be due to many different infectious and non-infectious agents. Unfortunately, these may all result in similar symptoms, which makes diagnosis somewhat difficult without in-depth investigation. The veterinary management of these different diseases varies tremendously so it is of utmost importance to establish the inciting cause as early as possible.

Structure of the nose

The nose comprises the rhinarium, the nasal cavity and the paranasal sinuses. The rhinarium is the moist hairless part at the tip of the cat's nose; it may be black, pink or a spotty combination of the two. A midline groove called the philtrum divides the rhinarium into two, each half containing a nostril (naris). Being made of cartilage, the rhinarium is relatively mobile and the nostrils can dilate during breathing; this is not as obvious in the cat as in the dog where the end of the nose projects further from the face.

From the nostrils extends the nasal cavity. This is a chamber split in two by a vertical midline sheet (septum) formed of cartilage and bone that stretches from the nose tip back to eye level. The floor of the nose is the hard palate. At the rear of the mouth, the hard palate is continued by the fleshy soft palate. In humans the soft palate is very short and ends in the dangling 'uvula' seen at the back of the throat. Air breathed in through the nose passes along both sides of the nasal cavity into an area of the throat called the nasopharynx. From here it moves through the voice box (larynx), into the windpipe (trachea) and then to the lungs. In panting dogs, and in some other species, air can bypass the nose, but a cat will mouth breathe only in severe respiratory distress, as occurs with some respiratory diseases, when the cat is hot or severely stressed, or, occasionally, following damage to the nasal cavities.

Each side of the nasal cavity is filled with very delicate scrolls of bone called turbinates. These are arranged in a complicated pattern but basically comprise three groups, each formed of many fragile sheets of bone coiled round on themselves. The turbinates reduce the air space within the nasal cavity to a series of narrow clefts and passages.

The rhinarium is covered by modified skin which ends a short distance into the nasal cavity. The rest of the internal nose, including the turbinates, is covered by nasal mucosa, a thin lining layer only one cell thick underlain by blood vessels and tough connective tissue which attaches to bone. The thickness of the mucosa varies with the amount of blood contained in the blood vessels. When people have a cold, the vessels fill up and the mucosa swells, partially occluding the air channels; hence the stuffiness we feel at this time. The same process occurs in the cat with flu.

The turbinates at the rear of the nasal cavity are where the sense of smell or olfaction occurs. The mucosal covering here contains special smell sensors (olfactory neurons) on its surface. When stimulated by an odour, impulses are generated in the neurons and travel along their length, passing through a skull bone (cribriform plate) that separates nasal cavity and brain. The neurons then travel to a nearby area of the brain called the olfactory bulb, which is responsible for the perception of smell.

Figure 58 Structure of the nose in section

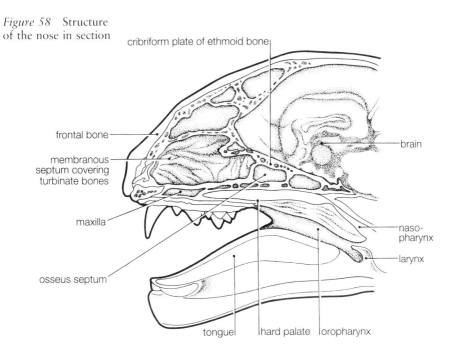

cribriform plate of ethmoid bone

frontal bone

membranous septum covering turbinate bones

maxilla

osseus septum

brain

naso-pharynx

larynx

tongue   hard palate   oropharynx

The nasal cavity has the important job not just of detecting smells but of changing the incoming air so that it is suitable for the lower respiratory airways. The air is warmed by the blood vessels in the mucosa and humidified by evaporation of secretions coating it. A component of these secretions is mucus, which is produced by glands in the mucosa and spread like a carpet throughout the nasal cavity. It traps particles that come in contact with it before it is swept back to the throat by millions of little hairs (cilia) on the mucosa that act in a synchronous fashion. Finally it is swallowed.

The paranasal sinuses are outpouchings or diverticuli from the nasal cavity that extend into the skull bones. The frontal sinuses are the only ones of significance in the cat; they are located at the junction between the nasal and cranial cavities. The narrow opening into the nasal cavity makes them prone to blockage when there is inflammation and thickening of the lining mucosa.

Nasal disease

SYMPTOMS

Before considering the specific diseases of the nose, it is important to look at the indicators of a nasal problem. Many of them are not specific for any one disease but, taken in conjunction with one another, they may narrow the range of possibilities quite considerably.

Nasal discharge

This is a common finding in association with most nasal diseases. However, it is not just its presence that is significant but also its character. The quantity and frequency of discharge must be considered as well as whether it is from one or both nostrils. Appearance is probably of most importance; discharges may be serous (clear), mucoid (containing mucus), purulent (mainly pus), mucopurulent (a combination of mucus and pus) or haemorrhagic (containing blood, Plate 24). Occasionally, diseases not originating in the nasal cavity can give rise to a nasal discharge; for example, a generalized bleeding disorder such as a clotting factor deficiency can result in nose bleeds (epistaxis).

Sneezing

Cats sneeze as an involuntary reflex in response to an irritating stimulus in the nasal cavity. Sometimes sneezing is repeated several times in short succession and is then termed paroxysmal. The presence of sneezing is common in many nasal disorders and is therefore not often much help by itself in reaching a diagnosis. Diseases that cause a lot of destruction of the lining mucosa, for example some tumours, may not result in sneezing because the receptors sensing irritation have been destroyed.

Stertor

Stertor is a snoring or snorting noise heard during respiration and usually originates from the throat (pharynx). It is sometimes due to foreign body entrapment but nasopharyngeal polyps are a common cause in cats.

Open-mouth breathing

Cats do not breathe through their mouths unless in severe respiratory distress, unlike dogs who pant as a mechanism for heat loss. Mouth breathing cats usually have severe lung disease, but occasionally they are heat-stressed. The other situation in which a cat will mouth breathe is when marked nasal obstruction is present, for example with a large nasal tumour; in this case there will be no other signs of lower airway disease. Similarly, swelling and discharge following nasal trauma can result in temporary mouth breathing.

Coughing

Generally regarded as an indicator of disease of the airways below the larynx, coughing can occasionally be as a result of nasal disorders. This is due to discharges from the nasal cavity draining into the lower airways where they stimulate a protective cough reflex.

INVESTIGATION

After a vet has learned all he or she can from discussion about the cat's symptoms, a superficial examination of the rhinarium and skull will be performed. Skin lesions and nasal discharges can be inspected. Non-patency (blockage) of the airways may be detected although not as easily as in dogs where the airflows are greater. Distortion of the skull bones overlying the nasal cavity may be apparent and the hard palate may also be abnormally shaped. However, these changes are not always sufficient to yield a diagnosis and further tests, usually under general anaesthesia, may be required. X-rays of the skull, including the nasal cavity and frontal sinuses, can be taken (Fig. 59 on page 186) and endoscopic examination of the back of the throat and nasal cavity performed. This is a procedure utilizing a rigid or flexible narrow telescope with an illuminated tip through which the vet can see otherwise inaccessible structures. It is not generally possible to see all the turbinates, the frontal sinuses or the middle of the nasal cavity with an endoscope, which is unfortunate as several diseases start in these areas. In addition to these procedures, some tissue from the diseased area may be removed for examination under a microscope; this is termed a biopsy. Biopsies can be removed from within the nasal cavity via a nostril or from round the back of the soft palate, or entry may have to be gained through the overlying bones in an operation called a rhinotomy. Blood samples and nasal discharges may also be collected to aid diagnosis. As soon as the results from the relevant tests are evaluated, an accurate diagnosis can be formulated and appropriate treatment started.

The conditions responsible for nasal disease, their diagnosis and of course their treatment will now be outlined.

Diseases of the rhinarium

TUMOURS

Of the various types of tumours seen on the tip of the nose, squamous cell carcinoma in white-nosed cats is one of the most common. It most frequently appears as a nasty ulcer on the rhinarium and tends to bleed spontaneously. In some cases it becomes extensive enough to involve both nostrils. As in man, growth of this tumour may be triggered by the ultraviolet light in sunlight, and other white areas, particularly the ear flaps, may be affected. It doesn't spread to other areas of the body very quickly but it causes extensive nasal destruction. Unfortunately it is difficult to remove all of the tumour so it often recurs following surgery unless the whole of the tip of the nose is removed. Some vets may try cryosurgery, where the affected tissue is frozen to destroy it. Since the success of this depends partly on how early it is done, it is of utmost importance to seek professional help as soon as any suspicious areas on the rhinarium are noted.

The prognosis for other tumours depends very much on the type of cell involved; a biopsy may be required to indicate the best therapy and the long-term outlook.

ULCERATION

There are several auto-immune conditions in the cat that may result in ulceration of the rhinarium. Although rare, it is important to distinguish them from tumours because treatment is quite different. In these conditions antibodies are produced by the cat against 'own' tissues; these 'auto-antibodies', as they are known, then attack specific tissues believing them to be the enemy. The rhinarium is one such site of attack. Diagnosis may necessitate a biopsy and blood samples. Treatment is usually the administration of steroids to suppress the abnormal immune system.

Diseases of the nasal cavity

These may be broadly categorized under the headings of congenital, traumatic, infectious and cancerous diseases. Infectious agents may be viral, bacterial or fungal but all result in inflammation of the nasal cavity which is termed 'rhinitis'.

CONGENITAL DISEASES

Cleft palate

As discussed previously, the hard palate is the roof of the mouth and the soft palate is a fleshy sheet of muscle covered with mucosa which continues the hard palate into the throat. The palate closes off the throat from the nasal cavity during swallowing; a defect in either hard or soft palates permits the passage of food and liquids into the nasal cavity. Here, damage to the nasal mucosa occurs, partly as a result of rubbing by food particles and partly because of bacterial infection. The contents of the nasal cavity also have a tendency to be inhaled and set up infection in the lungs. Cleft palates may either be present at birth (congenital) or occur as a result of trauma (acquired). Acquired cleft palates will be discussed later. With congenital cleft palates, it may be evident in the first few days that the kitten is failing to thrive. Very little milk is taken in because the kitten cannot develop the necessary force for drawing milk from the teat; any milk that enters the mouth tends to come back down the nose. A severe pneumonia may develop if the kitten lives for long enough. Surgery to repair the defect may be possible if the kitten survives but the prognosis is unfortunately rather grave.

TRAUMA

Trauma to the nasal cavity is often as a result of a collision with a moving vehicle. Haemorrhage into the chamber is invariably the initial response although this will stop given time. However, obstruction of the airways may persist for several days afterwards due to the presence of blood clots and inflammation in the nasal cavity. The cat may be forced to mouth breathe during this period. Facial bone fractures may have occurred and repair of these might prove necessary. If the cat is unable to eat because of injuries, feeding by an alternative route will be provided by the veterinary surgeon, often by a gastric or pharyngostomy tube, and this will obviously require hospitalization of the cat. Given time, the tissues will heal but it is important that vital intensive care is provided in the early stages when the cat is in most trouble.

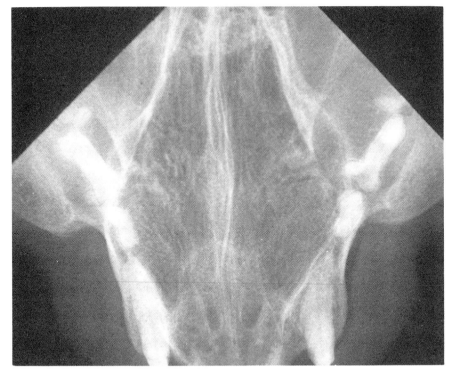

Figure 59 Radiograph of the normal nose showing the fine bones that make up the bulk of the contents of the nasal cavity

Acquired cleft palate

This is the most common cause of cleft palate in the adult cat and usually results from a road accident. The effects are identical to those of congenital cleft palates – the passage of material into the nasal cavity resulting in a rhinitis. Surgical repair of the defect is necessary if it is too wide to heal by itself. This may be done by wiring the upper canine teeth together to pull the two halves of the palate into apposition. Other surgical procedures are also available if wiring is not suitable. The prognosis for this sort of cleft palate is very good.

INFECTIOUS RHINITIS

See also Chapter 22, Infectious Diseases.

Viral rhinitis ('cat flu')

The two main viruses involved in infectious rhinitis are feline herpesvirus (FHV) and feline calicivirus (FCV). These are very important agents and in fact about 80 per cent of all cases of infectious rhinitis can be attributed to

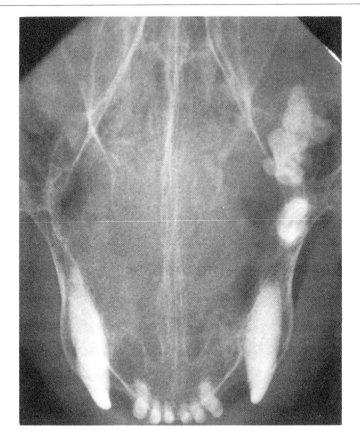

Figure 60 Radiograph of a nasal tumour. The tumour has destroyed the fine turbinate bones and the tumour can be seen as a white opacity

these two alone. Vaccines are available against both viruses and have contributed enormously to the decrease in frequency of disease seen in recent years. However, cat flu is still common and the viruses are widespread in the cat population.

Infection is most common in cats less than 6 months old and in households with several cats. Symptoms include dullness, being off food, bouts of sneezing and a nasal discharge that is serous initially but later becomes purulent with secondary bacterial infection. There may be conjunctivitis with a mucky discharge from the eyes. In the case of FHV, coughing due to infection of the larynx and windpipe is seen fairly frequently. FCV often causes severe ulceration of the mouth but it must be stressed that there is a range of severity of symptoms and much overlap and similarity between the two viruses. The great majority of cats will recover from infection although very young or debilitated cats may need special care. Factors influencing the severity of disease include not only the age and health of the cat but also its environment, such as the ventilation and available airspace, and the individual 'nastiness' (virulence) of the virus. Since treatment is identical for both viruses, it is not usually important to distinguish between them; a breeding cattery with a bad cat flu problem may be the exception.

The treatment of a cat in the early stages of the disease is mainly limited to nursing care because the viruses cannot be killed by the drugs available to us at the moment. Although antibiotics do not act against viruses, they are usually administered to keep bacterial invaders at bay. They may need to be given as a syrup or by injection because swallowing tablets can be very painful.

Nursing care is often best provided at home where the cat is happier and can be given undivided attention. A sick cat should be kept in a clean, warm environment, out of draughts but with good ventilation. Obviously it is important to isolate sick cats from other cats. With severe disease, the cat may be unwilling to eat because his throat is sore and he has no sense of smell to stimulate his interest in food. Hand feeding with smelly food, such as sardines or tuna, will encourage the cat to eat – try to feed him little and often. Warming the food also makes it more appetizing. Those cats with ulcerated mouths may benefit from liquidized food. Discharges from around the eyes and nose should be removed with moist cotton wool before they build up. Some cats with sore mouths will drool saliva which should also be wiped away gently. If the discharges are copious, Vaseline can be applied to the skin around the nose and under the chin to stop these areas becoming raw and irritated. Placing the cat in a steamy bathroom for a while will clear his airways and help his breathing (but don't leave him alone with a bath full of hot water). If he has stopped washing himself, grooming his coat will help keep up his morale. All this care and attention will play a major part in giving some cats the will to recover and its importance cannot be overemphasized.

Despite this care, some cats may become dehydrated and require fluid administration by the vet. Hospitalization is necessary in these cases until the cat is able to hold his own again. If the cat is unable to eat for a long time, feeding through a tube placed in his gullet by the vet may well be desirable. Even cats with such severe disease tend to make a successful recovery and the short-term prognosis for the disease is good.

Although the majority of cats will make a good recovery, unfortunately this is not the end of the cat flu story. Many cats will go on to develop a chronic rhinitis because the mucosa of the nasal airways is permanently altered. The mucous glands grow much bigger than normal and produce a copious discharge. There may also be some bacterial infection, although this is not the major problem. The cat sneezes and snuffles and always has a runny nose. The sinuses retain mucus because it cannot drain through the narrowed airspaces. Many different treatments, both medical and surgical, have been tried with little success and most cases are actually best left alone if the problem is tolerable.

Another left-over of viral rhinitis is the subsequent development of the 'chronic carrier state'. This is a term which describes the inability of many cats, up to 80 per cent in fact, to cure themselves completely of viral infection. Instead they carry the virus around with them and release it at certain times.

FHV carriers resemble people with cold sores; the virus spends most of its time sitting in nerves of the head in a latent state and when the cat is stressed the virus moves to its original site of infection and is released from there into the environment. Kittening and lactation are common stresses which stimulate virus movement and, of course, at this time there are a lot of susceptible kittens about for the virus to infect. Cats releasing virus may or may not develop sores at this time.

FCV is different in that it does not have a latent state but lives in the lining of the throat and is shed continuously. Both sorts of carrier state are thought to continue for periods of months to years and these cats act as a reservoir for infection. This is one of the reasons for the continuation of cat flu in cat populations.

Vaccination will not prevent infection but it radically reduces the severity of disease so that many cases will go totally unnoticed. An initial course of injections at 9 and 12 weeks of age followed by annual boosters is recommended. There are also nasal vaccines available that are administered by drops into the nose.

Bacterial rhinitis

The nasal cavity of the normal healthy cat is heavily populated with many different types of bacteria. These live in relative harmony unless some other agent causes sufficient damage for them to invade and multiply out of control. Bacteria are therefore secondary invaders and they tend not to cause disease by themselves. Viral infections and foreign bodies are most commonly responsible for the initial damage but in many cases it is the superimposed bacterial infection which causes a lot of the symptoms. A mucopurulent nasal discharge and mucky eyes are seen and the cat becomes ill and goes off his food. The cat will have a fever. These infections can become very serious and occasionally life threatening so antibiotic therapy is recommended in any cat with nasal disease. However, since the bacteria didn't cause the initial problem, it is also important to try to diagnose and treat the first disorder. If not resolved rapidly, the cat can be left needing intermittent courses of antibiotics throughout life.

Feline chlamydiosis

The one type of bacterium that can actually initiate nasal disease without another agent first causing damage is *Chlamydia psittaci*. However, its role in rhinitis is minor compared to FHV and FCV and its significance lies in its ability to cause a severe and long-lasting conjunctivitis. Any nasal discharge and sneezing is mild. Prolonged antibiotic therapy is necessary to treat the cat but even then symptoms may persist for up to 6 weeks. Vaccines against this organism have recently become available in this country.

Fungal rhinitis

This type of infection of the nasal cavity usually occurs in older cats and is most commonly due to the fungus *Cryptococcus neoformans*. Sometimes the disease is not limited to the nose and other tissues, such as the eye and skin, become involved. Nasal infection results in a nasal discharge which may come from one or both nostrils and is usually mucoid in nature. The cat may also suffer from persistent sneezing and intermittent nose bleeds. It is a very destructive disease and invasion of the overlying nasal bones may cause bumps to appear on the outside of the face. X-rays may demonstrate this destruction but a biopsy may be required to make a diagnosis. Unfortunately, fungal rhinitis is often secondary to some other disease causing poor functioning of the immune system, for example FeLV infection. In these cases, although treatment of the fungal infection may be possible, the other disease may have no cure.

TUMOURS

In this site they may be benign or cancerous. Benign tumours can be removed but cancerous growths tend to recur very soon following surgery. Cancerous growths usually occur in older cats and may arise from several tissue types including glandular, cartilage, bone and lymphoid (immune system) tissues. Symptoms include sneezing, mouth breathing, nasal discharge, nose bleeds and bumps appearing on the face over the nose. The turbinates are often destroyed and the facial bones may become involved. This destruction is usually quite obvious on an X-ray and the tumour mass can be seen in place of the turbinates (Fig. 60 on page 187) although endoscopy or a biopsy may sometimes be required to make a diagnosis. These tumours tend not to spread to the rest of the body although there is a lot of local destruction which will eventually cause suffering. When this occurs, euthanasia is the kindest course of action. Tumours of lymphoid tissue are different in that other organs are usually involved but they may respond to treatment with steroids and other drugs.

OTHER CONDITIONS

Two fairly common causes of nasal disease which do not fit into the categories above are foreign bodies and nasopharyngeal polyps.

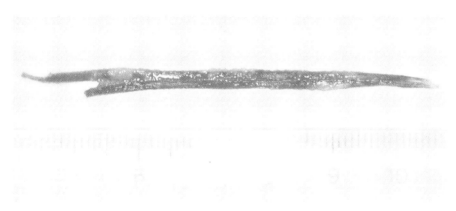

Figure 61   Blades of grass removed from nasal cavity

Foreign bodies

Blades of grass are among the commoner objects which find their way into the nasal cavity (Fig. 61) although many other strange items may be found. Initially the cat sneezes violently in an attempt to dislodge the foreign body but if he fails a chronic rhinitis may develop with permanent damage to the turbinates. Early removal to prevent this is obviously desirable.

Nasopharyngeal polyps

This condition is unique to the cat and there are still many things about it that are not well understood. It is seen mainly in young cats, sometimes as young as 2 months of age. The polyp consists of a dangling growth, usually on a stalk, that originates in the Eustachian tube, a channel running from the middle ear to the throat. The polyp passes out of the tube and into the back of the throat where it obstructs the airway and causes difficult breathing, sneezing and a nasal discharge. It consists of thickened mucosa with proliferation of all the mucosal layers. Quite why it occurs is not known although there is some correlation with middle ear disease. Similar polyps may also grow out of the external ear rather than down the Eustachian tube. Some unfortunate cats have polyps in both sites. Surgical removal is relatively straightforward and the prognosis is good.

Conclusion

Nasal disease is a common problem in cats and can be due to many different conditions. The symptoms may be very similar and diagnosis is not always straightforward. The age of the cat affects the types of disease that are most likely to occur, although this is not clear-cut. The treatment and long-term outlook very much depend on the individual disease but most diseases are easier to treat the earlier they are detected.

12

THE EYE

Ophthalmology is the study of eyes. It is a discipline which often uses long, complicated words. These scientific terms have been used in the text and there is a glossary at the end of the chapter to explain their meanings.

Problems involving eyes are a common everyday occurrence for the veterinarian in feline practice. Unlike dogs, cats have very few inherited eye conditions. The majority of feline eye problems are due to trauma, infection or neoplasia. There are some congenital eye diseases in cats but few are inherited. Most feline eye disease is classed therefore as non-inherited and acquired. Unfortunately most of the conditions to be discussed are not amenable to first-aid measures or home remedies. Therefore, if you are at all worried about your cat's eyes you should seek prompt veterinary attention.

Many of the conditions cause ocular pain and this can be recognized in your cat because it will show a combination of the following signs: blepharospasm, increased lacrimation and photophobia. Some of the diseases will result in loss of vision. If the loss occurs gradually the cat will slowly adapt, and it can be difficult for even the most observant owner to determine the degree of vision loss. A sudden loss of vision will be much more obvious, producing a sudden change in behaviour, but with time blind cats adapt and cope amazingly well in familiar surroundings.

To examine the eye properly, veterinary surgeons first use a bright light, which allows close examination of the lids, conjunctiva, cornea and iris. Using an ophthalmoscope in a darkened room allows a magnified view of these structures, and by using the lenses within the ophthalmoscope, it is possible to focus on the structures further back in the eye, such as the lens, vitreous and retina.

Structure and function

Looking at the eye from the front, the structures which are visible are the eyelids, the sclera, the edge of the third eyelid, the cornea, the iris and the pupil (see Plate 1).

The eyelids are made of skin and lined with conjunctiva. When closed they protect the eye, and by blinking they spread the tear film over the cornea, keeping it moist. The third eyelid or nictitating membrane is a piece of cartilage covered with conjunctiva and often has a pigmented edge. It sits at the medial canthus but can come across the front of the eye when the globe is pulled back into the orbit. Some cats may show third eyelid protrusion when they are ill, but in others it can be related to specific medical problems such as the condition called third eyelid and diarrhoea syndrome or the neurological condition of Horner's syndrome. There is also a gland in the third eyelid which contributes its secretions to the tear film. This gland can occasionally prolapse in young cats and needs to be replaced surgically.

The *cornea* is the clear circular area at the front of the eye through which the iris and pupil can be seen. Light passes through the cornea, the lens and then on to the back of the eye. Most of the focusing is performed by the lens but some is done by the cornea.

The *sclera* is the white fibrous coat of the globe which meets the cornea at the limbus. It is partially covered by conjunctiva and protects the more fragile internal structures.

The *iris and the ciliary body* are muscular, vascular structures which lie behind the cornea and in front of the lens. The iris is pigmented and gives the cat's eye its colour. Thus a blue iris is associated with little or no pigment in the anterior layer of the iris. Yellow and green develop as a result of varying concentrations of pigment cells. Together with the ciliary body and the choroid the iris makes up the uvea. The uvea is the vascular layer of the eye, and because of its vascular nature it is a common site for inflammation within the eye. Inflammation can occur in part or all of the uvea.

The *pupil* is the hole in the middle of the iris; in cats it is elliptical and its size can be altered by the action of the muscles of the iris. A wide, dilated pupil will let in more light than a small, constricted one; the pupil therefore acts like the lens aperture of a camera. In normal cats both pupils should be the same size and should respond equally to light.

The lens is a clear, disc-shaped structure suspended behind the iris by ligaments which emanate from the ciliary body. These suspensory ligaments contract and relax to change the shape of the lens and thereby focus light on the retina. The focusing system of a cat's eye is not as well developed as that in man. Cats' eyes are better adapted for following movement rather than focusing on detail.

The aqueous humour is a watery fluid which is constantly produced by the ciliary body and circulates through the anterior segment to drain out through a drainage angle behind the limbus. The aqueous is responsible for maintaining pressure within the eye.

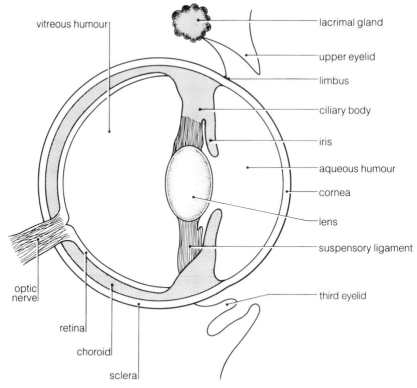

Figure 62　Cross-section of a normal eye

Looking at the eye in cross-section will enable you to see the internal structures of the eye as well as those already described. These are the vitreous humour, the retina and the choroid (see Fig. 62).

The vitreous humour is a jelly-like substance which fills the posterior segment. It is formed during the development of the eye and not constantly replaced like the aqueous.

The retina is at the back of the eye and is where the visual image is formed. It functions like the film in a camera. Light focused on receptor cells in the retina sets off a chemical reaction through a series of cells and results in a nerve impulse which travels along the optic nerve to the visual centres of the brain. In the brain the patterns of nerve impulses are converted to a visual image. The optic disc is the point at which the nerves converge to leave the eye as the optic nerve. The disc is visible as a white spot on the retina when viewed with an ophthalmoscope (see Plate 2).

Cats and dogs have another structure in their retina, the tapetum, which humans do not. It is a reflective layer which enhances any light entering the eye by reflecting it within the eye. This structure is present in the upper half of the retina and enables cats and dogs to see well in dim light and at night.

The choroid is the vascular layer which lies between the retina and the sclera and provides the blood supply to the retina. It is part of the uvea.

Diseases of the eye

THE ORBIT

The eye sits in a bony socket in the skull known as the orbit. Cats can be born with eyes that are microphthalmic, which is a non-inherited congenital condition. In short-nosed breeds the orbit is shallow and normal sized eyes bulge forward. This situation can predispose to a number of problems, such as exposure keratitis, overflow of tears and even prolapse of the globe. An abnormal enlargement of the globe, buphthalmos, is the end point of glaucoma.

The globe can prolapse out of the orbit following head trauma, a common injury for cats involved in road traffic accidents. A minor prolapse replaced early can result in restoration of normal function. However, there is often stretching of the optic nerve and tearing of the extra-ocular muscles. In these cases the eye may be permanently damaged and have to be enucleated. Applying a moist cloth to the prolapsed eye on the way to the surgery will help preserve it.

Problems involving the orbit behind the eye usually become evident when they cause the eye to bulge forward. Common retrobulbar lesions include abscesses, foreign bodies, tumours and occasionally haemorrhage (see Plate 3).

EYELIDS

The eyes of a kitten should open around 10–14 days of age. Once this has occurred, it is possible to see if the lids have been properly formed. Failure of all or part of the eyelids to develop is a rare congenital problem. Early infection in the eye may delay or even prevent eyelid opening; if this does occur the lids can be opened surgically under local anaesthesia. Before the eyes are due to open, bathing away discharge and giving appropriate medication may prevent the problem arising.

Common defects of the eyelids seen in dogs are entropion and ectropion. Fortunately these are rare in cats, but if they do occur can be corrected surgically as in the dog.

There are a number of eyelid defects which can arise as a result of feline herpesvirus (FHV) infection in very young cats. These include ankyloblepharon and distortion of the lids due to scar tissue formation. FHV infection can cause problems elsewhere in the eye and will be discussed later. Management changes and early vaccination programmes in colonies of cats where there is a known FHV problem will help prevent further problems.

Extra or abnormally positioned eyelid hairs are frequently seen as an inherited problem in dogs but fortunately are rare in cats. These can be known as ectopic cilia, distichiasis and trichiasis, depending on where they arise.

There are several types of tumours which can occur on the eyelids. The most common type is known as squamous cell carcinoma, which is more prevalent in white and part white cats. It is believed that ultra-violet light (sunlight) plays a part in causing this condition. This type of neoplasia is potentially treatable if caught early enough. Radiation therapy is the treatment of choice and is often very successful (see Plates 4 and 5).

CONJUNCTIVA

The most frequently encountered problem with the conjunctiva is conjunctivitis (see Plate 6). In cats most cases are caused by infectious agents such as bacteria and viruses, but there are also some non-infectious causes. An eye with conjunctivitis usually looks red and swollen with signs of ocular pain. There is usually a watery ocular discharge as a result of pain. However, if the discharge becomes yellow and sticky it usually indicates bacterial infection. Topical ointments and drops are often prescribed for cats with conjunctivitis. It is always important to clean away any discharges before applying treatment.

FHV is the most common viral cause of conjunctivitis in cats, and probably overall the most common cause of feline conjunctivitis. Infection is usually associated with signs of corneal damage and upper respiratory tract involvement. Infection of young kittens can result in symblepharon formation. Symblepharon can be treated surgically once the kittens are older. Feline calicivirus (FCV) can also cause conjunctivitis and is usually associated with other signs, such as upper respiratory tract signs and mouth ulcers. It is important to realize that both herpes and calicivirus infection can occur in cats which have been vaccinated. There are a number of reasons for this:

(a) They were infected with the virus before their vaccination was complete.
(b) There are some strains of FCV which are not covered by the vaccines currently available.
(c) The vaccine is not effective due to other technical reasons.

Another cause of conjunctivitis in cats is the bacteria *Chlamydia psittaci*, said to be responsible for up to 30 per cent of cases. Infection in individual cats can be effectively treated using the appropriate antibiotics. Infection in a multi-cat household can result in chronic and recurrent conjunctivitis, which requires thorough and prolonged treatment, management changes and, where appropriate, vaccination.

Mycoplasma spp. can cause a less severe conjunctivitis than *Chlamydia* spp. *Pasteurella* spp. can also be involved following cat fight wounds as this bacteria is found on cats' teeth and claws.

Non-infectious causes of conjunctivitis include tumours, dermoids, trauma, foreign bodies, allergic disease and pre-corneal tear film abnormalities.

One unusual form of conjunctivitis, which is not fully understood, is called 'Eosinophilic keratoconjunctivitis'. This disease involves invasion of the conjunctiva and often the cornea with white blood cells, primarily mast cells and eosinophils. These cells are responsible for inflammation and allergic reactions. Treatment is possible using topical corticosteroids, but very often long-term treatment is necessary to maintain an improvement.

Dermoids are elements of skin tissue that arise in abnormal places. Dermoids often, but not invariably, contain hairs and can form on the conjunctiva and/or cornea. One type is thought to be inherited in Birmans (see Plate 7). Dermoids act as foreign bodies in the eye, causing irritation and pain, and need to be removed surgically.

Several forms of neoplasia can affect the conjunctiva of cats and can be either primary tumours arising in the conjunctiva or secondary, spreading from elsewhere in the body.

SCLERA

Congenital defects of this structure are very rare. Inflammation (scleritis and episcleritis) is a problem in dogs but extremely rare in cats. The only problems seen with the feline sclera are associated with trauma (e.g. cat fights and road accidents) and neoplasia.

PRE-CORNEAL TEAR FILM

This forms from tears and is composed of three different layers. It moistens, lubricates and helps protect the cornea from infection. Decreased tear production occurs if the tear glands are not working properly and results in a condition called 'dry eye' or keratoconjunctivitis sicca (KCS). The cornea becomes dry and roughened leading to keratitis and ulceration (see Plate 8). There is a common problem in dogs, often breed related, but is much less common in cats. It can occur following FHV infection, trauma, facial paralysis and chronic inflammation.

Overproduction of tears can be seen as a result of ocular pain. There is a duct which runs from the inner corner of the eye to just inside the end of the nose called the naso-lacrimal duct. Cats can be born with congenital defects of this duct, such as a small opening which can result in an overflow of tears and staining of the skin around the eye. Tear staining is seen frequently in short-nosed breeds (typy or ultra-typy cats) because the duct is more tortuous and drainage is thus inadequate, a situation which is very difficult to improve surgically (see Plate 9). However, some of the congenital defects of the duct can be corrected with surgical intervention.

CORNEA

Congenital defects are rare but include micro and megalocornea. There is sometimes a transient cloudiness of the cornea following opening of the eyes but it should disappear by 4 weeks of age.

One of the most common problems involving the cornea is ulceration, where the top layer of corneal cells (the epithelium) is lost and the underlying stroma is exposed, resulting in ocular pain. The most common cause is trauma, primarily from fight wounds and foreign bodies. FHV is another frequent cause, resulting in inflammation of the stroma as well as loss of the epithelium. FHV infection can be difficult to diagnose and causes chronic eye disease, which is challenging to treat.

In short-nosed breeds with bulging eyes it may be difficult for the cat to close its eyelids fully, and in these cases exposure of the cornea can lead to ulceration and keratitis.

There is also a form of ulceration where the epithelium does not stick properly to the underlying stroma and can easily become detached. This is seen as a breed-related problem in dogs. In cats it is occasionally a problem in older animals, resulting in recurrent ulcer formation.

Fluorescein is a special stain which can be used to demonstrate ulcers. The stain will not attach to non-ulcerated cornea but will attach to and stain the exposed corneal stroma. An ulcer will show up as a yellow/green patch on the cornea (see Plate 10). If your cat has had this performed, you may have noticed the stain appearing at the end of its nose; this is because it drains down the naso-lacrimal duct and is a way of demonstrating that it is not blocked.

The cornea is very quick to repair ulcers and, provided that the initial cause is removed healing should only take a few days. Antibiotics are often applied to the eye while the ulcer heals to prevent bacteria infecting the exposed stroma. Ulcers do need prompt veterinary attention as they can deteriorate rapidly; deep ulcers can lead to rupture of the eye and may need surgical repair.

The cornea is a common site for cat scratch injuries and some may even penetrate the full thickness into the anterior chamber. If these wounds are repaired quickly and appropriate medical therapy is used, vision can usually be preserved.

The most common cause of keratitis is FHV, resulting in opacity of the cornea and invasion with blood vessels. This form of keratitis, often seen together with conjunctivitis, sometimes responds well to topical antiviral therapy (see Plate 11).

The cornea is often a site for foreign bodies; these usually result in ocular pain, but even those that are not painful need to be removed as they may penetrate into the eye causing internal problems.

Another unusual condition specific to cats is called 'corneal sequestrum' or necrosis. In this condition the stroma degenerates, turns brown/black and emerges through the epithelium, causing ulceration and a foreign body reaction with signs of ocular pain. These lesions usually need to be removed surgically because of the discomfort they cause, but a few will slough off naturally. Often a sequestrum will recur in the same eye or occur in the opposite eye at a later date (see Plate 12). This condition is most commonly seen in colourpoint Persians and is thought to have an inherited component. The next most common breed with sequestra is the Burmese.

Corneal stromal dystrophy can be seen as an inherited problem in Manx cats. A non-inherited epithelial dystrophy can occasionally be seen in domestic shorthaired cats.

Any corneal problem can result in the formation of a scar, which will show up as a white mark, but unless they are extensive they do not usually affect vision.

AQUEOUS HUMOUR

If the drainage angle is blocked and aqueous cannot drain away, pressure within the eye builds up and this is known as glaucoma. Glaucoma due to a narrowed or closed drainage angle is an inherited problem in many breeds of dog but is rare in the cat. When glaucoma does occur in cats, it is usually because the angle is blocked by inflammatory or neoplastic cells.

Anterior uveitis can result in white blood cells in the anterior chamber, which gives it a cloudy look known as aqueous flare. Infection in the anterior chamber with *Pasteurella* spp. can occur following cat fight wounds, and if pus accumulates in the chamber this is known as hypopyon. Trauma to the eye and intra-ocular tumours can result in bleeding into the anterior chamber, known as hyphaema. This blood usually forms a clot and is absorbed. Foreign bodies can also occasionally be seen in the anterior chamber.

IRIS AND CILIARY BODY

Congenital defects are rare but occasionally cats are born with pieces of the iris missing; this is known as iris coloboma (see Plate 13).

During a cat's life iris colour may change for a number of reasons:

(a) As young cats mature their iris colour may deepen.

(b) In older cats there is a loss of pigment and darker areas from the back of the iris show through. This is usually but not always a diffuse change, occurring slowly in both eyes. It must be differentiated from melanoma (see Plate 14).

(c) Melanoma is a tumour of the pigment cells which can result in either diffuse or nodular discolouration of the iris. It usually progresses quickly and only in one eye. This type of neoplasia has the potential to spread outside the eye and is usually treated by enucleating the affected eye.

(d) Inflammation results in reddening of the iris, due to an increase in blood vessel formation and engorgement, and is known as rubeosis iridis.

(e) The iris may also darken following inflammation, i.e. after anterior uveitis. This is a permanent colour change.

A difference in colour between the two irises in an animal is known as heterochromia irides. This can occur naturally in white or poorly pigmented breeds where there is one blue and one green or yellow eye (see Plate 15). In other cats it usually indicates a problem in one or other eye.

The ciliary body and iris are known as the anterior uvea, while the choroid is the posterior uvea. Uveitis will often involve both the anterior and posterior uvea. Uveitis has many causes in the cat, and the most frequently seen cases are those caused by infectious diseases. These include feline immunodeficiency virus (FIV), feline leukaemia virus (FeLV), feline infectious peritonitis virus (FIPV) and toxoplasmosis. The signs of uveitis for all these diseases are the same and include a constricted pupil, rubeosis iridis, aqueous flare, poor vision and ocular pain (see Plate 16).

It can be difficult to determine the cause in some cases despite thorough investigation. Even if the primary viral infection cannot be cured, cats with uveitis should be treated symptomatically to ease discomfort and attempt to maintain perfect vision.

Atrophy of the iris may occur as a result of ageing or as a result of previous inflammation. Cysts of the iris are sometimes seen, and look like black balloons. They form on the back of the iris but can detach and float through the pupil to rest in front of the iris. They are not neoplastic and do not usually need to be removed. Tumours of the iris can be a more serious problem. The most common tumour is melanoma but others can also occur.

LENS

A cataract is an opacity in the lens. Many forms of hereditary cataract are seen in dogs but not in cats. Congenital cataracts are occasionally found as a non-inherited problem. Most of the cataracts seen in cats are formed secondary to lens damage, e.g. blunt trauma, penetrating wounds, chronic anterior uveitis and lens luxation (see Plate 17). If cataracts involve the whole lens, light will not be able to get through to the retina and the eye will be rendered blind. If appropriate, cataracts can be surgically removed.

If the lens's suspensory fibres weaken or break, it will become dislocated and can fall either into the back or into the front of the eye. This is a common breed-related problem in terrier dogs and is only occasionally seen in cats, usually as a result of trauma, ageing or cataract. The lens is usually surgically removed in these cases or it may block the pupil and lead to glaucoma.

The lens condenses with age giving it a grey appearance, known as senile sclerosis. This is not a cataract as light can still pass through to the back of the eye and vision is not impaired.

VITREOUS HUMOUR

Like the aqueous humour, the vitreous can be infiltrated by haemorrhage and inflammatory cells. Foreign bodies (e.g. shotgun pellets) can occasionally be found in the vitreous. Inflammation of the vitreous, known as hyalitis, can be seen as part of a generalized uveitis. The vitreous may start to degenerate with age, giving a cloudy appearance to the back of the eye, but this does not usually affect vision to any great extent.

RETINA

Congenital retinal problems are rare in cats, but colobomas can occasionally be seen in the optic disc.

Inflammation of the retina usually occurs together with inflammation of the choroid and is called chorioretinitis or posterior uveitis. This can be caused by FIV, FeLV, FIPV, toxoplasmosis, parasites and fungal infections. Inflammation may lead to detachment, haemorrhage, degeneration or just scarring of the retina. It can be difficult to diagnose the cause of posterior uveitis but symptomatic treatment is generally given to try to maintain vision (see Plate 18).

The retina may also degenerate as a result of non-inflammatory processes. An inherited form of retinal degeneration has been described in Abyssinian and Siamese cats (see Plate 19). Another form of retinal degeneration is caused by a deficiency of taurine in the diet (see Chapter 7, Nutrition). This problem was discovered a few years ago when some popular diets were found to be deficient in this substance. This situation has now been corrected and the condition has become rare.

Retinal detachment occasionally occurs in cats (see Plate 20). There are many causes, the most common of which is hypertension. Hypertension in cats can be seen secondary to other diseases, such as kidney disease, hyperthyroidism and diabetes. These are more commonly seen in older cats. Inflammation and neoplasia may also cause retinal detachments. If the retina does not reattach in 24–48 hours there will be partial and possibly total blindness in the affected eye depending upon how much is detached. Symptomatic treatment is often given in an attempt to reattach the retina, but it is also important that the underlying cause is treated.

Retinal haemorrhages can occur as a result of hypertension, inflammation and trauma. They are not as sight threatening as detachments and will often be absorbed (see Plate 21). Once again it is important to find the underlying cause and treat it accordingly without delay.

Finally, if in any doubt regarding the condition of your cat's eyes, it is always worthwhile consulting your veterinarian. Even if you consider the condition relatively minor, it may not remain so!

Glossary

Acquired: develops after birth.

Adnexa: orbit, orbital contents, lids, lacrimal system, conjunctiva and third eyelid.

Agenesis: failure of all or part of a structure to develop.

Ankyloblepharon: fusion of the eyelids.

Anophthalmus: absence of the eye.

Anterior: to the front.

Anterior chamber: the space behind the cornea and in front of the iris (part of the anterior segment).

Anterior segment: space behind cornea and in front of the lens. Includes the anterior and posterior chambers.

Aqueous: watery fluid that fills the anterior and posterior chambers.

Atrophy: decrease in size or wasting.

Blepharospasm: blinking.

Buphthalmus: increase in the size of the globe.

Cataract: opacity (cloudiness) of the lens.

Chemosis: swelling of the conjunctiva.

Choroid: vascular layer between the retina and the sclera.

Ciliary body: thickened part of the vascular tunic between the iris and the choroid. Composed of the ciliary processes and ciliary muscles, it produces aqueous.

Coloboma: defect (hole).

Congenital: present at birth.

Conjunctiva: pink tissue lining the eyelids and the third eyelid, and covering the front of the sclera.

Cornea: clear circular structure at the front of the eye.

Dermoid: elements of skin which grow in abnormal places, e.g. on the cornea and conjunctiva.

Distichiasis: extra eyelashes.

Dystrophy: abnormal growth, non-inflammatory, developmental, nutritional or metabolic.

Ectopic cilia: extra eyelashes.

Ectropion: turning out of the eyelid.

Entropion: turning in of the eyelid.

Enucleation: removal of the eye (globe).

Epithelium: a delicate layer of cells lining and covering structures.

Exophthalmus: protrusion of the globe.

Fluorescein: special stain used for demonstrating corneal ulcers.

Glaucoma: increase in intra-ocular pressure.

Globe: the eye.

Haemorrhage: bleeding.

Hereditary: passed from parent to offspring in their genetic material.

Heterochromia irides: a difference in colour between the two irises of one animal or within one iris.

Horner's syndrome: a nerve deficit resulting in specific signs in the eye including third eyelid protrusion, drooping of the upper lid and constriction of the pupil.

Hypertension: increase in blood pressure.

Hyperthyroidism: increase in activity of the thyroid gland.

Hyphaema: blood in the anterior chamber.

Hypopyon: pus in the anterior chamber.

Inflammation: the body's reaction to damage, which manifests as redness, swelling, pain, heat and loss of function.

Iris: pigmented structure in front of the lens, with a hole in its centre known as the pupil.

Keratitis: inflammation of the cornea.

Lacrimation: tear production.

Lens: clear disc-shaped structure suspended behind the iris responsible for focusing light entering the eye onto the light sensitive retina.

Limbus: area where the cornea meets the sclera.

Lymphoma: cancer of lymphocytes (white blood cells).

Macrophthalmus: globe which is too big for the orbit.

Melanocyte: a pigment producing cell.

Melanoma: cancer of melanocytes.

Microphthalmus: globe which is too small for the orbit.

Miosis: constriction of the pupil.

Mydriatic: a substance which will dilate the pupil.

Neoplasia: 'new growth' or cancer.

Ocular: pertaining to the eye.

Ophthalmoscope: an instrument which enables inspection of the various structures of the eye.

Orbit: bony cavity in the skull containing the eyeball and associated muscles, blood vessels and nerves.

Photophobia: fear of light.

Phthisis bulbi: degenerative shrinkage of the eye.

Posterior: to the back.

Posterior chamber: space behind the iris and in front of the lens (part of the anterior segment).

Posterior segment: space behind the lens and in front of the retina.

Renal: pertaining to the kidney.

Retina: structure at the back of the eye containing photoreceptors.

Retrobulbar: behind the eye.

Sclera: white fibrous coat of the eye.

Stroma: middle layer of the cornea, below the epithelium.

Symblepharon: adhesion of the conjunctiva to itself and the cornea.

Synechia: adhesion of the iris to cornea (anterior synechia) or iris to lens (posterior synechia).

Tapetum: reflective layer below the retina.

Taurine: an amino acid, one of the building blocks of proteins.

Trichiasis: extra eyelashes.

Uvea: vascular layer consisting of iris, ciliary body and choroid.

Uveitis: inflammation of the uvea.

Vascular: composed of veins.

Vitreous: jelly-like substance which fills the space behind the lens and in front of the retina (posterior segment).

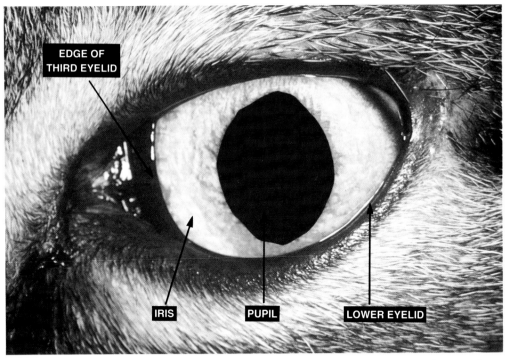

Plate 1 Normal eye, view from in front

Plate 2 Normal cat retina

Plate 3 Retrobulbar lesion

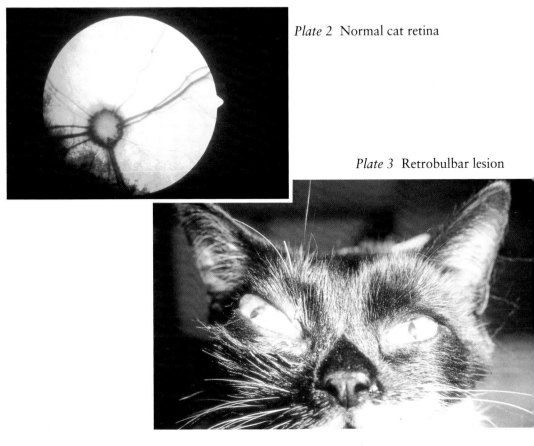

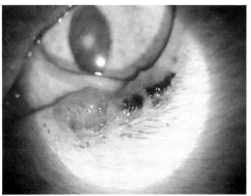

Plate 4 Squamous cell carcinoma

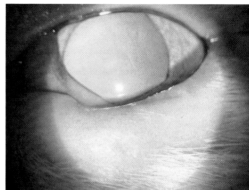

Plate 5 Squamous cell carcinoma after radiotherapy

Plate 6 Conjunctivitis

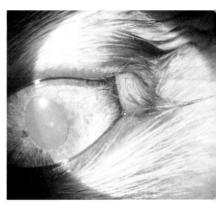

Plate 7 Dermoid in a Birman cat

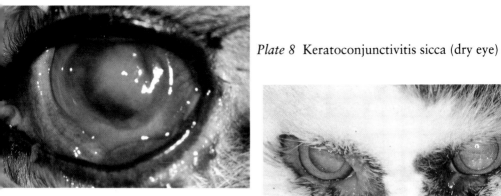

Plate 8 Keratoconjunctivitis sicca (dry eye)

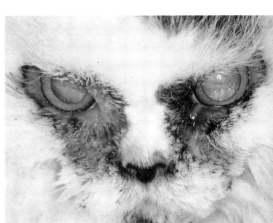

Plate 9 Tear staining

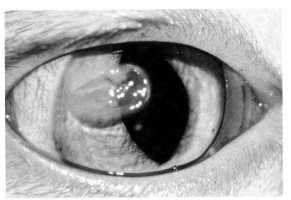

Plate 10 Fluorescein positive ulcer

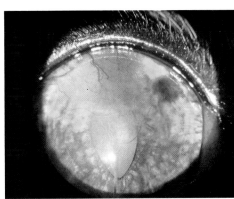

Plate 11 Keratitis

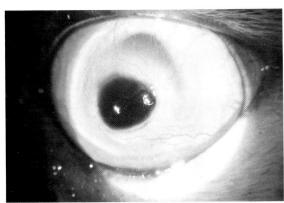

Plate 12 Corneal sequestrum

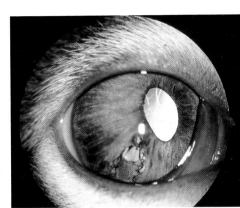

Plate 13 Iris coloboma

Plate 14 Iris 'freckles' associated with ageing

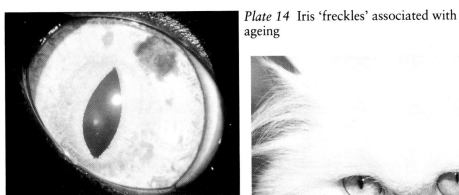

Plate 15 Heterochromia irides – odd colour eyes

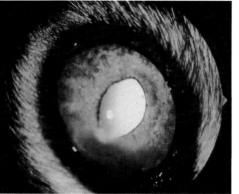

Plate 16 Uveitis

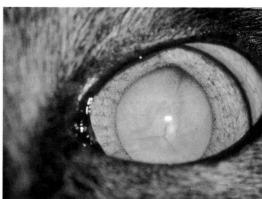

Plate 17 Cataract

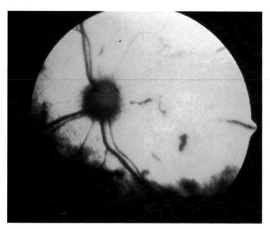

Plate 18 Chorioretinitis

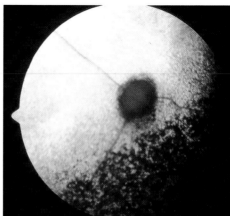

Plate 19 Retinal degeneration in an Abyssinian cat

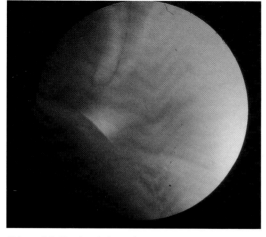

Plate 20 Retinal detachment

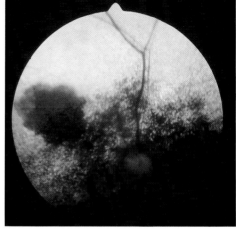

Plate 21 Retinal haemorrhage

13

THE SKIN

Structure and functions

The skin is the largest organ of the body and has a number of functions essential to life. It is the barrier between animals and their environment and protects against physical and chemical damage. It inhibits infection with micro-organisms – bacteria, fungi and viruses – and prevents loss of important materials especially water and mineral ions. This explains why the loss of a large area of skin following a physical injury or a thermal or chemical burn is potentially life-endangering. The skin is involved in regulation of body temperature and blood pressure. It is elastic and flexible to allow movement and is responsible for hair and nail production. Pigmentation protects against sunburn and the camouflage it affords helps prevent attack by predators. Skin is a reservoir for water, nutrients and mineral ions and is a site for vitamin D synthesis.

Skin has two main structural components, a thin outer component, the epidermis, and a thicker inner component, the dermis (Fig. 63). The epidermis is divided into a number of layers (Fig. 64). It is the major barrier restricting loss of water and other materials from the body and preventing entry of infectious micro-organisms, such as bacteria and fungi.

The dermis contains blood vessels, nerves, skin glands, hair follicles and connective tissue components, the latter mainly comprising collagen and elastic fibres, which confer mechanical strength and allow mobility. The main function of the dermis is to support and nourish the overlying epidermis, glands and hair follicles.

There are two types of skin glands in cats. Contrary to popular opinion, cats have large numbers of sweat glands in their skin. They do not open directly on to the surface via pores, as in man, but discharge sweat on to the skin surface through openings in the hair follicles. Sweat may have an important role in skin disinfection, but plays little part in temperature regulation in cats. Heat loss is via a number of other mechanisms (see

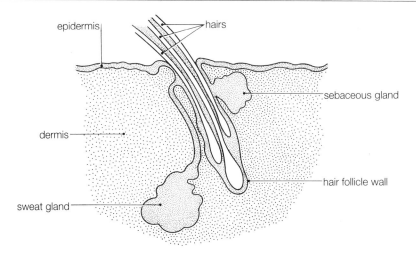

Figure 63 Normal hairy skin

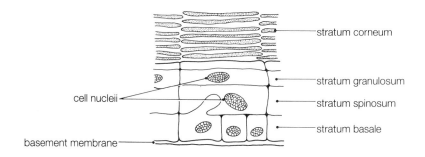

Figure 64 Epidermis

Chapter 8, Anatomy and Physiology). Sebaceous glands produce sebum, an oily material which is important in waterproofing the skin surface, maintaining skin pliability and resistance to infection. In cats, hairs are arranged in bundles of between 12 and 20 hair follicles, and all of the hairs within each bundle emerge from a common pore. There are between 800 and 1,600 such bundles per square centimetre. Two types of hairs are present, large, rigid primary or guard hairs and secondary or undercoat hairs, which are thinner and softer. Usually there are up to three primary hairs within each follicle group and the remaining hairs are secondary.

This is a typical arrangement in shorthaired cats. In Longhairs the guard hairs are often vestigial or totally absent, and the thinner, softer undercoat or lanuga hairs have been developed, sometimes to great length. Semi-long-haired breeds fit midway between these two types with a coat containing some guard hairs and undercoat hairs of moderate length which are thicker than those found in true longhair (Persian) breeds. In consequence Semi-Longhairs need considerably less coat attention since the thicker undercoat hairs are much less likely to matt than in the true Longhair (Persian) breeds.

Most cases of skin disease in cats are due to ectoparasite infestation. The most common parasite implicated in feline dermatology is the flea. Hence, many cases will be easily diagnosed and treated, although a percentage of problems will present a difficult and frustrating challenge to both owners and veterinary surgeons. The clinical signs of many different skin diseases are very similar and may require a wide range of laboratory tests and trial therapies in order to reach a diagnosis. In some instances this may take several months and is likely to be quite expensive. On occasion the underlying cause is impossible to discover and life-long symptomatic therapy is required. Insufficient space is available to discuss in detail the many disorders that can afflict the skin of cats. This account will therefore concentrate on the more common, troublesome and interesting diseases.

Parasitic skin disease

FLEA-RELATED DISEASE

The most important and common cause of skin disease in cats is probably the flea. Cat fleas (*Ctenocephalides felis*) are most commonly found on cats, although hedgehog fleas (*Archeopsyllus erinacei*) and rabbit fleas (*Spilopsyllus cuniculi*) may occasionally be present. The life cycle of the flea varies between 3 weeks and 2 years depending on the climatic conditions. The greater part of the life cycle is spent off the host animal in the environment, which is why treatment of the animal alone is usually ineffective in controlling flea problems. Eggs and immature fleas are found in the environment, but adult fleas live on the animal where they feed on blood. They may even feed on humans. Typically, skin disease is seasonal, coinciding with a peak in flea activity in late summer and early autumn, although with the widespread use of central heating it has become an all-year-round problem.

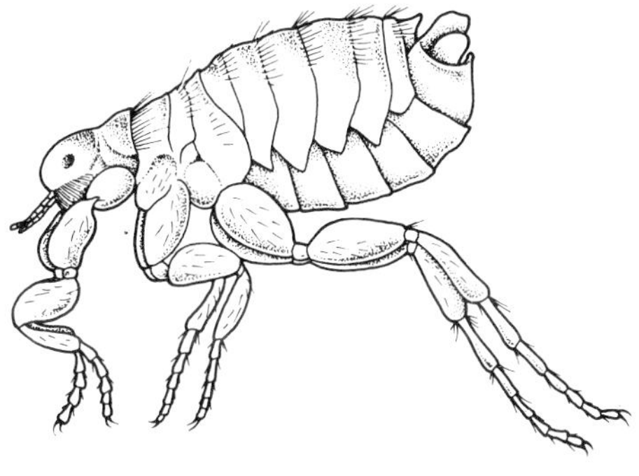

Figure 65   The cat flea

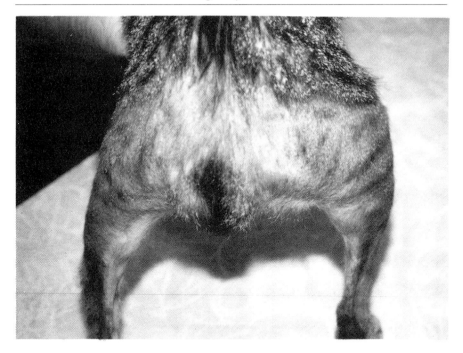

Figure 66   Self-induced hair loss due to flea allergy

It is likely that skin disease occurs as a result of an allergic reaction (see later) to flea saliva injected when the flea feeds, which leads to a sensation of itchiness (pruritus) and causes the cat to lick, chew or scratch. The response of the cat to fleas varies. In non-allergic individuals pruritus is absent or mild and results in few clinical signs. In allergic cats pruritus is marked especially at the base of the tail and posterior portion of the back, the abdomen, between the hind legs and sometimes the face and neck. Flea-allergic cats tend to increase the frequency and vigour of grooming, so removing hair, often without damaging the underlying skin. The skin damage (lesions) can vary and range from simple hair loss to the eosinophilic granuloma complex (see later) or miliary dermatitis. Miliary dermatitis (see later) is characterized by a widespread 'rash' with raised, red pinhead-sized lesions covered with a dry, brown exudate (or scab).

Diagnosis is based on the identification of fleas or flea dirt (excrement) in the coat, lesions in typical sites and response to a flea eradication programme. In some instances, fleas and flea excrement may be absent on clinical examination. This usually occurs when few fleas are present in the environment but the affected cat is highly allergic to them. In these cases an effective flea control programme (Table 2) is essential in providing a diagnosis. Veterinary surgeons will often initially recommend a strict flea eradication programme when confronted with cats with skin disease in

Table 2   Guidelines for flea control

1. All cats and dogs in the household should be treated regularly with residual insecticides such as sprays, dips, 'pour-on' and 'spot-on' preparations. Recommendations by the manufacturer regarding frequency of application and precautions for use should be carefully observed. Powders and flea collars are of limited use. Shampoos have no residual action as they are rinsed off after application and most cats are reluctant to allow bathing!

   Many insecticides are toxic to cats and so veterinary advice should be sought before purchasing these chemicals.

2. The environment (house or cattery) should be treated regularly (every 6–12 weeks) with a residual environmental insecticide after thoroughly vacuum cleaning (house dust is a breeding site for fleas). Again, the manufacturer's instructions should be followed. A professional pest control company may be needed to treat the environment in some cases. A new oral flea control product has recently become available which has the effect of 'sterilizing' fleas in the environment.

3. Some so-called 'flea-control' products such as flea traps and ultra sonic collars, may have little effect against fleas. Consult a veterinary surgeon for advice in selecting suitable products.

4. Recommendations for flea control vary with time of year, geographical location, severity of the problem and number and type of pets owned. Ideally, a flea control programme should be designed specifically for each individual case in consultation with a veterinary surgeon.

---

order to rule out this diagnosis at an early stage, even if no fleas have actually been seen.

EAR MITE INFESTATION

Ear mites (*Otodectes cynotis*) are one of the major causes of otitis externa in the cat (see Chapter 23, Parasites). They are just visible to the naked eye as white dots and are usually confined to the ear canal, although they can spread on to the skin of the head, tail and between the shoulder blades to cause dermatitis. Typically the disease is characterized by inflammation and a thick, waxy discharge from the ears. Head shaking and ear scratching may also be present. The disease is contagious between dogs and cats. Diagnosis is based on observation of the mites either on examination of the ear canal using an auroscope or by microscopical examination of ear wax. Treatment of all cats and dogs in the household with anti-parasitic eardrops for at least 3 weeks is usually effective, although it is sometimes necessary to treat the affected skin simultaneously with an insecticidal agent.

TICKS

These are grey, bean-shaped parasites, 5–10 mm (¼–½ inch) long, which infest animals in order to obtain a blood meal. They can affect all domestic animals and man, but are found on cats infrequently. The commonest tick involved in these instances is the hedgehog tick, *Ixodes hexagonus*. Cats usually tolerate ticks well, although pruritus and discomfort at the site of attachment may be present. Often cat owners will consult a veterinary surgeon about a 'cyst' or 'growth' which they have noticed on their cat only to be informed that the lesion is in fact a tick. The incidence of tick-related disease depends on climate, season and geographical location. Feeding ticks are particularly prevalent in south-west England and on the west coast of Scotland, especially in the spring and autumn.

Treatment is by manual removal after killing the tick with a parasiticidal agent. Care must be taken to remove the entire parasite as mouth parts left embedded within the skin may lead to infection. Traditionally, surgical spirit, dry-cleaning fluid or nail-polish remover on a piece of cotton wool have been used to loosen the mouth parts of the tick before it is pulled off. Lighted cigarettes have sometimes been employed, but none of these methods can be recommended. Insecticidal sprays should be employed and the ticks removed when dead. If in doubt, consult your veterinary surgeon.

LICE INFESTATION

The biting louse, *Felicola subrostratus*, is occasionally seen on cats. Clinical signs of lice infestation vary. Some individuals may be symptomless, whereas others may be pruritic. Lice are host specific, hence cat lice will not spread to other non-feline pets or man. Diagnosis is based on identification of lice within the coat and eggs ('nits') attached to the hairs.

Lice are easier to control than fleas as they live and breed on the host and are susceptible to most insecticidal agents.

CHEYLETIELLOSIS (*Cheyletiella* mite infestation)

These mites are just visible to the naked eye and live within scales and debris at the skin surface. Infestation is usually with *Cheyletiella blakei*, although *Cheyletiella parasitivorax* (usually found on rabbits) and *Cheyletiella yasguri* (from dogs) may also infest cats. The disease is contagious between cats and other animals and may transiently affect man. Clinical signs include mild to moderate dry scale, variable degrees of pruritus, eosinophilic granuloma complex (see page 218), miliary dermatitis (see page 217) or symptomless carrier status. Diagnosis is based on detection of mites or their eggs on microscopical examination of skin scrapings, plucked hairs and surface scales. Application of adhesive tape to the skin surface or collection of material obtained by brushing the coat will provide samples of scale and hair. Using a magnifying lens adult mites may occasionally be seen moving through the animal's coat or within the specimens described above.

Treatment with three applications of anti-parasitic shampoo at weekly intervals together with treatment of the environment is curative. In-contact animals should also be treated.

HARVEST MITE INFESTATION

In late summer and autumn cats in rural areas may occasionally become infested with the immature larval stages of the harvest mite *Trombicula autumnalis*. The feet and head, especially the ears, are usually affected, and the clinical signs vary from mild dermatitis to severe pruritus and self-trauma. Diagnosis is by identification of the mites as tiny (0.2 mm long) bright orange dots on the skin. Treatment with anti-parasitic sprays, powders or washes is curative, and it has been suggested that recurrence might be less likely if flea collars are used.

NOTOEDRIC MANGE (feline scabies)

This parasite is regarded as being virtually extinct in the United Kingdom. Infestation with this microscopic parasite leads to intense self-trauma and self-inflicted injury. Diagnosis is based on identification of the mite by microscopical examination of material scraped from the skin surface with a scalpel blade, a technique known simply as 'skin scraping'. Treatment of affected cats with insecticidal shampoos is curative.

DEMODECTIC MANGE

This is a rare disorder caused by the parasitic mite *Demodex cati*. Little is known of this disease, but some cases have occurred in cats suffering other immunosuppressive, neoplastic or systemic diseases, such as feline immunosuppressive virus (FIV) or feline leukaemia virus (FeLV) infection. Diagnosis is achieved by the use of skin scrapings.

Ringworm

This is a fungal infection of the dead components of the skin, the stratum corneum and occasionally the nails. Infection may be by a number of routes: direct contagion between cats, indirect spread by brushes and combs or by contact with infected hairs and skin scales in the environment. The infectious particles, fungal spores, may remain viable in the environment for extremely long periods. All ages and breeds of cat are susceptible to infection but young cats, cats housed in areas of high temperature and humidity, those with systemic disease or defective immune function (e.g. FIV, FeLV), those fed a deficient diet or those with skin wounds (bite wounds or cuts) are more prone to ringworm. A number of fungal species have been documented as causes of feline ringworm, but most cases in the United Kingdom are due to *Microsporum canis.*

The lesions of ringworm vary. Some cats, especially longhaired breeds, may be symptomless carriers of ringworm. Such cases can form a persistent source of reinfection in catteries and multi-cat households. Other cats will develop the classic circular ringworm lesion with hair loss and greyish, dry scale covering the skin surface. Miliary dermatitis may also be a feature of ringworm. Owners of affected cats may also become infected and are advised to consult their medical practitioners.

There are a number of laboratory techniques for the diagnosis of ringworm. Initially, veterinary surgeons will examine cats in which ringworm is suspected using filtered ultra-violet light. With this special filter (Wood's Lamp), at least 60 per cent of strains of *Microsporum canis* will fluoresce with an apple-green colour. In those cases in which no fluorescence is elicited, but ringworm is still suspected, the veterinary surgeon may pluck or brush hairs from lesions for laboratory culture. This is a specialized and difficult technique and many veterinary surgeons prefer to send specimens to a laboratory experienced in dealing with such specimens. Results may take up to 3 weeks. Microscopical examination of hairs from lesions may be diagnostic, but this is a technique that is seldom used in veterinary practice as considerable expertise is necessary to interpret such samples.

Recovery from ringworm often occurs spontaneously but may take several weeks. The time to recovery can be shortened by aggressive therapy which will limit the opportunity for spread to other animals and humans and reduce the likelihood of reinfection. Longhaired cats should be clipped and the clippings destroyed. An anti-fungal antibiotic should be administered by mouth and the animal re-examined and sampled monthly until it is free of symptoms and cultures are negative. All in-contact animals should also be examined for signs of ringworm and have hair specimens cultured. If ringworm is present they will need treatment as discussed above. If cultures are negative, it is advisable to treat with an anti-fungal antibiotic for a short period.

The Governing Council of the Cat Fancy (GCCF) are particularly concerned regarding the spread of ringworm among show cats. In consequence, any cat showing signs of skin lesions indicative of possible ringworm is rejected from a show under Section D of their rules. All exhibits from the same household or cattery are also rejected no matter whether the rejection takes place at vetting-in or later during the show day.

The exhibit(s) showing lesions must be examined by a veterinary surgeon within 7 days. Microscopical examination and cultures have to be carried out on material from any lesions present and also from brushings from the whole cat. If these prove negative the exhibitor obtains a clearance certificate signed by the veterinary surgeon, but the exhibitor may not attend shows nor exhibit any cat until the clearance certificate has been received and acknowledged by the veterinary officer of the GCCF. If ringworm is confirmed, no cat belonging to the exhibitor nor any in-contact cats may be exhibited, nor may the exhibitor attend shows. A clearance certificate in this case must be signed by a veterinary surgeon and state that all cats listed as belonging to this exhibitor and/or living at the same address have been examined and found to be clear of ringworm. To achieve this, microscopical examinations and cultures of material from whole cat brushing and from any lesions, if present, must have been carried out on two occasions 8 weeks apart with negative results.

Cats showing scars etc. of significant size which are obviously due to injury rather than any possible infectious cause may be rejected under Section A, which effectively means that the cat is withdrawn from that particular show on compassionate grounds. Owners are often worried that cats which have been clipped for blood samples will be rejected at vetting-in, but the GCCF guidelines make it clear that such cats should not be rejected.

Faced with such stringent regulations to prevent the spread of ringworm, it is surprising that so many exhibitors present cats at vetting-in with obvious lesions which may be indicative of this contagious condition. Once a cat has been rejected under Section D, it is time consuming and an expensive procedure to obtain a clearance certificate. Therefore, if in doubt regarding any skin lesion, it is sensible not to exhibit the cat.

Treatment of the environment is also important as fungal spores may persist for several months or even years. Disposal of bedding and grooming equipment, vacuum cleaning and disinfection using fungicidal agents are recommended. The elimination of ringworm from cat colonies is a difficult and expensive process requiring persistence and dedication on the part of both the veterinary surgeon and owner. Insufficient space is available to discuss the procedure here and readers are referred to their own veterinary surgeon for advice.

Hormonal skin disease

This type of disease in cats has recently become the subject of controversy in veterinary dermatology. In general, bilaterally symmetrical hair loss (alopecia) in an animal indicates that a hormonal problem is present. This has been assumed to be the case in cats, and large numbers of bald cats are treated with hormones by veterinary surgeons every year. Hormonal therapy is usually helpful, so reinforcing the erroneous view that a hormonal abnormality was to blame for the problem. In fact, the majority of bald cats do not suffer from exaggerated, hormonally induced, hair loss or moulting but actually remove the hairs themselves by grooming excessively. This process can be quite subtle and owners may not be aware of their cat's behaviour; many cats are secretive about grooming.

The distinction between self-inflicted hair loss, where cats are licking the hairs out, and that due to a hormonal abnormality is easily made by examining hairs from around the lesional area under a microscope. It is usually possible to differentiate normal healthy growing hair roots from broken hair shafts. Occasionally resting roots and normal tips are seen; in these cases the hairs are falling out and the diagnosis is likely to be feline symmetrical alopecia, which is a disease of unknown cause but may possibly be hormonal in origin.

The major causes of self-inflicted hair loss include flea allergy, ringworm, psychogenic alopecia (a behavioural problem of excessive licking – see Chapter 6, Behaviour Problems – which occurs in breeds such as Burmese, Abyssinian and Siamese) and other forms of allergy (see below). Hormonal therapy may help these cats in a number of ways: it may stimulate hair growth, have a sedative or calming effect, and may reduce skin irritation in the case of allergy, so minimizing the desire to lick at the affected area.

True hormonal skin disease is uncommon. Hypothyroidism (deficiency of thyroid hormone) has not been proven to exist in cats. Hyperthyroidism has recently been recognised as a fairly common problem in cats, but it causes only mild dermatological lesions (a greasy, matted, scaly coat may be present). Adrenal over-activity (hyperadrenocorticalism or Cushing's syndrome) is very rare in cats and leads to increased thirst, appetite and urination without causing many skin problems in the majority of cases. Diabetes mellitus can lead to a dry scaly coat and skin, with or without mild pruritus. These disorders are covered in detail in Chapter 20, The Endocrine System.

Allergic skin disease

This common group of diseases is difficult and frustrating to diagnose and treat. Allergic, or more correctly hypersensitivity reactions occur when the immune system makes an exaggerated response to a foreign substance leading to tissue damage. In cats, the main foreign materials, or allergens, involved are flea saliva (fleas are the commonest cause of allergic skin disease), other parasites, foods, drugs and pollens and dusts. Allergic reactions damage the skin by complex and, in many instances, poorly understood mechanisms, resulting in inflammation and pruritus. Cats are not born with allergies but develop them after repeated exposure to an allergen. Consequently a cat may develop food allergy dermatitis having been fed the same diet for many years. Animals may become allergic to more than one substance, which can make diagnosis and treatment difficult. Furthermore, they may develop *new* allergies after previous ones have been identified and controlled.

PARASITE ALLERGY

Flea-related disease has been covered in detail previously (see page 207). Other parasites, such as harvest mites and ticks, may also induce allergic states in cats.

DIETARY ALLERGY

This is a fairly uncommon cause of skin disease in cats. Foods implicated as allergens in this disorder include cow's milk, beef, mutton, pork, chicken, rabbit, fish and eggs. The clinical signs are very variable with generalized or localized pruritus and self-trauma being present. Often the head and neck will be severely affected with self-induced alopecia and excoriation of the skin. This is probably not due to the cat being more itchy in this area, but is more likely to be because this is an area that can easily be scratched by all four paws. Miliary dermatitis or the eosinophilic granuloma complex may occur (see pages 217-18). Gastrointestinal symptoms resulting from food allergy are rare.

Diagnosis is straightforward in cats which live indoors. A four-week-long dietary trial with a source of pure meat to which the cat has not been regularly exposed previously (a 'hypoallergenic' diet) will lead to improvement in cats which are allergic to their food. If the condition improves, then the cat should be challenged with the original diet to determine whether a relapse occurs, thus confirming the diagnosis. Obviously, the 'hypoallergenic' diet must be fed to the exclusion of other foods and only water should be given to drink. In the case of cats which have access to the outside world, the problem of diagnosis is more complex as some cats are regularly fed by neighbours or may hunt or steal food from dustbins and other sources. In some instances there is no practical way of making a diagnosis of food allergy in a cat without confining the animal for a month and feeding a strictly controlled diet. However, once the diagnosis has been made, the practical problem arises of how to prevent the problem recurring once the animal is released.

Treatment is based on feeding a diet that does not induce skin disease. Commercial hypoallergenic diets are now available for use in cats (see Chapter 7, Nutrition). These diets are convenient, but even they may contain ingredients to which the cat is hypersensitive. In these cases other sources of food must be tried and can be added sequentially to the test diet until a balanced, non-allergic home cooked diet has been formulated. Considerable dedication is required for the long-term management of cats with dietary allergy.

INHALANT ALLERGY (atopic dermatitis)

In this disease an allergic response occurs when an affected animal inhales dusts, pollens and moulds. This is similar to human asthma or hay fever, except that the target tissue is the skin, not the respiratory tract. Human eczema is analogous to feline inhalant allergy. The prevalence of this condition in cats is unknown, as reliable diagnostic methods are yet to be developed and the mechanisms leading to this form of allergy in cats are poorly understood at present.

Clinical signs may be seasonal (if, say, pollens are involved) or perennial (if the allergens involved are present all the time e.g. house dust). Pruritus and self-excoriation, particularly around the face, ears, neck and limbs, may be present, although miliary dermatitis and manifestations of the eosinophilic granuloma complex (see below) may be seen. Diagnosis is difficult and is usually based on ruling out other causes of pruritus such as parasite and food allergy. In some cases intradermal allergy testing might be undertaken. This complicated procedure involves the injection of small volumes of a range of liquid allergens into the skin. In some atopic cats one or more of these will elicit an allergic response at the site of injection. These tests are extremely difficult to undertake and interpret and currently are only performed by veterinary surgeons specializing in dermatology.

Treatment is difficult. In rare instances the cat can be isolated from the offending allergen although this is seldom practical as allergic cats are often allergic to more than one substance. Moreover, it may be difficult to determine which substances are involved as the results of intradermal skin testing can be unreliable in this species. Anti-inflammatory drugs, including glucocorticoids ('steroids'), antihistamines and essential fatty acids (such as evening primrose oil) are used to reduce inflammation, irritation and pruritus. However, antihistamines and essential fatty acids will not work in all cats and glucocorticoids may induce serious side effects.

DRUG HYPERSENSITIVITY (drug allergy)

Cats may occasionally develop allergic reactions to drugs given orally, by injection or applied topically to the skin surface. Theoretically, almost any drug could cause this condition. Clinical signs are variable, but a drug reaction should be suspected if a skin problem commences following the onset of therapy for another problem or if continued therapy leads to worsening of the dermatosis. If drug hypersensitivity occurs then the use of the offending drug has to be discontinued.

Bacterial skin disease

Abscesses and cellulitis (inflammation of the tissue beneath the skin) are among the commonest reasons for which cats are presented to veterinary surgeons. They occur following fighting injuries and most frequently affect entire males; castration reduces the incidence of these syndromes. The limbs, tail, head and face are the most commonly affected sites. Careful examination of the area usually reveals the presence of a pair of puncture wounds due to the bite of another cat. The skin becomes swollen, inflamed, tender and painful to touch. The lesion may burst to yield foul-smelling, blood-tinged pus. Affected cats may have an increased body temperature and be depressed and anorexic.

The bacteria isolated from the lesions are usually those which live in cats' mouths and so the cause is simple inoculation of bacteria into the skin following a bite. Antibiotics are usually administered, and many veterinary surgeons will lance and drain mature abscesses.

Diseases of unknown or uncertain origin

In both human and veterinary medicine there are many disorders for which no cause has been definitively identified. In this chapter only two such diseases are considered: miliary dermatitis (or MD) and the eosinophilic granuloma complex (or EGC). These are not true diseases but rather are the symptoms of the cat's reaction to a wide range of disorders and so can have many different causes. It is for this reason that the investigation and treatment of cats with MD or EGC can be prolonged, time-consuming, expensive and ultimately may be unrewarding.

MILIARY DERMATITIS

MD is readily recognized clinically as a widespread disorder with raised, red pinhead-sized lesions covered with a dry brown exudate. Often the lesions are more easily felt than seen within the skin. Affected cats often resent the affected area being touched or groomed and they may be pruritic. Examples of underlying diseases are given in Table 3, although in some instances it is possible that a diagnosis will not be obtained as medical knowledge does not yet have all the answers required for such cases. Treatment is usually based on identifying the underlying cause and correcting it. In undiagnosed cases symptomatic anti-inflammatory therapy may be necessary as in cases of atopic dermatitis (see page 216).

Table 3 Examples of causes of miliary dermatitis

Ectoparasites	Fleas
	Cheyletiella
	Ear mites
	Lice
Hypersensitivity	Fleas
	Dietary
	Atopic dermatitis
	Drugs
Infections	Ringworm
	Bacteria
Nutritional	Essential fatty acid deficiency

EOSINOPHILIC GRANULOMA COMPLEX

Three distinct but related clinical syndromes comprise the eosinophilic granuloma complex:

1. *Eosinophilic (or rodent) ulcer.* This may occur on the skin or in the mouth but usually affects the upper lips. The lesions are well-demarcated ulcers (Fig. 67).
2. *Eosinophilic plaque.* These are raised, moist, red, eroded or ulcerated areas with a well-demarcated border (Fig. 68). Pruritus is usually severe. Lesions usually occur on the underside of the cat (abdomen, brisket or inside the thighs).
3. *Linear granulomata.* These can occur at most sites, especially behind the hind legs and within the mouth. They are well-demarcated lesions which are raised and yellow to yellowish pink in colour. They are often long and thin, hence the name *linear* granuloma.

The mechanisms leading to the onset of this group of symptoms is unclear. However, it is known that cats with flea allergy, food allergy or atopic dermatitis may have EGC. It is probable that the underlying causes of EGC are similar to those of MD. Again, treatment is based on identification of the underlying cause or the use of anti-inflammatory drugs (glucocorticoids, essential fatty acids and antihistamines) in undiagnosed cases.

Miscellaneous diseases

CUTANEOUS ASTHENIA

This disorder is congenital (i.e. present from birth) and is characterized by excessive skin extensibility and fragility. The skin tends to tear readily and

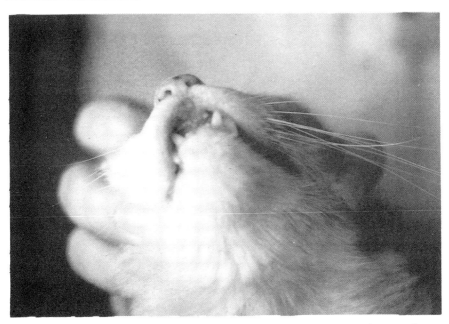

Figure 67   Collagenolytic (or 'rodent') ulcer on upper lip. A common feature of pruritic and allergic disorders

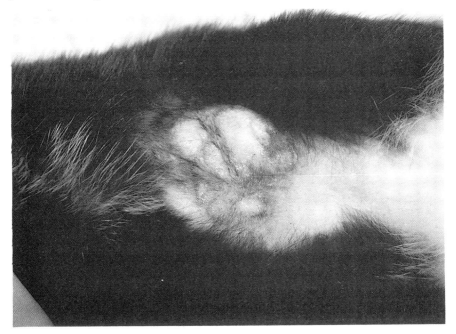

Figure 68   Eosinophilic plaque on abdomen. A common finding in allergic or pruritic disorders

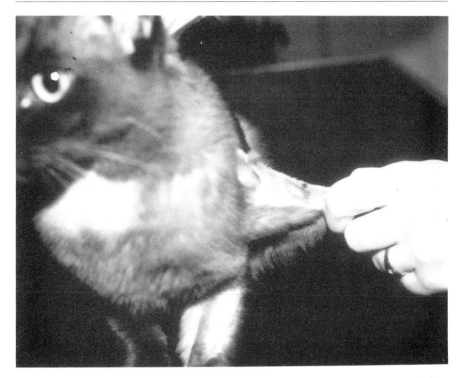

Figure 69   Burmese cat with cutaneous asthenia showing increased skin extensibility and scarring following previous tears

healing is usually impaired. It is also known as Ehlers–Danlos syndrome, dermatosporaxis or, graphically, as 'India-rubber disease' (Fig. 69). There is no cure.

FELINE POX VIRUS INFECTION

In recent years this has become a quite common problem in cats in the United Kingdom and the rest of Europe. The lesions are multiple, circular, crusted and raised above the skin surface. There may be pruritus and some cats are also systemically ill. In general affected cats recover spontaneously although recovery may be impaired if glucocorticoids are administered as these drugs depress the immune system.

Glossary

Allergen: foreign substance eliciting allergy or hypersensitivity.
Allergic reaction: an exaggerated response to a foreign material leading to tissue damage.

Alopecia: loss of hair.

Auroscope: instrument for examining the ear canal. Also known as otoscope.

Collagen: tough, fibrous protein of which the majority of the structural material of the body is composed.

Dermatitis: inflammation of the skin.

Dermatosis: any skin disease.

Dermis: thick inner portion of the skin.

Epidermis: thin outer portion of the skin.

Glucocorticoids: anti-inflammatory drugs used to control pruritus and pain.

Hypersensitivity: allergy.

Hypoallergenic diet: a food that does not elicit an allergic reaction in an individual with food allergy.

Lesion: any deviation from normality in a tissue.

Pruritus: the sensation of itchiness.

Skin scraping: laboratory technique involving the use of a scalpel blade to obtain material from the outer layers of the skin for microscopical examination. This procedure is particularly useful in the diagnosis of parasitic skin disease.

14

DENTISTRY

Veterinarians have been aware of feline dental problems for many years, but it is only recently that research has highlighted the unique problems associated with dental disease in the cat. Over the last three decades the cat has enjoyed increasing popularity as lifestyles have changed, and the importance of the feline patient has increased concomitantly. In consequence problems which were present but ignored 30 years ago are today assuming ever more importance.

Recent surveys have indicated that periodontal disease is present in over 80 per cent of the feline population over 3 years old. In addition to this single but widespread disease, there are two other dental problems that are specific to the felines:

1. The neck lesion or subgingival resorptive lesion is a problem that affects the neck or lower part of the tooth adjacent to the gum and is seen only in domestic cats. Worldwide the incidence of the problem is estimated at 52–65 per cent. This is in accordance with the only British survey currently available, which indicates an incidence of 57 per cent of cats over 2 years old having at least one tooth affected with the problem.
2. Chronic gingivitis/stomatitis is the second feline dental problem of importance. This disease can be extremely difficult to treat and is estimated to affect 2 per cent of the feline population.

Normal anatomy of the mouth

The feline dentition has many functions. It is designed for grasping, tearing and shearing, self-defence and for grooming. The adult cat has 30 permanent teeth, of which 16 are in the upper jaw and 14 in the lower jaw. Anatomically there are four different types of teeth:

1. *Incisors.* These teeth are in the front of each jaw and are very small with long single roots. Each tooth has three cusps with the central cusp most prominent. Their function is nibbling. There are six incisors in each jaw.
2. *Canines.* The canine, or cuspid, teeth are commonly called fangs. There are four of them, two in the upper jaw and two in the lower. They are the largest single-rooted teeth in the mouth and are normally used for holding and tearing. They are frequently damaged in fights and when biting hard objects, because of their prominence.
3. *Premolars.* These are the cheek teeth and are situated immediately behind the canines. There are ten in total, three on each side in the upper jaw and two on each side in the lower jaw. The first upper premolar has a single root and the third upper premolar has three roots. All the others have two roots. These teeth are designed for cutting and shearing.
4. *Molars.* There are four, two in each jaw. These are the 'back teeth', i.e. they are most caudal. The upper molars are very small, single-rooted teeth situated behind and central to the large upper premolars. The lower molars are the largest cheek teeth in the lower jaw. They have two roots. The function of the molar, like the premolar, is concerned with cutting and shearing.

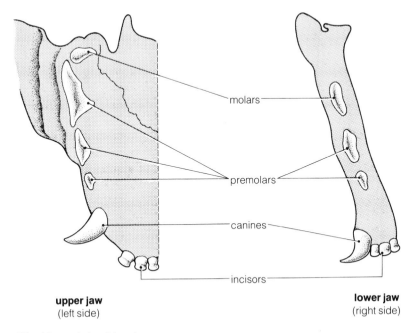

molars

premolars

canines

incisors

upper jaw
(left side)

lower jaw
(right side)

Figure 70 Normal dentition in a mature cat

The dental formula of the adult cat is as follows:

$$\text{I} \quad \frac{3}{3} \quad \text{C} \quad \frac{1}{1} \quad \text{P} \quad \frac{3}{2} \quad \text{M} \quad \frac{1}{1} \quad \times 2 = 30$$

I = incisor, C = canine, P = premolar and M = molar.

The primary or deciduous teeth start erupting during the second week of life, and the dentition is complete by the fourth week of life. There are 26 deciduous teeth, and the dental formula is as follows:

$$\text{I} \quad \frac{3}{3} \quad \text{C} \quad \frac{1}{1} \quad \text{P} \quad \frac{3}{2} \quad \times 2 = 26$$

The eruption dates of the permanent teeth are variable, but generally start at 12 weeks of age with the incisors. The full process takes approximately 3 months, so the kitten has a full dentition by the time it is 6 months old.

The anatomy of the individual tooth is similar in the cat and the dog. Each tooth consists of a crown, a neck and a root. The crown is covered with enamel, which is the hardest substance in the body. Underneath the enamel is the dentine which comprises the bulk of the tooth. The pulp cavity lies at the centre of the tooth and contains the nerves and blood vessels. The cells that line the pulp cavity, odontoblasts, send nerve fibres into the dentine, making it sensitive when exposed.

The root is that portion of the tooth hidden in the jaw. It is covered by cementum, which is similar in consistency to bone. The periodontal ligament binds the tooth to the jawbone and acts as a shock absorber during biting.

The gingiva, or gum tissue, is hard and fibrous and covers and protects the jawbones. It attaches to the tooth just below the neck at the cementum enamel junction (Fig. 71).

The hinge joint of the lower jaw is called the temporo mandibular joint (TMJ). It is classified as a gingymus or hinge joint and as such is only capable of working in one plane, i.e. opening or shutting. The anatomy of the joint allows no lateral movement, so the cat is unable to chew with a side-to-side movement, as in some animals. In the wild, the cat will kill its prey with the canine and incisor teeth and then tear bite-sized portions off the carcass with the premolars and molars.

The TMJ is frequently dislocated or fractured due to trauma of the skull, such as occurs as the result of a fall or road traffic accident.

The cat has fewer problems with its bite than the dog, although some variations do occur with skull types. The normal bite is a scissor bite where the canines should interdigitate with each other. The lower canines should occlude the space between the upper canine and the lateral or corner incisor. The premolars and molars in each jaw should have little or no contact as they are designed to act as scissor blades when gnawing.

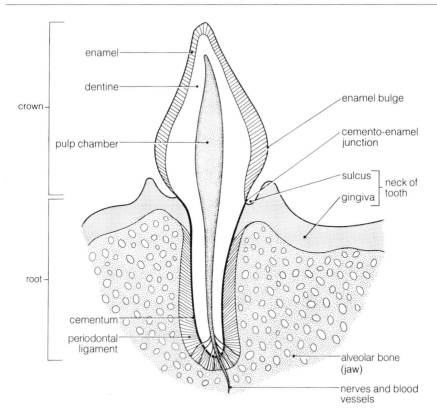

Figure 71 Cross-section of a tooth

MALOCCLUSIONS

Four variations of bite are commonly seen:

1. *Brachygnathism*: the lower jaw (mandible) is shorter than the upper jaw (maxilla). This is popularly known as overshot.
2. *Prognathism*: the mandible is longer than the maxilla – undershot.
3. *Wry-mouth*: one side of the mandible or maxilla is larger than the other side. The jaws are not symmetrical and an open bite, i.e. the incisors do not meet, may ensue at one side.
4. *Anterior crossbite*: one or more of the upper incisors may be situated behind its opposite tooth on the lower jaw.

Malocclusions are generally thought to be of genetic origin, but some can occur from a traumatic incident during kittenhood. One other source of malocclusion is the delayed loss (exfoliation) of the temporary teeth. As a general rule, temporary and permanent teeth of the same type should not be seen together.

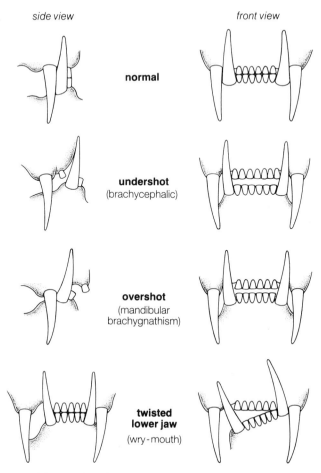

Figure 72　Normal bite and malocclusions

If you are worried about a possible malocclusion, consult your veterinary surgeon as soon as possible. Early treatment is much more likely to be successful than later.

Cats with malocclusions of possible genetic origin should be excluded from any breeding programme. Do remember that, whilst all cats are entitled to a healthy bite, not every cat may have a perfect bite.

Dental disease

CLINICAL SIGNS

What should the cat owner look for to determine whether or not dental disease is present? With the cat sitting on your lap, lift the upper lip gently with the thumb. The lip can be rolled up to reveal the canine teeth and the upper cheek teeth. The gum should be glistening, smooth and salmon pink in colour. The teeth should be white and firmly fixed in position. Anything other than this is abnormal and indicates dental disease.

COMMON PROBLEMS

Gums

These redden with inflammation. This can manifest itself as a red line where the tooth meets the gum, which is called marginal gingivitis. If the whole of the gum is inflamed, this can be very significant. It is worthwhile comparing one side with the other to determine how much gum tissue is present. If gingivitis (or periodontitis) is chronic the gum will recede away from the tooth. Inflammation is never normal. Seek veterinary advice if it is present.

Teeth

The teeth should be white and fixed solidly in their sockets. Tartar can be seen easily. If the teeth are coated with tartar (calculus) this will take the form of a brown stone-like covering. If extensive this tartar can cause ulceration on the lip where it abuts the tooth.

Plaque, on the other hand, is invisible to the naked eye unless it is stained with a special disclosing solution. This can be applied to the teeth with a cotton bud. The tooth surface is observed after 10–15 seconds. The amount of plaque present will be indicated by the depth of colour on the tooth. Do not wait too long or saliva will wash the bulk of the colour away.

A small pink spot on the outside surface of the tooth, near the gum margin, may indicate a 'neck lesion'. This is usually a small depression in the wall of the tooth, into which inflamed gums will grow. It is intensely painful and should be treated without delay.

Odour

Bad breath or halitosis is never normal in domestic animals. In the majority of cases halitosis indicates dental problems.

Salivation

Cats' mouths do not normally drip saliva. If excessive saliva is seen, especially on one side of the mouth, it is likely to indicate advanced dental disease.

Facial swelling

Some dental conditions can manifest themselves with facial swelling, and root abscesses from broken teeth are the commonest cause. However, infection due to other causes, such as fight abscesses, may have caused the swelling. Tumours usually also show initially as a firm swelling under the skin.

Difficulty in eating

This is called dysphagia, and cats that are unable to eat properly, although appearing hungry, are often suffering from dental disease. Some cats may eat on one side but not the other. Some may spit, back off or run away while trying to eat.

PERIODONTAL DISEASE

This is the most common feline dental disease. Most surveys place the incidence between 80 and 90 per cent in cats over 3 years of age. The progression of events is well documented and starts with an accumulation of plaque on the tooth surface.

PLAQUE = FOOD DEBRIS + SALIVARY PROTEINS + BACTERIA

These constituents of plaque are always present in the mouth, and if the plaque is not removed regularly it will change in character to cause inflammation of the soft tissues surrounding the tooth. In the wild, the cat will hold its prey and use its cheek teeth to rip the food into pieces small enough to swallow. This is an effective natural toothbrush. With the soft diets of today the plaque is never naturally removed. Studies have shown that when a cat has its teeth cleaned professionally no plaque is present. Within 10 days the invisible plaque that adheres to the teeth progresses from relatively innocent bacteria to strains that are capable of causing severe inflammation. Once plaque is established it will harden as minerals from the saliva stick to it, and calculus will form. This in turn leads to a roughened surface and further deposits of plaque.

The accumulation of plaque is generally more pronounced on the outside surfaces of the cheek teeth as these teeth are continually bathed in saliva. The inside surfaces also accumulate plaque, but the cat's rough tongue moving across the surface of these teeth limits the speed at which plaque can be deposited. The soft gum tissue surrounding the tooth reacts to this insult with inflammation. Initially only the margin of the gum is involved, but as the process progresses the whole of the gum tissue will redden and swell with inflammation. As the plaque advances down the tooth and the gum surface is pushed away from the tooth, the body's resistance is then reduced. Once infected pockets have been formed beside the tooth, periodontal disease is present.

Unless this disease is halted, the gums will recede, the bony support will disappear and the tooth loosen. Finally the tooth will be lost.

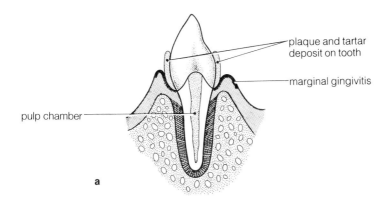

plaque and tartar
deposit on tooth

marginal gingivitis

pulp chamber

a

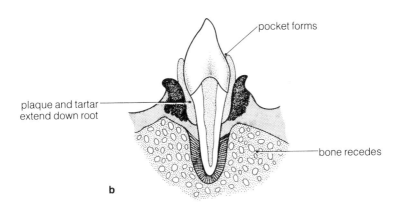

pocket forms

plaque and tartar
extend down root

bone recedes

b

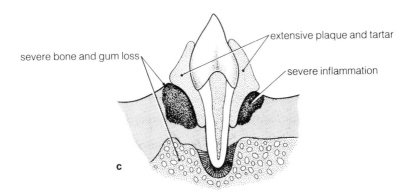

extensive plaque and tartar

severe bone and gum loss

severe inflammation

c

Figure 73 The progression of periodontal disease

Cats with periodontal disease show variable signs, depending on the progression of the disease. With mild disease the only signs may be small amounts of tartar, mild gingival inflammation and some halitosis. As the disease progresses and the tartar accumulates, the gums recede and halitosis becomes more pronounced. Some of the gum tissue may bleed with light finger pressure. Severe, advanced periodontitis presents with massive amounts of calculus and almost complete gum loss and debris (e.g. hair plus food material) can be found around loose teeth, and some teeth may be missing. The cat may be unwilling or unable to eat and will paw at its mouth or rub its face on the ground often accompanied by copious drooling.

Due to the pain involved, clinical examination is difficult without sedation or anaesthesia.

Treatment

Prevention is the best form of treatment. With people twice-daily brushing and regular twice-yearly check-ups prevent gingivitis progressing to periodontitis in the majority of cases, but even with these measures, many people over the age of 30 suffer from periodontitis.

Cats suffer the same pathological process, and since domestic cats do not function as they would in the wild, it is inevitable that their soft unnatural diet and lack of oral hygiene will cause periodontal disease.

Dental scaling and polishing is the basis of treatment. This requires a general anaesthetic if it is to be performed effectively. Gross tartar is removed manually or with an ultrasonic scaler, and the sulcus of the tooth must be probed to check for pockets, neck lesions and areas of subgingival tartar.

A small curette is used to smooth the subgingival tooth surface. Unless this hidden subgingival tartar is removed, it will continue to provide the focus for gingival inflammation, even if the crown appears to be perfectly clean.

Any loose teeth are extracted. If any neck lesions are present, the teeth should be X-rayed to determine whether treatment is possible. The teeth are then polished with a special paste. This is important since hand or powered instruments cause pits or fissures to form on the enamel surface. Unless the teeth are polished, using a special power-driven polisher, the rough surface will cause rapid plaque formation within a few days of scaling and polishing.

A final flush with a weak disinfectant solution, such as 0.1 per cent chlorhexidine, will remove any debris and excess paste from the sulcus area.

Finally the teeth are dried and treated with a fluoride mousse to harden the enamel, reduce the presence of bacteria and desensitize any dentine close to the enamel surface.

Follow-up home care

This is essential to prevent the progression of periodontal disease. Remember that the teeth will be coated in plaque after the first meal. Effective home care is designed to remove the plaque at regular intervals. This can take the form of a dietary change to more abrasive foods and brushing or rubbing the teeth with an effective agent to remove the plaque accumulation.

Special kits are available for cats, including a small brush and a sophisticated enzymatic dentifrice that can be swallowed and is reasonably palatable for the cat.

Many owners find this home care hard to do. Some cats will not allow it, but with gentle training and perseverance many cats will tolerate the procedure enough for it to be effective.

The benefits of home care were described in a survey, where it was noted that cats that had had home care daily had 95 per cent less tartar than those who did not. Even cats who had home care only once weekly had 76 per cent less tartar formation than those that did not.

Home care should be considered as oral maintenance by owners. As with coat grooming and ear cleaning, the more frequent and effective maintenance is, the less likelihood there is of a problem developing.

Cats who will not allow home care should have more frequent health checks and prophylaxis to maintain their dental health.

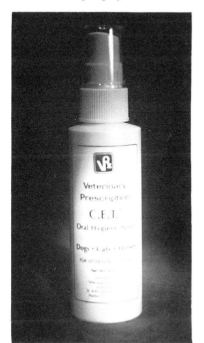

Figure 74   CET cat's toothbrush for home use – specially designed to brush small sulcus in cats

Figure 75   CET oral spray for home use

THE NECK LESION (SUBGINGIVAL RESORPTIVE LESIONS)

In the last few years the veterinary profession has become increasingly aware of the phenomenon known as the feline neck lesion. The term refers to damage to the neck of the tooth, and these lesions are also known as external osteoclastic resorptive lesions, subgingival resorptive lesions or cat caries. They are half-moon-shaped concavities in the structure of the tooth at the cemento-enamel junction. Histologically the destruction of the dental tissues is associated with cellular digestion by multinucleated giant cells analogous to osteoclasts, which are found in bony tissue and are associated with the continuous remodelling process that goes on with bone and other mineralized tissues. Tooth lesions are lined by these similar-looking cells and are invariably non-carious, i.e. are not undergoing decay. The fact that the dental margins are fully mineralized, hard and scalloped supports this fact.

Neck lesions are intensely painful and are associated with irritative, gnawing movements of the jaws during mastication. The early stages of neck lesions are associated with bacterial plaque. Soon the defect fills with oedematous, proliferative, fibrovascular connective tissue. The lesion then becomes coated with an ingrowing layer of collagen matrix cementum, and, in time, the healing tissue can become continuous with the connective tissue of the gum. However, the tooth is now damaged and weakened, which predisposes it to fracture.

The neck lesion affects the tooth where the enamel of the crown meets the cementum covering the root, the so-called 'neck of the tooth'. It can be hard to find in the early stages of the lesion, as the lesion is often covered by the gum margin.

With 'neck lesion' disease the tooth is digested by special cells called osteoclasts.

It should be noted that neck lesions are unique to domestic felines. They rarely occur in wild or feral cats.

Incidence

Several surveys of general feline populations over the last 10 years in various countries have indicated an incidence of feline neck lesions varying from 20 to 65 per cent, the cats examined exhibiting at least one or more lesions. A survey involving 152 cats conducted in the United Kingdom in 1990 indicated that 57 per cent of the cats displayed at least one lesion. A survey in the USA in 1992, involving 794 cats, conducted by Professor Colin Harvey, indicated that only 26 per cent of cats had one or more neck lesions, but in this survey the cats were checked for a number of factors by members of the American Board of Feline Practitioners. The cats were all examined under general anaesthesia, in the following percentages:

(a) 36.4 for periodontal disease treatment
(b) 26.4 for other dental or oral disease
(c) 37.2 for non-dental reasons

Thus 62.8 per cent of cats were anaesthetized for dental or associated reasons.

Of the cats anaesthetized, 97.6 per cent had a normal occlusional bite.

Diet was also investigated and it was found that 46.4 per cent of the cats were fed on dry food; 10.6 per cent on canned food; 39 per cent a mixed diet; and 4 per cent on a semi-moist diet.

The survey also revealed that 2 per cent of the whole survey population had stomatitis in addition to gingivitis.

A survey of cats' skulls in the British Museum, dating from 14 BC to 1958, revealed only one apparent lesion in 2,015 teeth examined, supporting the theory that this may be a new disease.

Causes of neck lesions

This condition was not described in veterinary literature until 1976. Whether or not these lesions existed before that date is difficult to say but the balance of probability indicates that they did, albeit in much smaller numbers than are found today.

Many theories regarding their cause have been advanced during the last ten years in an attempt to explain the astonishing rise in incidence in the last twenty-five years. Some of the early theories were essentially simplistic, but those currently in vogue are very complex.

In the periodontal pocket, or sulcus, where host defence mechanisms meet and confront micro-organisms, an environment is established in association with other factors. These factors are mechanical stress, underlying systemic and immune problems and nutritional imbalance. In this environment, bacterial products and inflammatory elements attract and activate odontoclasts and osteoclasts.

The accumulation of plaque, specifically *Porphyromonas* and *Peptostreptococcus* species of bacteria, plays an important part in initiating and establishing neck lesions in cats.

In addition, local mechanical trauma may be an important factor in initiating the resorptive lesion. Finally, the metabolism of calcium-regulating hormones and vitamins may be a secondary factor in the initiation and establishment of feline resorptive lesions.

In summary, the complex and multiple factors that are now thought to be involved in the initiation and establishment of neck lesions can be described thus:

1. Local immune response mediating cell and humoral factors
2. Release of biochemical components in dental tissues to attract odontoclasts

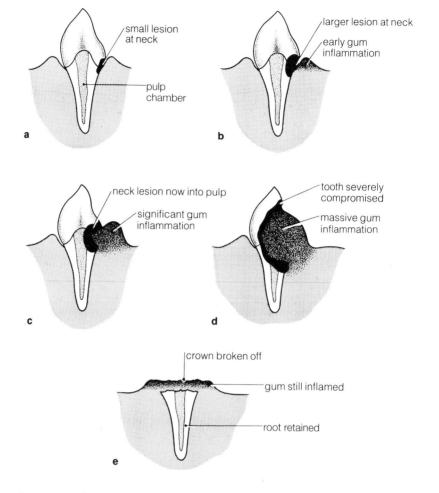

Figure 76 The progression of a neck lesion

3. Mechanical stress on the tooth tissues
4. Local and systematic calcium regulation including remodelling of mineralized tissue and dietary intake of calcium. From the above it will be obvious to the reader that this is not a simple subject!

Diagnosis

There are three main methods of diagnosis of the presence of neck lesions.

1. *Visual.* Neck lesions are commonly found underneath an area of local gingivitis. The area of inflammation is generally circular and highly vascular and oedematous. Although neck lesions can be found in any

feline tooth, the most common site is over the rostral (anterior) root of the first premolars (both upper and lower) and the caudal (posterior) root of the upper premolar 3 and the lower molar 1.

2. *Tactile.* During a standard dental check-up a tactile or 'touch' examination of the sulcus area is performed with a special explorer. The main reason for this examination is the detection of subgingival tartar, but it is possible to detect neck lesions, as the explorer tip will drop into small pits or depressions on the surface of the tooth. Due to the vascularity of the inflamed gingiva in and around the lesion, this may cause pronounced bleeding, and, if the lesions are at all advanced, some pain reaction may be noted, despite the fact the cat is anaesthetized.

3. *X-ray.* Radiography is the definitive method of diagnosis and should be used if either of the above two methods give rise to the suspicion that one or more neck lesions exist. Using specialized methods employed by veterinary dentists, areas of lysis (dissolution of tooth tissues) are usually obvious.

Classification of neck lesions

Neck lesions are usually progressive. They usually start in the sulcus at the cemento-enamel junction and progress apically into the root dentin and coronally into the enamel. To enable treatment of these lesions in a logical fashion, they must first be classified:

Stage 1. Early lesions appear as abrasions or shallow enamel or cementum defects near the cemento-enamel junction. They are usually less than 0.5 mm in depth and do not enter the dentin.

Stage 2. As the erosion progresses into the dentin, either through the enamel or through the cementum of the root structure, the tooth becomes painful. This is because the sensitive dentin tubules are exposed. These stage 2 lesions do not enter the pulp chamber.

Stage 3. As the progressive subgingival odontoclastic resorption continues through the dentin into the pulp chamber, severe loss of tooth structure may occur. These stage 3 lesions are very painful, and bleeding from pulp tissue will be evident on probing.

Stage 4. Chronic lesions will often have extensive gingival inflammation with cavitations in the root structure, complete root destruction, loss of crown and ankylosis of the retained roots as a result of periodontal ligament loss and cementum remodelling. Thus, to put it more simply, an erosion may go so far as to create physical separation between the root and the crown.

Stage 5. The crown is lost completely, and retained roots alkylosed to the alveolar bone are demonstrable on radiography. The oral mucose may well have healed over the root tips and may or may not be sensitive.

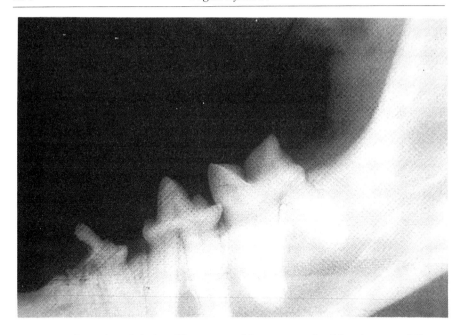

Figure 77 Stage 4 neck lesion. The crown of lower premolar 1 has been partially lost

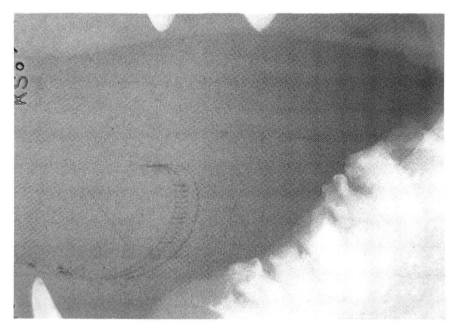

Figure 78 Stage 5 neck lesions. The crowns have been completely lost

Treatment

Neck lesions are intensely painful for cats, and it is essential they are treated once they are found. Treatment options open to the veterinarian have evolved over the last 5 years. Up until 1991 most lesions were restored using a glass ionomer filling material. This was thought to be an ideal material as it bonded chemically to both enamel and dentin and also leached fluoride ions into the surrounding tooth tissue. These ions, in theory, should help prevent further damage at the site.

However, work in 1991 by Harvey and Okuda has shown that the lesion continues to progress, and it was found that the most common cause of failure of treatment was continued resorptive disease (65 per cent) rather than simply loss of restoration (27 per cent). Therefore considerations relating to the choice of the restorative material are of doubtful significance. Today it is thought that the microscopic progression of this lesion and the unknown aetiology suggest that continued use of restoration of feline resorptive lesions as the major treatment technique is not effective.

What, then, can be done to treat these lesions? The use of the classification system outlined above is of considerable help in deciding the best form of treatment to apply.

Stage 1

The treatment of stage 1 lesions accompanied by a thorough dental prophylaxis and the polishing of the lesions with a non-fluoride flour grade pumice. The tooth is then air dried and painted with a fluoride cavity varnish. An important part of the treatment is to chart the lesion and re-examine by radiography at an interval of not more than 6 months.

Stage 2

These lesions are treated by the surgical removal of any gingival tissue which has covered the erosion or migrated into the defect. This is known as surgical gingivectomy. In deeper dentin erosions a hard-setting calcium hydroxide dressing is placed prior to any restoration being carried out. It is then possible finally to restore the lesion using a glass ionomer material, but clients have to be informed that there is an 81 per cent failure rate. Again, charting of the lesion and further radiographs taken at an interval of not greater than 6 months to monitor the progression, if any, of the lesion are imperative.

Stage 3

These erosions into the pulp cavity should be treated with a combination of full root canal filling and restoration as described for stage 2. However, the procedure is normally only carried out in an attempt to save the canine (cuspid or fang tooth), with extraction as the option for any of the other teeth involved to this stage.

Stage 4

Extraction techniques are the best option for teeth affected with chronic resorption to the level of stage 4. Alveoloplasty (reshaping of the alveolus) should be performed following extraction to eliminate any sharp bony margins.

Stage 5

This sort of lesion consists of retained roots with no crowns. In many cases these will be felt as hard swellings under the healed oral mucous membranes. If there is no pathology of the soft tissues over the swelling, and no sensitivity, no treatment is necessary. However, if soft tissue inflammation is present, or if the cat feels pain or sensitivity in the area, particularly when eating, removal of the retained roots is desirable. Once all the root tissue has been removed, the alveolar bone is smoothed and then the gums sutured with fine, absorbable suture material.

Summary

Neck lesions, feline subgingival resorptive lesions, appear to affect at least 30 per cent of the general cat population, and at least 60 per cent of those cats presented to veterinarians for oral cavity disease.

The true cause is yet to be established, but recent work indicates that chronic loading of the teeth with micro-organisms leads to enhanced immune response, resulting in osteoclastic differentiation or migration which thereby induces dental resorption at the cemento-enamel junction.

Treatment of neck lesions by restoration *per se* can no longer be supported, as recent studies indicate a long-term (greater than 6 months) failure rate of 81 per cent for any restoration on any one site. This failure rate is mainly due to the lesion continuing to progress around the restoration. However, if neck lesions are classified carefully, and the lesion is identified as an early stage 2, treatment by restoration may be acceptable, as long as follow-up examinations are diligent and post-operative home care is possible by the owner to reduce the burden of micro-organisms on the tooth.

However, careful assessment and effective treatment of the lesion are imperative, even if the cost appears to be high, which is likely, since general anaesthetic is always necessary for any feline dental work. The defect may seem insignificant, but if early methodical treatment is not carried out, and is not followed by regular reassessment, tooth loss and pain will inevitably follow.

FRACTURED TEETH

Cats can fracture their canine (fang) teeth and, less frequently, other teeth in fights or when crushing bones. Cats' teeth are easily fractured due to

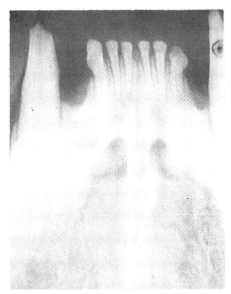

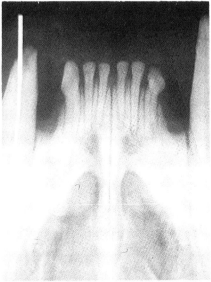

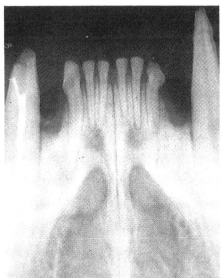

Above left: Figure 79 X-ray of left upper canine with fractured tip to show length and anatomy

Above: Figure 80 X-ray during excavation by filing of the pulp cavity

Left: Figure 81 Post-operative X-ray to show filling of root

their conformation (small size) and long, thin shape. Also, the pulp canal extends almost to the tip of the crown in the canine teeth, making any loss of structure in these teeth significant.

Whenever the pulp of the tooth is exposed it will die. Eventually, as the deeper pulp becomes involved, the likely outcome is an abscess at the apex of the tooth root.

Treatment is certainly possible in the larger teeth. It consists of removing the dead or dying pulp and, after thorough cleansing of the pulp cavity, refilling the tooth with an inert and disinfectant material. In cats it is preferable not to use phenol-based derivatives, such as eugenol, which are frequently used in humans for root fillings.

Once the pulp cavity has been filled, the access point is sealed with a special restoration material which restores the integrity of the tooth so that the filling is virtually invisible. The long-term results are excellent.

CHRONIC GINGIVITIS/STOMATITIS

This is the second most frequently seen dental condition in cats. This condition, also known as lymphoplasmacytic stomatitis (LPS), affects the gum tissues and often the lining membranes of the mouth and throat. It can be extremely difficult to treat and can affect cats from a very young age. All breeds are susceptible, but certain lines of pedigree cats, especially Abyssinian, Siamese and some Longhairs, seem to be predisposed to the condition. It is estimated that 2 per cent of the feline population is affected, to such an extent that only control rather than cure can be expected from treatment.

The main presenting signs are inflammation of the gums and sometimes other oral tissues; poor appetite and difficulty in eating; weight loss; and halitosis.

Cause

The precise aetiology is unknown. Examination of damaged gum and other tissue together with other laboratory findings indicate that there is an exaggerated response by the affected cat, or in some cases the immune system appears unable to respond to the presence of bacteria normally found in the bacterial plaque in the mouth.

The maintenance of a healthy mouth is based on an equilibrium between bacterial challenge in the mouth and the defences of the host. Disease will occur when the balance is changed by increasing the amount or the virulence of the bacteria, or decreasing the host cat's defences. An acquired immune deficiency has been shown to be associated with feline dental disease. Two main viruses of cats are associated with lowering of immune response, feline leukaemia virus (FeLV) and feline immunodeficiency virus (FIV). Although studies have shown that the proportion of FeLV-infected cats with oral disease is low, the most common reported symptom of cats with FIV is gingivitis/stomatitis.

Furthermore, when cats with chronic gingivitis/stomatitis are investigated, a high proportion of those infected with FIV are also found to be positive for feline calicivirus (FCV), which is one of the viruses commonly associated with the cat flu syndrome. The exact role of FCV is unclear, as it has not been possible to reproduce chronic gingivitis/stomatitis by inoculating normal cats with FCV. However, it has been postulated that the action of FIV and FCV is synergistic and the effect together is much worse than the action of FIV alone.

In addition to immunosuppression many immune-mediated causes of host tissue destruction have been shown to be significant, especially failure of immune response against the microbes associated with plaque production. In this case a type of 'allergic' reaction known as delayed hypersensitivity reaction will cause destruction of tissue, and the damaged tissue will be quickly colonized by bacteria. This is similar to the problem seen in the progression of periodontal disease in man.

Classification

Due to the many factors involved, feline gingivitis/stomatitis has been separated into four distinct syndromes based on the age of onset and the cause of the disease.

Feline juvenile gingivitis

Frequently pure-bred cats, especially Abyssinian and Longhairs, are affected. Cats are frequently affected just as the adult teeth are about to erupt. The main symptom is a hyperplastic gingivitis, where the gum tissue becomes intensely inflamed and actively proliferates and 'grows' up the teeth so that the crowns of the cheek teeth can be completely covered with gum.

Feline juvenile onset periodontitis

This frequently affects Siamese and domestic shorthaired cats. Many are physically small and have a history of being sickly kittens with chronic respiratory disease. Again, symptoms begin with the eruption of the adult teeth. Plaque and tartar build up very quickly, and rapid gum loss takes place with periodontal pockets and eventual bone loss around the tooth.

Feline adult onset periodontitis

This group are often infected after years of plaque and tartar accumulation without the benefit of professional dental prophylaxis or home care. This is the easiest group to treat as the response of the immune system is more predictable and typical.

Feline gingivostomatitis

This group affects adult cats and has no breed predilection. It appears to be the culmination of chronic immune-mediated processes resulting from immune suppression or hyper-responsiveness. In this group the processes have often been present since before adulthood, but because of lack of awareness or neglect the problem is not detected until the disease is advanced. Commonly there are excessive accumulations of plaque and tartar with missing teeth and exuberant granulation tissue. Those cats which are immunosuppressed show a low white blood cell count and low to normal serum globulin despite plaque accumulation, pus and dramatic oral inflammation. Cats which hyper-respond have more extensive and dramatic oral inflammation, involving gums, lips and throat. It can be difficult to differentiate the two categories as biopsy findings can be similar in both types.

Treatment

The initial treatment for all categories is a thorough dental prophylaxis followed by aggressive home care by the owner. Antibiotics are a useful addition to this treatment, as is supportive nutrition. Additional help will be provided by investigation of blood biochemistry and FeLV/FIV testing. X-ray surveys of the mouth often help to assess bone loss, the presence of neck lesions and the location of missing teeth. Thus adequate diagnosis can be fairly expensive before treatment is even contemplated. In feline juvenile gingivitis a procedure called gingivectomy is useful to reduce the excess gum tissue. It may be necessary to scale and polish the teeth as frequently as every 2 or 3 months until the cat is mature and a more competent immune status is attained.

The other three categories may need scaling and polishing every 4–9 months. Again, since these procedures require general anaesthesia, such a prevention procedure can be fairly costly in the long term. Where this type of professional treatment is not possible, or where home care by the owner is difficult, if not impossible, the only practical solution is to extract all the teeth behind the canines. Occasionally the canines and the incisors may also need to be extracted.

Any sites that fail to heal should be re-explored and any diseased bone removed in order to allow it to heal normally.

Summary

The main cause of chronic gingivitis/stomatitis can be said to be a complete intolerance to bacterial plaque by affected cats. Some cats may be suffering from suppression of the immune system, while others suffer from an exaggerated immune response. If it is possible to differentiate which process is taking place, this should be done as staging of the treatment, and perhaps the use of corticosteroids is possible. However, on no account should corticosteroids be used on immunosuppressed cats, since this may only exacerbate the condition in the long term.

I hope this chapter goes some way to explain why cats with chronic dental disease require so many repeat visits to the veterinary surgeon, with the concomitant cost of general anaesthesia, X-rays and operations. The pathology of the cat's mouth is a challenge to the veterinary surgeon, and an undoubted challenge to the pocket of the owner if it is to be controlled with any degree of effectiveness.

15

THE ALIMENTARY SYSTEM

Introduction

The digestive system consists of a collection of organs designed to take in food and process it in such a way that it can be used by the body. Food is taken in by the mouth and passes through the *alimentary canal*, where it is digested. The food is broken down into its component parts. These are then absorbed through the wall of the gut by the body and are used for growth, bodily maintenance and repair, and to provide energy.

Basically the digestive tract consists of a long tube running from mouth to anus (Fig. 82). It is divided into various parts: oral cavity, pharynx (or oropharynx), oesophagus, stomach, small intestine (which comprises duodenum, jejunum and ileum) and large intestine (consisting of caecum, colon and rectum). Along the route are several accessory organs: teeth, tongue, salivary glands, pancreas, liver and gall bladder and anal glands (Fig. 83).

The digestive process

Cats pick up food by the front teeth or incisors and the tongue. The latter is used especially with soft foods, such as most canned preparations. Large pieces of food are crushed by the premolar and molar teeth (cheek teeth) with their scissor bite into manageable sizes and mechanically mixed with saliva using the tongue. Saliva lubricates the food, making it easier to swallow. Parcels of food are pushed to the back of the mouth (oropharynx) by the tongue. Here a reflex action is initiated, using the tongue and muscles of the pharynx. This process is swallowing.

Wave-like movements of *peristalsis* convey food down the *oesophagus* to the *stomach*. This acts as a temporary reservoir for the food, and is the first site of chemical digestion. Throughout the alimentary canal digestion has

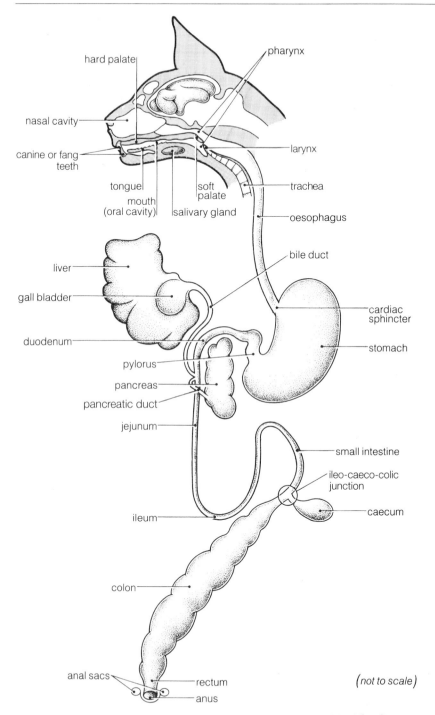

Figure 82 The digestive tract

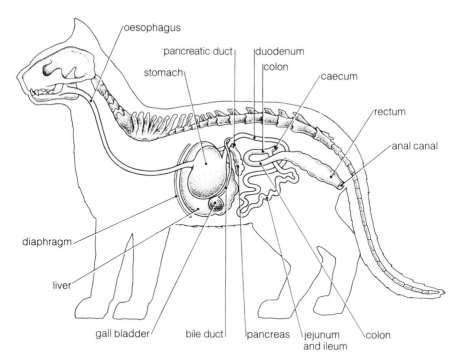

Figure 83 The digestive tract with accessory organs

two components: physical breakdown, by chewing, or churning by the stomach, or segmental contractions in the small intestine; and chemical breakdown, using *enzymes* which break food into constituents or 'building blocks' which can then be absorbed through the gut wall. These two processes occur in the stomach and result in the food being processed into a semi-solid fluid called *chyme*. This is periodically released into the small intestine by relaxation of the pyloric sphincter, a valve-like muscle under involuntary control.

The *duodenum* is the first part of the small intestine. It contains openings from the pancreas and gall bladder, allowing secretions from these organs to mix with chyme. The pancreas produces three types of enzymes which digest fats (lipases), carbohydrates (amylases) and proteins (proteases), which in this particular case are known as trypsin. It also manufactures hormones, such as insulin, which do not act in the gut (see Chapter 20, The Endocrine System). The gall bladder secretes *bile*, which is manufactured in the liver and stored in the gall bladder. Bile contains salts which render the acid passed from the stomach alkaline, and also helps to emulsify the small fat particles. It also contains pigments which colour the faeces.

Short waves of peristalsis move the chyme through to the second section of the small intestine, the *jejunum* and *ileum*. Food continues to be broken

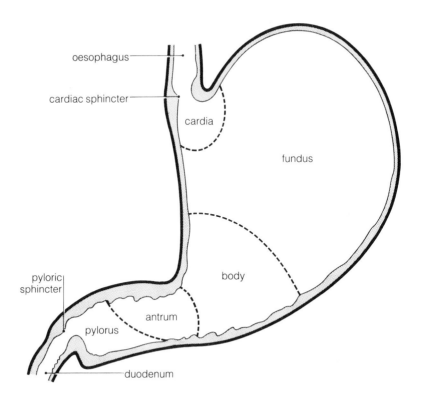

Figure 84 Parts of the stomach

down into its constituent parts: carbohydrates to simple sugars, proteins to amino acids and fats to fatty acids or glycerol (see Chapter 7, Nutrition). These substances are absorbed through the gut wall into the bloodstream, or into the lymphatic system in the case of fat digestion. Absorption is aided by the presence of thousands of finger-like folds or *villi*, which increase the surface area of the small intestine.

The contents of the alimentary system which pass into the large intestine are mostly fluid and are called *chyle*. The junction between the small and large intestines is the *ileo-caeco-colic junction*. The blind ending sac, the caecum, is present here. Cats do not possess an appendix. The *caecum*, *colon* and *rectum* form the large bowel. The semi-solid contents are now known as faeces and remain stored in the rectum until they are voided through the anus. The process of defecation has both voluntary and involuntary components.

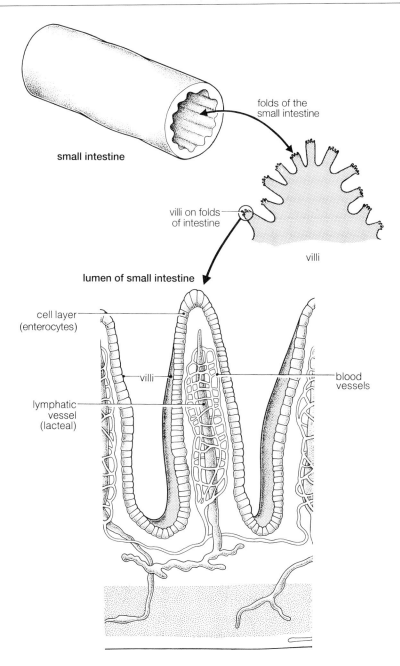

folds of the
small intestine

small intestine

villi on folds
of intestine

villi

lumen of small intestine

cell layer
(enterocytes)

villi

blood
vessels

lymphatic
vessel
(lacteal)

Figure 85 Villi are microscopic projections from the folds which line the wall of the small intestine, considerably increasing its surface area and thus the efficiency of absorption

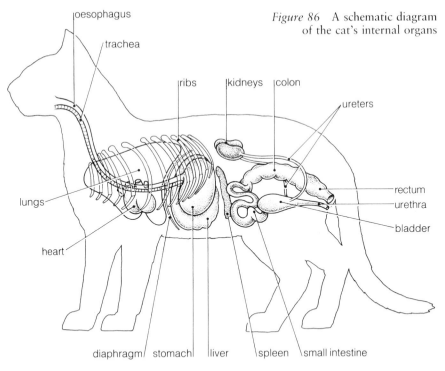

Figure 86   A schematic diagram of the cat's internal organs

The liver

In the cat, this organ is found in the cranial part of the abdomen, anterior to the stomach and adjacent to the diaphragm. It is the 'engine room' or chemical factory of the body, producing a number of enzymes and metabolizing many products of digestion. Once absorbed from the small intestine, most products go straight to the liver, as do chemicals that need to be removed from the body, such as toxins and drugs. Although some pathways are less efficient in the cat than in the dog, the liver plays a vital role in bodily function and health.

Anal glands

The anal glands or sacs are situated on either side of the anus. They produce a smelly discharge which is used to mark territory, and a little is released each time a cat defecates.

Disorders of the digestive system

THE MOUTH

The cat can suffer from a variety of problems within the mouth. *Dental disease* is extremely common and can result in cats refusing to eat because

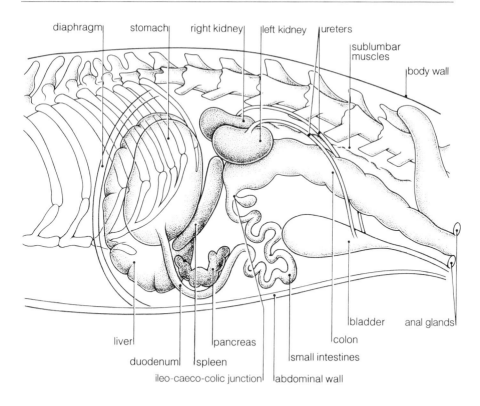

Figure 87 Diagram of the abdominal cavity

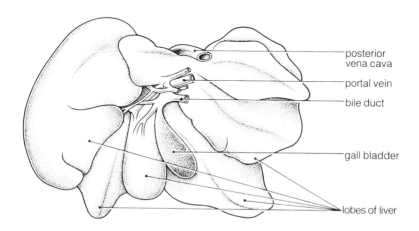

Figure 88 Liver and gall bladder

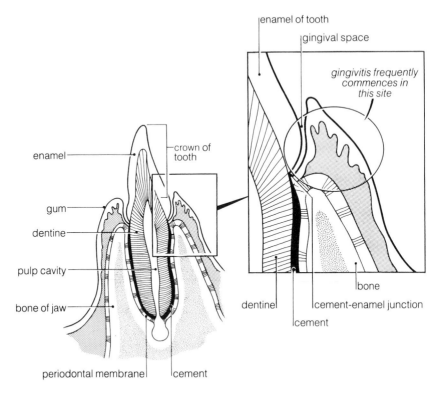

Figure 89   Structure of the tooth and the site of onset of gingivitis

of painful lesions. A build-up of tartar is very common in cats, especially those eating mainly soft tinned foods. Regular cleaning of the teeth can help limit calculus or tartar, usually by a combination of veterinary de-scaling and home brushing (see Chapter 14, Dentistry, for details).

Sore gums or *gingivitis* is very common. It can be due to dental problems or other causes, such as trauma, respiratory infections (part of the cat flu syndrome), cancers or part of a general illness, such as kidney failure. Cats with gingivitis have a bright red line along the base of their teeth on the gum margin. Some breeds of cat are prone to red gums and they do not seem to worry the cat, e.g. Siamese and Abyssinian cats. More serious gingivitis can cause the cat to stop eating, develop smelly breath, dribble or paw at the mouth.

The latter two symptoms are often present if a *foreign body* has become lodged in the mouth. Needles and thread, bones, pieces of string or even blades of grass can get stuck around the tongue, hard palate or oro- or naso-pharynx. They cause a great deal of distress to the cat and veterinary attention should always be sought.

Mouth ulcers also occur in cats. Viruses may be implicated, or general infections and illnesses. Sometimes the cause can be irritation, e.g. from licking the feet after the cat has walked across paint or creosote, or from chewing certain plants, e.g. dieffenbachia or poinsettia.

Other problems with the mouth include neoplasia, tongue injuries and blocked salivary glands. On occasion kittens can be born with a cleft palate, where the hard palate does not join in the midline.

A common condition is the 'rodent ulcer' or 'eosinophilic granuloma'. This has nothing to do with rats or mice, but is a sore that develops on the upper lip, alongside the portion where the lower canine tooth rests.

Unfortunately cats are often the victims of road traffic accidents, and head injuries are frequently incurred. A fractured jaw is not uncommon. Such injuries can usually be repaired using wiring techniques, and with careful nursing and treatment the cat can make a full recovery. However, sometimes the nerves supplying the face and mouth can be damaged, creating problems when picking up and swallowing food.

PHARYNX AND OESOPHAGUS

Foreign bodies, such as bones or needles, can lodge in the back of the throat (oropharynx) or pass around the soft palate into the nasal passages (nasopharynx) and cause problems as described above.

Nasopharyngeal polyps are benign growths which can occur at the back of the mouth. They slowly enlarge and eventually interfere with swallowing and can cause breathing difficulties. Usually they need to be surgically removed.

Diseases of the *oesophagus* are uncommon in cats. Typically a cat will regurgitate food (passively bring up food undigested). It may lose weight or if young be poorly grown. *Megaoesophagus* is sometimes encountered where the gullet has enlarged and widened excessively so that it cannot function normally. *Heart defects* in kittens can cause compression of the oesophagus as it passes through the chest. Narrowing of the oesophagus can also occur after injury, such as a lodged bone, since scar formation causes a narrowing or stricture.

STOMACH AND SMALL INTESTINE

Gastritis occurs less commonly in the cat than the dog. The usual sign of inflammation of the stomach is sudden vomiting, although there are many other things that make cats sick. For example, a sudden change of diet, eating grass, foreign body ingestion, worms, certain drugs or general illness can also cause cats to vomit.

Infections can cause vomiting, often with diarrhoea as well. There are two main causes of *infectious gastroenteritis*:

1. *Viral causes.* Of the viral causes, feline infectious enteritis caused by panleukopaenia virus is now thankfully rare due to widespread vaccination. The disease is highly contagious and affects all types of cats, including lions and raccoons. It causes sudden vomiting and a profuse, bloodstained watery diarrhoea. Affected cats dehydrate rapidly, and even with intensive care the condition can be fatal.

   Feline leukaemia virus (FeLV) and feline immunodeficiency virus (FIV or feline AIDS) can cause similar symptoms and cats are usually very ill.

   A condition commonly seen in young cats is mild diarrhoea with prominence of the third eyelid (haws). Again it is due to a virus (coronavirus), and it can take 2–3 weeks for the eyes to return to normal.

2. *Bacterial causes.* Bacteria can cause gastroenteritis where diarrhoea is the major problem. It can be chronic, i.e. long-lasting. Salmonella and Campylobacter have both been shown to make cats ill (as they do people). Again, there is a general ill-thrift and weight loss in affected animals.

Another cause of vomiting in cats is foreign body ingestion. This is surprisingly common when one considers that cats tend to be fastidious eaters! Solid structures, such as bones, needles or rarely hairballs, can obstruct the outlet of the stomach or the small intestine so that food cannot pass through. Linear foreign bodies, like string, wool or cotton thread, get caught at one end, yet waves of peristalsis continue. In the stomach these waves mix the contents with the digestive enzymes, while in the intestines they move the contents along. Since the foreign body is caught at one end, the small intestine gets squashed together like a concertina (Fig. 90). This is often extremely painful for the cat. X-rays and surgery are usually necessary to remove the item.

A somewhat similar condition is that of *intussception*, where one piece of bowel telescopes into the other (Fig. 91). This is more common in younger cats, and sometimes follows a bout of diarrhoea. It causes vomiting, weakness and scant passing of motions. Again, surgery is needed to remove the portion of damaged intestine.

Tumours of the intestine are fairly common in older cats. Straining with blood in the faeces along with weight loss and general debility are commonly noticed. More frequent tumour types are lymphosarcoma (often associated with FeLV infection) and adenocarcinoma, which appears more commonly in older Siamese cats. Sometimes these tumours are operable, but unfortunately they are often widespread by the time they cause the cat to become ill.

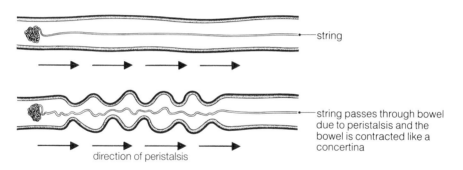

Figure 90 Schematic diagram of the consequences of a linear foreign body in the small intestine

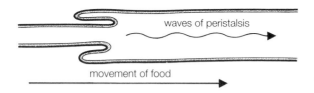

Figure 91 Schematic diagram of intussception, where one section of bowel telescopes into another

Diarrhoea can occasionally occur due to dietary problems, e.g. lactose intolerance or an inability to digest cow's milk, or dietary allergy can also occur. However, cats with food allergies more commonly have skin disease rather than bowel upsets, although these do occur (see Chapter 13, The Skin, and 7, Nutrition).

Parasites can cause digestive problems. Young kittens, especially, suffer from diarrhoea, ill-thrift and assume a pot-bellied appearance. Both roundworms and tapeworms can occur. Regular worming with a suitable agent is advisable for all cats. Sometimes protozoa (single-celled parasites) such as Giardia and Cryptosporidia cause a chronic, sometimes intermittent diarrhoea in infected individuals.

Small bowel inflammatory disease has been recognized in cats. Again, this results in diarrhoea, occasional vomiting and inappetence. The cause for this group of conditions has not been found, although an immune-mediated component has been suggested.

Pancreatic insufficiency results from an enzyme deficiency resulting in improper digestion of food.

Malabsorption syndrome is a condition where the body fails to absorb the food, once it has been digested. It can occur associated with small bowel inflammatory disease or with problems in the pancreas. Deficiency of pancreatic enzymes is rare in the cat, although common in dogs. Pancreatitis – inflammation of the pancreas – can result in malabsorption, especially if chronic. Usually cats lose weight despite eating well and produce voluminous fatty stools.

Vomiting and diarrhoea can also be due to general illnesses, such as kidney or liver disease or endocrine problems.

LARGE INTESTINE

Colitis is very common in dogs, but rare in cats. Constipation is a far more common problem in the cat (yet less so in dogs!). Inflammation of the large intestine occurs in a similar manner to small bowel inflammatory disease and causes straining with blood and mucus-stained faeces, which may be of normal consistency or loose.

Constipation is characterized by absent, infrequent or difficult defecation. Sometimes a change to a high fibre diet along with judicial use of laxatives will solve the problem. Cats are generally fussy about where they defecate so a change of environment, such as boarding, or a new cat in the household can trigger a bout of constipation. More serious causes include pain due to a fractured hip or pelvis, often after a road traffic accident or a fall. Healed fractures can result in a narrowing of the pelvic canal through which the rectum passes, thus obstructing it. Polyps or small tumours can also cause a physical narrowing of the rectum.

Another condition is *Key-Gaskell syndrome* or feline dysautonomia. Once fairly common this is now an exceedingly rare cause of constipation.

Sometimes constipation can be so severe as to cause permanent stretching of the rectum and colon, known as *megacolon*. This is a serious condition which requires specialized medical treatment or extensive surgery.

Faecal incontinence can occur, often as a result of nerve damage incurred during a road traffic accident. Sometimes a severe bite wound causes infection around the anus with abscess formation and leakage of faecal contents.

Anal gland problems do occur in cats from time to time. Usually they become impacted or infected, and the cat will wash the area excessively, and may scoot its bottom along the floor.

With all of these conditions specialized veterinary attention is required.

THE PANCREAS

As stated previously, deficiencies of pancreatic enzymes can cause malabsorption with weight loss and an excess of soft, fatty faeces despite normal food intake. Both acute and chronic pancreatitis are rare in the cat. The most common problem associated with the pancreas does not involve the bowel. This is diabetes mellitus caused by a deficiency of insulin production (see Chapter 20, The Endocrine System).

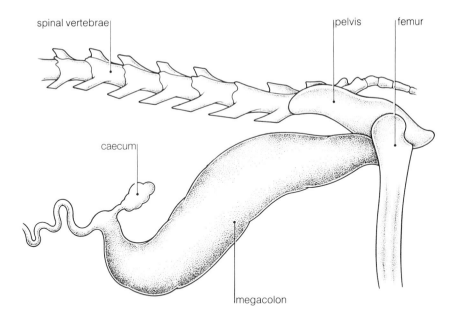

spinal vertebrae | pelvis | femur

caecum

megacolon

Figure 92 Megacolon as a result of severe constipation

THE LIVER

Jaundice is fairly common in the cat and is often an indication of problems with the liver. It may be associated with vomiting and diarrhoea or decreased appetite, increased thirst, weight loss and general ill health. It is usually due to Cholangio-hepatitis (CH) syndrome which results in inflammation of both the bile duct and the liver tissue itself. It is a chronic progressive disease and the end-stage is *biliary cirrhosis*. The cause is unknown, although in some cases suppurative CH is caused by bacteria ascending the bile duct from the bowel. Treatment with antibiotics often effects a dramatic improvement in these cases. Another type of CH is *chronic lymphocytic cholangitis*. This appears to be an immune-mediated disease and is often accompanied by ascites (dropsy). Treatment with antibiotics and corticosteroids will often stabilize the condition. Biliary cirrhosis is really the end-stage of many liver conditions and affected cats are typically thin, anorexic and jaundiced. Treatment can only be supportive, and unfortunately survival is only a few days to weeks from diagnosis. Tumours are quite commonly found in the liver, and some endocrine imbalances cause problems here, e.g. diabetes mellitus and Cushings syndrome (hyperadrenocorticalism).

Since the liver removes toxins from the body, any hepatic dysfunction can allow them to build up. This results in a variety of signs. Cats salivate, seem depressed or have a change of behaviour, and can show signs of hysteria, aggression or convulsions.

Feline infectious peritonitis caused by feline coronovirus, similar to the coronovirus causing protrusion of the haws in young cats is a fatal disease which attacks the liver among other organs. It causes leakage of fluid into the abdomen (ascites) giving the cat a pendulous abdomen. Cats are generally very ill at this stage.

OTHER PROBLEMS

Ruptured diaphragm is common in cats, especially after road traffic accidents. The diaphragm is the muscular sheet dividing the chest and abdomen. If it tears, abdominal contents which are more freely mobile than the heart and lungs, move forward into the chest. Respiratory distress is usually severe, but delicate surgery can be performed to restore normal anatomy. However, this condition is very serious, and a successful outcome cannot always be guaranteed.

Obesity is becoming more of a problem in domestic cats. Boredom, idleness and availability of food all contribute. Obesity can result in many problems. Among the most important are joint and movement difficulties, respiratory embarrassment, heart disease, endocrine problems, liver disease and constipation. If you think your cat is getting fat, consult your veterinarian, whatever the reason. Today there are many excellent remedies.

16

THE URINARY SYSTEM

Structure and function

Cats have two kidneys situated in the upper (dorsal) abdomen, just behind the liver, one either side of the midline, the left being a little less than half a kidney length behind the right (see Fig. 35, page 129). Both kidneys can usually be palpated in all but grossly obese cats and they should feel about equal in size, bean-shaped, smooth, firm and fairly mobile. Sizes vary slightly from one cat to another, but on average an adult cat kidney is about 4 cm (1.5 inches) long, 3 cm (1.2 inches) broad and 2.5 cm (1 inch) thick, and weighs 10–15 gm (up to 0.5 oz).

The kidney has a very rich blood supply, with blood entering at the hilus via the renal artery, passing through a complex network of arteries, capillaries and veins, finally returning to the hilus and leaving via the renal vein (Fig. 93). Intimately connected with the blood vessels is a complicated arrangement of tubules and ducts which carry fluid filtered from the blood vascular system. This fluid eventually becomes urine and leaves the kidney via the ureter, a thin muscular pipe which runs back through the abdomen to the urinary bladder, a highly distensible, bulb-shaped organ situated at the posterior end of the abdomen, and in which urine is stored prior to being voided. Urination is the process whereby urine is expelled from the bladder following relaxation of the bladder sphincter (outflow 'valve') and contraction of the bladder wall muscles, forcing urine into the urethra. In the female this opens into the floor of the vagina, and in the male it becomes the passage through the penis.

Filtration of the blood takes place in microscopic tufts of blood vessels surrounded by the bulbous beginning of the urinary tubule system. Each tuft is called a glomerulus and this, together with its associated tubules and blood vessels, is called a nephron. The glomeruli are positioned in the outer part (cortex) of the kidney, while the majority of the tubules and closely associated blood vessels are deeper, in the medulla. The tubules unite to

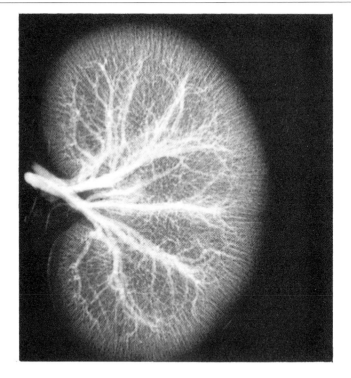

Figure 93   Cat kidney infused with contrast medium via the renal artery to show the large and complex vasculature

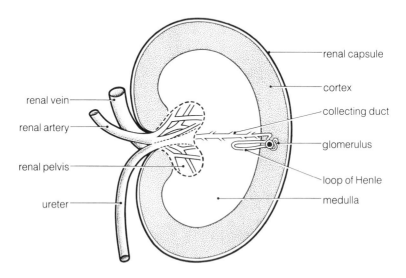

Figure 94   Diagrammatic longitudinal section of kidney to show complex structure

form collecting ducts which empty into the renal pelvis and thence into the ureter (Fig. 94). The glomeruli act as blood filtration units and permit the passage of water and small molecules into the duct system, and, under normal circumstances, prevent passage of blood cells, proteins and other larger molecules.

The kidneys perform several life-maintaining functions, and some others which are not so vital but still very important. Urine is the final outcome of the kidney's role in maintaining the body water at the correct volume, concentration and acidity (pH). In addition to ions, such as sodium and chloride, the urine contains large amounts of the soluble products of nitrogen metabolism, such as urea and creatinine. The kidneys play an important part in the control of blood pressure as their finely tuned vasculature close to the glomeruli quickly recognize and respond to any variations, especially lowering of pressure. This is in part due to the fact that filtration of the blood in the glomeruli can take place only if the blood pressure is sufficiently high, but not too high, otherwise destructive damage can occur. The kidneys have a more minor function in converting vitamin D3 to its final, useful form, thus providing a key factor in calcium metabolism. One further function is the production of a substance called erythropoietin releasing factor, which promotes the production of red blood cells in the bone marrow.

The ureters, bladder and urethra have no function apart from the passage, storage and expulsion of urine, although, in the male, the urethra is also used for the passage of seminal fluids formed in the testes, prostate and bulbo-urethral glands (see Fig. 34, page 127)

Mechanisms of kidney failure

To say that a cat is suffering from kidney disease conveys very little, and may in fact be misleading. Examination of the kidneys of cats after death has shown that a large number have suffered some form of kidney damage at some time during life, but it has been of a minor nature, probably never causing the animal to be ill. One reason for this is that the kidneys have a very large reserve capacity, so damage has to be severe and widespread before the cat shows clinical signs. Kidney disease is therefore not the same as kidney failure. Moreover, some of the tests for kidney function, e.g. measurement of the level of urea in the blood, will indicate changes that are the result of disease elsewhere in the body, leading to a secondary effect on the kidneys. Thus, extreme dehydration may cause a rise in blood urea levels because glomerular filtration is reduced as a result of dehydration. If the latter is corrected by means of replacement fluid therapy, then renal function continues as normal. This form of raised blood urea (termed *uraemia*) is called *pre-renal*. In other circumstances, uraemia may develop because the urea is unable to leave the body, e.g. in the case of a cat suffering from a urethral outflow obstruction (see feline lower urinary tract disease, page 277). Initially, urine is still formed by the kidneys, but the back pressure of urine in a maximally distended bladder quickly leads to renal failure. This is called *post-renal* uraemia. In both pre- and post-renal uraemia, the situation can be life threatening and requires immediate treatment, but is not primarily the fault of the kidneys. *Primary renal failure* occurs whenever there is a decrease in the rate of glomerular filtration due to disease, from whatever cause, actually within the kidneys. In some cases, as with the examples of dehydration and outflow obstruction given above, the kidney failure is potentially reversible provided rapid and appropriate treatment is given and the animal is still capable of responding. In other cases, the uraemia is irreversible and the cat will die. The same applies to cases of primary kidney disease, where recovery depends on the severity of the condition, the nature of the damage done to kidney tissues and the speed at which appropriate treatment is applied.

Acute and chronic renal failure

If primary kidney disease is sudden and severe, the cat is said to be suffering from *acute renal failure*, which in some may be fatal, despite treatment. In other cases there is complete recovery, while in others there is ongoing insidious damage and eventual loss of sufficient nephrons for the development of *chronic renal failure*. Clinical signs of chronic renal failure are not usually apparent until three-quarters of the total number of nephrons have been destroyed, so the process may continue over many months or years, and by the time signs do appear, the condition is well advanced. The loss of further nephrons will lead to increasingly severe illness but in some cats this process occurs extremely slowly and during this time appropriate treatment often allows the animal to lead a reasonably normal life. Clinical signs of acute renal failure are outlined on page 272, in relation to renal toxicity due to ingestion of ethylene glycol (antifreeze), and are further described and compared with the signs of chronic renal failure in Table 4.

Blood and urine samples taken from cats in acute and chronic renal failure will help to confirm the diagnosis, and the important laboratory results to be expected are shown in Table 5. Other helpful diagnostic procedures, such as radiography and ultrasonography, can be used to give an indication of kidney size, shape and position, and radiography can also help in demonstrating the demineralization of bone ('rubber jaw') that may occur in chronic renal failure due to the failure of the kidneys to excrete phosphate, although this latter manifestation is rare in cats.

It is clearly important to distinguish between acute and chronic renal failure both in terms of the choice of appropriate treatment and in prognosis (outlook). The broad outlines of treatment are given in Table 6.

Table 4 Clinical signs usually present in cats with renal failure

Acute renal failure	*Chronic renal failure*
sudden onset illness	usually gradual onset
dullness	increased thirst/polyuria
weakness	altered drinking habits
no appetite	reduced appetite
oliguria/anuria	weight loss
repeated vomiting	occasional vomiting
dehydration	increasing dullness
congested mucous membranes	pale mucous membranes
swollen painful kidneys	small firm kidneys

Uraemic signs
present in late stages of both acute and chronic renal failure

uraemic halitosis
gum and cheek ulcers
blood in vomit and faeces
muscle twitches
uraemic convulsions
coma and death

Table 5 Laboratory results commonly reported from cats with renal failure

Parameter	*ARF*	*CRF*
Blood samples		
packed cell volume	high (dehydration)	low (anaemia)
total white blood count	raised (infection)	usually normal
Plasma		
urea	high	normal* to high
creatinine	high	normal* to high
phosphate	high	normal† to high
sodium	high (dehydration)	normal to high
chloride	high (dehydration)	normal to high
calcium	normal to high	normal to high
potassium	high	normal† to high
Urine samples		
volume	less/none	increased
colour	dark	pale
protein content	variable	low to moderate
specific gravity	high	low

* Urea and creatinine levels only rise when more than 70 per cent of the nephrons cease functioning.
† Phosphate and potassium usually rise at a late stage in the process.

Table 6 Treatment and management of renal failure in cats

Acute renal failure	Chronic renal failure
rehydration (intravenous)	drinking water always available
encourage urine flow with fluids, diuretics	reduce dietary protein
control vomiting with anti-emetics, stop ingestion	vitamin replacement
peritoneal dialysis (rare)	anabolic steroids
specific treatment, e.g. antibiotics, antitoxic	periodic injections of antibiotic/steroids/vitamins

Nephrotic syndrome

We have already said that the glomerular filter acts as a barrier to large molecules in the blood, especially protein. If the glomerulus is damaged, either on its own (*primary glomerulonephropathy*) or in conjunction with generalized acute or chronic kidney failure, then substantial amounts of protein may be lost into the urine. In many cases the protein leak may not cause any trouble; in some, it will contribute to loss in body weight, but in others, if proteinuria is severe and prolonged, the blood protein becomes so depleted that the circulation loses the osmotic support that protein provides and fluid flows out of the blood vessels into the extracellular compartment of the body (i.e. the spaces between cells and the cavities of the abdomen and chest) to accumulate as oedema. When this happens, the cat is said to be suffering from the nephrotic syndrome. Prior to the development of the nephrotic syndrome the cat may have noticeably lost weight and been thirstier, but need not have been dull or inappetent. In cats, the oedema fluid nearly always gravitates first to the lower parts of the hindlimbs (Fig. 95) and then affects the skin of the lower body wall. In more severe cases there is a swollen abdomen (due to accumulation of ascitic fluid) (Fig. 96) and possibly breathing difficulties (due to hydrothorax), together with swelling of the head, neck and forelimbs (Fig. 95). At this point the cat looks bloated and may appear to have gained weight rather than lost it. Many nephrotic cats behave quite normally within the limitations of the fluid accumulations, but, if suffering from coexisting renal failure, they will show the associated signs.

Laboratory examination of blood and urine samples is particularly helpful and typical results are given in Table 7.

So far we have described kidney disease in general terms. This is possible because the kidney can only react in a few fixed pathways to a number of different insults, whether they are *congenital* (a disease present at birth or resulting from an inborn error), *metabolic, viral, bacterial, chemical,*

Table 7 Laboratory findings in cats with protein-losing nephropathy and nephrotic syndrome

Parameter	No renal failure	With renal failure
Plasma		
urea	normal	raised
creatinine	normal	raised
phosphate	normal	normal to raised
cholesterol	raised	raised
total protein	normal to low	normal to low
albumin	low to very low	low
globulin	normal to high	normal to high
Urine samples		
volume	increased	increased
protein content	very high	high
specific gravity	normal to high	low

Figure 95 Nephrotic syndrome. Oedema causing a thickened appearance of the forelimbs and hindlegs of a 4-year-old male neutered domestic shorthaired cat

Figure 96   Nephrotic syndrome. Severe abdominal distension and oedema of both thighs due to ascites (fluid transudate) in a 2-year-old female spayed domestic shorthaired cat. *Right:* The same cat after drainage of one litre of ascitic fluid. This cat did not respond to medical treatment with diuretic drugs and had to be drained every few weeks. She survived for nearly two years

immune-mediated, traumatic or *neoplastic* in origin. While this makes diagnosis of kidney disease in general relatively easy, it seldom permits a specific diagnosis, and in most cases the latter is difficult unless kidney tissue is examined by either a biopsy in the living animal or at post mortem. Even then, it is sometimes impossible to be precise, because the severity of the changes, e.g. in chronic renal failure, makes them indistinguishable.

Other clinical signs of urinary tract disease include straining and pain in attempts to pass urine (stranguria), irrespective of the amount of urine passed, and blood in urine (haematuria). Both of these signs will be dealt with in more detail with diseases of the urinary bladder.

'Classical' chronic renal failure

This is the commonest manifestation of kidney disease in the cat. Typically, it affects later middle-aged and old cats, although younger cats can be affected. It is usually progressive but development can be exceedingly slow and early signs are often insidious. One of the first signs is a slight to moderate increase in thirst and this may be shown by a preferential change from milk to water. The change may not be noticed, as frequently cats will drink water outside from ponds, puddles, watering cans, etc. Observant owners may notice an increase in the frequency of urination, or, if the cat uses a litter tray, an increase in the volume of urine, represented by an increased weight of wet litter. In other respects the cat may remain well, but, as the disease progresses, mild reductions in appetite and body weight may be apparent. Stressful circumstances, e.g. boarding in a cattery, anaesthesia and surgery (often dentistry in older cats), may lead to a sudden precipitation of more major clinical signs, simply because the kidneys have no reserve capacity to overcome insults to the blood circulation. In these circumstances, dullness, total inappetence, vomiting, foul-smelling breath (uraemic halitosis), mouth ulcers and even neurological disturbances, can develop (Fig. 97).

Cats diagnosed as having mild chronic renal failure are frequently treated with periodic injections of antibiotics, cortico- and anabolic steroids and vitamins, often with beneficial results, even though the reason for the response is not understood.

Figure 97   Chronic renal failure in a 3-year-old domestic shorthaired cat. This cat developed uraemic ulcers on the lateral borders and under the tongue (arrows)

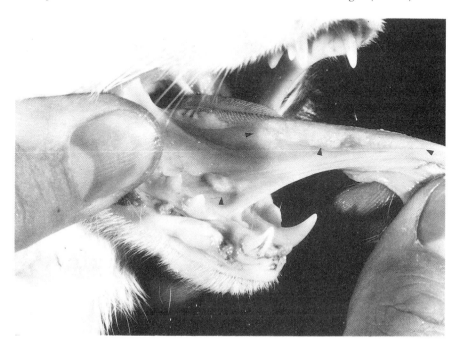

Congenital renal disease

A variety of congenital abnormalities of the kidney have been reported in cats but not all of them result in chronic renal failure and may be found incidentally. Examples include unilateral renal agenesis (i.e. one kidney totally absent; the existing kidney is quite capable of fulfilling the renal requirements on its own); ectopic kidney (i.e. one kidney in an abnormal position); and renal fusion (i.e. two kidneys joined together and having a single ureter or both ureters). These are rare conditions, and renal function usually remains normal unless another problem arises which causes renal damage. Unlike the dog, in which there are many breed-related familial kidney diseases, few have been described in cats.

POLYCYSTIC KIDNEYS

In this condition, one or both kidneys may contain multiple small and large fluid-filled cavities in both the cortex and medulla. Renal function is compromised and severely affected kittens do not live for more than a few weeks. Longhaired cats, both pure-bred and domestic, are more prone to this disease, which is characterized by stunted growth and unthriftiness, poor appetite, dullness, thirstiness and excessive urination. Careful examination will reveal the presence of enlarged, often irregular-shaped non-painful kidneys. Specific diagnosis is often difficult without the use of special X-ray techniques, or, better still, ultrasound examination of the kidneys. If only one kidney is affected, the cat may not show any clinical signs, although the affected kidney would be enlarged. Some cats develop polycystic kidneys later in life as a result of conditions leading to obstruction of urinary tubules, but again, if only one kidney is affected, the cat may remain normal. When disease does become obvious as chronic renal failure, it is then often difficult to differentiate between congenital and acquired polycystic disease, unless there is a previous history of a cat being investigated for kidney problems.

HYDRONEPHROSIS

This is similar in its effect to polycystic kidneys, except that the kidney becomes a single cystic cavity. The disease can arise congenitally, but it is more likely to develop later in life.

AMYLOIDOSIS

This is a rare familial kidney disease which has been seen in related young to middle-aged Abyssinian cats. It will be dealt with in greater detail later (see pages 273 and 412).

Kidney trauma

Injuries to the kidneys may follow road traffic accidents and other crushing incidents. The renal capsule may be ruptured and the kidney lacerated, or, if the capsule remains intact, there may be intra-renal haemorrhage, severely increased renal pressure and necrosis. In either case the situation is serious, especially if both kidneys are affected. Badly lacerated kidneys may contribute to severe internal haemorrhage and possibly death, in addition to whatever effects there may be from reduced renal function. When only one kidney is affected, the other should function more than adequately, provided it is normal. It may be necessary to remove the damaged kidney.

Clinical features

These will vary according to the nature and extent of the damage and which other organs are involved. There may be a history of an accident,

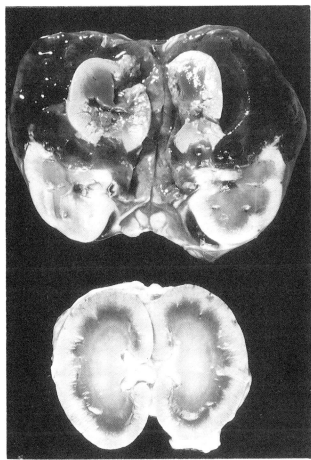

Figure 98 Left *(top)* and right kidneys from a 1-year-old cat which had a road traffic accident. The left kidney was severely traumatized. The right kidney was relatively normal. The cat died as a result of the massive haemorrhage surrounding the left kidney

and the cat is likely to be in a state of shock, collapsed and with very pale mucous membranes. Palpation of the abdomen may reveal either an enlarged, bulbous, painful kidney (or both), or an irregularly shaped mass in the kidney region. There may be mild distension of the abdomen if a large volume of free blood is present. This will gradually be reabsorbed into the circulation if the animal survives.

Diagnosis

This is based on the history, clinical signs and evidence of free blood in the abdomen (confirmed by needle aspiration of the contents), or of misshapen kidney shadows on an abdominal X-ray. Final diagnosis may require an exploratory laparotomy operation.

Treatment

Initially treatment will be directed at counteracting shock and giving intensive care. Fluid or blood transfusions may be required and antibiotic and corticosteroid drugs administered. Surgery will be performed as soon as the animal can stand anaesthesia. Sometimes lacerated kidneys can be repaired, and subcapsular or intra-renal haemorrhages drained to reduce intra-renal pressure. In cases of severe unilateral damage, inspection of the other kidney for normality and prior renal function tests will help to determine the feasibility of removing the damaged kidney. If both kidneys are hopelessly damaged, euthanasia will be necessary. Whenever a post-traumatic laparotomy is performed, the integrity of the bladder will always be checked as this organ is more vulnerable than the kidneys.

Prognosis

Traumatic renal damage is unlikely to heal without considerable scarring. However, many cats recover well. Those cats requiring unilateral nephrectomy also do well provided the remaining kidney is in good condition. The outlook is poorer when both kidneys are severely lacerated or contused, or if infection is involved, e.g. following deep wounds caused by fighting.

Kidney infections

Two broad types of infection can affect the cat kidney.

BACTERIAL INFECTIONS

Generalized or more localized bacterial infection can develop in one or both kidneys. In most cases the infection is caused by organisms in the lower part of the urinary tract, the bladder especially, migrating up the ureter(s) into the kidney(s) and becoming established in the renal pelvis and medulla. The commonest bacteria isolated from these infections are *Escherichia coli, Proteus* sp., *Pseudomonas* sp., and *Staphylococcus aureus*, all of which are capable of stimulating abscess production with resulting obstruction of renal blood and urine flow and destruction of kidney tissues. The condition is called pyelonephritis. However, bacterial infection of the lower urinary tract in cats is relatively uncommon by comparison with dogs. This is thought to be partly due to the fact that cat urine is normally highly concentrated, providing a very poor medium for bacterial survival and growth. This means that feline pyelonephritis is also relatively uncommon (see feline lower urinary tract disease, page 277).

While the ascending route is the most common cause, it is also possible for infection to be introduced to the kidneys from the bloodstream (haematogenous route) or directly, e.g. from deep penetrative bite wounds. Whatever the route the result may be the development of acute renal failure in the relatively few cases where infection is sufficiently severe and widespread. Cats so affected will become rapidly dull, fevered and have swollen, painful kidneys, as well as the other signs of acute renal failure (Table 4). There may have been previous evidence of lower urinary tract infection, recent generalized illness or recent kidney injury.

More commonly, the cat may have a milder, vague illness, if any at all, and eventually either recovers or progresses to chronic renal failure, with typical signs (Table 4). A relatively high proportion of cats in chronic renal failure have kidneys which show evidence of earlier bacterial infection, but this may never have been evident as an illness until the final decline into an irreversible state.

If diagnosed early, treatment with broad spectrum antibiotics for at least 10 consecutive days will often be successful. If there is acute renal failure, the cat will require more intensive treatment with intravenous fluids. Many cats will be treated with antibiotics for, and recover from, vague febrile illnesses in which the kidneys are involved, even though a specific diagnosis is never made.

VIRAL INFECTIONS

The second group of kidney infections are mainly of viral origin and the kidney involvement is only part of a much more widespread illness. The two major viral infections which can affect the kidneys are *feline leukaemia virus* (FeLV), which can sometimes cause either a protein losing glomerulonephropathy associated with viral antigen/host antibody complexes, or, more commonly, chronic renal failure due to lymphosarcoma of the kidneys; and *feline coronavirus*, responsible for *feline infectious peritonitis* (FIP), and leading to glomerulonephritis and chronic renal failure resulting from blood vessel disease in the kidneys (see Chapter 22, Infections).

Clinical signs depend upon the multisystem nature of the infections, and in some cats the kidney involvement will be relatively insignificant and only diagnosed on laboratory investigation. Renal lymphosarcoma often affects cats whose primary site of disease is the intestine, so a proportion of these cats will suffer from intractable diarrhoea. In coronavirus infections, either the 'wet' (effusive) form or the dry form may lead to kidney disease, but, especially in the former, other signs of feline infectious peritonitis will be more obvious (see Chapter 22, Infections). In other cats, the renal involvement is the major manifestation of the illness, especially in some cats with renal lymphosarcoma in which there is bilateral, irregular kidney enlargement, sometimes reaching 4–5 times normal size. This enlargement is due mainly to infiltration with malignant lymphocyte cells and their precursors (see Fig. 99). Some cats with quite enormous kidneys can remain surprisingly well despite the impairment to renal function and physical disability of such enlarged organs. Diagnosis can be confirmed by taking a fine needle aspirate from the kidney and looking at a stained smear under the microscope for the large numbers of lymphoid cells present. In the case of coronavirus infection, serum antibody titres are usually significantly high in affected cats.

Many cats with renal lymphosarcoma test negative for FeLV and treatment for renal lymphosarcoma is possible using anti-cancer drugs and

Figure 99 Lymphosarcoma in the kidneys of a 5-year-old Persian cat with more than half the kidney infiltrated by neoplastic cells. Between the arrows the kidney was relatively normal and would have permitted some normal function

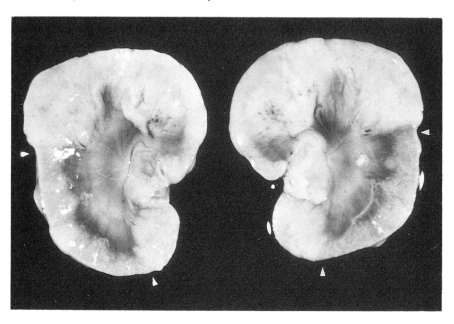

sometimes is highly successful, with periods of remission from a few months to several years. However, it is probably unwise to treat cats which are FeLV positive, because of the risk of infection spreading to other cats. Treatment of FeLV-related glomerular disease and feline coronavirus infection is usually unsuccessful.

Renal tumours

It is appropriate here briefly to mention kidney tumours, which, apart from those associated with renal lymphosarcoma, are very rare in cats. Primary kidney tumours, such as renal carcinoma, an aggressive localized malignant kidney tumour, usually affecting only one kidney, may occasionally occur, and affected cats usually show signs of vague abdominal pain and pass bloodstained urine. Much of the kidney substance is unaffected, so function remains reasonably normal. Diagnosis is difficult and there is no treatment. In some cases there is spread to other organs (metastasis), e.g. the lungs, and it may be the secondary tumour deposits which lead to clinical signs of disease.

Chemical and drug toxicity (nephrosis) and renal ischaemia

Kidney toxins can be classified in three broad groups:

1. Natural body constituents or products of metabolism which become toxic if normal levels are exceeded.
2. Drugs (including some antibiotics) which may be prescribed, or be given inadvertently or deliberately, e.g. paracetamol, or to which the cat may gain access.
3. Chemical or organic poisons which may be inadvertently ingested, e.g. ethylene glycol (antifreeze). Cats are by nature inquisitive creatures but are very selective in what they will ingest. Antifreeze appears to be naturally attractive to some cats.

Nephrotoxins in sufficient amounts cause acute renal failure, which is usually severe and often fatal. In addition, acute renal failure of a similar kind can result from the effects of reduced renal blood flow (renal ischaemia) in such conditions as kidney injury, prolonged anaesthesia, severe shock, extensive burns and extremes of temperature (hypothermia and heatstroke).

In most of these conditions the kidney tubules are the prime target and lining epithelial cells are destroyed in large numbers. Epithelial cell debris blocks the tubule lumen, preventing urine flow, resulting in reduction in or absence of urine in the bladder (*oliguria* or *anuria*) and back pressure on the glomeruli reduces glomerular filtration. If the cat survives and urine begins to flow again, it is very dilute and remains so until the tubular epithelium has been re-established. However, this pre-regenerative polyuria is a good sign that recovery is taking place.

Clinical features

Toxic nephrosis leads to classical acute renal failure and the cat becomes suddenly and severely ill, with swollen, painful kidneys. There is dullness, inappetence and repeated vomiting. If the condition lasts for more than 48 hours, uraemic changes may occur in the mouth, including foul-smelling breath and epithelial ulceration, and convulsions due to uraemic encephalopathy can occur. Urine output is reduced or ceases completely until the recovery phase.

Diagnosis

Unless there are predisposing underlying circumstances, e.g. a course of drug therapy, anaesthesia and surgery, severe shock, etc., or the cat has been seen to ingest toxic material, specific agents responsible may never be identified. Blood biochemistry will support the clinical findings of severe renal failure but tests for specific poisons, e.g. ethylene glycol, are not readily available, and even if they were, results are unlikely to be available until the cat is either dead or better. Ethylene glycol, one of the main constituents of anti-freeze used in car radiators, can be recognized as refractile crystals on microscopic examination of kidney specimens; however, the diagnosis is again usually retrospective. If the cat dies or is euthanased during the course of the illness, then microscopic examination of the kidneys will reveal the disruption of the tubules and necrosis of epithelial cells.

Treatment

Toxic nephrosis requires urgent and rigorous treatment. Intravenous fluid therapy for rehydration and encouragement of urine flow is vital but must only be continued if urine flow is established. *Diuresis* can be encouraged by using diuretic drugs or infusions with osmotic substances like mannitol. In some cases the use of *peritoneal dialysis* may be considered, whereby a large volume of concentrated electrolyte solution is infused into the peritoneal cavity and then removed one hour later. The idea is to attract water and solutes, including urea, through the peritoneum into the dialysed fluid, and these are then removed with the fluid, resulting in a reduction in blood urea levels. If the procedure is successful, it needs to be repeated several times if it is to be of lasting benefit. Peritoneal dialysis requires intensive handling and may have detrimental effects on an already very ill animal; it is also very time consuming and expensive, so a careful prior assessment of its potential value in each individual case must be made.

Any drugs already in use must be stopped immediately and the cat intensively nursed. Specific treatments may be given if the underlying cause is definitely known. Repeated blood testing to measure kidney function will give a good indication as to the success or otherwise of the treatment.

Prognosis

Toxic nephrosis is serious but if the cat recovers from the acute illness, complete restitution of renal function is possible. In other cases, there is residual damage which, if severe enough, may lead to chronic renal failure.

Glomerular disease

For many years it was thought that the only disease regularly affecting the renal glomeruli was *amyloidosis*, in which non-inflammatory proteinaceous material becomes deposited in the glomeruli. This may be confined to the kidney, where it is associated with the breakdown of certain immunoglobulin proteins, or more widely distributed in a number of vital organs as a reaction to certain chronic infectious, inflammatory or neoplastic diseases.

However, during the last 25 years it has been recognized that cats can also develop *glomerulonephritis*, resulting from damage initiated by the formation or deposition of immune (antigen-antibody) complexes in the capillary walls of the glomeruli (*membranous nephropathy*) or in the mesangium – the structure holding the tuft of capillaries together (*proliferative glomerulonephritis*). Although the underlying cause has been discovered in some cases, e.g. cats with feline leukaemia virus infection and feline coronavirus infection (Chapter 22, Infections and page 268) sometimes develop clinical signs of membranous nephropathy, in the majority of cases the disease is of uncertain cause, for which the term *idiopathic* is used.

In both amyloidosis and glomerulonephritis, the damage to the glomerulus results in a leak of protein into the urine, which in many cases leads to the development of the *nephrotic syndrome* (page 262). At the same time, damaged glomeruli are being closed down, with the consequent death of nephrons, and resultant scarring and fibrosis. This progressive loss of nephrons and renal fibrosis leads inexorably to chronic renal failure. Thus cats with glomerular disease develop a *protein-losing nephropathy*, may become nephrotic, and often eventually succumb to renal failure.

Clinical features

The signs of a protein-losing nephropathy do not appear until large amounts of protein have been lost in the urine for a considerable time.

When urine protein loss plus normal daily requirements exceeds daily dietary protein intake (a *negative nitrogen balance*) the cat begins to draw on its own protein, largely from muscle, and so begins to lose weight. Protein in the urine tends to attract water, which means the animal will urinate larger volumes more frequently (*polyuria*) and consequently will become thirsty (*polydipsia*). Unless chronic renal failure occurs early on, the only signs of a protein-losing nephropathy are therefore weight loss, polydipsia and polyuria. When blood protein falls below a critical level, variable from one animal to another, the nephrotic syndrome develops and the cat becomes oedematous.

Oedema can spontaneously regress and later recur but more often requires to be dispersed with diuretic drugs (often called 'water tablets'). The intestine wall can also become oedematous and this may prevent absorption of digested food and water, leading to diarrhoea. In some cases of protein-losing nephropathy, large thrombi (aggregates of blood clotting factors) form in blood vessels, especially the pulmonary arteries which carry blood from the heart to the lungs. If a pulmonary artery is occluded, then the cat develops severe respiratory distress and may die within a few hours. There is no treatment for this particular problem. Most cats with a protein-losing nephropathy will, if not presented with it initially, develop chronic renal failure (Table 4), which is progressive.

Diagnosis

The hallmarks of a protein-losing nephropathy are: (a) *massive persistent proteinuria*; (b) *reduced plasma albumin*; and the nephrotic syndrome (a) and (b) plus (c) *oedema*, with or without evidence of chronic renal failure.

A definite diagnosis of the underlying disease can only be made by means of a renal biopsy, which involves either removing a small piece of kidney cortex using a special needle or cutting out a tiny wedge of kidney. The former can usually be done through a very small incision in the body wall whereas the latter requires a full surgical opening of the abdomen (laparotomy). Amyloid material can be readily recognized on stained sections by routine microscopy, while the immune-mediated diseases usually require examination using special stains, plus immunofluorescence and electron microscopy.

Treatment

There is no specific treatment for amyloidosis, but, dietary management may temporarily help to alleviate chronic renal failure, and diuretic drugs should be used if the animal becomes nephrotic. Corticosteroid drugs are unhelpful in this condition, while, for the immune-mediated diseases, it is thought that immunosuppressive drugs like prednisolone (a corticosteroid) may help to reduce the number of immune complexes. Such drugs have been used in the treatment of similar diseases in man but with only limited success, and there is no real evidence that they are beneficial for glomerulonephritis in the cat.

Cats losing protein but not in renal failure should be given reasonable, but not excessive, amounts of dietary protein. Egg is an ideal source of additional high-quality protein, if the cat can be persuaded to eat it.

Oedema is usually responsive to diuretic drugs, frusemide being the most useful, and treatment should be stopped once the fluid has been cleared. Cats on diuretic drugs are naturally thirstier, but excessive water intake should be discouraged in order to allow the drug to act as fully as possible on the oedema fluid.

When a cat has a combined protein-losing nephropathy and chronic renal failure, treatment is more difficult because maintenance of normal dietary protein intake will tend to exacerbate chronic renal failure. However, in most cases it has been observed that as renal failure progresses, proteinuria diminishes. This is presumably because the surface area for protein loss is steadily reduced as more glomeruli are lost. In these cats, therefore, renal failure is more of a threat than recurrence of the nephrotic syndrome, and so a reduced protein diet is usually prescribed.

Prognosis

Most cats with glomerulonephropathies live for only a few months following diagnosis. Those in renal failure have a poorer outlook than those with an uncomplicated protein-losing nephropathy or nephrotic syndrome, and some cats with membranous nephropathy have survived for several years. However, frequently recurring nephrotic episodes and intractable diarrhoea are bad signs and often necessitate earlier euthanasia.

Ureters

Although the ureters are vital to the flow of urine from the kidneys to the bladder, they seldom let the system down. Very rarely a kidney stone (renolith) becomes lodged in a ureter, and if the obstruction is not relieved quickly, hydronephrosis (see page 266) will develop in the associated kidney.

Rupture of the ureter with consequent leakage of urine into the peritoneal cavity would cause an acute, life-threatening illness, and this can occur if a ureterolith ulcerates the wall. Damage to ureters can also occur during abdominal surgery. External trauma leading to rupture of a ureter is also possible but very rare and would usually accompany other major skeletal and organ injuries. Treatment of these conditions would depend on circumstances but would probably require removal of the damaged ureter and associated kidney.

Urinary incontinence

Urinary incontinence is a distressing condition in which urine is unconsciously voided, either continuously or intermittently, depending on the underlying cause.

ECTOPIC URETERS

This is a relatively rare congenital condition affecting both male and female kittens, in which one or both ureters bypasses the bladder and empties into the urethra or, in females, the vagina and less commonly the uterus. The result is urinary incontinence and any young cat which suffers from genuine urinary incontinence, i.e. unconscious lack of control over urination, should be investigated for the condition.

The kitten is usually normal in every respect except that it dribbles urine frequently, but may also be capable of urinating normally. Urine may be passively passed on rising or as the cat changes position while washing. The rear end smells strongly of urine, is wet and the skin may become scalded.

This can be difficult and requires careful radiographic assessment following infusion of contrast medium into the female vagina, male urethra or intravenously.

Surgical repositioning of the ureters into the bladder is essential if both are ectopic but success is not guaranteed. If only one side is affected, it is often dealt with by removing the affected ureter and its associated kidney. The same procedure is required if reimplantation of a ureter into the bladder is unsuccessful.

PERSISTENT URACHUS

Another congenital condition seen occasionally in young kittens also involves urinary incontinence. The urachus is the tube which carries foetal urine from the bladder to the allantois (one of the foetal sacs making up the placenta) via the umbilicus. It should close automatically at birth and the tube withers, but in some kittens it remains patent, allowing urine to flow out at the umbilicus. Affected kittens will have a wet, urine smelling ventral abdomen and are often poor doers due to ascending infections. Surgical correction is possible but euthanasia is often preferred.

Urinary incontinence from other causes, such as neurological diseases affecting nerves supplying the bladder, or as sequelae to hind end trauma and spaying of female cats, is rare.

Diseases of the urinary bladder

The bladder is a highly resilient organ, capable of considerable expansion and contraction as it fills slowly with urine and then empties relatively quickly. However, it is also a very vulnerable organ, open to trauma (see bladder rupture, page 267), inflammation (cystitis) and the development of uroliths. The latter two are particularly important in the cat and are dealt with together in the section on feline lower urinary tract disease (below). Apart from this, bladder problems in cats are quite rare.

Tumours of the bladder do occur and have been reported in young middle-aged to old cats, with a history of blood appearing in the urine at the time of urination (haematuria). Sometimes bleeding into the bladder will cause the formation of blood clots, which lead to difficulty, straining, pain and increased frequency of attempts to urinate. Diagnosis of bladder tumours requires special X-ray techniques and possibly surgery to examine the bladder and take a biopsy. Surgical treatment is theoretically possible but often the tumour is too advanced or in an inoperable position. Then euthanasia is the only realistic option.

Feline lower urinary tract disease (FLUTD)

This condition is also known as feline urological syndrome, urolithiasis and 'blocked cat'. All these terms are used to cover a wide spectrum of lower urinary tract disease in cats, from mild cystitis through to total urethral obstruction. There are a number of specific causes of the condition, including bacterial infection (bacterial cystitis), trauma to the bladder, urolithiasis (hard crystalline stones which may form in the kidneys or bladder, but which are fairly uncommon in the cat), and tumours of the bladder. Any of these may lead to clinical signs of increased frequency of desire to urinate, pain on urination, straining and haematuria. If a specific diagnosis is made, appropriate medical or surgical treatment can be given.

However, in the majority of cases, the cause of the problem is none of those mentioned and the term idiopathic is used. There is an association in many cats, especially neutered males, between recurring cystitis and the formation of struvite (a mixture of a mineral compound, magnesium ammonium phosphate and an organic matrix), which can aggregate in the narrow urethra and plug it. Struvite rubbed between finger and thumb may feel like fine sand, but in the urethra it often forms plugs which are more like toothpaste in consistency, causing a serious blockage, which, in the small bore of the male cat's urethra, can be very difficult to remove.

CYSTITIS

Whatever the underlying cause, this is the simplest manifestation of FLUTD. Affected cats often remain well and continue to eat but make frequent, often pained, attempts to pass urine. Cats used to urinating outdoors will keep asking to go out; those trained to a litter tray will make frequent visits, and often only pass minute amounts of urine, which is usually bloody. Irrespective of normal habits, many affected cats will start to urinate in abnormal, unacceptable sites around the house, very often attempting to 'dig a hole' in a carpet prior to an attempt to urinate. Pain and discomfort is shown by apprehensive facial expression, excessive licking of the hindquarters, and crying. Bloodstains may be found at sites of attempted urination and there may be traces of blood on the fur adjacent to the prepuce or vulva.

Treatment

Usually by means of broad spectrum antibiotics, which should be given for at least 7 consecutive days, and probably longer, irrespective of the fact that in many cases there is a dramatic and early improvement. This is because if the cystitis has a bacterial cause, it is important to remove the organisms effectively and permanently. Short courses of antibotics will be inadequate and the infection is likely to recur.

Diagnosis

This rests on examination of urine samples, carefully taken via a urinary catheter passed into the bladder, for the presence of disease producing bacteria in significant numbers and microscopic examination for struvite crystals and red blood cells. A strip test for urine pH (cat urine should be acid) may reveal alkaline urine, which favours bacterial growth and struvite formation, so in these cases the urine must be acidified. This can be achieved by feeding a diet which is low in protein, magnesium and phosphorous but high in salt, with or without the addition of urinary acidifiers, many of which are not very palatable. Affected cats should be encouraged to drink as much water as possible, in order to keep the urine dilute, thereby minimizing the formation of struvite crystals. If a cat is reluctant to drink, additional water can be mixed with its food.

Other factors

It has been shown that many cats which develop recurrent lower urinary tract diseases are overweight, neutered males, having a particularly sedentary lifestyle and urinating relatively infrequently. In these cats, it is helpful if the owner can be persuaded to encourage the cat to be more active, drink more, urinate more, and eat a weight reducing diet. Cats which have several episodes of mild FLUTD are more likely to progress to serious disease, including urethral obstruction, so early remedial and preventive advice and treatment should be heeded.

OBSTRUCTIVE URINARY TRACT DISEASE

This is serious and can be life threatening. Affected cats show signs similar to those of cystitis, but, if blocked, strain to pass minute quantities of urine or none at all. If urine cannot be passed, the bladder fills up to an enormous size, increasing the abdominal discomfort already present. Pressure in the bladder prevents urine flowing down the ureters and back pressure in the kidneys causes renal swelling, pain and, quite quickly, the development of acute kidney failure.

Blocked cats require immediate and intensive treatment, involving reduction of bladder size by means of aspiration of urine into a large syringe via a fine needle inserted into the bladder through the body wall; intravenous fluid therapy to reduce the effects of kidney failure; and attempts to remove the urethral plugs (or, in rare cases, true stony uroliths). This is normally done by trying to pass a urine catheter into the narrow urethra and simultaneous flushing with saline. Anti-inflammatory drugs may help to reduce local swelling in the urethra and aid the catheterization process. Sometimes the plugs can only be removed from the bladder side after abdominal and bladder surgery (cystotomy).

Some cats become persistent blockers and require repeated extensive and expensive treatment. In some cases, the only lasting treatment is surgical removal of the penis and re-establishment of the urethral orifice in the perineal region.

Dietary control

For cats which suffer from struvite urological disease, specially formulated diets are often helpful, provided the cat will eat them and receives no other kind of food. Diets have been shown to be capable of removing struvite present and preventing more from forming (see Chapter 7, Nutrition).

17

REPRODUCTION AND BREEDING PROBLEMS

Introduction

There can be few people who have not heard the calls of a queen in heat and the clamour of rival toms. Reproduction in cats, as in any other animal, is essential for the maintenance of the species, and cats have developed a number of unusual features which help to maximize their reproductive potential. Most planned breeding takes place between pedigree cats, and a knowledge of the normal reproductive behaviour and physiology can be invaluable.

Fortunately, reproductive problems are generally less common in cats than in other domestic species, such as dogs. Nevertheless problems may arise, and it is important to know when to seek veterinary care and attention. Prevention of breeding is also important, particularly for many pet cat owners, and the ways this can be achieved are outlined at the end of this chapter.

The reproductive system

MALE

The male reproductive system comprises the scrotum, paired testes, epididymis and vas deferens, the urethra and associated glands (prostate, bulbo-urethral gland), and the penis contained within the prepuce (Fig. 100). (See also Chapter 8, Anatomy and Physiology.) Within each testis, germinal cells undergo constant division to produce spermatozoa (spermatogenesis), while other cells produce the male sex hormone testosterone. The epididymis, vas deferens and urethra allow for storage, maturation and transport of the spermatozoa, whilst the associated prostate and bulbo-urethral glands add important fluids which are present in semen. Successful spermatogenesis (production of sperm) requires

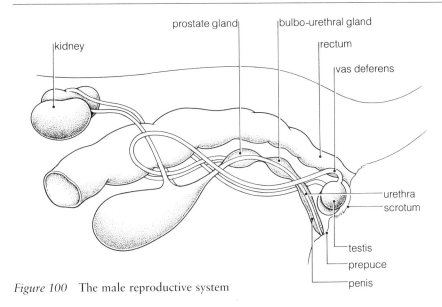

Figure 100   The male reproductive system

a temperature slightly lower than normal core body temperature, thus the testes migrate from their original abdominal position close to the kidneys and enter the scrotum just below the anus around the time of birth.

The penis allows delivery of sperm into the female's vagina during coitus. Uniquely among the domestic species, the end of the cat's penis is covered with between 100 and 200 small barbs or papillae. These point backwards, and the rasping action they produce in the female's vagina may assist in the process of ovulation (see page 285).

FEMALE

The female reproductive system comprises the paired ovaries and oviducts (fallopian tubes), the uterus, cervix, vagina, and the external opening of the vagina – the vulva (Fig. 101). The ovaries remain in the position in which they originally develop, which is close to the kidneys in the abdominal cavity. At birth the ovaries contain many thousands of oocytes, along with associated cells. Throughout life, under the influence of hormones, these develop into follicles which release mature eggs or ova formed from the oocytes. The ovaries also produce the important female sex hormones oestrogen and progesterone. Ovulation is the process of release of a mature ovum (egg) from an ovarian follicle. Following ovulation, the ovum passes down the oviduct (fallopian tube) into the uterus. The feline uterus is Y-shaped, having a body that divides into two horns which terminate in the oviducts. Between the vagina and the uterus lies the cervix, which can serve as a physical barrier, preventing access of micro-organisms to the uterus and escape of uterine contents.

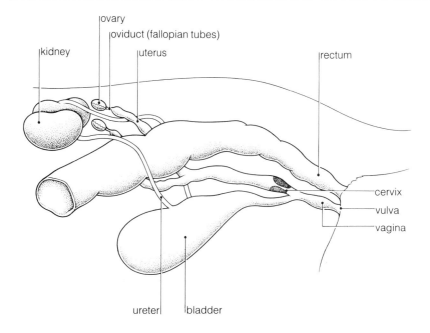

Figure 101   The female reproductive system

The reproductive cycle

MALE

Sexual maturity and production of spermatozoa usually occurs between 6 and 8 months of age. Spermatogenesis thereafter is essentially a continuous process, and males may remain fertile for more than 14 years. Spermatogenesis is under complex hormonal regulation. The pituitary gland, a small gland located at the base of the brain, secretes luteinizing hormone (LH) and follicle-stimulating hormone (FSH), both of which exert actions on and influence production of testosterone in the testes. These hormones are necessary for the stimulation and maintenance of spermatogenesis, and testosterone is also important in the development of male physical and behavioural (including sexual) characteristics.

FEMALE

Female cats usually attain sexual maturity between 4 and 12 months of age, dependent in part on the time of year they were born. However, pedigree cats show great variation, some reaching puberty as young as 3 or 4 months, whilst in others it may be as late as 18 months. Breed differences have been suggested, but there is little objective information available on this. Queens may remain fertile for 10 years or more, with many continuing to show oestrous cycles beyond this age.

Cats are described as seasonally polyoestrous, i.e. they have repeated oestrous (heat) cycles for a period of the year, and are anoestrous (sexually inactive) for the other part. Although there are individual, and probably breed differences, in general cats begin to cycle in January or February, and then will continue to have oestrous cycles until the breeding season ends, which may be between June and November. In most cats anoestrus appears to be quite short, usually lasting from October to December. The peak in sexual activity is generally seen in February and March, leading to the usual high number of spring-born kittens (in April and May). The seasonal nature of oestrous cycles is primarily dependent on the length of daylight hours (which affects production of pituitary gland hormones), and because of this cats kept indoors or in housing with artificial light may not necessarily experience the usual season pattern. For example, if queens are kept in conditions where there is a constant 12 hours of light per day, they may cycle throughout the year with no anoestrous period. Longhaired breeds also tend to show less dependence on length of daylight hours than shorthaired and Foreign breeds.

During the breeding season, a healthy non-pregnant queen will have repeated oestrous cycles comprising a period of oestrus and a period of non-oestrus or inter-oestrus. The length of the cycle is highly variable (around 1–5 weeks) but is usually about 2–3 weeks. The cycles occur due to repeated sequential maturation of follicles in the ovary, which develop under the influence of FSH secreted by the pituitary gland. As a follicle matures it secretes the hormone oestrogen, which causes the commonly seen signs of oestrous in the queen and her receptiveness to the male. The oestrous period generally lasts from 5 to 8 days and is only very rarely longer than 10 days. Many queens will display very dramatic signs of oestrous during this time. These can include vocalization, rolling, rubbing of the head and neck against objects and also the characteristic movements of the legs known as 'treading'. Queens may also adopt a position ready for mounting, e.g. crouching with pelvis raised and tail deviated to one side to display the vulva, especially if stroked around the base of the tail. In contrast to dogs, cats rarely have a vulval discharge during oestrous cycles.

Unlike most other species, cats are induced rather than spontaneous ovulators. This means that ovulation will generally only occur if the cat is successfully mated during an oestrous period. In the absence of ovulation, oestrous cycles continue uninterrupted throughout the breeding season with inter-oestrous periods typically lasting 10–14 days.

Normal breeding

HUSBANDRY PRACTICES

Throughout the spring and summer months many unplanned matings of domestic stray and feral cats can be heard in most localities, but planned breeding of cats usually involves the confined management of queens and toms, and generally takes place between pedigree cats.

The chances of successful breeding are increased if the male is not intimidated by being introduced to unfamiliar surroundings. It is usual practice therefore for queens to be taken to the tom; however, a queen in unfamiliar surroundings may also fail to show overt signs of oestrus, especially if she is timid. Consequently the queen should be kept in familiar surroundings until oestrous behaviour is clearly observed. The onset of oestrus may not be obvious in all cats, as some show relatively undramatic changes, while others are particularly friendly and display some of the characteristics of oestrous behaviour at any time. Careful observation of some queens is thus necessary to determine the correct time for mating.

When overt signs of oestrus are being displayed, the queen may be taken to the tom. If mating a queen for the first time, it is wise to use an experienced tom and vice versa. Also, if the queen shows signs of nervousness and reluctance to allow the tom to mount, she may need a day or two alone in the new environment to settle down.

The breeding of cats often involves their transport from one household or cattery to another. This process carries with it some risk of transmission of infectious diseases, and it is therefore essential that all cats involved are fully vaccinated against the 'cat flu' viruses (feline herpesvirus and calicivirus) and panleukopaenia virus (feline infectious enteritis). Vaccination against *Chlamydia psittaci* (an ocular infection) is also now possible and is likewise desirable, particularly with breeding cats. The cats should also be tested (by means of a blood sample) for feline immunodeficiency virus (FIV) and feline leukaemia virus (FeLV) infections. Cats with either of these diseases, even if apparently healthy, should not be bred from. It is also now possible to vaccinate against FeLV, and this too should be considered.

MATING

As well as being shy or nervous, some queens may refuse to allow a tom to mount in very early oestrus or pro-oestrus. As with a shy queen, keeping her away from the tom for a day or two should overcome this problem.

Although courtship or pre-mating behaviour between two unfamiliar cats may be quite prolonged, it generally lasts no longer than a few minutes, and may be very rapid with experienced cats. The queen may roll, vocalize and adopt a receptive posture (crouching with elbows and chest on the ground, pelvis raised, tail deviated and sometimes treading with the hindlegs), while the tom approaches and circles the queen. Mating involves the male grasping the back of the queen's neck (neck biting), followed by him mounting her first with his forelegs and then his hindlegs. After arching his back and treading with his hindlegs, he will begin pelvic thrusting, which is followed by penetration and ejaculation. The time from neck bite to penetration may be very short or last up to 5 minutes, but penetration and ejaculation are usually complete within a few seconds. Successful mating is signalled by the post-coital reaction or 'after-reaction': the queen lets out a piercing scream, the post-coital yell, during or immediately after withdrawal by the male, and she will try to free herself from him, turn round, and strike out at him with her claws. The prudent tom will anticipate this and retreat to a safe distance while the queen will often lie on her side vigorously rolling and rubbing. The queen will also lick her vulva obsessively, while the male may lick his penis. This after-reaction may continue for many minutes during which, and for a variable time afterwards, the queen will warn off the male if he tries to approach.

REPEAT MATINGS AND OVULATION

Following the after-reaction, the queen will gradually become more receptive to the tom again, and repeat matings will occur. Initially the intervals between matings may be short (5–30 minutes), but with each successive mating the interval becomes longer. Up to 30 matings have been reported between a queen and a tom over a 24-hour period.

The repeat matings that occur serve an important physiological purpose: during mating the barbed penis of the male stimulates the vagina of the female, inducing a reflex release of LH from the pituitary gland. A surge of LH is necessary for the final maturation of ovarian follicles and the release of ova (induced ovulation, see above). However, in many queens the LH production after a single mating is insufficient to induce ovulation, but subsequent matings occurring over a limited period of time enhance the LH production and will result in ovulation. To maximize the chances of successful ovulation and subsequent pregnancy, a queen and tom should therefore be allowed multiple matings, and are commonly kept together for 1–3 days.

PSEUDO-PREGNANCY

Following ovulation, the remaining cells of the ruptured follicles in the ovaries will form *corpora lutea*, which secrete progesterone, a hormone important in the maintenance of pregnancy. However, if the mating, for whatever reasons did not result in fertilization of the ova, *corpora lutea* still form and secrete progesterone, which leads to a false or pseudo-pregnancy. The duration of pseudo-pregnancy is highly variable, but is commonly between 40 and 50 days (i.e. usually a little shorter than true pregnancy), during which time the cat will not cycle.

Pregnancy

FERTILIZATION

During mating the tom ejaculates a small volume of semen (usually around 0.05 ml) containing some 100 to 1000 million spermatozoa. Several copulations within a few hours ensures a high peak in LH levels, which in turn induces ovulation in most queens 24–36 hours later. Usually, between three and eight ova are released from the two ovaries, but this is dependent on many factors, including the breed and age of the queen. Induced ovulation has the advantage of ensuring maximum likelihood of fertilization of some or all of the released ova. The spermatozoa migrate up through the cervix, which is open to allow their passage, and reach the ova whilst they are still in the oviducts. After fertilization the embryos continue to migrate down the oviducts and into the uterine horns.

IMPLANTATION

The embryos arrive in the uterus around 4–6 days after ovulation, where migration continues to enable even spacing of the embryos. Progesterone produced by the *corpora lutea* promotes changes in the uterus to allow implantation of the embryos (between 12 and 14 days), with the subsequent development of the placentae.

GESTATION

The average duration of gestation in the cat is 66 days, but the normal range is very wide (e.g. 61–70 days or more). However, the previously suggested average gestation length of 63 days is almost certainly incorrect and is probably based on the duration of pregnancy from the *last* of many matings over several days.

During pregnancy the queen should be fed a high-quality commercial cat food, and her intake may increase by some 10–25 per cent towards the end of gestation. Care should be taken to ensure she does not become obese, however, as this can cause problems with parturition (queening). Queens should ideally receive vaccinations and be wormed prior to mating. It is generally unwise to vaccinate pregnant queens, and some vaccines must never be used (e.g. live attenuated panleukopaenia virus vaccines) as they may harm the developing kittens. Likewise, many drugs can potentially damage the kittens, and therefore medications should only be used strictly under the guidance of a veterinary surgeon.

PREGNANCY DIAGNOSIS

Fortunately, pregnancy diagnosis is relatively straightforward in the queen. If a queen is taken to the veterinary surgeon between days 20 and 30 of the pregnancy, the vet will be able to gently palpate (feel) the uterus through the abdominal wall, and pregnancy is confirmed by detecting the small (pea to walnut-sized) foetal swellings. The care and experience of a veterinary surgeon are necessary with this technique to avoid any potential physical damage to the foetuses.

A veterinary surgeon may also be able to use an ultrasound machine (as used in human pregnancies) for pregnancy diagnosis in cats. Using this, pregnancy can be confirmed as early as day 15, and it may be used throughout pregnancy to monitor the kittens if necessary. Radiographs (X-ray pictures) may also be taken, and from day 45 these will show the skeletons of the foetuses; however the use of radiographs is neither necessary nor desirable to confirm pregnancy.

PARTURITION (QUEENING)

Towards the end of gestation, a complex series of hormonal changes take place which prepare the queen for parturition, and ultimately initiate the process.

Around 1–2 weeks before parturition the queen may become restless and look for a suitable place to give birth. A wooden or cardboard box or a cage should be provided in a quiet, warm, secluded place away from other cats. Newspaper, blankets and specialist acrylic material, such as Vetbed, make suitable bedding for the queen. As parturition approaches the queen's vulva and nipples should be gently cleaned with warm water, and some hair may be usefully trimmed from these areas in longhaired cats to allow easier access for the kittens to suck.

Parturition is divided into three stages. The first of these is the preparatory stage, where the cervix dilates and uterine contractions begin; the second stage consists of delivery of the foetuses; and the third stage is the delivery of the placentae. In the queen, as in many other species that give birth to more than one foetus, the second and third stages are not separate events but are combined together.

The queen will usually exhibit active nesting behaviour for the 12 or 24 hours before parturition starts, and at this time, or during the final stage of parturition, the rectal temperature may also fall by a degree or so, i.e. to 99–100°F (37–38°C), but this is very variable. Stage one parturition may last for between 2 and 24 hours or so. The signs may vary between individuals, but include restlessness (pacing), vocalization, rapid breathing, persistent licking around the vulva and tearing up of the bedding. There may also be a clear or blood-tinged discharge from the vulva. The progression to second-stage parturition is marked by the onset of more forceful, regular uterine and abdominal contractions. The first kitten is usually born within 60 minutes of the onset of second stage, and kittens may be delivered either head first or rear first (breech) – either is perfectly normal. Further kittens may follow very rapidly after the first, or there may be intervals of up to 60–120 minutes. Individual placentae (brownish in colour) are usually passed after each kitten is born, which the queen will usually eat if not removed, without any deleterious effects. The queen will remove the foetal membranes and umbilical cord from each kitten after birth, and also clean herself. She may suckle newborn kittens before the next is delivered depending on how rapidly the birth is proceeding. Occasionally, particularly with a first litter, a queen may not appear to know what to do with the kittens. It is generally best to interfere as little as possible, but it may be necessary to remove foetal membranes from a kitten if the queen is reticent and they would otherwise obstruct breathing. The entire litter is usually born within 2–10 hours of the first kitten, although occasionally a queen may give birth to a litter of one or more kittens, only to resume parturition again after 24 hours or more and deliver further healthy kittens. Sometimes this happens if the queen is disturbed during parturition, but often there is no obvious reason and it is regarded as normal behaviour.

The average litter size in cats is between four and five, but may range between one and more than ten. Oriental breeds (e.g. Siamese) tend to have larger litters, while the opposite is true of some of the longhaired cats. Age will also affect the litter size with older queens having smaller litters.

It is a wise precaution to have the queen and litter examined by a veterinary surgeon within 24 hours of completion of parturition, but if there are problems this is usually indicated by a distressed or lethargic queen and/or kittens. A blood-stained vaginal discharge is normal for around 7–10 days post-partum, but if it is very heavy, veterinary attention should be sought (see page 292, post-partum haemorrhage).

Kittens will initially suck from the queen at regular intervals (e.g. three or four times an hour). The stress of lactation, particularly with a large litter, can be very high and the queen should therefore be provided with a plentiful supply of premium quality commercial cat food. Special 'high density' foods are available. Your veterinarian will be able to advise you. Vitamin and mineral supplements are generally *not* needed or advisable except under veterinary supervision. First foods (e.g. commercial kitten foods) may be introduced to the kittens from around 3 weeks of age, in fact as soon as possible after their eyes have opened, and these can also provide a suitable high-calorie food for the queen during lactation. Weaning of the kittens can usually be completed by week 7 or 8.

Breeding/reproductive problems

INFERTILITY

This condition appears to be quite rare in cats. Good management practices will overcome many of the potential causes of infertility, whilst others will require investigation with the help of a veterinary surgeon.

Toms

The most common form of infertility in toms is simple lack of libido, and therefore failure to mount. This can be due to the stress of a change in environment, or a particularly aggressive queen (especially if the tom is inexperienced). Careful management of the tom and queen is usually sufficient to overcome these problems.

Failure to produce, or production of abnormal or insufficient numbers of spermatozoa will also result in infertility. This is normal in most tortoiseshell toms, whose genetic make-up usually prevents the development of normal testes and spermatozoa. Other than this, abnormal spermatogenesis appears to be rare, but can result from systematic diseases of various kinds, obesity and nutritional problems. Investigation of sperm abnormalities requires examination of a semen sample obtained either through the use of an artificial vagina, through electro-ejaculation or by taking swabs from a queen's vagina after mating. Collection of semen in the cat is not easy compared with other species, e.g. the dog.

Queens

Some queens may fail to come into oestrus. Causes of this include immaturity (failure to reach puberty), lack of adequate light (e.g. less than 12 hours of light per day), lactation (most lactating queens will not cycle until a few weeks after weaning) and pseudo-pregnancy (see page 285: in occasional queens ovulation and pseudo-pregnancy may be induced simply by handling and stroking her during oestrus). Additionally some queens kept in isolation may fail to cycle, but will come into oestrus normally under the stimulating presence of other cycling queens or toms. Also, nervous, young or intimidated queens, especially, if not allowed time to settle after travelling to the tom, may not sanction the approaches of the tom even when in full oestrus.

Other uncommon causes of infertility in the queen include failure to ovulate after mating, and failure of implantation of fertilized ova. The latter of these two disorders requires very specialist investigation, but failure to ovulate can be confirmed by looking at progesterone levels in a blood sample taken 3 days or more after mating. Successful ovulation will result in high levels of progesterone (released by the *corpora lutea*). A queen who consistently fails to ovulate may be treated successfully by an injection of an LH-like drug given on the day of mating.

ABORTION, RESORPTION, STILLBIRTHS AND KITTEN MORTALITY

The first two of these are probably the major types of pregnancy failure encountered in domestic cats. In this situation mating, fertilization and implantation of the embryos occur normally, and pregnancy may be confirmed by one of the techniques described above. Later in the pregnancy, a problem leads to death of the foetuses and results in abortion or resorption. Whether the kittens are resorbed or aborted depends in part on the stage of gestation when death occurs – abortion being more common later in the pregnancy and resorption more common earlier. Depending on the underlying cause, the queen may or may not appear ill, and although a discharge may be present both with abortion and resorption, this may not always be noticed if the queen cleans herself thoroughly, and similarly aborted foetuses may not be apparent if the queen eats them. In some cases, the first sign that all is not well may be a reduction in abdominal swelling or failure of the abdomen to swell normally during pregnancy. Important causes of resorption/abortion include:

(a) *Infections of the queen*:
(i)   feline leukaemia virus
(ii) feline panleukopaenia virus
(iii) feline immunodeficiency virus
(iv) Chlamydiosis (infection with *Chlamydia psittaci* has been suggested but not proven as a cause of abortion/resorption).

(b) *Endometrial hyperplasia/Endometritis*. An abnormality of the lining of the uterus related to hormonally induced changes which may lead to secondary bacterial infection (endometritis) is perhaps one of the most common causes of foetal losses. A variety of bacteria may be implicated in this disease, which can result in infertility, resorption, abortion and stillbirths. In some queens, a low-grade chronic endometritis may eventually progress to a condition known as pyometritis. This is a severe and potentially life-threatening infection of the uterus which requires careful treatment.

(c) *Foetal defects*. Defects in the foetuses may arise from a variety of causes, including the use of teratogenic drugs (i.e. drugs that harm the foetus), inherited traits, exposure to X-rays during early development and some infections. Severe defects may result in early death of the foetus followed by abortion/resorption.

(d) *Other problems*:
(i)   inadequate progesterone levels
(ii) poor nutrition (including taurine deficiency) (see Chapter 7, Nutrition)
(iii) trauma
(iv) abnormalities of the reproductive tract.

Because of the many different causes of foetal losses, it is essential to seek veterinary advice as soon as any problems are suspected. If, despite appropriate investigation and treatment, a queen continues habitually to lose her litter, she should not be used for breeding.

In a large survey conducted in the USA, involving cats from 28 different breeds, around 9 per cent of kittens were stillborn. Most of the causes of abortion and resorption listed above may also result in stillborn kittens, but the occurrence of just one or two stillborn kittens in a litter is likely to be due to the presence of lethal defects, to overcrowding of the uterus in a large litter or to hypoxia (lack of oxygen) during parturition. Sometimes partially resorbed or mummified foetuses will be born along with other healthy kittens.

Kitten mortality within the first 1–2 weeks of life can represent a major problem. In the survey from the USA, 13 per cent of kittens died in the first week of life, although most breeders would expect losses to be considerably less than this. The causes of neonatal death are extremely diverse and include both infectious and non-infectious causes. Non-infectious causes can include inadequate care by the queen, lack of milk and congenital defects. Heavy or unexpected neonatal losses should be reported immediately to a veterinary surgeon, and it is helpful to keep detailed records of all births and the progress of individual kittens.

DYSTOCIA (DIFFICULTY GIVING BIRTH)

The relatively uniform size and shape of the domestic cat is probably one of the major reasons why feline dystocia is quite rare, and so much less common than canine dystocia. Dystocia may arise with very large kittens, queens with a small pelvic canal, torsion (twisting) of a uterine horn, or most commonly uterine inertia (lack of uterine contractions). Uterine inertia is more common in older and obese queens, and may sometimes follow a prolonged labour, where the uterus becomes exhausted.

Dystocia is a serious condition for both the queen and kittens, requiring prompt veterinary attention. Treatment may include the use of drugs, such as oxytocin, to increase uterine contractions, or in some cases a Caesarian section may be required. It may sometimes be difficult to decide whether or not a queen is having problems with parturition. However, if there is any doubt, it is always wise to contact the veterinary surgeon. As a rule of thumb a queen should not be allowed to go longer than 2 hours with strong ineffectual contractions. Also, if contractions are gradually getting weaker but the queen is showing signs of unease or distress, then again prompt veterinary attention should be sought.

POST-PARTUM HAEMORRHAGE

This type of haemorrhage (reddish-black vulval discharge) is relatively light, and usually clears between the fifth and tenth day. Continuous heavy discharge, discharge beyond 3 weeks or malodorous discharge should all be investigated further. Potential causes include infections and failure of the uterus to contract down normally after birth.

RETAINED PLACENTA(E)

Although often considered a major worry, retained placentae are very rare following feline pregnancies, and even when they do occur they can be very difficult to diagnose. Generally if a retained placenta is suspected, all that needs to be done is to keep a close watch on the queen. The placenta will usually be passed (complete or in pieces) within a few days, and only rarely will it lead to uterine infection.

METRITIS

Acute metritis (infection of the uterus) may be seen within 1–4 days of parturition, and may sometimes be associated with a retained foetus or placenta. The queen will usually be depressed, lethargic, inappetent, pyrexic (high temperature) and perhaps vomiting. There is typically a foul-smelling vaginal discharge. Urgent veterinary treatment should be sought, and in severe cases ovario-hysterectomy (surgical removal of the uterus and ovaries) may be necessary.

MASTITIS

Infection in one or more mammary glands is relatively rare in queens. Signs include lethargy, depression, anorexia and pyrexia. One or more mammary glands will be hot, painful, firm and swollen. Most cases respond well to treatment, which includes poulticing and the use of antibiotics.

ECLAMPSIA

'Lactational tetany' is rare in cats, but may occur either during late pregnancy, or (more often) during lactation due to heavy calcium demands.

Affected queens develop low blood calcium levels and may show difficulty in getting up or walking. This may progress to muscle tremors or even fits. Immediate veterinary treatment is essential for this life-threatening but readily treatable condition.

HAND REARING KITTENS

This is sometimes necessary if they are rejected by the queen (rare) or if the queen cannot feed them (e.g. eclampsia, mastitis, etc.). Kittens should be kept together in a draught-free warm environment at a temperature of between 90–95°F for the first 5 days and around 80–85°F subsequently. Special feeding apparatus is available from veterinary surgeons and pet shops, but the choice of feed must be made carefully. Wherever possible specific commercial kitten milk replacer powders should be used, reconstituted and fed according to the manufacturer's instructions. In an emergency, and as a temporary measure, a mixture of 20 g of skimmed milk powder, 10 ml olive oil and 90 ml water warmed to 98–99°F will suffice. Newborn kittens will need approximately 1 ml of milk or milk replacer per hour, and need to be fed at least 3–4 times during the night, initially increasing by around 0.5 ml per feed per day. Gradually larger and less frequent feeds may be given, so that by 10–14 days there is a 6-hour gap during the night. However, this is only possible if frequent feeds are given during the day and correct temperatures (see above) are maintained during the night. By 4 weeks around 6 milk feeds are given during a day and supplementation with kitten food begins. Kittens must be groomed regularly, and warm wet cotton-wool should be used to clean the genitals and anus after each feed to help stimulate defecation and urination.

Control of reproduction

MISMATING

Unwanted/unplanned matings happen frequently in queens that are allowed outside, especially young queens that become sexually active before their owners are aware of it. It is possible to prevent establishment of pregnancy after mismating by the use of hormones which either inhibit transport of oocytes in the oviducts (oestrogens) or perhaps prevent ovulation (progesterone-like agents). These drugs have to be administered within a few hours of the mismating, however, and both carry some risks of side-effects. Their use in cats is therefore often discouraged. A safe alternative is to spay (neuter) a queen when she is 3 or 4 weeks pregnant if she is not required for further breeding (at this stage the early pregnancy does not complicate the operation), or allow her to carry the litter to term.

SURGICAL NEUTERING

Any cat, either male or female, that is not going to be bred from should be neutered, i.e. castrated if it is a male, or spayed if female. Castration involves removal of both testes, and spaying entails removal of both ovaries and the entire uterus. Neutering cats has many advantages for both sexes. In males it reduces inter-male aggression, and roaming behaviour. Sexual behaviour is absent or reduced, as is urine marking. In females, there is an absence of oestrous cycles and no risk of unwanted pregnancy, with reduced risk of mammary tumour development. The benefits of neutering to both pet and owner far outweigh the small risk associated with any routine anaesthetic. Cats (both male and female) are generally neutered when they are between 4 and 6 months of age.

PHARMACOLOGICAL CONTROL

The management of a multi-cat household with several breeding queens can sometimes prove difficult, and the use of drugs to control (suppress) the oestrous cycle temporarily appears attractive. Progestogens (progesterone-like drugs) are available from your veterinarian and are licensed for this use in the United Kingdom, but they have some potential side-effects. Amongst other effects progestogens may increase the risk of uterine infections (pyometritis), cause weight gain and alter behaviour. They can also induce diabetes in a small number of cats, and sometimes suppress the activity of the adrenal glands (see Chapter 20, The Endocrine System). Although progestogens can be useful for short-term oestrous control, because of this array of potentially serious side-effects, prolonged or repeated use is generally discouraged.

Another potential way of temporarily controlling oestrus is to make use of the fact that queens are induced ovulators and produce an 'after-reaction' of the vagina by sufficiently stimulating it with a non-traumatic probe, e.g. a glass thermometer. If this is done several times during a single day when the queen is in ovulation, it will quite reliably induce ovulation and pseudo-pregnancy, during which she will not cycle. Ovulation can also be induced during oestrus by an injection of LH. Such a procedure will provide satisfactory temporary control of cycling in a queen; however its repeated use is not recommended as recurrent induction of pseudo-pregnancy may also induce undesirable side-effects such as making the uterus more susceptible to infections, and thus reducing overall fertility.

18

THE CARDIOVASCULAR SYSTEM

Introduction

The cardiovascular system consists of the heart, which pumps oxygenated blood to all tissues of the body via arteries, and removes the waste products of cellular metabolism, particularly carbon dioxide, via the veins. Heart failure occurs when this system is unable to meet the body's needs. This may be because of disease of the cardiovascular system itself or because of excessive demands placed upon it as a result of malfunction of other body systems. This chapter will discuss the normal anatomy and physiology of the cardiovascular system, the mechanisms involved in heart failure and the particular diseases which may be seen in the cat.

Anatomy and physiology

THE HEART AND BLOOD VESSELS

The heart essentially consists of two muscular pumps which function simultaneously, referred to as the right and the left sides of the heart respectively. Venous blood containing carbon dioxide and waste products of cellular metabolism is carried from the tissues via veins to the right side of the heart (see Fig. 102). The venous blood collects in the thin-walled right atrium and is then pumped into the right ventricle, which has thicker muscular walls and pumps the blood to the lungs via the pulmonary arteries. As the blood flows through the capillaries lining the air sacs in the lungs, the carbon dioxide is released and oxygen binds to the haemoglobin in the red blood cells. The oxygenated blood flows back to the heart and collects in the left atrium, which pumps the blood into the left ventricle. The left ventricle is the main pump of the heart and has a thick muscular wall to pump the blood to the whole body via the aorta and the arterial

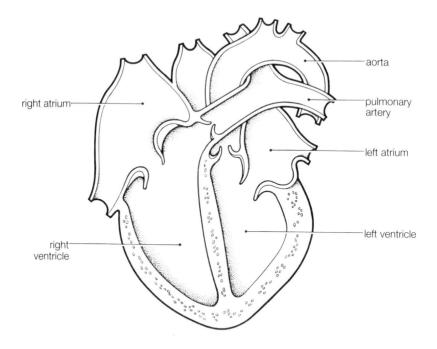

right atrium

aorta

pulmonary artery

left atrium

left ventricle

right ventricle

Figure 102 A diagrammatic representation of the four heart chambers and major blood vessels

system. Valves in the heart and blood vessels ensure that blood can flow only in a forward direction. The large valves dividing the atria from the ventricles have two leaflets (or cusps) on the left, the mitral valve, and three leaflets on the right, the tricuspid valve. Backflow into the ventricles is prevented by the smaller semi-lunar valves situated at the exit of the pulmonary artery from the right ventricle and where the aorta leaves the left ventricle. The elastic properties of arterial walls help the forward flow of blood away from the heart. Thin-walled veins act as collecting ducts and allow the blood to run back towards the heart.

THE LYMPHATIC SYSTEM

Due to the high pressure in the arteries, some tissue fluid (serum) moves through the capillary walls into the spaces between cells. This fluid then drains into thin-walled vessels called lymphatics and passes through the lymph nodes (glands). In the lymph nodes, any foreign material in tissues, such as infectious organisms, is recognized by specialized cells which contribute to the immune response to such foreign material. After flowing through the lymph nodes, the fluid (lymph) flows into larger lymphatics draining into large veins and thus rejoins the main circulation (see Chapter 8, Anatomy and Physiology).

Pathophysiology of heart failure

The volume of blood pumped by the heart per minute is known as the cardiac output and is calculated as the volume of blood pumped per beat times the number of beats per minute (heart rate):

cardiac output = heart rate × stroke volume.

When the body requires more oxygen, for example during the physiological stress of exercise, the cardiac output can be increased by the body in two ways. Firstly, the volume of blood per beat can be increased by a stronger contraction of the cardiac muscle. Secondly, the heart rate can be increased.

Figure 103   The renin-angiotensin system

decreased arterial blood pressure triggers the system
↓
RENIN
released by cells in the kidney
↓
converts **ANGIOTENSINOGEN** in the blood
↓
ANGIOTENSIN I
↓
converted in the lungs by
Angiotensin Converting Enzyme (ACE)
↓
ANGIOTENSIN II

blood pressure and **cardiac output increase**

ANGIOTENSIN II causes:
1. **vasoconstriction** of arterioles –
　　　　　increases blood pressure
2. release of **aldosterone** from adrenals –
　　　　　salt and water retention by kidneys
　　　　　increases circulating blood volume
　　　　　increases cardiac output
3. release of **antidiuretic** hormone –
　　　　　decreases water loss in urine
　　　　　increases body water
　　　　　increases cardiac output

Heart failure can be defined as a failure of cardiac output to meet the body's demands for oxygen.

This may be due to excessive demands by the body, as in hyperthyroidism, where the metabolic rate of the body is increased, making additional demands for oxygen. More commonly, heart failure is due to failure of the heart to pump blood effectively. In diseases such as cardiomyopathy, the heart muscle is unable to pump with sufficient force to be effective. Where the heart valves are diseased or deformed there may be backflow of blood, which creates a volume overload too great for the heart to pump effectively.

When cardiac output falls below the body's demands, several compensatory mechanisms are activated in an attempt to relieve the situation. One of the first responses is an increase in heart rate. Another early mechanism is constriction of the blood vessels, especially the arteries, to decrease the overall volume of the vascular system, so that the heart does not have to work so hard to maintain blood pressure. The most important mechanism for improvement of cardiac output is the renin-angiotensin system which is activated by the kidneys to increase the overall volume of blood in the vascular bed (see Fig. 103). Renin is a substance released by the kidneys when the blood flow to the kidney decreases, as in heart failure. Renin then acts on other hormone systems to cause constriction of blood vessels and to conserve salt and water from being excreted by the kidney in urine. This conservation increases total body water, and hence blood volume and blood pressure.

OVER-COMPENSATION

When heart failure persists in spite of these mechanisms, over-compensation can occur, which can of itself be deleterious to the body. When the heart rate reaches approximately 300 beats a minute, there is insufficient time for the ventricle to fill between beats, and thus the cardiac output starts to fall again. Constriction of the blood vessels may be such that the oxygen supply to the muscles is so poor that the animal becomes weak and unable to exercise. Water retention may become so marked that the vascular system is unable to contain it and fluid leaks into body cavities or tissues causing ascites (free fluid in the abdomen) or oedematous swelling of limbs and other tissues (see Fig. 104, page 300)

Investigation of patients with suspected cardiovascular disease

A variety of information and test results are required to assess the severity of disease of a patient with heart failure, and to attempt to diagnose the cause of such failure.

HISTORY

Any previous disease or treatment of the cat should be considered for possible contribution to the current problem. Details of the onset and progression of clinical signs may help to elucidate the cause of the condition. Deformities caused by genetic defects often affect more than one individual in a litter or close family.

CLINICAL EXAMINATION

A full clinical examination of all body systems should always be carried out before concentrating on a detailed assessment of the cardiovascular system. The heart failure may be secondary to another disease such as hyperthyroidism due to a thyroid tumour. The heart rate and pulse rate should be recorded. In cases of cardiac rhythm disturbance, there may not be a pulse (effective stroke volume) generated by every heart beat and so the rates will differ. Careful note should be made of the heart sounds. Any abnormal sounds such as murmurs, their point of maximum intensity and the area of radiation of the sounds indicate the likely cause of the problem. The mucous membranes of the mouth and eyes should be examined. Paleness may be due to vascular constriction, especially in cardiogenic shock. Where oxygen and carbon dioxide exchange is severely affected in the lungs, the mucous membranes may appear bluish or cyanosed.

The degree of free fluid accumulation can be assessed. The cat may be breathing fast and shallow owing to either free fluid in the chest cavity or tissue fluid filling the alveoli (air sacs) of the lung. An enlarged liver or free fluid in the abdomen may also be felt.

RADIOGRAPHY

Chest radiographs can be useful in assessing the severity of heart disease (see Fig. 105). The heart is commonly enlarged in cases of failure (see Fig. 106). Enlargement of the major blood vessels or free fluid in the chest or abdomen may also be diagnosed radiographically. The full extent of such fluid accumulation may not be apparent during the clinical examination. Some congenital defects show characteristic changes on X-ray.

ELECTROCARDIOGRAPHY

An ECG (electrocardiogram) is a graphic interpretation of the electrical changes which occur within the heart muscle during the course of the cardiac cycle of contraction and relaxation for each beat. The ECG can be used to show disturbances of heart rate and rhythm as well as problems of electrical conduction caused by heart muscle disease or blood electrolyte imbalance (see Fig. 107).

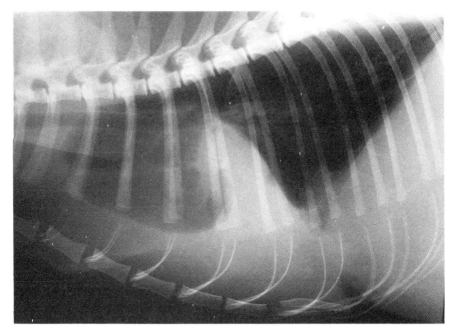

Figure 104 Thoracic radiograph of a cat with free fluid in the chest cavity. The presence of the fluid obscures the detail of the lungs and the silhouette of the heart

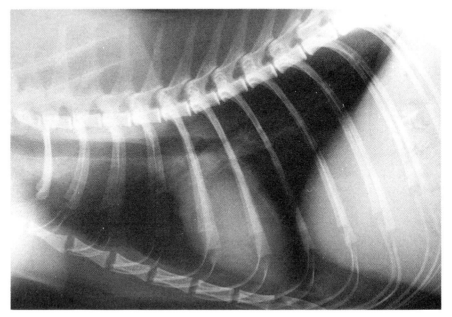

Figure 105 Thoracic radiograph of a normal cat. The white silhouette of the heart can be seen against the black (air-filled) lung fields within the rib cage

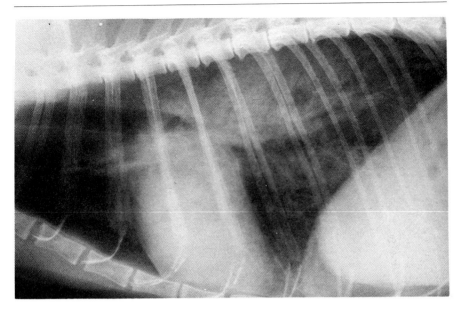

Figure 106 Thoracic radiograph of a cat with cardiomyopathy showing enlargement of the silhouette of the heart. Increased density (whiteness) of the lung fields indicates oedema (free fluid in the lung tissue and the air sacs)

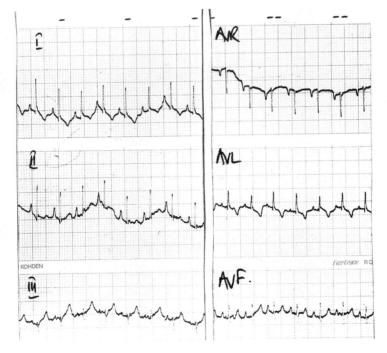

Figure 107 A six-lead ECG tracing from a cat with congenital heart disease

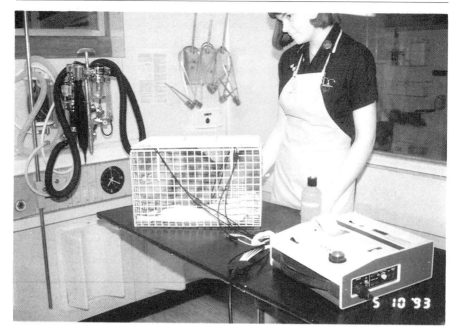

Figure 108 Recording an ECG from a cat without the distress of physical restraint

To obtain the recording, electrodes are placed on each of the four legs, usually using blunted crocodile clips. Ideally the cat should lie on its right side during recording, but if it is distressed by this it may be placed in a basket to settle down with the clips in place before a recording is made (see Fig. 108). If the latter method is used then the tracing cannot be used to infer changes in heart size, but as this information can usually be gained from the radiograph it is not essential.

ULTRASOUND EXAMINATION

Anatomical details that cannot be seen on radiographs may be gained by using ultrasound examination. Sophisticated techniques and interpretation of data can also provide details on cardiac function, as well as basic anatomy. Such examinations are usually only carried out at specialist referral centres.

Principles of treatment of cardiovascular disease

There are a variety of methods and drugs available for the management of heart failure. Simple measures such as weight and exercise control may suffice for mildly affected cases. In severe cases multiple drug therapy and cage rest may be needed. Many cats do not show notable signs in early heart failure, simply adopting a more sedentary lifestyle.

DIET

Any overweight animal is placing an extra load on its heart function. It may be difficult to control food intake for a cat unless the animal is confined to the house. Otherwise the cat will hunt or beg from neighbours and so defeat all efforts made by the owner to restrict its intake. Food with a low salt content can help to reduce salt and water retention in heart failure. However, as such diets are often unpalatable and are refused by sick animals, this aspect of dietary management may have to be abandoned. Some of the new commercially available diets are low in salt and palatable – but individual cat tastes vary!

In the mid-1980s it was discovered that cats with a dietary deficiency of the essential amino acid taurine suffered from dilated cardiomyopathy. Since that time all commercial sources of cat food are adequately supplemented with taurine, to the extent that this form of cardiomyopathy has now become rare in both Europe and the USA. It is important to consider supplementation if the cat has a homemade diet. Taurine can be obtained from pharmacists or health food shops and should be fed at the rate of 250–1000 mg daily.

EXERCISE

As mentioned earlier, exercise increases the amount of work the heart has to perform. In heart failure, exercise should be restricted. Most cats will naturally tend to sleep more with heart failure. When an animal is severely affected it may be useful to confine it to one room or even a small basket or kennel to reduce the extra strain on the heart.

DRUG THERAPY

Most of the drugs available for the treatment of heart failure are marketed to treat man. Cat owners will be warned by their veterinarian that many of the drugs have not been specifically tested for the treatment of cats. Nevertheless, over the years, clinicians have used many of the drugs in cats and are able to predict, with some accuracy, whether undesirable side effects might be encountered.

Diuretics

These drugs are the mainstay of therapy for heart failure. They reduce total body water by increasing urine output by the kidneys. Frusemide is the drug of choice, but care must be taken with dosage levels as cats readily become dehydrated. Maintenance therapy is usually only given on alternate days.

Digitalis

Compounds of this substance are traditionally used in heart failure in many species to slow the heart rate and to increase the force of contraction. However, the cat is particularly sensitive to the toxic side effects of these drugs and may show anorexia, vomiting and abnormal cardiac rhythms. As a result these drugs are not commonly used in cats.

Beta-blockers

These drugs, particularly propranolol, are used to decrease excessive heart rates but do not increase the force of heart muscle contraction. They are well tolerated by cats and side effects of bronchial constriction are uncommon.

Calcium channel blockers

This group of drugs is also used in the cat to decrease the heart rate. The drugs affect the rate of movement of calcium through the cell wall during contraction of the heart muscle and thus affect heart rate. There is recent evidence from American veterinary schools that diltiazem may be preferred to verapamil in the cat as a calcium channel blocker of choice for the treatment of cardiomyopathies. In addition to decreasing heart rate, these drugs also act to dilate blood vessels. This has the effect of improving blood flow to essential tissues and decreasing the blood pressure so that the ventricles can empty more easily, hence increasing the stroke volume and cardiac output.

Vasodilator drugs

These compounds may be used to dilate blood vessels and lighten the workload for the heart. Drugs such as prazosin and hydralazine have been used but many clinicians prefer angiotensin converting enzyme inhibitors in the cat.

Angiotensin converting enzyme (ACE) inhibitors

These drugs are used to block the activating mechanism of the renin-angiotensin system (see Fig. 103). They block the cascade of reactions so that constriction of the blood vessels and water retention by the kidneys are restricted. Captopril is the drug in this class most commonly used in cats. Side effects of anorexia or kidney failure can usually be controlled by decreasing the dose levels.

Anti-arrhythmic drugs

Abnormal heart rhythms are treated with these drugs but they are not commonly used in cats as they frequently have undesirable side effects.

Lignocaine hydrochloride may be used in emergencies for ventricular fibrillation. The beta-blocker propranolol, discussed previously, is most frequently used for abnormal rhythms in cats.

Anti-coagulants

These are indicated in cases of thrombosis associated with heart disease. Heparin may be given intravenously in the acute situation. Low doses of aspirin at the rate of 75 mg (¼ tablet) every 3 days may be given for long-term treatment.

Common congenital cardiac defects

A congenital defect is one which is present from birth. Such a defect may be caused by a genetic abnormality or may have arisen when a particular event affected the dam during pregnancy; for example, some drugs administered to pregnant females can cause malformations of the foetus.

Approximately 2 per cent of all cats may be affected by a congenital cardiac defect.

Familial patterns of disease incidence suggest a genetic defect but to date only endocardial fibroelastosis in the Burmese cat has been proven to have a genetic cause. Other conditions that have been recognized as familial include aortic stenosis, patent ductus arteriosus, atrioventricular malformations and ventricular septal (wall) defects.

There is wide variation in the severity of defects. Some animals may be stillborn; others may die around the time of weaning; others only show signs later in life as young adults; and still others may never show any clinical signs of their defect. Common presenting signs of congenital cardiac disease include: failure to thrive; stunting compared with littermates; marked respiratory efforts and difficulty in breathing; lack of play behaviour and spontaneous exercise; early onset of signs of congestive heart disease usually associated with audible heart murmurs.

Although most of the congenital cardiac defects cannot be treated, some animals will live almost normal lives in spite of them. It is important to note that it is not yet possible to determine whether an affected individual has resulted from a genetic abnormality. For this reason it is advisable not to breed from any cat in which a congenital defect has been diagnosed.

ATRIOVENTRICULAR MALFORMATIONS

These are the most commonly encountered congenital defects in cats, resulting in malfunction of the valves between the atrium and the ventricle on either the left or the right side, or both. There is subsequent backflow of blood during ventricular contraction which increases the heart work and finally results in congestive failure.

VENTRICULAR SEPTAL DEFECTS

In these cases the wall that separates the right and left ventricles fails to close completely so that blood can pass directly from one to the other. As the left ventricle is usually at a higher pressure than the right, oxygenated blood flows back into the right side so that less goes to the rest of the body, in other words a reduced cardiac output. Whilst this condition can quite commonly be treated surgically in children, the problems of providing cardiopulmonary bypass for open heart surgery in animals as small as kittens preclude surgery from being a treatment option in cats.

AORTIC AND PULMONARY STENOSIS

The aorta is narrowed at the level of the semilunar valves or just above or just below those valves at the exit from the left ventricle. This means that the left ventricle has to work harder to eject sufficient blood into the circulation and the left ventricular muscle usually thickens (hypertrophies) as a result. Where the narrowing is severe, the muscle may finally fail and the animal shows weakness and fainting due to insufficient cardiac output. The 'fainting' is of course because of the effect of insufficient oxygenated blood reaching the brain.

Pulmonary stenosis is simlar to aortic stenosis where the right ventricular exit is affected.

PATENT DUCTUS ARTERIOSUS

The foetus is supplied by oxygenated blood from the placenta via the umbilicus. Consequently there is no need for all the blood from the right ventricle to flow through the foetal lungs. A blood vessel called the ductus arteriosus connects the pulmonary artery directly to the aorta in the foetus. Within a few days of birth the ductus normally closes off so that all the outflow from the right ventricle passes through the lungs. If the vessel fails to close off because of genetic or environmental factors, blood flows back from the high pressure aorta into the pulmonary circulation and causes congestion of the lungs and overload of the right ventricle. If the effects are not too severe it is possible to treat this defect by tying off the vessel surgically. The animal may then live a normal life.

ENDOCARDIAL FIBROELASTOSIS

In this condition there is an excess of non-elastic fibrous tissue lining the chambers of the heart. This prevents dilation of the chambers when they fill with blood and so limits the stroke volume. This condition is known to have a genetic basis in the Burmese cat.

VASCULAR RING ANOMALIES

In some animals congenital defects of the major blood vessels in the chest occur. The most common of these is where the aorta runs down the right side of the chest instead of the left. This results in constriction of the oesophagus between the trachea, the base of the heart, the aorta and the closed-off ductus arteriosus. Kittens with this condition present with vomiting or more correctly regurgitation of food after weaning. Usually it is possible to correct the condition by surgery if there is no permanent damage to the oesophagus.

Acquired cardiac disease

Some surveys have shown that heart disease affects up to 15 per cent of the total cat population. Again it is important to note that some affected individuals will never be recognized as they will simply adopt a more sedentary lifestyle in order to avoid distress. Poor appetite or anorexia are common early signs of heart disease in cats. Clinical signs vary. Some cats may sleep a lot and take very little voluntary exercise. Frank signs of congestive heart failure may be present due to fluid accumulation. Fluid in the chest cavity or lungs results in breathing difficulties and animals may become severely distressed and cyanosed. Excess fluid in the abdomen can result in enlargement of the liver and a pot-bellied appearance. Such animals may show such gastro-intestinal disturbances as anorexia, vomiting or diarrhoea.

CARDIOMYOPATHY

In most cases of acquired heart disease in the cat the heart muscle itself is affected – cardiomyopathy. Such conditions may be primary or they may be secondary to some other disease process. *Primary cardiomyopathies* can further be subdivided into dilated or hypertrophic forms. In the *dilated* form the heart becomes enlarged and the ventricular walls become thin and unable to contract with much force. The cardiac output goes down. In the mid-1980s it was discovered that most cases of dilated cardiomyopathy in cats were caused by diets deficient in the essential amino acid taurine. Since that time commercial diets have been supplemented such that the condition is now unusual. Affected animals require treatment for congestive heart failure, usually for the rest of their lives, but can show marked improvement when taurine deficiencies are made good.

Hypertrophic cardiomyopathy describes the condition where the ventricular muscle becomes excessively thickened. This results in less space for blood to fill the chamber and the thick muscle becomes too stiff to contract with much force. These features lead to reduction of cardiac output. Hypertrophic cardiomyopathy is often a feature of *hyperthyroidism* although in many cases the cause of the cardiac disease cannot be determined.

In many cases the changes in the heart muscle are neither clearly dilated nor obviously hypertrophic. Such cases are classified as *intermediate* or intergrade. Often the cause of such cases is not determined.

Secondary cardiomyopathy may be associated with a number of different conditions, for example toxicity, cancers, bacterial or viral infections, high temperatures, hormonal disorders, kidney failure or dietary abnormalities. Management of such cases involves treating the underlying disorder where possible, as well as the signs of heart failure.

THROMBOEMBOLIC DISEASE

Thrombosis is a frequent sequel to heart disease in the cat and is often the first sign that a problem is present. Disease and damage to blood vessel walls (atherosclerosis) is not a feature of cardiovascular disease in animals as it is in man. Thrombosis occurs in cats with heart disease apparently due to pooling of blood in the atria when cardiac output fails. Spontaneous clots occur which can then break off and flow into the general circulation causing arterial blockage. Most commonly one or both of the main arteries to the back legs are affected and the cat presents with lameness or apparent hindleg paralysis. Severe pain is associated with acute thrombosis and often both owners and the veterinarian may think that such animals have been involved in a road traffic accident. Less commonly, one of the front legs may be affected or the animal may appear to suffer a 'stroke' or a coronary thrombosis. Many cases can be treated conservatively with pain killers and anti-coagulants but the problem of the underlying heart disease can often not be solved and thrombosis recurs.

Non-cardiac disease causing heart failure

HYPERTHYROIDISM

This disease is caused by a tumour of the thyroid tissue resulting in overactivity of the gland. In most cases the tumour is benign. Cats over 6 years of age are affected with an insidious but progressive onset of clinical signs. Animals become hyperactive and usually lose weight in spite of an increased or ravenous appetite. Fluid intake and urine output may be increased and gastro-intestinal signs such as vomiting or diarrhoea may occur. Usually the owner regards the changes as the natural onset of old age. The increased metabolic rate causes an increase in heart rate and hypertrophic cardiomyopathy. Signs of congestive heart failure may be the initial reason for the owner seeking veterinary advice. In most cases a cure can be effected by surgical removal of the tumour. If this is not possible there are several cytotoxic drugs which can be used to alleviate the signs.

HYPERTENSION

Until recently high blood pressure has not been recognized as a clinical problem in domestic animals due to the difficulties of measurement without invasive arterial catheters. Blood pressure can now be accurately assessed at referral clinics using sophisticated Doppler ultrasound techniques. Hypertension has been recorded in cats with hypertrophic cardiomyopathy but it is currently unclear whether this is cause or effect.

HYPERKALAEMIA

High levels of potassium in the blood can cause abnormal heart rhythms which may be life threatening. In cats, very high circulating potassium levels may occur in urinary obstruction. In these cases it is most important to lower the potassium levels to avoid cardiac arrest during the surgery for relief of the obstruction.

ANAEMIA

Heart murmurs may be heard in cats with severe anaemia. The lack of red blood cells decreases the viscosity of the blood to such an extent that turbulence may occur in major blood vessels and be heard as murmurs at the body surface. These murmurs are not usually of significance with respect to heart function and disappear once the anaemia has been treated.

Other cardiovascular conditions

PORTOSYSTEMIC SHUNTS

These physical abnormalities of the cardiovascular system may be either congenital or acquired. The veins draining blood rich in absorbed nutrients from the gut usually pass via the portal vein into the liver. Here the portal vein divides into small capillaries throughout the liver so that absorbed nutrients and toxins can be metabolized. The capillaries then merge into a vessel joining the caudal vena cava to flow into the right atrium. A variety of abnormalities can occur, such as the blood in the portal vein bypassing the capillary system in the liver. Affected animals are often stunted due to poor use of their food and may show toxic signs, in particular central nervous system derangements such as excessive drowsiness or excitation and even seizures, because of the toxins which have not been rendered harmless due to lack of action by the liver.

PERICARDIAL DISEASE

Diseases affecting the pericardial sac which surrounds the heart are uncommon in cats. Rarely, bacterial pericarditis may occur, probably following bite wounds to the chest. Free fluid may accumulate in the sac subsequent to congestive heart failure or feline infectious peritonitis. Usually other signs are referrable to the underlying disease rather than the accumulation of fluid in the pericardial sac. A congenital deformity of the pericardium and diaphragm is sometimes seen which allows organs from the abdomen to move into the pericardial sac. This may be corrected surgically. It is relatively rare in the cat.

CHYLOTHORAX

This is a condition where fluid from the major lymphatic ducts in the chest drains freely into the pleural cavity. In the cat this most commonly occurs in association with lymphosarcoma. In recent years it has been recognized that chylothorax may also occur in severe right-sided congestive heart failure where the flow of lymph into the major blood vessels draining into the right atrium is obstructed. Lastly, chylothorax sometimes occurs as a result of trauma, for example following a road traffic accident.

Conclusion

In cats, as in other species, primary heart disease is usually incurable. However, many cats live near-normal lives for a number of months or even years before their cardiac condition becomes sufficiently severe that clinical signs are noted by their owners. At that point there is a variety of treatment options which can improve the quality of the animal's life for quite some time before the signs are irreversible.

19

HAEMATOLOGY – THE BLOOD

Haematology as a science deals with the morphology, function and diseases of blood and blood forming organs. Clinical haematology is important as an aid to diagnosis of many feline conditions. A blood sample can easily and repeatedly be taken from a suitable vein. Blood circulates through the various organs of the body and is altered during circulation. Established normal parameters of the blood may change significantly in disease and these changes can be measured by a number of laboratory tests. Interpretation of the results of these tests can help the veterinarian to reach a diagnosis, plan treatment and thus help many cats.

Blood

Blood is an organ. The only difference between it and other organs is that the cells of the blood are suspended in a fluid matrix called plasma and not suspended in a solid or semi-solid matrix, e.g. the liver.

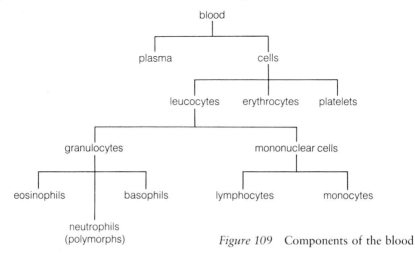

Figure 109 Components of the blood

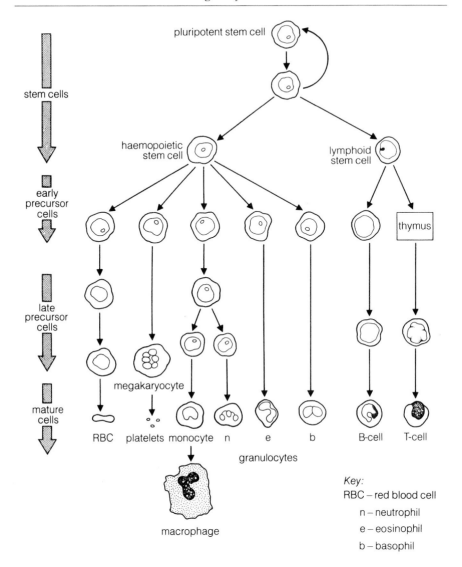

Key:
RBC – red blood cell
n – neutrophil
e – eosinophil
b – basophil

Figure 110 Formation of blood cells

PLASMA

A clear, slightly yellow fluid consisting mainly of water and a complex mixture of proteins and other components. Albumins, globulins and fibrinogen are the most common proteins in the plasma. Albumins are involved in the control of fluid balance of the body and globulins have an important role in immunity. Fibrinogen is a coagulation factor; it has the highest concentration of any of the coagulation factors which circulate in an inactive form in the blood. After activation, e.g. after withdrawing blood from a vein, coagulation factors undergo a cascade of reactions resulting in the clotting of blood. A clotted blood sample contains no fibrinogen and the fluid is called *serum*. Cells of the blood will be trapped in the clot. Therefore, a clotted sample is useful only if estimation of serum components is required. For any other haematological test an anticoagulant (e.g. EDTA) has to be added to the blood sample in order to prevent clotting.

CELLS OF THE BLOOD

The cells normally found in the circulating blood are of three main types: erythrocytes, leucocytes and thrombocytes (see also Chapter 8, Anatomy and Physiology). Erythrocytes or red cells are largely concerned with oxygen transport. Leucocytes or white cells play various roles in defence against infection and tissue injury while thrombocytes or platelets are immediately involved in maintaining the integrity of the blood vessels and in the prevention of blood loss.

Three types of leucocytes can be distinguished. These are the granulocytes, the monocytes and the lymphocytes. In the granulocytes, the cytoplasm is packed with enzyme-containing granules which are essential to the cells' phagocytic and other functions. Monocytes are also actively phagocytic but have other specialized functions as well. The lymphocytes are potent mediators of the immune response to a wide range of infections and a variety of tissue injuries.

Haemopoiesis or formation of blood cells

Before birth, in the embryo, the liver is the main blood forming organ. Later the spleen and finally the bone marrow take over this role.

After birth, the main site of haemopoiesis is the bone marrow. In growing animals, the active bone marrow occupies the shafts of the long bones and has a red colour. With increasing maturity, the active red marrow is replaced by fatty yellow marrow. Active haemopoiesis, however, continues throughout life in all flat bones, e.g. sternum, ribs, vertebrae.

In adult life, if there is a great demand for more cells, haemopoiesis may be re-established in the long bones or even in the spleen and liver. Formation of blood cells outside of the marrow is referred to as extramedullary haemopoiesis (EMH). EMH is a frequent finding in cats in cases of *regenerative anaemia* (see page 321).

Most blood cells have short lifespans and new cells must be produced continuously in adult life to maintain appropriate amounts of these cells.

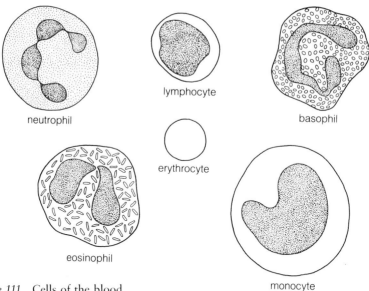

Figure 111 Cells of the blood

The widely differing functions of the circulating blood cells make their production very complex.

Proliferation, maturation and release of mature cells from the bone marrow are regulated by a number of circulating regulatory factors and by the microenvironment of the bone marrow. Red cell production is regulated by the hormone called erythropoietin (EPO), which is produced by the kidney. Tissue hypoxia, a lack of oxygen to the tissues, triggers EPO production, which in turn induces red cell precursors to proliferate. Development of granulocytes, monocytes, megakaryocytes (these are the cells from which the platelets are derived) and lymphocytes is also regulated by a number of haemopoietins or growth factors which are proteins. The sources of these growth factors are the T lymphocytes, monocytes and the specialized stromal cells of the bone marrow.

CELLS OF THE BONE MARROW

Three populations of cells are present in the marrow:

1. *Stem cells.* These are multipotential, small lymphocyte-like cells capable of becoming the early precursors of any of the cell lines.
2. *Early precursor cells.* These are also small lymphocyte-like cells but already committed to produce certain cell lines.
3. *Late precursor cells.* These are the proliferating and maturing cells of the various cell lines. These morphologically recognizable cells make up the large majority of cells in the marrow.

There is experimental evidence that all blood cells are derived from one primitive multipotent stem cell which arises in the embryo. The development of blood cells is as follows.

The original stem cell gives rise to two types of stem cells, the so-called *lymphoid* and *haemopoietic* stem cells. These cells proliferate and make up two pools of stem cells for lymphopoiesis and haemopoiesis. Under the influence of various regulatory factors, early precursor cells of the lymphoid and haemopoietic cells will develop from the above stem cells. Early precursor cells are already committed to produce a particular cell type, e.g. early erythroid precursors under the influence of EPO will produce only erythrocytes, and so on. Early precursors of the haemopoietic cell lines undergo a number of divisions and after each division, the size of the cells and the shape of their nuclei will change. These dividing and maturing cells are the late precursor cells. Eventually, the cells reach a stage where they become mature cells. In health, only mature cells are released into the circulation. The presence of immature cells in the blood is associated with a haematological abnormality (see below).

ERYTHROCYTES

Those of the cat are smaller than those of the dog and have an average diameter of 5.8 micrometres. The feline mature red cell has no nucleus in the circulating blood. Similarly, none of the red cells of the other mammals is nucleated. Birds, fish, amphibia and reptiles, however, have nucleated red cells. Feline red cells appear as biconcave discs under the scanning electron microscope.

In the cat, the lifespan of erythrocytes is relatively short, ranging between 66 and 78 days.

Red cells are the most numerous cell type in the blood and 7.5 million are found in every cubic millimetre (mm^3).

The main function of erythrocytes is to transport oxygen from the lungs to the tissues, and carbon dioxide, one of the end products of metabolism, from the tissues to the lungs. In order to do so, erythrocytes contain a large amount of haemoglobin. Haemoglobin is a protein which consists of globin and an iron containing substance, haem. By its iron component, haemoglobin is an oxygen carrier; one haemoglobin molecule can combine with four molecules of oxygen. Any deficiency or lack of iron interferes with haemoglobin synthesis and may lead to iron deficiency anaemia (see page 322).

The number of circulating erythrocytes is kept constant and aged erythrocytes are replaced by new ones.

At the end of their lifespan, aged erythrocytes are removed by phagocytic cells chiefly in the spleen but also in the liver and bone marrow. Phagocytosed red cells are broken down into globin and haem. The iron component of haem is retained in the body and transported back to the bone marrow for new haemoglobin synthesis. The other component of haem is converted into bilirubin. Bilirubin is released into the blood and transported to the liver where the liver cells, after processing, excrete it into the bile. Hence bilirubin is a bile pigment. In conditions of excessive red cell breakdown, i.e. in haemolytic anaemia, the liver may not be able to cope with the increased demand and the concentration of bilirubin in the blood may remain high causing jaundice. In a jaundiced animal, the normally pink mucous membranes become yellow and this can be detected by the examination of the lining of the mouth.

Erythropoiesis or formation of erythrocytes

This takes place in the bone marrow and is regulated by EPO. Red cell precursors make up approximately half or one-third of the cells in the bone marrow. The time required for erythropoiesis to proceed from the stem cell to the reticulocyte is about 7 days. The nucleated precursor cells undergo three or four divisions and after each division become smaller and show changes in the nucleus and in the cytoplasm. After the last division, the cells lose their nuclei and their cytoplasms become fully haemoglobinized. These young red cells are the reticulocytes.

Reticulocytes

These are larger than mature circulating red cells and stain bluish with normal haematological stains. With special stains, e.g. with methylene blue, the cells show a fine net of reticulum due to the presence of proteins, hence the name reticulocyte. With final maturation young cells lose their staining property and reach normal size. Most reticulocytes mature in the bone marrow but some are released into the blood. In normal cats, approximately 0.5–1.0 per cent of the circulating red cells are reticulocytes. The number of reticulocytes may rise significantly in the blood in cases of increased erythropoiesis associated with regenerative anaemias. Normal bone marrow can increase its production up to 10 times. Therefore, counting of reticulocytes in the blood and the resulting reticulocyte count is essential for the assessment of bone marrow activity.

LEUCOCYTES

The number of feline leucocytes in the blood is extremely variable; $5.5–19.5 \times 10^3$ cells can be found in one cubic millimetre of normal blood.

The leucocytes of the peripheral blood are of three main types: granulocytes, monocytes and lymphocytes. Monocytes and lymphocytes are known as mononuclear leucocytes because their nuclei are not lobed.

Granulocytes

These have lobed nuclei and granulated cytoplasm. According to the colour of the cytoplasmic granules, three types of granulocytes can be distinguished. These are the neutrophils, eosinophils and basophils.

Neutrophils

Mature feline neutrophils have twisted coil-like nuclei. The lobulation of the nuclei is not as prominent as that of the dog. Neutrophils are often referred to as polymorphonuclear leucocytes or polymorphs because of their multilobed nuclei. Band neutrophils, which are slightly immature, have smooth U-shaped nuclei. The cytoplasm is pale with very fine pink granulation. The granules contain enzymes and other active materials. Approximately 60–70 per cent of all leucocytes are neutrophils. There is, however, a significant age-related change in the proportion of leucocytes, and in young kittens lymphocytes are the predominating cell type.

The primary function of neutrophils is to phagocytose and digest bacteria that invade the body. In order to perform this function, neutrophils do not remain in the circulation during their lifespan. They spend only 6–10 hours in the blood before emigrating into the tissues where they may either be immediately destroyed or may survive for 10–30 hours.

Eosinophils

The nucleus of a feline eosinophil has two lobes (bilobed) and the cytoplasm contains numerous fine rod-shaped, orange-red granules. Normally, only 1–5 per cent of circulating leucocytes are eosinophils.

Eosinophils are phagocytic cells. They are involved in reactions to foreign protein and to antigen–antibody complexes. Their number increases (which is termed eosinophilia) in certain parasitic infestations and in immune-mediated diseases, such as asthma, hay fever and eosinophilic gastroenteritis.

Basophils

This leucocyte is rarely seen in the blood. The nucleus is slightly lobed or twisted. In the cytoplasm, pale pinkish-purple granules are present. In other species, basophilic granules are more prominent. The granules are rich in histamine, heparin and other substances which act as initiators of inflammation. Basophils play a role in inflammatory and allergic reactions.

Monocytes

These are the largest of the mature leucocytes in the blood. The nucleus is either round or ovoid, or may show various degrees of folding, but it is not as bizarre as the canine one which can assume any shape. The cytoplasm is blue-grey and has a ground glass appearance, and may contain phagocytic vacuoles. From 1 to 4 per cent of leucocytes are monocytes. Monocytes are precursors of tissue macrophages. The monocyte-macrophage has three functions: (1) defence against microorganisms; (2) removal of damaged cells and debris; and (3) interaction with the immune system.

Lymphocytes

In adult cats approximately 30 per cent of leucocytes are lymphocytes. These have round or slightly indented nuclei and a thin rim of cytoplasm.

Two distinct types of lymphocytes are recognized, the B-cells and the T-cells. Lymphocytes are involved in cell-mediated and humoral immune reactions (see Chapter 24, Feline Immunology).

LEUCOPOIESIS OR FORMATION OF LEUCOCYTES

All types of granulocytes are produced in the bone marrow under the influence of a number of growth factors (see page 313, Haemopoiesis). Late precursor cells proliferate and after each cell division the size of the cells and the shape of their nuclei change. At a certain stage, the specific granules appear in the cytoplasm. These proliferating cells make up the *mitotic pool* of the bone marrow. After mitotic activity ceases, cells undergo further maturation and the nuclei become U-shaped (band cells) and finally multilobed. Proliferation and maturation of granulocytes take 4–7 days. Mature cells enter the *storage pool* of the bone marrow which ensures that a ready supply of cells is at once available to meet urgent demand, as in acute infection. Dogs have larger storage capacity than cats and this explains the fact that dogs have a higher number of neutrophils in the blood when responding to infection.

After entering the blood, granulocytes either circulate in the blood (*circulating pool*) or adhere to the walls of the blood vessels (*marginal pool*). In the cat, three times more granulocytes are in the marginal pool than in the circulating pool. In a blood sample only the granulocytes of the circulating pool are present.

The number of granulocytes in the *peripheral blood* can rapidly change, i.e. increase or decrease, due to the fact that cells are either shifted from the bone marrow or from the marginal pool into the circulating pool. Cells may leave the circulation and enter the tissues more rapidly than they are being replaced by the bone marrow, particularly if the marrow's storage pool is already exhausted by great demand.

Production of mature monocytes requires 24 hours. They appear transitorily in the blood, circulate for 1–3 days and emigrate into the tissues. In the tissues, monocytes are transformed into actively phagocytic macrophages. Macrophages occur in many organs but they are particularly numerous and active in the spleen, liver, lung and in the thoracic and abdominal cavities.

Production and function of lymphocytes are discussed below.

PRODUCTION OF LYMPHOCYTES

Bone marrow is the site of production of all blood cells. All cells are derived from multipotential primitive stem cells. The myeloid stem cells have the capacity to produce precursor cells of erythrocytes, granulocytes, monocytes and megakaryocytes (these are the platelet producing cells). The lymphoid stem cells produce the early precursors of T lymphocytes (T-cells) and B lymphocytes (B-cells).

T-cell precursors leave the bone marrow and migrate to the thymus during foetal development. B-cell precursors remain in the bone marrow and arise continuously throughout life.

Mature T-cells and B-cells are produced in the thymus and bone marrow respectively, hence the thymus and the bone marrow are regarded as the primary lymphoid tissues. The primary lymphoid tissues provide the microenvironment for the maturation and differentiation of T-cells and B-cells. In this differentiation, both the T-cells and B-cells acquire their repertoire of specific antigen receptors, i.e. T-cell receptors on T-cells and immunoglobulins on B-cells, in order to cope with the antigenic challenges the individual receives during its life. A diversity of T- and B-cells are generated with receptors to recognize an essentially infinite number of antigens. T-cells also learn to discriminate between self antigens, which are tolerated, and non-self antigens, which are not.

T lymphocytes are the major contributors of cell-mediated immunity. On the basis of their cell surface receptors and function, T-cells can be divided into sub-populations. These are the helper, cytotoxic and suppressor cells. Helper T-cells help B-cells in the production of antibodies, and cytotoxic cells are responsible for killing tissue cells infected with viruses or intracellular bacteria. Suppressor cells possibly have a regulatory role in suppressing the immune response.

In the primary lymphoid tissues, lymphocytes are not exposed to antigens; therefore, their differentiation and maturation is *antigen-independent*.

After maturation, T-cells and B-cells leave the thymus and bone marrow and migrate into the specific T-cell and B-cell dependent areas of the secondary lymphoid tissues, which include the lymph nodes, spleen and mucosal associated tissues, e.g. tonsils and Peyer's patches of the gut. The secondary lymphoid tissues create the environment in which lymphocytes can interact with each other and with antigens. Once in the secondary tissues, the lymphocytes do not remain there, but many of them move from one lymphoid tissue to another through blood and lymphatics. The overall

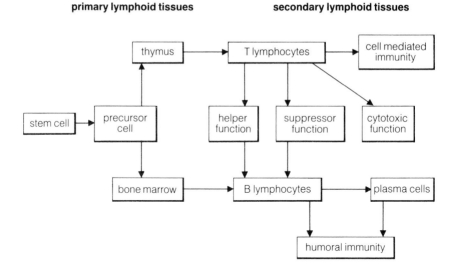

Figure 112　Origin and function of lymphocytes

effect of this process allows a large number of antigen-specific lymphocytes to come into contact with their appropriate antigen.

T-cells are activated by antigens in the paracortical areas of the lymph nodes, where the activated cells increase in number and become effective or memory cells.

B lymphocytes are involved in humoral immunity, i.e. in the production of antibodies, which are large protein molecules secreted into body fluids by plasma cells.

B-cells are activated by the binding of a specific antigen to the surface receptors. Multiplication of activated B-cells produces a clone of cells specific for that antigen. This clone of cells differentiates into plasma cells and also into B-memory cells. Memory cells are extremely long-lived and can subsequently be reactivated by contact with the same antigen to produce more plasma cells and antibodies in secondary immune responses.

Clonal expansion of activated B-cells takes place in the follicles of the lymph nodes. Activated cells migrate out of the follicles into the medullary cords, where they differentiate further into plasma cells and secrete antibodies. Activated cells (plasmablasts) migrate to other sites as well, such as the bone marrow, where they differentiate into plasma cells. Hence, plasma cells can be found in the bone marrow and their number may increase in cases of infection. Normally, plasma cells are not encountered in the peripheral blood.

In multiple myeloma, which is a rare lymphoproliferative disorder, a clone of neoplastic (cancerous) plasma cells replace the bone marrow, and in such cases plasma cells may be found in the blood.

Disorders of the blood

The main disorders of the blood are anaemia, polycythaemia and leucocyte abnormalities. These are discussed below. Disorders associated with bleeding problems and cancers of the blood cells will be considered in the following sections.

ANAEMIA

This is defined as a reduction in the number of circulating erythrocytes or in the haemoglobin concentration of the blood, or both. Anaemia is rarely a primary disease; usually it is only the result of a generalized disease process. Anaemia is a fairly common finding in cats and severely affected animals often die.

The clinical signs of anaemia are associated with the reduced oxygen carrying capacity of the blood. The clinical signs in the cat are the same as in other species, i.e. weakness, lethargy, pallor, cold sensitivity and occasionally jaundice. Anaemic cats often eat earth, or other unnatural materials, which behaviour is referred to as *pica*. Because of their relaxed lifestyle, cats may become severely anaemic before the condition is recognized by the owners.

Clinical investigation and examination of a blood sample are required to determine the cause of anaemia. Anaemias can be caused either by increased red cell loss or destruction, or by decreased red cell production. Anaemias may be described as regenerative or non-regenerative.

The term 'regenerative' indicates that the bone marrow is responding to the anaemia by increased red cell production, i.e. the bone marrow is hyperplastic.

Examination of a blood film under the microscope shows changes characteristic of a regenerative blood picture, e.g. many young bluish red cells, and, particularly in the cat, numerous nucleated red cell precursors which are released from the spleen where extramedullary haemopoiesis is re-established. The most important finding is the high reticulocyte count.

The term 'non-regenerative' describes the fact that the bone marrow is not responding to the anaemia for a variety of reasons, i.e. the bone marrow is hypoplastic or aplastic. Examination of a blood film reveals no significant changes and reticulocytes are scant or totally absent.

Regenerative anaemias

Haemorrhagic anaemia

This type of anaemia is due to direct loss of blood which can be acute or chronic.

If the blood loss is large and sudden, there is a drop in circulating blood volume and hence the onset of shock. Coma and death may follow.

In chronic cases, the blood loss is not severe but goes on for a long time and may lead to the depletion of the iron stores of the body. Lack of iron interferes with haemoglobin synthesis. In this situation, in addition to the loss of red cells, the new cells formed in the bone marrow become smaller and contain very little haemoglobin. Such cells are not able to carry adequate amounts of oxygen and consequently an *iron deficiency anaemia* develops. Only this type of anaemia requires iron supply as a therapy. Causes are as follows:

(a)   Trauma/surgery.
(b)   Infestation by blood sucking parasites: fleas, lice and coccidia in young kittens.
(c)   Rupture of fragile tumours causing bleeding into the abdominal cavity, e.g. haemangioma, haemangiosarcoma.
(d)   Coagulation and platelet disorders, which will be discussed later.

Haemolytic anaemia

Excessive breakdown of red cells may occur either in the blood vessels or red cells may be phagocytosed by macrophages outside the circulation. The former process is termed *intravascular lysis* and the latter *extravascular lysis*. In both cases, destruction of red cells takes place within the body and iron is not lost but reused for new red cell production. Consequently, in haemolytic anaemia iron deficiency will not develop and the bone marrow is able to increase maximally the rate of erythropoiesis resulting in a very high reticulocyte count.

In case of severe intravascular lysis, jaundice and dark-coloured urine may be present due to the large amount of haemoglobin released from the burst erythrocytes into the circulation.

In the case of extravascular lysis, enlargement of the spleen (splenomegaly) may develop due to increased cellularity caused by excessive phagocytosis of erythrocytes and to extramedullary haemopoiesis.

Examination of a stained blood film may help to establish the cause of haemolysis because, in addition to a regenerative blood picture and high reticulocyte count, other features may be present, such as the blood parasite called *Haemobartonella felis*, which can be recognized on the surface of the red cells as small, purple, round or rod-shaped structures.

Lysis of erythrocytes may be caused by infectious agents, toxic oxidant compounds and by antibodies in an immune-mediated process.

The commonest types of haemolytic anaemias in the cat are listed below.

(a)   *Infectious.* Feline haemobartonellosis or feline infectious anaemia (FIA) is caused by parasitism of erythrocytes by an organism known as *Haemobartonella felis*. It is presumed that the disease is transmitted by biting insects such as fleas. Many cats are infected without becoming anaemic, and these are the silent carriers. FIA has been considered to be stress-related, with the implication that stress or intercurrent disease could precipitate the clinical disease in carriers. In fact, there is a correlation between FIA and feline leukaemia virus (FeLV) and feline immunodeficiency virus (FIV) infections. FIA is characterized by recurrent episodes of severe anaemia which may be accompanied by fever or jaundice. Parasite levels in blood seem to increase to a peak value and then decrease spontaneously, sometimes to a point at which blood films become negative. Therefore, infected cats may need to be examined several times in order to make a definite diagnosis.

(b) *Toxic.* Drugs and chemical agents may cause haemolysis by several mechanisms. Use of urinary antiseptics containing methylene blue, phenol compounds and paracetamol intoxication are reported to cause haemolytic anaemia in cats.

(c) *Immune-mediated.* Autoimmune haemolytic anaemia (AIHA) is seen in cats but not nearly as often as in dogs. The disease is caused by sudden appearance of auto-antibodies which are directed against the animal's own erythrocytes. Erythrocytes may be destroyed by intra- or extravascular lysis depending on whether the antibodies are IgG or IgM type (see Chapter 24, Feline Immunology).

Auto-antibodies can react with red cells either at body temperature (warm antibodies) or at lower than body temperatures (cold antibodies). Most AIHA are warm antibody induced. The rare cold antibody AIHA is termed *cold haemagglutinin disease*. In this condition, the IgM type antibodies are activated by low temperature (in cold weather) causing agglutination of red cells within the skin capillaries. Blood flow is impeded and due to lack of oxygen the skin becomes necrotic, particularly on the extremities such as tips of ears, tail and feet.

Non-regenerative anaemias

Anaemias due to reduced red blood cell production are common in cats. These include the secondary and the hypoplastic/aplastic anaemias.

Secondary anaemias

As the name implies, the anaemia is only the consequence of a primary disease which has to be treated first in order to re-establish normal erythropoiesis.

The commonest disorders associated with secondary anaemia are the following:

(a) *Anaemia of chronic inflammatory disease.* This is frequently seen in feline infectious peritonitis (FIP),* chronic abscessation, pyometra and in cancerous diseases, e.g. in lymphosarcoma. Certain substances are

* Feline infectious peritonitis (FIP) is caused by a feline coronavirus (FCoV).

released from the inflammatory lesions which interfere with iron utilization for haemoglobin synthesis, thus causing non-regenerative anaemia.

(b) *Anaemia of chronic kidney failure.* As discussed, erythropoietin is produced by the kidney and it is essential for erythropoiesis. In chronic renal disease, erythropoietin levels fall in the circulation causing depression of erythropoiesis and a non-regenerative anaemia. Other cell lines of the bone marrow are not affected.

(c) *Anaemia associated with replacement of the bone marrow (Myelophthisic anaemia).* Malignant transformation of one, two or all haemopoietic cell lines may occur in the bone marrow, which condition is referred to as leukaemia. Leukaemic cells proliferate and eventually replace the normal haemopoietic cells causing not only anaemia but low neutrophil numbers (neutropaenia) and reduced platelet numbers (thrombocytopaenia).

Tumours, such as lymphosarcoma, adenocarcinoma, from other parts of the body may also invade the bone marrow causing similar changes.

(d) *Anaemia associated with FeLV infection.* A large proportion of anaemic cats are FeLV positive. FeLV infection can induce haemolytic or hypoplastic anaemia. Due to its immunosuppressive effect, FeLV infection also predisposes cats to infection by *Haemobartonella felis*.

Haemolytic anaemia is moderately severe and often transient. It is believed to be immune-mediated.

Hypoplastic anaemia is the commonest finding in FeLV-infected cats. FeLV selectively affects the precursor cells of erythrocytes in the bone marrow causing erythroid hypoplasia and severe non-regenerative anaemia. Granulocytes and platelets are not affected. The long-term prognosis of these cases is very poor.

Hypoplastic/aplastic anaemias

The terms 'hypoplastic' and 'aplastic' imply that the cellularity of the bone marrow is moderately or severely reduced. Aplastic anaemia is caused by certain toxic agents, irradiation and drugs such as chloramphenicol and phenylbutazone, which should always be used with care. Cat marrow is particularly sensitive to aspirin and aspirin therapy should only be given under strict veterinary supervision. All toxic drugs should be withdrawn in any cases of non-regenerative anaemia.

Examination of a blood sample shows no reticulocytes. The main finding is pancytopaenia.

Pancytopaenia is the reduction or absence of platelets, granulocytes and erythrocytes in the circulating blood. The consequences of pancytopaenia are haemorrhagic problems, recurrent infections and anaemia. Occasionally, only one cell line may be affected (see FeLV infection).

SUMMARY OF ANAEMIAS

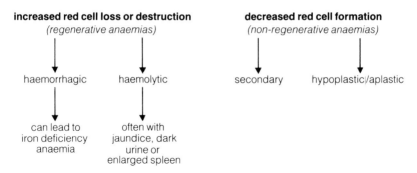

Figure 113 Summary of anaemias

POLYCYTHAEMIA

Polycythaemia is an abnormal increase of mature erythrocytes in the circulation. It can be absolute or relative. Absolute polycythaemia is the result of excessive levels of erythropoietin which is either produced by certain tumours of the kidney or is the consequence of constant lack of oxygen associated with diseases such as congenital heart disease or chronic lung disease.

Relative polycythaemia is due to low plasma volume which occurs in dehydrated animals as a result of high fever, severe diarrhoea or vomiting.

ABNORMALITIES OF LEUCOCYTES

A routine haematological test gives information about the numbers of all circulating leucocytes (total white blood cell count) and about the numbers of the various types of leucocytes (differential count). The former is expressed in absolute numbers, e.g. WBC $12 \times 10^3/\text{cm}^3$, and the latter is expressed either in percentage or in absolute numbers, e.g. neutrophils 60 per cent or $7.2 \times 10^3/\text{cm}^3$. On the basis of the cell counts, the following leucocyte abnormalities can be established.

Leukopaenia

If the number of leucocytes is below the established normal range the term leukopaenia is used.

Leukopaenia is common in cats and is often severe. Leukopaenia is frequently due to a low neutrophil count (neutropaenia) and sometimes to a low lymphocyte count (lymphopaenia).

In *panleukopaenia*, all types of leucocytes are depressed. Panleukopaenic cats should always be investigated for the viral disease known as feline infectious enteritis (FIE). In the cat, leukopaenia may be associated with severe, overwhelming bacterial infections or viral infections such as FIE, FeLV and FIV infections. The FeLV (feline leukaemia virus) and FIV (feline immunodeficiency virus) status of all leukopaenic cats should be determined.

Leukopaenia may also be the consequence of bone marrow hypoplasia/aplasia or acute leukaemia, or myelodysplasia which is a preleukaemic condition (see page 332).

Leucocytosis

This term is used when there is an increase in the number of leucocytes above the established normal range. Leucocytosis may be physiological or it may be a response to inflammation.

Physiological leucocytosis is a frequent finding in young cats. It may be induced by fear, excitement or rough handling and the numbers of lymphocytes and neutrophils are equally elevated. In inflammatory conditions, leucocytosis is caused by increased numbers of neutrophils, i.e. by neutrophilia.

Neutrophilia

The main cause of this condition is bacterial infection. Usually immature neutrophils are present in the blood, which is termed a left shift. Often toxic changes, such as blue inclusions (Döhle bodies), are seen in the cytoplasm of the neutrophils.

Neutrophilia is also a common finding in cases of trauma, necrosis, haemorrhage and haemolysis.

Stress-induced leucocyte changes

The main findings include low lymphocyte and eosinophil numbers (lymphopaenia and eosinopaenia) and neutrophilia, which is due to shifting of neutrophils from the marginal pool into the circulating pool, hence there is no left shift. Increased monocyte count (monocytosis), which occurs in dogs, is not a prominent feature in cats.

Haemostasis – haemorrhagic disorders

Haemostasis is the physiological process which arrests haemorrhage and it is achieved by complex interactions between coagulation factors, platelets and the blood vessels. Abnormalities of each of these three main components of the haemostatic mechanism can cause haemorrhagic disorders. Before discussing individual haemorrhagic disorders, a brief and simplified account will be given of the normal mechanism which prevents spontaneous haemorrhage and blood loss from injured vessels.

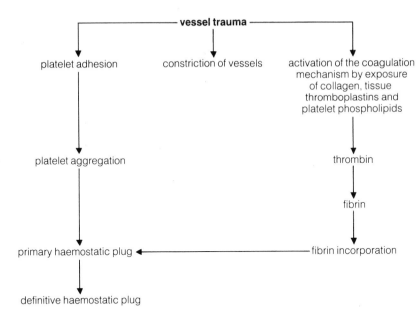

Figure 114   Normal haemostatic mechanism

Immediately after injury, platelets aggregate at the site of the damage to the blood vessel and form a plug to prevent escape of blood. This primary platelet plug is loose but it becomes stabilized by deposition of fibrin. From the site of damage, a substance called thromboplastin is released. At the same time, from the granules of the platelets, active materials, such as phospholipids, are also released. Thromboplastin and platelet phospholipids activate the coagulation mechanism which ultimately results in fibrin formation.

DISORDERS OF THE PLATELETS

Platelets or thrombocytes are formed in the bone marrow. The precursor cells of the platelets are the megakaryocytes, which are derived from the multipotential haemopoietic stem cell. Megakaryocytes are very large cells with multilobed nuclei and extensive granulated cytoplasm. Platelets are formed by the fragmentation of the cytoplasm, hence platelets do not have nuclei. Proliferation and maturation of megakaryocytes and release of platelets from the bone marrow are regulated by a number of growth factors.

Platelets of the cat are small round bodies with a central cluster of purple-reddish granules enclosed in a delicate membrane. The size is variable, and some of them may be as large as an erythrocyte.

Upon entering the circulation platelets are concentrated in the spleen for 3–4 days. At any one time, approximately one-third of platelets are in the spleen. Platelet survival time is between 10 and 12 days.

Thrombocytopaenia

In the cat, this is the commonest platelet disorder. Thrombocytopaenia is caused by an abnormally low number of platelets in the blood. If there is a deficit in platelets the primary platelet plug cannot be formed and bleeding is not stopped at the site of vessel injury.

Thrombocytopaenia is associated with small pin-point type of haemorrhages (petechiae) on the mucous membranes and with a prolonged bleeding time.

Thrombocytopaenia may occur either as a result of increased destruction (immune-mediated), increased utilization (DIC, see below) or decreased production of platelets due to deficit or absence of megakaryocytes in the bone marrow (marrow aplasia, leukaemia).

DISORDERS OF THE COAGULATION MECHANISM

Platelets, ionized calcium and a number of coagulation factors are required for an unimpeded coagulation mechanism. The majority of coagulation factors are proteins and are synthesized in the liver. Their production is dependent upon an adequate supply of vitamin K. Coagulation factors are often referred to by Roman numerals, e.g. Factor I, II, III, and so on. The individual factors normally circulate in an inactive form and the product of their activation is fibrin.

Disorders of the coagulation mechanism include the acquired and the hereditary deficiencies of coagulation factors. In acquired conditions, deficiencies of multiple coagulation factors occur, while in hereditary conditions, only a single coagulation factor is deficient or absent.

Abnormalities of the coagulation mechanism result in prolonged fibrin formation, and in such cases the primary platelet plug cannot be strengthened by fibrin deposition. It will eventually be broken up by the blood flow resulting in prolonged bleeding.

The clinical signs of coagulation defects are fairly typical; these are protracted bleeding from minor wounds and spontaneous and deep haematomas.

Acquired coagulation abnormalities

Acquired defects are most commonly due to certain drugs, vitamin K deficiency, vitamin K antagonists (coumarin) or to liver disease.

The rat poison Warfarin contains coumarin derivatives. It is widely believed that cats, unlike dogs, will not eat bait but this is certainly untrue and cats may even eat poisoned vermin. The commonest presenting sign is haemorrhage into the lungs, but bleeding from other sites is also present and the bleeding may be present in skin and gums as well as in internal organs.

Congenital coagulation abnormalities

In the cat, deficiencies of Factors VIII, IX and XII have been recorded but these are rare conditions.

Haemophilia is deficiency or absence of Factor VIII. It is inherited in such a way that only male animals manifest a bleeding tendency, which can be detected at a very young age.

In order to establish the cause of haemorrhagic disease, first the number of platelets should be estimated. If the platelet count is within normal range, the coagulation mechanism should be investigated by performing coagulation tests which will show prolonged clotting time in case of a disorder.

COMBINED PLATELET AND COAGULATION DISORDER

Disseminated intravascular coagulation (DIC)

Any disease causing stagnation of the blood flow or breakdown of the inner (endothelial) layer of the small blood vessels may contribute to the development of DIC which is a life-threatening condition.

In the case of DIC, spontaneous clot formation occurs in the small vessels affecting the whole vascular system. Circulating platelets and all the coagulation factors are used up by the excessive clotting process causing thrombocytopaenia, prolonged clotting time and consequently a haemorrhagic problem. In order to break down the fibrin clots, automatic activation of the fibrinolytic mechanism takes place resulting in increased amounts of fibrin degradation products (FDP) in the blood. Presence of FDP aggravates the situation because they interfere with primary platelet plug formation and increase the bleeding tendency.

Activation of coagulation in DIC may be caused by a number of factors, such as vascular damage, bacterial endotoxins, release of thromboplastins from necrotic and malignant tissues and overdoses of cytotoxic drugs used for treatment of cancer. The changes seen in DIC can result in mild or severe spontaneous bleeding, in shock and in obstruction of small vessels leading to tissue necrosis and organ failure, such as 'shock lung' and acute renal failure.

Few cases of DIC have been reported in cats. In feline infectious peritonitis, chronic DIC syndrome may develop with thrombocytopaenia, lowered levels of coagulation factors and elevated FDP levels.

Since DIC is secondary to a severe disease, the primary disease has to be treated first. After this, blood transfusion and anticoagulant (heparin) therapy can be tried but the prognosis is poor.

Neoplastic diseases of the haemopoietic system

Haemopoietic tumours (neoplasms) may arise either from the lymphoid or from the haemopoietic (myeloid) cell lines and these are the lymphoproliferative and myeloproliferative disorders.

Haemopoietic tumours are common in cats and are strongly associated with feline leukaemia virus (FeLV) infection. FeLV can affect each of the haemopoietic cell types causing abnormal proliferation of cells resulting in neoplastic diseases. More frequently, however, FeLV infection induces non-malignant haemopoietic disease, such as anaemia, marrow aplasia/dysplasia and immunosuppression.

LYMPHOPROLIFERATIVE DISORDERS

In the cat, approximately 90 per cent of haemopoietic tumours involve the lymphoid cells. Lymphosarcoma and lymphoid leukaemia are the main presenting forms.

Lymphosarcoma or malignant lymphoma

These are the solid tumours of the peripheral lymphoid organs. Lymphosarcoma is the commonest neoplasia of cats. Lymphosarcoma may develop in any of the peripheral lymphoid organs and, depending on the localization, the following forms may occur:

(a) *Multicentric*. Bilateral enlargement of the lymph nodes. Average age of affected cats is about 4 years.
(b) *Alimentary*. Tumour mass is present in the bowel or stomach. Associated with weight loss, anorexia, wasting and vomiting or diarrhoea. It occurs in older cats.
(c) *Thymic*. Mass is present in the upper frontal area of the chest causing displacement of the windpipe (trachea) and consequently difficulty in breathing, and exercise intolerance. Young animals are mainly affected.
(d) *Other rare forms*. Skin, kidney or eye may be the only organ affected. Lymphosarcoma of the kidney is the commonest type seen in cats.

Many cases of lymphosarcoma are FeLV negative and most of these cases are the alimentary type. The role of FeLV in the development of such tumours is not known.

Lymphoid leukaemias

The term 'leukaemia' implies that neoplastic (cancerous) haemopoietic cells are present in the bone marrow and in the peripheral blood. Leukaemic cells arise in the bone marrow and replace the normal haemopoietic precursor cells causing anaemia, neutropaenia and thrombocytopaenia. The ensuing severe anaemia, increased susceptibility to infection and haemorrhagic problems are the fatal consequences of leukaemia.

Leukaemic cells are released into the circulation and may be present in low, moderate or very high numbers. Examination of a blood sample, including a blood film, is essential for the diagnosis of leukaemia. In some cases, additional examination of the bone marrow is required.

The two main groups of leukaemias are the myeloid and the lymphoid leukaemias (myeloid leukaemia is discussed below). Leukaemias may also be described as acute or chronic.

In the cat, lymphoid leukaemia is usually acute lymphoblastic characterized by the presence of immature lymphoblasts in the blood and bone marrow and by a rapid course of disease.

Occasionally, chronic lymphocytic leukaemia is seen characterized by a high number of mature lymphocytes in the blood and bone marrow. The onset of the disease is more insidious and it has a more protracted course than the acute lymphoblastic type.

In most cases of lymphosarcoma, no neoplastic lymphoid cells are present in the blood, but in some cases secondary involvement of the bone marrow and development of leukaemia may occur.

MYELOPROLIFERATIVE DISORDERS

These include the acute and chronic myeloid leukaemias and myelodysplasia. The latter is considered to be a preleukaemic condition. Myeloproliferative diseases are less common than lymphoproliferative conditions.

Myeloid leukaemias

These are the cancers of the cell lines which are derived from the haemopoietic (myeloid) stem cell, i.e. granulocytic, monocytic, erythroid and megakaryocytic cell lines. The term 'myeloid' is often used as a synonym for 'granulocytic' because granulocytic leukaemia is the commonest myeloid leukaemia.

Acute myeloid leukaemias are characterized by proliferation of blast cells and other immature cell forms while chronic myeloid leukaemias are characterized by proliferation of well differentiated mature cells.

Often more than one cell line is involved, e.g. granulocytes and monocytes in myelomonocytic leukaemia, and granulocytes and erythroid precursors in erythroleukaemia. The spectrum of cell types may change in time in a particular animal. Cancer of red cell precursors (erythroid myelosis) may change into erythroleukaemia and eventually into acute granulocytic (myeloid) leukaemia in a particular cat.

Table 8 Myeloid leukaemias encountered in cats

Type	Frequency
Acute granulocytic (myeloid) leukaemia	rare
Monocytic leukaemia	rare
Myelomonocytic leukaemia	rare
Erythroid myelosis	rare
Erythroleukaemia	rare
Megakaryocytic myelosis	rare
Chronic granulocytic (myeloid) leukaemia	most common type
Chronic eosinophilic leukaemia	rare

Presenting signs and consequences of myeloid leukaemias are similar to those of lymphoid leukaemias. They are caused by interference with normal haemopoiesis which leads to the development of progressive anaemia, recurrent bacterial infections and, if thrombocytopaenia develops, haemorrhages on mucous membranes.

Myelodysplasia/preleukaemia

This is a condition characterized by unexplained, transient low cell counts, such as anaemia, low white cell count and low platelet count. No abnormal cells are present in the blood but examination of the bone marrow shows evidence of abnormal maturation of the cell lines. This condition can last for weeks, months or even years, depending on the severity of the disease. Leukaemia may develop in some cases.

Myelodysplasia is relatively common in cats. Many cats, but not all, are FeLV positive. Affected animals usually die from complications such as anaemia, bacterial infections or haemorrhage.

Haematological tests

The main, and simplest, techniques used in clinical haematology are aimed at enumerating the different cell types of the blood and estimating the amount of haemoglobin both in the blood and in the individual erythrocyte.

The tests normally performed are as follows:

(a) Haemoglobin estimation
(b) Haematocrit (packed cell volume) estimation
(c) Red cell count
(d) White cell count
(e) Differential white cell count
(f) Reticulocyte count
(g) Platelet count

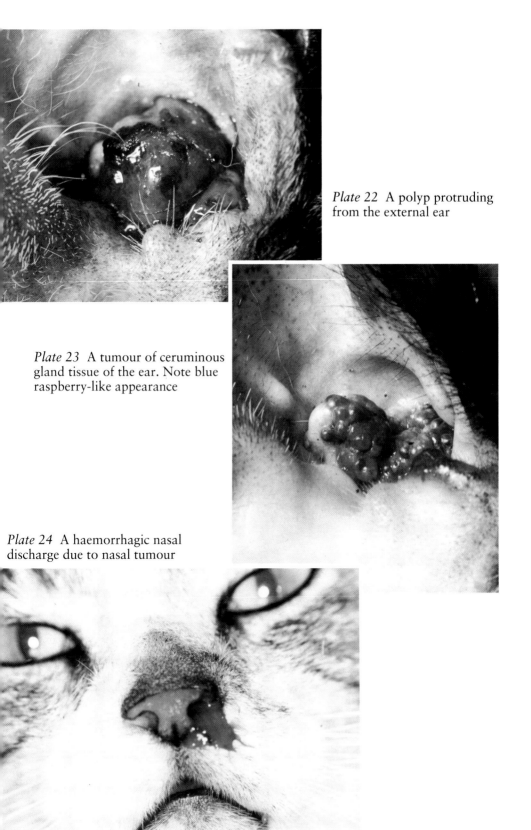

Plate 22 A polyp protruding from the external ear

Plate 23 A tumour of ceruminous gland tissue of the ear. Note blue raspberry-like appearance

Plate 24 A haemorrhagic nasal discharge due to nasal tumour

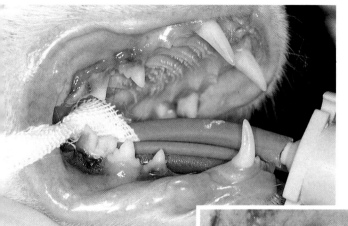

Plate 25 Periodontal disease – moderate to severe accumulation of calculus with gingivitis, pocketing and recession

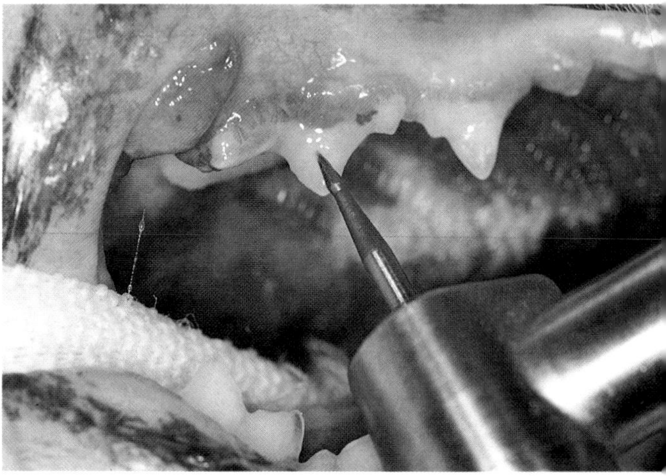

Plate 26 Rotosonic scaling of teeth with periodontal bit in high speed hand piece

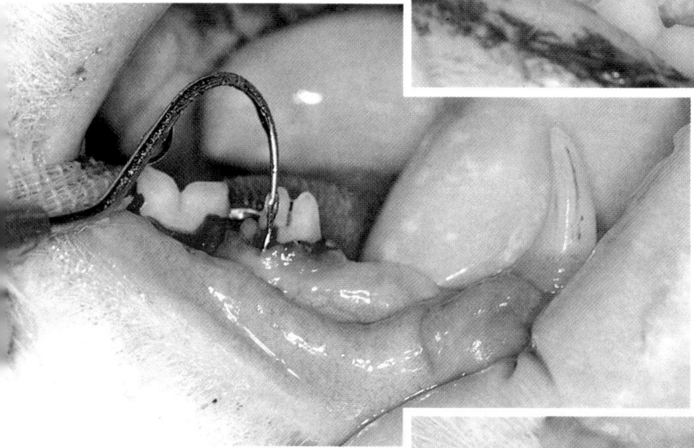

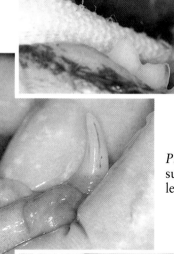

Plate 27 Probing sulcus for subgingival tartar and/or neck lesions

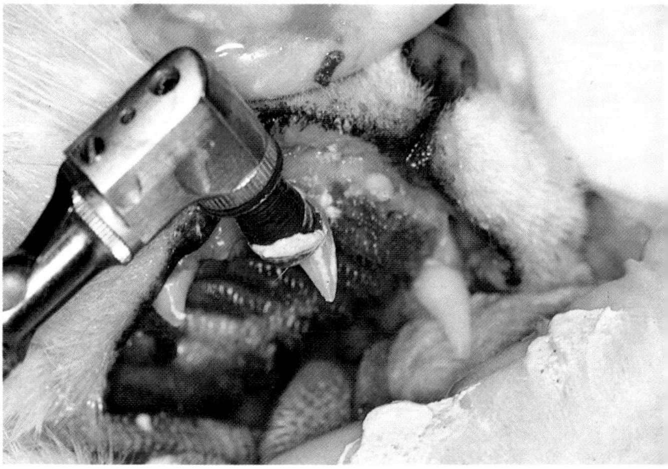

Plate 28 Polishing teeth after scaling with prophy paste and rubber cup in slow hand piece

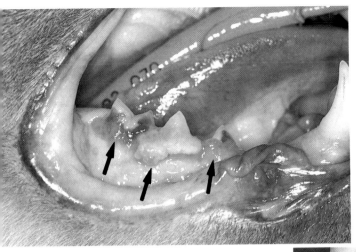

Left: Plate 29 Neck lesions on lower premolars and adjacent molar

Below: Plate 30 Left upper canine showing fractured tip. Gumboil is result of root abscess (see also X-rays on page 239)

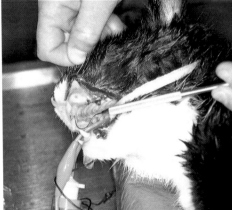

Below: Plate 31 Cat with conjunctivitis resulting from cat flu infection

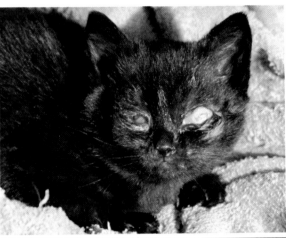

Below left: Plate 32 Corneal ulcer due to feline herpesvirus (FHV)

Below: Plate 33 Ulcers on the tongue caused by feline calicivirus (FCV)

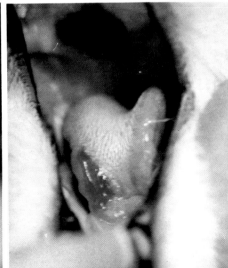

Plate 34 Cat with a swollen abdomen due to feline infectious peritonitis (FIP)

Plate 35 Inflammation of the iris (iritis) due to feline infectious peritonitis

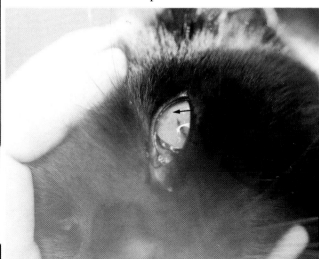

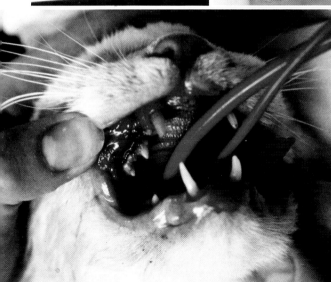

Plate 36 Gingivitis associated with feline immunodeficiency virus (FIV)

Plate 37 Shaved base of tail area showing burst abscess

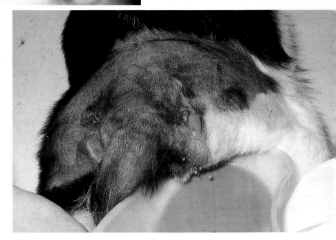

Where haematological abnormality is suspected, most or all of these are performed.

There are other specific tests which can be carried out if required, e.g. clotting tests, estimation of fibrinogen and fibrin degradation products, cross-matching of blood for blood transfusion and many others.

BLOOD TRANSFUSION

Erythrocytes of domestic animals possess several species specific antigens belonging to many different blood group systems. Blood group antigens vary in antigenicity, i.e. they may evoke either strong or weak antibody response. Naturally occurring antibodies to some red cell antigens are also present in the blood.

Unlike man, animals have weak antigens on their erythrocytes and naturally occurring antibodies are rare in the serum. Therefore, most animals can be transfused on a single occasion without great risk. If, however, more than one transfusion is required and if the recipient is a female animal, the blood of the donor and recipient should always be cross-matched in order to ensure that the donor and recipient belong to the same blood group. Cats are less frequently transfused than dogs because donor cats are not as readily available as donor dogs.

20

DISORDERS OF THE ENDOCRINE SYSTEM

As has already been described in Chapter 8, the cat, in common with other mammals, possesses 7 major endocrine glands, the positions of which within the body are illustrated in Figure 115. The secretions of the endocrine glands, known as hormones, generally act at a number of different sites in the body altering the rate at which particular reactions take place. Consequently disorders of hormone production frequently produce a variety of clinical signs. Although other organs, such as the stomach, kidney and liver, also produce hormones they are not regarded *primarily* as endocrine glands. The role of the ovaries in producing the female hormones oestrogen and progesterone, and that of the testes in producing the male sex hormone testosterone, is bound up with the subject of reproduction, and disorders of reproduction are therefore best dealt with under that heading (Chapter 17). Disorders of the other major endocrine glands are dealt with in this chapter.

The predominant endocrine disorders in the cat are hyperthyroidism and diabetes mellitus. Although other endocrine conditions do occur they are much less prevalent than in the dog.

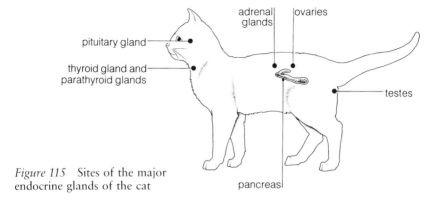

Figure 115 Sites of the major endocrine glands of the cat

Disorders of the thyroid gland

The major thyroid disorder of the cat is hyperthyroidism; the contrary situation, hypothyroidism, can occur but does so much less frequently.

HYPERTHYROIDISM

This condition is caused by the excessive and unregulated secretion of the metabolic hormones thyroxine (otherwise known as T4) and tri-iodothyronine (T3) by a tumour of the thyroid gland. Collectively these two hormones are usually referred to simply as thyroid hormone. Hyperthyroidism is the most common endocrine disorder of the cat.

Hyperthyroidism arises in cats in or beyond middle age; their average age at the time of diagnosis is 13 years. No case has yet been diagnosed in a cat under 6 years of age. There are no breed or sex predispositions.

In 98 per cent of cats the tumour responsible for this increased output of hormone is of the benign type (an adenoma) rather than malignant (a carcinoma). This means that usually the tumour does not spread to other parts of the body, either those nearby or more distant organs, as is common in cancer. One or both of the thyroid lobes may be affected.

The presence of a tumour results in discernible enlargement of the affected lobe(s) in almost every case (96 per cent). This enlargement is termed a goitre, but it is seldom readily visible, particularly in longhaired cats. Detection of the goitre needs to be made by careful palpation of the neck, feeling up and down the jugular furrows, but even then, because the thyroid lobes are very loosely attached, they may at times slip behind the trachea or even down into the chest (thorax). To detect an intrathoracic goitre can require the use of general anaesthesia or heavy sedation to allow the cat to be held vertically with its head downwards so that the affected lobe falls back into a position where it can be felt.

The underlying problem of the increased output of metabolic hormones increases the cat's metabolic rate, i.e. the rate of working of the body's tissues and organs, with an increased demand for, and use of, energy. It results in a number of signs, especially loss of weight and increased appetite. Weight loss may however be slow and insidious so that it is first noticed by occasional visitors rather than the owners. Finicky eaters may develop tremendous appetites, even raiding dustbins and stealing their owner's food. In many cases the coat is unkempt with some hair loss (see Fig. 116) and these cats seldom groom themselves, presumably because they find it difficult to settle.

Muscular weakness, trembling, intolerance of heat (seeking cool places to lie), hyperactivity, nervousness, panting, diarrhoea, vomiting, an anxious facial expression and aggressiveness can all result from the increase in metabolic rate. Because of the effect of thyroid hormone on the

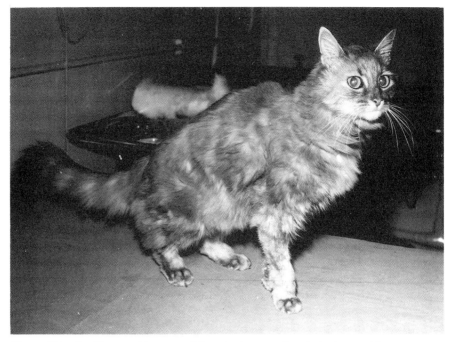

Figure 116   An 11-year-old neutered female domestic longhaired cat with hyperthyroidism. A bilateral goitre is present and the cat has a typically unkempt appearance. (Courtesy of Dr K. L. Thoday)

kidneys, many cats produce more urine, and then drink an increased amount of water to compensate, i.e. to prevent dehydration. Unfortunately it seems likely that in the past the combination of increased drinking and deteriorating bodily condition led to many hyperthyroid cats being diagnosed as cases of renal disease. Heart failure and diabetes mellitus are common complications of feline hyperthyroidism.

Although it may seem paradoxical, 8–10 per cent of hyperthyroid cats are brought to veterinary surgeons because of contradictory signs, i.e. apathy and a decreased appetite. These indicate a deteriorating stage of the condition, usually associated with severe heart disease.

Diagnosis of hyperthyroidism is made on the finding of increased concentrations of thyroid hormone in the blood, though in early cases additional test procedures may be required.

Usually the preferred treatment is surgical removal of the affected thyroid lobe(s), and this is best preceded by a period of drug treatment to reduce the output of thyroid hormone and to control excitement and the rapid heart rate. There are complications, although these are treatable, where bilateral surgery is required, because not only is all thyroid tissue removed but also all the parathyroid glands. Animals that are a poor anaesthetic risk may be *permanently* maintained on such drug therapy, although long-term side effects are common and recurrences of hyperthyroidism may occur. In such animals, therefore, the administration of radioactive iodine to reduce the amount of functional thyroid tissue may give better results, but this procedure can only be performed at licensed centres.

HYPOTHYROIDISM

Spontaneous hypothyroidism in the cat is a rarity and the majority of cases result from bilateral thyroid lobe excision, or excessive dosage with radioactive iodine, as treatment for hyperthyroidism. The reduction in metabolic rate which follows most frequently results in lethargy and obesity. Alopecia is one of a number of skin changes that can develop. Classically it is a bilaterally symmetrical, non-pruritic alopecia, meaning that the pattern of hair loss is more or less identical on both the right and left sides of the body and that the animal shows no signs of itching and scratching. This typical endocrine alopecia is also seen in other hormonal disorders, e.g. Cushing's syndrome (see page 341). In all these conditions, rather than a few hairs 'dying' at any one time and being replaced by new hairs growing from the same hair follicles, most of the hairs, particularly in certain areas, 'die' simultaneously but still remain in the follicles because there is no new hair growth to push them out. Initially the sides of the neck, chest and abdomen are affected. The skin is thickened and the coat is dry and lustreless. Queens may also fail to have normal reproductive cycles.

The recommended therapy for hypothyroidism is daily supplementation with thyroid hormone (usually thyroxine), which is capable of reversing all the clinical manifestations.

Endocrine disorders of the pancreas

DIABETES MELLITUS

This is a complex disorder of carbohydrate, fat and protein metabolism caused by the inability to produce, or to utilize, adequate amounts of insulin. It can arise in cats of any age or breed but most cases are diagnosed in cats of 6 years of age or older, and it is felt that there may be a predisposition in the Siamese breed. It also appears to be more common in males.

Two major types of diabetes mellitus are recognized. The classic form is Type I (or insulin-dependent) diabetes mellitus which arises from a lack of functional beta cells resulting in a deficiency of the hormone insulin (hypoinsulinism). In the cat the cause of this loss of functional cells is unclear; in over half such cases an inert glycoprotein, amyloid, is deposited in the beta cells but this is now thought to be a *result* of diabetes mellitus rather than the cause. It is believed that a combination of genetic susceptibility and environmental factors, such as a viral infection, are necessary for Type I diabetes mellitus to develop.

In recent years it has become clear that diabetes mellitus can also develop when body cells fail to respond to insulin, i.e. when the body develops insulin resistance. This type of diabetes mellitus (Type II or non-insulin-dependent diabetes mellitus) may involve an inherited predisposition to insulin resistance as well as factors which create resistance. It can result from overeating (because in obesity the number of receptor sites where insulin can act is reduced) or from an excess of other hormones. In the cat thyroid hormone in particular is known to interfere with the action of insulin, and a high proportion of cats suffering from hyperthyroidism develop diabetes mellitus secondarily. Also progesterone-like drugs (progestagens) such as megestrol acetate (which may be given to prevent or postpone oestrus and to treat certain types of skin disorder) can induce diabetes mellitus, and the signs (see below) persist throughout the period of treatment.

All of these situations are best dealt with as soon as they are recognized, i.e. animals with obesity should be dieted (when weight is lost the number of insulin receptor sites increases again) and cases of hyperthyroidism or Cushing's syndrome should be appropriately treated. If nothing is done to correct the insulin resistance the beta cells eventually give up the struggle to produce more insulin, i.e. become exhausted, and this can result in permanent Type I diabetes mellitus, i.e. hypoinsulinism.

It is thought that some cases of Type II (non-insulin-dependent) diabetes mellitus in cats can exist in a compensated state for long periods of time without showing any abnormal signs. Only during episodes of concurrent illness and/or severe stress, when resistance to the effects of insulin is increased, do the signs of diabetes mellitus appear.

Regardless of the type of diabetes mellitus the clinical signs are virtually identical in all cases. The inability to utilize or store glucose means that high levels accumulate in the blood, and so much is filtered out by the kidneys that it cannot all be reabsorbed (in normal cats reabsorption is complete). Consequently some glucose is excreted in the urine and, since it needs to be in solution, takes more water with it. Thus there is increased urine production and a compensatory increase in thirst. There is also muscle wasting and weight loss in most cats, despite an increased appetite. Other common findings are jaundice, dehydration, a poor coat and enlargement of the liver (due to accumulation of fat). Some diabetic cats may walk in a characteristic manner with their hocks touching the ground. Unfortunately none of these signs occurs only in diabetes mellitus and they can arise in various combinations in a number of other illnesses. Even finding a high level of glucose in the blood (causing glucose subsequently to appear in the urine) can prove misleading in the cat, since many normal cats respond to the stress of handling and the collection of blood by temporarily increasing their output of adrenaline substantially and thereby raising their blood glucose levels.

Eventually, in an attempt to obtain a source of energy the body increases the breakdown of its fat stores, and fatty acids are released faster than they can be metabolized. Instead they are converted into three substances, collectively referred to as ketones, which accumulate in the blood, and their appearance causes a dramatic change in the clinical picture. Effectively the onset of ketosis marks the beginning of the end. Ketones are toxic to the brain and cause a loss of appetite, vomiting, marked dehydration and listlessness, progressing to coma and death. This condition of keto-acidosis is a major cause of death in cats with diabetes mellitus.

The correction of those conditions (obesity, hyperthyroidism, megestrol acetate therapy) which promote insulin resistance is clearly an important first step in treating non-insulin-dependent diabetes mellitus. Type I diabetes mellitus, almost by definition, requires treatment to be by the injection of insulin, with the daily dose being adjusted according to the level of glucose in the urine, or, if it is possible to measure it routinely, the level in the blood. Generally the longer-acting types of insulin, injected once or twice a day, are most suitable for the cat. The inadvertent administration of *excess* insulin leads to a severe fall in the blood level of glucose (hypoglycaemia), ultimately resulting in a coma. At the first signs of drowsiness, weakness or staggering, a solution of sugar in water, or some honey or syrup, should be administered by mouth or rubbed on to the gums and lips for the cat to lick off. The effect is very dramatic with the cat becoming normal once more in a very short time.

To achieve successful control of diabetes mellitus with minimum fluctuations in insulin requirements, the amounts of exercise and food, and the type of food, should be kept as constant as possible. Both types of diabetes mellitus benefit from being maintained on a diet containing a restricted amount of fat, complex carbohydrates (such as starch) and increased amounts of soluble and insoluble fibre. The last two features slow down the liberation and absorption of glucose in the gut, thereby avoiding temporary high peaks of glucose in the blood which will require higher levels of insulin to control. Obviously those animals which are obese or underweight need to have these problems corrected with appropriate diets.

Recently it has been found that cats with non-insulin-dependent diabetes mellitus can be controlled combining this type of diet with drugs (hypoglycaemic drugs) given by mouth to stimulate additional insulin production. After initial insulin therapy some diabetic cats can even be controlled using diet alone (i.e. without the use of either insulin or drugs).

The soft-moist type of feline diet is unsuitable for diabetics because it contains large amounts of sugars as preservatives. Adequate water should always be available.

HYPERINSULINISM

In *dogs* (usually above 6 years old) tumours, generally malignant, of the pancreatic beta cells can develop which secrete excessive amounts of insulin quite unrelated to the animal's requirements. As a result the glucose level in the blood falls disastrously low and the animal shows appropriate clinical signs. Such tumours are referred to as insulinomas; they are not common but occur often enough to be well recognized.

However, only one such case has so far been reported in a cat – a 12-year-old male Siamese. He developed restlessness, incoordination and seizures due to the low blood glucose concentration, and these signs could be controlled by using a glucose solution administered intravenously. Surgical removal of the tumour is usually successful, although in this case it was not, perhaps because there were other insulin secreting cells elsewhere in the body.

Disorders of the parathyroid glands

HYPERPARATHYROIDISM

This refers to the increased production of parathyroid hormone and has four possible causes. Primary hyperparathyroidism, the uncontrolled over-secretion of the hormone by an abnormal gland, is a very rare condition, usually due to a benign tumour, but it can result in a very high blood calcium level. Pseudo-hyperparathyroidism is more common. This is the excessive production of parathyroid hormone, or a substance which has exactly the same effect, by a malignant tumour located in some organ *other than* the parathyroid glands. Malignant tumours of the lymphoid tissue (lymphosarcomas) or bone marrow are particularly likely to act in this way. Surgical removal of the offending tumour is the preferred treatment, assuming that this is possible.

In the remaining two causes the increase in parathyroid hormone production is a response to a marked fall in the blood calcium levels. One of these, renal secondary hyperparathyroidism, is associated with kidney failure; the kidneys find themselves unable to eliminate phosphate from the blood efficiently, with the result that it accumulates and produces a reciprocal fall in the calcium level. In the other condition, nutritional secondary hyperparathyroidism, the problem is caused by feeding young kittens a diet containing large amounts of meat or offal, which are notorious for containing relatively far too much phosphate and far too little calcium. (The recommended dietary ratio of calcium to phosphate is approximately 1.2:1, whereas in beef heart the ratio is 1:20 and in beef liver 1:50.) This condition develops in kittens after consuming a diet of beef heart for 1–2 months. The high phosphate content of the diet results in a high phosphate level in the blood, and again a reciprocal fall in the calcium level.

Affected kittens become quiet, reluctant to move and show lameness or staggering in the rear limbs. They tend to sit or lie with their hindlegs splayed out.

In the last two conditions described above the low blood calcium level stimulates increased parathyroid hormone output, a mechanism which is often extremely successful in restoring the calcium level to within, or only just below, the normal range.

Treatment of hyperparathyroidism requires correction of the underlying cause, and in the case of the secondary conditions the feeding of an appropriate balanced diet, usually one which has been commercially produced.

In all four hyperparathyroid disorders the abnormally high level of parathyroid hormone causes excessive amounts of calcium to be removed from the bones resulting in them becoming structurally much weaker. Often comparatively trivial accidents will result in severe fractures.

HYPOPARATHYROIDISM

This term denotes reduced output of parathyroid hormone. In the cat it most commonly results from complete removal of, or damage to, the parathyroid glands when the thyroid gland is being removed to treat hyperthyroidism. Spontaneous hypoparathyroidism appears to be extremely rare. The resultant fall in the blood calcium level increases the 'excitability' of nerve-muscle junctions and animals become liable to show muscular twitches, incoordination and weakness (especially when handled). This may progress to muscle tremors and convulsions, which can persist for long periods of time. The administration of calcium is necessary to control these signs.

Disorders of the adrenal glands

HYPERADRENOCORTICISM

This disorder, also known as Cushing's syndrome, the name of its human counterpart, arises comparatively rarely in the cat. It develops in middle or old age and females account for some 85 per cent of cases. In the majority of instances (85–90 per cent) the disorder is attributable to the excessive output of the hormone ACTH from the anterior lobe of the pituitary, which stimulates the adrenal cortex to produce excessive amounts of cortisol. In the remaining natural cases the cause is a tumour of the adrenal cortex, usually in one gland alone, which, quite uncontrolled, secretes large amounts of cortisol. In all these cases it is cortisol that is responsible for the many clinical signs that appear. However, the same effects can be produced by administration of a corticosteroid (particularly the more potent, long-acting preparations), although they do need to be given for a long time in high dosage.

Whatever the cause, the clinical signs are similar, but as with other endocrine disorders, not all of the signs will appear in every case. The most consistent features are excessive urination and thirst (polyuria and polydipsia) and a good, or even excessive, appetite. Gradually the abdomen becomes distended giving a 'pot belly'. This is due in part to weak abdominal muscles. Muscle wasting is also obvious in the limbs, leading to difficulties in jumping. Skin changes are common including a generally unkempt and rough hair coat, bilaterally symmetrical hair loss and thinning of the skin.

Three-quarters or more of affected cats also develop diabetes mellitus, which requires appropriate therapy as described previously.

Surgical removal of one or both adrenal glands (according to the underlying cause) has so far proved to be the most effective means of treating feline hyperadrenocorticism. The use of drugs to suppress the activity of the adrenal cortex has met with variable success, sometimes providing efficient suppression and at other times not.

HYPOADRENOCORTICISM

Spontaneously occurring hypoadrenocorticism, with in consequence a deficient output of both cortisol and aldosterone, is a very unusual condition in the cat. It can be given the name of its human counterpart, Addison's disease. When it does occur it seems likely to be the result of an immune defect that destroys the adrenal cortex. The principal signs are lethargy, loss of appetite, weight loss, weakness and dehydration.

These signs can also appear in cats following the administration of progestagens, e.g. megestrol acetate, or corticosteroids if the drug is withdrawn abruptly or the cat is subsequently acutely stressed. In addition a complete lack of all adrenal hormones will necessarily follow the surgical removal of both adrenal glands.

Diagnosis can be a major problem, since the signs are often vague and resemble those seen in disorders of the digestive tract or kidneys. Treatment involves supplying the hormone(s) of which there is a deficiency, and this is usually a lifelong requirement.

Disorders of the pituitary gland

As will be apparent, the following conditions are seldom encountered in the cat.

PITUITARY DWARFISM

A lack of growth hormone during the normal growth phase of development will result in an animal which is stunted, though perfectly proportioned, and which retains a fluffy hair coat and its first (milk or deciduous) teeth. The head can appear more square and chunky. Although growth proceeds normally for the first 1–2 months of life (consistent with the finding that early post-natal growth is not dependent on growth hormone), by 3–4 months of age it is obvious that the affected kitten is the runt of the litter. Fortunately dwarfism appears to be a rare condition in cats.

Frequently a lack of growth hormone is associated with a lack of other hormones also, particularly thyroid hormone and the gonadotrophic hormones. Although treatment with growth hormone is possible, it would be expensive and, judging by experience in the dog, probably disappointing.

ACROMEGALY

The excessive production of growth hormone in mature cats (usually 8–14 years old and most commonly male) results in this relatively rare disorder. It is most often caused by a growth hormone secreting tumour of the pituitary gland. There is overgrowth of both soft and bony tissue, especially involving the face and extremities. There may be an increase in body size with weight gain, enlargement of the abdomen and face, excessive thickening and folding of the skin, especially around the head and neck, and sometimes exaggerated spaces between the teeth.

Most animals develop insulin-resistant diabetes mellitus due to the diabetogenic action of growth hormone, with accompanying increases in their output of urine and their thirst. Enlargement of the liver, kidneys and heart are common, with a profound weakness of the heart muscle causing signs of developing heart failure.

Surgery has not been evaluated as a treatment, and drug therapy has so far proved disappointing. Currently radiation therapy appears to offer the best chance of effective control.

DIABETES INSIPIDUS

The kidneys are continually filtering water from the blood passing through them and then reabsorbing (i.e. putting back into the blood) a greater or lesser proportion of it in order to keep the water content of the blood plasma relatively constant. Efficient reabsorption requires an adequate level of antidiuretic hormone (ADH); the more ADH there is released, the more water is reabsorbed and the less urine is formed. In the rare condition of diabetes insipidus the synthesis of ADH is deficient, so that a high proportion of the water filtered from the kidney is *not* reabsorbed but passes out as urine. The cat drinks a correspondingly large amount of water (polydipsia) to compensate for the increased loss in its urine (polyuria), and the large volume of urine produced over a long time span (e.g. overnight) often exceeds the capacity of the bladder, so that the animal is obliged to urinate in the house. Tests may be required to distinguish this condition from others in which polyuria and polydipsia are features, but an important characteristic is that the urine is only marginally more concentrated than water. Successful treatment may be possible by injecting ADH, or by administering it as nasal or conjunctival drops.

21

THE NERVOUS SYSTEM

Introduction

Veterinary medicine and surgery have seen many significant advances in recent years. One of the areas of specialization that has most benefited from these advances is *neurology*, in particular *feline neurology*. For many years, the cat was considered to be the clinical equivalent of a small dog. However, there are many important differences between the species in all aspects of medical sciences. So great are these differences that there is a plethora of literature concerning feline diseases, including neurological disorders.

Many animal owners extrapolate from human experience when they recognize signs of disease in their pets. This leads to many misconceptions about what is actually occurring. For example, diagnoses of 'stroke' and 'heart attack' are frequently made in pets, but in fact, cerebrovascular and coronary artery disease hardly ever occur in dogs or cats. Similarly, the range of diseases seen in cats differs markedly from that in dogs. Thus, a syndrome in a cat that appears similar to a presentation in dogs can be caused by a completely different disease. A common example in neurology is acute paralysis of the hindlimbs. Barring trauma, the most likely diagnosis in a dog is intervertebral disc disease ('slipped disc'). In cats, disc disease rarely causes clinical signs. It is far more likely that a paralyzed cat, which has not been the victim of trauma, has either experienced an interference to the blood supply to the limbs or has a tumour of the spine. Thus, those who consider cats to be small dogs are treading a hazardous diagnostic path.

This chapter is divided into the following sections:

Neurological signs and syndromes
Diagnosis in feline neurology
Diseases of the nervous system: diagnosis and treatment

It is hoped that the information presented will alert the informed cat owner to the clinical manifestations of neurological disease seen in cats, the performance and limitations of the neurological examination, the tests and investigations that are available in neurology, and the diagnosis and treatment of the most common neurological diseases in cats.

Neurological signs and syndromes

SEIZURES

A seizure or 'fit' in an animal is the physical manifestation of an abnormal electrical discharge in the brain, and usually takes the form of an attack lasting a couple of minutes. Cats typically become unaware of their surroundings, lie down, paddle, and may urinate, defecate and salivate uncontrollably. The seizure is usually followed by a period of drowsiness that is termed the *postictal period*.

Recurrent seizures are termed *epilepsy*. A state of continual seizures is termed *status epilepticus*. Neither seizures nor epilepsy are specific diseases; rather, they are signs of brain malfunction.

Seizures can be caused by conditions within the brain (intracranial causes) or outside the brain (extracranial causes).

In the diagnosis of a cat with seizures, much depends on the observations and history given by the owner, as the veterinarian is unlikely to see the episodes. Information such as age, breed and lifestyle is important. Also, an accurate description of the episodes is useful, particularly if there is any abnormal behaviour before the seizure, how the seizure appears and how long it lasts (as timed by a clock). If the episodes are related to any activity, for example feeding, this should be noted. If the owner can make a videotape of the episodes this is very useful.

Reaching a diagnosis depends largely on the neurological examination and use of the tests described below. In dogs, the most common cause of seizures is *idiopathic epilepsy*, that is, there is no identifiable disease. However, an identifiable cause is often present in feline epilepsy.

Status epilepticus is a genuine emergency and a cat so afflicted should be dealt with immediately. Many conditions can cause status epilepticus, particularly toxicity, trauma or decompensated idiopathic epilepsy where medication is abruptly stopped. The priority in such a patient is to control the seizures rather than discover the cause. This requires use of drugs and other measures such as administration of oxygen.

BEHAVIOURAL CHANGE, ALTERED CONSCIOUSNESS, BLINDNESS AND CIRCLING

This combination of signs is usually indicative of brain dysfunction, particularly involving the cerebral cortex or *forebrain*. The signs are often accompanied by seizures.

Acute onset of forebrain signs is usually caused by trauma or ischaemic encephalopathy, where the blood supply is 'cut off'. A more chronic onset is typical of inflammatory or neoplastic diseases. Extracranial disease, particularly liver failure, can cause forebrain signs, caused by an increase in toxic substances in the blood, which affect the brain.

PUPIL ABNORMALITIES

Bilaterally dilated pupils are typical of feline dysautonomia (Key–Gaskell syndrome). Other signs of this disease include regurgitation, dry nose and eyes, and constipation. *Anisocoria* or asymmetry of pupil size may be seen in a variety of diseases. Diseases of the eye itself may cause this (see Chapter 12, The Eye). The most common neurological causes of anisocoria involve interruption to the nervous supply to the pupil, usually resulting in a small pupil (Horner's syndrome) (Fig. 117). Diseases of the middle ear, damage to the neck and damage to the forelimb nerves may cause this sign.

HEAD TILT, ATAXIA AND NYSTAGMUS – THE VESTIBULAR SYNDROME

The vestibular system is based in the ears and brain; it provides information about the position of the body and head. The characteristic

Figure 117 Cat with Horner's syndrome. Note small pupil and protruded third eyelid in right eye

Figure 118   Cat with vestibular disease; note marked head tilt

signs of the vestibular syndrome are well recognized, that is, head tilt, ataxia and the rhythmic movements of the eyes termed *nystagmus* (Fig. 118). The important clinical differentiation is between central vestibular disease (a lesion within the brain) and peripheral vestibular disease (a lesion of the nerve or receptors). Central lesions are usually neoplastic or inflammatory and carry a poor prognosis. Peripheral lesions often involve the ear and, with the exception of tumours, may respond to treatment.

GAIT ABNORMALITIES – ATAXIA

An ataxic or 'wobbly' gait is a feature of many neurological diseases. Cats with forebrain lesions described above may be ataxic, particularly after seizures. Vestibular diseases often cause ataxia.

Cerebellar diseases are important causes of ataxia. Cerebellar hypoplasia in kittens is caused by virus infection of the queen during pregnancy. The other important causes of cerebellar dysfunction are lysosomal storage diseases, which are of genetic origin (see page 354), and inflammatory conditions.

Diseases of the spinal cord and peripheral neuromuscular systems are also important causes of ataxia.

In most situations (other than cerebellar disease), ataxia is often accompanied by weakness and deficits of conscious proprioception. The latter feature is a subtle indication of neurological dysfunction and may be noted as a tendency to 'knuckle' the paws. This sign indicates that the problem is neurological rather than the result of other causes of weakness such as orthopaedic disease. However, it is not specific for any location in the nervous system, as diseases of brain, spinal cord and nerves can all cause such deficits.

PARALYSIS

All limbs

Paralysis of all four limbs (tetraplegia) or weakness of all limbs (tetraparesis) may be caused by a lesion in the brain or cervical spinal cord, or by a generalized peripheral neuromuscular disease (see below). The neurological examination will indicate which is present in an individual cat.

Acute onset of tetraparesis or tetraplegia of spinal origin is usually the result of trauma. Tumours tend to grow more insidiously, but the onset of clinical signs associated with spinal tumours is often acute. Hypervitaminosis A, a nutritional disease, is an important cause of chronic cervical spinal disease and can cause tetraparesis (see Chapter 7, Nutrition).

Hindlimbs

Acute paraparesis or paraplegia in cats is usually the result of one of the following: trauma, spinal tumours or ischaemic neuromyopathy – a vascular disease. Owners are usually aware if their cat has had a road accident, but sometimes a cat will be found paralyzed and the cause is not apparent. The diagnostic features of ischaemic neuromyopathy are cold, firm limbs and a lack of a pulse in the femoral arteries. Many spinal tumours have a surprisingly acute history and must be considered in any paralyzed cat. Spinal pain is a feature of fractures and some spinal tumours.

One limb

This sort of paralysis is relatively uncommon. Trauma can damage the nerve supply to the limb, either with or without fractures being present. In the forelimb, brachial plexus root avulsion occurs following road accidents. In the hindlimb, sciatic nerve injuries can result from injections or following orthopaedic surgery. Pelvic fractures also may damage the nerves to the hindlimb.

BLADDER DYSFUNCTION

Diseases of the urinary tract are important causes of urinary dysfunction (see Chapter 16, The Urinary System). Neurological diseases can interfere with normal bladder function. Spinal injuries may interfere with the ability to empty the bladder, and it is important that in this situation the bladder is emptied regularly. Urinary incontinence may result from trauma to the caudal spine, pelvis or tail. Cats with dysautonomia also suffer from urinary incontinence.

GENERALIZED STIFFNESS AND WEAKNESS

A number of important conditions cause these signs. Muscle diseases or nerve transmission diseases are the most common. Electrolyte imbalances, such as low potassium, and toxicities, such as organophosphate overdosing, are examples. Other signs related to toxicity may be seen in the latter, for example increased excitability or salivation.

EPISODIC WEAKNESS

Myasthenia gravis is the disease that classically causes collapse on exercise in many species, and the cat is no exception. Regurgitation also may occur. The disease is immune-mediated with dysfunction at the neuromuscular junction. (See page 358.)

Diagnosis in feline neurology

The most important diagnostic tools available to the clinician are taking a history, the clinical or physical examination and the neurological examination. The amount of information available from the neurological examination varies with the species. In man, much can be gained from the patient's subjective impression of the disorder – the *symptoms*. Clearly, this information is not available to veterinary clinicians; rather, we have to depend on observation of *signs*. Many signs indicate nervous system dysfunction, and some of these have been described above.

Performance of the neurological examination can be difficult in cats. Many of the tests that dogs respond to in a predictable fashion are less reliable in them. Thus, the clinician must be familiar with the reflex tests and their expected responses *in cats* when interpreting the examination.

Much can be learned by careful observation in a quiet room, once the cat gets used to its surroundings. Abnormalities of head position, gait and balance can be observed. Tests to evaluate cranial nerve function and vision are then performed. Conscious proprioception is tested in the limbs (see above). Limb reflexes are limited in availability in animals, but the patellar reflex ('knee-jerk') and reflex response to a toe pinch can be tested. The presence of pain in the spine is determined.

The information gained from the neurological examination is used to determine whether the disorder is in the nervous system, and if so, in which part. Also, some information regarding prognosis may be gained.

Once the location of the lesion has been identified, a provisional differential diagnosis can be reached. Further identification requires use of certain ancillary tests.

Routine laboratory evaluations, for example a complete blood count, serum biochemistry analysis and urinalysis, are valuable in assessing the general health of the cat. However, rarely will these tests provide a specific diagnosis in neurological disease. The feline leukemia virus (FeLV) and feline immunodeficiency virus (FIV) status of the cat should be established in most instances. Clinical pharmacology is necessary in monitoring anti-convulsant therapy.

Cerebrospinal fluid analysis is a useful indicator of nervous system disease. With the high prevalence of inflammatory and neoplastic central nervous system diseases in cats, cerebrospinal fluid analysis is valuable. Collection of cerebrospinal fluid requires general anaesthesia and some experience on the part of the clinician.

Radiology is a useful ancillary aid in evaluation of many neurological cases. Radiographs of the skull are useful in trauma. Most other intracranial lesions require computed tomography to reveal them. Spinal radiographs are valuable in trauma, but myelography is required to demonstrate most tumours. Again, general anaesthesia is required for radiographic examinations, except where trauma has occurred recently.

Diseases of the nervous system: diagnosis and treatment

BRAIN

Cerebral cortex

Idiopathic epilepsy is less common in cats than in dogs. A diagnosis of idiopathic epilepsy can only be reached after all other possible causes of seizures have been eliminated. Careful evaluation of epileptic cats reveals a high incidence of structural brain diseases.

Anticonvulsant therapy is required in idiopathic epilepsy. Phenobarbitone and diazepam are the most useful; other anticonvulsants are not suitable in cats. If phenobarbitone is prescribed, it is important that serum concentrations are checked periodically, at least twice yearly and two weeks after any change in dosage. Idiopathic epilepsy can be managed successfully in cats, provided that medication is given regularly and is carefully monitored.

Ischaemic encephalopathy causes an acute onset of neurological signs. Behavioural change, seizures, altered personality and circling are typical. There is an interruption of the blood supply to the cerebral cortex. Treatment with corticosteroids is indicated in the acute phase. Anticonvulsants are given if seizures occur. The prognosis is good, but residual neurological deficits may remain.

Cerebral trauma causes various neurological presentations, including seizures, coma and locomotor disability. Usually, the diagnosis is apparent from historical or physical findings. Complications can arise some time after cranial trauma. There is a tendency for the pressure within the brain to increase, which can be a life threatening situation. Affected cats show worsening clinical signs, with progressive tetraparesis, reduced consciousness, slow pupillary reflexes and respiratory depression.

Management of the cat with cranial trauma must consider all body systems, not only the nervous involvement. Other life threatening injuries must be treated. Seizures should be controlled and the airway must be maintained. If raised intracranial pressure is suspected, this can be managed by oxygen therapy and drugs. Skull fractures may require surgical treatment. General nursing care is vital, with particular attention to the bladder, nutrition and fluid balance. The prognosis for forebrain injuries is relatively good, even when marked deficits are present.

Brain tumours. The central nervous system (CNS) signs caused by brain tumours depend on the location. Meningiomas are the most common. Typically, they involve the cerebral cortex and they may be multiple. Diagnosis is based on the clinical signs and the progressive nature of the disease. Radiographs may reveal an area of thickened bone in the calvarium over the neoplasm, but the best method of diagnosis is by computed tomography. Treatment by surgical resection is effective.

Hydrocephalus is usually secondary to CNS diseases obstructing the flow of cerebrospinal fluid. Often there is an underlying cause such as inflammation or neoplasia. Identification of hydrocephalus is best achieved by computed tomography.

Hepatic encephalopathy causes various clinical signs, including behavioural changes, seizures, visual deficits, pupillary abnormalities and increased salivation. Hepatic dysfunction caused by blood being diverted past the liver leads to increased concentrations of neurotoxic substances in the circulation. Laboratory tests provide the diagnosis. The liver may appear small on radiographs. Treatment with a low-protein diet, oral neomycin or lactulose is useful, and surgical ligation of shunts is useful in many patients.

Occasionally cats with underlying hepatic disease become comatose, particularly following an additional stress, for example anaesthesia. Oral protein intake should be stopped, neomycin and lactulose given by enema, and attention paid to fluid and electrolyte balance.

Vestibular disease

There are several important conditions that cause vestibular syndrome (Fig. 118).

Peripheral

Otitis media/interna is a common cause of peripheral vestibular disease. In addition to the vestibular signs, facial nerve paralysis and Horner's syndrome may be present. External evidence of otitis may be seen, and radiographs may show evidence of involvement of the middle ear cavity.

Many medications and topical agents used in ear cleaning and treatment can damage middle and inner ear structures. For this reason, saline is the best fluid for ear irrigation; antiseptics and detergents should be avoided. Irrigation must be performed gently, as vigorous flushing or massage can cause eardrum perforation.

Idiopathic vestibular syndrome. Signs of peripheral vestibular disease are seen where no underlying disease process can be detected. Signs are usually acute in onset and non-progressive. Specific causes must be eliminated before a diagnosis of idiopathic vestibular syndrome is reached. Otoscopic examination with the cat under anaesthesia and bulla radiographs are the minimum requirements. The prognosis is good; some of the features resolve in time, but the head tilt may persist.

Polyps arising from the auditory tube are found in the nasopharynx and the middle ear, the latter causing vestibular signs. Otitis may occur secondary to the presence of the polyp. Physical, otoscopic and radiographic examinations will confirm the diagnosis. Treatment is by surgical resection.

Neoplasia. Squamous cell carcinoma may arise within the middle or inner ear. These tumours are usually aggressive, destroying bone in the skull. External evidence of a discharge may be seen. Radiography is useful, and collection of tissue by surgery provides the definitive diagnosis. The prognosis is poor.

Ototoxicity. Systemic medications, particularly some antibiotics, may be toxic to the auditory and vestibular systems. As mentioned above, direct application of antiseptic solutions into the middle ear can be toxic.

Congenital vestibular disease. Rare cases are seen in some pure-bred cats. The signs may resolve, but residual deficits may remain.

Central

The conditions causing central vestibular disease generally have a progressive nature and carry a poor prognosis. Thus, the differentiation between central and peripheral disease is important. Inflammatory diseases, neoplasia, toxicities, thiamine deficiency and storage diseases may present with signs of central vestibular dysfunction.

Cerebellum

Cerebellar hypoplasia. In utero infection of queens with panleukopaenia virus causes cerebellar hypoplasia in affected kittens. Characteristic cerebellar signs of ataxia, tremor and hypermetria are seen. The condition is seen at a few weeks of age but is not progressive. Treatment is not possible, but affected cats can lead a relatively contented life.

Lysosomal storage diseases are disorders of young cats, with abnormal accumulations of waste material within cells. The accumulations cause loss of function, primarily in the nervous system. The diseases are a result of specific genetic defects. There is no treatment and the prognosis is poor.

Inflammatory conditions may cause cerebellar dysfunction and can be diagnosed by evaluation of cerebrospinal fluid.

Neoplasms of the cerebellum are relatively uncommon in cats.

MULTIFOCAL DISEASES

Inflammatory, neoplastic and degenerative diseases tend to cause multifocal signs, that is, the disease affects multiple parts of the nervous system. Also, other body systems may be involved.

Inflammatory diseases

Virus infections

Feline infectious peritonitis virus is a relatively common cause of nervous system infection, usually in the dry form of the disease. Seizures, vestibular signs, cerebellar signs and paraparesis are common, and the progression is insidious. There is no definitive treatment and the prognosis is poor.

Feline leukaemia virus and *feline immunodeficiency virus* may cause non-specific neurological syndromes related to brain, spinal cord and nerve. Serological testing is appropriate in any cat with neurological disease of obscure aetiology.

Rabies virus infection. Behavioural changes are early signs, usually followed by the furious form and later paralysis. Rabies must be considered in the differential diagnosis if environmental circumstances are appropriate.

Pseudorabies (Aujesky's disease) can cause neurological signs in cats, usually causing pruritus and self-mutilation. The disease progresses rapidly, and the prognosis is poor.

Bacterial infections

These are rare in the nervous system but should be considered, particularly following skull trauma. Treatment with appropriate antibiotics may be beneficial.

Mycotic infections

Several fungal diseases have a predilection for the nervous system. *Cryptococcus neoformans* is the most common, often in association with upper respiratory infection. Serological tests are available for some organisms. The possibility of immunosuppression related to FeLV or FIV should be considered. Treatment with systemic anti-fungal drugs may be useful, but the prognosis is generally poor.

Protozoal infections

Toxoplasma gondii is an unusual cause of nervous system inflammatory disease. Infections may be related to virus-induced immunosuppression. Serological testing may be useful in reaching a diagnosis. Treatment with clindamycin may be useful, but the prognosis is guarded.

Parasitic infections

Rare cases of parasitic migration cause CNS signs in cats.

Degenerative diseases

Storage diseases

Storage diseases are important causes of multifocal signs.

Spongiform encephalopathy

A multifocal neurological syndrome has recently been reported in cats. Gait abnormalities, behavioural change and hypermetria predominate in the multifocal presentation. The disease is progressive and the prognosis is poor.

SPINE

Spinal trauma

This is usually caused by road traffic accidents. Most cases are readily recognized by historical or physical information but accurate owner information regarding trauma is relatively less common in cats than dogs. Radiography will confirm the diagnosis (Fig. 119). Many cats respond well to conservative treatment by cage rest or application of a body cast (Fig. 120). Surgical intervention may be appropriate if there is evidence of cord compression, the fracture is unstable or the cat is in severe pain. Acute spinal injuries may benefit from short-term treatment with high-dose corticosteroids, but prolonged use is not indicated.

Ischaemic neuromyopathy (aortic thromboembolism)

This is a common cause of acute paraplegia in cats. Acute paraplegia, areflexia, absent pain sensation, cold limbs, absent femoral pulses and

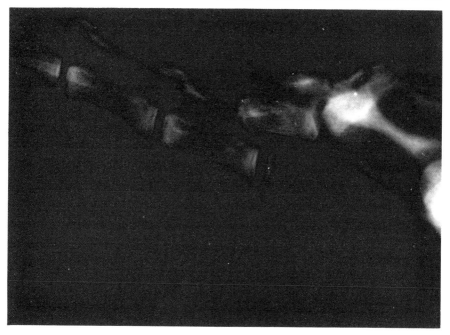

Figure 119 Radiograph of lumbar spine following road accident. The seventh lumbar vertebra is fractured

Figure 120 Cat with spinal fracture in body cast

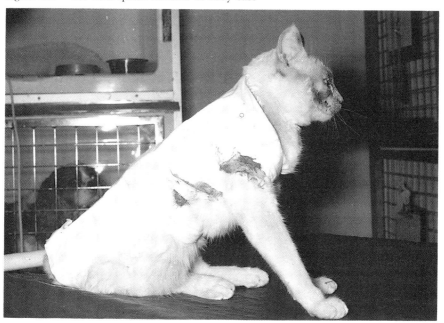

swollen painful limb muscles are the most common features. Affected cats have cold extremities in the hindlimbs, with cyanotic nail beds and toes that do not bleed with needle prick. Diagnosis is based on the typical clinical signs.

There is an underlying heart disorder in affected cats, which leads to the thromboembolic episode (see Chapter 18, The Cardiovascular System). The presence of a thrombus does not entirely explain the clinical signs, but there appears to be a failure of collateral circulation caused by release of vasoactive substances from the area of the thrombus.

Treatment is aimed at stabilizing the cat with suitable fluid therapy and cardiac medications. Drugs aimed at promoting reperfusion have been recommended but all have potentially severe side effects. Surgical removal of thrombi has been described but is rarely indicated.

Whatever method of treatment is selected, the prognosis is guarded. The neurological status will improve in approximately 50 per cent of cats, but the underlying cardiac disease may be difficult to resolve and recurrences can occur.

Tumours

These are common in the spinal cord and associated structures. Lymphosarcoma is the most prevalent; vertebral tumours are rare.

Most cases of spinal lymphosarcoma occur in cats less than 3 years old, and the progression of the clinical signs is relatively acute (Fig. 121). Thus,

Figure 121 Two-year-old cat with one week progression to paraplegia. Diagnosis – spinal lymphosarcoma

neoplasia must be considered in all paralyzed cats, regardless of age or acuteness of signs. Thoracic and lumbar tumours are most common, causing neurological signs in the hindlimbs.

Diagnosis of spinal tumours in cats depends largely on myelography. Cerebrospinal fluid may be abnormal but is unlikely to provide definitive information. In spinal lymphosarcoma, systemic signs may not be apparent, but the great majority of these cats are FeLV-positive.

The diagnosis is based on a compatible clinical course, positive FeLV test and myelographic evidence of a mass. Biopsy and surgical removal may be performed if definitive pathological confirmation is required.

Surgical removal alone is not adequate and must be accompanied by other treatment modalities. Combination chemotherapy and radiation therapy are beneficial. The neurological status may improve with treatment, but most cats succumb to the systemic effects of the disease in time.

Disc disease and discospondylitis

Disc protrusions occur in cats, but clinical signs related to the disc are rare. Discospondylitis (infection of the intervertebral disc and adjacent vertebrae) is also rare in cats and is generally seen with other manifestations of infection, for example subcutaneous abscesses.

PERIPHERAL NEUROMUSCULAR SYSTEM

Myasthenia gravis

This condition may cause typical episodic weakness related to exercise, regurgitation, muscle tremors, altered voice and neck flexion. Aspiration pneumonia may develop with megaoesophagus. Congenital and acquired forms of the disease are seen, and Abyssinian and related breeds may have a relatively high incidence. The diagnosis is based on the clinical signs and is confirmed by the edrophonium response test, in which cats with acquired myasthenia gravis rapidly become normal for a period of several minutes with administration of the drug edrophonium hydrochloride. The disease is immune-mediated, with antibodies directed against part of the junction between nerve and muscle. Treatment with pyridostigmine hydrochloride and corticosteroids is indicated.

The congenital form of the disease is rare and is caused by a defect in the neuromuscular junction.

Insecticide poisoning

Organophosphorus, carbamate and fenthion are widely used as insecticides in small animals and can be toxic to cats. The compounds interfere with neuromuscular transmission. There is autonomic overstimulation and neuromuscular dysfunction. With organophosphorus and carbamate toxicity, there is muscular stiffness and a rigid gait with tremors and fasciculations. In fenthion toxicity, weakness predominates. Treatment is by reducing further absorption, by bathing or gastric lavage as appropriate. Atropine is used to counteract the parasympathetic signs.

Potassium-depletion myopathy

This complaint is the most commonly recognized muscle disease of cats reported during recent years. Affected cats show acute muscle weakness with a typical posture of neck flexion and the head carried low. The gait is stilted and the cats are reluctant to walk. Muscles may be painful on palpation and exercise induces collapse. The diagnosis is confirmed by demonstrating a low serum potassium in a clinically affected cat.

Potassium is necessary for maintenance of normal muscle membrane potentials; depletion causes muscle weakness and eventual paralysis. The origin of the potassium depletion is a combination of reduced dietary intake and increased renal loss in cats with renal disease. The potassium depletion is chronic, but the onset of clinical signs may be acute.

Treatment depends on the severity of the clinical signs. Severely affected cats require aggressive intervention. Careful intravenous potassium supplementation is required. When the crisis is resolved, or in less severely affected cats, oral potassium supplementation is adequate with potassium gluconate. If renal insufficiency is present, oral potassium supplementation is required for life. The prognosis for recovery of muscle function is good.

Peripheral nerve diseases

Traumatic avulsion of the brachial plexus nerve roots is an important peripheral nerve injury. This usually occurs without limb fractures but can occasionally complicate such cases. In addition to the limb deficits, an ipsilateral Horner's syndrome or loss of the panniculus reflex may be seen. The prognosis is poor.

Neoplasia. In chronic cases of forelimb paralysis, neoplasia is the most likely diagnosis. Most tumours occur in the nerve roots and may invade the spinal cord substance. Diagnosis can be difficult, but there may be myelographic abnormalities if the tumour infiltrates the spinal cord.

Traumatic pelvic fractures are the most common cause of hindlimb peripheral nerve injury. Care must be taken in repairing pelvic fractures as *iatrogenic damage* can occur.

Sciatic nerve injury occurs in two particular situations: during intramedullary pin fixation of a fractured femur and in injections into the thigh. Placement of a pin in the femur can inadvertently damage the sciatic nerve. Pins can migrate proximally after placement, usually causing marked pain and neurological deficits. If sciatic damage occurs, the offending pin must be removed and an alternative method of fixation used if the fracture has not healed. The sciatic nerve can be explored and debrided; if it is transected, anastomosis or grafting may be required. The prognosis for traumatic sciatic neuropathy is guarded.

The second situation where iatrogenic sciatic neuropathy occurs is following intramuscular injections in the caudal thigh. This site should not be used for intramuscular injections; an alternative site should be chosen. Affected cats usually show signs at the time of injection. The prognosis depends on the material injected and whether the injection was near to or into the nerve. The prognosis is guarded or poor.

Tail fractures cause tail paralysis, but they are often complicated by urinary and faecal incontinence and even hindlimb paresis. The site of the fracture does not account for these neurological signs. In fact, there is avulsion of the nerve roots from the caudal aspect of the spinal cord. This complication should be considered in any tail fracture. The prognosis can be good with appropriate management. It is important to empty the bladder regularly.

Infectious Diseases

22

INFECTIONS

Introduction

WHAT ARE INFECTIONS?

Infections are not synonymous with disease; for example, most cats which become infected with feline coronovirus will show no signs of illness at all. Infections are not necessarily contagious – in other words they do not always spread to other animals.

The infections that will be dealt with in this chapter are caused by viruses, bacteria, fungi and other organisms which do not fall into these categories. Parasites are dealt with elsewhere.

Viruses are tiny organisms which consist of a genetic blueprint of DNA or RNA for making new viruses and a protein container to protect the genetic material. They have no way of harnessing energy to multiply or make new protein for themselves, therefore they depend on getting into the cells of animals or plants and hijacking their equipment for this purpose. Viruses are so small they can only be seen by means of an electron microscope.

Bacteria are cellular organisms with a nucleus and cell walls. They can ingest and digest food and reproduce themselves, therefore they don't necessarily have to get inside the cells of plants or animals. Unlike viruses, they are susceptible to antibiotics. Bacteria can usually be seen with a light microscope.

Chlamydia are organisms which used to be classed as viruses, because they are very small and live inside cells, but, like bacteria, they have a cell wall and are susceptible to tetracycline (antibiotics) so they are now regarded as highly specialized bacteria.

Recently, an infectious particle even smaller than a virus has been discovered, called a prion, the cause of bovine spongiform encephalopathy (BSE) and feline spongiform encephalopathy (FSE). The nature of the prion is still controversial but many believe it to consist solely of protein. Prions are extremely difficult to destroy.

Fungi are classified as members of the plant kingdom, have rigid cell walls and are visible by light microscopy. The natural home of many fungi is in the soil, where they perform the important task of breaking down decaying materials. Unfortunately some can infect animals, often by chance, and cause disease. These are termed opportunistic infections. Others, like *Microsporum canis* (one of the causes of ringworm), have specialized in parasitizing animals. Cats are fairly resistant to fungal infections. In the United Kingdom, fungi other than those which cause ringworm are rarely isolated, and in the USA they are only isolated occasionally. Fungal infections occur most commonly when the cat's immune system is impaired by concurrent infection with feline leukaemia virus (FeLV) or feline immunodeficiency virus (FIV).

Infection with feline panleukopaenia virus seems to predispose cats to aspergillosis.

Many fungal infections can result in granuloma formation. Granulomata are masses which can appear similar to tumours and can form in any organ. The result is similar to cancer: the cat loses weight and has clinical signs relating to the organ(s) affected.

ANTIBODY AND ANTIGEN

In considering the immune response of animals to infectious organisms, the terms 'antigen' and 'antibody' must be understood (see Chapter 24, Feline Immunology). Antigens are proteins which induce antibody formation. Any protein can potentially be an antigen: if scrambled eggs were injected into an animal it would be antigenic and antibodies against it would be made. Antigen may be the whole or only part of a virus, bacterium, fungus, etc. Most FeLV ELISA* tests are for a single protein antigen, not for the whole virus.

The main mechanism of protection that the body uses against many infections is antibodies. Antibodies are small proteins produced by white blood cells called B-cells. Some antibodies function by binding to an invading organism and physically preventing it from doing any damage (see Fig. 122). Antibodies can also function by attracting certain cells or molecules (such as complement) which will destroy the invading organism.

Antibodies are as specific for each antigen as a particular lock is for its key. In Figure 122 viruses are represented simplistically with spikes ending in either triangles or squares. It can be seen that antibodies to virus 1 will not fit the spikes of virus 2 and vice versa. One method of preventing infection is to elicit antibody formation by injecting viruses which have been made harmless in some way. This technique is called vaccination. Antibodies, like any body protein, are eventually broken down and disappear, which is why booster vaccines must be given.

* Enzyme-linked immunosorbent assay

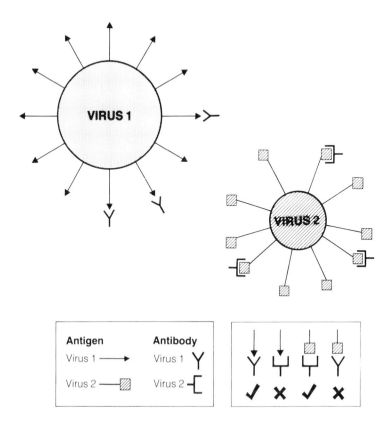

Figure 122 Virus antigen/antibody reactions

TRANSMISSION OF INFECTIOUS DISEASES

Infectious organisms can pass from one cat to another either directly (i.e. the cats meet, sniff, lick, mate or fight with each other) or indirectly (an uninfected cat contracts the infection from a cage or basket, food bowl, litter tray, hands, etc. which have been touched by an infected cat). The specific mode of infection for each condition is described in the appropriate paragraph.

Cats which spread viruses or bacteria may be clinically ill, but can also be in the early stages of infection before illness is apparent. Also, they may be healthy carriers (even though they may have been vaccinated, as can occur, for example, in cat flu). So prevention of infection is not always achieved simply by keeping your cat away from a sick cat.

CONTROL OF INFECTIOUS DISEASES

Obviously the ideal way to control disease is simply not to have the animal encounter the infection at all, as practised in the United Kingdom in the control of rabies. Many cat breeders attempt to isolate their cats by keeping them indoors all the time, and by testing new animals before they arrive, or at least isolating new cats until their test results are known. This is the ideal method of control for FeLV, FIV, feline coronavirus (FCoV), cat flu, *Chlamydia* and ringworm in closed households.

Breeding and rescue establishments should safeguard young, susceptible kittens from sources of infection by isolating the queen and her kittens from all other cats and kittens. Early weaning and isolation of kittens is especially recommended in control of cat flu and feline coronovirus, the cause of feline infectious peritonitis (FIP).

A routine should be established whereby susceptible 'clean' animals should be fed and their litter changed first. Older, vaccinated animals should be seen to next, and the sick ones last of all. The person tending the cats should not go back in to the susceptible cats after dealing with the sick ones. Each cat should be equipped with two sets of litter trays and bowls, so that while one is being cleaned and disinfected, the cat is using the other. Hands should be washed between touching each cat. The most hygienic catteries will even have an overall to wear for each pen and overshoes or a foot bath and rubber gloves.

Pens should be thoroughly disinfected between cats inhabiting them using one of the disinfectants in Table 9. Pens should be left empty for as long as possible between occupants.

Rescue establishments should ideally house cats individually, or, where this is not feasible, no more than two or three cats should be housed together at a time. They should home every cat in a group and disinfect the pen before introducing a new batch of cats. Cats should not be introduced to an existing group simply because one has been homed and there is a 'vacancy'. The new cat can be subject to overwhelming doses of infection from the other cats, which may have had time to become healthy carriers.

People thinking of building a cattery should consult the Cat's Protection League, 17 King's Road, Horsham, West Sussex RH13 5PN, UK, or the Feline Advisory Bureau, 235 Upper Richmond Road, Putney, London SW15 6SN, UK, for advice on sneeze barriers, pen construction and dimensions to minimize disease spread.

TESTING

Tests exist for some of the infections described in this section. Most catteries will have specific disease control policies (these are described

Table 9 Safe disinfectants for use near cats

Use	Active ingredient	Product name	Recommended concentration
Hands	Chlorhexidine gluconate	Hibiscrub	neat
	Chlorhexidine gluconate and Cetrimide	Savlon	1 in 40
	Alcohol	Surgical spirit	neat
	Hydrogen peroxide (H_2O_2)	Hydrogen peroxide	neat
	Halogenated tertiary amine	Trigene Surgical Hand Scrub	neat
Equipment, floors	Sodium hypochlorite*	Domestos, Milton	1 part in 650 (Domestos) 1 Part in 130 (Milton)
	Cationic detergent	Tego	1 part in 100
	Glutaraldehyde	Parvocide spray	undiluted
		Parvocide concentrate	1 part in 50
	Oxidizing agent	Virkon	1 part in 100 (2 parts in 100 for FPV)
	Halogenated tertiary amine	Trigene	1 part in 10-100

* Sodium hypochlorite will only disinfect areas that are already clean; it is inactivated by organic matter (e.g. faeces).

under the headings of each specific disease), but because all possible infections can rarely be tested for, the hygiene precautions outlined above must be a major priority in rescue and boarding catteries where there is a high turnover of cats.

VACCINATION

This is available for certain, but not all, conditions and is a useful adjunct to hygiene and testing in disease prevention. Some vaccines (e.g. feline panleukopaenia (FIE)) are almost 100 per cent efficacious, but others may only work in some cats or may only decrease the severity of a disease once caught. Cat owners should have all their cats vaccinated and boosters should be kept up to date. Boarding catteries should insist on up-to-date vaccination for at least FIE, cat flu and rabies (in countries where appropriate). Some cattery owners may also insist on Chlamydia and feline leukaemia virus (FeLV) vaccines.

Viral infections

CAT FLU

This is caused by either feline calicivirus (FCV) or feline herpesvirus (FHV) – also known as feline viral rhinotracheitis virus (FVR) – or, uncommonly, a combination of both. The most serious cases are caused by FHV.

The main method of spread of the cat flu viruses is by direct contact of one cat with another. Large amounts of virus are present in saliva, tears and nasal secretions (FCV may also be shed in urine and faeces). Thus it can be spread by cats sniffing each other, mutual grooming and sharing feeding bowls. Sneezed droplets may travel 1–2 metres, Cat flu can spread rapidly through a cattery unless cats are housed individually with sneeze barriers. Both of the cat flu viruses are relatively fragile: FCV lasts about a week outside the cat and FHV lasts a day. Plainly, however, these viruses can be spread within a cattery on cages, food dishes, litter trays, people, etc., so good hygiene precautions should be taken (see the introduction).

Cats cannot catch flu from humans with flu nor can humans or other animals catch cat flu.

The main signs of cat flu, as in human flu, are sneezing and runny eyes, which may progress to a mucous discharge (Plate 31 shows a cat with conjunctivitis resulting from cat flu infection). Just before sneezing begins, the cat's temperature will increase, sometimes to as high as 105°F. The cat feels ill and is unable to smell its food because of its blocked nose, so cats with flu are often anorexic. FCV also causes mouth ulcers (Plate 33) which make eating very painful, and may cause the cat to salivate. The lymph nodes under the chin commonly swell up and it may be possible to feel them. These signs generally last only for a week or two in adult cats, longer in kittens, and most cats recover.

In very young kittens or immunosuppressed cats (e.g. those coinfected with FeLV or FIV, or on long-term corticosteroid or treatment with progestagens (e.g. Ovarid)), cat flu can progress to a severe pneumonia. The cat loses weight and may not eat for such a long time that it has to be fed by intravenous drip or stomach tube by the veterinarian. The cat will have difficulty breathing and will breathe through the mouth and may make a wheezing sound.

Chlamydia infection also causes conjunctivitis and may be mistaken for cat flu. In early feline coronoviral infection, catteries often report a transient, mild, flu-like condition passing through the cats despite, perhaps, the cats being vaccinated against flu.

In very young kittens a few days or weeks old, FHV can cause the fading kitten syndrome. The kittens stop eating, lose weight and die. At post mortem they are found to have pneumonia.

FHV can cause ulceration of the cornea (the front of the eye, see Plate 32), and if left untreated, the eyeball may rupture. Some kittens which have bad cat flu may continue into adulthood with chronic sinusitis or rhinitis. Their breathing is more audible than that of normal cats, they snore when asleep, the eyes and nose run continuously or occasionally and the cat may sneeze. One or both eyes may be distorted by adhesions from the eyeball to the inner eyelid.

Older cats which develop chronic rhinitis are often immunosuppressed by concurrent FeLV or FIV infection. In the USA, certain fungal infections can also cause chronic rhinitis: these are *cryptococcus, aspergillus* and *blastomyces*. Certain bacteria can be associated with chronic rhinitis such as *Pasteurella* and *Haemophilus felis*. When chronic rhinitis occurs, cats should be tested for immunosuppressive viruses and fungi.

FCV is associated with chronic gingivitis (when the gums are red and inflamed). In some cats, FCV has been reported to cause a limping syndrome. Cats are lame on one leg, then another, and are off-colour and have a high temperature but do not necessarily have respiratory signs. In rare cases, this syndrome occurs a few days to a week after vaccination and may be caused by the FCV in the vaccine. This condition generally disappears in a few days.

Diagnosis of cat flu can be confirmed by your veterinary surgeon sending a throat swab in viral transport medium to a laboratory, where the virus will be identified.

Owners of cats with flu should always seek veterinary advice, as many cats will require antibiotics to control secondary bacterial infections. The cat should be frequently tempted to eat with small portions of aromatic foods, such as sardines, roast chicken or liver. Brand's Essence is a good food for ill cats, and today there are special liquid foods available from your veterinarian. In order to clear the nasal passages, it is good if the cat can be confined to a hot, steamy bathroom for an hour each day. Vick's Vaporub may help if applied to the chin of some cats. The cat should gently be cleaned with a cloth and warm water, especially if it can no longer groom itself, and kept warm until dry.

Cats with eye discharges should have their eyes bathed 3–4 times a day with a solution of salt and water using one teaspoon of ordinary table salt (sodium chloride) in one pint (half a litre) of water. Veterinary surgeons may prescribe antibiotic eye ointment for cats with secondary bacterial conjunctivitis or a special antiviral ointment, idoxuridine, for cats with FVR eye ulceration. Occasionally in kittens, the eyeball may rupture and need to be removed, as happened with the kitten in Plate 31. However, most ulcerated eyes will recover in 6–8 weeks with treatment.

Cats with chronic rhinitis are notoriously difficult to treat, and many have to stay on antibiotics all their lives. Some veterinarians offer radical surgery, removing the small bones inside the nose in really severe cases which is sometimes very successful.

After cats have been infected with cat flu viruses, whether or not they have shown clinical signs, they continue to excrete virus. In FHV, the carrier state will be lifelong, even in spite of vaccination. Cats do not shed FHV continually but intermittently, particularly in times of stress, e.g. when they are rehomed, or go to boarding cattery or cat show, when they have kittens or if treated with corticosteroids. Virus shedding begins about a week after the stress has taken place and lasts 1–2 weeks. Animals may show mild signs of flu at the time. If mother cats have only low levels of anti-FHV antibodies in their milk, their kittens may be protected from showing disease but are not sufficiently protected not to get infected, so that they can become carriers without having shown disease.

Carriers of FCV, by contrast, shed virus continuously. However, they may spontaneously recover and eliminate the virus. FCV is present in 8 per cent of household pets, 25 per cent of cats at cat shows, 40 per cent of colony cats and 85 per cent of cats with chronic gingivitis.

Fortunately, there are many vaccines available for cat flu. Kittens are routinely vaccinated from 8 or 9 weeks of age, receiving a second dose at 12 weeks, or 3 weeks after the initial injection. Cats should receive a regular annual booster dose.

Most vaccines have no side effects whatever, but some cause mild sneezing and watery eyes for a few days. As stated above, some vaccines have been associated with limping. If a vaccine is used when the cat is already incubating cat flu, it will not benefit the cat. This is why vaccines sometimes appear not to work or appear to cause the condition. It is often a good idea to keep a new cat for 1–2 weeks before vaccinating it so that any diseases it is incubating have time to show.

Vaccination for FHV is straightforward because there is only one type of FHV. However, there are many different types or strains of FCV and vaccination will not necessarily protect against all of them.

Carrier cats can be vaccinated with no ill effects, but vaccination will not stop them from excreting virus.

Cat breeders often have difficulty eliminating cat flu from their stock. One regime is to wean kittens early, at 3–4 weeks, when the antibodies they will have received in the colostrum will be declining. The kittens should be isolated and vaccinated, preferably with the intranasal vaccine, every 3 weeks until they are 12 weeks old.

Cat/cow pox – see section on skin disease.

FELINE CORONAVIRUS/FELINE INFECTIOUS PERITONITIS

Feline coronavirus (FCoV) is a virus whose natural home is in the intestine of the cat. In about 90 per cent of cats it lives and replicates there causing no ill effects, except occasionally some diarrhoea. However, in 10 per cent of cats, the virus leaves the intestine and causes inflammation of the blood vessels (vasculitis). In about half of the cats which develop vasculitis the major sign is peritonitis, hence the name feline infectious peritonitis (FIP) (see Plate 34). The course of the disease in these cats is only a few weeks. In some cats the disease takes a more chronic course, with the cat initially having 'off' days when it doesn't want to eat and is running a high temperature. Gradually the cat loses weight and becomes very listless. Abnormalities may be noticed in one or both eyes: the colour may change; a reddish area may appear on the iris (Plate 35); there may be bleeding into the front chamber of the eye or it may appear cloudy; and white precipitates may form on the cornea (the front of the eye). The cat may develop kidney failure, jaundice or signs of brain damage.

Any age of cat can be affected but the disease usually occurs in cats and kittens less than 18 months old. Often these are pedigree cats or have a history of recently coming from a multi-cat environment, such as a breeding cattery or rescue shelter. When the infection initially gets into a cattery, all or most of the cats may show sneezing or runny eyes or diarrhoea for a few days. In some cats the diarrhoea may be quite severe, the third eyelids may protrude and the diarrhoea may last weeks to months. These cats will need a bland diet of minced white meat, brown breadcrumbs and natural yoghurt or Felizyme or a special diet available from your veterinarian.

Cases of FCoV vasculitis (FIP) invariably die, though some will enjoy weeks or months of quality life under veterinary treatment before the end. There is no cure.

Many other conditions can cause similar signs, so it is vital that a veterinarian be sure of the diagnosis before euthanasing a cat. At the time of writing, there is no commercially available test for the virus itself, but tests exist which detect antibodies to FCoV. In Britain, around 50 per cent of cat breeders have FCoV infections in their cats, as shown by the presence of antibodies. This makes it difficult for a veterinarian to differentiate FIP from other conditions in their cats, e.g. a cat with a swollen abdomen could actually be pregnant, but if she coincidentally has a high antibody titre (titre means count), the mistaken diagnosis of FIP could be made. Fortunately, only 10 per cent of cats from homes with only one or two cats have antibodies. The titres of these cats tend to be low (less than 40), so that high antibody titres in this group are much more significant.

FCoV is a very infectious virus. Over 90 per cent of cats which are exposed to it become infected and make antibodies, though, as stated above, only a very small proportion of these become ill. Cats get infected mainly by meeting a cat which is shedding virus. It is possible that infection also takes place by inhalation of sneezed droplets (e.g. at cat shows) and may occur by sharing the litter tray or food bowl of an infected cat. FCoV survives from a few days to 7 weeks outside the cat but is easily killed by any disinfectant. After losing a cat to FIP one can obtain another cat 3–4 weeks later, unless there are other cats in the household, in which case these should be tested negative for antibodies before obtaining a new cat. If they test positive, wait 3–6 months then retest. It may take months to a few years before they become negative.

There is no vaccine available in Britain against FCoV. In the USA a vaccine which is given as droplets into the nose has recently been invented.

Owners of FCoV-free cats can prevent introduction of the virus into their catteries by testing any new cats *before* they come on to the premises. Breeders must remember that this should apply to stud and queen cats who are only visiting for a short time. Owners of FCoV-positive breeding animals should use their own studs or queens or those of other positive catteries and not infect negative catteries. The kittens of such matings can be prevented from becoming infected by keeping the queen and kittens isolated and weaning the kittens at 5–6 weeks or younger and then keeping the litter isolated from *all* other cats and kittens in the cattery. These kittens should be tested at 12 weeks of age before being sold. If kittens have not been completely isolated or were isolated too late, and test positive, they should then be isolated and retested 1–2 months later. A positive kitten has a one in ten chance of developing FIP.

About one in three cats with antibodies to FCoV excretes virus, but it is not known for how long this goes on. A few cats remain carriers for years. One-third of catteries with FCoV become negative in 18 months to 3 years and these tend to be the catteries which keep their cats in groups of three or less.

There is currently no test which can detect the virus itself, and existing tests detect antibody to FCoV. Available tests include the immunofluorescent assay and the ELISA. These tests often contain some cell culture, and since vaccines sometimes contain cell culture components, cats may produce antibodies against cell culture and therefore have a false positive result on the feline coronavirus test. It is important therefore to make sure that the test used allows for this.

FCoV cannot infect humans. Both dogs and pigs have similar viruses called canine coronavirus and transmissible gastroenteritis virus of pigs which cause diarrhoea, but neither dogs nor pigs get vasculitis as a result of infection.

FELINE IMMUNODEFICIENCY VIRUS (FIV)

This used to be known as feline T-lymphotrophic lentivirus (FTLV). FIV was discovered in 1986, but has been associated with cats for a very much longer period.

FIV, like FeLV, is a type of virus known as a retrovirus. In the infected cat, a copy of the viral genes is inserted into the cat's genes. Once the virus is established in the cells these infections are permanent.

FIV is a fragile virus, living for a short time outside of a cat's body. For this reason it cannot be transmitted indirectly (i.e. on food bowls, litter trays, hands, etc.). Transmission is mainly by biting when virus from the saliva of the infected cat is inoculated into the skin of its victim. This is probably why infection is commonest in older unneutered male cats which have had lots of fights. When many cats are being injected for any reason (e.g. vaccination), it is vital that a new syringe and needle be used for every cat.

Sexual transmission is not believed to occur, but it must be remembered that the tom holds on to the scruff of the queen with his teeth during mating (see Chapter 8, Anatomy and Physiology), so that mating an uninfected cat with an infected cat would be unwise.

Infection rarely crosses the placenta to the unborn kittens, and the majority of kittens born to FIV-infected queens are not infected. It is possible, but not common, that the queen could infect the kittens within the first few weeks of life when grooming them with her infected saliva. FIV poses no danger to other animals or humans.

FIV is more commonly found in middle-aged or older cats (over 5 years of age) and is most prevalent in feral cats. It has been isolated in all countries which have looked for it. Similar viruses occur in larger wild felidae, including pumas, cheetahs and African lions.

Clinical signs of FIV infection are very variable. At 6–8 weeks after they have been infected, cats often develop raised lymph nodes and may have a high temperature. They are sometimes also lethargic and have diarrhoea or conjunctivitis. These signs may last days or weeks, then the cats return to normal.

Most FIV-positive cats are apparently healthy for years. My FIV-positive cat is exceptionally fond of her basket by the radiator, but other than sleeping more, is as healthy as my two negative cats. The effect of the virus on the body is to deplete the number of white blood cells called T-cells, which eventually impairs the cat's ability to fight off infection. The most commonly reported sign of FIV is gingivitis (see Plate 36), and about one-third of cats with gingivitis are FIV positive. Other common signs are sneezing, snuffling, discharge from nose or eyes, raised temperature, diarrhoea or kidney failure. The eye and brain may be affected with changes in character reported in about 5 per cent of cases, which may include the cat becoming more aggressive. Finally, the cat may be overwhelmed by an infection.

Treatment consists of dealing with whatever signs the cat exhibits: if the cat has gingivitis, your veterinarian may need to remove some bad teeth and clean the others. Antibiotics will be needed for infections. Terminally, the cats lose weight and go off their food and will have to be humanely euthanased.

The routinely used FIV test is a test for antibody. Cats become positive from about 4–6 weeks after infection. One complication of this test is that when kittens suckle an FIV-infected mother they obtain antibodies in her milk, and so the kittens will be positive on the FIV test. These antibodies disappear in most kittens by around 12 weeks of age, so the kitten will then be negative. *Young kittens should never be destroyed on the strength of an FIV test.* Some veterinary laboratories are able to test cats for the virus itself, but this is difficult and takes longer to do than the antibody test.

No vaccine currently exists though researchers all over the world are trying to develop one. FIV-positive cats should be vaccinated for cat flu, enteritis, etc. so that they have an optimal chance of fighting natural infection should they meet it.

The question of whether an infected cat should be allowed access to the outside world is an ethical one which really only its owner can decide. If the cat is an habitual fighter, then it is not fair to other cats to allow it outdoors.

FIV is easily killed by all disinfectants. *Boarding catteries should have no qualms about taking in an FIV-positive cat*, though it should obviously not be allowed to mix with other cats. However, owners must remember that FIV-positive cats may suddenly become ill and deteriorate very rapidly. Whether or not cat rescuers should home an FIV-positive cat is again ultimately their own decision, but it must be borne in mind that the cat has a very guarded prognosis, and the home might be better used by a cat with a longer life expectancy. Also, the new owner of an FIV-positive cat would then be unable to take in any other cats until the cat died.

An owner of several cats who finds that one cat is FIV positive and the others negative must decide whether or not to segregate the positive and negative cats. Infection rates amongst contacts of infected cats range from 0–100 per cent. The reason for this variation may be that some strains of FIV are more virulent than others, or that some cats are more able to live peaceably together.

FIV cannot infect humans.

FELINE LEUKAEMIA VIRUS (FeLV)

This is a retrovirus which was discovered in Glasgow in 1964.

FeLV is fragile and cannot be transmitted on hands, bowls, cages, etc. It is mainly transmitted by direct contact of one cat with another, particularly if they lick each other. FeLV is found in the saliva of infected cats. Kittens under 4 months of age are particularly susceptible to infection by FeLV. After 4 months of age there is a gradually increasing resistance to infection. However, this resistance can be overcome by prolonged exposure to infection or by large doses of virus (e.g. when an adult cat enters a multi-cat household in which large numbers of cats are infected).

FeLV can cross the placenta to the unborn kitten and usually all kittens born to an FeLV-positive queen will be FeLV positive. It is possible, though rare, for a queen to have the virus in her mammary glands (and therefore in her milk) but not in her bloodstream, so that although she tests FeLV negative, her kittens will become infected as they suckle.

There is a long incubation period (months to years) from infection with FeLV to development of disease. Eighty-five per cent of infected cats die within 3.5 years of infection. One effect of FeLV infection is to suppress the immune response, leaving the cat more susceptible to infections, such as cat flu, diarrhoea, feline infectious anaemia or feline infectious peritonitis. Whenever a young to middle-aged cat keeps getting ill or doesn't recover in a normal time from an infection, or gets a fever and is listless for no apparent reason, it should be tested for FeLV (and FIV).

FeLV also causes anaemia, leukaemia and solid tumours called lymphosarcomas (see Chapter 19, Haematology for more details). The lymphosarcomas most commonly associated with FeLV infection are thymic lymphosarcoma (a tumour in the chest which generally affects young cats), multicentric lymphosarcoma (in which masses arise in the lymph nodes and are palpable under the chin, behind the knees, in front of the shoulder and elsewhere) and alimentary lymphosarcoma (where the tumour is in the small intestine or colon, causing weight loss and diarrhoea), but lymphosarcomas can arise in any organ. The kidney, nervous system and eye are the next commonest organs to be affected. Lymphosarcoma is the commonest tumour of the eye of the cat.

FeLV is also associated with infertility, abortion, resorption of kittens and stillbirths.

Treatment involves dealing symptomatically with whatever manifestation of the disease the cat shows. The outlook for FeLV-positive cats is always poor. Cats with lymphosarcoma may be treated by chemotherapy. In a report of 103 cases of lymphosarcoma in cats which were treated by chemotherapy, the tumour regressed in 62 per cent who survived an average of 7 months. About 20 per cent survived more than 12 months. However, treatment of lymphatic or myeloid leukaemia is generally unsuccessful.

Although vaccines are available, none is 100 per cent effective and FeLV testing remains the main method of FeLV control. The FeLV test detects viral antigen (see introduction). Most veterinarians can perform a quick ELISA test on a sample of blood, saliva or tears. The ELISA test detects an antigen of the virus called p27. All positive FeLV ELISA results should be confirmed by virus isolation (where the virus is grown in cell culture) or immunofluorescence. In around 5–10 per cent of cats with positive ELISA results, no virus can be detected on virus isolation. Cats should *never* be euthanased on an FeLV ELISA result alone.

Cats which are positive on ELISA but negative on virus isolation become either positive or negative on both tests a few months later, although some continue to have a 'discordant' result, possibly because they have a latent infection. This is when a cat has no whole virus in its bloodstream, and therefore is not infectious to other cats, but has virus lurking in the bone marrow or other organ, producing p27 which can go into the bloodstream and be detected in the ELISA. Latency may be confirmed by bone marrow biopsy, but this procedure is complex and expensive.

An important method of control in FeLV infection is the separation of virus-positive infectious cats from negative non-infectious cats. If cats have only been recently infected, they may not yet have virus in their blood. The time from getting infected to producing virus in the blood can be as little as 2 weeks or as long as 8. For this reason, when cats are tested for the first time, it is recommended that they be tested twice, 12 weeks apart. Cats which test positive twice at a 12-week interval will be permanently infected.

In nature, many adult cats which are exposed to FeLV recover from the infection. Recovered cats have no FeLV antigen in their blood but may have antibodies to the virus. There is a test for these (virus neutralizing) antibodies, and it is important not to confuse this test with either the ELISA or the virus isolation test. A positive virus neutralization test means that the cat has recovered from infection and is immune.

Over 80 per cent of cats with thymic lymphosarcoma are FeLV positive, 66 per cent of cats with multicentric lymphosarcoma are FeLV positive and only one-third of alimentary lymphosarcoma cases are FeLV positive. The reason that some are negative is unknown, but since these conditions are more prevalent in houses where FeLV is endemic, all cats in contact with a cat which has a lymphosarcoma, whether or not it is FeLV positive, should be FeLV tested.

Many vaccines are available in the USA and Europe, but only two, Leucogen and Leukocell 2, are licensed for use in the UK at the time of writing.

Leucogen is one of a new generation of vaccines made by genetic engineering. The gene for the FeLV protein which induces the protective immune response in cats, was isolated and incorporated into special bacteria. The bacteria multiply and produce large quantities of the protein which is then purified and formulated into a vaccine. The vaccine is very safe because it contains only the viral protein and does not contain whole virus.

Leukocell 2 is derived from a cell culture which produces FeLV, so it contains lots of viral proteins, including a protein associated with FeLV infection, called FOCMA (feline oncornavirus-associated cell membrane antigen). Antibodies to FOCMA may be able to prevent formation of the tumours which sometimes occur in FeLV-infected cats, however they do not prevent non-FeLV tumours. Although Leucogen does not contain FOCMA, vaccination with Leucogen also stimulates anti-FOCMA antibodies. Leukocell 2 is made safe by chemical inactivation of the virus.

The initial course of FeLV vaccination consists of two injections 15 to 21 days apart in kittens and cats over 9 weeks of age and then a booster should be given every year to maintain immunity. Vaccination of FeLV negative female cats prior to mating should protect her kittens until they are weaned. Sick or pregnant cats should not be vaccinated with Leucogen but pregnant cats can be vaccinated with Leukocell 2.

The manufacturers state that both vaccines can be given at the same time as other vaccines (such as cat flu and enteritis) but some veterinarians feel that to give too many vaccines at once is a lot to impose on a cat and so prefer to give the FeLV vaccine a few days apart from other vaccines. After FeLV vaccination, some cats may be off colour for a couple of days or may develop a small lump at the site of vaccination.

The manufacturers of Leucogen recommend that cats and kittens to be vaccinated should first be tested for FeLV. This is not because vaccinating a positive cat would be harmful to it, but because positive cats derive no benefit from vaccination. There is also the danger that people will feel a false sense of security if they introduce a vaccinated cat to their own FeLV negative cats. *You must never assume that an FeLV vaccinated cat is not shedding FeLV.* Both vaccines are highly efficacious, but it must be remembered that no vaccine is 100 per cent effective, that is, not all of the cats which are vaccinated against FeLV will be immune. Vaccination is not a substitute for testing.

People who rescue cats should ideally *never mix foster cats with their own cats*. Remember that cats which carry FeLV or other lethal viruses can *appear* to be perfectly healthy. In practice, some fosterers have no alternative but to mix their own cats with those they are rescuing, in this case they must have their own cats FeLV tested. FeLV positive cats should *never* be allowed to mix with foster cats and FeLV negative cats should be vaccinated.

Reputable cat breeders have so far kept their cats free of FeLV by rigorously ensuring that only cats with FeLV negative certificates come into their catteries. It is important not to accept vaccine certificates instead of test certificates. To do so would, sooner or later, allow FeLV into your cattery.

FeLV vaccines do not cause cats to have positive FeLV tests.

FeLV does not infect humans or non-feline animals.

FELINE PANLEUKOPAENIA VIRUS (FPV)

This virus, feline infectious enteritis (FIE) or feline parvovirus, was the earliest cat virus to be discovered. It is found all over the world. FPV used to claim many feline lives until the advent of a most successful vaccine and is now seen only rarely. FPV can infect any age, breed or sex of cat which has not been vaccinated. It is extremely infectious and in an unvaccinated cattery will become endemic. It only infects members of the cat family (including the large cats).

Like canine parvovirus, FPV is a most hardy virus and can exist in the environment for a year or more. It is more likely that cats contract the disease from infected premises than from infected cats, because the course of the disease from infection to death may be as short as 3–5 days. The virus can be killed by sodium hypochlorite (household bleach) and disinfectants, such as Virkon or Parvocide. Some recovered cats do become carriers and continue to excrete virus.

FPV virus is usually eaten by the cat. The virus multiplies preferentially in dividing cells and for this reason infects the lining cells of the small intestine, which have a rapid turnover, and the bone marrow where red and white blood cells are produced.

Many infections are asymptomatic and it is usually kittens which have lost their maternal antibodies which will be most susceptible. Clinical signs occur 2–10 days after infection. The first signs are usually a high temperature, extreme depression, anorexia and dehydration. A sign of dehydration is that when the skin over the nape of the neck is pulled up it does not immediately fall back into place (compare it with the skin on the back of your own hand). Some cats with FPV have a sudden onset of vomiting blood (vomited blood is not necessarily bright red, but may look like coffee grounds in a pool of liquid). Many cats appear to be thirsty but unable to drink. Despite the name feline infectious enteritis, enteritis may not occur in all cases. Some cats will die within 2 or 3 days of starting to vomit or even without developing either vomiting or diarrhoea. In those animals which have enteritis, diarrhoea is copious, watery, foul-smelling and may or may not be tinged with blood.

In the growing foetus the virus affects the dividing cells of the cerebellum, which is the part of the brain controlling balance. Kittens born to mothers which were infected or vaccinated with a live vaccine during pregnancy may have cerebellar hypoplasia (underdevelopment of the cerebellum).

The signs of cerebellar hypoplasia are usually apparent by about 2 weeks of age. The signs vary from a slight tremor of the head, which becomes more noticeable when the animal attempts to eat or drink, to complete loss of balance and inability to walk properly. There is no cure, but the condition is not progressive, so the kitten will not get any worse.

Cats and kittens suffering from FIE always require intensive veterinary care, to be put on an intravenous drip and kept warm. If recovery begins, they should carefully be given boiled water, or electrolyte mixtures available from veterinary surgeons. When they are able to manage solid food, they should be given only a light diet of boiled fish or chicken for several days.

All kittens should be vaccinated against this disease from 8 weeks of age, with a further injection at 12 weeks. When a cattery has an outbreak of FIE, kittens may also be vaccinated at 4 and 6 weeks to confer extra protection. Both live and inactivated (killed) vaccines are available, and only the latter should be administered to pregnant females or to kittens under the age of 4 weeks, because of the risk of cerebellar hypoplasia. Kittens suckling an immune mother cat will receive antibodies in the colostrum which will protect them for up to 12 weeks. Booster vaccinations should be given every 1–2 years.

Feline poxvirus – see Chapter 13, The Skin.

PSEUDORABIES OR AUJESKY'S DISEASE

This is an acute disease which can affect cats living in piggeries. It is caused by a pig herpesvirus. The cat may suddenly be found dead. Prior to death, cats may become anorexic, listless, have pica (desire for unusual foods, often shown in cats by licking concrete, cat litter etc). They may salivate excessively or have an intense itch, especially around the head. Seizures and coma precede death, which usually occurs within 48 hours of the initial signs.

RABIES

Rabies occurs in almost every country in the world, although it is not present in the United Kingdom or Australasia. It is caused by a virus which attacks the central nervous system. All mammals (including humans) and some birds are susceptible.

Rabies virus is present in the saliva of infected animals and is most commonly spread by biting. Although the virus cannot penetrate intact skin, it can get through mucous membranes (e.g. the lining of the eyelids, mouth, etc.) and of course can enter open wounds or scratches if licked by an infected cat, dog or other animal. The virus is present in the saliva before the animal shows clinical signs. The interval from infection to first clinical signs may be from 9 to 51 days (average 18) in the cat. The first clinical sign the cat shows is abnormal behaviour. Cats become more friendly or aggressive or may become withdrawn and attempt to hide in dark places. This stage usually lasts no more than a day after which the cat may become quite vicious, biting and scratching without provocation. This phase ('furious rabies') lasts 2–4 days. Some cats have 'dumb rabies' and have difficulty eating and drinking, because of paralysis of the muscles of swallowing. Unlike the dog, it is unusual for a rabid cat to have its mouth hanging open drooling saliva.

Convulsions, paralysis, coma and death ensue in 2–4 days. No animal can recover from rabies and there is no treatment. In the United Kingdom rabies is a notifiable disease and the Ministry of Agriculture, Fisheries and Food must be informed if rabies is suspected.

Certain poisons, such as metaldehyde (slug pellets), lead, organophosphorous (in a lot of insecticides), morphine, phenols (e.g. Jeyes fluid), benzoic acid (used sometimes to preserve meat), can mimic some of the clinical signs described here. See also tetanus.

Vaccination against rabies is not permitted in the United Kingdom unless the cat is in quarantine, when it is compulsory, or is about to be exported. Rabies is prevented from entering the United Kingdom by compulsory quarantine of immigrating pets for 6 months. This period allows any animal incubating the disease to show clinical signs without spreading it to other animals. In countries where rabies is endemic, there is a reservoir of infection in wild mammals. In Europe the red fox is the main source, while in North America the raccoon, striped skunk and fox are reservoirs. In future a method of control of rabies in wild life in these countries is likely to be oral vaccination by vaccine in bait placed in appropriate locations. A problem with this strategy has been that the raccoon and skunk are both harmed by the live vaccine, but new vaccines have been made to overcome this difficulty. It is possible that rabies may be eradicated from western Europe in this way.

Should you or your cat be bitten by an animal suspected of being rabid, the area of the bite should be immediately washed with disinfectant (e.g. cetrimide 'Savlon') and water and rinsed copiously with water. Medical advice should be obtained *as soon as possible* so that therapeutic vaccination can be carried out.

FELINE SPONGIFORM ENCEPHALOPATHY

Feline spongiform encephalopathy (FSE) or bovine spongiform encephalopathy (BSE) is included in the virus section, although it is not caused by a virus but probably by a prion. A prion is a protein capable of reproducing itself. It is believed that cats get FSE by eating meat from cattle infected with the BSE prion or sheep with the scrapie prion.

Clinical signs result from degeneration of nerve cells in the brain. Fifteen cases had appeared in the United Kingdom by summer 1991. The signs included difficulty in walking, or loss of balance; abnormal behaviour (e.g. aggression or timidity, loss of house training, failure to groom or excessive grooming); exaggerated response to stimuli, especially sound; drooling saliva; muscle tremors; and abnormal head posture. As the degeneration increases in the brain, the cat becomes more deranged until finally it has to be put to sleep. Any age of cat can be affected and signs will take weeks or months to develop.

There is no diagnostic test which can prove that a cat has FSE while alive, diagnosis being by examination of the brain post mortem. Under the microscope, the pathologist can see spaces in the brain which are characteristic of this disease and which give it the name 'spongiform'. There is no cure and no vaccine. Prevention is by feeding proprietary tinned cat food, fish and meat from reputable butchers. Humans and other animals are in no danger of catching FSE from an infected cat, unless, of course, they eat it.

FELINE SYNCITIUM-FORMING VIRUS

This virus is a very common infection of cats yet little is known about its effects. The virus has been isolated from cats with a number of conditions, but it is unknown if it causes these conditions or is there coincidentally as an opportunist. It has, however, been implicated in a lameness syndrome where young male adult cats, usually 1.5–5 years of age develop limping of one or more limbs. These cats get arthritis of several joints, and the joints may swell up and become stiff. Cats may also have large lymph nodes. The condition often gets worse and response to treatment is generally only temporary.

Feline syncitium-forming virus infection is probably life-long. Infected cats have antibodies to the virus but these do not appear to give an effective protection against the signs.

TOROVIRUS (DIARRHOEA AND THIRD EYELID SYNDROME)

The diarrhoea and third eyelid syndrome has long been recognized in cats and recently a torovirus was isolated which is thought to be the cause. Cats have diarrhoea for days to many weeks, though they are bright. Their third eyelids (haws, nictitating membranes) protrude part of the way across the eye. The condition is not serious and is self-limiting. Antibiotics are rarely helpful, and it is more important to keep the cat on a bland diet of roast chicken or fish mixed with brown breadcrumbs and a teaspoon of natural, living yoghurt. Milk and red meat should not be given, since these are likely to exacerbate the diarrhoea.

Bacterial and fungal infections

ABSCESS

The most common bacterial infection is the abscess (see Plate 37) caused usually by a bite from another cat. Bacteria from the mouth of the feline assailant are inoculated into the skin of the unfortunate victim, where they multiply rapidly. The most common bacteria found in abscesses are *Pasteurella multocida, Bacteroides species, Fusobacterium species* and *Peptostreptococcus species*.

Within hours to days of the bite, the cat may develop pyrexia (a raised temperature), become lethargic and be unwilling to eat. A swelling will gradually develop over the site of the bite and will be painful to the touch. In a longhaired cat the swelling may be difficult to detect. The swelling is soft and feels full of fluid – a hard swelling is unlikely to be an abscess. In the course of a few days, the abscess may rupture and a greenish yellow, grey or blood-tinged pus will discharge.

Chronic abscessation, where the abscess(es) will not clear up, can occur when the immune system is depressed, e.g. by FeLV or FIV infection or long-term treatment with corticosteroid or progestagens (e.g. Ovarid). Chronic abscessation can also occur due to L-form infections. L-forms are a kind of bacteria without cell walls. The appearance of the discharge in L-form infections is not like that in Plate 37 but is watery and bloody.

One form of chronic abscessation is called a mycetoma. A mycetoma is caused by a chronic infection by bacteria or fungi and is characterized by the presence of granules (which are often black) composed of bacterial or fungal filaments. The infections involved are usually *Actinomyces species, Nocardia species, Cryptococcus neoformans, Blastomyces dermatitidis* (not United Kingdom), *Coccidioides immitis* (not United Kingdom), or *Sporothrix schenckii*. These organisms normally live in the soil and infection results from wound contamination. In mycetoma there are frequently sinuses which discharge granules and pus through the skin. All cats which have chronic abscessation should be checked for the presence of FeLV and FIV and should not receive immunosuppressive drugs such as corticosteroid or progestagen (e.g. Ovarid).

An abscess which has already burst should be bathed three or four times daily with a solution of salt water made by dissolving a teaspoon of ordinary table salt in one cup of water. The cat should be taken to the veterinary surgeon, who will prescribe appropriate antibiotics and will lance an unruptured abscess. Where chronic abscessation occurs, further investigation to establish the exact nature of the infection will be necessary.

If you see that your cat has been bitten (or, indeed, if you yourself have been bitten by a cat) apply surgical spirit immediately to the wound. Although it stings, it is a lot less painful than an abscess. Domestic disinfectants other than surgical spirit should be avoided as many are toxic to cats.

BORDETELLOSIS OR 'KENNEL COUGH'

The bacterium responsible for kennel cough in dogs, *Bordetella bronchiseptica*, can also cause coughing, sneezing with or without runny nose and eyes in cats for a few days. Affected cats usually have a history of being exposed to a dog with a cough. The condition is easily treated with the antibiotics oxytetracycline or doxycycline, or sulphonamides.

An experimental vaccine has been developed, but, at present, is not commercially available.

BUBONIC PLAGUE

This has not been seen in the United Kingdom for many years. It has been reported in the cat as recently as 1987 in the USA. The cat had lost a lot of weight, had a raised temperature and had a huge abscess. It was treated successfully with penicillin. Plague is caused by a bacterium called *Yersinia pseudotuberculosis var pestis*, which exists all over the world except in Australia and the United Kingdom.

Y. pestis occurs in wild birds and small animals (most notoriously, of course, black rats). The cat can become infected by eating an infected rodent, but *Yersinia* species are uncommonly isolated from cats. Susceptible cats have a high temperature, anorexia, depression, diarrhoea, weight loss and may show respiratory signs or raised lymph nodes, usually in the neck area. Cats which develop septicaemia die in 1–2 days, while others can be ill for several weeks.

People and other animals are susceptible, so where *Yersinia* is isolated all animals (including humans) should be checked and treated if infected. People are mainly infected by flea bites (the cat can transport infected fleas), but bites by infected cats can infect other animals. People may get septicaemia or abscesses in the lymph nodes ('buboes').

CAMPYLOBACTER INFECTION

Campylobacter jejuni has been associated with diarrhoea in cats, although it can also be isolated from normal cats. As it can multiply during diarrhoea caused by other agents, it is difficult to know for sure that it is the cause of diarrhoea when it is present. It may cause diarrhoea in healthy cats, but in most cases it makes illness worse when the gut is already weakened, e.g. by feline panleukopaenia, coronavirus, worms, etc. Cats are less susceptible than humans, who can get severe vomiting and diarrhoea and abdominal pain for 1–2 weeks following infection.

Cats only remain carriers for a short while. Infected cats shed the bacterium for 1–4 months. The organism can survive up to 1 month in the environment, especially in moist and cold conditions. Flies may spread it by landing on infected faeces, then on food. Fortunately it is easily killed by any household disinfectants. Campylobacters from the faeces of diarrhoeic cats could infect humans but the cleanliness of cats means that their faeces are rarely a source of infection. Diarrhoea and contaminated litter should be cleaned up with care.

When both humans and cats (or dogs) in a household have diarrhoea, then a faecal sample should be examined for *Campylobacter* and appropriate antibiotic treatment instituted.

CANDIDIASIS

Candida albicans is a yeast which normally inhabits the mouth, nose, ears and genitalia. Uncommonly, it can spread from these places and cause illness, particularly if the cat is immunosuppressed. *Candida* has been reported to cause eye changes (such as iritis, bleeding into the eye and precipitates in the front of the eye), head tilt, tremor and internal granulomas in a cat. Thus the signs can be very similar to feline infectious peritonitis. *Candida* can cause pyothorax (pus in the chest). The treatment is ketoconazole, but this drug can be toxic to the cat. Therefore this is a very serious and often fatal condition when it arises.

CAT SCRATCH FEVER

Also known as cat scratch syndrome, cat scratch disease and benign lymphoreticulosis, this is an uncommon condition of humans which have been scratched or bitten by a cat. The cat itself is usually perfectly healthy.

Seven to 20 days after the scratch or bite, the person becomes feverish, sweating and aching, as if suffering from flu. About half of affected people develop pustules or red swellings at the site of the wound. Frequently the affected limb swells up and the nearest lymph nodes also become painful and swollen. The lymph node most commonly affected is the one in the axilla (armpit) because the scratch is often on the hand or arm. The syndrome can last up to 2 months. One bacterium which causes this condition is *Afipia felis*, discovered in 1991 by a team at the Center for Disease Control in Atlanta, who have devised a test to detect it and are currently searching for an antibiotic which will cure the condition. Another possible cause is *Rochalimaea henselae*. Treatment is usually carried out at present with tetracyclines.

CHLAMYDIA

Previously called feline pneumonitis, *Chlamydia psittaci* infection of cats does not in fact cause pneumonia but is most often associated with conjunctivitis (inflammation of the linings of the eyelids). *C. psittaci* causes different signs in sheep and birds.

C. psittaci is a tiny, bacterium-like organism which lives mainly inside the cells of the conjunctiva. It generally passes directly from one cat to another in discharges from the nose and eye. It may possibly be spread in sneezed droplets and on food bowls, hands, etc. Any age of cat may be affected, but it is most commonly reported in young kittens, even as young as 2 weeks of age when their eyes have just opened.

Clinical signs occur 3–10 days after infection, with only one eye at first, then both, having a watery discharge. The cat may also sneeze or have a runny nose. If secondary bacterial infection complicates the infection, the discharge thickens and becomes yellow or green. The conjunctivae are inflamed and swollen. The cat's temperature may rise for a few days initially, but most cats continue to eat and are otherwise well, so that this condition is not as severe as cat flu. Unfortunately it is a persistent infection, lasting at least 6–8 weeks, and is often recurrent, clearing up for a while but then coming back, especially in colonies of cats. *C. psittaci* causes abortion in sheep but at the time of writing has not been proven to cause abortion in cats. *C. psittaci* has been demonstrated in chronic diarrhoea of kittens.

C. psittaci is resistant to many antibiotics and the most successful are oxytetracycline or doxycycline (Ronaxan), which must be used for at least 4–6 weeks in all cats (unless pregnant) in the household, *whether symptomatic or not*.

A live vaccine has been available for many years in the USA and was introduced in Britain in 1991. Two doses are given 3–4 weeks apart in cats over 9 weeks of age. A yearly booster is required. The vaccine should not be used in pregnant queens.

When chlamydia is suspected, three diagnostic tests are available: antibody testing reveals whether or not a cat has been exposed to chlamydia, but not whether there is active infection present at the time of testing. Swabs from the eye can be examined for the chlamydia organism, but this is much more difficult. Special transport media are required and the sample must be taken to the laboratory within 12 hours of sampling. Smears or swabs from inside the eyelid can be stained to reveal chlamydia inside the cells.

C. psittaci can cause conjunctivitis in man, though the strains which affect humans and the cat may differ. However, hands should be carefully disinfected after handling an infected cat.

CRYPTOCOCCOSIS

Although rare in the United Kingdom, cryptococcosis is probably the most common fungus to infect cats (other than the fungi which cause ringworm) in the USA. *Cryptococcus neoformans* is a yeast found all over the world. It is frequently associated with pigeons and can survive up to 2 years in pigeon excreta.

Cryptococcus can affect the skin, nose, lungs, eyes and nervous system. Infected cats will become chronically ill and may have many clinical signs: weight loss, anorexia, depression, fever, sneezing, a runny nose and swellings which resemble tumours. Sometimes a flesh-coloured mass can protrude from the nostril. In the eyes, the colour of the iris may change (iritis or uveitis) and one pupil may be bigger than the other. The cat may bleed into the front of the eye or it may go cloudy. Blindness can occur. If the nervous system is affected, the cat can become paralyzed in one or more limbs.

The veterinarian may diagnose this infection by checking a smear or a biopsy for yeasts, or he may send off a blood sample for an antibody test.

Unfortunately, despite treatment, many cats die of this infection. There is no vaccine.

Rarely, humans can get cryptococcosis, particularly if they are immunosuppressed. Like cats, humans tend to catch it from the environment.

HAEMOPHILUS FELIS

This recently recognized bacterium has been associated with conjunctivitis, chronic rhinitis (sinusitis), pneumonia and infertility in cats. It is a delicate organism and often dies if mailed to a laboratory, so when infection is suspected, a swab must be taken from the cat and delivered directly to the laboratory. USA strains are unfortunately resistant to many antibiotics, but United Kingdom strains are relatively easy to kill.

Leprosy, feline – see Chapter 13, The Skin.

LYME DISEASE (BORRELIOSIS)

Lyme disease is caused by the spirochaete *Borrelia burgdorferi*. Cats acquire the infection by being bitten by the sheep tick (*Ixodes ricinus*, see Fig. 123) in Europe, or the deer tick (*Ixodes dammini*), in the USA. *I. ricinus* feeds on animal hosts at the larval, nymph and adult stages of its life. Tick bites tend to occur from spring through to autumn in the United Kingdom and clinical signs occur weeks to 3 months after the bite. Obviously this condition only affects cats with access to fields grazed by sheep, cattle or deer and does not occur in city cats.

Clinical signs include acute or recurring lameness, raised temperature, lethargy and swollen lymph nodes. The cat may seem reluctant to jump. The skin, heart and kidney may also be affected. The clinical signs may recur.

Figure 123 Sheep tick *Ixodes ricinus*

Searching for *B. burgdorferi* in the laboratory is often unrewarding, but various tests exist which detect antibody to it. The cat should be treated with antibiotics from the veterinarian for at least 4–5 weeks. No vaccine is currently available. Prevention of Lyme disease can only be effected by preventing tick bites. Spraying the cat with a reputable flea spray once a week during the months of peak tick activity will reduce its chances of being bitten.

Human beings may also contract Lyme disease by being bitten by ticks. There is probably no danger from an infected cat, though it should be borne in mind that *B. burgdorferi* may be excreted in the urine. The clinical signs in humans are a skin rash, with or without concurrent flu-like symptoms (aching joints, headache and raised lymph nodes). Later on signs similar to rheumatoid arthritis occur: hot, swollen, painful joints. Treatment with antibiotics at the skin rash stage prevents later symptoms.

MYCOBACTERIUM INFECTION

The best-known mycobacterium infection is *M. tuberculosis*, the cause of tuberculosis (TB). Before the eradication of TB in cattle in the United Kingdom, cats used to have infections of the gut through drinking contaminated milk. *M. avium* and other species of mycobacteria may occur in cats concurrently infected with FeLV.

PERITONITIS

See feline coronavirus/feline infectious peritonitis.

Bacterial peritonitis is uncommon but may occur in young kittens when infection has ascended the umbilical cord. The abdomen enlarges with pus, which may conceal the fact that the cat or kitten has lost weight. The cat will not want to eat or suckle. The veterinarian makes a diagnosis by draining some of the fluid and will institute treatment with antibiotics. This condition is often fatal.

PLEURISY (PYOTHORAX)

Cats may have fluid in their chests due to a variety of reasons – tumours, FCoV, heart failure, ruptured thoracic duct or diaphragmatic hernia – but in all of these conditions the fluid is sterile. When the fluid is pus, then the cause is a bacterial infection. Many species of bacteria and fungi are able to cause this (including *Bacteroides species, Nocardia species, Streptococci, Staphylococci* and *Pasteurella multocida*). How these bacteria get into the thorax is a mystery. In a few cats the cause has been a chest wound or an inhaled or swallowed object (such as a twig) which has penetrated the windpipe or oesophagus, while in others infection may have been blood-borne.

The cat shows increasing difficulty breathing. The sedentary lifestyle of the cat means that the condition can get quite severe before an owner will notice. The cat may mouth-breathe, and any sudden exercise will result in panting, with the mouth open and a wide-eyed distressed appearance. Sometimes the cat may go off food, lose weight and have a raised temperature before it gets to the breathless stage.

The veterinary surgeon will detect fluid in the chest by X-ray and by hearing that the heartbeats are muffled with his stethoscope. Fluid may be drained from the chest to determine its nature, because, as stated above, the type of fluid gives a clue to its cause. Antibiotic treatment will be instituted and probably the chest will be drained quite frequently. However, many cats do not respond to treatment and die of this condition.

A cat with pyothorax will not be infectious to other cats or other animals in the household. There is no way of preventing the occurrence of pyothorax; however, it is a fairly uncommon condition.

Ringworm – see Chapter 13, The Skin.

SALMONELLA INFECTION

Salmonella has become a household name since the scare concerning infected eggs. Fortunately, cats seem to have a high natural resistance to infection by salmonellae. Infrequently, they may become infected through eating contaminated foodstuffs. Infected humans should be sure to wash their hands carefully before feeding their cats.

Salmonellae are bacteria which inhabit the gut. *Salmonella typhimurium* is the type most commonly isolated from infected cats.

As in humans, it is the very old, very young or immunologically compromised (i.e. those infected with FeLV or FIV, or on long-term corticosteroid or progestagen treatment) who are most at risk. The signs are lethargy, a high temperature, anorexia, diarrhoea and/or vomiting and weight loss. Persistent vomiting can lead to dehydration. There may be blood and mucus in the faeces. Some cats may succumb. Salmonella infections may remain localized as abscesses after the initial disease has resolved.

Confirmation of diagnosis is made by sending a faecal specimen to a laboratory. Most cats cease to shed salmonellae in the faeces by about 10 days after recovery; however, some may continue for 4 weeks.

Antibiotic treatment reduces the numbers of organisms shed and prevents septicaemia in kittens; however, it may make the cat more likely to become a carrier. Carriers remain chronically infected and shed salmonellae whenever stressed, becoming a hazard to humans and animals around them. Fluid therapy, kaolin and good nursing are important in salmonellosis.

There is no vaccine against salmonellae currently licensed for cats. Prevention of spread within a cattery will depend entirely on good hygiene precautions. Salmonellae can be killed using the disinfectants recommended in the introduction. No new cats should be introduced until all the cats are negative. Breeding and rescue catteries should not home kittens or cats until they are negative and boarding catteries must fully explain the situation to owners collecting their cats and refer them to their own veterinary surgeons and doctors.

Clearly, humans and other animals can be infected by infected cats. As well as wearing rubber gloves for dealing with litter trays, remember that salmonellae will be present in the mouth of an infected cat and will be transferred to the fur during grooming. Whenever possible, the source of infection should be traced to prevent further contamination.

SPOROTRICHOSIS

Like the other fungi described in this section, sporotrichosis is an uncommon infection of wounds by a fungus whose normal home is in the soil. It is not found in the United Kingdom. A scratch by a contaminated claw can introduce infection into the body. Unlike the other fungi, however, this one is found in large amounts in the exudates and faeces of infected cats and can be transmitted to humans. Infected humans develop skin wounds such as ulcers and abscesses which can take 1–10 months to heal. People should wear plastic gloves when handling cats suspected of having *Sporothrix* and should wash their hands and arms carefully with a povidone-iodine solution.

As stated above, *Sporothrix* infection in cats is often manifest as a chronic abscess or cellulitis. The wound can become so deep that bone and muscle are exposed. The fungus can be spread to other parts of the body by the cat grooming and it can become internal, damaging other organs. The cat may therefore become anorexic, thin, feverish and depressed.

As with the other fungi, the veterinarian can make a diagnosis by examining a smear of the exudate or can send a blood sample for an antibody test. Treatment is difficult because some anti-fungal treatments are toxic to cats; however, new anti-fungals are constantly being developed which are safer. There is no vaccine.

TETANUS

We all know that if we step on a rusty nail we get whisked off to the local hospital for a tetanus shot. Yet whoever heard of the same for a cat? The reason that cats and dogs (unlike horses) are not routinely immunized against tetanus is that they are relatively resistant to tetanus toxin.

Tetanus is a disease which results from the effects of a toxin produced by a bacterium called *Clostridium tetani* which lives in the soil. *C. tetani* is an anaerobe (i.e. it dislikes air) and hence tetanus is most likely to occur where there is a deep, penetrating wound rather than one that is open.

The first signs tend to occur in the limb where the wound occurred: the muscles close to the site of injury become persistently rigid. Gradually, rigidity will spread to other limbs and then to the face. The lips are pulled back, the head is held arched along the back. (It is important not to confuse these signs with hypocalcaemia in nursing queens, in which similar signs appear in a matter of hours.) Cases of tetanus which has only affected one limb have been documented in the cat. Signs occurred some days or weeks after the initial wound so that it had healed by the time the signs of tetanus occurred. When the front leg is affected, it is typically held rigid and pointing towards the tail, with the paw bent under. When only one limb is involved, the prognosis is good, and eventually, in up to 3 months, the cat should regain use of its leg. Treatment includes cleaning and irrigation of the wound, tetanus antitoxin, antibiotics, diazepam and physiotherapy. There is no test so diagnosis depends on eliminating other possible causes by X-ray and clinical examination.

23

PARASITES

Parasites are organisms which live on the surface of, or within, an animal's body. They obtain their food and other essential requirements from the animal, which is known as the host. The parasite benefits from the relationship and the host suffers. If they live on the surface, they are known as ectoparasites (e.g. fleas), whilst those that live within the body are known as endoparasites. The most common endoparasites are, of course, worms.

Ectoparasites

The common ectoparasites of the cat are shown in Table 10 (see also Chapter 13, The Skin). It should be remembered that the flea, apart from causing skin problems, is the intermediate host for the most common cat tapeworm, i.e. *Dipylidium caninum*.

Some parasites spend all their life on the host and are known as permanent parasites whilst others spend only part of their time on the host and the rest as free-living organisms. These are known as temporary parasites. The difference between the two types has to be borne in mind when programmes are being carried out to free the cat of the parasite.

Table 10   Ectoparasites of cats

Common name	Scientific name
Flea	Ctenocephalides felis
Louse (biting)	Felicola subrostratus
Ear mite	Otodectes cynotis
Fur mite	Cheyletiella blakei
Harvest mite	Trombicula autumnalis
Notoedric mange	Notoedres cati
Ticks	Ixodes sp.
Maggots	Calliphorid fly larvae
Ringworm fungi	Microsporum canis (most important)

FLEAS AND LICE

Probably the most common ectoparasites found on the cat are fleas. Some cats can harbour a considerable number but show virtually no clinical signs whilst others, especially the white or light-coloured animals, need only have a single flea to show severe pruritis (itching). Although the fleas obtain their food by biting and the wounds caused by this can cause irritation, more commonly the clinical signs are due to an allergic reaction set up by the flea's 'saliva'.

Both fleas and lice are classified as insects and as a result have a number of similarities, e.g. three pairs of legs, but there are also differences between them. Important is the fact that the flea is a temporary parasite whilst the louse is a permanent one. Lice can be of two types, biting and sucking, but those that affect the cat always belong to the biting group. Unlike many of the other parasites the cat harbours, both the flea and the louse are large enough to be easily seen with the naked eye.

The adult flea does not spend all its time on the cat but jumps off and lays its eggs on the ground or in crevices in the house, returning to the animal to feed. The egg hatches to a larva which is free-living and its food is organic material, often the excreta of the adult that was passed at the same time the eggs were laid. The larvae grow and undergo several moults before they become new adults, at which time, by means of their well-developed legs, they jump back on to the host. Under suitable conditions of temperature and humidity, the whole life cycle, from eggs being laid until new egg producing adults are produced, can be accomplished in approximately 3 weeks. Under unfavourable conditions for development, a highly resistant larva is produced which can persist until conditions become suitable for further development. In these cases the life cycle can take up to two years.

The louse, being a permanent parasite, lays its eggs on the host. The eggs are sticky so they become attached to the hairs and are known as nits. When the eggs hatch the young resemble the adults and undergo moults to become adults.

Treatment for fleas and lice is effective using parasiticidal sprays and this is much preferred to the use of traditional powders. It must be emphasized that instructions for their use should be *carefully* followed and they should not be used in conjunction with flea collars. Modern flea control now includes effective oral preparations and also liquids which are applied to the skin in small quantities.

MITES

Several mange mites can cause disease in the cat, the clinical signs depending on the mite involved. *Otodectes cynotis*, probably the most

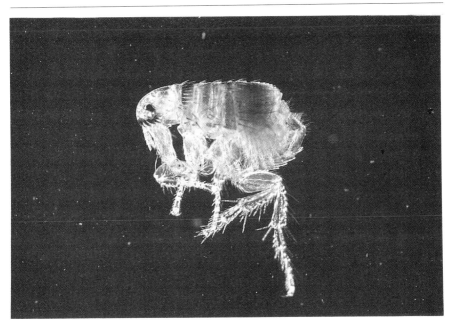

Figure 124 *Ctenocephalides felis*, the cat flea (2 to 4 mm in length)

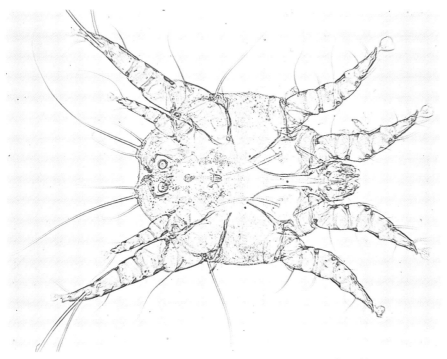

Figure 125 *Otodectes cynotis*, the ear mite (male) (0.4 mm in length)

common mite in the cat, is found in the external auditory canal. It is readily transferred from cat to cat and kittens are often infected from their mothers whilst they are suckling. Owners often confuse the presence of the mite for dirty ears. The mites attach themselves to the mucous membrane of the canal and cause damage to it. Once the mucous membrane has been damaged it is very susceptible to secondary bacterial infection.

Notoedres cati is a very uncommon mite to affect the cat but it can cause a form of mange which is associated with bald, pruritic areas usually found on the head, particularly above the eyes. The disease is hardly ever encountered in the United Kingdom.

Cheyletiella blakei is sometimes known as the fur mite. If the cat is affected with this mite the owner often believes the animal is suffering from dandruff. This mite is larger than the others and is just visible to the naked eye. Apart from its size it can be distinguished from other mange mites by its 'hairiness'.

The harvest mite, *Trombicula autumnalis*, differs from the other mites since not all stages of its life cycle are parasitic. It is the developmental larval stage that causes clinical signs in the cat and it usually causes problems in the autumn, hence its name. This mite is only found in areas where there is a high chalk content in the soil. The larva is scarlet in colour and can be seen with the naked eye on the animal as a minute red speck. Some owners confuse these mites with specks of blood. They are usually found on the feet and lower parts of the legs as cats are infected by walking over ground infested with larvae. Once on the animal, they start burrowing into the skin and cause severe irritation. This leads to the animal licking and chewing its feet and hence to a secondary dermatitis.

TICKS

These are frequently found on the cat. They are sometimes called sheep ticks, which, if they live in an urban area, causes owners to wonder how the cat has contracted them. Although ticks that infest sheep will also infest the cat, much more usually the cat is infested with hedgehog ticks. It is usual for just one or two to be seen on the cat but occasionally a multiple infestation can occur. They appear as bluish swellings and comparatively quickly grow to a considerable size. Their colour is due to the fact that they suck blood. After a period of time, if not removed, they will drop off. However, they should be removed and care must be taken when this is done. They have very strong mouth parts which, if the ticks are pulled off, can be left in place and subsequently cause more clinical problems. Before attempting to remove a tick, it must either be killed or anaesthetized, as occurs when a veterinarian places a swab of spirit over the tick before removing it. Regardless of whether it is killed or anaesthetized the mouth parts will release their grip and can be removed in their entirety. Once a tick has been removed it should always be checked to ensure the mouth parts are complete and it is dead, since ticks can survive off the host for months, living off the remains of their blood meal.

MAGGOTS

Those from the blowfly can cause very severe problems in the cat. The flies are attracted to the animal by the presence of discharges, which can be faeces adhering to the coat or, on occasions, discharges from wounds. It is unusual for a pet animal with good coat attention and fly control in the home to become affected, but it is comparatively common in feral colonies. The maggots burrow into the skin and form tunnels which can run for considerable distances. Toxins are produced to aid the burrowing and these are toxic to the cat.

If maggots are present, thoroughly clean the animal to remove all visible maggots. It may be impossible for an owner to get rid of them all if tunnels have been formed and frequently the veterinary surgeon has to complete the task under general anaesthesia. The problem may not be completely overcome even if the maggots are all removed and the wounds treated since the toxins are absorbed by the cat and can have severe effects on the liver.

RINGWORM

The fungal parasites that cause this condition are very important since the condition is zoonotic. There are several species of fungi that can cause this condition although the clinical signs exhibited are virtually identical regardless of the causal fungus. The fungi cause damage to the hair in the follicles and as a result the protruding hairs at first appear broken and then bald areas appear. Lesions can be found anywhere on the body surface. The condition is highly contagious and is zoonotic (causes disease in man). It can be spread by direct or indirect contact via utensils, combs, etc. Very often the cat shows no signs of irritation. Although in man the lesions are seen as distinct rings, these are not usually evident in the cat. Spores are formed as part of the life cycle, are very resistant to disinfectants and can remain viable for years on inanimate objects. A blow torch is considered the best method of eliminating them if the surface on which it is to be used can withstand such treatment.

Diagnosis of the condition is based on history, the clinical signs shown by the cat and laboratory tests. The use of a special filtered ultra-violet light (Woods Lamp) can be useful but is not 100 per cent diagnostic as only some of the causal fungi will fluoresce under the light. The fluorescence which occurs from *Microsporum canis* is lilac green in colour. This can be confused with fluorescence that occurs with other substances. For example, urine stains will fluoresce as will bits of cotton, Vaseline and the base of some ointments. It is important, if a Woods Lamp is being used for diagnostic purposes, that the patient is properly cleansed prior to its use. Other laboratory tests are carried out on hair samples when the fungi are grown in culture. It can take considerable time for the results to become available since culture will sometimes take 10 days, some of the fungi being very slow-growing. Positive results are often available earlier.

Treatment of ringworm today usually involves the use of tablets, usually grizeofulvin, and this is more effective than the use of ointments or skin dressings, although occasionally washes and lotions are also used.

Endoparasites

The most common worms found in the cat in the United Kingdom are listed in Table 11. In addition to endoparasitic worms, there are, of course, other endoparasites. A coccidial organism, *Toxoplasma gondii*, is also an important endoparasite of the cat in Britain since it is zoonotic, i.e. can cause disease in man. Sensible hygiene reduces the risks of transmission considerably.

Cats are presently quarantined on entry to the United Kingdom for 6 calendar months. This is chiefly to prevent the entry of rabies into the country, but, since cats are routinely wormed during the quarantine period, it also bars some of the parasites commonly found abroad from entering the country.

The adult stages of most of the worms that occur in the cat in the United Kingdom are found in the small intestine. Exceptions are *Aelurostrongylus abstrusus*, the lung worm, which is found in the lungs and bronchii, and *Capillaria plica*, which is found in the bladder but is relatively rare.

Toxocara cati and *Toxascaris leonina* are the common roundworms.

Dipylidium caninum, *Taenia taeiniaformis* and *Echinococcus granulosus* are tapeworms found in cats in Britain.

Echinococcus is an uncommon tapeworm in Britain although it occurs more commonly in the dog. It is an important worm because it can infect man.

The non-scientific names used for worms are very descriptive: roundworms are cylindrical in cross-section whereas tapeworms are flattened or ribbon-like in appearance.

ROUNDWORMS

Adult roundworms living in the gut are of separate sexes. After fertilization by the male, the female produces eggs which develop into larvae. These undergo several stages of development in both *Toxocara cati* and *Toxascaris leonina*. The first and second larval stages remain encased

Table 11 Endoparasites of cats

Common name	Scientific name
Roundworm	Toxocara cati
Roundworm	Toxascaris leonina
Tapeworm	Dipylidium caninum
Tapeworm	Taenia taeiniaformis
Lungworm	Aelurostrongylus abstrusus
Coccidia	Toxoplasma gondii

within the egg. If either a newly voided egg or an egg containing a first-stage larva is ingested by a cat, no further development takes place and it is either killed within the gut or passes out of the cat with the faeces. Eggs containing second-stage larvae will however, upon ingestion, continue development and such eggs are described as infective, i.e. the contained larva is at the infective stage. Once the infected larva has been ingested, development differs depending on whether it is a larva of *T. cati* or that of *T. leonina*. Although *T. cati* is probably the most common roundworm of the cat, nevertheless the life cycle of *T. leonina* is more simple and will therefore be described first.

Once swallowed, the wall of the egg containing the infective second-stage larvae of *T. leonina* is dissolved. The larva then undergoes a moult to become a third-stage larva before it passes within the chyme into the small

Figure 126 Roundworms passed by a cat with a heavy worm burden. Please worm regularly

intestine. Once there it undergoes another moult and becomes a fourth-stage larva and this in turn develops into a new adult worm.

Some of the eggs may be eaten by a mouse or a rabbit and if these species are then in turn eaten by the cat the larvae develop to adults within the digestive system.

The development of *T. cati* is more complex. Once the second-stage larva has entered the digestive tract it is released from the egg and then undergoes a migration around the animal's body before it becomes an adult. The second-stage larvae burrow into the wall of the small intestine and then either enter a blood vessel or go through the entire thickness of the wall to enter the abdominal cavity.

Regardless of whether they are in the abdomen or the blood system, the larvae then migrate or are carried to the liver. Having reached this organ they are then carried via the bloodstream to all parts of the body. In any but very young kittens most of the larvae then encyst in the muscles and do not become active again until the animal becomes pregnant. In late pregnancy stress and hormonal changes influence the larvae to migrate once more and re-enter the bloodstream from whence they are carried to the lungs and become trapped in the fine capillaries surrounding the alveoli of the lungs. They then burrow out into the respiratory system where they undergo another moult to become third-stage larvae.

They then migrate up the trachea and pass into the pharynx where they are swallowed and enter the stomach. Once in the stomach they undergo another moult to become fourth-stage larvae and pass into the small intestine where they become adults. Unfortunately, the life cycle can be even more complex since some of the larvae which have passed into the pharynx are not swallowed but pass out of the queen's mouth and can be transferred to her kittens when she is washing them. If this occurs, these third-stage larvae, once they pass into the kitten's stomach, will moult, become fourth-stage larvae and then adults. Another complication is that some of the larvae harboured by the queen will pass out of her body through the colostrum and the milk and infect the young suckling kitten. Eggs are passed from the host with the faeces and thus are always present on the ground. In addition to their being eaten by cats, they can also be ingested by birds, earthworms and other small animals. If these eat the eggs, no further development of the larvae takes place but if they in turn are subsequently eaten by the cat further development will take place, without any further migration, in a similar manner to that described with *T. leonina* if the cat has eaten a rodent.

If the kitten ingests larvae from the dam through the colostrum, or milk, development to the adult, capable of producing eggs, will be complete within a few weeks without encystment in the muscles. Larvae encysted in the muscles of male cats are thought to remain dormant for life.

LUNGWORMS

Contrary to common belief, lungworms are comparatively common in the cat. A survey which was carried out some time ago showed that approximately 25 per cent of all domestic cats harbour them. Many cats show no clinical signs of their presence, and it is only if the animal becomes ill with a respiratory infection or anaesthesia is undertaken that clinical problems arise.

The adult worms are very small and are often said to resemble tiny bits of black cotton thread. They are found in the lung alveoli and the bronchioles. The adult worms lay their eggs in these sites and the first-stage larvae are released from the egg. They then start migrating up the respiratory passages and eventually reach the pharynx. Once there they are either swallowed and pass into the digestive tract or they pass out of the mouth on to the ground.

The larvae that are swallowed develop further within the digestive tract and in the small intestine. They burrow into the blood vessels and are then transported back to the capillaries in the lung alveoli where they leave the bloodstream and develop to adults.

The larvae that are passed on to the ground are eaten by slugs and snails. These in turn can be eaten by birds, rats or mice, in addition to small wild rodents. The cat then becomes infected by eating its prey following hunting.

TAPEWORMS

The life cycle of tapeworms in general varies in certain respects from that of roundworms. For example, the sexes are not separate, each worm containing both male and female organs. Although the eggs are passed on to the ground, the cat cannot reinfect itself by eating these eggs since with every tapeworm species part of the life cycle has to be spent in an intermediate host, not the cat, whilst it undergoes development. These hosts include fleas, rodents and many farm animals. The tapeworm in these species is often known as a bladder worm as 'the worm' (larva) is surrounded by a fluid-filled sac.

The most common tapeworm in the cat is *Dipylidium caninum*, the common tapeworm of the dog. The most common intermediate host for this tapeworm is the flea. The cat does not usually deliberately eat fleas but may do so when it is grooming. Another relatively common tapeworm that infests the cat is *Taenia taeiniaformis*. The intermediate hosts for these tapeworms are mice and other small rodents. A tapeworm that is believed to affect the cat on rare occasions is *Echinococcus granulosum*. Although comparatively rare, it is important as in addition to the usual intermediate hosts, chiefly sheep, man can also act as an intermediate host and become infected from cats.

Contrary to popular belief, clinical signs often are not shown by cats harbouring sometimes high worm burdens regardless of type. Sometimes an owner thinks that worms are the cause of illness when this is not the case. The animal can be ill with an unrelated problem and coincidentally may vomit or have profuse diarrhoea when worms may be seen. If an animal is infected with tapeworms the owner may see what appear to be grains of rice around the anus. These are in fact segments of the worm containing eggs. In severe cases worms may be associated with retarded growth, a pot-bellied appearance and other rather non-specific signs. Cats should be regularly treated with anthelmintics, i.e. worming medicants. Obviously the cat is better free from parasites but, in addition, regular worming reduces the possible risk of infection to humans.

As stated in the anatomy section (Chapter 8, Anatomy and Physiology) the liver of the cat cannot detoxicate products as readily as other animals and therefore only preparations that are recommended and licensed for use in the cat should be used. Regrettably there is no one product that will destroy all the adult and development stages of all the worms with which the cat may be infested. Preparations come in the form of tablets, liquids and the veterinary surgeon may even use an injection if the cat is difficult to dose. In view of the life histories of the worms described and that it is the nature of cats to go hunting, they should be dosed regularly. In addition they should also be treated for fleas when they are being dosed for tapeworms. With modern deworming preparations there is usually no need to starve the patient before administration. Often owners wonder if they have been effective since it is unusual for parasites to be seen when faeces are passed following treatment when modern anthelmintics are used.

Apart from worms, cats can also become infested with other endoparasites which belong to the group of organisms known as coccidia. These are microscopic organisms and cannot be seen with the naked eye. The most important coccidia to infest the cat is *Toxoplasma gondii*.

COCCIDIA

The life cycles of coccidia are very complex and different from those of the worms. Coccidia have developmental stages both within hosts, which can be either final or intermediate hosts, and also outside the body on the ground.

A structure known as an oocyst is passed within the faeces from the final host. This undergoes development on the ground to become a sporocyst. Within the sporocyst development takes place and sporozoites are formed. This process is usually complete in 1–5 days after the oocyst has passed from the body.

A similar situation occurs with coccidia as with worms in that certain larval stages will only undergo development when eaten by a host. If the host eats an oocyst no further development takes place. It is only when a sporocyst containing sporozoites is ingested by a host that further development takes place. When the sporocyst reaches the intestine in the final host (the cat), trophozoites are released. These pass into the bloodstream and are carried to all parts of the body. Once lodged in the tissues development takes place and many merozoites are formed. After about 3 weeks some, but not all, of these pass back into the intestine, when oocysts are subsequently produced.

Sporocysts are ingested by species other than the cat including man, farm animals, rats, mice and birds. These species act as intermediate hosts. The sporocysts at first develop as in the cat, namely the trophozoites are released in the intestine and then pass to all parts of the body, when they develop and increase in number but do not pass back to the intestine.

If the cat either eats one of these intermediate hosts, following hunting, or is fed raw meat contaminated with trophozoites, further development will then continue and oocysts very quickly form which pass from the digestive tract.

In all the hosts the trophozoites, after a period of development, can form minute 'cysts' which can remain in the animal's tissues for the rest of its life and may never cause any clinical problems. On the other hand, the animal may from time to time release trophozoites from these 'cysts'. In intermediate hosts, but not in the final host, trophozoites may pass through the placenta and continue to develop in the foetus. Recent studies have shown that about 30 per cent of all cats tested pass oocysts in their faeces.

Toxoplasmosis

The disease caused by the trophozoites is known as toxoplasmosis and the clinical signs can vary, being dependent on where the trophozoites are causing damage, which they do by destroying the cells in which they are multiplying. In the cat the disease they cause may be acute or chronic. In the acute form the clinical signs are usually those of pneumonia, but diarrhoea and vomiting can sometimes occur. With the chronic form the intestinal signs are the more common ones, but blindness and nervous signs can also occur.

Since man can act as an intermediate host, and trophozoites can pass across the placenta in the intermediate host, the zoonotic implications of toxoplasmosis are not without concern. However it should be remembered that it usually takes 3–5 days for sporocysts to be formed after the oocysts have been voided; therefore it is important that pregnant women take sensible precautions such as wearing rubber gloves, particularly when clearing cat litter trays, which should be cleared as soon as they are soiled. In this way there is little danger of inadvertent contamination.

Cats normally cover their faeces when voided and therefore the pregnant should perhaps avoid gardening if it is well populated with cats. However, the risk is really very slight and, provided rubber gloves are worn and scrupulous hygiene adhered to, there is really little danger.

Other types of protozoan flagellates, e.g. giardia, also occur in the cat but do not usually cause any clinical signs.

Feline
Immunology

24

FELINE IMMUNOLOGY

Cats, like ourselves and other animals, have two lines of defence mechanisms to protect them from diseases caused by the invasion of foreign organisms, tissues or other substances. The first line includes the skin, mucus and mucous membranes and the liver. The healthy skin acts as a barrier to microbes and other potentially harmful substances. Mucous membranes in the nose trap substances that are breathed in. Coughing prevents the passage of invaders to the lungs, while the mucus lining the airways acts as a further barrier. Stomach acid and the mucus produced by the small bowel are defence mechanisms, as is the liver when it destroys toxins produced by bacteria.

The second line of defence is the immune system, and this is activated when the primary defence mechanisms fail and potentially harmful organisms or substances (antigens) enter the body.

Structure

The immune system consists of the lymph nodes together with the spleen, thymus, lung, liver and white blood cells, known as leucocytes. These cells are formed in the bone marrow and circulate in the blood. They can be recognized from their appearance (see Chapter 19, Haematology), and there are five types: lymphocytes, polymorphonuclear leucocytes or neutrophils, monocytes (which are also called macrophages when they are found in tissues), eosinophils and basophils. Lymphocytes, neutrophils and monocytes are the most important in defending the body against invasion by micro-organisms.

Neutrophils and monocytes (macrophages) are scavenger cells. They engulf particulate matter such as bacteria by a process called phagocytosis. Once engulfed, the bacteria are killed and broken down by enzymes released within the scavenger cells. Neutrophils are highly mobile and generally arrive first at the site of inflammation or tissue injury, while the monocytes (macrophages) arrive later in the inflammatory process. Macrophages are often found within tissues through which large numbers of potentially pathogenic organisms pass, hence there are large numbers of macrophages in the lung to remove airborne micro-organisms and in the liver to filter out harmful bacteria (pathogens) arriving in the blood from the gut.

Non-specific immunity

A healthy cat is protected from potentially harmful micro-organisms in the environment by a number of effective mechanisms that have been present since birth. These primary defences do not depend on the cat having any previous experience of a particular infection and are generally effective against a wide range of potentially infective agents. Thus they are truly non-specific. Such defences may be physical, as in the case of the tough waterproof layer of skin on most of the body's surfaces. The layer of mucus coating the surface of the respiratory tract also acts as a physical mechanism for trapping small particles. The action of the fine, hairlike cilia within the mucus moves the particles in the direction of the mouth, from where they may be swallowed or coughed out.

Other primary, non-specific defences may be chemical in nature. The acidic juices present in the stomach kill many micro-organisms in the gastro-intestinal tract. Natural lubricants such as saliva, tears and nasal secretions contain substances capable of deactivating some viruses, as well as lysosymes, which are enzymes capable of killing some types of bacteria. Anti-fungal agents can also be present in the secretions, as well as cells such as neutrophils and macrophages capable of engulfing bacteria and killing them.

Specific immunity

The circulating white blood cell population of the cat consists of 20–25 per cent lymphocytes. These are present in particularly large numbers in those tissues engaged in the production of antibody, i.e. the lymph nodes, the spleen and the bone marrow. At these sites pieces of the infective agent consisting of large molecules called antigens are presented to special small lymphocytes known as B-cells. The antigens become bound to the B-cells at special receptor sites on the cell surface and this stimulates the B-cell to divide, producing a group of cells known as a clone of plasma cells, each of which is capable of producing a specific substance that can combine with the antigen and render it harmless. This substance is known as antibody and antibody molecules are specific to a particular antigen. The analogy of a lock and key perhaps explains this more easily. If the antigen is thought

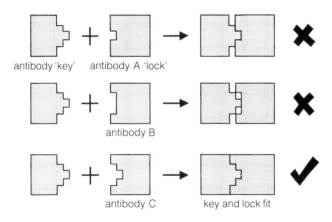

antibody 'key'   antibody A 'lock'

antibody B

antibody C   key and lock fit

Figure 127   Lock and key analogy of antibody specificity

of as a key then there is only one lock, or antibody, that the key will fit (see Fig. 127). In other words antibody produced by a particular antigen combines with that antigen only. The number of antigens that can result in an antibody response is immense, running into many millions. Simply, antigens can be thought of as any form of foreign protein, i.e. not of the body, and may be parts of bacteria or viruses or other foreign proteins that have entered the body.

Antibody molecules produced may have one of a number of functions. They may (a) render inactive or neutralize the bacterial toxins, (b) promote breakdown (lysis) of bacteria, viruses or protozoa, (c) promote ingestion (phagocytosis) of particles by scavenger cells by coating the particles and making them more 'sticky', and (d) trigger other defence enzyme systems, e.g. the complement system. This consists of complex protein enzymes occurring in normal serum which interact to combine with the antigen/ antibody complex to destroy the antigen when it happens to be a complete cell.

The production of antibody is known as the humoral response. At the same time there is also another response taking place, known as the cell-mediated immunity (Fig. 128). While the small lymphocytes (B-cells) are producing antibody, antigen is also presented to large lymphocytes known as T-cells. This triggers the production of sensitized (aggressive) T-cells specific for a given antigen. These sensitized T-cells are capable of recognizing antigen on cell surfaces and can directly kill these target cells, e.g. virus-infected cells, tumour cells, etc.

The production of such a specific immune response is a slow process. Detectable amounts of antibody cannot normally be demonstrated in the circulation until at least 5 days after the antigen is first presented. Peak levels are not reached for approximately 2 weeks. However, when the same antigen or infection occurs on a second or subsequent occasion, the

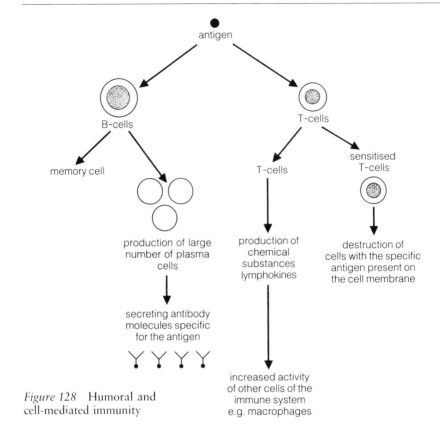

Figure 128 Humoral and cell-mediated immunity

animal's immune system responds rapidly and peak response is usually present within 2 or 3 days and very much greater than the initial response. It is upon this immune response that vaccination depends for its success.

Although, as previously mentioned, the physical defences are present in the kitten from birth, immunologically the kitten is incompetent for some weeks. Protection is afforded by the queen providing some of her circulating antibodies. Small amounts are transferred across the placenta before birth and much greater quantities absorbed across the gut in early life from the first milk or colostrum. The presence of this antibody, which is called passive antibody since it has not been produced by the kitten itself, gives the kitten protection against those diseases that the queen herself has encountered or been protected against by vaccination. This maternally acquired immunity is only of a temporary nature and starts to fade as the kitten's own immune system becomes competent. However, its presence can sometimes interfere with the development of immunity and the production of antibody by the kitten at the time of vaccination against one of the major diseases, and thus necessitates the use of two or more doses of vaccines several weeks apart. This commonly occurs in the case of feline infectious enteritis (FIE) where vaccination may be commenced at an early age but the final dose must be given after 12 weeks of age.

The presence of high circulating antibody levels does not necessarily guarantee protection from infectious disease. In certain circumstances the production of local antibody gives better or more rapid protection. An example of this is the intranasal vaccine against cat flu which gives more rapid protection than those vaccines given more conventionally.

Protection may also be a function of some aspect of cell-mediated immunity, i.e. the stimulation of T lymphocytes.

Auto-immunity

The immune system is primarily concerned with the elimination of antigens from the system. These are usually foreign proteins and may be bacteria, viruses, parasites or other pathogens. Similar proteins are present as part of the body's own tissues and therefore it is important that the immune system recognizes 'itself' from what is 'non-self'. At some stage during the development of the kitten an inventory of all the antigenic material present is taken and this is designated as 'self'. Any proteins (i.e. antigens) introduced in later life are then recognized as 'foreign' and an immune response is mounted against them. Utilizing this method of recognition, disease producing organisms (pathogens) that do invade the body are usually eliminated rapidly and it has long been recognized that individuals who recover from attacks of disease are spared further attacks. An example of this was smallpox in man. We know today that the disease did not recur in the recovered individual due to the development of immunity against the foreign protein (antigen), in this case the smallpox virus.

When an immune response is mounted against self 'tissue' it represents a severe breakdown in the finely tuned immune system. Diseases caused by such a breakdown are termed auto-immune. They include such conditions as auto-immune haemolytic anaemia (AIHA), immune-mediated thrombocytopaenia (IMT) and systemic lupus erythematosis (SLE).

In all these diseases 'self' protein is mistaken for a foreign antigen. There are thought to be a number of reasons for the lack of recognition of the self tissues. These include:

1. The presence of certain viruses, e.g. feline leukaemia virus (FeLV) and feline infectious peritonitis virus (FIP), also known as feline coronavirus (FCoV), in association with some of the body cells can stimulate an immune response which not only damages the virus but leads to the destruction of the cells with which it is associated.
2. Drug molecules, themselves too small to stimulate an immune response, may become attached to protein molecules in cell walls or free proteins

in plasma, increasing their overall molecular size and then stimulating an immune response. The resulting immune response can be directed against both the drug and cell protein, or the response can result in the production of circulating antigen-antibody complexes. These can become bound to circulating red blood cells, blood platelets or body tissues and so result in their damage. Examples of drug-induced auto-immunity are well recognized in the cat.

3. Formation of new antigens during the animal's development. Such potential antigenic substances as spermatozoa and lens protein from the eye are normally shielded from the body's immune system, but when such barriers break down auto-immunity can result.

4. Neoplastic conditions (cancers) of the lymphoid or immune system itself.

Now let us look at some of the more important auto-immune diseases encountered in the cat.

AUTO-IMMUNE DISEASES

Systemic lupus erythematosis (SLE)

This disease affects many systems of the body and is associated with the formation of antibodies to the nucleus (antinuclear antibody) or cytoplasm of body cells (anticytoplasmic antibody). It is uncommon in cats but those cases reported resemble the condition as it occurs in man and the dog.

Clinical signs include arthritis affecting several joints, skin conditions of the face and at the junctions of the mucous membranes and normal skin, central nervous system disorders, including encephalitis and meningitis, and kidney damage leading to protein loss in the urine (protein losing nephropathy). In some individuals anaemia (lack of red blood cells), leukopaenia (lack of white blood cells) or thrombocytopaenia (lack of white platelets) may occur. Diagnosis is made on the basis of laboratory tests demonstrating the presence of antinuclear or anticytoplasmic antibody.

Treatment is with corticosteroids and/or immunosuppressive drugs.

Polyarteritis (periarteritis) nodosa

In this condition circulating antibody-antigen complexes are deposited in the walls of large- and medium-sized arteries and arterioles, giving rise to thickening and nodular swelling in these blood vessel walls, and reducing blood flow. Most organs can be affected. Clinical signs include fever, lethargy, loss of appetite, muscle wasting, joint pain, inflammation of the inner structures of the eye (uveitis), kidney failure and mouth ulcers. Diagnosis is made from examination of tissue samples. Many cats with such clinical signs have FIP and are positive for FCoV and treatment is unrewarding.

Auto-immune haemolytic anaemia (AIHA)

This occurs less frequently in the cat than in the dog. AIHA is the production of antibodies against circulating red blood cells (erythrocytes), leading to the destruction of these cells in the liver and spleen. In the cat it is most commonly associated with the presence of a foreign antigen on the cell membrane, most often that of the feline leukaemia virus, and also seen in haemobartonellosis and some forms of neoplasia (cancers) of the lymphoid tissue or bone marrow.

Clinical signs include progressive weakness and lethargy, raised heart and respiratory rates, sometimes fever and the development of jaundice. Diagnosis depends on laboratory testing and treatment is with corticosteroids and other immunosuppressant drugs.

Immune-mediated thrombocytopaenia (IMT)

IMT is a rare condition in cats. It has been reported to occur with SLE and after infection with the feline leukaemia virus (FeLV). Antibodies are directed against blood platelets (thrombocytes), which are the small blood cells whose function is to plug the gaps in any damaged blood vessels. Clinical signs include excessive bruising or bleeding from the slightest blow, knock or wound, the presence of small haemorrhages on the gums, nose bleeds and the presence of blood in urine or faeces. The clinical signs are similar to those seen after the ingestion of warfarin, a commonly used rat poison, in some circumstances. Diagnosis depends on the use of laboratory tests. Treatment is with corticosteroids, but the response may depend on the underlying cause. Many cases are FeLV positive, although some are drug related.

Chronic progressive polyarthritis

This disease is associated with a dual infection with feline leukaemia virus and the feline syncitium forming virus (FeSFV), leading to the production of antigen-antibody complexes in the synovial structures of the joints. The small end joints of the toes are more often involved than the larger joints further up the limb, but these too may be affected. More male cats than females are reported to be affected and two forms are recognized. The first affects mainly young to middle-aged males, giving rise to stiff swollen joints with a progressive loss of movement in the joints. The second form affects older cats of both sexes, giving rise to joint instability and progressing to joint deformity. Diagnosis is made by examination of radiographs of the affected joints and laboratory examination of samples of joint (synovial) fluid. Response to treatment of both forms is poor. Corticosteroids and cytotoxic drugs are only palliative.

Myasthenia gravis

The form of myasthenia gravis seen resembles the late onset form in man. It involves the formation of auto-antibodies against the acetylcholine receptors on skeletal muscle fibres. Acetylcholine is an important transmitter of nerve impulses to the muscles and the antibodies formed sit on the acetylcholine receptors, blocking its action and therefore nerve transmission. Clinically this appears as muscle weakness aggravated by exercise and improved by rest. Whilst oesophageal dilation (megaeosophagus) is common in dogs with this condition, this is rare in the cat. Treatment is with corticosteroids to decrease the formation of auto-antibodies and with long-acting acetylcholinesterase inhibitors. These prolong the action of the acetylcholine.

Glomerulonephritis

When antibody reacts with antigen (foreign protein) under conditions where the number of antigen molecules greatly exceeds those of antibody, large networks of so-called antigen-antibody complexes are formed. Glomerulonephritis occurs when antigen-antibody complexes are deposited in the capillary walls of the kidney glomeruli (filtration units). They then trigger the series of complex enzyme reactions known as the complement cascade, resulting in irreparable damage to the cells of the kidney filtration system. Such immune complexes may be formed in the circulation or locally and in the cat this is often associated with the formation of antibodies to viruses, e.g. FeLV, FIP (FCoV).

Loss of protein into the urine (proteinuria) is usually less of a problem than in the dog, but blood protein levels fall (hypoproteinaemia) and may lead to the formation of oedema (accumulation of fluid in the tissues). Treatment is with corticosteroids and immunosuppressive drugs, but as the condition is most often associated with concurrent viral infection, most cases have a poor long-term outlook.

CONSIDERATIONS OF THE TREATMENT OF AUTO-IMMUNE DISEASE

The treatment of cats with auto-immune disease is complicated by the role of the feline leukaemia virus and feline infectious peritonitis virus (feline coronavirus) in their development. In cases not complicated by the presence of these viruses treatment very often does not result in cure but rather in the suppression of the clinical signs of the disease. The aim is to provide a reasonable quality of life for the cat, but this requires a great deal of owner dedication.

The drugs used are themselves not without side effects; many will reduce the cat's ability to heal after minor surgery, make the cat more susceptible to other infections or produce side effects which cannot be controlled and therefore make them unsuitable for use in that particular patient.

Poisoning
and First Aid

25

POISONING

Poisoning is a frequent occurrence in the cat, but not as common as some owners believe, since at times the clinical signs of poisoning can be confused with those of infectious diseases, e.g. severe vomiting.

It is sometimes debated whether cats are more susceptible to poisoning than dogs, some people arguing that the dog is more susceptible because of its scavenging nature. On the other hand, as was mentioned in the anatomy and physiology section, the liver of the cat is much less efficient in carrying out detoxification than in other species. This increases the chances of toxicity occurring and the signs of poisoning being presented. These signs can appear even if only small amounts of a substance enter the cat's body, amounts which would be harmless in other species.

Definition

For the purposes of this chapter, a poison is defined as a substance which, when taken into the cat's body in sufficient quantity, will cause illness or in some cases death.

There is a large range of substances that can cause poisoning and a brief list of them is shown in Table 12. They include household substances which can be found in any room of the house, plants, both house and garden, products for use in the garden, such as slug killers or fertilizers, and pest killers, including those used for vermin control, as well as many DIY materials and materials used for the car in the garage.

Poisons can enter the body by the mouth, through the skin and via the respiratory tract, the mouth being the most common route. Cats are fastidious animals and if contaminated with any substance will invariably attempt to clean themselves. If a poisonous substance is being absorbed through the skin, this cleansing will exacerbate the situation by causing the poison to be ingested.

Table 12   Common poisons

Poison	Source	Clinical sign or systems affected
Domestic		
Acrolein	Fumes of overheated fat	Respiratory
Benzoic acid	Food intended for human consumption	Nervous
Alkalis and acids	Disinfectants, polishes, DIY products	Burns; digestive
Carbon monoxide	Inefficient heating boilers	Respiratory and nervous
Medicants	Human and veterinary tablets, medicines, etc.	Various
Household plants	Poinsettia, oleander Diffenbachia	Various. Chiefly digestive but also nervous
Pesticides		
Alphachloralose	Rodenticide	Nervous
Warfarin	Rodenticide	Anaemia
Calciferol	Rodenticide	Digestive
Fluoracetate/ fluoracetamide	Rodenticide	Circulatory, nervous
Methiocare	Slug killer	Nervous
Metaldehyde	Slug killer	Nervous
Garden		
Creosote	Fluid for preserving wood	Burns; digestive, nervous, renal
Chlorate, paraquat, diquat and others	Weedkillers	Various
Garage		
Diesel and oil	Car sump	Burns; digestive, hepatic/renal failure
Acids and alkalis	Car battery, DIY repair materials, cleaning agents	Burns; digestive
Ethylene glycol	Anti-freeze	Nervous and renal

'Secondary' poisoning can also occur if the cat catches and ingests prey, usually vermin, that has itself been poisoned. Rodenticides slow down rats and mice, making them easier to catch.

It is the cat's natural habit to nibble grass and other vegetation, and if confined to the house cats will often nibble at household plants, many of which are poisonous. Dumb cane, or Diffenbachia, is a good example. It contains oxalates that can cause renal failure. It should be remembered that many substances taken as medicants become poisons if taken in overdose. Aspirin is a good example of this. Felines are particularly sensitive to the effects of aspirin and if they are given a comparable human or canine dose poisoning will very rapidly occur. Nevertheless aspirin is still useful in the cat if given in suitably small, suitably spaced doses, i.e. twice a week. It can have extremely beneficial effects particularly in the case of certain blood clotting disorders and is used in the cat mainly for this purpose. (See Chapter 7, Nutrition and Feeding; also Chapter 8, Anatomy and Physiology.) Like aspirin, Warfarin is useful in small doses. Used normally as a rodenticide, in very much smaller quantities it can be used in cases of blood disorders.

If you are at all concerned that your cat may have been poisoned, do not hesitate to contact your veterinary surgeon, for although an owner can carry out first aid for a case of suspected poisoning (see page 418), these cases are always emergencies and the sooner the animal is seen by a veterinary surgeon the better are the chances of survival.

Clinical signs

The sort of first-aid treatment administered by an owner depends primarily on the clinical signs exhibited by the cat, which in turn depend on the type of poison ingested.

In broad terms poisons may affect the nervous system, the digestive system, the skin and the respiratory system, but in some cases, e.g. when some rodenticides are ingested, the blood clotting mechanism may be disrupted.

If the digestive system is affected the cat will probably have diarrhoea, vomit and show acute abdominal pain. There may be behavioural change, e.g. hyper-excitability or fits, or the cat may become quiet, depressed and then become unconscious and comatose.

It should be remembered that, depending on the type of poison and its effect on the nervous system, death can follow as the result of severe convulsions or as the result of depression, unconsciousness and coma.

Poisons absorbed through the skin will often cause severe irritation and redness. It should be remembered that the cat will invariably lick itself and cause the mucous membranes of the larynx and throat to be affected.

First aid treatment

The type of first aid that can be rendered by the owner will depend upon the type of poison. The method of ingress into the body is also important. Clearly, if the cat has been gassed there is little point in making it sick, but assuming the condition is the result of eating a toxic substance, the administration of an emetic is a sensible course of action, with the exception of substances which are either corrosive or anticoagulant.

In the case of a corrosive poison, i.e. one that causes burning of the tissues, making the cat sick is likely to exacerbate the situation since the poison will pass through the throat and mouth a second time and can cause further damage. Similarly, anticoagulants, which prevent blood clotting, can cause minute haemorrhages which can be made worse by the act of vomiting.

Obviously, it is unwise to try to vomit a cat which has become drowsy or unconscious. However with these exceptions it can be said that if the animal vomits within half to one hour of ingesting the poison the chances of recovery are greatly increased as there will not have been time for the material to pass into the small intestine and be absorbed through its wall.

Making a cat vomit in an emergency is not as difficult as many owners think since there are several everyday materials which can be used, providing they are available. These include a small spoonful of salt thrown at the back of the throat or a strong solution of salt in water; a piece of washing soda pushed down the throat; a solution of mustard and water or even a strong solution of washing up liquid.

It is advisable to wrap the patient in a thick towel or blanket while attempting to perform this necessary first aid since the cat is likely to be frightened and will no doubt fight tooth and nail. Firmly but gently pulling the head back as far as possible with a firm grip on the skull will usually result in the mouth being opened sufficiently to insert the necessary substance. If you are not successful on the initial attempt it is probably preferable to contact your veterinarian and take any advice offered rather than persist with futile attempts.

Noxious materials on the coat should be removed as quickly and effectively as possible. If necessary cut off some of the fur and wipe away and absorb as much as possible of the contaminant using absorbent tissue, paper towels, etc.

Many of the substances we use for removal of fats, creosote, paint, diesel oil, etc. are themselves toxic to the cat and under no circumstances should turpentine, paint brush cleaner or paint stripper be used in first aid.

Having removed as much of the substance as possible by wiping, the cat can then be washed using such products as Swarfega, LOC (Amway Products Ltd) or a good-quality washing-up liquid. If the poison is known to be corrosive, do not make the cat vomit. Wipe away as much of the substance as possible from around the mouth. Wet cotton wool placed between the jaws will often dilute any material that is causing injury to the mucous membranes of the mouth and gullet. This latter procedure is possibly preferable to attempting to neutralize the corrosive using acids or alkalis since obtaining these often causes delay and they are in any case of doubtful value.

Inhalant poisons affecting the respiratory system are usually gases but occasionally aerosols may be the culprit. The most commonly inhaled poison in the cat is carbon monoxide. Despite cars being a common source of this gas the most common cause of poisoning is inefficient solid fuel or oil-fired boilers. Cats appreciate the warmth from the boiler, particularly in winter, and are often put to bed in such a situation, only to be found in distress or dead the next morning if the boiler is working inefficiently.

It should be remembered that natural gas does not contain carbon monoxide and therefore gas leaks are unlikely to be responsible for making pussy poorly unless there has been considerable deprivation of oxygen.

Smoke inhalation will also cause considerable distress. This is due to oxygen deprivation and to the toxic substances and particles within the smoke. In addition, the increased temperature can cause serious injury to the airways and lungs.

First-aid treatment is similar in all cases of poisoning by inhalation. The patient should be removed from the source as quickly as possible and a good supply of fresh air ensured. If necessary the cat can be confined in proximity to an electric fan, if available. If the cat is not breathing, artificial respiration by gentle chest compression and relaxation may be tried but may be of little avail.

In all cases of poisoning or suspected poisoning it is advisable to contact your veterinarian as soon as possible.

Sensible ancillary first-aid measures involve keeping the cat warm, quiet and comfortable. If there are burns on the mouth or severe irritation on the skin try to prevent the situation from being worsened by self-mutilation. Often this will mean wrapping the animal in a towel or blanket and physically holding it until such time as you manage to get the cat to the veterinarian.

Veterinary attention

Frequently owners are unable to provide much information to the veterinarian when cats suspected of being poisoned are presented. If there is a suspicion concerning a particular substance, taking along the container or as many details of the product as possible can be very helpful. History can be vital and sometimes owners feel they are being asked irrelevant or rather personal questions when a history is being taken. For example, questions regarding 'do it yourself' activities, gardening and car maintenance are often asked. The responses often give the veterinarian some idea of what products might be causing the presenting signs in the cat.

Frequently owners expect specimens to be sent away for forensic analysis and are often upset when this is not done. There are three reasons why laboratory analysis is not more commonly employed.

Firstly, it will be at least several days before a reliable result is to hand and in that time the animal either dies or recovers.

Secondly, toxological work is very specialized and the laboratory must have some guidelines and usually will only test for two or three substances. Therefore a tentative diagnosis must first be made.

Thirdly, because of the work's specialized nature, and the fact that the results often have to be used in courts of law, charges are invariably high. Thus the veterinarian is unlikely to advise laboratory help unless there is evidence that the poisoning was a deliberate act by another person and legal action is anticipated, or several animals in a colony are affected.

From a veterinary standpoint, treatment involves three considerations:

1. The prevention of further absorption of the poison.
2. The administration of an antidote if one is known and available.
3. Supportive treatment according to the clinical signs exhibited.

In the first case the owner will frequently have done all that could be done to prevent further absorption of the poison by giving an emetic, washing the cat, and so on, but often the veterinarian will give some substances that, in the case of ingested poisons, will combine with the poison to prevent further absorption.

All veterinarians have access to the Central Poisons Bureau, which, although basically dealing with poisoning in man, will provide very helpful veterinary advice. However, it should be remembered that this advice has to be paid for by the veterinarian and is not cheap, and regretfully still has to be paid for whether the advice followed is successful or not.

The Central Poisons Bureau can be extremely helpful in the area of antidotes but it should be remembered that antidotes are usually uncommon clinical substances and frequently have to be obtained by the veterinarian, and in any case of poisoning time is of the essence. If any antidote is to be effective it should be given as soon as possible after the ingestion of the poison.

Supportive treatment depends on the clinical signs exhibited. Often, poisoned cats are shocked or unconscious and in those cases intravenous fluid therapy is often life saving. Alternatively, if there are chemical burns affecting the mouth and pharynx, the cat may be unable to eat and therefore will be hospitalized in order that fluids and nutrients may be administered by an alternative route.

If the poisoning has resulted in a convulsive state, anti-convulsants or tranquillizers may be needed.

Many poisons will cause extreme discomfort, if not severe pain, to the cat and supportive treatment will, in these cases, involve the administration of analgesics of which there exist today several that are eminently suitable for the cat.

Cats poisoned as the result of inhalation of fumes or other gases will often apparently quickly recover once removed from the source of the poison, and owners often believe, mistakenly, that the animal has returned to normal. Regretfully, this is not always the case. Due to the central nervous system being deprived of oxygen, deafness or reduced hearing, blindness or impaired sight, together with a change in character or behaviour pattern, can all follow apparent recovery. It is therefore very worthwhile consulting a veterinarian as soon as possible following any suspected poisoning, however slight.

Prevention of poisoning

Obviously it is far preferable to avoid poisoning than have to treat it. As far as the pet cat is concerned a series of simple measures can be undertaken that will greatly reduce the chances of poisoning occurring.

Access to hazardous areas can be limited. This can often be achieved by merely shutting a door and preventing the cat from entering the danger zone. Garages and garden sheds are areas where many potential poisons for the cat are kept and care should be taken to exclude the pet from this area. Stuffy kitchens in winter, particularly in houses with oil-fired or solid fuel boilers, should also be regarded with some suspicion. If in doubt have the boiler checked or ensure there is always adequate ventilation.

Any potential poison should be kept in a sealed, cat-proof container and any excess product or the used container should be disposed of safely where it can cause no hazard. This particularly applies to used motor oil. Every veterinarian in feline practice will remark on the number of cats that are brought in having fallen into open containers of motor oil. What the attraction is for such a fastidious, sure-footed animal is unknown. The effects can be disastrous if not fatal for not only are the toxic substances contained within the oil absorbed through the skin but they are also ingested in large quantities while the animal endeavours to rid itself of the noxious substance on its coat. In these cases, if the animal is to be saved, treatment has to be immediate, intensive, is invariably expensive and can be prolonged. Prevention is simple. Ensure that all oil storage tanks are covered and if any such substances have to be kept in open-topped containers ensure that there is no feline access.

Households owning cats must consider the choice of products that are to be used within the home. For example, non-toxic house plants should be selected in preference to those of known toxicity to the cat, particularly if the cat has no, or limited, access to the garden. 'Window box' grass can be obtained today to satisfy those feline fancies which cannot be catered for by a wander round the garden. A rare but real source of poisoning can be some preservatives used in human foodstuffs that are actually toxic to cats. These are commonplace in some prepared meats intended for human consumption. Many cats like these but instead of providing a treat they can, on occasion, have quite the reverse effect.

Remember that medicines intended for human use or even for the pet dog may be actually toxic if given to a cat, basically because of the restricted detoxification pathways available in the liver of the cat, as mentioned in the chapter on anatomy and physiology (Chapter 8). Therefore only give feline medicines which have been prescribed by your veterinarian. These will be safe for your cat.

Most flea sprays specify that they should be used for a very short period of time and that it is dangerous to exceed this. In addition flea sprays should not be used if a flea collar is also being worn as this can increase the toxicity. The same principle applies with the new 'spot-on' flea preparations. These should be applied strictly according to the manufacturer's instructions and should not be applied more frequently, nor should flea sprays be used in conjunction with them.

Known poisons are not infrequently used in the home for the eradication of vermin or as garden pesticides. If used, care should be taken to ensure that cats do not have access to the area. Not only should your own cat be denied access to the area but it is worthwhile warning any neighbours with wandering animals of the potential hazard.

The saying goes: 'Curiosity killed the cat'. Fastidious though she may be, pussy is not averse to having a good nose around the refuse. Therefore ensure that any dustbins and refuse sacks are stored where the cat cannot gain access.

26

FIRST AID

First aid is the care and treatment given to an individual in an emergency. The principal purpose is to preserve the life of the patient, but other important aims are to reduce pain and discomfort (i.e. to alleviate suffering) and to minimize the risk of permanent disability or disfigurement by preventing further damage to already injured tissues. In the context of first aid, an emergency can be defined as any situation, usually unforeseen and rapid in onset, such as a serious injury or illness. The following signs are characteristic of emergencies, and are a major cause of concern:

(a) the absence of breathing, or severe difficulty in breathing
(b) severe bleeding
(c) signs of severe shock.

Figure 129 How to carry your cat

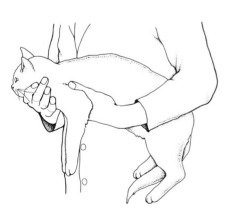 

To carry the uninjured cat, place one hand beneath the cat's chest with your fingers between its legs. Close your arm into your side to support its rear end. Gently restrain its head

An alternative way to carry a pregnant cat is in the 'sitting-up' position. One hand takes the weight of the body, whilst the other holds the front legs

The following conditions are equally serious:

(a) unconsciousness and/or convulsions
(b) signs of poisoning.

These are dealt with in Chapters 21, The Nervous System, and 25, Poisoning.

In these emergency situations it is essential that assistance be given promptly and maintained until the help of a veterinary surgeon is available. The veterinary surgeon may subsequently urge euthanasia of the injured animal as the most humane course of action, but until he or she does so first-aid efforts should be directed towards keeping the animal alive.

Priorities

With all emergencies it is important to remain calm and not give way to panic. Remember that all injured animals need to be adequately restrained before they can be provided with help. Therefore the approach to and restraint of the injured cat is a vital preliminary (although, the greater the damage the less likely it is that an animal will offer serious resistance). The ABC approach is a useful way of remembering the priorities in giving first-aid treatment. These are:

A Airway – ensure that the animal's airway is not obstructed, which will impede its breathing.
B Bleeding – control major, and therefore life-threatening, haemorrhage.
C Collapse, convulsions and lack of consciousness – in these situations treatment for shock may be required, and it becomes particularly important to ensure that the animal is in a place where it will not suffer further injury.

The treatment of these life-threatening signs must receive priority, and always leave the cleaning of wounds and other non-essential procedures until afterwards. The help and advice of a veterinary surgeon is essential in virtually all emergencies and should be obtained as soon as possible. Therefore the first-aid measures subsequently described are designed to precede, not to replace, proper veterinary attention. The initial contact with the veterinary surgeon is best made by telephone to make sure he or she will be ready to deal with the animal when it arrives.

RESTRAINT

After a major injury a cat, unless unconscious, will be bewildered, extremely frightened and will usually resent handling, and will often be aggressive. However, since handling is essential for examination and subsequent treatment, the cat will have to be restrained. Restraint also avoids the animal inflicting further damage on itself and injuring those trying to help it.

If the animal is in a dangerous situation, e.g. in the roadway following an accident, it is of course imperative for it to be first of all moved to a safer, and preferably sheltered, position.

The approach to an injured cat should be calm, quiet and yet purposeful. It is valuable to have the help of one or two sensible people, and to have handy a cat basket or other container into which to place it. Noisy and hysterical onlookers should be asked to leave. By talking to the animal in a quiet, reassuring voice you may be able to get close enough to restrain it, at least temporarily. Be cautious if the cat is above ground level or is cornered because it may try to attack.

The next step is to extend your hand and make a few tentative stroking movements, and then, if possible, take a firm grasp of the scruff of the neck. Keep your hands clear of the animal's mouth because if you touch any obviously injured parts you may be bitten. Watch the cat carefully and be prepared for a struggle. Do not let go unless you absolutely have to because a second attempt to restrain the cat will probably be less successful. And be warned, a cat held by the scruff may endeavour to twist round very violently and dig the hind claws into your arm and wrist.

Ideally, have an assistant to hand with an already opened cat carrier into which you can quickly place the cat. To avoid personal injury, hold the cat at arm's length with its back towards you. If it is clear that the cat is winning the battle and you will be injured, try to push it down on to a rug, blanket or old coat etc. into which its claws will catch. This, together with the cat, can then be placed in the carrier before the animal disentangles the material from its claws. If there is no readily available carrier and the cat is very violent, it is sometimes possible to wrap it in the material on to which it has been pushed for a short time until a suitable box can be found in which to secure it. If, when held by the scruff, the cat does not struggle too much, you can use your other hand to support its body. It can then be placed into the container for transport or carried a short distance in order to perform essential first aid. If the animal proves very difficult to handle, even vicious, it is best to drop an old coat or blanket over it, then quickly tuck the edges under the animal, taking care not to get your hands underneath as well, and to lift the whole bundle. Quickly place the bundle into the cat basket or other container and immediately close and secure it.

It should be remembered that some frightened or injured cats can be extremely vicious towards strangers, and you should take as many precautions as possible to ensure your personal safety. On the other hand, despite the difficult circumstances and your possible panic, you have to try and ensure the animal is able to breathe, and therefore should take care that it is not wrapped up too tightly.

If you are unable to gain the animal's confidence sufficiently to take hold of it, you may be able to apply a 'slip noose' made from a strong, flexible dog lead by passing the end with the clip through the looped end, or by running a narrow trouser belt or dress belt through the buckle. Without making any sudden movement, the slip noose should be dangled in front of the animal's head and slowly manipulated backwards to a position around its neck. A quick pull will then tighten it; and the lead should be held high. Now you can drop a coat or blanket over the cat and lift it into the container.

If all your attempts at catching the animal fail, telephone for professional assistance, e.g. from an animal welfare society, veterinary surgeon or the police, who will probably then employ devices specially developed for catching stray animals. Do not chase the animal, and do not bother to tempt it with food or drink. These approaches are not likely to succeed and only waste time. Cats are unlikely to want to eat or drink in this situation, and if they did it might well interfere with subsequent treatment. Above all, do not trust the animal, even if you are the owner; if it is frightened, it may still bite and try to escape.

AIRWAY PROBLEMS

If a cat is breathing irregularly or with difficulty, it is important firstly to ensure that its airway is unobstructed, and, if it is not, or if clearing it produces no improvement, artificial respiration should be applied.

If breathing appears to have completely stopped and yet the animal is still alive, as established by checking for its heartbeat and so on, artificial respiration is essential.

When breathing ceases all the body organs, including the brain and the heart, are deprived of their normal continuous supply of oxygen. After a few minutes without air they become unable to function normally, and then the animal loses consciousness and eventually dies. Depriving the brain of oxygen for longer than four minutes can produce irreversible damage, and for this reason artificial respiration should take precedence over every other procedure in an emergency. Once it is under way, attention can be directed towards other problems.

Ensuring a clear airway

Any foreign material in the air passages (respiratory tract) or in the lungs must first be removed. If a cat has drowned the most common cause is steep walls preventing its escape from the water, as in swimming pools, canal locks or even rainwater butts. It is important firstly to wipe away any oil or mud from the mouth and nostrils, and then to allow as much water as possible to drain from the lungs by holding the cat upside down by its thighs.

Check that there is nothing around the neck (e.g. a collar or rubber band) that is causing compression. A cat can be strangled if a non-elastic collar catches on a projection and leaves it dangling in midair. Obstructions in the throat usually produce choking, coughing or gulping. Foreign bodies, such as bones or broken teeth, should, where possible, be quickly removed with the fingers (be careful) or a pair of fine-nosed pliers, and if the problem is vomit, mucus or blood at the back of the throat, it should be carefully wiped away. After opening the jaws and pulling the tongue well forward, the back of the throat should be checked with a torch.

Artificial respiration will be ineffective if there is a penetrating chest wound. If this is present, air can usually be heard passing through the opening and frothy blood appears from the wound. Also, bloodstained froth is coughed up and appears at the mouth and nostrils. Quickly seal the wound in the chest by plugging the opening with a clean, preferably sterile, piece of gauze or cotton wool, or, in an emergency, any other clean piece of material, such as a handkerchief. Ideally this plug should then be covered by a further thick pad which is bandaged in place. However, the immediate aim is to obtain an airtight seal.

Checking for signs of life

If breathing appears to have stopped completely, i.e. there is no obvious rhythmical rise and fall of the chest in a cat which is showing no other signs of life, it is sensible to check for the heartbeat, because artificial respiration will obviously be of no value if the animal is already dead. The heartbeat can be detected chiefly on the left side by passing a hand around the lower part of the chest between, or just behind, the forelegs. With finger and thumb positioned on opposite sides of the chest, the heartbeat can be felt between them.

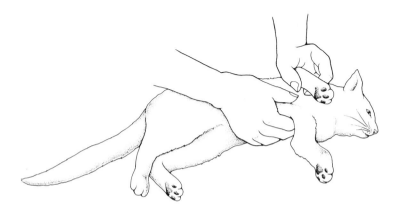

Figure 130 How to find your cat's heartbeat

If a heartbeat can be felt, proceed immediately with artificial respiration. The cessation of breathing may be caused by an existing lack of oxygen to the brain (asphyxia), as can occur if the animal is obliged to breathe smoke or carbon dioxide or has an obstructed airway (see above). Also, following electrocution, the respiratory muscles may be paralyzed.

Bear in mind that there may be no movement in an unconscious animal for a long time, making it resemble a dead one. During this time it may not respond to noise or movement. It should be appreciated that a cat's eyes do not automatically close in death, so a cat's state cannot be judged from them. In both death and unconsciousness the muscles relax, which includes the sphincters of the bladder and the anus, perhaps causing urine and motions to be passed. Of course, in death the body gradually becomes colder and after 3–7 hours the muscles become rigid (rigor mortis).

Administering artificial respiration

Lie the cat flat on its side, remove any collar and make sure that its head and neck are stretched well forward. In the case of a drowned animal the head should ideally be lower than the rest of the body, and if the animal has a wound then that should be uppermost. Place both hands on the chest wall over the ribs, and apply firm downward pressure to expel the air from the lungs. (Avoid using excessive pressure because it is easy to crush the ribs.) Immediately release the pressure and allow the chest wall to expand again and the lungs to fill with air. Repeat this procedure at approximately five-second intervals. Applying pressure more rapidly will prevent oxygen remaining in the lungs long enough to diffuse into the blood.

Provided that the heart continues beating, artificial respiration can keep the animal alive almost indefinitely – certainly long enough for veterinary help to be obtained. Check the heartbeat at intervals and ensure that the

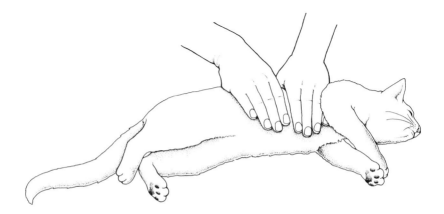

Figure 131   How to give artificial respiration

airway remains clear. If the cat is transported to the veterinary surgeon's premises, artificial respiration may be required throughout the journey. Mouth-to-mouth resuscitation ('kiss of life') has been attempted in the cat, but, because of the shape and size of its mouth, it is usually not very effective. Probably, a better procedure is to close the animal's mouth with your hands and to blow firmly and regularly into its nose with your lips closely applied to its nostrils. Blow for about three seconds, allow a two-second pause, and then repeat the sequence continuously.

Bleeding

CONTROLLING SEVERE HAEMORRHAGE

When a large blood vessel is severed, the flow of blood is vigorous enough to wash away quickly any clot which begins to form. This is especially likely when an artery is damaged, since it carries blood under high pressure, and a separate spurt of blood can be seen to emerge with each heartbeat. The recommended method for controlling severe haemorrhage is to apply pressure to the cut end of the blood vessel using a pressure bandage (pressure pad, pressure wrap). This works well with wounds on

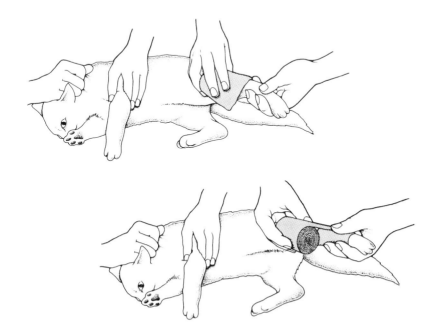

Figure 132 How to control severe bleeding from a limb

the limbs (see Fig. 132). A half-inch thick pad of clean (preferably sterile) absorbent material, such as cotton wool, or in an emergency a clean handkerchief, is quickly and firmly applied to the cut end of the blood vessel and swiftly and firmly bandaged in place. The rough surface facilitates clot formation. A crêpe bandage, which gives more certain and even pressure, is preferred for bandaging, but in an emergency a scarf or handkerchief etc. can be used. It is difficult to apply pressure pads too tightly except where a wound is around the neck. If a pad becomes soaked with blood another should be applied, usually more tightly, on top of the original until a veterinary surgeon is able to examine the animal. As an alternative, if no materials are to hand, the sides of a large wound can be tightly pressed together. Care should be taken not to push fragments of foreign bodies, such as glass or metal, further into the wound, and any obvious pieces should be removed.

To control severe haemorrhage whilst appropriate materials are being assembled and the pressure bandage is being put in place, direct pressure should be applied to the cut end of the bleeding vessel, or, as an alternative, pressure applied to specific pressure points. The three main pressure points are:

1. On the inside of the thigh at the point where the femoral artery crosses the bone, to control bleeding from the lower part of the hindlimb.
2. On the inside of the foreleg, just above the elbow joint, where the brachial artery crosses the humerus, to control bleeding from the lower part of the forelimb.
3. On the underside of the tail, where the coccygeal artery passes beneath the vertebrae, to control bleeding from the tail.

There is also a pressure point on the carotid artery at the lower part of the neck in front of the foreleg, which may help control bleeding from the head and neck, but it is difficult to find and control of bleeding is often unsatisfactory.

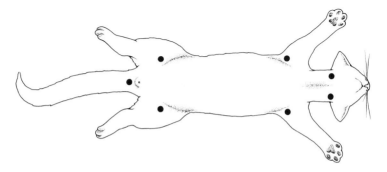

Figure 133   Pressure points

The use of a tourniquet to stop bleeding is not recommended for routine use, because totally cutting off the blood supply to tissues can result in their death. For this reason, applying pressure to pressure points, or the use of a tourniquet, should be limited to a maximum of 15 minutes at a time. In an emergency a tourniquet can be made from a narrow strip of cloth 1–2 inches wide (e.g. a tie or handkerchief) or a thick rubber band, which is then firmly tied or clipped around a limb or the tail nearer to the body of the animal than the wound. The efficiency of the tourniquet can be improved by tying a short stick, such as a pencil or ruler, on top of the first knot and then twisting it until the bleeding stops.

Special first-aid treatment is needed to arrest bleeding from sites around the head, although in all cases it is best if the animal is restrained lying down, with the site of the haemorrhage uppermost, and is kept quiet.

If bleeding is from the eyeball or from the nostrils, a pad of lint or cotton wool soaked in clean, cold water should be applied and held in place. Bandaging is not successful here, and attempts should not be made to insert materials into the nostrils. If the bleeding is from the mouth, keep the head low to prevent clots forming at the back of the throat, and if the animal is unconscious, regularly wipe out blood and clots from the mouth and throat. Haemorrhage on the inside of the lips or cheek may be controlled by squeezing the part between the fingers and thumb. With bleeding from the ear flap, place a pad of cotton wool either side of the flap, producing a 'sandwich', and then fold the ear flap flat across the top of the head so that the ear tip points towards the opposite side. The flap should then be firmly bandaged in place, using a crêpe bandage passing around the head, but not too tightly. The same procedure can be used if there is bleeding from the ear canal, although it is advisable first of all to place a small piece of cotton wool in the canal to assist clotting. In all such cases the animal should be prevented from rubbing or pawing at the lesion, or shaking its head.

Internal haemorrhage (i.e. bleeding into the chest or abdominal cavities or into hollow organs) may produce no visible sign until shock develops, unless blood is seen to pass out of the mouth or nostrils or appears in the urine, vomit or motions. It usually follows crushing or severe impact injuries, such as falls or kicks, and especially road traffic accidents. There is little that the lay person can do to control internal haemorrhage apart from keeping the animal quiet, treating the signs of shock if they appear (see page 433) and wiping away any blood that might appear in the mouth or nostrils so as to keep the airway clear.

Minor haemorrhage, even if extensive (e.g. with abrasions – 'scrape' injuries) will stop on its own after a while as a blood clot forms. Clotting can be facilitated by applying a fine powder, such as talcum powder or flour, but clots which have already formed should not be disturbed because this can bring about fresh bleeding.

COLLAPSE, CONVULSIONS AND LOSS OF CONSCIOUSNESS (COMA)

Collapse is a non-specific term, but it encompasses conditions in which the animal is usually conscious as well as some in which it is not. Collapse follows the sudden onset of complete unconsciousness, as occurs in the following examples:

(a) Physical damage to the brain, i.e. with head injuries
(b) Heart failure, e.g. with weakness of the heart muscle
(c) Stroke, i.e. blockage of the blood supply to the brain by a blood clot
(d) Some types of poisoning and snake bite
(e) The effects of 'natural poisons', such as bacterial toxins and accumulated waste products as occur in advanced cases of kidney disease or diabetes mellitus
(f) Heatstroke
(g) Hypothermia (an exceptionally low body temperature)
(h) Asphyxia (interference with breathing)
(i) Most forms of severe shock, e.g. electrocution
(j) Convulsions.

Cats may also collapse, but remain conscious to a varying degree, when these causes are present to a lesser extent, and also when animals are extremely weak (as with anaemia or severe fluid losses) or are unable or unwilling to move because of great pain or mechanical difficulty (e.g. after suffering fractures, spinal lesions or extensive muscle wasting).

Collapse

If possible, leave the cat where it has collapsed, provided that it is not in a dangerous situation, such as in a roadway or a smoke-filled room, and that it will not become very cold. Otherwise move the animal to a safe and sheltered place where there is plenty of fresh air, to avoid further injury. Do this gently and carefully, especially if there are head or back injuries. It is best not to raise the animal's head or to prop it up, e.g. by putting a cushion under it, because saliva and blood or vomit could pass to the back of the throat and block the airway. Check that the animal is breathing satisfactorily (as described above) and treat for haemorrhage and shock where necessary.

Loss of consciousness (coma)

It is important to check a cat's breathing; clear the airway and apply artificial respiration if there appears to be difficulty or if breathing has temporarily stopped. Where breathing appears to have ceased completely, check for other signs of life as described earlier. Individuals that remain unconscious for 48 hours after an accident rarely recover.

Convulsions (fits, seizures)

This is a series of violent and uncontrolled spasms of the muscles accompanied by partial or complete loss of consciousness. It begins with a series of muscle tremors that is followed by muscle contractions. It can occur when the animal collapses and shows 'paddling' and 'chewing' movements. Often the cat will salivate and froth at the mouth and pass motions and urine. Upon recovery the animal may be dazed, confused and unable to see properly. Many cats are extremely frightened and wish to hide; some become quite vicious. Most convulsions are over in 15 minutes, but there may be several attacks in one day. At times the convulsions can be continuous (*status epilepticus*). The causes include:

(a) Convulsive poisons (e.g. organochlorines, lead and metaldehyde)
(b) Brain tumours
(c) Head injuries
(d) Encephalitis (inflammation of the brain) and meningitis (inflammation of the covering of the brain), which may result from infection
(e) Diseases of the liver and kidneys where there is accumulation of toxic substances
(f) Low blood levels of glucose or calcium.

An abnormally low blood calcium level (hypocalcaemia) may occur in the nursing queen and the convulsive state which develops is termed eclampsia.

A convulsing animal is best left where it has collapsed, unless it is in a dangerous situation, e.g. near to a fire, when it is best to lift or carefully drag the animal to safety. However, to avoid getting bitten in the process, it is best to throw a blanket or coat over the cat beforehand. Otherwise the animal should be kept as quiet and undisturbed as possible; certainly do not attempt to nurse it or to give it anything by mouth. At home, move small pieces of furniture away from the animal, draw the curtains, and turn off gas or electric fires and the radio, television, hi-fi or computer.

Arrange for veterinary treatment as soon as possible and if the fit turns out to be continuous (as with some poisons), there may be no alternative but to transport the animal whilst in the convulsing state. This is best done by covering and picking it up in a blanket and then transferring it to a cat basket or other receptacle. If, as is more usual, the fit ends spontaneously, confine the cat in the same cool, dark room until it is sufficiently recovered for it to be taken to the veterinary surgeon or veterinary instructions are received. Any urine or faeces on the coat and any froth around the mouth can then be cleaned up.

Shock and its treatment

This is a clinical state in which there is an inadequate flow of blood to the body tissues, leading to a lack of perfusion with oxygen, an accumulation of acids (acidosis) and ultimately death of the cells. There are three major causes:

1. Hypovolaemic shock, resulting from a markedly reduced volume of blood in the circulation. This arises from:

(a) acute blood loss, i.e. severe haemorrhage;
(b) the loss of large amounts of fluid from the body as with diarrhoea and vomiting;
(c) the movement of massive amounts of fluid out of the circulation, such as follows crushing injuries, electrocution and the destructive effects of corrosive poisons and burns.

Internal bleeding can result in 'secondary shock' occurring some 4–6 hours after an injury.

2. Cardiogenic shock, due to reduced output of blood from the heart, which is a feature of many types of heart disease.
3. Vasculogenic shock, caused by the dilation of blood vessels. This may be the result of either of the following causes:

(a) local release of toxic substances, as with septic shock (in peritonitis or pyometra) or anaphylactic shock, as occurs following stings from wasps or bees;
(b) effects on the autonomic nervous system following damage or depression, such as very deep anaesthesia (neurogenic shock); this type is rare in animals.

The tell-tale signs of shock are as follows:

(a) The animal is weak, collapsed and almost always lies down. It is often semi-conscious and does not respond to stimulation.
(b) Breathing is rapid (more than 40 breaths per minute) and also shallow (i.e. panting).
(c) The lips, gums and tongue appear pale and greyish and feel cold and clammy, the main exception being in septic shock when they may appear reddened.
(d) The paws feel cold, even though the animal is in warm surroundings, and it often trembles or shivers. Its body temperature, when taken, is found to be subnormal. Again the only exception to this general rule is in septic shock where fever may exist.
(e) The heart beats more rapidly (i.e. more than 180 beats per minute).
(f) The pupils are often dilated (i.e. wide open) and the eyes appear glazed and unseeing.
(g) The cat may vomit.

Any problems with breathing or haemorrhage should be attended to first, as mentioned previously. The cat should be kept horizontal if possible to ensure effective blood circulation, and it should be kept warm. If the animal is wet it should be dried and not allowed to lie directly on a cold or wet surface. Body heat should be conserved by covering it with blankets or aluminium foil and providing it with a *warm* hot-water bottle, but it should *not* be subjected to direct heating in front of a fire or radiator, or on a heating pad. Such animals are not able to regulate their body temperature effectively. Although the aim is to maintain normal body temperature, animals do survive moderate hypothermia better than overheating.

If the cat is sufficiently conscious to drink and wants to do so, it may be given small amounts of warmed liquids (e.g. milk or water, possibly with added glucose). However, withhold liquids if the animal begins to vomit and never attempt to force them into the cat. Particularly avoid giving any form of alcohol, such as brandy; although this may prove beneficial in certain types of shock, it is extremely harmful in others. In general, keep the animal quiet and undisturbed.

Shock is a serious condition and veterinary attention for it should be obtained quickly. An important part of treatment is fluid therapy, preferably given intravenously, to restore the circulating blood volume, together with, in some cases, specialist stimulant drugs.

Specific problems in first aid

The general principles, as described above, apply in all cases, but at times there may be specific problems.

ROAD TRAFFIC ACCIDENTS

Undoubtedly, this type of accident is the most common emergency in which cats are involved, especially in urban areas. Nevertheless, in rural areas the speed of the vehicle on impact, and the resultant trauma, are often greater. There are many different types of injuries and multiple injuries are common. At times, these are so severe as to cause the death of the animal immediately or within 24 hours. This is an inevitable consequence of allowing a cat the freedom to wander at will. In the 1980s it was estimated that in Baltimore, Maryland, USA, a city of 800,000 people, 5,000 cats were killed by motor vehicles each year, of which well over half were unneutered males. A majority of deaths occurred during the summer months. The animal may be struck a direct or glancing blow, not only from the front bumper or a wheel, but also from a low-slung part of the chassis, transmission or exhaust system as the vehicle passes above the cat. It may suffer crush injuries as a wheel passes over part of the body, and it may at times be dragged behind the vehicle for a considerable distance. In addition to shock, a road accident can produce a variety of external and internal wounds with varying degrees of haemorrhage, fractures, dislocations, concussion or paralysis. Head and pelvic injuries are very common, and sometimes there is diaphragmatic hernia (passage of the abdominal organs into the chest cavity through a ruptured diaphragm), which causes great difficulty in breathing. Almost all cases of diaphragmatic hernia are due to road traffic accidents.

At times, the only external evidence of a cat's involvement in a road accident may be frayed or splintered claws, resulting from its attempt to grip the road surface, and possibly some loss of hair, with oil and dirt on the coat. Despite the minimal external signs, there is often serious internal bleeding.

The animal may remain at the scene of the accident, frequently dazed or unconscious, or it may run away in a blind panic, only to return home, if at all, several hours or even days later. First-aid treatment for road traffic accidents consists primarily of treatment for shock, plus attention for whatever other serious sign(s) might be present, e.g. severe haemorrhage, difficulty in breathing, fracture, paralysis, etc. before the cat can receive veterinary attention.

HIGH-RISE SYNDROME

Falls from a great height are more common in cats than in dogs. They enjoy sitting on balconies and window ledges, but are sometimes distracted (e.g. by birds or insects) or are suddenly woken from sleep (e.g. by a loud noise) and lose their balance. The worst injuries are sustained by cats that fall 5–9 storeys. Damage to the chest on impact with the ground results in pneumothorax (air in the chest), and fractures of the forelegs, face and hard palate are common.

FRACTURES

These are breaks or cracks in bones caused by the application of physical force. Most fractures are the result of road traffic accidents and falls, and in the cat the bones most often affected are the femur (thigh bone) and pelvis, the vertebrae in the tail and the mandible (lower jaw).

Fractures are described as 'open' or 'closed', depending upon whether or not the skin surface is also disrupted; sometimes the broken end of the bone protrudes through the skin. Such 'open fractures' are more likely to become infected.

Fractures are also classified on the basis of the number of breaks, on the fragments of bone or on the damage to the surrounding tissues, but from a first-aid point of view such classification is unimportant, the only type worth special mention being a 'greenstick fracture', in which the bone is not completely broken but merely cracked and bent. This type usually occurs in young animals where the bones are still flexible.

The six major signs of a fracture (not all of which may necessarily be present) are:

1. Pain at the fracture site, which can make the animal resent handling and provoke shock.
2. Swelling due to bleeding and bruising.
3. An unnatural degree of movement in the lower part of the limb or the tail, which may swing freely or even be dragged along.
4. A loss of function, so that the animal may be unable to move or to use the fractured part normally, thereby appearing lame.
5. Some deformity, which may be obvious, such as shortening or twisting of the limb, or which may only become apparent when felt, such as a protrusion or sharp edge along the bone.
6. A grating sound (crepitus), heard when the animal moves or is handled, due to the broken ends of the bone moving against each other. Of course this noise is absent in greenstick fractures.

If you are uncertain as to whether the shape of a bone is abnormal, or whether there is undue movement present, compare it with the same part on the opposite side of the body.

In addition to applying the general principles of first aid, movement of the fractured bone should be limited to minimize pain and to prevent further damage to surrounding tissues. The cat's movements should be severely restricted, and the limb or other affected part not handled unnecessarily. Support and immobilize it as far as is possible, particularly if the animal has to be transported.

Fractures and dislocations of the spine can result in paralysis of the hind quarters, demonstrated by the cat's inability to move its hindlegs. To avoid further damage, it is important that such animals are lifted with the spine perfectly straight, e.g. on a tray or something similar. Regrettably the long-term outlook for such cases can be poor.

DISLOCATIONS

This condition occurs when one of the bones which forms a joint moves out of place. Usually considerable force is required for this to occur; it frequently follows a road traffic accident, and dislocation of the hip joint is the most common example. The lower jaw can also be dislocated, resulting in an inability to close the mouth.

Although there are many features in common with fractures, useful distinguishing signs of dislocations are that pain and swelling are usually confined to the region of the joint, movement is restricted rather than increased and there is no grating sound or penetration of the skin. However, it can be difficult to make a complete distinction, especially when fractures occur near to joints, and of course at times they may occur together. In general the same basic advice applies as in cases of fracture.

FOREIGN BODIES

Any solid object or fragment which enters part of an animal's body (e.g. a needle, grass seed, or a piece of bone or glass) is classified as a foreign body. Young cats are more likely to swallow objects than older ones. Some foreign bodies penetrate the body tissues, either passing through the skin or through the wall of the digestive tract. Others merely become lodged in a part of the body, usually part of the digestive tract, e.g. mouth, stomach or intestines, but also in the ear or nose, beneath the eyelids or between or in the pads.

Foreign bodies in the mouth cause profuse salivation, often gulping, frantic rubbing and pawing at the mouth, with movements of the tongue and jaws, and, if the airway is blocked, choking and gasping. Kittens may attempt to eat balls and toys made of wool or foam rubber, and this can result in obstruction and choking. If, after opening the mouth, the foreign body can be seen, it should be firmly grasped with fine-nosed pliers and removed. Occasionally, a small cooked bone, such as a vertebra, may be speared by a canine tooth, or a piece of bone may become wedged between the teeth. Again it may be possible to remove these with pliers.

Barbed fish hooks which have penetrated the lip or tongue cannot, because of the barbs, be drawn out the same way as they went in. These hooks need to be pushed all the way through with the animal under a general anaesthetic, and then the barbs cut off with wire cutters so that the shank can be withdrawn.

Foreign bodies (often grass seeds) up the nose or in the eye or ear should be removed (if protruding) with tweezers. In each instance the affected part will be rubbed by the animal; foreign bodies in the nose tend to cause sneezing and those in the eye result in increased tear production. If they cannot readily be removed, a veterinary surgeon should be consulted, and meantime a little warm olive oil or liquid paraffin can be dropped into the eye or ear. However, do not attempt to place anything up the nose.

The occasional swallowing of foreign bodies seems to be related to the hunting and play behaviour of cats. Most commonly these are string, fish hooks, pins, needles, bones, small toys, and, of course, hair – a consequence of poor grooming in longhaired cats. If hairs are not combed or brushed out the cat will remove them as it washes itself, and, because of the backward-pointing rough processes on the cat's tongue, it is difficult for the hairs to be passed forward out of the mouth. It is much easier for the hairs to pass backwards so that they gradually work their way into the throat and are swallowed. The hair then accumulates and forms a hairball. A cat with a hairball in the stomach can feel hungry and yet full at the same time and consequently makes frequent trips to the feeding bowl, but eats very little.

Apart from hairballs, needle and thread foreign bodies are the most frequently found, although in 90 per cent of these thread alone is present.

Solid objects may be arrested in the oesophagus (causing gagging, salivation, repeated swallowing or difficulty in swallowing) or in the stomach (causing loss of appetite and perhaps vomiting, sometimes with blood) but rarely in the intestine. Needles that have been swallowed may penetrate the digestive tract or at times pass right through it only to turn just before moving out of the anus, thereby lodging in the rectum. The animal licks at the anus and strains and there may be bleeding.

The major problem in the intestine is so-called linear foreign bodies, usually lengths of thread or string, one end of which becomes trapped around the base of the tongue or at the exit from the stomach. The normal contractions of the intestinal musculature cause the intestine to move forwards over the fixed string, becoming bunched-up or pleated in the process. Eventually, the pressure of the string on the folds in the intestine will result in complete perforation at a number of points, the consequence of which is peritonitis.

If one end of the string is seen in the mouth, around the tongue (present in 50 per cent of cases) or hanging from the anus, *do not* pull on it as serious damage could be caused; instead, take the cat to a veterinary surgeon as soon as possible.

Foreign bodies in the paws and skin, such as glass fragments, drawing pins and pieces of tar-covered grit from roads, should be pulled out, using fingers, tweezers or pliers wherever possible. If the foreign body has temporarily to remain in the wound, because it is impossible to remove, covering the wound with a thick pad of cotton wool, lightly bandaged in place, can help to limit further injury.

BURNS AND SCALDS

Burns are caused by dry heat (a flame or hot surface) and scalds by hot liquids (boiling water or hot fat), although their treatment is identical, and for practical purposes both can be described as thermal burns. Because blistering of the skin is not a feature, burns are best not classified as first-, second- and third-degree but as superficial, partial-thickness and full-thickness burns. A major burn is a partial-thickness or full-thickness injury, which involves more than 20 per cent of the total body area.

Scalds are more common in cats than dry heat burns, resulting from boiling water or hot cooking oil being spilled or splashed on to the animal, generally in the kitchen. Frequently, it is not appreciated that scalding has occurred until a day or so later when one or more scabs are felt when the cat is stroked or groomed. Examples of dry heat burns are those on the feet and tail of cats that walk on cooker hotplates or the embers of bonfires or barbecues.

Fortunately, burning-building burns are usually confined to the pads, face and ears of cats, because other parts are protected by their thick hair coats. The majority of fire-related deaths that occur are in fact due to inhalation poisoning by carbon monoxide and other noxious chemicals produced by burning materials (e.g. the oxides of nitrogen and sulphur, acrolein, benzene and cyanides). The tendency of cats to hide in a place of previous security, such as under the bed, rather than to attempt to leave the premises, increases the risk of this happening.

Excessive heat can damage the lining of the mouth and upper respiratory tract, causing a degree of swelling which obstructs the airway. Inhalation of live steam or explosive gases (which is mercifully rare) can inflict damage throughout the respiratory tract. Super-heated particles of soot and other substances may also be inhaled during fires.

Burns are painful, produce shock and later exude plasma. They may become infected and cause contraction of the skin due to scar formation. Malicious burns, caused by fireworks or following dousing in petrol or paraffin, produce the most extensive and horrific burns, and their immediate treatment requires the smothering of any flames by covering the cat with a blanket, rug or coat.

With all thermal burns water should be liberally applied for 5–10 minutes to remove residual heat. This should be done as soon as possible, using a spray attachment or hose, or water can simply be poured or sponged over the area. Any constriction around the site, such as a collar, should be removed because the area will swell, but any burned material which is adherent to the skin should be cut away and not simply pulled, which will also remove skin layers. Subsequently severe shock is a problem and hypothermia must be prevented; animals should be wrapped in clean sheets and blankets for both warmth and comfort during transport.

It is not necessary for the temperature to be very high for skin cells to be destroyed (70°C for one minute will suffice), and the cause can be apparently trivial, such as holding a hair-dryer too close to the skin or contact with a hot-water bottle, something which is a risk if the animal is unconscious.

Oils and greasy preparations should not be applied because they delay healing.

In all cases the help of a veterinary surgeon should be sought, and obviously this should be done immediately in cases of major burns.

In addition to thermal burns there are also freezer burns, chemical burns (corrosives such as bleach, creosote, melted road tar, acids and alkalis), electrical burns, sunburn, radiation burns and frictional burns (due to the heat of friction in addition to abrasion of the skin surface, e.g. when an animal is dragged along the ground or contacts a rapidly moving wheel).

Electrical burns most often occur when flexes are playfully chewed. Usually this results in unconsciousness for a time followed by muscle spasms and difficulty in breathing. The localized burns which result, e.g. to the hard palate, may not be evident for several days. When a cat remains in contact with the source of current, switch it off before handling the animal, although with relatively low voltage domestic supplies, i.e. up to 250 volts, some dry material (e.g. a dry coat, blanket or rug) can be used to cover the animal and provide insulation as it is pulled or pushed away. However, this should not be attempted with a high voltage supply, because *you* may be electrocuted as well. In severe cases of electrocution, artificial respiration is essential to reinstate breathing.

HEATSTROKE

This can affect cats kept for a period in extremely hot, poorly ventilated surroundings, especially if they are also without water. Many cases occur when a cat is left inside a cat carrier within a car parked in the hot sun; there is a tremendous build-up of heat even if the car windows are left fully open.

Although cats seem better able to tolerate high temperatures than dogs, eventually they are unable to maintain their normal body temperature and this gradually rises. They become increasingly distressed and weak, panting rapidly and drooling saliva, with the tongue and lips appearing bright red. Eventually such animals will collapse, go into a coma and die. This condition sometimes arises in cats that have been accidentally, or maliciously, shut inside a clothes drier.

First-aid treatment aims at lowering the body temperature quickly by the application of cold water to the skin. The animal should be carefully placed in a large water-filled bowl (e.g. washing-up bowl) or bath, with its head above the water; alternatively water can be sprayed from a hose or simply poured or sponged over the body surface. Successful treatment is rewarded by an obvious improvement in breathing and the cat's improved appreciation of its surroundings within 5–10 minutes.

Do not overdo the cooling process, because the normal temperature-regulating mechanism of the brain has been severely impaired, and once the body temperature has begun to fall it may continue to do so. In some cases it may be necessary to apply artificial respiration.

After cooling, the cat should be dried and left to rest in a cool place with adequate drinking water, but it is usually desirable to seek veterinary advice. Veterinary surgeons may resort to using cold water enemas if bathing alone does not bring about a sufficient fall in temperature.

HYPOTHERMIA

A significant fall in the body's core temperature can occur in cats exposed to severe chilling and/or wetting, especially the old, injured, debilitated or unconscious. Shivering ceases at body temperatures below 90°F and animals appear lethargic, stiff and bemused and can only walk with difficulty. In extreme cases, breathing, and even the pulse, can be difficult to detect and cats may be thought to be dead.

Kittens under 2 months of age are particularly susceptible to hypothermia, because their thermoregulatory mechanisms are poorly developed.

All such cats must be gently handled, because it is easy to induce cardiac arrest. Re-warming is best begun by wrapping the cat in blankets rather than exposing it to sources of intense heat, which may provoke cardiac irregularities and collapse. Subsequently, a veterinary surgeon may employ the infusion of warmed liquids to warm the animal internally.

PROTRUSION/PROLAPSE OF ORGANS

In all cases where body organs are displaced and appear externally they should be covered with a suitably large piece of clean (preferably sterile) cloth that has been soaked in clean, cold water and wrung out. This should be held or bandaged in place to prevent further injury to, and drying out of, the organs until veterinary assistance is available. Do not apply any dry material, which will stick and cause damage when removed. Fortunately these situations seldom arise, but when they do they are very dramatic and frightening.

Following damage to the abdominal wall (usually in a road accident, but sometimes in fights or as doors are closed), the intestines may protrude. There should be no attempt to push the contents back in place, but the cat should be restrained on its back or side, with the organs covered as described above and held in place with a wide bandage.

At times the eyeball may be forced out of its socket due to increased pressure behind it. After prolapse the eyeball swells rapidly and cannot readily be replaced in its socket. Do not attempt to replace the displaced eyeball yourself or to allow the animal to rub the eyeball on the ground or with its paw. Instead, hold a damp pad in position over the eyeball and try to keep the animal calm until it receives veterinary attention.

Veterinary Nursing

27

VETERINARY NURSING

The veterinary nurse, or VN, that cat owners encounter at the vet's surgery has been professionally trained and has had to pass two stiff examinations to qualify for the title. Generally people are sure the VN has been around as long as the vet, and are surprised to learn that the sort of VN they know has only really existed since the 1960s, having come into being after a long, haphazard development, which it is interesting to trace.

Very few pet animals received veterinary attention until well into the last century. Veterinary knowledge of them was relatively sparse and it just did not occur to owners to seek veterinary attention. Both cats and dogs usually spent most of their lives outdoors and slept in outhouses.

With the rise in popularity of the 'lapdog' among society ladies in the last century things began to change, and it was perhaps the care of these animals that formed the basis for pet animal practice as we know it today. It was often the lady's maid's task to assist the vet by holding the animal or to administer any subsequent treatment he ordered.

From such beginnings, small animal practice, i.e. that aimed at pet animals and not horses, cattle and sheep, started to develop, and by the end of the last century there was a canine hospital in Neasden, north-west London, with facilities for 200 patients. This is quite remarkable when one considers that few veterinary surgeons today hospitalize more than 30 dogs at a time and even large boarding and quarantine kennels seldom exceed 200 animals. This Neasden hospital was run on similar lines to a general hospital and there were even male and female wards, according to an article in a magazine called *Homechat* in January 1899. A dog bathing pool was provided and the magazine published a photograph of two dogs swimming with three men in attendance. Were these the first male veterinary nurses?

An eminent veterinary surgeon, Sir William Hobday, established a practice in Kensington, west London, at the beginning of this century and reference is made in his book *Surgical Diseases of the Dog and Cat*, published in 1906, to his small 'infirmary' at the practice. However, there is no mention of personnel.

A Canine Nurses Institute (CNI) was in existence prior to the First World War and the nurses employed by it wore uniforms and a CNI badge embroidered in red on a white background. At this time nursing sick dogs was considered a means of 'opening up a new line of work to women'. The rules of conduct of the CNI were very similar to those we present-day VNs follow and which appear in our contracts of employment, particularly those relating to professional conduct towards the animal patients and the owner.

This CNI would provide qualified nurses when required for £1 5s 0d (£1.25) per week, plus board, lodging and travelling, which made them considerably better paid than many other employees at that time. They may have priced themselves out of business, since no further references can be found to the Canine Nurses Institute. Training covered treatment of sick animals, setting and bandaging broken limbs and giving medication. Tuition on coat care and even showing was included, together with care of cats.

It seems that the south of England was undoubtedly the place for these forerunners of our veterinary nursing scheme, for in 1913 in Middlesex the Ruislip Dog Sanatorium published an illustrated brochure with what appears to be a 'lady nurse' sitting outside a door labelled 'Surgery and Office'. The Sanatorium was under the direct supervision of a veterinary surgeon, William Kirk. Today the site is part of a modern housing estate.

In 1933 a cigarette card in a series issued by Churchman's cigarettes depicted Mrs Florence Bell, the Head Nurse at the Royal Veterinary College in London's Camden Town. I was told by two vets who were on the staff at the College at the time that she was very respected, and even feared by some members of the staff. They recall her as a very dedicated person.

An entire book on canine nursing was published in 1938 by veterinary surgeon David Wilkinson. Throughout reference is made to the unpleasantness of the tasks, the strong disinfectants needed and the necessity for the nurse to wear thick gloves for protection. At that time few small animal diseases could be positively cured and only devoted nursing could help the fortunate ones.

Prior to the Second World War an attempt was made by two vets in small animal practice in Mayfair, in London's West End, to 'train women nurses for dogs'. They approached the Royal College of Veterinary Surgeons (RCVS), the governing body for veterinary education in Great Britain, and asked them to recognize the designation of 'canine nurse', which a person would be entitled to assume after they had passed appropriate examinations based on the study of a syllabus to be approved by the RCVS. This approach to the RCVS was the first serious attempt to establish a national veterinary nursing course as we know it today. It did not come to fruition until 1961, nearly 30 years later, by which time small animal practice had become an established part of the veterinary scene.

In 1957 the British Small Animal Veterinary Association (BSAVA) was established by a group of veterinary surgeons particularly interested in 'specializing' in small animal matters. These forward-looking veterinary surgeons were aware of the need for staff trained to a basic standard who could assist and support them in their work. Only four years after the formation of the BSAVA such a scheme was officially commenced by the RCVS.

The early years presented many problems. A syllabus was organized but there were difficulties in determining the level of knowledge that would be required and the standard that should be set. There was resistance to the need for qualified nurses from vets who had lay assistants, trained in the ways of their particular practice, and, having worked with them for years, considered them very competent. Many held the view that their home-trained staff were better than any 'outside trained' personnel would be – and, moreover, why should their staff not be considered 'qualified'?

Then there was the problem of the name – the simple, elegant, descriptive title 'veterinary nurse' could not be used. The title 'nurse' was protected by the Royal College of Nursing and could only apply to a person trained in human nursing. Difficulties were encountered in the use of the term 'veterinary' so the rather demeaning title 'Registered Animal Nursing Auxiliary' (RANA) was agreed as a compromise and RANAs we remained until 1984.

Figure 134   The RANA VN and BVNA badges

The Nurses, Midwives and Health Visitors Act of 1979 and the Nurses Act of 1957 were due for repeal in July 1983 and this opened the way for the official recognition of the title 'Veterinary Nurse'. The RCVS moved swiftly and effected the necessary changes, so with effect from 1 November 1984, those qualifying could legally use the term veterinary nurse and bear the letters VN after their name. Those of us who qualified as RANAs were able to convert from 1 November 1984, so many of us possess two certificates, one as a RANA and the other as a VN, and two similar badges, one inscribed VN and the other RANA.

A statutory register for veterinary nurses, giving them official recognition as a professional body, was the next step to be taken and had to wait until there was an amendment to the Veterinary Surgeons' Act. This took place on 1 July 1991.

From that date, the change made in the law enabled qualified veterinary nurses to 'carry out any medical treatment or minor surgery, not involving entry to a body cavity, on a companion animal under the direction of a veterinary surgeon'.

For all those who had long campaigned for the recognition of the importance of the role of VNs in the care and welfare of animals and as vital support staff for the veterinary surgeon, this was a most satisfactory development. The RCVS is now required by law to maintain an up-to-date list of all VNs so that only those suitably qualified and experienced (and in good standing as the professional bodies put it) will be entitled to exercise the right to undertake minor surgery and medical treatment. Naturally these rights can only be exercised under the supervision or direction of a registered veterinary surgeon.

The list of VNs is based on the existing register maintained by the RCVS and on this list are entered all who pass the veterinary nursing examinations, complete with the two years' training, and pay the registration fee. The old register will now be closed.

Commencing in 1993 and annually thereafter those on the new list will be required to pay a modest annual retention fee to help defray the costs of maintaining and publishing the list. As only those appearing on this list will be permitted to exercise the new rights to carry out minor surgery and medical treatment, it is imperative that the list is available to veterinary surgeons so they can check that any VNs they employ are legally entitled to carry out their duties.

These new powers effectively designate VNs as veterinary para-professionals and with their new status, of which they are justly proud, have come new responsibilities. With the responsibilities will come a disciplinary system administered by the RCVS similar to the present disciplinary system exercised for veterinary surgeons. The expectation is that such a system will not often be needed.

At present minimum entry requirements are 4 GCSE passes at A, B or C grades or acceptable equivalents. There is also a Pre-veterinary Nursing course available. The minimum age for enrolment is 17 but there is no upper age limit. The student must be in full-time employment for a minimum of 35 hours a week at a training centre approved by the RCVS. Approved training centres (ATCs) are usually established veterinary

Figure 135 Qualified VN preparing surgical swabs prior to sterilization

Figure 136 Veterinary nurses are trained to carry out many laboratory procedures in practice

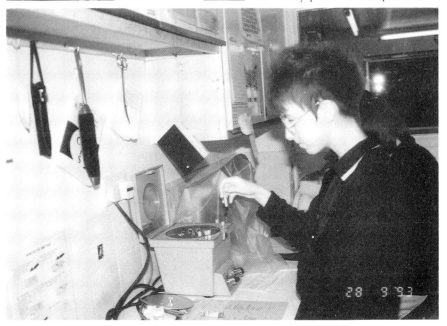

practices with a high component of small animal work, although certain other establishments such as the Dogs' Home, Battersea, London Zoo, the Royal Army Veterinary Corps and Wood Green Animal Shelters are also approved training centres. The student has to work for at least two years in an ATC and be successful in both the professional examinations, one at the end of each year, before qualifying as a VN. The Part I examination is taken at the end of the first year and deals basically with anatomy, physiology, kennel and cattery management and first aid. The successful candidate then embarks upon the syllabus for the final examination which many regard as veterinary nursing proper, with subjects such as radiography, surgical and medical nursing as well as intensive care, anaesthesia and laboratory work. The Part II examination incorporates an exhaustive practical test.

Full details of the requirements for entry to the veterinary nursing scheme, lists of approved training centres and enrolment forms are available from the BVNA office on receipt of a large stamped addressed envelope.

The veterinary nursing qualification is not easily acquired. It requires tremendous dedication to study subjects which appear, superficially at least, unrelated to the day-to-day work, particularly after a long working day in practice. This is very apparent in the case of the Part I syllabus, when the finer aspects of anatomy and physiology are hard to reconcile with a day spent scrubbing out a ward of cats with diarrhoea!

There are currently approximately 1500 approved training centres in Great Britain. Some employ several trainees while others may engage only one at a time. In addition to the minimum entry requirements, some ATCs require trainees to be 18 or over, especially if they are living away from home. Others demand a higher academic level of entry. There are many qualified VNs today who commenced training with one or more GCSE A level. There are also many of us who have trained as mature students.

Training methods vary but all have to follow the guidelines issued by the RCVS in the current 'Guide for Persons Wishing to Train as Veterinary Nurses'. This is obtainable from the BVNA on payment of the appropriate fee.

The aim of the course is to produce practical VNs trained to a minimum standard so therefore much of the training is covered by normal day-to-day duties in the ATC with additional formal tuition. Some ATCs provide this in the form of lectures at the practice given by the staff and sometimes outside lecturers. There are various part-time courses, some on a day release basis and others run as evening classes. Full-time residential courses are available at several agricultural colleges and in conjunction with some veterinary schools, as well as block release courses. In addition, the BSAVA run day and weekend courses for VN students on various parts of the syllabus and the British Veterinary Nursing Association (BVNA) arranges scientific meetings which are often of value for trainees.

Figure 137 Student veterinary nurse tube feeding a kitten. Note approved striped uniform

A correspondence course is available to those who are unable to travel to formal lectures and this has veterinary surgeons and VNs as tutors.

The examination consists of multiple choice written papers and Part II has an emphasis on practical components of the course as well as a written section. Examiners are veterinary surgeons and VNs appointed by the RCVS Veterinary Nursing Committee.

The scope of work open to veterinary nurses continues to widen but the majority are still employed by veterinary surgeons in small animal practice. It is recognized that our training allows us to carry out nursing duties competently and efficiently and this is endorsed by the change in the Veterinary Surgeons' Act.

Many VNs today are employed in commerce, working as veterinary representatives, managing drug wholesalers' warehouses or working as product managers for drug companies. Also many of us are involved in practice management where we undertake stock control and general practice administration, or run practice laboratories. VNs with business qualifications are increasingly in demand as practice managers. VNs are also employed as kennel managers in boarding, breeding and quarantine kennels, as lecturers on veterinary nursing and related courses at agricultural colleges, as well as nurses, counsellors and administrators in small animal practices and welfare organizations. Several dog wardens have veterinary nursing qualifications. The opportunities are endless and thus criticisms in the past that there is no career structure are now clearly confounded.

Although predominantly a women's profession, men are encouraged to qualify and there are many career prospects available.

Responsibility in general practice can vary from head nurse over two or three others to being part of a senior nursing team in a larger practice with responsibilities in one area only, such as the operating theatre, client counselling, or, if your interest lies in laboratory work, you may find your *métier* in charge of the practice laboratory. It is impossible accurately to define a career structure in such a wide range of workplace situations. Promotion in the accepted meaning of the word is often impossible in practice, but a change in jobs *is* possible and, with the variety of openings that exist, a more senior position attainable.

In 1989 the introduction of the Diploma in Advanced Veterinary Nursing (Surgical) was introduced. This is a further qualification for those qualified two or more years. The Diploma course covers two years with a structured tutoring course, residential course and oral and practical examinations in anaesthesia, radiography and intensive care. The standard is extremely high and the first 18 obtained this further qualification in the summer of 1992.

In 1965, two years after the first final examination, there were 46 qualified nurses, or RANAs to use the official but hated title. The scheme was a success! There are now over 4000 RANAs and VNs with over 2500 on the new register. Students in training number approximately 2500.

The next logical step was the formation of an official Veterinary Nursing Association and this came into being on 13 March 1965 as the result of the efforts of a group of RANAs considerably aided by a minority of veterinary surgeons committed to the concept. The name selected by the original committee was the British Veterinary Nursing Association (BVNA), another sign of the distaste for the officially assigned designation. The aims of that original committee were commendable and should be acknowledged. Sadly, the establishment prevailed and before long the association's name was changed to British Animal Nursing Auxiliaries Association (BANAA). The President was, until 1984, a veterinary surgeon but subsequently a VN was elected to this office. Trevor Turner, editor of this book and the last veterinary surgeon President, was committed to the concept of future BVNA presidents being drawn from the veterinary nursing profession.

The early development of the BVNA was similar to that of all new and numerically small associations. Newsletters were typed, duplicated and issued sporadically. Meetings were few and far between. Membership grew, however, and before long the BANAA was invited to attend the BSAVA's annual congress. Uniforms were organized and approved and exhibited at veterinary congresses.

The approved uniform for the VN was suggested by the BSAVA. Qualified VNs wear a bottle-green dress and belt and a white apron. Student nurses wear green and white striped dresses with a black belt for the first year and a grey belt for the second plus similar white aprons. In the

Figure 138 The format of the BVNA journal has changed over the years

early days of the scheme a white cap was worn but this has been discontinued since the hat was not very suitable in such a practical job. Similarly, uniform cuff frills are seldom seen today.

After the title VN was approved and the demeaning title 'auxiliary' lost, the Association was able to revert to its proper title of BVNA, which marked a tremendous increase in membership.

Today the BVNA publishes a highly professional journal every two months. This has scientific articles, news items, details of forthcoming meetings, branch news, etc. There are over 30 BVNA branches around the country and meetings take place approximately every two months. Support for the branches comes from BVNA members and anyone else interested in veterinary nursing.

The BVNA flourished even before its change of name. During the 1970s the first all-day scientific meeting was held to coincide with the AGM. This became an annual congress. Its popularity led to its outgrowing the long standing venue at the Berkshire College of Agriculture and in 1987 it moved to the National Agricultural Centre at Stoneleigh. At the centre facilities to cater for 325 delegates were reserved and nearly 100 potential delegates had to be turned away. Therefore in 1988 a larger facility was booked at the National Agricultural Centre and nearly 500 delegates attended. In 1989, for the first time, a dual presentation took place with simultaneous lectures in two different lecture rooms. The congress now expects around 900 delegates every year and in 1990 was spread over two days. The flourishing commercial exhibition that accompanies the congress now boasts over 100 stands at each congress.

And still BVNA goes from strength to strength with its annual congress. The first International Veterinary Nursing congress was held in 1993, again at Stoneleigh, but this time a three-day programme was attended by over 1000 delegates.

The inaugural International Veterinary Nursing meeting took place at the World Small Animal Association Congress in Vienna in 1991. There were several representatives of BVNA present and delegates from Canada, USA, Germany, the Netherlands, Switzerland, Australia and Romania as well as one from Australia who had trained as a VN in England before emigrating. In 1993 BVNA congress hosted the first International Veterinary Nursing congress with over 70 overseas delegates from 11 countries.

The BVNA is now established as the voice of the veterinary nursing profession and is self-supporting. However, help for the BVNA from the veterinary profession as a whole continues unabated, with consistent additional support from the 'trade', those drug companies, pet food suppliers, equipment manufacturers and pet insurance houses who realize that it is the VN in practice they should contact to generate business. All in veterinary nursing are grateful for this support.

Until 1988, BVNA, like so many other associations, was run by its Council Members meeting at a central venue every 6 to 8 weeks but carrying out most of the work from their homes. As membership increased so the need for an established office became apparent. Legal advice was taken and a decision was made to establish an independent office in Essex. Now all BVNA business including council meetings is conducted there. In less than a year the office was being used to its capacity and so there was another move to larger premises on the same site. Today BVNA is in the process of assuming responsibility for more and more of the veterinary nursing scheme presently administered by the RCVS. Hence even larger office space is required and the search is now on for a more permanent home, either as a result of purchase of premises or on a long lease.

Membership details are available from the office. There are several categories of membership ranging from the qualified VNs, who are full members with voting rights, to student members and also associate membership for those working in veterinary practice or allied fields who are supporters of the Association.

ADDRESSES

British Veterinary Nursing Association, The Seedbed Centre, Coldharbour Road, Harlow, Essex CM19 5AF. Tel. 0279 450567.

Royal College of Veterinary Surgeons, 32 Belgrave Square, London SW1X 8QP. Tel. 071 235 4971.

28

NURSING THE SICK CAT

The aim of this chapter is to outline broad principles. Specific conditions will only be mentioned when examples are required.

Cats when sick have different needs from when healthy and it is important to recognize these in order that nursing can be correctly undertaken. Owners are frequently too emotionally involved with their pets to realize how important it is for certain instructions from the veterinarian to be carried out precisely and it may be preferable for the cat to be nursed in the veterinary practice rather than at home. If this is suggested, it will be because it is considered to be in the patient's best interests.

Considerable differences exist between nursing the cat in the home and in the veterinary practice. At home the pet is in familiar surroundings, with noises from household appliances, radio, television and sometimes nearby traffic. In the practice the patient will be placed in a comfortable cage, but it will be surrounded by strange people and strange noises. Even stranger smells come from disinfectants, medication and other animals. Surprisingly, cats seem to cope very well under these circumstances, probably because they are adaptable and the dedicated attention from the veterinary personnel reassures them. Since the majority of the cats are pets, they respond to voice and touch as they do with their owners at home. One of the main functions of a veterinary team is to provide the stimulus to get well by 'touch and talk' (see Fig. 139) although early in the course of treatment when the animal may be quite ill, the veterinarian may feel that even this stimulation must be denied. However should this be so, it will be only for a short period in the majority of cases.

It is a matter for the veterinarian to decide where best the animal should be nursed. It makes sense that the cat returns home to familiar surroundings as soon as possible because, as with people, recovery is usually that much more rapid at home. However there are some situations where home nursing is just not possible.

Figure 139   Tender loving care

If a cat requires intravenous feeding or fluids, i.e. is on a drip (see Fig. 140), home nursing would be virtually impossible. The cat must be in an environment where movement is strictly curtailed and trained personnel are available to adjust flow rates, change solutions and ensure the cat is comfortable. Restriction of movement in a hospital cage helps to ensure that the intravenous line is not dislodged. In practice there are various methods to ensure the drip remains in place but few owners could undertake this. Animals are great at interfering with dressings and drips and cats are no exception. Interference with a drip could cause physical damage to the vein as well as disrupting treatment if it went unnoticed.

Intravenous fluids are usually administered into the cephalic (radial) vein in the foreleg or the jugular vein in the neck. It is done by the insertion of a fine plastic or metal tube (catheter) into the vein which is then carefully strapped or bandaged in place (Fig. 141). The choice of vein depends on the cat, its condition, and sometimes the veterinarian's preference.

While the cat is very ill, it is not worried that there is a catheter conveying life-giving fluids into the bloodstream, but once there is improvement, there will be a concerted effort to remove this strange object. Even an owner with some medical training would find it difficult to cope in such circumstances.

The administration of medication in tablet or capsule form can be undertaken by most owners (see Chapter 29, Administration of

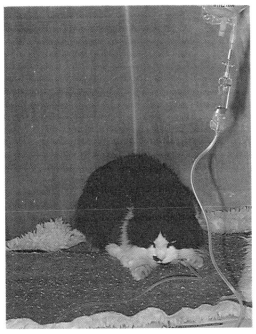

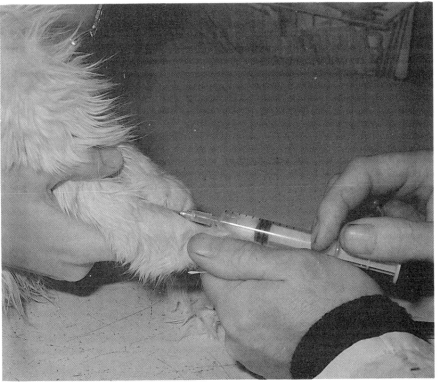

Figure 140 Intravenous drip

Figure 141 Intravenous injection

Medicines). Some tablets are specially formulated to be palatable for cats, which does help. Cats, unlike dogs, do not respond as well to bribery as an aid to medication. However certain aids in the form of 'pill poppers' are available and can be useful. It is important to follow instructions carefully and ensure that all medication is given as instructed. If in doubt, do not be afraid of asking. Tablets to be given three times a day should be evenly spaced out at 8-hourly intervals to ensure a correct level of the drug is available for maximum effect. Many labels now instruct owners to give medication every 8 hours rather than three times a day or every 12 hours rather than twice a day. This is less ambiguous. If instructions are given for medication to be administered before or after meals, it is important these instructions are followed. Different drugs need different regimes. Be guided by your veterinarian and follow instructions precisely.

Some medication needs to be given by injection and most owners cannot cope unless some training has been given. Owners who have diabetic cats which are dependent on insulin injections are taught the procedure and usually become very competent in a surprisingly short time.

Drugs may be given on an out-patient basis depending on the cat's condition and owners then attend a clinic with the cat on a regular basis. However if very frequent injections, sometimes on a daily basis, are needed, it may be more practical to hospitalize the cat. Please do not worry if this is suggested; it often leads to a speedier recovery which is in everyone's best interests, not least the cat's.

There are occasions when medication, other than fluids, needs to be given intravenously. If this medication has to be repeated frequently, the intravenous line, or catheter, may be capped between injections and the site bandaged to prevent self-trauma. Do watch your cat in these circumstances, bearing in mind that once feeling better, the cat is likely to try to remove the dressing and catheter. Should you be worried contact your practice for advice without delay.

If your cat has received an intravenous injection a small quantity of hair may have been clipped from one or both forelegs or the neck. This is in order to see the skin over the vein into which the intravenous injection is to be made and ensures the site can be aseptically prepared. An intravenous injection is really a skilled surgical procedure and surgical cleanliness is most important.

Some owners who exhibit their cats request that no hair is clipped from the site. Veterinary personnel endeavour to cooperate but this is not always possible. Some cats have very small veins and we do need a clear field of vision in order to enter the vein smoothly. With some longhaired cats it is virtually impossible to find the vein if the hair is not clipped (see Fig. 141). If some drugs are injected perivascularly, i.e. outside and around the vein, they can cause irritation and pain at the site. The resultant self-trauma can be more serious than the removal of a small amount of hair. It will be obvious to any show judge that the site has been clipped for an intravenous procedure and it is unlikely the cat will be penalized.

Your veterinarian may advise hospitalization for your cat in order to restrict movement. This is often important when orthopaedic procedures are involved. In the practice the cat will be confined in a cage with sufficient room to stretch out and turn round, and have a litter tray and feeding and water dishes but little more than this. Think of what would happen if you had the cat at home. Even in the smallest kitchen there are worktops on to which the cat can jump and possibly slip. Such behaviour could cause more damage! The only way you can cope in the circumstances is to place the cat in a tea chest with a wire front or use a puppy or kitten pen. Even in such a confined space, the general household activities of the family will stimulate the cat to move around more than if hospitalized at the practice.

Hospitalization is only suggested to ensure restoration to normal health as soon as possible.

Road traffic accidents are not uncommon with cats. The most common injuries are fractures of the pelvis, lower jaw and limbs (see Chapter 26, First Aid). Cage rest is essential when the pelvis is fractured irrespective of whether surgery has been carried out or not. Sometimes there is minimal displacement of the bones and close confinement is all that is needed but frequently wiring and pinning of the bones is essential. If the cat jumps, even on to a chair, the 'hardware' can become displaced and the cat will need further surgery. Cats cope incredibly well with fractured lower jaws. The usual surgical procedure is to repair them with wires. Although they heal rapidly, initially the cat cannot eat or drink and my own experience is that feeding via a pharyngostomy tube (see Fig. 142) speeds up recovery enormously.

Figure 142   Cat being fed via pharyngostomy tube

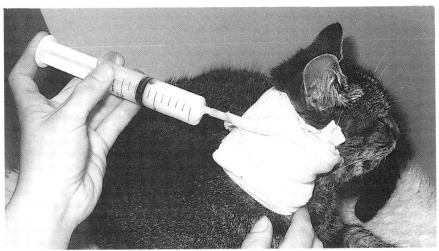

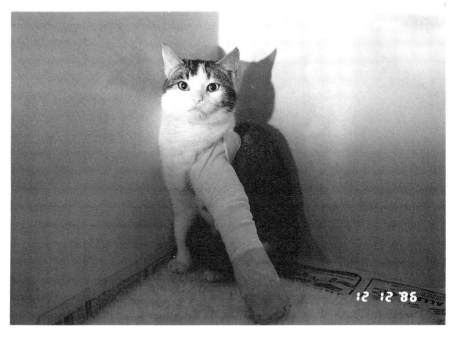

Figure 143   Orthopaedic dressing

Protein requirements are high after surgery and we must ensure adequate nourishment is readily available. In addition a cat with a full stomach feels more comfortable and will relax and sleep which also aids recovery.

Hardware in the form of pins, plates or wires is often left in situ unless it causes problems. However wires used for the stabilization of mandibular fractures are usually removed as soon as healing has occurred. To remove any hardware, a further general anaesthetic is normally necessary and sometimes further radiographs.

If your cat is sent home from the veterinary practice with a dressing, please try to ensure that this does not get wet (see Fig. 143). A wet bandage shrinks and causes constriction at the site. Cats should be kept indoors with a litter tray until you are advised otherwise.

Infectious conditions are assessed according to the condition of the cat and the type of infection. Cat viruses are usually airborne and a sneezing cat needs to be isolated to prevent spread to other cats (see Fig. 144). It will depend on the circumstances whether your cat will be hospitalized or whether you will be given instructions on home nursing. Cats loathe being unable to breathe through the nose and most respiratory viruses result in eye and nasal discharges (see Fig. 145). Careful, frequent cleansing of eyes and nose is imperative. Your veterinary surgeon will instruct you but generally attention is required several times a day, to clean the discharges and apply ointment or drops to the eyes or nose as required. All cleansing materials

Figure 144   Kittens with viral infection

Figure 145   Chronic sinusitis

should be disposed of by burning or placed in sealed plastic bags and you should make sure that you wash your hands thoroughly before and after each procedure.

The patient will need to be kept warm and comfortable and if you have other cats, it will need to be isolated to prevent the spread of infection. If the cats normally live together, it may be too late but until you are sure, separating the affected cat is sensible. Seek advice from your veterinarian if in doubt.

Cat bite abscesses are common and usually need lancing under a general anaesthetic. Infiltration with antibiotic or antiseptic solutions may be needed for several days together with the administration of antibiotics. It is essential that any accumulation of pus is drained. This can be very unpleasant at home because of the cat's tendency to walk over worktops and most feline patients' disinclination to tolerate any form of dressing when at home.

Home nursing should not be a problem following elective surgery, i.e. neutering, dental attention etc. Following neutering, male cats are usually confined to the house for a few days and female cats until the sutures are removed, which is usually about 10 days after the operation. The cat will have been starved for about 8 hours prior to surgery and can usually be fed a small quantity of the normal diet when first returned home and then fed normally the next day. Following surgery, bowel movement may not return to normal for a few days but if you are worried, do ring your practice for advice. Following dental attention, soft foods are usually advised for a few days. Specific instructions will be given following any surgical procedure, when you collect your pet. These should be meticulously followed.

Following Caesarian section, the queen is usually returned home as soon as she has recovered from the anaesthetic and is showing interest in her kittens since it is less stressful for her to be at home feeding her kittens than in the practice. Keep her in quiet, familiar surroundings, and offer her frequent meals and drinks. Contact the practice if worried and follow instructions.

Gentle grooming of a sickly cat helps enormously with a patient's wellbeing. Sick cats are disinclined to groom themselves and gentle combing and brushing will aid recovery. Any discharges from the eyes or nose should be wiped away at this time.

High energy foods greatly aid recovery. The need for a high protein intake has already been mentioned (see Chapter 7, Nutrition and Feeding). Your cat, when sick, may need a great deal of tempting to ensure it is eating sufficiently to maintain recovery. Offer favourite foods. Try warming the cat food, or giving sardines, pilchards or other strong-smelling foods. Chicken or fish cooked so that the cat can smell it cooking, then fed finely chopped but still warm, often works wonders. Finger feeding may be needed. Dipping your finger in the food and wiping it round the cat's

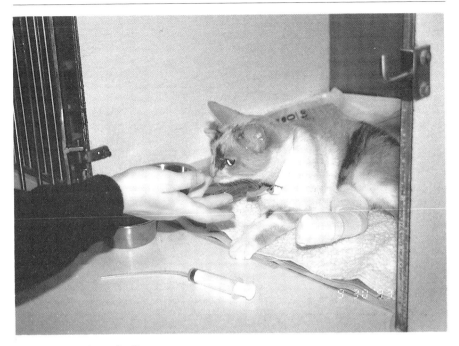

Figure 146   Finger feeding

mouth often helps (see Fig. 146). Stroking the patient while tempting it with food is another nursing tip.

Today there are several specially formulated feline convalescent and recovery diets as well as liquid foods available from your veterinarian. These are generally very palatable and one or two may be attractive to your cat. In any case keep trying. At this stage do not worry what the cat eats; anything is better than nothing until on the road to recovery when it can be returned to more normal food.

Special diets may be subsequently prescribed for longer term recovery. Follow instructions carefully and never hesitate to contact your veterinary surgeon if you have any worries about caring for your sick cat at home.

A more specialized form of nursing involves first aid and this is dealt with separately in Chapter 26. For further information on the administration of medicines see Chapter 29.

29

ADMINISTRATION OF MEDICINES

Tablets or capsules

Although a course of drug treatment for your cat may be initiated when you visit your veterinary surgeon, usually this means that you will be asked to give doses of the required medicines at home, as it is seldom practicable to return each time another dose is due. The medicine may be solid (e.g. tablets or capsules) or liquid.

Exceptionally, a cat will accept a tablet or capsule concealed in a titbit of minced meat or fish, especially if hungry; this may be worth trying first. When a tablet is placed in a dish of food, usually the food is eaten and the tablet left. Crushing the tablet and mixing the powder in with the food is equally unsuccessful in most cases, especially if the tablet tastes unpleasant; occasionally, disguising its flavour with strong-smelling substances (such as fish oils, yeast extract or evaporated milk) *may* work. Certain tablets contain very bitter drugs surrounded by an innocuous coating, and if these are crushed the cat will salivate profusely when this bitter material contacts the inside of its mouth. As a result the mouth frequently becomes filled with froth, causing great distress. Consequently, if your veterinary surgeon tells you not to crush or break a tablet before giving it, do follow this advice.

In most cases, the tablet has to be placed at the back of the cat's mouth before it will swallow it; this is particularly true where repeated dosing is required. You may be able to do this single-handed, if the cat is reasonably good-tempered, although with someone else's assistance in holding the cat it becomes easier. Where the cat is difficult to handle, some assistance is essential.

First of all place the cat on a table or kitchen worktop about 3 feet high, with its mouth facing a good source of light. If you are right-handed, grasp the cat's scruff (the loose skin at the back of the neck) gently but firmly in your left hand and hold the tablet or capsule between the thumb and index finger of your right hand. (If you are left-handed, reverse these instructions.) Hold the animal so that it is lying or sitting upright. Your assistant should prevent the animal from scratching by holding its front legs down on the table. If necessary the cat can be firmly wrapped in a towel, or placed inside a pillow case or shoe bag with only its head protruding, and then held down on the table. It helps to have a pencil or ballpoint pen within reach,

Rotate the hand which is grasping the scruff so that the animal's nose points upwards at roughly 45° to the horizontal, but at the same time press down on the cat to prevent it rising. Usually its mouth will open, but if necessary the second finger of the hand holding the tablet can push down slightly on the lower front teeth. Now place the tablet into the mouth as far back as possible.

Immediately take up the pencil or pen and with its blunt end quickly, but gently, push the tablet over the back of the tongue into the throat (you could use a finger to do this, but there is the risk of being bitten).

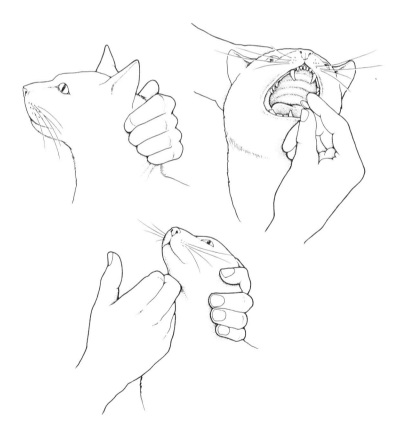

Figure 147   How to give your cat a tablet

Now relax the grip on the scruff, close the cat's mouth quickly and stroke its throat. Wait for it to gulp and lick its nose, which indicates that the tablet has been swallowed. Do not let the cat put its nose down *before* swallowing; the tablet will simply be spat out again.

An alternative way to open the mouth, with your helper restraining the cat in a lying or sitting position, is to put one hand over the cat's head, your index finger and thumb well behind the large canine teeth on either side, and then to push down on the lower teeth with those fingers. As the mouth opens, introduce the tablet into the throat with the other hand, close the jaws quickly afterwards, and again stroke the throat.

It is possible to purchase plastic 'pill-givers' from veterinary practices and pet shops to introduce small capsules and tablets or parts of tablets into the mouth. Essentially they consist of a flexible plastic tube, the end of which will accept the whole or part of a tablet. When it is in position in the cat's mouth, pressure on a 'plunger', which runs down the inside of the tube, pushes out the tablet into the throat. Veterinary surgeons often use a pair of forceps to place a tablet at the back of the throat. Consult your veterinarian regarding the acquisition of such an instrument.

Whichever method is adopted, the aim is to be firm, quick and efficient. With successive attempts the animal will become more restless and the job more difficult, so try to get it right first time. Watch the cat afterwards to check that the tablet isn't spat out; of course, if it is the procedure will need to be repeated.

Tablets are much simpler to give than capsules, because the outer gelatin shell of a capsule becomes sticky on contact with moisture, so if the capsule is not put down the throat successfully at the first attempt it usually becomes sticky and adheres to your fingers or the inside of the cat's mouth. Successive attempts then become progressively more difficult. Do not attempt to crush tablets and introduce them directly into the cat's mouth, because it is virtually impossible to get a cat to swallow and the cat responds by producing copious amounts of saliva.

Liquids

Giving a liquid medicine is usually more difficult than giving a tablet, unless a syringe is employed. Again, the cat should be restrained, lying or sitting, on a tabletop or worktop. Your helper should stand behind the cat and hold its front legs down to prevent it scratching, or again it can be rolled in a towel or placed in a pillow case or shoe bag with only its head protruding.

With a good-tempered cat it may only be necessary to hold its nose pointing slightly upwards; if a cat is more difficult to handle, it becomes necessary to grasp the scruff firmly to direct the nose upwards.

Figure 148 How to give your cat liquid medicine

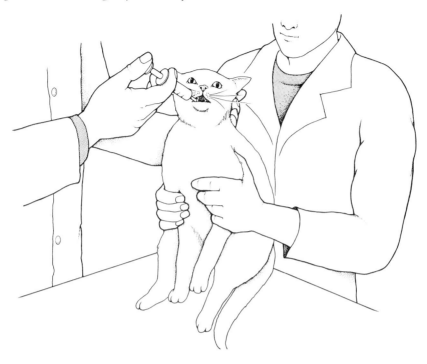

Figure 149 Syringe-feeding a semi-liquid diet, with the syringe tip inserted between the incisor teeth. (Courtesy of Hill's Pet Nutrition Ltd)

A disposable plastic syringe is the best container for a liquid medicine, a liquid or semi-liquid diet, or even water, that needs to be administered. It is much easier to handle, avoids spilling of the liquid, is easy to introduce between the teeth and causes the cat less distress than, for example, a metal spoon. Your veterinary surgeon will be able to supply you with the appropriate type of syringe. With the cat's head held, the tip of the syringe can be placed between its lips at the side of the mouth, or between the incisor teeth at the front of the mouth, and the liquid trickled out by gentle pressure on the plunger. This should be done slowly so that the cat is able to swallow without coughing or spluttering. If that should occur allow a pause for the cat to put its head down to recover before administering any more. Do not try to hold the mouth open and spray the liquid on to the back of the throat, because this readily leads to choking.

If a syringe is not available, a spoon or eye dropper may be used, preferably plastic, because then it is of less concern if it is chewed. Take particular care if a glass eye dropper is used.

Eye preparations

A similar method of restraint (the cat sitting or lying) will be required for bathing a cat's eye and/or applying drops or ointment into it. Bathing is useful as a first-aid measure to help flush pieces of grit or a grass seed etc.

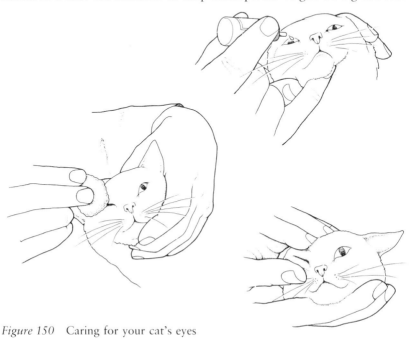

Figure 150   Caring for your cat's eyes

out of the eye, or where the eyelids have become gummed together by discharges. Either a human eye lotion can be prepared as directed by the manufacturer or a warm (not hot) boric (boracic) acid lotion made by dissolving two level teaspoons of boric acid crystals in half a tumbler of lukewarm water. In an emergency, or if nothing else is available, just use warm water. (Don't add salt to the water; if too much is added the resultant brine will be very irritant and damaging.)

With the cat restrained, soak a small pad of cotton wool or lint in the water or eye lotion and squeeze the liquid out on to the lids (if stuck together), or on to the surface of the eyeball. Wet cotton wool twisted into a spiral can be gently used to brush away any foreign body from the surface of the eyeball, provided that this isn't repeated too frequently. With eyelids that are stuck together, the wet pad should be gently wiped over the outer surface, mainly using an outward movement, i.e. from the nose towards the side of the face, until the lids gradually become free. Then the surface of the eyeball can be bathed. Repeated re-soaking of the pad may be necessary. The eye baths used by humans are the wrong size and shape for use with cat's eyes. Finally, the surrounding skin area should be dried, but never let any dry material (cotton wool, lint, etc.) contact the surface of the eye, because it will stick to the moist surface and will remove the outer layer of cells when pulled off.

If infection is revealed beneath the eyelids, or a foreign body cannot be removed, then veterinary help must be obtained.

To apply eye drops or eye ointment, the head should be turned so that the eye faces upwards. Usually drops are squeezed from a squeegee bottle or dropper held half an inch above the eye; generally apply two or three drops. Eye ointment (which will flow more easily if the tube is gently warmed beforehand) should be applied as a short 'ribbon' about an eighth of an inch long on the inside of the lower lid near to the inner corner of the eye. In an emergency, e.g. if there is grit in the eye which cannot be removed, one to three drops of warm (not hot) olive oil can be dropped into the eye with an eye dropper, or in an emergency dropped from the *blunt* end of a pencil.

Gently rub the eyelids together afterwards to distribute the medicament. Discourage the cat from undue rubbing of its eye.

Breeding
and Genetics

30

BREEDING

Do I want to breed cats? This question probably never occurred to you when you bought your first kitten. It certainly did not occur to me. But sooner or later just about every cat owner seems to wonder whether or not they should. Thirty years after deciding my answer was 'yes', I still get as much pleasure from seeing a new litter born as I did when I was an anxious novice with my first litter, consulting my handbook every five minutes!

Many people who buy a female kitten are told, 'You must let her have one litter, queens are much better afterwards'. Let me dispel this idea straight away; it is just not true. A queen who is spayed at 7 months is probably much happier than if she has been through the months of producing and feeding a hungry brood. Moreover, we really need to reduce the number of kittens being born, for far too many end up in rescue homes.

If you have chosen a pretty household pet queen, I would advise you to have her spayed. She will no longer be pestered by feral tomcats and your garden will benefit. The same of course applies to a pedigree queen, unless she was bought with future breeding in mind. I have to admit that I came to breed cats purely by chance. My younger daughter had been given a female Siamese kitten and friends persuaded me to breed from her. I have bred several breeds over the past thirty years and have played an active part in Britain's Cat Fancy, all of which activities have brought happiness, and quite a few tears. So, if you have really considered the pros and cons then do it but don't be dispirited if there are problems on the way!

Whatever the breed, a queen intended for breeding must be chosen with special care. She must be strong and healthy and come from a line that is not too inbred.

Inbreeding is often confused with line breeding, which involves the mating of cats with common ancestors. Inbreeding involves mating closely related cats, e.g. father to daughter, brother to sister, etc. Such close breeding will soon emphasize good points but if there are any defects these will also show up.

Well-known geneticist Roy Robinson has said, 'To inbreed is acceptable but the progeny must be outcrossed to different lines' (see Chapter 31, Genetics). I have proved his point by personal experience. It is frightening to find that one is responsible for the occurrence of health defects, and unfortunately it can happen, especially when inbreeding is practised.

To find a good queen in the breed you have chosen is not always easy and it may be some time before the right one is available. It is advisable to join a club that caters for the chosen breed. These clubs, which should be affiliated to the Governing Council of the Cat Fancy, are listed every month in the official journal *Cats*. Having joined a club, discuss your problems with some of the more experienced members, most of whom will be pleased to share their knowledge with a novice.

The brood queen

When you have at last located a suitable queen, try to choose a kitten rather than an adult. In this way a close bond is formed between kitten and owner. As mentioned in Chapter 1, Should I Have a Cat? the usual care must be taken over the choice. Even experienced breeders are sometimes unaware of defects in their cats. Others know but endeavour to conceal the defect.

When selecting the queen of your chosen breed, enquire if there are studs of compatible lines within a reasonable distance. If a queen begins to 'call' (the usual term for a queen in oestrus) and then has a long journey to the stud, she may well be off call by the time she arrives. While the queen is still young, try to visit the stud of your choice. This really is important since some studs are kept in less than ideal conditions, often with no separate pen for the queen. If the quarters are satisfactory, arrange a provisional future booking.

Most queens come into oestrus for the first time at about 7 months of age. Queens of Siamese and 'Foreign' breeds may be slightly younger. A careful watch must be kept on any young queen after the age of 5 months. Whilst Siamese usually tell you in fairly strident tones when they need a male, many Persians do not make a sound. If these queens have the freedom of the garden, or if there is a young male in the household, they may be mated and leave the owner blissfully unaware of the fact. I institute a daily examination of my queen when I know that oestrus is imminent. If the queen is stood on a table, the tail lifted and the vulva examined, the vaginal orifice, which usually appears like a small slit, may be round and slightly pink and moist. The queen may also react by moving her tail or arching her back when the hindquarters are touched.

It is probably not advisable to take the queen to stud on the first day of oestrus, and besides most stud cat owners prefer to have them on the second day, by which time the queen will probably be 'treading' (lifting her back feet up and down when her back is stroked). When ready, she should be taken in her travelling box or basket to the stud owner's home.

The stud owner will take down the particulars of the visiting queen and will ask to see the certificate of vaccination against feline infectious enteritis and cat flu. Most stud owners will also ask to see proof that the queen has had a blood test which has proved negative for the feline leukaemia virus. This subject is fully dealt with in another chapter (see Chapter 22, Infections).

It is now known that feline leukaemia virus infection can cause many problems in cats. Responsible breeders now test their stock to ensure that they are free from the disease. The tests are reliable, provide rapid, accurate results and only involve the taking of a small sample of blood. Many of them can be carried out at the veterinary surgeon's premises. I have all my breeding cats tested each year. Pet cats should be tested if they are 'outside' cats and have free range of the neighbourhood and possible contact with neighbourhood strays. If you have seen a cat die from one of the FeLV related diseases, you are not likely to forget it. At the same time it is worth discussing deworming preparations with your veterinary surgeon. The queen should be wormed before she is taken to the stud and then later during her pregnancy. This is discussed more fully in the chapter on endoparasites.

If your queen's papers are in order, the stud owner will place her in a pen next to that of the stud cat and you can return home. The stud owner will watch the behaviour of the queen and will allow the stud access when she is obviously ready for him. Thus the mating of cats is a more humane procedure than with dogs, where the bitch is often given one mating and then sent home immediately.

Most stud owners keep the queen for three or four days, depending on how the affair progresses. Usually the queen's owner checks on her progress by telephone, returning to collect her when the stud cat owner advises. On collection, the stud owner should supply a copy of the stud's pedigree together with a certificate of mating and the probable date on which the kittens will be born. Most stud owners offer the queen a repeat mating if she does not conceive.

It is not unusual for a 'maiden' queen to fail to conceive from the first matings, often because of her immature hormone balance. However, if she fails to conceive after repeated matings this may be due to abnormally low levels of circulating leutinizing hormone (LH). Cats are induced ovulators, that is they only ovulate in response to the stimulus of mating. Ovulation depends on the correct blood level of LH, and if it is unusually low the queen will not ovulate despite successful matings.

Providing the queen is fit and free from infection, an injection of an LH drug given on the day of mating may resolve the problem.

Queens should not be allowed to call continuously without being mated since there is evidence that ovarian cysts may result, which can in turn lead to sterility. This happened to one of my Siamese. She was a lovely Seal Point who had won two Challenge Certificates and needed one more to become a Champion. I was still not very experienced and was desperately keen to 'make her up'. I allowed her to call too often. As a result she became quite neurotic in her behaviour, and then developed a slight vaginal discharge. An exploratory examination discovered ovarian cysts and she had to be spayed. I learned the hard way!

Today this sequence of events can be avoided. Oestrus can be controlled or suppressed with the use of progesterone-like drugs, progestagens, which are available from your veterinary surgeon in the form of tablets or as an injection. However, they are not without side effects and should not be used irresponsibly. Administered under strict veterinary supervision they are safe and effective and can be used to suppress oestrus for many months after which time the queen may be bred from successfully. It is worthwhile ensuring a young queen establishes her cycle, that is has several calls, before any progestagens are administered. A persistent caller can be mated after the age of 10 months. There are some queens that do not have their first oestrus until they are 2 years old but even then it is still advisable not to mate until after the second call, which will usually be three weeks or so after the first.

Sometimes queens never make a sound, even when in full oestrus. One of the easiest ways to detect this is when local toms begin to wait outside the garden fence. It is essential that local toms do not have access to a queen, as they will often force mate her before she shows any signs of calling, and often such queens will conceive from one quick mating!

After the queen has been mated to the chosen stud and has settled down again at home, she will show no signs of pregnancy for 3 weeks. Then, about 21 days after a successful mating, her nipples will change from a normal skin colour to a rosy pink. This is almost certainly a definite sign of pregnancy, a moment of real excitement for the owner. It is known as 'pinking up'.

The requirements of a queen during pregnancy are unlike those of a dog where the main weight gain occurs in the last third of pregnancy. In the queen the energy requirement increases by around a third during the whole of gestation and then by up to three to four times as much during the period she is suckling her kittens. Unlike most other animals, the pregnant queen begins to eat more and her weight steadily increases within a week of a successful mating. It is normal for the pregnant cat to lay down fat which can be used later during pregnancy or when she is suckling her large brood. It is therefore essential that sufficient food is offered to her, particularly from the fourth week of pregnancy onwards. However, the amount of room in the abdomen is restricted by the growing foetuses and the rule tends to be 'little and often' with highly palatable, highly nourishing meals being offered. Remember she could be carrying up to nine kittens and this causes a great drain on her energy resources. If she will take milk she can be given a small saucer of evaporated milk at bedtime.

A normal pregnancy lasts for approximately 65 days, the range being from 61 to 70 days. I have found that a kitten born on the 61st day will, with care, survive. Those born earlier than this usually die, however hard one tries to hand rear. I have never yet had the courage to have such a premature kitten put to sleep, but in fact it is the kindest thing to do.

Figure 151   Kittening box

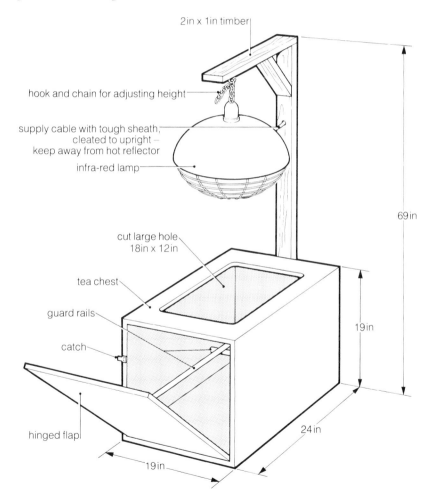

2in x 1in timber

hook and chain for adjusting height

supply cable with tough sheath, cleated to upright – keep away from hot reflector

infra-red lamp

69in

cut large hole 18in x 12in

tea chest

guard rails

catch

19in

hinged flap

19in

24in

IMPORTANT – use only cable with toughest possible sheathing because of cat's claws and teeth

I have known queens who will wait until the 70th day before going into labour and still produce a normal healthy litter. The important thing is not to panic and call the vet. Call him only after considered assessment.

Assess the situation carefully. If the queen is straining continuously, and has been doing so for two hours, veterinary assistance is required. If, on the other hand, there has only been the occasional contraction it is better to be patient and wait, provided the queen is not distressed.

From the sixth week of pregnancy most queens will be choosing the place where they intend the litter to be born. This is often the most impossible place! I have had queens decide to have their kittens in the fireplace, in cupboards or in a dark corner. It is a good idea to prepare at least two large cardboard boxes and place in easily accessible but quiet

Figure 152 Kittening

The queen straining in second stage labour

The water bag (amniotic sac) appearing through the vulva

The queen breaks the amniotic sac with her teeth

The queen chewing through the umbilical cord and eating the afterbirth

places. These boxes should be about 2 ft square and should be well lined with newspaper since queens frequently like to prepare the nest by tearing up paper. A large wooden box, such as a tea chest, turned on its side can also be used. Figure 151 shows approximate dimensions.

Nail bars of timber approximately 2 ins × 2 ins (5 × 5 cm) round the inside at about 3 ins (7–8 cm) from the floor. The bars allow a kitten to be pushed against the sides without the danger of being squashed, something which can happen with a weak kitten. Also prepare and leave by the box a tray holding surgical spirit, sharp scissors, cotton wool and tissues.

When parturition is imminent, the queen will become restless, walking from room to room, and sometimes crying. The owner should previously decide where kittening is to take place and then, when the queen shows signs of needing her owner, as many queens do, escort her to the right box and lift her in while stroking her gently and talking to her soothingly. Some

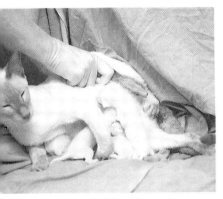

e head being born

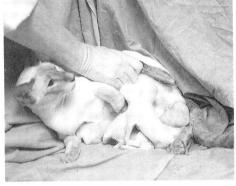

The kitten, anterior presentation, is born within the amniotic sac

um cleans and stimulates the new born . . .

. . . and relaxes for suckling

queens prefer another cat in the household to act as their companion and this should not be discouraged. There may be several false starts but eventually she will show signs of pushing or contracting. This is the first stage of labour. There is really no rule regarding the length of this stage; it can last an hour or several hours.

There is no need to panic if the queen seems to be contracting with periods of rest in between. Normally within two hours the contractions become more frequent, the queen may pant and then what appears to be a dark 'bubble' appears in the vulva. This is the sac which holds the kitten. The sac is fluid filled and is ruptured by the queen's hard licking. Several layers of newspaper are necessary to soak up the fluid. Each kitten is enclosed within a separate sac except when identical twins share one sac.

The second stage begins with the expulsion of the kitten. If the cat is a maiden queen she will probably yell at this stage since there is a lot of tension on the vulva. Kittens are born with either the head and forelegs presented (anterior presentation, the most common form), or hindlegs, tail and rump presented (posterior presentation). It is not uncommon for kittens to alternate between these two forms of presentation.

Breech presentation is posterior presentation with the legs forward so that the rump and tail are presented. Sometimes this presents problems and requires realignment of the kitten in order that a normal posterior presentation can be achieved. If in doubt consult your veterinarian.

As soon as a kitten appears the queen will usually lick it quite roughly, which can alarm novice breeders, but usually she is instinctively doing the right thing. However, sometimes kittens are born and apparently ignored by the queen. She does not even bother to sever the cord so that the kitten is still attached to the placenta, which may not have been expelled. If this occurs, it is important that the membranes are removed from the kitten's mouth and nose as quickly as possible. Here cleanliness is all-important, so only proceed with freshly washed hands. The kitten should be held in the palm of the hand with a finger and thumb pinching the cord an inch or so away from the body. It is important that the cord is not pulled away from the kitten as this can cause damage.

Using clean, preferably sterile, scissors cut the cord approximately one inch from the body and pinch the end for a few moments between the finger and thumb, which should prevent any haemorrhage. If you are concerned about haemorrhage, the end of the cord can be ligated using a piece of clean thread.

The kitten should then be placed on a towel on the palm of your hand and gently rubbed with the towel in order to stimulate it. Most of the rubbing should be on your hand and not on the kitten. The friction will both warm and stimulate the kitten. At the same time blow gently into the mouth and nostrils and if necessary turn the kitten upside down and gently swing it to remove any fluids in the mouth and nasal chambers. As soon as the kitten starts to mew the mother usually becomes interested and it is then safe to leave her to carry on with its care.

If the queen still appears disinterested, as soon as the kitten is moving or crying place it in a small box on a warm water bottle covered with a towel. Drop another towel on top of it so it is totally enclosed. In this way it will be kept warm until the kittening is finished. Some queens prefer not to be bothered with the kittens until they have produced their entire litter and finished the process of parturition.

The next stage in parturition is the expulsion of the placenta or afterbirth and many breeders are concerned to ensure the same number of placentae as kittens are expelled. However, since most queens eat the placentae, keeping tally is often impossible. The placenta contains many nutrients that are beneficial to the queen, and in addition it is rich in the hormones which aid the let-down of milk and help contractions to continue. If afterbirths are retained it is unlikely to cause problems in the majority of cases.

Very occasionally problems can arise due to malpresentation. Perhaps a tail and one leg are presented at the vagina and the sac is already ruptured. This situation calls for fairly immediate attention. If the kitten is not born very soon, and its blood supply via the umbilical cord and placenta has been compromised due to pressure in the birth canal, it will be unable to breathe naturally and death will supervene. Experienced breeders are often able to manipulate the kitten and bring about a live birth, but if you are in doubt consult your veterinarian without delay.

For this reason it is always worthwhile taking the pregnant queen to your veterinarian for a check-up and to discuss the whelping service. Most vets like to be called when owners think the queen is about to kitten and are then prepared for any emergency calls later on, even at entirely unsocial hours.

Many breeders prefer to remove the kittens as they are born and place them in the traditional cardboard box which contains a warm water bottle and towels. It really depends upon the queen. Experienced queens will happily cope with newborn kittens and further ones. Young mothers may not be able to cope so easily and in those cases it is advisable to remove the kittens until she appears to have finished and has settled down. Usually the queen relaxes and cleans up thoroughly after the birth of the final kitten and this is the time to introduce the kittens back to her if they are not already with her.

Kittening can take anything from 2 to 24 hours and it should be remembered that stages two and three in the queen cannot be accurately separated. Stage 3 is the expulsion of the placenta and this can occur either after each kitten or after two or three.

When the new mother appears to have settled offer a saucer of warm milk or her favourite food if she seems interested. Delivering babies is a thirsty business and mother and owner deserve a drink at this time!

It is usually easier to differentiate the sexes when the kittens are still damp with the foetal fluids. If they are dry it is probably better to wait a week or so when the differences will be more obvious. Colours in those breeds that throw a variety of colours are also checked. In some breeds it is fascinating to see the wide variety of colours that may be presented in the litter. For example, in the Siamese, where, for example, a chocolate male carrying blue was mated to a red female carrying both blue and chocolate, the resulting litter could contain blacks, blues, tortoiseshells, creams, chocolates and lilac. Lilac needs a combination of chocolate and blue genes on both sides.

During the days immediately after the birth a careful watch must be kept on the family, which should be housed in a darkened area of the room. Although the queen cleans the kittens, it is wise to change the bedding every alternate day or the mother may try to move her babies to another room. This behaviour is due to an inherited instinct that a dirty nest may be scented by predators. It is also important to make sure that every kitten is feeding well. Occasionally, a slightly weaker kitten will be pushed out by its stronger litter mates. If this happens, the owner should try to hold the stronger kittens back whilst helping the weak kitten to latch on to a teat. I have spent hours doing this only to lose the battle in the end. I personally never like to lose a life although some breeders accept the fact and do not trouble to try and keep the weak kitten alive.

Very rarely, the queen produces insufficient milk for her kittens. Another queen with kittens at this time will usually be glad to foster two or more kittens. Sometimes there may be a breeder in the neighbourhood with a queen with very young kittens who will agree to foster the kittens.

If you have the kittens fostered, try to ensure as far as possible that the health of the queen and the status of the premises are satisfactory. It is all too easy for kittens to return with one of the feline viruses, flu or something worse and infect your own stock.

One method of avoiding this is to hand rear the kittens. Cimicat, obtainable from most veterinary surgeons, is a simulated queen's milk, which is much richer than cow's milk. Using this together with one of the special feeders that are also available from veterinary practices or good pet shops gives a reasonable chance of success with hand rearing, providing you have the dedication. It is an exhausting job because for the first couple of weeks it has to be carried out at two to three hourly intervals including night feeds. Eye droppers etc. should not be used as this can result in air being swallowed and colic supervening. However, in an emergency it is possible to use a small paint brush and allow the kitten to suck the milk-laden bristles. This should minimize the ingestion of air.

In an emergency, if no simulated queen's milk is available, evaporated milk will suffice. Dilute three parts of milk with one of boiled water. It is important to remember that the queen's milk contains less sugar (carbohydrate) and approximately twice the fat content of cow's milk.

Caesarian sections

Over the last two decades anaesthesia and surgery have become a great deal safer due to the development of new drugs and techniques. If a queen has been unsuccessfully contracting for one and a half to two hours to expel a kitten, it is certainly time to consult the veterinarian, and it is for this reason that it is a good idea to alert the practice to the imminent parturition, especially if the subsequent emergency occurs in the middle of the night. Initially drugs may be given to relax the queen and increase the force of the contractions. If this is not successful a Caesarian section may have to be carried out without delay. The queen is premedicated, anaesthetized and prepared just like a human. The actual operation will probably only take 20–30 minutes but the preparation and cleaning up afterwards can easily treble that time. The kittens often need resuscitating at birth particularly if the labour has been a protracted one, and they need to be dried and stimulated since the mother is in no fit state to carry out these tasks. With luck the kittens will be as strong as any that have been normally born.

However, the queen does not always readily accept the kittens. The operation can upset her maternal instinct and it can take some days for things to get back to normal. Veterinary surgeons usually try to present the kittens to the queen before she goes home and in this way can check that she is accepting them. If there are problems, it is worthwhile trying certain ploys, such as rubbing a little of her favourite food on the kitten, which will often stimulate her into licking the kitten she has previously ignored. Remember that sometimes milk is not let down for a little while after a Caesarian and it may be necessary to supplement the kittens' diet for a day or two.

After a Caesarian the owner has to decide whether or not the queen will be a good breeder. If there was no physical obstruction preventing normal parturition, such as a badly presented kitten, she may have suffered from primary uterine inertia, in other words never really started to contract, which makes her one of those rare queens who will never be a good breeder. The questions are then whether or not to have her spayed and whether to find her a good pet home or keep her as a neutered pet. In either case her welfare must be the prime concern.

The growing kitten

The first three weeks of the kittens' lives should be happy and tranquil ones. The kittens may be weighed daily to ensure that they are growing, although it is usually obvious if they are not. By the age of three weeks the kittens will begin to try to climb out of their nest. This is the time to transfer them to a large, clean cardboard box which should be placed in a strong wire mesh kitten pen with a fitted top so that the kittens cannot escape into the room. The pen should be placed on newspaper and given a shallow filled litter tray. The kittens will soon learn to use the tray, copying Mum. The queen will be glad to have periods away from her kittens and they can be confined within the pen while she has some relaxation outside it. If she has already used the tray the kittens will soon follow suit.

Now come some of the most fascinating times in the kitten days – the early reactions and learning from them. Since this is the time when the kittens' characters are forming, it is very important that they should become used to everyday sounds, such as the vacuum cleaner, the washing machine, the radio and television. These will all be part of their future lives, and if they become used to them in the early weeks of life, and they can be connected with pleasant feelings, so much the better.

I usually leave the vacuum cleaner running whilst I stroke and cuddle the kittens. At first they will shiver but within a matter of hours they become used to it. Television time can be fun, especially if wildlife films are showing, as the kittens will usually try to chase a running animal and then search behind the television to discover where it has gone!

Ideal toys in the early weeks are spiders, made at home by twisting together four pipe cleaners and winding a length of wool around the centre to form a body. The kittens adore these, at first catching them in slow motion and then finding they can carry the spiders by one leg! Another toy is a cloth mouse stuffed with catmint with which they will play for hours. Rolled-up newspaper balls will also provide hours of fun.

Of course, once the kittens have their freedom they will want to use their owner's legs as scratching posts. This can be discouraged by a firm 'no' and a gentle pat on the nose with a folded newspaper.

If the litter is a large one, weaning should commence as soon as the kittens are about 3 weeks old. If there are only two or three kittens they will probably refuse any food as the mother will still have sufficient milk. She will have a tremendous appetite and should be fed on demand. Her intake will probably be three times that seen normally.

Although some breeders prefer to use a milk substitute to commence weaning, I find they take more easily to one of the stronger smelling canned kitten foods. Probably the hardest part is for the kitten to learn to stand on four legs to eat the food from a saucer. For this reason I put the food into a tablespoon and hold it up to the kitten, which will then take it quite easily. Within two days it should be able to bend down to a saucer with ease.

At first two solid meals a day are sufficient. As the kitten grows the meals should be increased to four and then a small amount of dried food should be mixed in, giving the kitten something to chew on.

Worming the kittens for roundworms is essential. The first dose should be given at about 2–3 weeks of age, repeating the dose weekly until approximately 6 weeks of age when it should be given monthly until the age of 6 months. The mother and any other adult cats or large kittens should also be dewormed at this time if the cats have free access to a garden. Worm eggs and insect larvae are often found in the earth, and they live for a long time. The earth should be frequently turned.

By the age of 6 weeks the kittens should be fully weaned. At this time it is unkind to keep them in a pen. Free range of the living room is enjoyed but great care must be taken to ensure that there are no electric cables for them to find. A young kitten will eagerly bite an interesting looking cable, possibly with fatal results.

The first vaccination against feline enteritis and flu can be given at 9 weeks with a further injection at approximately 12 weeks. Feline leukaemia virus and chlamydia can also be inoculated against.

All kittens should be registered with the Governing Council of the Cat Fancy. When the queen was registered in the owner's name forms for registering her kittens will have automatically been sent. The registration fee for each kitten is small and it means that all the breeder's stock will be recorded. Should the breeder prefer some kittens not to be used for breeding these can be registered on the non-active register. Of course, this cannot prevent unscrupulous people from breeding from such kittens but they cannot obtain papers for any progeny, which provides some safeguard.

If a breeder intends to breed several litters it is well worth registering a prefix. This means that any kitten bred by that breeder carries the distinguishing prefix. It is the way good breeders become well known as cats with their prefix may have great success on the show bench. It is not easy to register a prefix as the name, which must not consist of more than 26 letters, must be one that has not been used before. All prefixes are listed on computer in the offices of the Governing Council of the Cat Fancy (GCCF), making it comparatively easy to check if a name has been used in the past 50 years. The cost of a prefix may initially seem high but it is a sum well worth paying. Not only does the prefix distinguish the owner's stock, but the cost of registering each prefixed kitten is slightly less than those without one.

The vaccination course should be complete by the time the kittens are 12 weeks old, which is the age recommended by the GCCF that the kittens can go to their new homes. I always feel a pang of regret when they leave and I do everything possible to ensure that they go to good homes.

Once a prefix becomes well known, a breeder usually has a waiting list for kittens. However, an unknown novice breeder will have to advertise their kittens, which can be costly. If the kittens are only to be sold as pets, an advertisement in the local paper will usually bring many enquiries. If, however, the kittens are to be sold as breeding stock, it is advisable to advertise in one of Britain's two specialist cat magazines. *Cats* is published weekly and *Cat World* monthly. Both magazines contain helpful articles but are not often found on bookstalls. To obtain them it is best to take out a subscription for 6 months or a year (the addresses may be found at the end of this chapter).

Invite prospective buyers to come and view the kittens. Never sell a kitten to someone unknown and unseen. Do not sell an entire litter to one buyer since the chances are they will be resold, often via a dealer.

When a prospective buyer comes to view the kittens, watch their reactions. If the buyer wants the kitten solely as a decorative addition to the house, he or she will not trouble to watch the kittens' reactions but will usually point to one, saying 'I'll take that one'. When this happens to me I always find an excuse for not selling them a kitten. But when the buyer wants to stroke a kitten, to play and talk with it, then you can be fairly sure the kitten will have a loving home. When each kitten is collected, a copy of the pedigree, transfer form, vaccination certificate and a current diet sheet should be provided.

If a prospective owner asks you to reserve a kitten, ask for a deposit. In my early days of breeding, I was caught like this and found myself holding on to kittens for a long time. Needless to say, the buyers never returned!

When the last kitten has gone it is advisable to clean thoroughly the rooms where the kittens played. However healthy the cats appear, frequent breeding in the same premises can cause a build-up of infection which could cause illness in future litters. It really is advisable to allow the premises – as well as the queen – to rest.

I am often asked, 'How often should I breed from my queen?' One litter a year is the ideal answer but some of the Foreign breeds seem constantly to be in season, becoming frustrated if they do not have kittens. With these one litter every 10 months is a good solution. If, however, a queen calls almost continuously, and even 'sprays' around the house like an entire male, use of oestrus suppressing drugs should be considered. The queen will get some rest and the owner will be saved from having a nervous breakdown!

There is no definite age when a queen stops breeding. I had one Rex queen who had her last litter of two at the age of 12. However, after 8 years of age a queen tends to call less frequently and finally ceases to come into oestrus. There is no need to have her neutered unless she has any vaginal discharge, which may mean she has a uterine infection. After she ceases to breed she usually becomes chief nursemaid to kittens from other queens. In fact, like people, she reaches an age of sexual tranquillity!

The stud cat

Owning a stud cat is no easy task, as it needs time, patience and skill. I always advise breeders not to consider taking on the responsibility of a stud cat until they have been breeding for at least 5 years. During that time they will have been able to observe other breeders' studs and have come to understand something of the problems that can arise.

If owning a stud seems attractive, time must be taken in finding just the right one. It is not an easy task.

If possible, as I mentioned earlier, it is advisable to buy a future stud when it is still a kitten but old enough to be sure that he is entire, having both testicles descended into the scrotum. Cats with only one testis (monorchid) will probably sire kittens but it is a hereditary condition and monorchids may not be shown.

Buying a stud whilst still a kitten ensures the forging of a great bond between the cat and the owner which will be of great help when he is mature and working.

Again, pedigrees must be studied and those containing cats of the breed which are known to be healthy and of good type are probably the best ones to choose. Sometimes a cat may have been imported in order to bring new blood lines into breeds which have become too inbred. If these cats have been shown to be producing good kittens, it may be worth considering buying a kitten from the new line. Prices of such kittens may be higher than with old stock but will be worth investigation.

As when choosing a queen, the future stud's home should be visited. Ask to see the kitten's parents, if possible. If both are available judge if they are strong and healthy and if they are of a friendly temperament. Certificates of vaccination against feline leukaemia, feline leukopaenia (feline infectious enteritis) and the flu syndrome should be available for the parents on the premises.

It is essential to ensure that not only are the parents free from leukaemia, but that the kitten you buy has been tested and vaccinated, as he could have been infected by contact with another cat. This will add to the expense but it will be a safeguard against possible future tragedy.

When the new kitten reaches his future home he must be introduced carefully. Allow him to smell around the house in peace before he meets the other cats. The best time for introductions is at feeding time. Care must be taken to ensure that he is only given foods he had in his first home, otherwise you could precipitate a bowel upset.

The new kitten usually adjusts easily to a home where there is genuine loving care. At the age of about 4 months he should be introduced to his future stud house. This should have been constructed with care. It will be his home for the rest of his 'working life' so it must be large, comfortable and with a good-sized run where he can actually run if he wants to and, if possible, climb a tree or climb several shelves, which should be included. It must be warm in winter and cool in summer. For the sake of those who intend to build their own stud quarters, I will describe this in some detail. However much the stud is loved he cannot occupy a spare room in the family house. I have visited many owners who do exactly this, assuring me that their dear tom does not spray. Such owners must have lost their sense of smell! No mature entire male will entertain and mate his queens without some spraying. There are very few people who can tolerate the very strong tomcat smell for long, unless their senses have been dulled in some way.

A well-built stud house and run is the answer. The best houses are constructed of cedar wood and should measure 8 feet × 6 feet approximately, with a queen's sleeping quarters of no less than 3 feet × 6 feet. The walls should be insulated with glass fibre covered with hardboard, sealed with a good non-lead paint. All joints should be sealed with special tape to eliminate the risk of leaving a flea breeding ground. The ideal floor covering is urine resistant vinyl, bonded to the floor and extending 2 feet up the walls to prevent any spray seeping under it. The queen's quarters should be constructed in the same way, but should have a large window looking into the stud's room and covered with wire, through which the two can communicate.

A cat flap should open into the run, which should measure not less than 12 feet × 10 feet. The ideal material for the walls of the run is Weldmesh, which is more expensive than wire netting but is much stronger and more durable. The wire walls should be fixed to strong wooden or metal frames with a door to allow access for the owner. Both the house and the run should be 6 feet high so that the owner can clean and supervise in comfort.

I have always had an extra 'entrance hall' to the stud house where the queen could be welcomed and examined. This should be large enough to accommodate a chair and a strong shelf.

Inside the stud house should be several shelves at different heights to allow the stud exercise on cold days and also for him to retreat immediately after the mating, when the gentlest of queens may be quite vicious. Although there are very smart cat beds in all pet stores, I prefer to use large cardboard boxes for both stud and queen as these can be burnt after each queen's visit thus ensuring that risk of infection is reduced to a minimum. Blankets can be used for bedding but acrylic bedding of the VetBed type is preferable. It is easily washed and allows any fluid to drain through without dampening the bed.

The stud house should have an ample window to allow him to watch all that is going on. Even the best-kept stud has a fairly lonely life, so I prefer to have the stud house within easy sight of the kitchen so that the stud still feels part of the family.

Whether the stud is a longhaired Persian or sleek-coated Siamese, both he and the queen will need some form of heating in winter. I have found the safest and most economical heaters are tubular electric heaters fixed to the wall and controlled by a thermostat. Whilst Longhairs can be perfectly comfortable at a temperature of 8° C (46° F) a Foreign-type Shorthair needs a temperature of at least 14° C (58° F). The queen needs at least an equal temperature as she has probably been used to living in a sitting room, enjoying her place next to the radiator. My own studs always had a 'top up' form of heating for really cold weather in the form of a heated pad placed beneath the bedding.

It is necessary to clean the stud house every day to prevent any possible lingering infection. This need not be a lengthy process since vinyl flooring is easily cleaned. There are many good and safe disinfectants on the market today but I have always used a solution of bleach, which is known to kill all bacteria and most viruses. I usually make a solution of approximately 1 fluid ounce of bleach per gallon of water. A fluid ounce of liquid detergent may be added.

If infection is confirmed on the premises one of the special disinfectant preparations available from your veterinarian should be used according to instructions.

If the stud has become used to his house from the age of 5–6 months, by the time he is fully mature he should feel perfectly happy in his quarters, although he will still need plenty of affection from his owners. His first queen should be mature and used to the ways of a stud. Once he has accomplished a couple of matings, he will become fairly confident but will still need encouragement and an adequate diet. I always feed a stud three times a day as he uses a lot of energy in courting and mating his queens. When he has successfully mated two queens, he can be allowed one queen every 3 weeks for the first 6 months. After this a virile stud can happily mate two queens a week but this should not be exceeded.

If an owner decides not to take any visiting queens for any reason, the problem then is that the stud may not have sufficient queens to keep him happy and his fertility may drop. This is another reason why the decision to keep a stud should not be taken lightly.

The stud's run should have a concrete base into which is fixed a tree trunk or some type of climbing frame so that he can use his frustrated energy in playing solo games. A neutered cat in the household will often make a good companion for an entire male. I found that a neutered companion eased the solitude of a bored stud. Occasionally there are a few disagreements but it is very unusual to find the companion suffering any real injury. Most of the scuffles were due to high spirits.

Stud work is fascinating but is genuinely hard work. Not only must the stud house be kept warm and clean but the amount of work arising from visiting queens is considerable. Having made the arrangements with the queen's owner, her quarters must be ready to receive her.

If possible she should not be brought through the family home but accepted at a side entrance. The stud owner should ask to see the blood test certificate and the certificate of vaccination before handling the queen. Having been brought into the stud's entrance 'hall' she should be gently examined to check that she is free from external parasites and that her ears and eyes are clean. If there is any suspicion of ear mites it is better to refuse access rather than risk infection of your stud.

If she appears free from problems she can be put into her own pen to take her time to get to know the stud. Meanwhile all her details and those of her owner should be entered in the stud book with the date of her arrival. This book is invaluable for keeping a record of the stud's performance. The queen's owner should be asked to notify the study owner of the arrival of the kittens, their sex and colours so that these can be recorded. I still have stud books kept 30 years ago and they are of great interest in tracing the breed's history.

The queen's movement towards the stud will show when she is ready for mating. This could be within a couple of hours after her arrival or it could take a whole day. If she is in oestrus she will not be able to control herself for very long and can then be safely admitted to the stud quarters. The two should be allowed to mate as soon as they are willing after which the queen will usually scream loudly before turning and trying to hit or scratch the stud. For this reason it is important to ensure that the stud can easily jump away (see Chapter 17, Reproduction and Breeding Problems). An inexperienced stud should only be given a mature, proven queen for his first experience. If the queen is willing he may prove to be an excellent stud but one vicious queen during his early days at stud could ruin his future prospects.

Some studs allow their owner to assist in a mating by putting a hand beneath a queen, whilst others object and tend to lose interest. When I first started stud work, I was told all kinds of stories about 'correct positions'. The fact is that the two cats will find their own ways of mating in much the same way as people. I am certain that, with some cats, there are true 'love matings' whilst others simply regard it as a business to be accomplished!

Most stud owners allow queens to run with the stud, to mate as frequently as they wish, as would happen in nature, but, if the stud is a very popular one, it is obviously wise to ration the number of matings, although I believe that all queens need at least three matings for a successful litter (see Chapter 17, Reproduction and Breeding Problems).

Agree to inform the queen's owner when the first successful mating has taken place as people are generally genuinely concerned to know. When the queen is collected the stud owner should supply a copy of the pedigree of the stud and a certificate of mating, with the expected date of parturition. It is normal procedure to offer a repeat mating if the queen fails to conceive. This should be written on the certificate. The owner of the queen should inform the stud owner when the kittens arrive.

Most studs are rested during November and December. They usually lose all interest in sex although some of the Foreign breeds remain sexually active throughout the year. Studs do not have any particular age at which they will lose their potency. My own studs were still raring to go at the age of 14 when I would retire them.

When it is decided to 'retire' a stud, he should be neutered but kept in his stud house for at least a month to 6 weeks, since he will still be capable of mating and impregnating queens during this period. I always hoped with my studs that upon retirement I would be able to integrate them back into the house where they had lived in their kitten days. Unfortunately my queens had different ideas and usually absolutely refused to accept them. On one occasion they not only turned on the stud but became quite belligerent towards me and some even began spraying up the walls. Clearly the colony was being highly stressed.

Discussing the problem with other breeders, I discovered I was not unique and that the usual solution is to rehome the ex-stud. I used to wait until I found a caring family prepared to take an elderly cat as a family pet and my boy then went on approval. Perhaps I was lucky for in every case this worked out and my ex-stud became a placid, gentle, fireside pet.

It should be remembered that, if a neutered male does integrate back into a house with queens, he will still mate with them when they are in oestrus and that although not fertile he can still cause them to ovulate since queens only ovulate under the stimulation of copulation. This can be disastrous because if the queen then visits a working stud she may still not conceive since she has already ovulated. On the other hand, keeping such a teaser tom with queens you do not wish to breed from removes the need to use progestagen therapy with all the possible side-effects.

Never sell a cat as a working stud to another breeder. This is seldom successful. The stud feels resentment and usually fails to work in a new environment. If his stud days with you are finished try to find a good home. There are so many lonely people who are only too happy to share their homes with an elderly retired stud where he can end his days in peace. A stud certainly earns it!

Cats, 5 James Leigh Street, Manchester M1 6EX
Cat World, 10 Western Road, Shoreham by Sea, West Sussex BN4 5WD

31

GENETICS

If you plan to breed pedigree cats, unless you aim to have just the occasional litter under the guidance of a more experienced breeder, a basic knowledge of genetics is essential. This does not mean learning the symbols for all the different genes but it does mean recognizing the fact that a kitten inherits a great many things from its parents.

It is also helpful to have a basic knowledge of colour genetics, for unless you know how a particular colour is inherited you might never breed the colours you wish to produce.

The Basics

Inherited characteristics are passed on via genes. A cat has 38 pairs of chromosomes, each of which can be considered to consist of a string of genes; the cat receives one of each pair of genes from each parent. Thirty-seven of the chromosome pairs have identical chromosomes but the thirty-eighth pair are the sex chromosomes: a female has an identical pair – XX – whereas a male has two dissimilar chromosomes – XY. The genes found on this pair of chromosomes are known as sex-linked genes and, as well as those for the characteristics which make the cat male or female, include the gene for 'orange' which can produce a red or ginger cat.

The gene governing a particular characteristic will always be found in the same position, or locus, on a particular chromosome. However, the genes on the two chromosomes of the pair may be the same or may be different; if they are different, the effect of one will often override the effect of the other. The gene whose effect is displayed is known as the dominant gene, the other being known as the recessive gene. The dominant gene is symbolized by an upper case letter, the recessive gene by a lower case letter. This can be illustrated using the recessive dilute gene that makes the cat's coat blue instead of black. A black cat will either be DD or Dd; the first is a cat which does not carry the dilute gene and is said to be homozygous for black; the second is a black cat which carries the dilute gene and is said to be heterozygous for dilute. A blue cat must have two recessive dilute genes, dd, and must therefore be homozygous for this gene; it cannot carry black (gene D) at all.

In some cases there is a choice of more than two different genes at one locus; here some of the genes are symbolized by superscript letters. Using a colour example again, a double dose of the recessive brown gene, b, turns a black cat into chocolate-brown, as in a Havana or a Chocolate Point Siamese. A double dose of the even more recessive light brown gene, b^1, will produce a Cinnamon instead. A black cat may have at this locus the genes BB (homozygous for black), Bb (heterozygous for, or carrying, brown/chocolate) or Bb^1 (heterozygous for, or carrying, light brown/ cinnamon). A chocolate-brown cat may be bb (homozygous for brown/ chocolate) or bb^1 (heterozygous for light brown/cinnamon) and a cinnamon cat must be homozygous b^1b^1. As there can only be a pair of genes for a particular characteristic a black cat cannot carry both brown and light brown.

Some genes show incomplete dominance over each other as can be illustrated using yet another gene which affects colour. A full-coloured cat may be CC (homozygous), Cc^b (full colour heterozygous for Burmese colour distribution) or Cc^s (full colour heterozygous for Siamese colour distribution). However, unlike the previous example, a Burmese must be c^bc^b and a Siamese must be c^sc^s. A cat which is c^bc^s is Tonkinese, having colour characteristics in between those of the Burmese and the Siamese, because the Burmese gene is incompletely dominant to the Siamese gene. Again, the full-coloured cat cannot carry both Burmese and Siamese genes.

The above are examples of genes which have distinct and visible effects on their own, but many genes will only produce an effect in conjunction with other genes; an obvious example is any gene that affects the descent of the testes since it can only have an effect on a male cat.

Other genes act together to have what is known as a polygenic effect, each individual gene contributing only a small amount; an example of this is the genes affecting the richness of colour of a red cat, which varies from the deep auburn colour of the Red Self Persian to the pale ginger seen in some non-pedigree cats.

In many cases the actual inheritance of a characteristic is unknown but a hereditary basis is strongly suspected because the characteristic occurs far more frequently in related cats than in other unrelated cats living under the same conditions. For instance, if a particular condition is far more common in one breed than another, there is good reason for believing that it has a hereditary component.

General considerations

Before you look for a future breeding queen you should learn something about the breed and you should most certainly have decided what breed you want. Visit cat shows to see what the various breeds and their winners look like, both as adults and as kittens, and buy a copy of the Standards of Points from the Governing Council of the Cat Fancy. This describes the desirable visual characteristics of the breed and also lists those features considered to be faults; as both good and bad characteristics are inherited you will need to know which are which before you buy the kitten.

Before you go to look at a kitten you should make it clear to the breeder that you are looking for a good female kitten because you wish to breed; there is no point travelling a long way to look at a pet quality kitten or to be fobbed off with a male kitten instead. When you visit, take an experienced breeder with you if you can and if you are not entirely happy with the kitten do not be afraid to say so. Do not allow yourself to be talked into having a 'breeding pair'. The male would need his own stud accommodation and would almost certainly not be happy with just the one queen; you would either have to buy in further queens yourself or accept outside queens and neither of these is a good idea for a novice breeder.

The most visible things that a kitten inherits are its 'type' (shape), colour and length of coat but there are many other qualities that are sometimes forgotten, such as temperament, size, stamina and fertility. All of these have some genetic component so they should all be considered when selecting a kitten for breeding and, later, when deciding on the stud to which she will be mated. The aim should be to start with a kitten which is a good specimen of her breed, has a good temperament, will grow to be a good-sized healthy cat and will produce, with no problems, a litter of kittens with these same qualities.

In addition to checking the kitten you should always look carefully at the mother and the other kittens in the litter. If the kitten you are contemplating is the one outstandingly good kitten in an otherwise mediocre litter from a mediocre dam think very carefully; she may have been produced by a 'freak' combination of genes it will be difficult to reproduce. You will probably do better to select the best kitten in a good litter from a good dam, even if this kitten is not as good as the former, because she will be more likely to pass on her characteristics.

TEMPERAMENT

Temperament varies from breed to breed and is also influenced by the environment in which a kitten is brought up, but there is some evidence that a kitten inherits its temperament from its sire. If the breeder of your potential kitten also owns the sire you can ask to see him, but in most cases the queen will have gone elsewhere to stud and you will only have the opportunity to see the litter and their dam. When the time comes to select a stud for your own queen, however, make sure that you check his temperament as well as his appearance.

SIZE

Consider the size of the kitten, her littermates and her dam. Although there is always some size variation within a breed, it is better to breed from a queen who is the average size for the breed or slightly larger, rather than from one at the small end of the scale; if you start with a small queen you will need to select a stud very carefully to make sure you do not produce kittens which are smaller still. Disregard the fact that the dam may be rather thin after rearing her litter, but try to assess the size of her skeletal structure. If the breeder has kept any kittens from previous litters assess these as well and make sure you are happy that your kitten stands every chance of being a sturdy specimen of her breed. If you are buying a Siamese or Oriental do not be deluded into buying the smallest kitten in the litter because it looks the typiest; it may remain small and typy and lack stamina when it is an adult or it may lose its looks when it grows to normal size.

HEALTH AND STAMINA

Although any cat may acquire an infection, in cats, as in humans, some individuals have greater powers of resistance to disease than others. As there is almost certainly some hereditary component to stamina, or the lack of it, you should try to find out what you can about the health of your kitten's line. Ask whether the cats in her pedigree are still alive and, if not, how old they were when they died and what they died of. If few of the cats lived to a ripe old age, unless they were unlucky enough to be involved in accidents, think twice about buying the kitten.

If several cats in the pedigree suffered from the same medical condition, such as kidney problems or mammary tumours for instance, although this may not be directly hereditary there may be an inherited tendency to succumb to that particular condition and, again, it might be safer not to buy that kitten.

ABNORMALITIES

Various abnormalities have a genetic basis. Some, such as an umbilical hernia or a retained testicle or testicles, do not appear to be caused by a single gene and are probably the result of a combination of genes. Others have been shown to be caused by single genes: hydrocephalus, for instance, is caused by a recessive gene. Progressive retinal atrophy, which causes blindness, occurs in two forms and may be caused by either a dominant or a recessive gene. A large number of other more obscure abnormalities have been shown to be inherited. Yet more, such as pyloric stenosis (an obstruction to the outlet of the stomach), corneal mummification or corneal sequestrum (a dark spot on the cornea, especially found in Persians and also known as focal superficial necrosis or keratitis nigrum) and epibulbar dermoids (cysts growing on the eyeball), are suspected of having a hereditary basis because they occur more frequently in related cats, but their genetic basis has not yet been proved.

Some dominant genes cause relatively minor abnormalities when only one such gene is present (i.e. the cat is heterozygous for the gene). For example, the gene for folded ear, when the cat is heterozygous for it, causes neatly folded ears; however, a cat which has two of these genes (homozygous) has deformed legs as well as folded ears. The Manx gene, when heterozygous, produces a Manx cat, but the kitten which is homozygous for the Manx gene does not survive long enough to be born, that is, the genes are lethal when homozygous.

When you select your kitten it is always worth trying to find out if any abnormalities have occurred in related cats. Any breeder who has been breeding for some time is likely to have produced at least one abnormal kitten since these occasionally crop up in all lines of all breeds. However, if you discover that the same abnormality has cropped up many times in the particular line you should think hard before buying the kitten. If some of the kittens in the litter have umbilical hernias you may be told that the queen dragged the kittens round by their placentas or bit the cord off too short; this is unlikely to have been the cause so, again, beware.

FERTILITY

A good breeding queen should mate easily, produce a good-sized litter without assistance and rear them unaided, calmly and efficiently, until they are weaned. A queen who does not do this is, at best, annoying and, at worst, a very expensive investment; repeat visits to the stud necessitate repeat blood tests and travel expenses, problems at parturition can require expensive veterinary attention at unsocial hours and failure to look after the kittens properly may mean that, instead of a week or so, you will have to take several weeks off work to help rear the litter. For this reason it is essential to find out as much as you can about the breeding history of the dam and others in the line as, again, there is probably a hereditary component to fertility.

If the dam had to go to stud several times before she conceived, if she needed a Caesarian, or even injections, to produce the litter, or if she was unable to rear them herself, think twice before buying her daughter. Ask about the total number of kittens in the litter and in the dam's own litter; if there were only one or two you should again think hard before buying, but on the other hand, a queen who produces very large litters can also be a problem.

THE STUD

Having selected your future breeding queen you must consider the stud cat to be used for mating. All the above considerations apply just as much to the selection of the stud as to the selection of the queen but you will probably have a better opportunity of assessing them.

Many studs are shown or are placed on exhibition, so you will be able to see them for yourself. In addition, their offspring are shown and this gives you an even better idea of the potential of the stud. When you visit a show always buy a catalogue and study not only the results but the breeding of the winners.

If you find that a particular stud is siring a large number of winners for different breeders, or to many different queens, consider him favourably, particularly if some of these queens are related to your own queen. The stud himself may not even be a Champion but this does not necessarily mean that he is not of Champion quality – he may have had an accident of some kind or may simply not enjoy being shown. Even if the stud himself is not top show quality, provided that this is not because he has a defect of some kind, still consider him favourably as it is his offspring that you are interested in rather than the cat himself.

There is often a temptation to rush to use the latest Grand Champion but this is not always wise: the cat may be young and may not have sired sufficient kittens to prove whether or not he is passing on his good qualities. Why not consider his sire instead?

INBREEDING OR OUTCROSSING

The basic difference between the two is that when inbreeding you are mating related cats together and when outcrossing you are trying to mate unrelated cats together.

Within any breed there will almost certainly be some degree of inbreeding because there will be some cats in common if you look back far enough on the pedigrees. This is necessary for the development of a breed since all cats within that breed are striving to look like the cat described in the standard of points; if all the cats within the breed were unrelated they would be unlikely to look similar.

However, there are various degrees of inbreeding and, obviously, the closest inbreeding involves such matings as brother to sister, mother to son and father to daughter. These matings may sound far too close but, although it would not be wise to use them to start with, they do have their uses; these very close matings are sometimes used to test for unwanted recessive genes and there is no reason to avoid them in a pedigree, provided that the cats come from a line with known good health and that the mating did not reveal any recessive defects.

Slightly less close matings, such as grandfather to granddaughter or half-brother to half-sister, are often done for various reasons. A cat may have been outcrossed to a different breeding line to improve eye colour or coat length or to introduce a different coat colour, but in the process some 'type' may have been lost; the offspring is then mated back to a fairly close relative to try to regain this type whilst retaining the new characteristic.

Line-breeding is another form of inbreeding which is even less close; here cats with common ancestors are mated together. This is the breeding pattern used by most breeders since, as I have said, in any breed there are very likely to be common ancestors and these are often only a few generations back in the pedigree.

Inbreeding should always be used with great care and all factors of the cat must be considered when selecting the kitten to breed on from. Inbreeding, because it increases the number of homozygous pairs of genes, will 'fix' characteristics within a line but it must always be remembered that it will *fix bad features as well as good ones*; it is all too easy to breed for type, coat and colour and forget all about size, fertility, stamina and temperament.

Outcrossing, as mentioned before, may be used to introduce a new or improved characteristic. It may also be used if the size, fertility or stamina of a particular line has declined. Any complete outcross needs as much careful thought as inbreeding since it may improve the sought-after characteristic but destroy other characteristics built up over generations, and it may take many more generations before these are restored.

The safest mating is, therefore, one involving line-breeding, having first made sure that the line you are trying to maintain is sound in all ways. Line-breeding is then a 'safe' middle of the road way forward.

The final word on mating your cat is a warning to think seriously before you do so. Have you the time to look after the queen and her kittens properly, particularly if the birth and rearing do not go as planned? Can you afford to keep all the kittens until they are at least 3 months old and have them vaccinated? If you do not have as many suitable owners as you have kittens, can you afford, and have you the space, to keep the surplus kittens?

If the answer to any of these questions is 'no' you should not mate the queen. You may have bought her for breeding, and her breeder may wish you to breed from her, but any kittens she produces are your responsibility for life. You are responsible for ensuring, so far as you can, that all the new owners will look after the kittens properly and keep them for life. Ensure that they are aware of the 'naughtiness' of Siamese, Burmese or Orientals

Figure 153 British Blue kitten

or that they are aware of the daily grooming required by Persians. Should one of these new owners be unable to keep the kitten, or grown cat, it is your responsibility to help to find it a suitable new home, even if you are unable to take it back into your own home at that time. If some of the kittens are not sold you will have to keep them until you are able to give them away to good homes, or may have to keep them for life. It is certainly not acceptable to hand the kittens over to a pet shop, to a rehoming service or to an already overworked cat charity, and such behaviour is considered reprehensible in a breeder.

If you cannot face these responsibilities you should have your queen spayed.

The Breeds

Cats are divided into 'breeds' more on a historical basis than on a purely logical one and the breed numbers allotted to the various breeds reflect this. They are first divided into breed groups by their type and hair length, then, in most cases, further subdivided by colour into separate breeds.

The basic colours to be found in the majority of cat breeds are black, blue, chocolate, lilac, red and cream. White is also found in many breeds; this is caused by a dominant gene (W) which covers up the basic colour of the cat with a white 'overcoat'.

The basic genetics of the first four colours have been touched on earlier. The dilute gene 'd' dilutes black to blue and also dilutes chocolate to lilac.

A cat with the gene configuration 'BbDd' will be a black carrying (heterozygous for) both chocolate and dilute and a cat that is 'bbdd' will be lilac. A cat should not be stated to 'carry lilac' since the colour is produced by a combination of two genes, not by one single gene.

Red and cream act in a rather different manner since the 'O' gene is carried on the X chromosome and is therefore sex-linked. A normal male cat can only have one of these genes whereas a female can have two. A male cat with 'O' will be red or cream whereas a male cat with 'o' will not; he will be whichever of the basic colours his other genes tell him to be. A female cat with 'OO' will be red and, as before, a female cat with 'oo' will not. However, a female cat with 'Oo' will be a tortoiseshell; again, she will be whichever colour of tortoiseshell her other genes tell her to be – Black Tortoiseshell, Blue Tortoiseshell (known as Blue-Cream in some breeds), Chocolate Tortoiseshell or Lilac Tortoiseshell (known as Lilac-Cream in some breeds). The dilute gene acts on red to dilute it to cream, so a cat with 'ddO' (male) or 'ddOO' (female) will be cream instead of red.

From this it will be seen that, unlike the old wives' tale, 'ginger' females are perfectly normal, but tortoiseshell males are not. A tortoiseshell male is a form of genetic abnormality that sometimes crops up, either due to an XXY configuration, that is, with an extra chromosome, in which case he will almost certainly be sterile, or to a mixture of different sets of XY cells in which case he may be fertile, although he will probably breed as either black or red and not both.

In addition to all 10 of the above colours (excluding white) a cat may also be tabby. A tabby cat is produced by two separate sets of genes, one of which decides whether a cat will be plain or tabby and the other of which gives it a particular pattern of tabby. A white cat may also be a tabby genetically but that is, of course, hidden by its white overcoat.

The gene that causes a cat to be tabby or plain is known as the agouti gene 'A' and is dominant. 'AA' or 'Aa' is an agouti or tabby cat, 'aa' is a non-agouti or non-tabby cat. The tabby pattern itself is determined by a series of genes: T^a, ticked pattern; T, mackerel pattern; or t^b, blotch or classic pattern. T^a is dominant to both the others and T is dominant to classic. The spotted pattern is not produced by a gene in this series but is probably caused by a separate gene or group of genes which break up the mackerel or classic pattern into spots.

All cats possess the genes that give them a particular tabby pattern but the pattern will only be revealed clearly if the cat also has the agouti gene 'A' or the orange gene 'O'. It is for this reason that all red cats have some tabby markings even if these have been reduced to a minimum by selection over the generations. It also explains why you cannot tell visually whether or not a red cat is genetically agouti, but will need to examine the pedigree or test-mate the cat to find out. In other colours of cat the tabby pattern may appear as 'ghost markings', especially in kittens.

As well as being one of the above 20 colours (ten plain, ten tabby, again ignoring white) a cat may possess the dominant inhibitor gene 'I' which causes the coat to be silver. A non-agouti cat which is also 'II' or 'Ii' becomes a Smoke (of any of the 10 colours) whereas an agouti cat becomes a Silver Tabby. In many of the breeds only the Black-Silver Tabby is recognized (and is known simply as the Silver Tabby) whilst in other breeds all 10 Silver Tabby colours are recognized.

All 40 of the above colours may also be the basic colour of the Bi-Coloured cat which is produced by the presence of the dominant white spotting gene 'S'. This gene is completely independent of the dominant white gene W. A cat with 'SS' will have more white on it than a cat with 'Ss', while a cat with 'ss' will not be a bicolour at all. The correct degree of white for a breed is selected for and not all kittens produced will have this correct white spotting pattern.

The coat colour of a cat may also be altered by the presence of one of the genes in the 'C' series described in the previous chapter. In the great majority of breeds, if coat colours produced by the Burmese or Siamese genes are accepted at all they are only accepted in the 10 basic colours plus the 10 tabby colours.

Luckily, the more obscure and complicated combinations of colour genes are only accepted in a few breeds, usually those in which coat colour is not an important feature. For instance, 'AabbDdIIOoSsTt^b' will be a chocolate silver tortie tabby and white of mackerel pattern, carrying non-agouti, dilute and classic pattern, but is only likely to be encountered in Cornish or Devon Rex!

In addition to colour, breeds are also distinguished by their coat length. The gene which produces a longhaired cat 'l' is recessive: 'LL' is a shorthaired cat, 'Ll' is a shorthaired cat carrying longhair and 'll' is a longhaired cat.

In all breeds a particular characteristic or group of characteristics defines the breed and distinguishes it from other breeds or from the average non-pedigree cat.

PERSIANS

Most of the longhaired breeds recognized in this country are Persian in type. They should be solid cats with a cobby body, sturdy legs, a short tail and a broad round head with a short nose, small ears set wide apart and large round eyes; the whole effect is one of roundness and substance. Persians generally have good temperaments and make good indoor cats, happy to lie on a comfortable bed and rarely destructive, even as kittens.

The different breeds are distinguished by their coat colour and markings and their eye colour, all of which are important features of the individual breeds.

Figure 154   Longhaired odd-eyed White

Figure 155   Blue and Blue-Cream Longhairs

The self-coloured cats are each defined as a separate breed – White, Black, Blue, Red, Cream, Chocolate and Lilac. The different tabby colours, which are only accepted in the classic pattern, are also defined separately; the Brown Tabby (genetically black), Red Tabby and Silver Tabby have Championship status, whereas the Blue Tabby, Chocolate Tabby, Lilac Tabby and the four colours of Tortie-Tabby are at their earliest stage of recognition. The Tortoiseshell and the Blue-Cream are also separate breeds, as are the Chocolate Tortoiseshell and Lilac-Cream although the latter two do not yet have Championship status.

Smoke Persians are recognized in the six basic colours and Bi-Colours are now recognized in the majority of basic colours, although the silver and smoke colours are excluded. They are recognized both in the ordinary, slightly more coloured than white, pattern and also in the Van pattern, where only the head, ears and tail should show any colours, the rest of the cat being white.

In addition to these colours, certain breeds of Persian are created by the presence of the dominant wide-band gene which restricts the colour on the hairs of an agouti cat. The Chinchilla is the extreme example of this, being genetically a Silver Tabby in which the colour has been moved so far to the end of the hair that it only shows as a minute tipping of black to give a sparkling effect; this has been created by two genes for wide band plus rigorous selection over many generations. A lesser expression of this effect produces a shaded cat such as the green-eyed Shaded Silver or the orange-eyed Pewter. A Cameo is the Red, Cream or Tortie example of this gene and is recognized in both Shell and Shaded versions. The non-silver example of the effect of this gene is the Golden Persian, bred from Chinchillas, where the tips of the hairs are black but beneath this the hairs are a rich apricot.

The Siamese coat pattern is represented in Persians by the Colourpoints, which are recognized in 20 different points colours, but the Burmese coat pattern is not accepted at all.

In the majority of Persians the eye colour is copper or orange but there are some exceptions. White Persians may have blue eyes or may be odd-eyed with one blue and one copper or orange eye. Chinchillas, Shaded Silvers and Golden Persians have green eyes and Silver Tabbies have green or hazel eyes. Colourpoints, as in other cats of this coat pattern, have blue eyes.

Persians are enhanced by their beautiful coats, which should be long, dense and silky and need daily grooming to keep them in good condition. A properly groomed Persian is magnificent but an ungroomed Persian is a very sorry looking creature; the coat starts to mat up very quickly if it is not groomed daily, right from kittenhood, and once this starts it can be very difficult to remove the knots. Many Persians have to be groomed or clipped under general anaesthesia because their coats have become so matted that it is extremely painful (to both cat and owner) to try to groom them in any other way.

Exotic

An Exotic is the ideal cat for someone who likes the shape and temperament of a Persian cat but cannot cope with the grooming required. They are, in fact, shorthaired Persians and are bred in all of the Persian colours.

SEMI-LONGHAIRS

Birman

This was one of the earliest Semi-Longhair breeds to be recognized. Although, like the Persian, it should be massive and well-rounded, the body, legs and tail are a little longer than in the Persian and the ears slightly larger, while the nose is straight and of medium length. The coat is long and silky but does not usually mat up like that of the Persian, so is easier to keep groomed.

The coat colour of the Birman is the same as that of the Siamese, being created by the same gene, and it is recognized in the 10 basic points colours plus the 10 tabby points colours; the eyes are almost round and must be deep blue. The unique characteristic of this breed is its white feet, the front feet having white 'gloves' to cover the toes and the hind feet white 'gauntlets' covering the paws and tapering up the back of the leg to the hock. These white feet are caused by a recessive 'white gloving' gene, not by the dominant white spotting gene.

Turkish Van

This breed is still less Persian in type, with a long sturdy body, medium-length legs and tail and a wedge-shaped head with large upright ears and a long nose. The long silky coat is again far easier to groom than the Persian, especially in the summer when Turks tend to lose much of their coat and look almost shorthaired except for their tails.

The coat is pure chalk white with coloured patches on the face and a coloured tail, this Van pattern being created by the breed being homozygous for the white spotting gene 'SS', together with careful selection for the correct degree of white. Turkish Vans are recognized with either auburn (red) or cream patches and their round eyes are either a light amber colour or blue or one of each.

Maine Coon

This breed originated in the USA and, when mature, is one of the largest of pedigree cats. It has medium Foreign type, far removed from that of the

Figure 156 Blue Point Birman

Figure 157 Seal Point Birman kitten

Figure 158 Maine Coons

Persian, and is bred in black, blue, red, cream, tortoiseshell and blue-cream, and the tabby, silver and bicoloured versions of all of these, plus white. However, the coat colour and pattern are far less important than the impressive build of the cat and its glossy weatherproof coat.

Ragdoll

Another Semi-Longhair with a moderately Foreign type head, a long muscular body, fairly long legs and a long tail. The basic colour is that of the Siamese, with Seal, Blue, Chocolate or Lilac points and, of course, blue eyes. However, in addition to the Colourpointed variety there are Mitted with white feet and undersides, and Bi-Colour with a far larger amount of white including a white triangle on the nose.

Norwegian Forest Cat

This Semi-Longhair breed of medium Foreign type originated, as its name suggests, in Norway. They are similar to the Maine Coon but have a triangular head with rather high-set ears, giving them a totally different expression. They are bred in the same colours as the Maine Coon, the only colours not accepted being chocolate, lilac and Siamese pattern, but colour is not an important feature of the breed.

British Shorthairs

A powerful, compact cat with a sturdy body and legs, a shortish tail and a round head with small, widely spaced ears, large, round eyes and a short, straight nose. The coat is short and dense, not fine and close like the Siamese, but with no fluffiness to it. Because of this density it requires more grooming than the very fine-coated Foreign breeds, but considerably less than the longhaired breeds.

British Shorthairs are bred in almost all the same colours as Persians, although some of the Bi-Colour colours are not recognized for competition, and their eye colour corresponds closely to that of the Persians, although deep gold is acceptable as well as copper or orange. In addition to the Classic tabby pattern, British Shorthairs are bred in Mackerel and Spotted patterns.

Manx

This is the only breed in the British Shorthair section that does not have true British type. The major difference, of course, is the complete absence of tail, but there are other minor points – the back is short and the hindlegs are longer than the front ones, the nose is longer than in the British and the ears are taller. The coat also has a slightly different quality as the hairs of the outer coat are longer than those of the thick undercoat. The coat and eye colour should, preferably, conform to those of other British Shorthairs (with the exception of the Siamese pattern), but are of less importance than the other features of the breed.

Figure 159 British shorthaired tipped

FOREIGN BREEDS

Russian Blue

This breed has a long, graceful body and legs with a fairly long tail and a medium-length head with a short straight nose. The 'Russian' look is created by the large ears set on top of the head, the prominent whisker pads either side of the nose and the almond-shaped, vivid green eyes. However, the truly distinctive feature of this breed is its short, thick, fine, clear blue coat which stands up from the body and shows a beautiful silvery sheen.

Russians are friendly cats and very good companions, but less talkative and demanding than Burmese or Siamese.

The Russian Blue has been bred as a 'pure' breed for very many years but they are now also bred with White or Black coats, still with the same vivid green eyes, but these are rarely seen.

Abyssinian

This cat has a similar medium Foreign build to the Russian, but with a very different expression, the ears being set wide apart on the gently curved, medium wedge head, while the large oriental eyes are amber, hazel or green. Abyssinians are lively cats, well mannered but wriggly. The coat is very short and fine, requiring minimal grooming.

The distinctive feature of the breed is that it invariably has the ticked tabby pattern, each hair having two or three bands of colour on it. The

Figure 160   British Oriental

Usual Abyssinian should be a rich golden brown with an apricot base colour and black ticking, black tail tip and black markings up the back of the hind paws, while the Sorrel Abyssinian is a lustrous copper-red with deep apricot base hair and chocolate brown ticking, tail tip and hindleg markings. The Usual is genetically a brown (black) tabby and the Sorrel colour is caused by the light brown gene. Abyssinians are also bred in Blue, Chocolate, Lilac, Fawn (dilute Sorrel), Red, Cream and all six Tortie colours, plus Silver versions of all except the red, cream and torties.

Somali

The Longhair version of the Abyssinian. It is the same shape and has a similar temperament. They are bred in the same colours as Abyssinians, with the ticked hair so distinctive of the breed. The coat is fairly long, silky and flowing, completely unlike the long, thick Persian coat, and requires relatively little grooming.

Cornish Rex

This is another breed with medium Foreign body type but with particularly long legs and tail. The head is a medium wedge with a straight nose, large rather high-set ears and oval eyes.

The coat, which is produced by a recessive gene, is short and plushy with a highly characteristic curl or wave to it, producing ripples all down the body to the tip of the tail; even the eyebrows and whiskers are crinkled. The coat may be any colour, since colour is not an important feature of the breed, so some of the more intricate colour gene combinations mentioned previously may be found in Cornish Rex.

Devon Rex

It looks quite unlike any other breed of cat. The slender body is of medium length, the tail and legs are long, especially the hindlegs, and the elegant neck tends to emphasize the head which has full cheeks, a short muzzle, prominent whisker pads, a strongly marked stop to the nose, big wide-based low-set ears, and large oval eyes.

The coat is very short, fine, soft and waved, this being caused by another, and completely separate, recessive Rex gene. Again, all colours are accepted as colour is not important.

Korat

Another breed of medium Foreign type with a glossy close-lying coat but the hair is short to medium in length, slightly longer than in the majority of Foreign Shorthairs. The type differences between this and other breeds are that the back is gently curved and the head is heart-shaped when viewed from the front; the ears are large and set high and the nose has a slight downward curve. The eyes, which are particularly large and luminous, are a brilliant green, although an amber cast is acceptable. The coat of the Korat is blue but, unlike that of the British, Russian or Oriental blue breeds, shows a silvery tipping to it.

Burmese

This breed also has medium Foreign type, neither as cobby as the British nor as extreme as the Siamese, but highly distinctive. The tail tapers only slightly and the head has a gently rounded look to its blunt wedge, with a distinct nose-break. The medium-size ears are set well apart and tilt slightly forward and the gently slanting eyes, neither round nor oriental, vary in colour from chartreuse, through the ideal golden-yellow, to amber. The coat is short, fine and very glossy and requires minimal grooming.

Burmese cats are lively, noisy and demanding and are excellent company but easily bored if left on their own.

The distinctive colour of the Burmese is produced by a double dose of the Burmese gene 'c^b' which reduces the colour slightly on the body of the cat and also reduces black to brown. Burmese are bred in all 10 basic colours, but none of the tabby colours is accepted.

Asians

These breeds were originally developed from a cross between Burmese and Chinchillas and they have the same type, coat and character as Burmese. They are bred in all 10 basic colours, plus the additional colours of caramel and apricot, together with the Burmese versions of all of the colours, in a vast range of patterns including shaded and tipped Burmillas, Smokes and all four Tabby patterns. The Asian group also includes the Bombay, a self-black Burmese-type cat.

The Tiffanie is the semi-longhaired Asian and is bred in the complete range of Burmese and Asian colours.

Tonkinese

Essentially a cross between Burmese and Siamese that is recognized in all the Siamese colours. In both type and colour it is midway between its two parent breeds, although after the initial cross Tonkinese are bred together to try to maintain type. The eye colour, again, lies between that of the Burmese and Siamese breeds, being a blue-green colour.

ORIENTALS AND SIAMESE

Orientals

These cats have extreme Foreign type identical to that of the Siamese, with the same elegant length of head, neck, body, legs and tail and the very short, glossy coat which requires little grooming. They are very lively cats

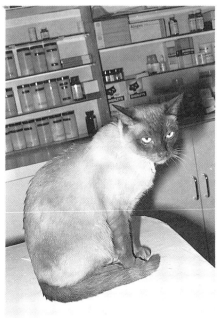

Figure 161 Brown Burmese   *Figure 162* Cream Burmese

which demand attention, often at the tops of their voices, and are excellent company.

They are bred in all 10 basic colours plus Cinnamon (produced by the light brown gene), Fawn (caused by the combination of the dilute gene and light brown), Caramel (a brownish-bluish-lilac colour caused by the presence of the dominant 'dilute modifier' gene in a blue or lilac cat), plus the tortie versions of these three colours. All colours, including their silver versions, are bred in all of the tabby patterns and in the tipped or shaded pattern, but bicolours are not accepted. The eye colour should be a vivid green in all colours, but yellow eyes are acceptable in red, cream and tortie Tabbies and Shadeds.

The Foreign White, which is not mated to the other Oriental breeds, is genetically a Siamese with the dominant white gene giving it a pure white coat to contrast with its brilliant Siamese-blue eyes.

Angoras

An Angora is the Semi-Longhair version of an Oriental, with the same type and characteristics, and is bred in all of the Oriental colours and patterns. It was originally developed from an Oriental line which happened to carry the Longhair gene and from outcrosses between Orientals and Balinese, so it is completely unrelated to the Turkish Angora which is recognized in some countries overseas.

Figure 163   Oriental Lilac

Siamese

The Siamese type is the most elongated of all breed types, but beautifully balanced, with a long svelte body, fine legs and feet, a long tapering tail and an elegant neck. The head is a long wedge, the large ears following the same straight lines, and the oriental eyes slant towards the nose. The coat of the Siamese is very fine, short, glossy and close-lying, requiring minimal grooming. As with the Oriental, this is a friendly and demanding cat and excellent company.

The colour is highly distinctive, the eyes being clear bright blue and the beauty of the coat lying in the contrast of the darker points and paler body colour, this coat pattern being caused by a double dose of the Siamese gene 'c'. Siamese are bred in all 10 basic colours plus their tabby versions; cinnamon, fawn and caramel colours are also recognized.

Balinese

This breed is the Longhair equivalent of the Siamese, being identical in shape and bred in all the recognized Siamese colours, except cinnamon, fawn and caramel, with the same blue eyes. The coat is fairly long, silky and flowing. These cats are bred from Siamese and are completely unrelated to other Longhair 'pointed' breeds such as Colourpoints, Birmans and Ragdolls.

The
Show World

32

SHOWING YOUR CAT

The First Steps

At its best, the show life can lift you to tremendous heights of happiness; at its worst it can plunge you into the depths of depression and despair. I have tried to understand the reasons for the tremendous differences but I think there is no easy solution.

I entered the show world entirely by accident. Having been given a pedigree Siamese kitten, friends suggested entering her into a big show. She won two third prizes and I felt as if I had a Crufts winner! My daughters were even more delighted by the fact that the local paper featured her photo. So, of course, when Melissa had kittens we showed some of them. By that time as a family we were truly bitten by the bug and were surprised to find how many delightful, helpful friends we had.

We registered our prefix, Annelida, which entitled us to sole use of names accepted to be registered with our prefix. After 5 years I decided to buy a stud cat, probably one of the best decisions I ever made as it ruled out the risk of infection to our queens when they were mated. My husband built roomy stud houses and runs, my nursing training enabled me to maintain strict hygiene practices and before long we were breeding our own stock!

People enter the show world for all sorts of different reasons. For instance, there are 'professionals', show competitors who read a number of books and then often spend a great deal of money on kittens or adult stock that have already distinguished themselves on the show bench. These people are only interested in show success and if they do not attain it the show world loses its attraction for them as swiftly as it arose.

Other exhibitors start at the bottom with a healthy female kitten of medium type. They register their kittens with the Governing Council of the Cat Fancy (GCCF) and breed their queen to a stud chosen for his blood lines. They may keep one kitten for breeding and will often register the other kittens on the non-active register. In this way kittens that are not quite 'up to scratch' cannot be bred from, so cats registered under that prefix become known for their good points and the breeder gradually gains respect in the Cat Fancy.

To describe the show world I will first discuss it from the exhibitor's angle and then from that of show management.

It is first necessary to decide how soon you want to show your kitten or cat and at what show, remembering that kittens may not be shown until they are at least 4 calendar months of age. They are eligible to be shown as adults from 9 months of age onwards and may be shown as entires or neuters. I believe it is best to start showing a kitten as young as possible. In this way they lose any nervousness and come really to enjoy their show days. When the baskets were prepared, my cats used to know this meant a show and would start to become excited. If a kitten is miserable and frightened at its first show, perhaps a show career should not be considered. There is no point in forcing a kitten to endure something it detests, for it will not do well. If such a kitten continues to be shown, as it grows older it may become vicious and could bite a show steward or a judge. In such cases this is noted and recorded at the GCCF. If the cat bites again at a future show, the GCCF have the power to order the animal not to be shown again. If the order is contravened, the owner will be disciplined.

When the decision about the time to show again has been made, then the show must be chosen. For the first attempt it is probably easiest to attend a small one, perhaps a club show for your own chosen breed. Having said this, I must admit that I entered my first kitten in the great National Cat Club Show at Olympia, London. I was extremely lucky to win third prize at my first attempt, as it does not often happen.

Probably the best way to decide is to ask the advice of the breeder of your kitten, who will doubtless belong to a breeder club. Your breeder should be able to advise you authoritatively and will be able to tell you where to apply for a show schedule. Another excellent way to get to know all show details is to subscribe to the weekly *Cats* magazine, the official journal of the GCCF, or to the other feline journal, *Cat World* (monthly)*.

These magazines list all shows licensed by the GCCF and also those run by the new group, the Cat Association, although cats registered with the GCCF may not be shown at these, the reason being that the strict rules ensuring that no cats are shown more than once in 13 days are difficult to enforce. This 13-day rule has been made to prevent the transmission of infectious diseases as most illnesses will show signs in less than this time if a cat has been in contact with one that is sick.

So, the day arrives when your first show schedule is in your daily mail delivery. The schedule will contain a full list of rules plus details of a bewildering number of classes in which your kitten may be entered. It

*For addresses, see page 491.

really is necessary to read the rules. Complicated though they may seem, if they are not read and understood a mistake can easily be made which will mean that your entry will be disqualified, a great disappointment after all the anticipation, not to mention the cost, for exhibiting is not cheap today.

The most important point to remember is that you must enter your kitten in its Open, or Breed, class. Should it win this, it may be entitled to be nominated for Best in Show if this event takes place. I have known exhibitors win Best in Show at their very first show, but it is rare; you will have done well if you win a third prize, as I did.

Usually entrance to a show is a 'package', i.e. you will pay your fee to include the penning, the Open class and three other 'miscellaneous' classes. With these you will be given a range of choices, such as Debutante kitten, for those which have never won before, Novice kitten for kittens which have not won a first prize before, Visitor's kitten for owners travelling over certain distances to the show, and Any Variety Shorthair or Longhair kitten. Then there will be club classes. Once again it is wise to ask the kitten's breeder to which club he or she belongs so that you may join the club and subsequently be eligible to enter its classes, in which there is a good chance of winning as entries will probably be fewer.

Carefully enter all the kitten's details on the entry form, including the registration number, or, if this is not yet known, you may write R.A.F. (Registration Applied For). The kitten must have been transferred to its new owner at least 3 weeks before the show and it must be fully vaccinated against feline infectious enteritis at least 7 days before the show. When you attend the show, the certificate of vaccination must be available as the veterinary surgeon who examines all exhibits before they are admitted to the show hall has the right to examine it.

Having filled in all the details, re-read the rules, check your form and then sign the statement that you are willing to comply with all the rules. It is a good idea to enclose with your entry a stamped, self-addressed postcard on which you have written 'entries received and accepted'. The show manager will sign this and return it to you so that you can be certain that you are entered and the form is not lost. After this you can relax for the next few weeks, although the kitten must be groomed daily. I like to give extra nourishment in the weeks preceding the show, including either a vitamin preparation or a treat such as a small saucer of real cream as this gives a kitten's coat an extra sheen.

Preparing the cat

Preparations for a show vary according to the breed. Shorthairs require much less preparation than Longhairs. Longhairs need regular bathing if their coats are to remain fresh and free from parasites and should be trained to enjoy bathing from an early age. I will deal with the various types as fully as possible.

SHORTHAIRS

British and most Foreign Shorthairs need a week of intensive brushing and combing. The pale-coloured breeds may be bathed about a week before the show. A good-quality baby powder can be used in the coat when it is dry. Since the British Shorthairs should have a crisp coat, brush out every trace of powder at once. The coats of a few Shorthairs do not respond well to bathing. For these and especially for Rex cats, a bran bath is the answer. To give this, warm two handfuls of normal bran (such as that used for feeding horses) to about 100°F. Stand the cat on the kitchen table and rub the bran well into and against the flow of the coat. Leave it in for as long as the cat allows and then carefully brush it out. After this, sprinkle on talcum or baby powder as usual. Beware of the mess bran can make, especially if you have a lively cat. For the safety of all concerned clip all claws the day before the show. Thoroughly clean ears and eyes as these will be examined by the vet. If the kitten has a favourite 'treat' such as Kitzymes or Pet-Tabs, it is a good idea to give this reward after preparation and also at the show.

LONGHAIRS

The preparation of these lovely cats is altogether more complicated, but if it is made into a routine, it really is not that difficult.

Regular bathing of Longhairs with a suitable shampoo is essential. To prepare for a show the important bath should be given about 5–7 days before the show as this gives the coat time to 'settle'. Baby shampoos are suitable but special shampoos are available for Persians and your veterinary surgeon may be able to help in getting them, but it is not wise to try one out at this time. Do not try any new shampoo when a show is imminent in case it does not suit your cat's coat. Special shampoos are obtainable from accessory stalls at the larger shows, where individual advice is freely given.

Having found a suitable shampoo then stick to it and use it frequently. Cats used to regular bathing will not be worried and many quite enjoy bath time. A spray is best for rinsing but the temperature must be carefully monitored. Pay special attention to eyes, ears and feet. There are special rinses available, also often on sale at cat shows, which are claimed to add the final sparkle. Reckitts blue is often used on white cats.

Use a quiet hair dryer until the coat is almost dry. At the same time it should be lightly brushed, always with an upward movement. Whatever the colour of the coat, the next step is to drench it liberally with simple talcum powder or fuller's earth. The latter is very light and some exhibitors prefer it. The excessive powder should be brushed out, leaving a fair amount in the coat. Each morning of the week before the show a little more powder should be brushed in. Use a soft toothbrush to brush the 'furnishing' hair around the base of the ears into place. Carefully pinch out the hair on the tips of the ears to give each tip a neat, rounded appearance. Many owners of white Persians protect their cats' coats at feeding times during the week before the show by tying a baby's bib around the neck. This ensures that there is no staining under the chin. There are many preparations available to prevent staining under the eyes and if in doubt a word with your veterinarian will be helpful.

At the show

The final preparations must be completed twenty-four hours before the show. Both long- and shorthaired cats should receive a thorough brushing so that the coat is sparkling. Foreign Shorthairs should be sleek, and the Longhairs like puffballs. Make sure that the tips of all claws are clipped so that there is no chance of even a tiny injury to a judge or steward.

With your precious exhibit now ready for the show, the show basket or carrier should be checked for cleanliness. It is a good idea to keep a show suitcase or carrier always ready so that when each show comes around you only need top-up on the night before. I am sure that once you have been bitten by the show bug, there will be many shows. This case should contain the following items (under show rules, items (a)–(d) must be white so that anonymity of exhibits is preserved for judging):

(a) Two blankets or pieces of VetBed, whichever your cat prefers
(b) Litter tray (litter can either be carried or purchased at the show.)
(c) Water container for the pen
(d) Dish for food
(e) Container to carry food (and in this connection remember dry foods are the easiest to carry)
(f) Brush and comb
(g) A few swabs of cotton wool
(h) Small bottle of Savlon or other disinfectant
(i) Cloth for wiping the pen before your kitten is put in it
(j) Pair of scissors
(k) Narrow white ribbon or the round type of elastic (for tying the tally number round your kitten's neck)
(l) Container for sandwiches for yourself
(m) Thermos flask
(n) The certificate of vaccination, which must be dated not less than 7 days before the show

All this probably seems a lot for just one day but it is all needed, and if it is ready on the night before show day there should be no panic in the morning.

Calculate your journey time carefully as many shows are held in rather inaccessible places, and on the important day be up in good time. It is advisable not to feed your kitten before the journey as some kittens tend to be car sick, in which case all the preparations will be ruined. You can offer just a little food after penning but only the water dish may be left inside the pen whilst judging takes place.

On arrival at the show hall you will see a queue following a sign which says 'Vetting-In'. As I mentioned previously, all competing cats and kittens must be examined by a vet and this will be thorough, so you must be absolutely certain that your kitten is free from fleas and is in perfect health. It is not only unwise but foolish to take a cat or kitten which is not in good health as you can be sure that the vet will spot any symptoms. The ears and eyes will be examined and must be sparkling and clean. Be certain that your kitten has no sores in his coat as these will be classed as skin lesions and the kitten rejected or put into an isolated room. Show regulations are very strict regarding skin lesions because of the incidence of ringworm in show cats in recent years. This disease is not only contagious but is communicable to man. Ringworm is not a killer disease but it is troublesome to both cat and owner. If suspected, the kitten will have to be checked by the owner's vet, and if positive, all the owner's stock will have to be checked. Showing or selling of stock is not allowed until clearance is obtained. GCCF rules state that this quarantine period lasts until 6 weeks after all the cats in the household have been given clearance.

Once your kitten has been passed by the vet, you will be given its tally and, usually, a card bearing the letter 'V'. This is fixed on to the pen door to show that your kitten has been passed by the vet.

On finding your pen, it is wise to wash it over with disinfectant, even though it is supposed to have been sterilized by the penning firm. They can be surprisingly dirty. Remember to use a disinfectant safe for cats – your veterinarian will advise here. Arrange the blankets in the best position for your kitten, fill the water pot and fix it to the wires at the back if possible. At this stage you may offer your kitten a small plate of food but this must be removed before you leave the hall.

Now is the time to give your pet its final grooming, so, if you possess a folding chair, it is a good idea to bring it with you, so that you can groom in comfort. Otherwise you will have to put the cat in the pen and groom there. Remember that no powdering is allowed in the show hall, but you may clean the eyes to make them sparkle. Finally, attach the tally to the ribbon or elastic and settle the kitten in the pen, making sure that no identifying object is in the pen. I always stay with my cats until the owners are asked to leave so that judging may commence. All your personal belongings may be stored in your carrier beneath the pen. If there is to be a Best in Show judging, make certain that your kitten's carrier is beneath its pen as there is always the possibility that it could be nominated for a best exhibit.

Outside the hall you will meet all the other exhibitors and there is usually a restaurant where you can have a cup of coffee and light refreshment. Sometimes the halls have galleries from which you can watch the judging, although it may be difficult to find a viewpoint near to your own kitten's pen. Excitement can be felt on all sides at this time.

Judging usually starts at 10 a.m. and continues through the day. At most British shows judges have trolleys which the steward wheels from pen to pen as each cat or kitten is judged. The first class to be judged is always the Open Breed class or the Champion of Champions class in which only full champions may compete. Every judge has an individual way of judging and a good steward soon learns them. After each exhibit has been judged, the steward washes the top of the trolley with disinfectant before writing notes on each cat in a book supplied by the manager. These books are very important as it is from them that the judge writes a full report that is later published in the cat press.

Figure 164 Alison Ashford judges a Russian Blue

A judge should carry the official standard of points when judging. This is a small bound book which lists the standards of all recognized pedigree cats. Now that there are over 100 varieties the judge has a formidable task to remember every standard. For this reason no judge is appointed to judge all varieties on the initial appointment. She, and I say she advisedly since the percentage of female judges is much higher than the male, has to satisfy the Breed Advisory Committee that she has a good knowledge of her own breed. On appointment she judges only those Open classes but she will be expected to judge other varieties in the numerous side classes which exhibitors can enter. She then has to write reports on all these cats. If these are satisfactory she can apply to judge another breed, but only as a probationer judge, i.e. she cannot award the coveted Challenge Certificates until she has been a probationer for at least 2 years. Even then her judging may not have been entirely satisfactory, in which case she will be 'deferred' for another year before permission is granted.

There is one show each year which is completely organized on continental lines. This is the Supreme Show, which is a 'qualifying' show. This means that each kitten or cat must have qualified by winning its Open Breed class prior to entering the Supreme Show. No owner can cheat as all entries are checked against the show record filed on the computer at the GCCF office.

The Supreme Show is the most attractive to view as the cat pens may be decorated in any way the owners wish. Some pens are really artistic masterpieces and there is a prize for the best-decorated pen. The cats are penned according to breed numbers, so can be identified fairly easily with the help of a catalogue. The judges are allowed to sit at tables (a much appreciated luxury) surrounded by a ring of pens into which each separate class is moved. The judge examines each cat on the table before deciding on the final placings and the prizes allotted are from one to six. On the completion of each class, the stewards take the cats back to their own pens, disinfect the ring of pens and then bring the next class.

Cats may only be entered in their breed classes, there being no miscellaneous or side classes. Some owners complain that they may only win one rosette, and rosettes are very highly prized by exhibitors. However, should their cat win Best of Breed they may then continue to be judged in the Best of Variety class and the lucky owner may then be considered for the prestigious Best in Show award. This event, judged on a platform in the centre of the hall, is both colourful and exciting and the lucky winner receives many valuable prizes.

The hall of the Supreme Show has the added attractions of clubs and commercial stalls. The overall effect is of a giant fair. It is an eagerly awaited event and is attended by visitors from every corner of the world.

At the end of a show day, whether it is a normal show or the Supreme, the bars are usually filled with elated winners or with losers drowning their sorrows. The conversation will be of great interest to newcomers. Invariably the topics are the cats and their judges. According to the disillusioned owners, half the judges don't know what they are looking for! In fact, as you will appreciate from the foregoing, the rules concerning the appointment of judges are very strict and no applicant is considered unless he or she has bred good kittens for a minimum of 5 years. The probationary period is lengthy so that by the time a fully fledged judge emerges he or she certainly knows the breed being judged.

Obviously, rules for judge qualifications vary slightly in countries outside Britain and most other countries adopt the 'ring judging' as used at our Supreme Show. I believe this to be a better system but the GCCF in Britain is democratic and up till now, whenever a suggestion has been made at a council meeting that all shows should use the ring system, delegates have voted by a large majority to retain the old trolley walking style.

Let us return to the cats, which are, after all, the most important part of any show. They are likely to be fairly exhausted by the end of the day when they are safely home again. Since, despite all precautions, there is always the possibility they may have been in contact with an infectious disease, it is a sensible precaution to keep exhibits away from any young, unvaccinated stock for a couple of weeks. Ideally a well-equipped spare cat house is useful for keeping the show cats isolated. I know this sounds hard, especially if your cats are lap cats, but it really is a wise precaution. Ringworm, the fungal skin disease, can be picked up at shows and, should your cats develop it, they could be off the show bench and forbidden to breed for up to 6 months. A kitten starting its show career at the age of 4 months soon becomes used to these periods of quarantine providing it is given plenty of affection during that time.

If you just do not have the facilities for isolating your show cats, take all possible precautions when you return home from the show. On re-entering the house, let the cats run in the garden or wherever you normally exercise them while you change out of the clothes you have worn at the show. The cats' show blankets should be put straight into the washing machine or, if you do not have one, in a bucket of disinfectant. Give the cats a good brush and a really nourishing meal and allow them to sleep it off. During the 2 weeks following the show, keep a specially watchful eye on the cats and if any develop snuffles, runny eyes, diarrhoea or any skin problems a visit to the veterinarian is essential. During my 30 years of showing, my cats have occasionally been infected with tummy upsets, but, by being careful, I have avoided the major feline infections.

There is no doubt that regularly shown kittens and cats really enjoy their show outings. They seem to know when they have done well! They also build up a good immunity to the show bugs and their happiness and contentment result in beautiful-looking cats. By careful selective breeding there is no reason why you should not, in time, produce Champions and

Grand Champions, but never forget in all the excitement that those winning cats are your pets and they need your love and encouragement to give of their best. I am always concerned when I come to judge a cat that is nervous and afraid of being handled because usually the reason is that the cat is not being given the love and attention it needs. If showing your cats ever becomes an obsession, then it is time to stop and review the situation before things get out of hand. If you keep cat shows in perspective, as a pleasant hobby to be shared by both cats and family, then you can be assured of many happy years with your hobby.

The organization of shows

The Governing Council of the Cat Fancy was founded in May 1910 after much bickering between the National Cat Club, which was founded in 1887, and the Cat Club, which was founded in 1896 by Lady Marcus Beresford. The first cat show was held in 1871. Organized by Harrison Weir, the man whose idea it was that there should be a cat fancy, it was a gentle affair with well-dressed ladies leading their darling pets on beribboned leads! There are many tales of cats being handled by menservants and arriving in carriages, whilst others say that cats were carried to the Crystal Palace in sacks! However, this little social affair was the forerunner of today's great shows in which up to 2,000 cats may compete and which take a full year to prepare.

The management of a cat show is a different world from exhibiting cats for management requires entirely different skills and personalities.

Most show managers begin their careers by helping to work 'on the table'. This 'table work' involves double-checking all show results, entering them in the records and releasing the judges' awards slips, which will be posted on to the award boards for anxious competitors.

For the show manager the show commences when the club applies to the GCCF for a show licence. Practically all championship shows are run by clubs and the expenses are covered by club funds.

Only affiliated clubs may be granted a GCCF show licence. Other shows may be held in Britain but no other body can issue the prestigious GCCF Challenge Certificates which are only offered at Championship shows.

The Executive Committee of the GCCF has the unenviable task of appointing the dates for the shows. With the number of clubs today there are shows on most Saturdays of the year, and often there may be two on the same day in different venues. With the numerous side classes a club needs to invite a great many judges, since the arrangement is that no judge should have to handle more than 60 cats in one day. However, this ideal seldom works in practice.

A club that decides to hold shows must proceed up a well-defined ladder of experience before it is allowed to handle a Championship show. This may sound unnecessary, but in fact it is very important because shows involve the welfare of a great many cats.

The first step is to hold an Exemption show, which is fairly uncomplicated to arrange. Here the manager must estimate how many cats can be accepted and must decide on a suitable show hall, which is not easy. All cats must be registered and all entry forms must be correctly filled in with the cat's name, parents and registered numbers. Exhibitors may enter their pet cats which are non-pedigree cats without registration numbers. These classes always attract a great deal of interest.

The GCCF rules state that once a club has organized three Exemption shows it may then run a Sanction show. The rules are more strict for Sanction shows and classes must exactly mimic those at a Championship show. At Sanction shows the spirit of competition runs high. Money prizes are not often offered but beautiful rosettes and cups are.

After having successfully run three Sanction shows the club may then apply to the GCCF to run its first Championship show. For the smaller breed clubs this requires great effort from all those involved. The show manager needs a reliable assistant and a hard-working show committee. The club secretary plays an important role but it is the club treasurer who perhaps has the most onerous task of all since it is their job to satisfy the GCCF that the club has sufficient funds to pay all expenses. Expenses include paying for the judges' travel and pre-show hotel accommodation, the hire of the hall, the rosettes and advertisements as well as the hidden expenses a show involves.

It is the show manager's responsibility to arrange the preparation of the show hall and also the dismantling afterwards. Few club members appreciate the sheer hard work and long hours necessary in show preparation, not only before the show but also in the immediate post-show period when dismantling has to be carried out to a tight schedule. These tasks invariably fall on the shoulders of the show manager and a few dedicated committee members and it is always the plea of every show manager for more dedicated volunteers. Work is, of course, entirely voluntary, although these days the clubs which hold larger shows are often able to donate a small honorarium to their show manager. Although it in no way compensates for the months of hard work and late nights needed to produce a successful show, it nevertheless is a much appreciated gesture.

A conscientious show manager is concerned with the wellbeing of all attending the show, the judges and stewards, the table workers, the exhibitors and, above all, the cats.

From all that I have written I hope I have made it clear that the Cat Fancy's aims are for the general improvement of cat care. At one show where I was judging, members of the Animal Rights Movement, shouting abuse at the officials, forced their way in and proceeded to open the cats' pens, proclaiming they needed their freedom. Fortunately there were enough club members and workers present to recapture the cats and eject the trouble-makers. This incident caused me to wonder if we in the Cat Fancy really care for our pets' welfare. And the answer I am sure is 'yes', for the great majority of us devote much love and care to our cats. There are a few who see the cats only as a means to making a name for themselves but they eventually find that cats used only as breeding machines do not live long and they lose interest.

Most cats thrive on the attention they receive at shows and when show day comes round again they are ready to jump into their carriers, preening themselves for the judge's admiration.

That is what showing should be – a mutual source of satisfaction for owner and cat. When it ceases to be enjoyable it is time to put the travelling boxes away and remain at home.

33

VETTING-IN

The purpose

To many exhibitors, be they novices or old hands at the game, vetting-in is regarded as a major hurdle to be overcome at any show. I, on the other hand, with over three decades of experience of vetting-in at cat shows, consider it an irksome necessity. To me it is a sensible precaution to have a veterinary check of cats before entry to any show in order to ensure that some form of contagious, or worse, infectious disease is not introduced and spread to other exhibits. It was only when I had one of my own exhibits rejected at vetting-in that I began to view the veterinary examination more critically, and I, too, became fearful of the procedure!

For the majority of exhibitors their cats are akin to children. To have one rejected, irrespective of the reason, is therefore taken as a personal reflection on the owner's ability to care and thus is regarded very personally.

What is the purpose of vetting-in?

When I first qualified over 30 years ago, both dogs and cats at all major shows had to undergo a veterinary examination before they were admitted. Originally this examination had been instituted in order to reduce the risk of spread of disease. Disease control via inoculation was in its infancy. Distemper was rife with dogs, and cats had feline enteritis and flu.

With the introduction of more effective vaccination veterinary examination of dogs at shows was dropped, but due to the more complex nature of feline infectious and contagious diseases, the Governing Council of the Cat Fancy (GCCF) have, very wisely, retained vetting-in at cat shows.

It should be borne in mind that vetting-in is only a rough screening test. No detailed diagnosis is expected or required and no attempt at treatment is made except in an emergency situation. The screening nature of the examination becomes very obvious if a little time is taken to watch the veterinary routine as performed by experienced veterinary surgeons at any of the larger cat shows. It appears that a cat receives a very cursory examination and within a few seconds has been returned to the carrier and the all-important entry slip signed. However, although the inspection and examination appear cursory, if you watch more carefully you will realize that the veterinary surgeon is quite thorough and is examining each cat methodically.

Some veterinary surgeons prefer to work on their own, while others will work with a steward. I have no particular preference and often feel that the cat is given more confidence if it is handled by the owner. Unfortunately vetting-in often takes place in an area where escape is all too easy and some cats will attempt a bid for freedom. It is therefore essential that the animal is gently but firmly held, and if I have any doubt regarding an owner's ability to do this, I much prefer to enlist the help of a steward who is fully aware of the stresses being imposed upon the exhibits, and sometimes has more experience than owners in judging the way stress is affecting a particular cat.

The first obstacle to successful vetting-in is removing the exhibit from its container. In this connection I make a plea for top opening carriers! Cats can be lifted out without any of the unseemly and undignified fights which sometimes occur when trying to extricate a reluctant exhibit through the small door of a seemingly vast carrier. Invariably it is to the far end of this that poor frightened Felix has fled in an attempt to forego the indignity of being looked at by the veterinarian.

Fear of rejection is certainly uppermost in each exhibitor's mind whilst waiting in that seemingly endless vetting-in queue. Therefore it might be worthwhile to consider next the reasons for rejection.

According to the Code for Veterinary Inspection at Cat Shows, issued by the GCCF, the reasons for rejection are broadly split into four sections.

Section A contains a collection of conditions, none of which is catching. These include pregnancy and lactation, monorchidism or cryptorchidism, fleas, poor condition or undersize, signs of obvious trauma, such as a clawed eye, which would be sufficient to reject the cat on compassionate grounds, severe distress, any signs indicating the presence of drugs (including some travel sickness remedies), ataxia, an inability to handle at vetting-in, and any gross malformation. In addition, cats which have been declawed are rejected under this section.

Section B includes ear mite infestation and/or dirty or waxy ears, which are indicative of possible infection, and may be contagious.

Section C is the true 'infectious conditions' section. Cats with ocular discharge, nasal discharge, mouth or tongue ulcers, evidence of gastro-intestinal disturbances, i.e. vomiting or diarrhoea, are rejected under this section. Other reasons for rejection under section C are generalized lymph

Figure 165   The vetting-in area of a large championship show

node enlargement and any other signs of transmissible disease. However, cats showing pyrexia, i.e. an elevated temperature, and general malaise are given every chance in case the elevated temperature and general feelings of malaise are solely stress-related. The exhibitor is advised to take the cat to a quiet corner to try to calm him down for a few minutes and then return for another examination. If the temperature has come down, and there are no other signs of illness, puss is 'in', although a record is made of the exhibitor number just in case the duty veterinarian is called to the same cat later in the day.

Section D is concerned with rejection of cats showing skin lesions, which could be indicative of possible ringworm. The GCCF stresses to examining veterinary surgeons that a disease should not be stated as a reason for rejecting; merely to state the signs is all that is required.

An official rejection form must be completed when a cat is rejected from a show by the veterinary surgeon. Rejection can either be prior to the show, i.e. at vetting-in, or during the show by the duty veterinary surgeon, who remains at the show after vetting-in has been completed. Frequently, during the show the services of the duty veterinary surgeon will be requested by stewards or judges. This is directed through the show manager, to whom all requests for veterinary assistance have to be made. Sometimes, as a result of these in-show examinations, cats have to be rejected and the procedure is similar to that at vetting-in: an official rejection form has to be completed so that the owners know precisely the reason for the rejection. Copies of these rejection forms have to go to the show manager who in turn forwards a copy to the GCCF.

At large cat shows 20 or more veterinary surgeons will take part at vetting-in, which usually commences at 7.30 a.m. in order that all the exhibits can be safely penned before the hall is cleared of exhibitors before judging of the open classes commences, usually at 10 a.m. Show managers are very conscious of the fact that, if there are not sufficient veterinary surgeons available at vetting-in, long queues of exhibitors can form, particularly as the time for judging approaches. This is stressful both for exhibitors, exhibits and not least the veterinary surgeons, and therefore every effort is made to avoid this situation. However, if a lot of exhibitors arrive together by train or coach, for example, sometimes some delay is inevitable.

The veterinary surgeons carrying out the vetting-in examination usually leave the show at around 9.30–10 a.m., but at least one designated 'Show Duty Veterinary Surgeon' remains throughout the show. GCCF regulations state that the duty veterinary surgeon 'must remain until 1 p.m. and preferably until 4 p.m. after which time the show manager must have made arrangements with a local veterinary practice for emergency attendance'. I believe that the duty veterinary surgeon should remain until the close of show, which is usually 5 p.m. I can recall emergency situations which have arisen quite late during the show. One occasion which springs to mind involved a cat with a fairly severe tail injury caused when the tail was caught in the carrier door when the exhibitor was removing the cat from the show just after it had closed. On another occasion I had to deal with a cat with a torn claw, sustained as it was being removed from the pen at close of show.

Cats are always handled gently and at vetting-in no cat is 'scruffed' (except by exhibitors themselves) unless it is essential either to prevent the cat from escaping or in self-defence.

Once removed from the container, the vet has a look at the cat's general condition. The coat should be clean and shiny and, although not a veterinary matter, I do like to see longhaired cats free from obvious knots and matts. Cats in such a condition cannot really be excluded under the sections explained above except possibly on the grounds of poor condition. Nevertheless I am always surprised when presented with such poorly turned-out exhibits. After all, just as I notice it at vetting-in, so do the judges subsequently. Entry to a show today is an expensive business and you should make every effort to make it worthwhile.

Next, a rapid but nonetheless thorough examination of the animal takes place. I always start at the head and look for evidence of any parasites, ringworm or mange. The ears are carefully examined on the outside for parasites and then internally for any dirt, wax, mites or discharges. Cats with dirty ears are rejected under section B. Since signs and not diagnoses have to be stated, there is really no need to use an auriscope to look for mites except in ears that have obviously been recently cleaned and are causing the cat some irritation. I also sometimes use an auriscope as a source of illumination! Regretfully vetting-in often takes place in relatively poorly lighted areas, and the light in an auriscope serves as a useful torch to let me see if there is any wax or dirt present!

The eyes are next examined and again discharges, swelling or the presence of conjunctivitis are noted, since these are reasons to reject the cat under section C. However, in this connection some discretion has to be exercised. Longhaired cats often have watery eyes due to conformation problems, resulting in blocked or distorted tear ducts. Also, some of the dilute colours (e.g. lilac-point Siamese) may show permanent pinkness of the eyes with or without a slight, pinkish, non-purulent discharge. These are clearly not infectious conditions and not a reason for rejection. However, to be able to differentiate these conditions requires experience, and it is for this reason that a suspected problem noted by the examining veterinary surgeon has to be referred to the duty veterinary surgeon for opinion before rejection can take place.

The duty veterinary surgeon's decision is final, and therefore it is usually veterinary surgeons of considerable experience who are selected. Sometimes exhibits referred to the duty veterinary surgeon during vetting-in will be admitted after examination, but a careful note of the condition and exhibit number is made in case any problems develop subsequent to admittance.

Continuing the methodical examination, the nose is then examined for any signs of discharges. A clear discharge which may be due to excitement or nerves is not regarded on its own as a reason for rejection.

The mouth is opened and a check made for signs of any ulcers on the tongue, gums or palate. Gingivitis is particularly prevalent in some breeds and is not necessarily infectious. Here again judgement based on experience is necessary. However, pharyngitis accompanied by enlarged lymph nodes may be indicative of infectious respiratory disease, and therefore the cat has to be rejected under section C.

I then go on to examine the skin and hair coat rather more thoroughly, brushing my hand through the coat to detect any signs of fleas or skin lesions.

I then prefer to have the cat turned round and will palpate the body gently but firmly for any signs of pain or other abnormalities. It is important in the female that a check is made for signs of lactation or pregnancy. If the queen appears plump, her abdomen has then to be palpated carefully for signs of any kittens. Lactation and pregnancy are reasons for rejection under section A.

Male cats over 9 months of age must have both testicles descended and in a normal position in the scrotum. It is easy to check the anus at this time to see if there are any signs of diarrhoea. Sometimes cryptorchid cats, i.e. those with both testes retained, are mistaken at vetting-in for neuters and

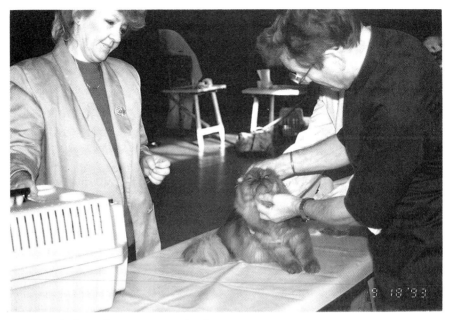

Figure 166   Screening a cat at vetting-in

are not rejected. However, with the virtually infallible 'fail-safe' systems which have over time developed within cat shows, these animals will be detected at judging since they will be judged in the wrong classes.

Kittens under 9 months of age are not rejected or disqualified for this fault, but it should be remembered that they should not be selected as future studs. In most cases, if the testes are not descended by 3 months of age, they are unlikely to descend. Occasionally, late descent of testes does occur, but these animals should not be bred from, since late descent is a fault. The norm is for the testes to be fully descended and in the scrotum by the time the cat is first shown at 4 months of age. A male cryptorchid cat, i.e. with neither testis descended, is unlikely to be fertile. However, if one testis is descended the cat is capable of siring. A retained testis is at risk of developing cancer, and therefore monorchid as well as cryptorchid cats should be neutered, although the operation is frequently more complicated than spaying a female cat.

Finally I examine the animal's legs and feet, checking for any skin lesions, and also checking for declawing or polydactyly, i.e. extra digits. Both are reasons for rejection under section A.

During this screening temperatures may be taken and the auriscope used, but only occasionally.

Both with instruments and hands strict hygiene has to be observed. Hands are always washed between exhibits and the table cleaned. Hand disinfection is important not only for the vet but for the steward as well.

Cleaning the table can present problems with longhaired cats since it is often difficult to dry it rapidly between the examination of exhibits. It is hardly surprising that exhibitors who have spent a long time on coat preparation view the vetting-in procedure with something less than pleasure if hours of preparation are ruined due to contact with a damp table with judging only minutes away! Under these circumstances I find it useful to use the blanket or bedding material in the carrying box to cover the table. Frequently I find the exhibits prefer this to the cold, damp, hard surface of the improvised examination table.

Any exhibit is regarded as a kitten for exhibition purposes up to 9 months of age, and these young animals can be ruined for showing if vetting-in at their first few shows is not undertaken with gentleness and understanding. Kittens unused to the vetting-in procedure are easily frightened and will remember that experience. I attempt to spend a little time with these novices, unfortunately often to the detriment of the lengthening queue if the kitten has arrived during the last rush before judging starts. However, I am sure most exhibitors are sympathetic and realize I am really trying to make the experience as enjoyable as possible for the kitten.

Rejection

Now let us examine the rejection procedure. First of all, if you are a caring exhibitor and have prepared your cat carefully, try not to be too upset if your exhibit is rejected. It is far better to be safe than sorry, and you can easily miss the minor skin lesion that we are trained to find. Similarly, conjunctivitis/rhinitis can easily develop en route to the show, but the vet would not be considered competent if such conditions were overlooked. As has been explained, the veterinary surgeon at vetting-in may become concerned about an exhibit and the duty veterinary surgeon then has to be consulted. If the suspicion is confirmed, the exhibit then has to be rejected under one of the sections. A GCCF veterinary rejection form has to be completed in triplicate, the top copy of which is given to the exhibitor and the other two copies retained by the show manager, who forwards one to the GCCF. The rejection form has to be correctly filled in with the name of the show, the date and the exhibit number(s). Any in-contacts also have to be declared together with the name of the exhibitor. Finally, the time has to be put on.

Cats rejected under section A do not have to obtain a clearance certificate before being exhibited again, but the exhibitor must ensure that the reason for rejection is no longer present.

Animals rejected under sections B, C and D have to have a clearance certificate signed by a veterinary surgeon before they can be exhibited again. If the rejection is under section B, i.e. ear mite infestation and/or dirty ears, all exhibits at the show belonging to that exhibitor have to be examined using an auriscope, and those cats which, in the opinion of the examining veterinary and/or the duty veterinary surgeon, show no signs of ear mites or dirty ears can be admitted to the show. The exhibitor must obtain a clearance certificate dated not less than 7 days after rejection for the rejected exhibits, and this certificate must state that all the cats belonging to the exhibitor and/or living at the same address have been examined and that on the date examined showed no evidence of ear mite infestation. No cat may be exhibited by that exhibitor until the clearance certificate has been received at GCCF headquarters and has been acknowledged.

Section C, as mentioned previously, is the section under which cats with possible infectious or contagious disease are rejected. All exhibits belonging to the exhibitor must be rejected from the show and a clearance certificate, again dated not less than 7 days after rejection, must be obtained and state that all cats belonging to the exhibitor and/or living at the same address have been examined and on the date of examination showed no evidence of the symptoms stated on the rejection form or other signs of infectious disease. Again, no cat may be exhibited by the exhibitor, whether or not that cat normally resides at the exhibitor's address, until the clearance certificate has been received and acknowledged by the GCCF.

Section D is the section for rejection of cats showing skin lesions indicative of possible ringworm. Cats showing scars which are obviously due to injury rather than any possible infection are rejected under section A unless the scars are so small as to be of no significance. All other skin lesions must be rejected under section D and not section C, although there is provision under this section for 'signs of transmissible disease'. However, skin lesions are regarded very seriously by the GCCF, because of the ever-present threat of ringworm.

Clearly, some of the skin lesions rejected under section D prove not to be ringworm on subsequent examination, but it is impossible to say with certainty on the show day whether they are due to ringworm or to other causes such as Cheyletiella etc.

Possible rejection under section D is something that is never undertaken lightly by the examining veterinary surgeon, and often causes a certain amount of disharmony between the duty veterinary surgeon and the exhibitor. Although all cats from the same exhibitor must be rejected from the show, it is only the exhibits with lesions which have to be examined by a veterinary surgeon within 7 days. The clearance certificate must state that the exhibit was examined within the statutory 7 days, and that microscopic examination and culture carried out on material from any lesions and also from 'whole cat' brushings showed no evidence of the presence of ringworm. No cat may be exhibited by the exhibitor, nor may the exhibitor attend shows, until this clearance certificate has been received and acknowledged.

If ringworm is confirmed, no cat belonging to the exhibitor or any in-contact cat may be exhibited, nor may the exhibitor attend shows. A clearance certificate in this case must be signed by a veterinary surgeon and state that *all the cats listed as belonging to the exhibitor and/or living at the same address* have been examined and that microscopic examination and culture of material from whole cat brushings and from any lesions have been carried out and the cat or cats appear clear. Before the clearance certificate can be signed, the tests have to be repeated at an interval of 8 weeks, thus providing two sets of negative tests 8 weeks apart.

With those conditions hanging over you, exhibitors become upset if there is a suggestion of rejection under section D!

If cats are rejected under this section, yet another special form has to be handed to the exhibitor. This explains the procedure after rejection under section D, and Part I, completed by the duty veterinary surgeon, lists the usual data regarding the show, breed number, name, etc., and also has outline diagrams of left and right, dorsal and ventral areas of the cat in order that skin lesions can be precisely pinpointed. Part II of this form has to be completed by the owner/exhibitor's veterinary surgeon, who has to record when the initial examination of the cat took place and the date on which samples were taken together with the final results and dates. Part III, completed by the owner/exhibitor, confirms that the cat named in Part I was the cat examined within 7 days of the show date and is the cat referred to in Part II.

If all the above tests prove negative, this completed form and the veterinary rejection form have to be sent to the GCCF veterinary officer, but if any of the results prove positive, all the cats belonging to the exhibitor then have to be examined.

Thus, in summary, vetting-in is a screening test, particularly for infectious and contagious diseases and in particular for skin lesions that may be attributable to ringworm. However, cats are also rejected for more general reasons under section A, as has been outlined.

Once vetting-in is over the duty veterinary surgeon's work really begins. It is unusual if there are more than half a dozen rejections during vetting-in, even at a large championship show. However, once judging commences the duty veterinary surgeon is frequently in demand to give opinions on conformation as well as conditions that may have occurred subsequent to vetting-in. Cats can become distressed during a show for a whole variety of reasons. Inadvertent and totally unexpected injuries can occur, and occasionally opinions have to be given on animals that are judged to be undersized or distressed by the show atmosphere.

Exhibitors are required to leave the hall while judging of the Open classes takes place. They are not usually readmitted until approximately midday. Thus if cats have to be removed from their pens and placed in isolation during this period, the duty veterinary surgeon frequently has to assume the role of counsellor, explaining to distressed owners the reason why a particular exhibit had to be removed from the pen.

Veterinary surgeons who undertake this work are clearly dedicated. Payment is only in the form of a token honorarium. At the end of a busy show the duty veterinary surgeon usually feels completely shattered. I well remember one large show where I wore a pedometer and found that I had walked nearly 19.5 miles between 7 a.m. when I started vetting-in and 5.15 when I finally left the show at close.

Even vetting-in without the responsibilities of duty vetting can be onerous. It is not unusual to have to leave for the show before 6 a.m. and you seldom get back before midday. Nevertheless, participating veterinary surgeons enjoy vetting-in and feel it is a worthwhile part of the show scene. Due to the complexity of feline diseases, particularly feline viruses, I feel that vetting-in should be retained despite the emergence of new and ever more effective vaccines. Cats nevertheless still have a number of infectious conditions which often show only subtle signs. These conditions can spread rapidly in the atmosphere of a cat show, and if vetting-in goes some way to reducing this risk, all the effort is worthwhile.

INDEX